Erich S. Gruen
Constructs of Identity in Hellenistic Judaism

Deuterocanonical and Cognate Literature Studies

Edited by
Friedrich V. Reiterer, Beate Ego and Tobias Nicklas

Volume 29

Erich S. Gruen

Constructs of Identity in Hellenistic Judaism

Essays on Early Jewish Literature and History

DE GRUYTER

ISBN 978-3-11-060944-8
e-ISBN (PDF) 978-3-11-037555-8
e-ISBN (EPUB) 978-3-11-038719-3
ISSN 1865-1666

Library of Congress Cataloging-in-Publication Data
A CIP catalog record for this book has been applied for at the Library of Congress.

Bibliographic information published by the Deutsche Nationalbibliothek
The Deutsche Nationalbibliothek lists this publication in the Deutsche Nationalbibliografie;
detailed bibliographic data are available on the Internet at http://dnb.dnb.de.

© 2018 Walter de Gruyter GmbH, Berlin/Boston
This volume is text- and page-identical with the hardback published in 2016.
Printing and binding: CPI books GmbH, Leck

♾ Printed on acid-free paper
Printed in Germany

www.degruyter.com

Overview

Preface

Constructs of Identity in Hellenistic Judaism:
Essays in Early Jewish Literature and History
Erich S. Gruen

Volumes of essays by retired (or nearly retired) scholars have proliferated in recent decades. How does one account for this phenomenon—let alone justify it? Publication of a scholar's *kleine Schriften* is, of course, not a new institution. But most of those that appeared in the past served as memorials to those who had already departed from the scene, a final legacy to the *epigoni*. The assemblage of pieces by authors still alive and kicking needs fuller explanation. A matter of ego? That inevitably plays a part, and it would be disingenuous to deny it. But a more respectable motivation can also be put forward. The multiplication of conference volumes, Festschriften, companions, handbooks, anthologies, and edited selections around a theme has become increasingly conspicuous, if not predominant. Many of the articles in this collection first appeared in such publications. Works of that sort are by no means an unworthy enterprise, especially as some of them reach out at a high level to a readership beyond the specialist. But they have a serious drawback. The volumes generally receive little promotion by publishers, and numerous individual contributions contained in them are overlooked or unknown by the large majority of scholars in the field. Unless one knows in advance where to look, the pieces are unlikely to be stumbled upon by accident. The present volume, by gathering scattered essays between two covers, will give them a wider circulation, make for more convenient consultation, and bring them to the attention of those who are otherwise unaware of them. Whether they merit the attention may be left for others to decide.

More than thirty years ago I was approached by a publisher who wished to produce a selection of my published essays as a book. That was a most flattering suggestion, and I considered it seriously. In the end—and with some reluctance—I declined that generous invitation. I felt at the time that my corpus of essays lacked both the quantity and the distinction to merit publication as a self-standing book. To approve such a project might seem (indeed would have been) an act of arrogance. Now, many years later, one can at least make a case for the quantity. And the added years could make the arrogance a little more forgivable.

The passage of time has had another significant consequence. An assemblage of my pieces in the early 1980s would have been heavily weighted toward Roman history, especially Roman political history. That is the area in which I cut my scholarly teeth, and I have never regretted it. But I have long since moved in other directions, for good or ill. I drifted into Hellenistic history and became heavily engaged with it, much to my pleasure and gratification. And the focus soon turned away from political and diplomatic history to cultural history, more particularly the interaction of Hellenic culture and Roman society that occupied much of my work for a decade and more. The exploration of means and media whereby Romans appropriated Hellenism to reformulate their own cultural identity led me in a natural progression (natural, at least, in retrospect) to investigation of a comparable subject, i. e. the relationship of Hellenism and Jewish identity. I regarded the shift in topic as an organic intellectual development— even though some of my colleagues and friends, especially those in Israel, interpreted the new direction as "a return to my Jewish roots." Whatever the alleged unconscious drive, however, engagement with Jewish history and literature in the Greco-Roman period has held sway in my research for the last two decades.

That focus also helped to prompt this publication. In reconsidering the proposition made three decades ago, I realized that there were now more than twenty articles that would come under the heading of Second Temple Judaism alone, thus providing a reasonable body of work on various aspects of the subject. Moreover, the collection could have a coherence often lacking in assemblages of one's favorite little gems.

The twenty-three papers collected here fall into five separate but interrelated categories. The volume opens with two contributions under the heading of "general reflections." The first is, in fact, the earliest piece, delivered originally as the presidential address to the American Philological Society in 1992. It served as a form of clarion call to Classicists to expand their horizons and look to the interconnections between Greek and Roman societies and the cultures of the Near East. This was hardly a new idea, but it stressed the means whereby cultural identities were defined by exploiting and appropriating the myths, legends, and tales of other societies, thereby enriching one's own. As prime illustrations, I called attention to Jewish stories that linked their traditions to those of the Hellenic world and thus enhanced their own self-esteem. That venture represented my initial steps into the realm of Jewish studies, and the theme itself augured much of my subsequent work in that field. Less than a decade later, I was asked by the eminent Jewish historian David Biale (who was also a good friend) to contribute a chapter on Hellenistic Judaism for his monumental *Cultures of the Jews* (2002). This afforded a welcome opportunity to provide an extended overview of the subject, but one that did not restrict itself to delivering a mainstream consensus. The medium served as a vehicle for presenting a number of my ideas on Jewish encounters with Hellenism, investigating a range of literary genres that illustrated Jewish commandeering of Greek forms to convey their own expressions of identity, and analyzing the complex relationship between an integrated existence in the diaspora and allegiance to the homeland. I remain deeply grateful to David Biale for extending to a relative newcomer to the field the opportunity to expose his ideas to a wider (but occasionally unforgiving) audience.

Part 2 consists of five essays that explore in some detail particular instances of the themes adumbrated in Part 1. Each of them illustrates facets of the construction of Jewish identity in the circumstances of Greco-Roman society. One offers a close analysis of the fascinating legend (a Jewish composition) that has Jews and Spartans both derive from the seed of Abraham. A second recounts the diverse reconstructions in which Greek writers depicted Jews as philosophers and Jews in turn conceived Greek philosophy as drawn from Mosaic teachings. Another calls attention to the instances of intermarriage and constructed kinship relations between Jews and non-Jews that underscored commonality rather than separateness. Still another examines the literary and epigraphic evidence that shows Jewish adaptation of pagan practices and the permeability of boundaries between Jewish and non-Jewish societies. And one other explores a range of fictive creations stressing the dynamic interchange between the cultures and undermining the simplistic dichotomy of "Hellenism" and "Judaism."

The five papers in Part 3 fall in the category of "reciprocal perspectives." They consider depictions of Jews by non-Jews and vice-versa, exposing concocted images and complex attitudes that marked mutual perceptions. An essay on manipulation of the Exodus story in the Hellenistic and Roman eras attempts to unravel the confusing strands that were fashioned less by hostile or favorable writers than by ingenious rewritings that complicated the tradition in the interests of self-representation. The portrait of Persia by Second Temple Jewish authors is also more ambiguous and subtle than might be expected from beneficiaries of Achaemenid power and ostensibly benign overlordship. The range of portrayals included mockery of Persian princes and subversive claims of Persian dependence on Jewish moral and intellectual superiority. By contrast, so another article argues, Tacitus' notoriously negative representation of Jews is far from simplistic or one-sided. The great historian's pages on this subject are suffused with irony and deliberate paradoxes that serve more as cynical commentary on contemporary Roman attitudes than serious characterization of Jews. Irony, furthermore, was no monopoly of pagan authors. An equally controversial essay in this section maintains that Josephus' expressed scorn for Greek writers in the *Contra Apionem* employed them as contrived foils for his own rhetorical purposes. At a more general level, one other contribution draws upon a variety of Jewish texts that illustrate inconsistent and heterogeneous approaches to Greeks and Greek culture, mirrored by similarly polyvalent views of Jews by Hellenic authors. And a final essay in this company, one composed for the volume, questions the proposition that Judeophobia contributed to certain horrific experiences Jews suffered at the hands of Greeks or Romans in the Second Temple period.

Part 4 moves from attitudes and images to historical facts on the ground. One essay tackles the critical and probably intractable problem of why Antiochus IV wrought horrific havoc upon the Jews in the unprecedented persecution that led to the Maccabean uprising. The article offers a radical solution that has by no means won the day, but may still stir reaction and discussion. A second piece addresses the equally difficult question of how to understand the meaning of the new Jewish temple that rose at Leontopolis in Egypt in the mid 2nd century BCE, often interpreted as a rival to Jerusalem. The article provides an alternative analysis that sees the shrine in Leontopolis as a complement to the Jerusalem Temple, a reinforcement of its authority in troubled times, and an assertion of continuity rather than schism. Another paper takes a fresh look at the notorious Jewish king Herod. It challenges two widely held readings of his career: that he was a compliant client of Rome, and that he utilized his influence to become a generous benefactor of Jews all over the eastern diaspora. It argues that Herod successfully cultivated the image of a partner rather than a subordinate. And it shows that the notion of Herod as champion of diaspora Jews rests largely on a single episode prompted by contingent circumstances, not a matter of considered policy. The central image that he presented was that of a successful Hellenistic ruler. A monarch of even greater notoriety and potential destructiveness for the Jews was the maniacal Roman emperor Gaius Caligula. The collection includes a piece that dissects Philo's account of Caligula's apparent effort to install a statue of himself as Jupiter in the Temple of Jerusalem. The essay points out numerous problems and puzzles in Philo's account that generate grave suspicions about its reliability, and it casts doubt upon the emperor's alleged motivations of hatred for the Jews and a drive for his own divinization. One other article takes a much wider scope. It stresses that the Jewish diaspora in antiquity cannot be characterized as enforced exile, an involuntary expulsion from the center that rendered its victims longing for a restoration to the homeland. The paper contends that most Jews had departed of their own accord for a whole range of reasons, had settled quite contentedly in the diaspora, but retained an abiding commitment through pilgrimage, tithes, and cultural identification with Jerusalem and the Temple.

The final segment trains its focus upon a diverse group of literary texts that range in genre, design, and form, but exhibit the ingenuity and inventiveness with which Jewish writers expressed connection or confrontation with the cultural world of Greeks and Romans. An article on the Letter of Aristeas calls attention to its subtly subversive depiction of Ptolemy, ruler of Egypt, the comic touches that pervade the table-talk of the symposium, and the playing with Hellenic genres that contributed to the advancement of Jewish self-esteem in the cultivated circles of Hellenic society. The clever compositions of Artapanus are the subject of another study in this assemblage. His work survives now only in fragments, but enough to show his idiosyncratic take on biblical tales, the weaving of enticing narratives that had more to do with pleasure than piety, and the entertainment value of writings that drew on folklore and myth from both Hellenic and Near Eastern traditions. Another rewriting of the Bible, in more sober fashion, occurs in the work of Pseudo-Philo whose version takes the tale from Adam to David. The paper on that author endeavors to cast him in a somewhat different light, points to numerous instances in which he applies a somewhat subversive tone, including rebukes of the Lord for failing to keep His own covenant, advice to Him to look to His own reputation, and the distrust of divine assistance even by some of the author's heroes and heroines. The work does not undermine the authority of God but calls upon its readers to challenge His actions and to engage in lively dialogue with His precepts and their fulfillment (or lack thereof). A very different form of writing exists in the Sibylline Oracles. An article on the subject in this volume devotes itself to the Third Sibylline Oracle, the earliest in that corpus, and one predominantly Jewish in composition. It seeks to shift the conventional approach of finding historical allusions and political implications in the work to an emphasis on its literary context and its eschatological character. The last piece in the collection discusses four different Jewish authors or works in relation to the revival of Greek literature in the early Roman Empire, the so-called Second Sophistic. The treatment of Philo of Alexandria, 4 Maccabees, Pseudo-Phocylides, and Joseph and Aseneth, addresses the tensions that existed between adherence to Jewish heritage and participation in the broader literary and philosophical culture of Hellas. The essay underscores the complex, occasionally difficult, adaptation to or commingling of the traditions and genres.

I am grateful to Tobias Nicklas who first suggested to me in 2010 the idea of republishing my articles in the area of Jewish studies. My earlier reluctance on this issue still lingered, and three years passed before I could persuade myself that the endeavor might have some value for the profession. When I contacted Tobias once more in 2013, he was gracious and generous enough to say that the offer still stood, and he was more encouraging than ever. He then kindly transferred this enthusiasm to Albrecht Döhnert and Sophie Wagenhofer whose expert work and whose helpfulness in every regard were instrumental in seeing the book through to publication. The indispensable person, however, was my outstanding research assistant Ashley Bacchi who put all the pieces together, brought uniformity to the whole, and accomplished the unenviable but inescapable chore of compiling the index. The book would not have been possible without her. And deep gratitude goes also to my friend Martin Goodman, a giant in this field, who agreed, without flinching, to contribute an introduction to the volume, thus lending it prestige—but not necessarily concurrence.

First Publications of Essays

The following articles have been reprinted with gracious permission of the original presses. Minor updates have been made to citations in the footnotes.

"Cultural Fictions and Cultural Identity (Presidential Address to APA)," *Transactions of the American Philological Association*, 123 (1993), 1–14.

"Hellenistic Judaism," in David Biale, *Cultures of the Jews: A New History*. New York: Schocken Books, 2002., 77–132.

"Fact and Fiction: Jewish Legends in a Hellenistic Context," in Paul Cartledge, Peter Garnsey, and Erich Gruen, *Hellenistic Constructs: Essays in Culture, History, and Historiography* Hellenistic Culture and Society. Berkeley: University of California Press, 1997., 72–88.

"Kinship Relations and Jewish Identity," in Lee I. Levine and Daniel R. Schwartz, *Jewish Identities in Antiquity: Studies in Memory of Menachem Stern* Texts and Studies in Ancient Judaism = Texte Und Studien Zum Antiken Judentum. Tübingen: Mohr Siebeck, 2009., 101–116.

"Hellenism and Judaism: Fluid Boundaries," in Zeev Weiss, O. Irshai, J. Magness, and S. Schwartz, *Follow the Wise: Studies in Jewish History and Culture in Honor of Lee I. Levine.* Winona Lake, Ind.: Eisenbrauns, 2010., 53–70.

"Jews and Greeks as Philosphers," in Daniel C. Harlow, K.M. Hogan, M. Goff, and J.S. Kaminsky, *The "Other" in Second Temple Judaism: Essays in Honor of John J. Collins*. Grand Rapids, Mich.: W.B. Eerdmans Pub. Co., 2011., 402–422.

"The Purported Jewish-Spartan Affiliation," in Robert W. Wallace and Edward M. Harris, *Transitions to Empire: Essays in Greco-Roman History, 360–146 B.C., in Honor of E. Badian* Oklahoma Series in Classical Culture. Norman: University of Oklahoma Press, 1996., 254–269.

"Jewish Perspectives on Greek Culture and Ethnicity," in John J. Collins and Gregory Sterling, *Hellenism in the Land of Israel* Christianity and Judaism in Antiquity. Notre Dame, Ind.: University of Notre Dame, 2001., 62–93.

"The Use and Abuse of the Exodus Story," *Jewish History*, 12 (1998), 93–122.

"Persia Through the Jewish Looking-Glass," in Erich Gruen, *Cultural Borrowings and Ethnic Appropriations in Antiquity* Oriens Et Occidens. Stuttgart: F. Steiner, 2005., 90–104.

"Greeks and Jews: Mutual Misperceptions in Josephus' Contra Apionem," in Carol Bakhos, *Ancient Judaism in its Hellenistic Context* Supplements to the Journal for the Study of Judaism. Leiden; Boston: Brill, 2005., 31–51.

"Tacitus and the Defamation of the Jews," in J. Geiger, H. Cotton and G. Stiebel, *Israel's Land:Papers Presented to Israel Shatzman on his Jubilee.* Jerusalem: The Open University of Israel, Israel Exploration Society 2009., 77–96.

"Diaspora and Homeland," in Howard Wettstein, *Diasporas and Exiles: Varieties of Jewish Identity.* Berkeley: University of California Press, 2002., 18–46.

"Was There Judeophobia in Classical Antiquity?", composed for this volume.

"Hellenism and Persecution: Antiochus IV and the Jews," in Peter Green, *Hellenistic History and Culture.* Hellenistic Culture and Society. Berkeley: University of California Press, 1993., 238–264.

"The Origins and Objectives of Onias' Temple", *Scripta Classica Israelica*, 16 (1997), 47–70.

"Herod, Rome, and the Diaspora," in David M. Jacobson and Nikos Kokkinos, *Herod and Augustus: Papers Presented at the Ijs Conference, 21st-23rd June 2005.* IJS Studies in Judaica. Leiden; Boston: Brill, 2009., 13–27.

"Caligula, the Imperial Cult, and Philo's *Legatio,*" *Studia Philonica Annual*, 24 (2012), 135–147.

"The Letter of Aristeas and the Cultural Context of the Septuagint," in Martin Karrer and Wolfgang Kraus, *Die Septuaginta – Texte, Kontexte, Lebenswelten: Internationale Fachtagung Veranstaltet Von Septuaginta Deutsch (Lxx.D), Wuppertal 20.–23. Juli 2006.* Wissenschaftliche Untersuchungen Zum Neuen Testament. Tübingen: Mohr Siebeck, 2008., 134–156.

"The Twisted Tales of Artapanus: Biblical Rewritings As Novelistic Narrative," in Ilaria Ramelli and Judith Perkins. *Early Christian and Jewish Narrative: The Role of Religion in Shaping Narrative Forms.* Wissenschaftliche Untersuchungen Zum Neuen Testament. Tübingen: Mohr Siebeck, 2015., 31–44.

"Jews, Greeks, and Romans in the Third Sibylline Oracle," in Martin Goodman, *Jews in a Graeco-Roman World.* Oxford; New York: Clarendon Press; Oxford University Press, 1998., 15–36.

"Subversive Elements in Pseudo-Philo," in M. Mor, et al. *For Uriel: Studies in the History of Israel in Antiquity Presented to Uriel Rappaport.* Jerusalem: The Zalman Shazar Center for Jewish History, 2005, 37–52.

"Jewish Literature and the Second Sophistic," in William A. Johnson and Daniel Richter. *The Oxford Handbook of the Second Sophistic (forthcoming).*

Introduction

To be asked to review a quarter of a century of work by a great scholar by, and in the presence of, the great scholar himself is a great compliment but no less daunting from the knowledge that the scholar in question is as genial and kindly as he is learned and acute. What follows is an attempt, undoubtedly inadequately, to put into some perspective the unique contribution, in the studies reprinted in this volume and in a series of major monographs since the mid 1990s, that Erich Gruen has made to the study of Jews in the Hellenistic word and in the early Roman Empire.

As Erich has frequently stressed, he came to the study of Jewish history in this period as something of an outsider. That deep immersion in the study of Greece and Rome in classical antiquity as a young scholar should have included more or less nothing about Jews of that period except when they impinged on the political and military history of the wider Mediterranean world (usually as a result of rebellion) was a direct product of the disciplinary boundaries erected in European and American universities in the nineteenth century which allocated the study of Jews to Christian theologians (as background to the New Testament) or to orientalists seeking continuities in the languages and cultures of the Near East. The texts of Josephus and Philo had been rediscovered and edited by European Christian and Jewish humanists in the sixteenth century, and the Jewish scholars of the *Wissenschaft des Judentums* movement in the nineteenth century studied their works with enthusiasm as material for their attempts to reconstruct a national history for the Jews as coherent and rational as those of other European national movements, but the Greek Jewish writings were rarely studied either for literary style or (except in a Christian theological context) for moral edification, and none of the works of ancient Jews became part of the core set of texts adopted in the teaching of Greek and Roman history. Classical historians occasionally raided the Jewish material for data on the wider non-Jewish world, especially as evidence for the amalgam of Greek and Jewish culture defined as the essence of the Hellenistic culture postulated for the Near East after Alexander the Great, but they rarely saw it as part of their role as classicists to study the culture of Greek Jews in its own right.

The decision of Erich Gruen, as already a major scholar in the field of ancient history, to turn his attention in the early 1990s to the Jewish material from Alexander to Hadrian was thus rather a surprise. Other ancient historians of Jewish origins had strayed into Jewish history in earlier generations, but in most cases their interest in the topic seems to have reflected the remains of their knowledge derived from a traditional Jewish religious education which they sought to reconcile with the very different training in the classics to which they had devoted their scholarly lives. Erich, born in Austria in 1935 but educated, after Bible study as a child in Hebrew School, in an essentially secular fashion in the United States and Oxford, had neither the advantage of close acquaintance with rabbinic materials nor the disadvantage of an instinctive tendency to rely too much on such materials for Jewish history, which such an education often brings, and for him it was natural to make the Greek Jewish texts not just an adjunct to rabbinic history but the main focus of his studies. Of these Greek Jewish texts, the writings of one author, Josephus, were beginning by the early 1990s to be treated as a more mainstream object of interest for ancient historians: Pierre Vidal-Naquet in the 1970s had used the example of Josephus caught between two political systems as a source of ruminations about contemporary politics, and Fergus Millar had used his writings as a major source for his study of the Roman emperor in 1977. But very few classicists were working on the rest of Jewish Greek literature, and questions of Jewish identity in a Greek world were still much bound up for most scholars with the issue, still fraught after the convulsions of the mid twentieth century, of the Jewish roots of Christianity.

When a classicist like Erich Gruen turns his gaze onto this material he sees quite different issues from those noted by New Testament scholars, let alone those who start from the rabbinic traditions. It is partly a question of perspective: we may know a great deal about Jews from this period because so much written by and about them was preserved by the continuous religious traditions of either Christians or Jews to the present day, but they were only a small group in a much larger and complex world, and we need to be constantly aware that what appears peculiar about the Jews may be a phenomenon more widely shared in the variegated cultures of the Mediterranean world even if it is only fully attested in the Jewish evidence. No less important is the instinct of classicists to subject texts not just to close reading but to sensitive analysis in light of genre and audience: the temptation of theologians, both Christian and Jewish, to raid the ancient evidence for proof texts to uphold a thesis runs counter to the principle of classical historians that each piece of evidence is to be judged on its merits even if the resulting picture of what actually happened is complex and confused.

Erich has brought these classicist's skills to bear on this material with masterly precision and infectious enthusiasm. His brilliant proposal in this volume that we should be aware of the strong possibility of irony in the depiction of the Jews by Tacitus cuts through centuries of discussion as to whether Tacitus was or was not anti-Jewish, and his sceptical re-reading of the presentation of Caligula's antipathy to Judaism in Philo's *Legatio* shows how much can be achieved by going back to look with fresh eyes at passages which have been intensively studied and mined for many decades. In his numerous studies of identity issues, it makes all the difference that he is constantly aware that Romans in the Middle and Late Republic were no less engaged than Jews in negotiating their own identity in relation to Greek traditions, and that integration of Jews into a Greek world will have been fluid and complex in light of shifting Greek views of Jews as well as shifting Jewish views of Greeks.

To such nuanced historical analysis Erich also brings some distinctive personal concerns and instincts. It is striking how often he chooses to emphasise the contingent over the general—in marked contrast to the great constitutional and legal theorists of the nineteenth and early twentieth centuries like Jean Juster, who sought to demonstrate the formal position of Jews in gentile societies in antiquity against a background of increasing legal restrictions on Jews in their own world, Erich emphasises the temporary and specific reasons both for state persecutions and for the actions in favour of diaspora Jewish communities attributed to the Jewish politician Herod. It is tempting to interpret Erich's depiction of Jewish life in the diaspora as essentially benign, with issues of identity expressed in literary genres often intended primarily to entertain, as a reflection of the far more cheerful position of Jews within the Californian society where Erich has made his home for the past fifty years. An insistence on the viability of diaspora Jewish life runs through many of these studies, as does an insistence on a humorous side to much Jewish Greek literature which had passed by unnoticed by previous generations of scholars (and remains unrecognised by some even now, despite Erich's best efforts). Not everyone will be persuaded to learn to read the *Letter of Aristeas* not just as evidence for a foundation myth about the origins of the Septuagint but as a repository of light comedy, or the strange assertion by the Jewish writer Artapanus that Moses introduced to the Egyptians their distinctive worship of animal gods as a product of mischievous wit, but scholars and students will undoubtedly much benefit from Erich's ingenuity and cheerful encouragement to understand these texts with such possibilities in mind.

Well over half of the studies in this volume were published in the last ten years, and Erich shows no sign whatever of slackening his pace in retirement. Not least through Erich's own teaching of numerous doctoral students, the number of classicists who share his interest in the Jewish Greek materials has burgeoned over recent decades, and his writings have sparked a conversation across the field of ancient history which should ensure that the topics to which he has contributed so much will continue to elicit studies both from him and from others. That study of Jewish Greek culture has now entered the mainstream of ancient historical studies is in no small measure due to him, and to the essays included in this volume.

Martin Goodman
December 2014

General Reflections

1. Cultural Fictions and Cultural Identity

Cultural identity is a hot topic in the academy these days. The phenomenon has swept through the halls of ivy. Courses, curricula, programs, and departments have undergone wholesale transformation in recent years. The affirmation of ethnic, racial, or religious roots has translated itself into new catalogue offerings, lecture series, majors, undergraduate degrees, and graduate specializations—not to mention scholarly conferences by the score. At Berkeley, an Ethnic Studies Division encompasses separate units for African-American studies, Native American studies, Asian-American studies, and Chicano studies, each offering a raft of courses and seminars. Nor is this an instance where Berkeley is so far in the vanguard as to have lost claim to representative status. In fact, the reshaping of academic disciplines in terms of cultural identity is a nationwide development, firmly entrenched in numerous institutions and in process of implementation in many others.

Where does Classics fit into this? Sadly, our discipline too often regards the development as a threat, girding its loins for retrenchment or resistance. And, sadder still, Classics frequently supplies a prime target for attack, labeled as the quintessential representative of elitism, the custodian of western tradition, the pillar of Eurocentrism. The current drive for multiculturalism appears in this light as the enemy, a menace to those old dead languages, that bygone civilization, that one-dimensional and stodgy academic pursuit that largely studies and is studied by aging white males of European extraction.

Certainly our discipline does not need additional enemies. At a time when tight-fisted administrators face budgetary shortfalls and receive directives to cut expenditures, Classics departments become inviting victims. Too many programs have already been reduced, amalgamated, or eliminated, too many individuals reckoned as expendable. This is hardly the time for retreat into the bunker, a rear-guard action to preserve hoary values against the presumed barbarian. Multiculturalism should, in fact, serve as a challenge and a stimulus, an occasion to reach out to concerns that swirl about the academy.

I do not here suggest truckling to the trendy. Nor do I refer to ad hoc strategies for survival, a mania for mounting enrollments. Tactical moves are not the issue. Many are already in place, and have been for more than a generation. They include, of course, Classics in translation, Classical Civilization majors, or courses in mythology—very successful, entirely legitimate, and altogether laudable enterprises—even though they have not always prevented the shutting down of departments or the laying off of personnel.

My point is a different one. The proposition that multiculturalism and the study of classical antiquity are somehow at cross-purposes strikes me as peculiar and paradoxical.

Few societies have ever been more multicultural than those clustered about the Mediterranean. The worlds of the ancient Near East, Greece, and Rome encompassed a bewildering range and diversity of peoples, races, colors, languages, attitudes, conventions, and beliefs. As Dio Chrysostom observed, with reference to the population of Alexandria in the late 1st or early 2nd century C.E., the inhabitants consisted of Greeks, Italians, Syrians, Libyans, Cilicians, Ethiopians, Arabs, Bactrians, Scythians, Persians, and Indians.[1] No need to devise artificial constructs in order to meet the tests of political correctness or to stave off the predatory dean. Far from being a threat to the study of antiquity, multiculturalism stands at its very core. This is precisely the area that can and should excite research, writing, and instruction—without defensiveness and without romanticizing.[2] The ancient world did not constitute a melting pot, some congenial mixing bowl that blended and integrated its pieces to form the origins of western civilization. The ingredients came from east as well as west, from north as well as south. And the differences among ancient societies are at least as striking as the similarities, the confrontations at least as significant as any assimilation. A sense of cultural identity, after all, can hardly take form unless defined against or with reference to other cultures.

The treatment of cultural identity as applied to ancient societies in recent years has not always been salutary. Emphasis can be misplaced, and false or unproductive issues have taken precedence. Take, for instance, the matter of cultural theft. Who stole what from whom? A singularly pointless debate. Cultures do not become impoverished if their creations are borrowed by others. This is no zero-sum game. Interaction enriches the legacy, rather than diminishing the contributors. Or, to cite another bustling enterprise, excessive energy has been expended in searching out origins. Our understanding of the Hellenic achievement is no more enhanced by postulating an occupation of Boeotia by the Hyksos than by belief in a Dorian invasion of the Peloponnese. Speculation along these lines can rapidly degenerate into polemics, with unwelcome overtones of politics and ideology. A decision on whether or not Cleopatra was black would bring us no insight into her character or accomplishment—let alone those of con-

---

1 Dio Chrysostom *Orat.* 32.40.
2 The wise words of Molly Myerowitz Levine, "Multiculturalism and the Classics," *Arethusa* 25 (1992) 215–220, deserve attention.

temporary blacks, whites, Greeks, or Egyptians.[3] Or consider a different line of inquiry that is quite familiar: the tracing of cultural influences from one society to another. That has long been a staple item of classical scholarship, and it can occasionally be fruitful and interesting. But it generally presupposes a rather passive recipient, thus posing a distinction between cultural benefactor and beneficiary. It also implies an unspoken privileging of one culture over another. And it ignores or suppresses what should capture attention: the dynamics of the interchange and the active transformation of a cultural inheritance into a new entity.[4]

Emphasis needs to be shifted. I want to place stress on the development of a cultural consciousness through experience with and by reference to other cultures. Antiquity supplies an especially rich repository for such an investigation. How did ancient societies come to articulate their own identities? The question presents numerous difficulties and stumbling blocks. One topic of inquiry, however, may bring some useful results. I refer to the manipulation of myths, the reshaping of traditions, the elaboration of legends, fictions, and inventions, the recasting of ostensibly alien cultural legacies with the aim of defining or reinforcing a distinctive cultural character. Research into this subject encounters intricate and involved tales of national origins, of borrowings, kinship, and interconnections among societies, of common heritage, and of intercultural associations.

Scholarly interpretation of such stories, of course, has a long history. But it has not always taken the most promising direction. That is to say, interpreters have exercised undue ingenuity in attempting to determine the historicity of these tales, efforts that can be debated endlessly without approaching a consensus. Yet the stories are no less intriguing—indeed more so—if they are imagina-

---

3 Reference, of course, is to the heated debate still raging over Martin Bernal's ambitious, admirably learned, occasionally brilliant, and productively provocative Black Athena, a projected multi-volume work, of which two have appeared; Black Athena: The Afroasiatic Roots of Classical Civilization, vol. 1: The Fabrication of Ancient Greece, 1785–1985 (New Brunswick, 1987); vol. 2: The Archaeological and Documentary Evidence (New Brunswick, 1991). Numerous discussions and disputes have found their way into print, with Bernal frequently offering rebuttal. See, especially, The Challenge of 'Black Athena', special issue, Arethusa (1989), ed. by M. M. Levine and J. Peradotto; and a range of articles in Journal of Mediterranean Archaeology 3 (1 990). Note also the trenchant remarks of Edith Hall, "When is a Myth not a Myth? Bernal's 'Ancient Model'," Arethusa 25 (1992) 181–201, with Bernal's response, 203–214. A valuable bibliography on the controversy may be found in M. M. Levine, "The Use and Abuse of Black Athena," AHR 97 (1992) 440–460.
4 Cf. the salutary comments of H. von Staden, "Affinities and Elisions: Helen and Hellenocentrism," Isis 83 (1992) 578–595.

tive inventions. For they thereby raise the more important questions about motives for adoption and adaptation of the fables, the context in which they were framed, the attitudes they reveal toward other cultures, and the role they played in forming a people's sense of cultural distinctiveness.

The present occasion forbids a detailed exploration of this topic. But certain revealing examples can bring it into vivid focus. I want to pursue the matter on two fronts, one quite familiar to Classicists, the other rather less so. It might be noted, with some relief, that neither one involves the debate about the origins of Greek civilization nor the competing claims of Egyptians, Semites, and Indo-Europeans on those origins. Rather, I look first at the legends of Rome's connection with Troy, and then at some of the fascinating tales that associate the Jews with the traditions and peoples of Greece. Each represents an illuminating case of appropriation and adaptation of alien traditions, in order, on the one hand, to establish a place within a broader cultural framework and, on the other, to assert superiority within it.

First, Rome and Troy.[5] It is no secret that the legends associating the forebears of Rome with the survivors of the Trojan War were conceived by Greek writers and intellectuals. They generated what was later to become the canonical tradition on Rome's beginnings. The orthodox tale, of course, has the city derive from a settlement of Trojan refugees, remnants of a people defeated by the Achaean expedition that sacked Troy. Aeneas holds center stage in this version, leader of the Trojans who survived that calamity and who, after countless setbacks and detours, successfully reached the shores of Italy. The progeny of Aeneas eventually carried out their destiny, the founding of Rome, via the cities of Lavinium and Alba Longa. Vergil's *Aeneid* enshrines the tale, and Livy's history encapsulates it.

What is not so well known, however, is the fact that this version took quite a long time before it attained canonical status and that it had some very different and very strong competitors along the way. The earliest Hellenic explanations, in fact, had Greeks themselves, not Trojans, as the ancestors of Rome. As might be expected, the stories began to take shape in the era of Greek colonization, a process that naturally sparked Hellenic interest in the west. Greeks, in characteristic fashion, inclined to interpret the western past in light of their own national traditions. The circumstances would readily call attention to legends like the western adventures of Herakles or the settler-heroes of the Nostoi—most particularly, the wanderings of Odysseus.

---

5 For what follows, see the much fuller treatment in E. S. Gruen, *Culture and National Identity in Republican Rome* (Ithaca, 1992), 6–51.

One intriguing item appears very early in the record. The concluding lines of Hesiod's *Theogony* register the union of Odysseus and Circe, a union that produced as offspring Agrius and Latinus, future rulers over the Tyrrhenians.[6] Those lines disclose early Hellenic interest in central Italy, possibly Etruria and certainly Latium, and the introduction of those lands into the Greek legendary complex. More significant, Odysseus takes the role of ultimate ancestor to the rulers of those regions. The passage appropriately exemplifies the Greek penchant for reshaping foreign experiences by imposing Hellenic lore.

A strong Greek component continued to cling to the legends of Rome's beginnings. Heracleides Ponticus, for instance, a pupil of Plato writing in the mid 4th century B.C.E., referred to Rome simply as a "Greek city".[7] Aristotle himself endorsed a version that had Achaean, not Trojan, warriors driven by storm to Italy while trying to return home after the fall of Troy. They got no further. Their ships were burned, an act of defiance by the Trojan women brought as captives from Troy. The stranded Achaeans had to remain in Italy and took up permanent residence in a site, which Aristotle called "Latinium".[8] Aristotle's pupil Heracleides Lembos was more precise: the shipwrecked Achaeans settled a city on the Tiber named for the woman who had set their ships ablaze, Rhome.[9]

The foregoing are but a small sample of the abundant tales of Rome's origins that trace those origins to Greek founders. The phenomenon is a familiar one, a form of Hellenic cultural imperialism, a spinning out of tales in accord with Greek legends, and ascription of foreign cities to Greek colonists—a standard characteristic of the Hellenic mentality.

That ingredient had a tenacious quality. One finds it still present and, in even more vivid form, in a contemporary of Vergil and Livy, the Greek rhetorician and historian Dionysius of Halicarnassus. For Dionysius, Rome was a Greek city many times over. He postulated successive waves of migrants from the east: Arcadians, Pelasgians, yet more Arcadians, then the followers of Herakles.[10] Dionysius engaged in a form of Hellenic over-kill, swamping Rome with eastern settlers in order to reinforce its role as torchbearer of Greek civilization. He even went so far as to have Romulus defend the rape of the Sabine women by assuring the victims that this constituted hallowed Hellenic practice.[11]

---

6 Hes. *Th.* 1011–1016.
7 Plut. *Cam.* 22.2.
8 D.H. 1.72.3–4.
9 Heracleides Lembos, *Festus* 329 L.
10 D. H. 1.31, 41–44, 60, 89.
11 Ibid., 2.30.

The orthodox version that has Aeneas as ancestor of Rome is, in fact, a later and, initially at least, a less prevalent one. It appears among Sicilian Greek writers who propagated the tales of Trojan migrants to their island. Western Greeks, on the edges of the Hellenic world, had a special incentive to attach their own pedigrees to the great legends that grew out of the epic tradition and that had served to define a common Greek culture. And when such writers perceived Romans expanding their influence into the Greek-speaking areas of central and southern Italy in the 4th century B.C.E., they extended those tales to encompass the new emerging power. It is not surprising that the earliest extant historians to associate Aeneas with the origins of Rome are Sicilian historians.[12]

The traditions subsequently overlap, becoming amalgamated or blended in confusing fashion. The eponymous creation Roma or Rhome took on a number of roles in the hands of various creative writers. Some gave her solid Greek lineage as granddaughter of Herakles, or Telemachus, or Odysseus. Others made her wife of Aeneas or Ascanius, or granddaughter of Aeneas.[13] One bizarre combination of traditions has Aeneas come to Italy together with Odysseus and become founder of the city, which he designated as Rome, taking the name from one of the Trojan women who set fire to the ships.[14] That version evidently patches together a variety of independent traditions: the western migration of Odysseus, the flight of Aeneas, the burning of ships after return from Troy, and the foundation story of Rome.

All of these tales derive from the Hellenic imagination. But it is the Roman response to which I seek to call attention. When Greek accounts of Rome's origins first impinged upon Roman consciousness, they came, as we have seen, in several different varieties. And many of them gave a greater role to Achaean than to Trojan heroes. Yet it was the Trojan tale that eventually prevailed, an outcome that could not have been forecast from the beginning. How does one explain it? Why did the Romans, in their own estimation, become Trojans rather than Greeks? The question goes to the heart of Rome's cultural awakening and its own sense of identity.

The canonical tale in its full-blown form associated Rome most closely with two Latin towns: Lavinium and Alba Longa. As the story has it, Aeneas established a Trojan settlement at Lavinium, and, after an interval of thirty years, his son Ascanius departed to found a new city at Alba Longa. Ascanius thereby instituted the line of Alban kings who reigned for three centuries until the birth of the

---

12 Gruen, *Culture and National Identity*, 14–16.
13 Plut. *Rom.* 2.1–3; *D. H.* 1.72.6; *Festus*, 326, 328 L; Serv. *A.* 1. 273.
14 D.H. 1.72.2

twins Romulus and Remus who would be the creators of Rome. The special prestige accorded to the Latin towns in this narrative supplies a vital clue.

Appropriation of the legend by Rome can reasonably be set in the late 4th century B.C.E. That period brought a convergence of political and cultural circumstances that made the Trojan connection in a Latin context particularly attractive. This was the era in which Rome defeated the forces of the Latin League and extended military and political control over the cities of Latium. It was also the era in which Rome spread its influence into Campania and entered into diplomatic relations with Greek cities like Naples. The time proved propitious for adoption of the fables that linked Rome and Latin cities to the heritage of the Hellenic past. Rome found especially welcome benefits in the legends. They lent a cultural legitimacy to its position of authority in Latium. Rome was now heir to the region's glorious past—not just its conqueror and suzerain but its cultural curator. And, equally important, the assimilation of the legends announced a connection with the Hellenic world, thereby to validate Rome's association with the Greek cities of Italy.[15]

This brings us back then to the central question. Why did the Romans choose to consider themselves as descendants of Trojans rather than Greeks? Were they drawn to Aeneas rather than to Odysseus because the latter had a reputation for sly shrewdness, a dubious quality, whereas the former exemplified pietas, the preeminent Roman virtue? An unsatisfactory solution. The Romans were not shopping for heroes in some divine supermarket, weighing respective qualities and selecting their favorite. The embrace of Troy had more subtle and more significant meaning. It enabled Rome to associate itself with the rich and complex fabric of Hellenic tradition, thus to enter that wider cultural world, just as it had entered the wider political world. But at the same time it announced Rome's distinctiveness from the dominant element in that world.[16] Rome's literate classes welcomed incorporation into the cultural legacy of Hellas—but preferred to carve out their own niche within it. They thereby sharpened a sense of their identity and laid the foundations for a national character.

Troy supplied an especially attractive ingredient in that endeavor. The celebrated Trojan past lay in remote antiquity, its people no longer extant, the city but a shell of its former self. Troy, unlike Greece, persisted as a symbol, not a current reality. So Rome ran no risk of identification with any contemporary folk whose defects would be all too evident and all too embarrassing. The Romans

---

15 Gruen, *Culture and National Identity*, 26–29.
16 Cf. A. Momigliano, *Settimo contributo alla storia degli studi classici e del mondo antico* (Rome, 1984) 109, 447, 459.

could mold the ancient Trojans to suit their own ends. As in so much else, they astutely converted Hellenic traditions to meet their own political and cultural purposes. In short, the successful and enduring version that made Trojans the forebears of Rome owed its origin to Greek inventiveness, but its reformulation to Latin ingenuity. The Greeks imposed the Trojan legend upon the west as a form of Hellenic cultural imperialism, only to see it appropriated by the westerner as a means to define and convey a Roman cultural identity.

The embrace of Troy made its mark on the international scene during the next century and more. That development has led scholars to render a familiar negative verdict on Roman character. Rome, so it is asserted, exploited the Trojan legend in order to facilitate interventionism and expansionism in the Greek east.[17] Such a verdict misplaces the emphasis and misconceives the motivation. The Romans had larger aims in view: they advertised this association to announce their credentials as legitimate participants in a broader Mediterranean civilization. To that end, for example, they installed a temple to Venus Erycina on the Capitoline in 215, a cult whose origins lay in Sicilian Eryx where, so legend had it, Aeneas had dedicated a shrine to his mother.[18] Similarly, the Romans transferred the worship of Magna Mater, protective deity of the Trojans, from her locus on Mt. Ida to her new home on the Palatine. The striking festival inaugurated for the goddess exhibited the high value that Romans placed upon public proclamation of their cultural legacy.[19] Roman commanders in the east reinforced that objective when they made a point of offering sacrifice to shrines in Ilium. The gesture was accompanied by carefully orchestrated and mutual expressions of joy delivered by Romans and Ilians at the common heritage that bound them to one another.[20] Such acts had purposes other than conventional aggrandizement. Contemporary Ilium was an utterly insignificant town that could hardly supply substantive assistance to expansionism. Nor is it likely that other Greek cities would render allegiance to Rome on the basis of a Trojan connection. The symbolic connotations took precedence—and the cultural, rather than the political, meaning was central. Rome shunned the label of barbarian and struck the pose of heir and standard-bearer of an antique civilization shared by Trojans and Achaeans. The words of T. Quinctius Flamininus, victor over Philip V of Macedon and self-proclaimed liberator of Greeks, epitomized the posture. Flamininus dedicated precious objects at Delphi inscribed with his own verses in

---

17 e.g. Momigliano, *Settimo*, 453.
18 Liv. 22.9.7 – 10, 10.10; 23.30. 13 – 14, 31.9.
19 Sources and discussion in Gruen, *Studies in Greek Culture and Roman Policy* (Leiden, 1990) 5 – 33.
20 Liv. 37.1 – 3; 37.9.7.

Greek, reminding the Hellenes that their liberation had come at the hands of a descendant of Aeneas.[21] That is a significant image. Flamininus had no military goals to achieve with this gesture; Roman martial supremacy had already been established. The conjunction of Greek freedom and Trojan ancestry delivered a different message. Flamininus not only enunciated Rome's claim to a place in the cultivated community of the Mediterranean but he declared Rome's centrality as the protector of that heritage.

The Jews approached Hellenism from an angle quite different from that of the Romans. The Romans, of course, held a political and military ascendancy. But the greater their success in those arenas, the more urgently they asserted an antique connection to that cultural world which they had, in fact, only recently entered. The Jews, on the other hand, constituted a numerical minority in the Diaspora and a subordinate state at home, dependent on the suzerainty of greater powers. Yet they too staked a claim on a shared cultural lineage with Hellenic society. And they too, like the Romans, propagated tales that both associated themselves with Greek traditions and reaffirmed their own special character.

An intriguing set of stories circulated declaring kinship between Greeks and Jews. As a notable example, consider the tradition that Jews and Spartans were both descended from the line of Abraham. That particular tall tale supposedly received acknowledgment in a letter by a Spartan king, Areus I, in the early 3rd century B.C.E. The evidence for his missive comes to us only in Jewish sources, I Maccabees and Josephus, reason enough for suspicion.[22] Scholars, however, have manufactured a host of ingenious hypotheses in order to establish the authenticity of the letter. They include theories that the Spartans had read the Scriptures and were familiar with the narrative of Abraham, that they employed Aramaic-speaking scribes, even that they hoped, by flattering the Jews, to recruit Jewish soldiers to fill the depleted ranks of the Spartiatai![23] No need to engage in lengthy refutation of these ideas. The tale that Jews and Spartans were kinsmen is plainly a Jewish invention. That is clear enough from the language of the supposed letter sent by Areus, which contains the very Biblical phrase "Your cattle and property are ours, and ours are yours".[24] No Spartan would have expressed himself in that fashion.

If the Jews invented this correspondence, to what end? Concoction of a fictitious kinship of this sort has been described as "a ticket of admission to the Hel-

---

21 Plut. *Flam.* 12.6 – 7.
22 1 Macc. 12.20 – 23; Jos. *AJ* 12.225 – 227.
23 W. Wirgin, *Palestine Exploration Quarterly* 101 (1969) 15. See J. Goldstein, *I Maccabees* (New York, 1976) 455 – 460.
24 1 Macc. 12.23.

lenic club."[25] If that were the objective, however, one would expect that the putative ancestor of both peoples would be a Greek divinity or a Greek hero, hardly a Hebrew patriarch. The naming of Abraham as the common forefather makes it plain that, while the Jews claimed links with the Hellenic community, they were bringing the Greeks within their own traditions rather than subordinating themselves to Hellenism. This attitude emerges unmistakably from the tone of the fabricated correspondence between Jewish leaders and the Spartan royal house. The Hasmonean High Priest Jonathan writes to the Spartans, reassuring them that the Jews remember them in their sacrifices and their prayers, thereby securing for the Spartans the favor of the true God. And they add that they seek renewal of their relationship not because they have any need of the Spartans, for they (the Jews) have recently emerged victorious over all their enemies through the aid of Heaven, but only to reaffirm their friendship and brotherhood.[26] The Jews, in short, are the benefactors, not the beneficiaries. The assertion of their συγγένεια goes beyond declaring links between the Jewish and Hellenic worlds; it announces the primacy of the Jews.

A comparable tradition appears in Josephus and Eusebius, ascribed to an otherwise unknown writer, Cleodemus Malchus, probably of the 2nd century B.C.E.[27] There it is reported that among Abraham's many children were three sons who joined with the Greek hero Herakles in his war on the Libyan giant Antaeus. After conclusion of that contest in which, according to Greek legend, Herakles conquered Antaeus and brought civilization to Libya, the Jewish version has the Greek hero marry the daughter of one of Abraham's sons, from whom the continent of Africa derived its name. A fascinating and illuminating tale. Whatever its provenance, it is plainly an *interpretatio Judaica*, not *Graeca*. The ultimate progenitor is again Abraham, given prime of place over Herakles. Hellenic tradition is neatly incorporated and appropriated: Herakles marries into the family, Abraham's sons share in his triumph, and one of them becomes the eponymous forebear of Africa. Once more, the kinship of Greeks and Jews places the Biblical patriarch in the center.

Nor are these the only allusions to connections between the two peoples that go back to remote antiquity. A presumed decree issued by the kingdom of Pergamum made reference to an ancient and warm friendship between Pergamenes and Jews that stems from the time of Abraham, "father of all Hebrews".[28] Here too the Hellenic people are put in the secondary category and the origins of

---

25 E. J. Bickerman, *The Jews in the Greek Age* (Cambridge, MA, 1988), 184.
26 1 Macc. 12.6 – 19.
27 Jos. *AJ* 1.239 – 241; Eus. *PE* 9.20.2 – 4.
28 Jos. *AJ* 14.247 – 255.

the relationship are defined in terms of the Biblical figure. A plethora of legends evidently made the rounds, a product of learned speculation that imagined ancestral bonds. One might cite, for instance, the conjecture that Jews derived from the island of Crete, an idea prompted by the similarity of the name *Judaei* with that of the *Idaei*, the tribe located near the Cretan mountain Ida. Or the theory that identified Jews with the nation of the Solymoi, a Lycian people celebrated in the Homeric epics, an identification suggested by the Jewish capital Hierosolyma (Jerusalem).[29]

In a somewhat different category, various attractive fables placed Jews in conjunction with prominent rulers of the Hellenistic world. In each case the story sets the Jews themselves in the most favorable light.

Perhaps the most memorable of such tales involves Alexander the Great. The Macedonian ruler, with the flower of his invincible army, marched in rage against Jerusalem because the Jews had maintained allegiance to Persia instead of switching to the Macedonian side. But the all-powerful Alexander was stopped dead in his tracks when the Jewish High Priest appeared, resplendent in blue and gold robes, a mitre on his head with a gold plate on which was inscribed the name of Jehovah. Thereupon the mighty Alexander prostrated himself before the Priest, declaring that the Jewish god was the great god who would lead him to victory over Persia. Alexander proceeded to sacrifice to Jehovah, to honor the Jewish priests, and to grant privileges to the land of the Jews.[30] The tale, of course, is a fiction; Alexander never went anywhere near Jerusalem. But it is a quite interesting fiction. The Jewish inventors did not concoct a tale that humiliated Alexander and rendered the Jews triumphant, as in many comparable stories. Alexander remains the great conqueror, but he turns from foe to friend. It is the Jewish god who guarantees him victory. The legend underscores a partnership between Jews and Greeks, with the Jewish faith authorizing the Macedonian conquest.

A more conventional tale of this variety occurs in III Maccabees. There the wicked Ptolemy IV attempted to force his way into the Holy of Holies in the Temple of Jerusalem, only to be felled by a stroke inflicted by God. Ptolemy then became more furious and instructed that all Jews in Egypt be rounded up and herded into the hippodrome in Alexandria, where they were to be trampled by five hundred intoxicated elephants. But Jewish prayers were heard again: two angels of the Lord suddenly materialized, and the elephants turned around to trample the soldiers of the king instead. Then, at last, Ptolemy saw the error of his ways,

---

29 Tac. *Hist.* 5.2.
30 Jos. *AJ* 11.317–339.

released the Jews, arranged a festival in their honor, and directed all his governors to assure their protection (III Macc. passim). This narrative plainly has a
sharper tone and a more hostile attitude toward Hellenistic rule than the
Alexander story. But the message is comparable: Jewish faith is vindicated
once again. The Hellenic king mends his ways, recognizes the magnitude of
the Jewish god, and becomes the protector of their community. Both tales acknowledge by implication a subordinate status for the Jews in the political
and military circumstances of the Hellenistic world—but a status to which the
rulers of that world pay respectful homage.

More telling still are the fictions that accommodate Jewish traditions to Hellenic culture. And, as one might expect, the Jewish contribution in these stories
takes central place. A noteworthy example exists in the fable composed by the
Egyptian-Jewish writer Artapanus in the 3rd or 2nd century B.C.E. It depicts
Moses not in the conventional mode as great lawgiver to the Israelites. Rather
he appears as author of most of the religious and cultural practices of other peoples, including the introduction of animal worship to the Egyptians and of circumcision to the Ethiopians. For the Greeks, according to Artapanus, Moses
was a revered figure, identified with the mythical Greek poet Mousaios, reckoned
as the teacher of Orpheus, and even made equivalent to Hermes in his capacity
as patron of literature and the arts.[31] So Moses emerges here as culture hero, a
source of inspiration to Hebrews, Greeks, and Egyptians alike.

The 2nd century Alexandrian Jew Aristobulus focused more pointedly upon
Hellenic culture and its putative Judaic roots. He had read widely in the works of
Greek authors—including some that they probably never wrote. And he repeatedly ascribed the wisdom and insights found therein to the Jewish lore that they
must have been familiar with. So, Plato found the source for his Laws in the Pentateuch, Pythagorean philosophy was an adaptation of Hebraic doctrine, Orpheus imitated Moses in his verses on the *Hieros Logos*, all Greek philosophy
with a monotheistic tinge derived from the Bible, and the Jewish reverence for
the Sabbath found its way into the verses of Homer and Hesiod.[32] Never mind
that the Septuagint was not composed until the Hellenistic period. Aristobulus
simply postulated some earlier unknown translation of the Pentateuch into
Greek, so as to have its doctrines available to Hellenic poets and philosophers
of the archaic and classical eras.[33] Once more the assimilation is not of Judaism
to Hellenism, but the other way around.

---

31 Eus. *PE* 9.8.1–2; Clement *Strom.* 1.154.2–3.
32 Eus. *PE* 7.32.16–18; 13.12.1–16.
33 Ibid., 13.12.1.

The reinterpretation of authentic statements and the invention of spurious utterances affords valuable insight into the motives of Jews learned in Hellenic literature and lore. Their activity goes beyond what is conventionally termed apologetic writing. This is no mere defensive posturing by a subordinate minority in an alien world. The Jews, to be sure, were in no position to challenge the political supremacy of Hellenic powers—nor did they do so. Indeed, many of the stories reaffirm that supremacy. But by selectively appropriating Hellenic culture, they redefined it in their own image, thus not only asserting their place in the larger community but also articulating their cultural identity in terms intelligible to that community.

On this broad level, therefore, Romans and Jews each gave their own spin to Hellenism. The cultivated elite among both peoples welcomed Hellenic traditions but reshaped them to sharpen their own identity and declare their own primacy. Two final illustrations can underscore the point.

First, from the Roman side. When that crusty old conservative, Cato the Elder, visited Athens, he came as a Roman officer in the campaign against Antiochus III. He delivered an address to the Athenian assembly, a brief and pointed speech in Latin, knowing full well that no one in the audience could understand a word of it. He then had a subordinate deliver a translation of that speech in Greek. The Greek version took twice as long to say the same thing. Cato thus exhibited the inferiority of Hellenic rhetoric to the forceful brevity of the Latin language. But he did more than that. He let it be known that he could have delivered the speech in Greek, had he wished to do so.[34] Whatever the truth of that claim, it emphasized that the Romans held the upper hand. Unlike his monolingual audience, so Cato implied, Romans had mastered both tongues, had the option of employing either, and chose the superior one. Rome's cultural confidence matched its military might.

Now, a final Jewish illustration, a quite irresistible one. As the story has it, a Ptolemaic army conducting a march to the Red Sea included a number of Jewish soldiers. Among them was a certain Jewish archer named Mosollamus. In the course of the march, the whole company halted because a bird was spotted overhead. The Greek seer who accompanied the army wished to observe its movements so as to be able to forecast what was in store. He proceeded to explain the rules that governed his divination: if the bird stays still, the army ought to wait; if it flies forward, the forces should advance; if it flies backward, the troops better retreat. When Mosollamus, the Jewish archer, heard this, he drew his bow and shot the bird dead. Of course, the Greeks were horrified, turned on Mosolla-

---

34 Plut. *Cat. Ma.* 12.4–5.

mus with fury, and demanded an explanation. "Look," he said, "if this bird was so smart and could predict the future, how come he didn't know I was going to shoot him?".[35] The setting of the story is authentic enough. Jewish soldiers served in the army of the superior power, the Ptolemaic rulers of Egypt, as participants in the larger Hellenistic enterprise. But the point of the tale, of course, lies elsewhere. The hard-headed, pragmatic Jew, like Cato the Elder, has gained familiarity with Greek practices—only to mock their fatuous superstition. The Jews have the upper hand not only in spirituality but even in street-smarts.

These diverse and miscellaneous examples share a common theme. In the heterogeneous society of the Hellenistic world, peoples strove to articulate their special qualities with reference to the dominant culture, but without succumbing to it. Indeed, it was precisely the ability to accommodate to that culture that supplied the tools whereby to express a distinct identity.

There is a lesson here for multicultural studies that hardly needs to be spelled out. A secure sense of one's own cultural identity depends upon engaging seriously with other cultures, gaining close familiarity with them, and perhaps even exploiting them to one's own advantage. The ancients did so all the time —or whenever they could. Ancient societies defined themselves by reference to "the other", but did so most effectively by expropriating "the other." That subject can stimulate some exciting research. And it will also play in the classroom—an extra dividend. Multiculturalism, in short, far from being a menace to the study of antiquity, is integral to it. This is not the periphery of our discipline but stands at the very heart of it. And it offers us as compelling a case as we can make, to administrators and to ourselves, for the enduring importance and the richness of our field.

---

35 Jos. *C. Ap.* 1.201–204.

2. Hellenistic Judaism

Alexander the Great burst like a thunderbolt upon the history of the Near East. Within a dozen years in the late fourth century B.C.E., he humbled the mighty Persian Empire, marching its length and breadth, defeating its armies, toppling its satraps, terminating its monarchy, and installing a Greek hegemony from the Hellespont to the Indus. It was a breathtaking achievement—and on more than just the military front. The conquests of Alexander provided a springboard for the expansion of Greek culture in the lands of the eastern Mediterranean. That world would never be quite the same again.

No direct confrontation occurred between the great Macedonian conqueror and the Jews of Palestine. Fanciful tales sprang up later in which Alexander paid homage to the high priest in Jerusalem and Yahweh sanctioned his subjugation of Persia. None of them has a basis in fact. Palestine was of small interest to the king who captured the great fortress of Tyre, then marched straight to Egypt and subsequently to Mesopotamia, on the way to the heartland of the Persian Empire. Judaea was spared—and largely ignored.

The long-term impact on Jewish culture, however, was momentous. Jews had hitherto lived under a Persian yoke, a light one and a relatively benign one. The centers of royal power lay at a great distance, in Susa and Persepolis, with little direct effect upon the society of the Jews. A major change occurred with the coming of the Greeks. Alexander's vast holdings splintered after his death, as his powerful marshals divided and fought fiercely over the territories he had claimed. In the new configurations of the Hellenistic kingdoms, Greco-Macedonian dynasts held sway, and Hellenism became the culture of the ruling class in the major cities and states, both old and new, of the Near East—in places like Sardis and Ephesus, Alexandria and Antioch, in Babylon, Tyre, and Sidon, and in the coastal communities of Palestine.

The political constellation affected Jews everywhere. Palestine itself came under the control of the Ptolemies of Egypt for about a century after Alexander's death, and, when power shifted in the region, the land entered the hegemony of the Seleucid monarchs of Syria from the beginning of the second century B.C.E. The Maccabean rebellion ushered in a Jewish dynasty, the Hasmonaeans, followed by the house of Herod, who provided ostensibly indigenous rule. But the Hasmonaeans, in fact, governed only under the shadow of the Seleucids, and the Herodians under the shadow (sometimes more than the shadow) of Rome. The Hellenistic monarchies continued to reckon Palestine within their sphere of influence, and Rome later undertook to supply its own governors of the region. In the Diaspora, Jews everywhere lived in circumstances where pagan power held sway. Through most of the third and second centuries B.C.E., the Ptolemies exercised authority in Egypt and usually in Cyprus and Cyrene; the Seleucids held power in Syria, Phoenicia, and at least nominally in the lands across the Euphrates; the Attalids ruled in Pergamum and extended their influence elsewhere in Asia Minor where a diversity of dynasts struggled for control; and in Greece itself contending forces from Macedon and various states and federations kept the Jews of their region in a politically subordinate position. The subsequent dominance of Rome in the eastern Mediterranean, beginning in the late second century B.C.E., brought Jews, among others, into direct contact with Roman governors, officialdom, and imperial power.

The Jewish Diaspora, to be sure, did not await Alexander. Jews had certainly found their way to Syria, to Egypt, and to the lands of the Tigris and Euphrates well before. But the arrival of the Greeks proved to be an irresistible magnet. Jews migrated to the new settlements and expanded communities in substantial numbers. A Greek diaspora had brought the Jewish one in its wake. Within a few generations, Jews had installed themselves in an astonishing array of places all around the Mediterranean and beyond. If one can believe the author of 1 Maccabees, composed in the late second century B.C.E., they could be found not only in Syria, Egypt, the Parthian empire, and throughout the cities and principalities of Asia Minor, but even in Greece itself, in various islands of the Aegean, and in Crete, Cyprus, and Cyrene.[1] This remarkable dispersal impressed itself even upon pagan writers like Strabo, who commented that the Jewish people by his day (late first century B.C.E.) had moved into almost every city and that hardly a place remained where they had not made their presence felt.[2]

The consequences are readily discernible. Jews became exposed to and thoroughly engaged with the Greek culture that prevailed in the various communities in which they settled. And not only in the Diaspora. Greek towns sprang up in Palestine itself, from Akko to Gaza on the Mediterranean coast, in the Lower Galilee, and in various sites on both sides of the Jordan.[3] Hence, even the Jews of Judaea could not and did not isolate themselves altogether from the pervasive aura of Hellenism. For many Jews, especially in the Diaspora, the close contact with the institutions, language, literature, art, and traditions of Hellas reached the point where they lost touch with Hebrew itself. The translation of the Hebrew Bible into Greek, probably in Alexandria sometime in the third or second century B.C.E., reflects the needs of Jews settled abroad for several generations for whom

---

1 1 Macc. 15:22 – 23.
2 Strabo, in Jos., *A. J.*, 14:115.
3 See, e.g., V. Tcherikover, *Hellenistic Civilization and the Jews* (New York, 1970), 90 – 116.

Greek was the primary, perhaps sole, language and for some of whom education gave greater familiarity with Plato than with Moses. The Jewish involvement with Hellenism in the period from Alexander the Great to the destruction of the Second Temple in 70 C.E. was a central, even a defining, characteristic.

But the involvement is rife with ambiguities. Indeed, ambiguity adheres to the term "Hellenism" itself. No pure strain of Greek culture, whatever that might be even in principle, confronted the Jews of Palestine or the Diaspora. Transplanted Greek communities mingled with ancient Phoenician traditions on the Levantine coast, with powerful Egyptian elements in Alexandria, with enduring Mesopotamian institutions in Babylon, and with a complex mixture of societies in Anatolia. The Greek culture with which Jews came into contact comprised a mongrel entity—or rather entities, with a different blend in each location of the Mediterranean. The convenient term "Hellenistic" signifies complex amalgamations in the Near East in which the Greek ingredient was a conspicuous presence rather than a monopoly.

"Judaism," it need hardly be said, is at least as complex and elastic a term. The institution defies uniform definition. And changes over time, as in all religions, render any effort to capture its essence at a particular moment highly problematic. "Hellenistic Judaism" must have experienced considerable diversity, quite distinct in Alexandria, Antioch, Babylon, Ephesus, Cyrene, and Jerusalem. Simplistic formulations once in favor are now obsolete. We can no longer contrast "Palestinian Judaism" as the unadulterated form of the ancestral faith with "Hellenistic Judaism" as the Diaspora variety that diluted antique practices with alien imports. Hellenism existed in Palestine—and the Jews of the Diaspora still held to their heritage. Each individual area struck its balance differently and experienced its own peculiar level of mixture. It is essential to emphasize that Jews were not obliged to choose between succumbing to or resisting Hellenism. Nor should one imagine a conscious dilemma whereby they had to decide how far to lean in one direction or another, how much Hellenism was acceptable before they compromised the faith, or at what point on the spectrum between apostasy and piety they could comfortably locate themselves.

A different conception is called for. Many Diaspora Jews and even some dwelling in Hellenistic cities of Palestine after a generation or two were already confirmed Greek speakers and integrated members of communities governed by pagan practices and institutions. They did not confront daily decisions on the degree of assimilation or acculturation. They had long since become part of a Hellenic environment that they could take as a given. But their Judaism remained intact. What they needed was a means of defining and expressing their singularity within that milieu, the special characteristics that made them both integral to the community and true to their heritage.

Jewish Creations in Greek Genres

How does one locate the boundaries between the cultures? The issue put in that form is itself problematic. The very metaphor of boundaries, even permeable boundaries, begs the question. The Jews, it might better be said, redefined their heritage in the terms of Hellenistic culture itself. They engaged actively with the traditions of Hellas, adapting genres and transforming legends to articulate their own legacy in modes congenial to a Hellenistic setting. At the same time, they recreated their past, retold stories in different shapes, and amplified the scriptural corpus itself through the medium of the Greek language and Greek literary forms. The challenge for the Jews was not how to surmount barriers or cross boundaries. In a world where Hellenic culture held an ascendant position, they strove to present Judaic traditions and express their own self-definition through the media of the Greeks—and to make those media their own.

This refashioning can be illustrated in a number of ways. Tragic drama is perhaps the quintessential Greek medium. This did not render it off-limits to the Jews. Quite the contrary. In one instance at least (and it can hardly be the only one), a Jewish writer named Ezekiel tried his hand in that genre, probably in the second century B.C.E. Working within the tradition of classical tragedy, influenced particularly by the plays of Aeschylus and Euripides, Ezekiel produced his own dramas, one of which—or at least a substantial portion of one—survives. The theme, however, is not drawn from Greek mythology or from the titanic clashes within Greek royal houses of distant and legendary antiquity. Ezekiel turned instead to material from his own people's legacy. The extant text, the *Exagoge*, is based on the story of Moses leading the Israelites out of Egypt. The choice of that tale clearly indicates an appeal to pride in national history and tradition produced in the most characteristically Hellenic mode.[4]

Ezekiel hewed closely to the narrative line contained in the Book of Exodus. He cast it in different form, of course, employing the conventions of the Greek

---

4 The surviving fragments of the play were preserved by the first-century-B.C.E. pagan writer Alexander Polyhistor and transmitted by the Church fathers Clement and Eusebius. Ezekiel wrote a number of tragedies on Jewish themes, as we know from Clement, *Stromata* 1.155.1. One may conveniently consult the fragments in the fine studies by H. Jacobson, *The Exagoge of Ezekiel* (Cambridge, Engl., 1983), 50–67, and C. Holladay, *Fragments from Hellenistic Jewish Authors: Vol. II: The Poets* (Atlanta, Ga., 1989), 344–405. The date and provenance of the work can be determined only within broad limits. Ezekiel employed the Septuagint version of the Pentateuch, as his language makes clear, and he must precede Alexander Polyhistor—thus sometime between the later third and early first centuries. The subject matter of the *Exagoge* does not suffice to fix the place of composition in Alexandria or elsewhere in Egypt. On these issues, see Holladay, *Fragments*, 2:308–13, with references to earlier literature.

theater, writing monologues and dialogues, keeping the battle scenes and the gore offstage, even bringing on the trusty messenger's speech to summarize events that transpired between dramatic episodes. But his tale diverges little from the biblical version. It was not Ezekiel's purpose to raise any doubts about the authority or adequacy of the Scriptures. The Septuagint, the Greek version of the Hebrew Bible, served as his text, and he conveyed its narrative faithfully. But Ezekiel was not wedded to it irrevocably. In a few key instances, he added new material to the mix. And they supply important clues to the tragedian's intent.

One item in particular merits special notice. Ezekiel inserted a remarkable scene that has no biblical prototype. Moses, in dialogue with his father-in-law, reports a puzzling dream in which he had a vision of a great throne high upon a summit extending to the cleft of heaven. There a noble man sat with diadem and a great scepter, summoned Moses to him, handed him the scepter and diadem, and departed from the throne. From that spot Moses had a view of the whole earth, both below it and above the sky, and a multitude of stars fell on their knees. Moses' father-in-law provides a most heartening interpretation of the dream: it is a sign from God that Moses will lift up a great throne, will issue judgments, and will serve as guide to mortals; the vision of the whole world, things both below and beyond God's firmament, signifies that Moses will perceive what is, what has been, and what will be.[5] This striking passage corresponds to nothing in the Book of Exodus. Indeed, no other tale anywhere in literature ascribes a dream vision to Moses. Furthermore, the very idea of a dream by a Hebrew figure rendered intelligible by a non-Hebrew figure is unparalleled. Ezekiel plainly aimed to capture his readers' attention here.

Greek tragedy could supply precedents of a sort. Certainly Attic plays include dream visions in sufficient quantity. And some approximations can be found in the Bible: a few fortunate figures received visions of God in their dreams, and still fewer actually glimpsed a throne. But nothing is quite like the sight seen by Moses in *Exagoge*. Nowhere does God relinquish his seat to anyone else.

The creativity of Ezekiel should receive its due. In the Book of Numbers, God announces that, though he reveals himself to others in visions and dreams, he speaks to Moses directly, face to face, without enigmatic messages.[6] Ezekiel chose to ignore or sidestep that message. It seemed a small price to pay. The playwright had a powerful scene in mind: the forecast of Moses' future through a dramatic dream that gave him access to divinity. Ezekiel employed forms and

---

5 Ezekiel, in Eusebius, *Praeparatio Evangelica* [hereafter *PE*], 9.29.4–6.
6 Num. 12:6–8.

material drawn both from Greek literature and from Jewish traditions, but he shaped them to convey an original conception. The dramatist not only intensifies the grandeur of Moses but also reconceives Moses' relationship with God.

Moses encounters a "noble man" with scepter and diadem on the great throne that extends to Heaven. The image here plainly presents God as sovereign power, ruler of the universe. The celestial realm appears as analogous to royal governance on-earth. God beckons to Moses to approach the throne, then bids him sit upon it, hands over the scepter and diadem, and departs. The meaning can hardly be that God has relinquished universal dominion. Rather, Ezekiel directs attention to the analogy. Moses' ascension to the throne and acquisition of royal emblems signals his appointment as the Lord's surrogate in governing the affairs of men. That meaning is reinforced when Moses' father-in-law interprets the dream. His reference to the great throne, to the exercise of jurisdiction, and to the leadership of men had clear resonance to the contemporaries of Ezekiel. Moses' role as executor of God's will on earth, with absolute authority, is modeled on royal rule in the Hellenistic realms.

Ezekiel deftly combined familiar conventions with striking novelty to create a complex portrait. He nowhere disputes or denies the biblical account. But the admixture of the dream episode both magnifies the Moses figure and renders it more accessible to the dramatist's own society. He expressed the powers of the Hebrew prophets in terms that applied to Greek seers. And he draped Moses in the emblems of royal power that would carry direct relevance to those who lived in the era of the great monarchies. The author reinvents the position of Moses on the model of Hellenistic kingship while making him the model and precursor of Hellenistic kingship itself. God places Moses upon his own throne, a symbolic assignment of universal authority, to sit in judgment and be a guide for all mortals. Those lines have telling significance: they betoken the application of the Law as a pattern for all nations. The Israelite hero thus becomes a beacon for humankind, a representative of the divinity on earth, described in phraseology that struck responsive chords among Ezekiel's Hellenic or Hellenized compatriots.

The tragic poet held scriptural authority in awe. But that did not prevent him from occasionally improving upon it. His most inventive scenes gave heightened force to Jewish traditions by commingling them with features arising from Greek culture and society. God's elevation of Moses to glory signified a royal dominion familiar to Hellenistic readers and a universal message that Jews could claim as their own. Ezekiel had effectively commandeered a preeminent Greek genre and deployed it as a source of esteem for his Jewish readership.

Jewish writers also adapted another and even more venerable Greek medium: epic poetry. Extant fragments are scanty and tantalizing—but also informative and illuminating. Record survives of a second-century-B.C.E. epic poet named Theodotus, whose remaining verses treated the tale of the rape of Dinah by Shechem and the consequent destruction of the Shechemite city by Dinah's brothers Levi and Simeon, the sons of Jacob.[7] The poet had obviously imbibed Hellenic culture and enjoyed thorough familiarity with Homeric language and epic technique. But he took as his text, at least in the surviving lines, an episode recorded in Genesis 34.

The biblical account has Jacob return to Canaan, after his lengthy absence in the land of Laban, and reach the city of Shechem. His daughter Dinah wanders into the city, only to be seized and ravished by the like-named Shechem, son of the ruler, Hamor. The event sets matters rapidly in motion. Shechem may have been initially overcome by lust, but he soon aims to make an honest man of himself. He obtains the intercession of his father, who speaks to Jacob about arranging a wedding. Hamor indeed goes well beyond that initial request. He generously proposes a host of marriage alliances between Jacob's people and his own, and makes his land and possessions available to the newcomers. The sons of Jacob, however, outraged at the defilement of Dinah, plot deception and revenge. They consent to the uniting of the peoples but only on condition that the Shechemites circumcise themselves, because intermarriage with the uncircumcised would be intolerable. Hamor and Shechem readily agree, and their example is swiftly followed; within a short time all the males in Shechem are circumcised. That provides the opportunity for Dinah's brothers. While the Shechemites still suffer the effects of the surgery, Levi and Simeon swoop down upon them, murder every male, loot the city, and carry off the women and children. The underhanded scheme and the ruthless butchering of a compliant people sits ill with Jacob. He rebukes his sons for making him vulnerable to the hostility of his neighbors. And he never forgives them. On his deathbed, he curses Levi and Simeon for their resort to the sword and their reckless yielding to animus and anger.[8] The tale hardly casts the Israelites' actions in the best possible light.

Theodotus's version adheres to the basic narrative but turns it in quite a different direction.[9] Both his elaborations and his omissions set the events in contrasting colors. Theodotus kept his eye on the Genesis narrative throughout.

---

[7] The text is contained in Eus. *PE*, 9.22.1 – 11. It can be conveniently consulted in A.-M. Denis, *Fragmenta Pseudepigraphorum Quae Supersunt Graeca* (Leiden, 1970), 204 – 7; H. Lloyd-Jones and P. Parsons, *Supplementum Hellenisticum* (Berlin, 1983), 360 – 65; and Holladay, *Fragments*, 2:106 – 27, with translation. Theodotus's date and provenance remain uncertain. For a survey of modern opinions, see Holladay, *Fragments*, 2:68 – 72, with notes.

[8] Gen. 33:18 – 34:31, 49:5 – 7.

[9] Eus. *PE*, 9.22.1 – 11.

Nothing in his account stands in flagrant contradiction to it. But he felt free to embroider or suppress matters, thus giving a distinctive slant and allowing for an alternative meaning.

The epic poet blended Greek elements with the Hebrew legend. Theodotus identified Shechem's founder with the son of Hermes, a feature that linked the city's story to *ktisis* (colonial foundation) tales and Greek mythology.[10] And he has the divine impetus for the attack on Shechem delivered through an oracular forecast, in Hellenic fashion.[11] The pagan trimmings were plainly congenial to the auditors of Theodotus's epic rendition of the Scriptures.

More important divergences, however, lay elsewhere. The biblical tale casts a cloud on the Israelites. Shechem's act of rape, to be sure, is hardly exemplary conduct, nor is it condoned in Genesis. But the young man hastens to make amends; his father is magnanimous toward Jacob's people; and the Shechemite males unhesitatingly subject themselves to circumcision—a stunning display of neighborliness. Yet it earns them only massacre, pillage, and captivity, the result of deception and a sneak attack. Theodotus puts a different twist on the tale. God implants the thought of revenge in the minds of Simeon and Levi. And the Shechemites get what they deserve, because they are a godless and disreputable people, maimed by God to set them up for the slaughter by Jacob's sons. Theodotus leaves out any calculated ruse on the part of the Hebrews. Nor does he suggest that the Shechemites had circumcised themselves and were still recuperating when attacked—although Hamor did encourage them to do so. The poet also omits any reproach or dissent from Jacob. The retaliation for Dinah's disgrace goes unquestioned.

What significance do these changes bear? Theodotus's revisions of Genesis do not so much excoriate the Samaritans as exculpate the Hebrew forefathers. The alterations are subtle rather than radical. Theodotus forbears from demonizing the Shechemites. In the poem, Hamor receives Jacob in welcoming fashion and provides him with land—thus going one better than the biblical version, which has Jacob purchase the lot.[12] Hamor further graciously meets Jacob's conditions and undertakes to persuade his people to circumcise themselves. Theodotus holds close to the biblical text here.[13] He avoids contradiction or challenge, let alone any suggestion of undermining the authority of the Bible. The selective omission had greater effect. No hint of duplicity on the Israelites' part, no actual circumcision by the Shechemites, no attacks while they were disabled, and no

---

10 Ibid. 9.22.1.
11 Ibid. 9.22.8.
12 Gen. 33:18–20; Eus. *PE*, 9.22.4.
13 Gen. 34:18–23; Eus. *PE*, 9.22.5, 8.

censure by Jacob of his sons. This rendition smoothed out some rough spots in the Genesis narrative. Theodotus's tale nowhere contravened the Scriptures; it left the Shechemites' behavior ambiguous but cleared the Hebrew leaders of acting deceptively, passed over their internal friction, and set the outcome as the execution of the divine will. Even though the fragments are few, they exhibit the skill of a Jewish poet employing a Hellenic genre to refashion his own people's history.

Epic poetry evidently had an audience among Hellenistic Jews. At least one other writer composed in that mode: the poet Philo, of uncertain date, a few of whose verses have reached us, produced a poem of substantial size with the title "On Jerusalem."[14] What survives may constitute no more than a tiny fraction of the whole. The few extant lines treat only Abraham, Joseph, and the waters of Jerusalem. And even they are expressed in tortured language enveloped in studied obscurity, with a variety of arcane allusions.[15] But a number of the preserved verses suggest that Philo, like Theodotus, may have endeavored to enhance the luster of the patriarchs.

Philo's inflated vocabulary, however pompous and pretentious, could serve that purpose. He hails Abraham in words either invented or refashioned as "widely famed," "resplendent," and "abounding in lofty counsels." He applies to the patriarch some striking terms to arrest the attention even of highly cultivated Jews conversant with the epic language of Hellenic literature.[16] Joseph receives comparable elevation. Philo depicts him not only as prophetic interpreter of dreams but also as holder of the scepter on the thrones of Egypt, a man who discloses the secrets of fate in the stream of time.[17] His extravagant language was more than mere bombast. Like Theodotus, Philo employed the genre to expand upon Scripture.

The re-inscription of biblical legend in Hellenic form had multiple manifestations. Perhaps the most extraordinary, however, came in the romantic story *Joseph and Aseneth*. This tale moves in a realm quite distinct from those discussed above, that of novelistic fantasy. Genesis provides barely a pretext for this inven-

---

14 Text in Denis, *Fragmenta*, 203 – 4; Lloyd-Jones and Parsons, *Supplementum Hellenisticum*, 328 – 31; and Holladay, *Fragments*, 2: 234 – 45. A single reference survives to one other Jewish presumed practitioner of epic poetry: a certain Sosates described as the "Jewish Homer in Alexandria" (C. Frick, *Chronica Minora* [Leipzig, 1892], 278).
15 The most valuable treatments of Philo may be found in Y. Gutman, "Philo the Epic Poet," *Scripta Hierosolymitana* 1 (1954): 36 – 63, and the exhaustive notes of Holladay, *Fragments*, 2: 205 – 99.
16 Eus. *PE*, 9.20.1.
17 Ibid., 9.24.1.

tion. The Scriptures report only that Pharaoh gave to Joseph as his wife Aseneth, daughter of Potiphar the priest of On, and that she subsequently bore him two children.[18] All else is embellishment. And *Joseph and Aseneth* embellishes in style.

The genre of the work has evoked discussion and controversy. Noteworthy affinities exist with Greek romances like those of Chariton, Heliodorus, Achilles Tatius, or Xenophon of Ephesus. One can, to be sure, find differences and contrasts. The erotic features usually prominent in Greek novels are subordinated in the first part of *Joseph and Aseneth* and altogether absent in the second. Parallels can also be found in Jewish fiction of contemporary or near-contemporary eras, like Judith, Esther, and Tobit. The mutual interactions and influences cannot be traced. But there is little doubt that *Joseph and Aseneth* emerged in the literary climate that also produced and encompassed the Hellenic novel.[19]

A summary of the yarn would be apposite. Joseph, gathering grain in the course of his duties as Pharaoh's agricultural minister at the outset of seven plenteous years, reaches the territory of Heliopolis. There he encounters the eminent priest Pentephres and his beautiful 18-year-old daughter Aseneth. The maiden, however, like Puccini's Turandot, scorns all men and rudely rejects suitors from noble houses in Egypt and royal families elsewhere. Pentephres immediately proposes to betroth Aseneth to the righteous, powerful, and pious Joseph. But Aseneth recoils in anger: she will have nothing to do with one who is a stranger in the land, a shepherd's son from Canaan, sold as a slave and imprisoned as an adulterer. The arrogant girl will accept marriage only with the son of Pharaoh. When she spies Joseph from her bedroom window, however, Aseneth is smitten—and overcome with self-reproach. Joseph in turn has his own reasons for reluctance. He first fears that Aseneth is yet another predatory female determined to bed him, like Potiphar's wife and a host of others. And then he recoils from Pentephres' arrangement on other grounds. The purist devotee of a sole deity will have no congress of any kind with an idolatress. Aseneth will have to mend her ways and acknowledge the true god.[20]

---

18 Gen. 41:45, 50–52, 46:20.
19 On *Joseph and Aseneth* as a Hellenistic romance, see M. Philonenko, *Joseph et Aséneth* (Leiden, 1968), 43–47; S. West, "Joseph and Aseneth: A Neglected Greek Romance" (1974): 71–77; and C. Burchard, *"Joseph et Aséneth: Questions actuelles,"* in W.C. van Unnik, ed., La *littérature juive entre Tenach et Mischna* (Leiden, 1974), 84–96. For parallels with Jewish fiction, see C. Burchard, *Untersuchungen zur Joseph und Asenath* (Tubingen, 1965), 106–7. See also L.M. Wills, *The Jewish Novel in the Ancient World* (Ithaca, N.Y., 1995), 170–84.
20 *Jos. Asen.,* 1–8.

The maiden turns her religious life around at a stroke. Much weeping and wailing ensue as she repents of former heresies, removed all the idols from her home, and falls to fasting and mourning, self-flagellation and humiliation, uttering desperate prayers to her newly found god, seeking forgiveness for past sins and rescue from the fury of spurned divinities. Aseneth's prayers are answered. An angel of the Lord materializes, offers her absolution, and bids her prepare for a wedding. Pharaoh himself presides over the ceremonies, places crowns on the heads of the couple, and sponsors a spectacular banquet that lasts for seven days. The marriage is consummated, and Aseneth subsequently produces two sons as Joseph's legacy.[21]

The happy ending, however, has not yet come. A second part of the tale, quite different from the love story, moves the narrative in a new direction. Internal friction shows itself both in the Hebrew patriarch's household and in that of Pharaoh. Joseph's brothers Simeon and Levi take joy in the company of Aseneth, while other brothers feel only envy and hostility. Further, Pharaoh's son determines to take her by foul means enlisting certain of the brothers in his nefarious enterprise. They lead Egyptian armed men in an ambush of Aseneth and her entourage, and plots are hatched to murder Joseph and his sons, while the heir to the Egyptian throne prepares to assassinate his own father. All the schemes, of course, are foiled. Benjamin, now a strapping lad of 18, protects Aseneth and launches 50 stones, each of which fells an Egyptian, including Pharaoh's offspring. His brothers wipe out the remaining foes. And when the wicked brothers make a final effort to slay Benjamin and Aseneth, their swords fall miraculously to the ground and dissolve into ashes. Aseneth then intervenes to urge forgiveness and concord. The peace-loving Levi stays Benjamin's hand when he attempts to finish off Pharaoh's helpless son. In gratitude, Pharaoh prostrates himself before Levi. The aging, ailing ruler subsequently turns his kingdom over to Joseph, bestowing upon him the diadem that signals royal authority. And Joseph goes on to reign as monarch of Egypt for 48 years.[22]

So ends the narrative, an agreeable and entertaining one. In fact, it consists of two narratives, a love story followed by air adventure tale, the two only loosely connected. The work has generated immense discussion, most of it concerned with language, date provenance, genre, and audience of the text.[23] We focus here on a different matter of broader consequence: the relation between Jew and gentile in the Diaspora. An initial impression might suggest that the tale

---

21 Ibid., 9–21.

22 Ibid., 22–29.

23 See the thorough and analytic review of the scholarship by R. D. Chesnutt, *From Death to Life: Conversion in Joseph and Aseneth* (Sheffield, Engl., 1995), 20–93.

pits the two cultures against one another. Joseph's insistence upon the purity of the faith and the pollution of idolatry, Aseneth's abject debasement and thorough break with her past to achieve absolution, the rigorous separation of Hebrews and Egyptians, and the favor of God supporting the faithful against the idol worshippers all seem to suggest a stark dichotomy between the forces of good and evil. But the breakdown is not so simple and the polarity not so sharp. Friction exists after all within each of the two communities. Joseph's brothers engage in potentially murderous activities against one another, and Pharaoh's son plots the assassination of the king. The fact that the wedding of Joseph and Aseneth takes place under the auspices of Pharaoh, who had not himself become a convert, holds central symbolic significance. The enemies of the faithful were forgiven, harmony and reconciliation followed, and the gentile ruler presided over the union of the Hebrew patriarch and the daughter of an Egyptian priest. The fable plainly promotes concord between the communities. Equally important, it asserts the superiority of Jewish traditions and morality —even against some Jews themselves.

Joseph exudes power and authority, more strikingly in this work than in Genesis or any other Hellenistic elaboration. The author of Joseph and Aseneth introduces Pentephres as chief of all satraps and grandees in the realm.[24] Yet, when he learns of Joseph's imminent visit, he is beside himself with excitement and goes to every length in preparing his household to receive so eminent a guest —one to whom he refers as "powerful man of God." Pentephres breathlessly describes Joseph to his daughter as ruler of all the land of Egypt and Pharaoh's appointee as all-powerful governor.[25] Joseph then enters the gates of his host's estate in a royal chariot, resplendent in purple robes and a gold crown with precious stones. Pentephres and his entire family hasten to prostrate themselves. The text could not make plainer the fact that, no matter how lofty was the position of Pentephres in the court and in the realm, he was far below the station of Joseph the Jew.[26] His crown radiated with 12 golden rays, emblematic of a sun god.[27] Aseneth's prayer to the Lord describes Joseph, as beautiful, wise—and powerful.[28] Joseph himself emphasizes his stature by dismissing Pentephres' offer to provide a wedding banquet. He would have none other than Pharaoh perform that task.[29] At the conclusion of the narrative, the dying Pharaoh pres-

---

24 *Jos. Asen.*, 1:4.
25 Ibid., 3:1–6, 4:8; cf. 20:7.
26 Ibid., 5:4–10.
27 Ibid., 6:2; cf. 5:6.
28 Ibid., 13:11, 18:1–2, 21:21.
29 Ibid., 20:6–21:5.

ents him with the diadem, and Joseph reigns as king of Egypt for five decades.[30] This goes well beyond the biblical tale and probably beyond any subsequent Hellenistic version of it.

The superiority of the Hebrews, their character, faith, and traditions, constitutes a central theme of the work. Joseph's contemptuous refusal to have a meal with Egyptians deliberately reverses the biblical passage that has the Egyptians shun any table occupied by Hebrews.[31] Aseneth's smashing of idols and her abject submission to the Lord accentuate the inferiority of her native religion. Pharaoh makes obeisance to Joseph's god when he conducts the wedding ceremony.[32] The second segment of the narrative demonstrates that the authority of the Hebrews is physical as well as spiritual. Pharaoh's son acknowledges that they are powerful men, beyond all others on the face of the earth.[33] And, in a climactic scene, Pharaoh descends from the throne to prostrate himself before Levi, who had spared his defeated son.[34] The harmonious relationship between Jews and gentiles stands at the core of the tale, but it is achieved only through the Egyptians' affirmation of the Hebrews' distinctiveness. This novel, therefore, fits a pattern that can be discerned again and again. Jews appropriated a genre familiar in the Hellenic cultural world, crossed conventional boundaries, underscored commonalties, but reiterated the special eminence they claimed for themselves.

Jewish writers in Greek entered still another realm preeminently associated with the Hellenic achievement: historiography. Here again, as in other modes, they utilized the conventions to present or to expand upon biblical material. They had no desire to compete with Greeks in recording the exploits of other peoples—let alone of the Greeks themselves. But they saw the virtue of borrowing the methodology to reproduce their own past.

A certain Demetrius, saw the advantages. He is one of the first Hellenistic Jews, perhaps the first (around the late third century B.C.E.), to venture into the arena of the historians. He is frequently called "Demetrius the Chronographer," a somewhat unfair label. His interest in chronological matters is clear enough. But the extant fragments of his work evince broader concerns.[35]

---

30 Ibid., 29:10–11.
31 Ibid., 7:1; Gen. 43:32.
32 *Jos. Asen.*, 21:4.
33 Ibid., 23:3; cf. 24:7.
34 Ibid., 29:5–7.
35 The most fundamental and thorough study of Demetrius is in J. Freudenthal, *Alexander Polyhistor* (Breslau, 1875), 35–82. The fragments can be usefully consulted in C. R. Holladay, *Fragments from Hellenistic Jewish Authors: Vol. I: Historians* (Chico, Calif., 1983), 51–91, with Holladay's valuable introduction and notes. See also the discussion by G. E. Sterling, *Historiography*

Demetrius composed an account, historical in form, that treated material in Genesis and Exodus. Three fragments at least, perhaps as many as five, attest to it. A sixth is ascribed to a work entitled *On the Kings in Judaea* and concerns subjects deriving from 2 Kings. Demetrius's attention was captured by problems and puzzles for which he could offer solutions. So, for instance, he addresses the issue of how Jacob managed to father 12 children in just seven years. The schedule is tight, but-Demetrius works out a timetable that includes all 12, produced by four different mothers.[36] Similarly, he confronts the question of why Joseph fed Benjamin five times what he offered his other brothers and bestowed four times the amount of clothing upon him. He supplies an answer: Leah had seven sons, Rachel but two hence Benjamin's five portions plus Joseph's two evened the balance. The disproportion appears in Genesis, but the explanation is Demetrius's.[37] When the historian moves on to Moses, he grapples with another puzzle: how is it that Moses could marry Zipporah, who like him traced her descent from Abraham, if Moses was six generations distant from the patriarch and Zipporah was seven? Demetrius's reconstruction answers the question: Isaac was already married when Abraham married Keturah and had a second son, who was thus of the same generation as the son of Isaac from whom Zipporah descended—a solution Demetrius evidently developed from a piecing together of biblical testimonies and some shrewd calculations.[38] And he also tackles a very different issue in the Exodus story: how did the Israelites, who left Egypt unarmed, manage to secure weapons, in the desert? An easy answer: they appropriated the arms of Egyptians who drowned in the sea. The conclusion plainly depends upon historical hypothesis, not any textual testimony.[39]

What ends were served by such exegesis? Demetrius's agenda surely had Jewish ends in view. That he was himself a Jew can hardly be questioned. Gentiles with an interest in the minutiae of biblical chronology or a concern about the disproportionate share meted out by Joseph to Benjamin would be rare birds indeed. But it is hard to detect, any apologetic purposes here. The narrative is sober, dry, and colorless. No hint of polemic exists in Demetrius's austere renditions, no embellishments of character, no syncretistic transformation of biblical personages into figures of universal significance. The exercise has a starkly academic quality. Demetrius may well have imbibed the exacting principles of

---

and Self-Definition: Josephos, Luke-Acts, and Apologetic Historiography (Leiden, 1992), 153 – 67, with excellent bibliography.

36 Eus. *PE*, 9.21.3 – 5.

37 Ibid., 9.21.14 – 15; Gen. 43:34, 45:22.

38 Eus. *PE*, 9.21.1 – 3.

39 Ibid., 9.29.16; cf. Exod. 13:18.

Alexandrian scholarship and put the techniques of Greek learning to the service of Jewish hermeneutics. Yet the extant fragments breathe hardly a hint of texts or traditions outside the Septuagint. Demetrius's narrative appears to be a rigorously internal one.

It does not follow that Demetrius provided exegesis for its own sake. His readership plainly consisted of Jews; why rewrite a historical narrative for those already familiar with it? In fact, Demetrius, as even the scanty fragments show, avoided a mere reproduction of Scripture. He abbreviated, streamlined, and modified the text—to the detriment of vividness and drama. He had other objectives. For Jews who read and spoke Greek, especially those attracted by Hellenic rationalism and critical inquiry, the Bible presented some vexing questions: inconsistencies, chronological disparities, and historical perplexities. Demetrius took up the tangles, reduced narrative to bare bones, assembled chronological data, straightened out genealogies, and supplied explanations for peculiar deeds and events. His work or works, therefore, offered reassurance on the reliability of the Scriptures. Demetrius engaged in ratiocination, not apologia. Nor did he offer an alternative to the biblical narrative. The authority of that narrative was taken for granted by the historian for whom it was the sole source of his reconstruction. He appealed to a sophisticated Jewish readership that posed tough questions but also sought edification. Demetritis's rewriting may have come at the cost of aesthetic quality and dramatic power. But it reinforced confidence in the tradition. Demetrius adapted the mode of Hellenic historiography to corroborate the record of his nation's past.

A more venturesome effort came from the pen of another Jewish historical writer, Eupolemus, who in the second century B.C.E. also composed a work entitled *On the Kings in Judaea*. Its scope extended beyond the limits suggested by the title, because even the scanty fragments include comments on Moses. The principal focus, however, evidently rested upon the era of the monarchy, at least to the inception of the Exile.[40]

Eupolemus took some interesting liberties in his narrative of David and Solomon. He records, for instance, a surprising string of military successes for King David. In his compressed account, David subdues Syrians dwelling along the Euphrates and the area of Commagene, Assyrians in Galadene, and Phoenicians; he further campaigns against Idumaeans, Ammonites, Moabites, Ituraeans, Nabataeans, and Nabdaeans. He then takes up arms once more against Souron the

---

40 For treatments of Eupolemus, see B. Z. Wacholder, *Eupolemus: A Study of Judaeo-Greek Literature* (Cincinnati, 1974); Holladay, *Fragments*, 1: 93–156; Sterling, *Historiography and Self-Definition*, 207–22.

king of Tyre and Phoenicia, makes the people tributary to the Jews, and frames a pact of friendship with Vaphres, the ruler of Egypt.[41] Questions arise about virtually every name in the text—not to mention a glaring omission: David's renowned conquest of the Philistines. Eupolemus departs drastically from the biblical narrative. The king's exploits in 2 Samuel include only a small portion of these victories. The Hellenistic historian extends David's territorial advance well beyond the scriptural testimony.[42] His conquests extend to the Taurus range in the north, the Euphrates in the east, and the Gulf of Aqaba in the south. Eupolemus takes a marked departure also in his treatment of Solomon. An exchange of correspondence between Solomon and Vaphres of Egypt appears in the text—a sheer invention. Solomon requests that Vaphres supply men to assist in the completion of his new temple, and the pharaoh responds with deference. He addresses Solomon as "great king," reports his joy at Solomon's accession, and expresses readiness to send workers from various parts of his realm.[43] The mutual messages are polite and cordial, drawing upon the Hellenistic conventions of royal correspondence. But, although Eupolemus takes care to affirm the independence and pride of the pharaoh, Solomon's ascendancy is clear and unequivocal.

Eupolemus's vision pierced beyond partisan politics and current events. The exaltation of Solomon through an ascendant relationship to pharaonic Egypt had wider significance. Vaphres not only acknowledges Solomon's superiority but even pays homage to the Israelite god.[44] The historian unhesitatingly "improved upon" the biblical account, depicting the ancient kingdom, at the time in which its sacred shrine was created, exercising widespread authority accepted even by the ruler of Egypt. Eupolemus may not have expected his Jewish readers to take the account literally, but it gave them the sense of a grand heritage, of a nation whose impressive history both reflected divine favor and earned the approbation of the great powers. For the Jews of Palestine and the Diaspora, that pride in their past buoyed the spirit and uplifted perceptions of national identity.

The fragment of Eupolemus on Solomon concludes in remarkable fashion. After the completion of the Temple, the king magnanimously restores the Egyp-

---

41 Eus. *PE,* 9.30.3 – 4.
42 The narratives of David's victories and annexations appear in 2 Samuel 5:17 – 25. 8:1 – 14, 10:6 – 19. Souron the king of Tyre, represented as a victim of David, is obviously equivalent to the biblical Hiram with whom David enjoyed a positive and productive association (2 Sam. 5:11). The Egyptian Vaphres has a place in the pharaonic royal genealogy but long after, any putative date for David.
43 Eus. *PE,* 9.31.1, 9.32.1.
44 Ibid., 9.32.1.

tian and Phoenician craftsmen to their native lands with enormous severance pay, dispatches lavish gifts to Vaphres, and to Souron of Phoenicia he sends a golden column, set up at Tyre in the temple of Zeus.[45] Here once more Eupolemus supplies details for which no scriptural authority exists, employing the occasion to embellish the wealth, power, and generosity of Solomon. The final item, however, deserves special notice. Would the devout Solomon, having just completed the most monumental act of piety, actually send a pillar of gold to stand in a pagan temple? No need for tortured explanations here. The Bible itself records Solomon's penchant for foreign wives and for foreign gods. Among the divinities whom he honored was Astarte, the goddess of the Sidonians.[46] Eupolemus simply pursued the point a step further: Solomon enabled the Phoenician king to honor Zeus with a handsome offering. The implications of this notice deserve emphasis. Eupolemus saw no inconsistency in presenting Solomon both as a dedicated devotee of the Lord and as a patron of foreign princes who honored alien cults. This is not "syncretism," as some have characterized it. Rather, it highlights Jewish superiority in the spiritual and material spheres. Solomon requisitioned the manpower of other kingdoms to erect his magnificent structure to the supreme deity; he could in turn take responsibility for subsidizing the worship of his compliant neighbors.[47] That theme supplies a leitmotif for Jewish depiction of ancestral achievements that extended even to the enhancement of foreign cultures. The Jews had successfully enlisted the craft of historiography to augment the accomplishments of their past.

Another form of Greek learning comes in for modification and manipulation by a very different Jewish text. *The Letter of Aristeas*, composed probably in the second century B.C.E., may be the most famous surviving product of Hellenistic Judaism apart from the Septuagint—its fame due in no small part to the fact that it recounts the creation of the Septuagint itself. The text describes the decision of Ptolemy II to have the Hebrew Bible rendered into Greek and added to the shelves of the library in Alexandria, the negotiations with the high priest in Jerusalem to send the most learned sages to Egypt to produce the translation, their collaborative work, and the end product that was so warmly received by Ptolemy and the Alexandrian Jews.[48] The tale, of course, should not be confused with his-

---

45 Ibid., 9.34.18.

46 1 Kgs 11:1–6.

47 A similar posture was taken later by King Herod, both rebuilder of the Temple and subsidizer of pagan shrines.

48 Among the more useful editions or commentaries, see R. Tramontano, *La Lettera di Aristea a Filocrate* (Naples, 1931); M. Hadas, *Aristeas to Philocrates* (New York, 1951); A. Pelletier, *Lettre d'Aristée à Philocrate* (Paris, 1962); and N. Meisner, *Jüdische Schriften aus hellenistisch-römischer*

tory. It is hardly likely that Ptolemy II marshaled the resources, commissioned the scholars, and financed the elaborate translation of the Books of Moses just to add some volumes to the royal library. That Hellenistic Alexandria was the site for a rendition of the Torah in Greek we may well believe. As late as the time of Philo, in the first century C.E., Egyptian Jews still celebrated an annual festival on the island of Pharos to mark the completion of that task.[49] The needs of Greek-speaking Jews who had lost command-of or even contact with Hebrew surely motivated the project to provide a Greek version for liturgical or instructional purposes or even for private worship. But little else in the *Letter of Aristeas* commands confidence as history. The yarn spun by its author is largely creative fiction.

The story of the translation, however, though central to the narrative, actually forms only a small part of it. For our purposes, another portion of the text, indeed a healthy chunk of it, holds special interest. When the Jewish elders, selected for their profound learning in both Hebrew and Greek literature, arrive in Alexandria, Ptolemy orders an elaborate welcome: an extended symposium, seven full days of formal banquets—all served with kosher food. In the course of this drawn-out entertainment, the king puts a different question to each of his guests, most of the questions concerning how best to govern a kingdom and to conduct one's life. Each of the sages responds promptly, includes a reference to God as principal ingredient in the answer, and receives warm compliments from Ptolemy, who is awestruck by their acumen.[50]

What is one to make of this? Ptolemy II, as portrayed by "Aristeas," is in control throughout: his power and authority go unquestioned. He issues the orders to write to the high priest and get the project under way.[51] It is his decision to have the Hebrew Scriptures translated into Greek, that he might add them to his library.[52] He even orders the kosher meal for his guests and partakes of it as well, a gesture of his good nature, but also of his authority, the entire banquet orchestrated at his behest.[53] The dependence of the Jews upon royal power is unequivocally acknowledged. This is not a subversive document.

Zeit, vol. 2 (Gütersloh, Germany, 1973), 1, 35–87. A general bibliography is in E. Schürer, *The History of the Jewish People in the Age of Jesus Christ,* rev. ed. by G. Vermes, F. Millar, and M. Goodman (Edinburgh, 1986), vol. 3.1, 685–87.
49 Philo, *Mos.,* 2:41.
50 *Let. Aris.,* 187–294.
51 Ibid., 11.
52 Ibid., 38.
53 Ibid., 181.

The *Letter of Aristeas* is thoroughly Hellenic in character, a fact of which the reader is repeatedly reminded. Greek men of learning and culture make an appearance or are referred to in the treatise. Even the Jewish high priest is described in terms that evoke a cultivated Hellenic aristocrat.[54] The scholars whom he sends to Alexandria not only command Greek as well as Jewish learning but express the noblest Hellenic ideal of striving for the "middle way."[55] The symposium in which the Jerusalemite sages are interrogated, of course, constitutes a fully Greek setting. And most of the sages respond with answers familiar from Greek philosophy or political theory—for example, they speak of the duty of the king to exercise restraint and honor justice; the definition of philosophy as reasoning well for every contingency, resisting impulses, and controlling the passions; and the designation of injustice as the greatest evil.[56] "Aristeas" has the high priest himself speak like a Greek philosopher.[57] The treatise plainly portrays Jews as comfortable in a Hellenic setting, attuned to Greek customs and modes of thought, and content under the protection of a Hellenistic monarch.

But to leave it at that is to miss the main message. The table talk of the symposium has a clear and unmistakable point: the superior wisdom of the Jews. Their representatives answer every question unhesitatingly, exhibiting their mastery of precepts familiar to the Greeks but incorporating in each response a reference to God as ultimate authority. The replies offer little that is distinctively Jewish—or even very specific. The sages never mention Moses, the Law, the Scriptures, or any practices peculiarly linked to Judaism. Indeed, God often appears in mechanical, even irrelevant fashion. The intellectual context is strictly philosophical, not at all theological—and rather superficial philosophy at that.[58] What matters is that the Jewish elders impress the king, over and over again. He commends every statement made, never moving from one interlocutor to the next without complimenting the speaker. The point of the episode, of course, is that the biblical scholars display an insight eclipsing anything that could be mustered by Greek philosophers. Ptolemy acknowledges it explicitly: the Jewish elders stand out in virtue and discernment, because the foundation of their rea-

---

54 Ibid., 3.
55 Ibid., 122.
56 Ibid., 209, 211, 222–23, 256, 292.
57 Ibid., 128–70.
58 On the banquet and the dialogue, see O. Murray, "Aristeas and Ptolemaic Kingship," *Journal of Theological Studies* 18 (1967): 344–61. Cf. P. M. Fraser, *Ptolemaic Alexandria* (Oxford, 1972), 701–3, and F. Parente, "La lettera di Aristea come Fonte pen la storia del Giudaismo Alessandrino durante la prima meta del I secolo a. C.," *Annali della Scuola Normale Superiore di Pisa*, 2, no. 2: (1972): 546–63.

soning lies in God.[59] More tellingly, the Greek philosophers themselves admit that they cannot equal the Jews' sagacity. The whole presentation has more than a touch of tongue-in-cheek. The narrator concludes his account of the seven banquets with a final dig at the Hellenic philosophers. In his own voice he observes that the scholars from Jerusalem were obviously worthy of the highest admiration from him, from those present, and especially from the philosophers.[60] That was no innocent remark.

The treatise of "Aristeas" is a complex, multilayered, and occasionally entertaining piece of work. No single purpose drove its composition. The idea, prevalent in modern scholarship, that it promoted a synthesis between Judaism and Hellenism is inadequate. The narrative implies that Jews are fully at home in the world of Hellenic culture. The use of a fictive Greek as narrator and admirer of Judaism carries that implication clearly enough. But the message has a sharper point: not only have Jews digested Hellenic culture but they have also surmounted it. Just as other Jewish writers displayed mastery of the tragic or epic art form, of romantic fiction, and of historiography, employing those Hellenic genres to embellish Israelite exploits, so the author of *The Letter* exhibits his familiarity with philosophic precepts and conventions while concocting a scenario in which all the advantage goes to the Jews.

Whether the texts discussed above typify Jewish attitudes cannot be said with certainty. But they (and other instances that could readily be cited) do represent a significant segment thereof. And the message rings loud and clear. The notion of a barrier that had to be overcome between Jewish and Hellenistic cultures casts precisely the wrong image. The Jewish intellectuals who sought to rewrite their past and redefine their traditions grew up in Diaspora or even Palestinian communities suffused with Hellenism. For them it was their culture. Their ideas and concepts expressed themselves quite naturally in Greek forms. But this in no way compromised, diminished, or undermined their sense of Jewish identity. On the contrary, Jewish thinkers and writers showed little interest in the Trojan War, the house of Atreus, the labors of Heracles, the customs of the Scythians, or the love of Cupid and Psyche. They mobilized the Hellenic crafts of epic, tragedy, philosophy, romance, and historiography to reproduce the record of their own people, to convey their conventions, and to enhance their achievements.

---

59 *Let. Aris.*, 200.
60 Ibid., 200–201, 235, 296.

The Jewish Construction of Greek Culture and Ethnicity

The embrace of Hellenic culture, as we have seen, served to reinforce rather than to dilute a sense of Jewish identity. But the broader the embrace, the more urgent it became to foreground those characteristics that distinguished Jews from the gentiles in whose lands they lived and with whose world they needed to come to terms. The Jews, in short, needed to establish their own secure, place within a Hellenistic framework and to make it clear that they were not swallowed up by that prevailing cultural environment. The construct of Jewish identity, an ongoing, complex, and shifting process, was tightly bound up with the construct of Greek ethnicity—that is, the character, values, and beliefs of the Greek *ethnos* in Jewish eyes.

That these were constructs is inescapable. Although Jewish intellectuals could draw distinctions among Greek peoples, communities, and conventions, they frequently lapsed into broad characterizations and stereotypes. The reasons are obvious enough. They had a definite agenda. In some form or other, Jews had to confront—or to formulate—those Hellenic traits from which they wished to disassociate themselves and, at the same time, to account for those characteristics that they had themselves adopted.

Greeks regularly reckoned other people, including Jews, as *barbaroi* (barbarians): they did not speak Greek and hence were unintelligible. But the Jews could turn the tables. The author of the Second Book of Maccabees was a Hellenized Jew of the late second century B.C.E., a writer thoroughly steeped in the traditions of Greek historiography, who composed his work in Greek.[61] His topic, however, was the background, circumstances, and consequences of the brutal persecution of Jews by the Hellenistic monarch Antiochus IV Epiphanes. The Jews resisted and retaliated under Judas Maccabaeus. According to 2 Maccabees, they fought nobly on behalf of Judaism and, though few in number, ravaged the entire land and drove out the "barbarian hordes."[62] So the author, well versed in the conventions of the genre, employed the standard Hellenic designation for the alien—but applied it to the Hellenes themselves. And it was not the only such occasion.[63]

A whole range of texts discloses the drive of Hellenistic Jews to brand the Greeks as villainous, or ignorant aliens, thus to distinguish more dramatically

---

61 The work itself is an epitome of the now lost five-volume history of the Maccabees by Jason of Cyrene, plainly also a Hellenized Jew (2 Macc. 2:19–31). For a recent register of scholarship on 2 Maccabees, see Schürer, *History of the Jewish People*, vol. 3.1, 536–37.
62 2 Macc. 2:21.
63 2 Macc. 10:4; cf. 5:22.

the advantages of being a Jew. Apocalyptic literature served this purpose. The visions of Daniel, which received their current shape in the very era of the persecutions, speak in cryptic but unmistakable tones of the catastrophic evils brought by the rule of the Hellenic kingdom. The terrifying dream that paraded four huge beasts in succession represented the sequence of empires, the fourth the most fearsome of all, a dreadful monster with iron teeth and bronze claws that devoured and trampled all in its path. That portent signified the coming of the Greeks. The forecasts given to Daniel, however, promised a happy ending: triumph over the wicked, a divine intervention to sweep aside the brutal Hellenic empire and bring about an eternal kingdom under the sovereignty of the Most High.[64] The Greeks here embody the mightiest of empires—and the one destined for the mightiest fall.

That theme is picked up in the prophecies of the Third Sibylline Oracle. The Sibyl had venerable roots in pagan antiquity, but the surviving collection of pronouncements stems from Jewish and Christian compilers who recast them for their own ends. The contents represent the earliest portion, which is almost entirely the product of Jewish invention, and some parts of which at least date to the era of the Maccabees.[65] The text repeats in varied form the sequence of empires: representing the Greeks as impious and arrogant; forecasting internal rot; condemning the Greeks for overbearing behavior, the fostering of tyrannies, and moral failings; and predicting that Hellenic cities all over the Mediterranean would be crushed by a terrible divine wrath.[66]

The portrait is hardly less severe in the First Book of Maccabees. That work, extant now only in Greek, appeared first in Hebrew, the product of a strong supporter of the Hasmonaean dynasty; it was composed probably in the late second century B.C.E.[67] The book opens with a harsh assessment of Alexander the Great, an arrogant conqueror whose campaigns brought slaughter and devastation in their wake, and whose successors over the years delivered multiple miseries upon the earth.[68]

The stark contrast between Jew and Greek receives dramatic elaboration in the martyrologies recorded in 2 Maccabees. Under Antiochus Epiphanes, the elderly sage Eleazer resists to the death any compromise of Jewish practice, calmly

---

64 Dan. 2:31–45, 7:1–27, 8:1–26, 11:21–45, 12:1–3.
65 The chronology is complex and contested. A valuable recent treatment may be found in J. M. G. Barclay, *The Jews in the Mediterranean Diaspora* (Edinburgh, 1996), 216–25.
66 3 Sib.Or. 166–90, 202–4, 341–49, 381–400, 545–55, 638–45.
67 On the date, see Schürer, *History of the Jewish People*, vol. 3.1, 181, and J. Sievers, *The Hasmoneans and Their Supporters* (Atlanta, Ga., 1990), 3.
68 1 Macc. 1:1–4, 9, 43–44.

accepting his agonizing torture. The same courage is exhibited by the devout mother who witnessed proudly the savage execution of her seven sons and joins them herself in death—memorable testimony to Jewish faith and Hellenic barbarity.[69] The stories were retold many generations later, in a text preserved in some manuscripts of the Septuagint under the title of 4 Maccabees, but at a time when the fierce emotions of the Maccabean era were a distant memory. The torments inflicted upon Eleazer and the unnamed mother with her seven sons were described in exquisite detail. The work was composed in Greek, probably in the first century C.E., by a Jew trained not in history but in Greek philosophy. He employed the martyrologies to illustrate Stoic doctrines of the command of reason over the passions. The author, therefore, ironically appropriated the Hellenic medium to express commitment to the Torah by contrast with the irrationality and atrocities of the Greeks themselves.[70] The schema that pits Jews against Greeks, the latter standing outside the bounds of morality and humane behavior, persists in all these texts.

A comparably sharp contrast surfaces in a most unexpected place. The *Letter of Aristeas* generally exudes harmony and common objectives between the cultures. Yet all is not sweetness and light even here. Eleazer the High Priest, when he responds to queries by Greeks about the peculiar habits of the Jews, affirms in no uncertain terms that those who worship many gods engage in foolishness and self-deception. Eleazer declares that Moses, in his wisdom, fended the Jews off with unbreakable barriers and iron walls to prevent any mingling with other nations, to keep them pure in body and soul, and to rid them of empty beliefs.[71] So, even the veritable document of intercultural concord, the *Letter of Aristeas*, contains a pivotal pronouncement by the chief spokesman for Judaism, who sets his creed decisively apart from the ignorant and misguided beliefs of the Greeks.

The contrast is elaborated at some length by Josephus. The Jewish historian of the late first century C.E. distinguishes unequivocally between the steadfastness of Jews and the inferiority of Hellenic practices and institutions. He records repeated interference by Greeks with the ancestral practices of the Jews and outright atrocities in Cyrenaica, Asia Minor, Alexandria, Damascus, Caesarea, and

---

69 2 Macc. 6:18–7:41.
70 4 Macc. 4–18. For discussions of the text, with bibliography, see H. Anderson, "4 Maccabees," in J. Charlesworth, ed., *The Old Testament Pseudepigrapha*, vol. 2 (Garden City, N.Y., 1985), 531–43, and Schürer, *History of the Jewish People*, vol. 3.1,588–93.
71 *Let. Aris.*, 134–39.

other cities of Palestine.[72] Josephus pulls no punches: the disposition of the Greeks is labeled "inhumanity."[73]

Elsewhere Josephus conceives the contrast on a broader front. He singles out Moses, as the most venerable of lawgivers and speaks with scorn of Greeks who take pride in such comparable figures as Lycurgus, Solon, and Zaleucus. He disparages Hellenic philosophy and education: the philosophers directed their precepts only to the elite, whereas Moses' teaching encompassed all. The study of Jewish traditions exposes the deficiencies and one-sidedness that inhere in both the Spartan and Athenian systems.[74] More important, he places particular weight upon the Jews' faithful and consistent adherence to their own laws. To the Greeks, such unswerving fidelity can hardly be imagined. Their history is riddled with inversions and deviations. Greek authors heap praise on the longevity of the Spartan system; for Josephus, that is preposterous. The endurance of that system was a mere trifle, not comparable to the 2,000 years that had elapsed since the time of Moses.[75] Josephus exploits Hellenic writings themselves to make a point about the foolishness and absurdity of their religious beliefs. The myths multiply deities without number, portray them in a variety of human forms, and have them engage in every type of licentiousness, misdemeanor, folly, and internecine warfare with one another. And, as if that were not enough, the Greeks grow weary of their traditional divinities and import foreign gods by the score, stimulating poets and painters to invent new and even more bizarre images of worship.[76] There could be no stronger contrast with the tenacity and constancy of Jewish practice.

The celebrated lines of the apostle Paul allude directly to the antithesis between the peoples: "there is neither Jew nor Greek, slave nor free, male nor female, for you are all one in Jesus Christ."[77] The string of antinomies makes it clear that the two nations represented conventionally opposite poles. The distinction held firm in Jewish circles.

The evidence to this point seems clear and consistent. Jewish compositions constructed the Hellenes as foils, as aliens, as "the Other," the better to set off the virtues and qualities of their own *ethnos*. But those constructs do not tell the whole story. The Jews' perceptions (or at least expressed perceptions) of

---

72 See, e. g., Jos., *A. J.*, 16:160–61, 18:257–60, 19:300–312, 20:173–84.
73 Ibid. 16:161.
74 Jos., *C. Ap.*, 2:154–56, 168–74.
75 Ibid., 2:220–31, 279.
76 Ibid., 2:239–54.
77 Gal. 3:28; cf. 1 Cor. 12:13.

the Greeks were more complex, varied, and subtle. In other texts, Greek character and culture acquire a more positive aspect, because they are conceived as owing those qualities to the Jews themselves.

Aristobulus, a second-century-B.C.E. Jew of philosophic education and pretensions, played with what became a favored Jewish fiction: that Hellenic ideas derived from Hebraic roots. A mere handful of fragments survive, and the identification of Aristobulus himself is disputed. But the emphasis on Jewish priority in concepts later conveyed by Greeks is plain enough.[78]

In Aristobulus's imaginative construct, Moses provided a stimulus for Hellenic philosophers and poets. The Torah inspired the loftiest achievements of the Greek intellectuals. Aristobulus asserts that Plato's ideas followed the path laid out by the legislation of Moses, indeed that he was assiduous in working through every particular contained in it. And he cites an earlier case still, an equally distinguished name, the sixth-century philosopher Pythagoras, who also found much in the Hebrew teachings that he could adapt for his own doctrines.[79] For any discerning reader, those pronouncements create some serious chronological problems. How would the Greek sages have had access to the Hebrew Scriptures generations or centuries before the Septuagint? Aristobulus has no qualms about fabricating one fiction to save another. He reassures potential skeptics by maintaining that translations of the Israelite escape from Egypt, conquest and settlement of the new land, and all the details of the law code were available long before the composition of the Septuagint.[80] Aristobulus compounds his creative fabrications.

That accomplished, Aristobulus proceeds with flights of fancy. He includes Socrates with Pythagoras and Plato among those whose reference to a divine voice in contemplating the creation of the cosmos derives from the words of Moses. And he goes well beyond. Aristobulus offers a broadly embracing doctrine that sweeps all of Greek philosophy within the Jewish orbit. He affirms universal agreement among the philosophers that only pious opinions must be held about God. And, since that view is embedded in Mosaic law, it follows that Jewish conceptualizing supplied the wellspring for Hellenic philosophizing.[81]

If Jewish inspiration could be claimed for Greek philosophy, why not for poetry? Aristobulus and others had no hesitation in extending the Jewish reach into

---

78 An up-to-date edition of the fragments, with translation, thorough notes, and comprehensive bibliography has been produced by C. Holladay, *Fragments from Hellenistic Jewish Authors: Vol. III: Aristobulus* (Atlanta, Ga., 1995).

79 Aristobulus, in Eus. *PE*, 13.12.1; Clement, *Strom.* 1.22.150.1 – 3.

80 Aristobulus, in Eus. *PE*, 13.12.1; Clement, *Strom.* 1.22.150.2.

81 Aristobulus, in Eus. *PE*, 13.12.3 – 4, 8; Clement, *Strom.* 5.14.99.3.

that realm. References to the number seven in Greek poetry were seized upon as evidence that the institution of the Sabbath had seeped into Hellenic consciousness. Aristobulus goes back to the beginning. He summons up the verses of Greece's premier epic poets, Homer and Hesiod, to affirm that they endorsed the biblical sanctification of the holy day. This requires some fancy footwork. Aristobulus or his Jewish source exercise special liberties in twisting the texts to his will. Hesiod's reference to a seventh day of the month becomes the seventh day of the week, and a Homeric allusion to the "fourth day" is transformed through emendation to the "seventh day." Other lines quoted by Aristobulus but not attested in the extant texts of Homer and Hesiod may also have been tampered with or simply invented.[82] The subtle—or not so subtle—reworking had Homer and Hesiod acknowledge the consecration of the Sabbath. From the vantage point of Aristobulus, it is all for a good cause: to demonstrate the dependence of Greece's most ancient bards upon the teachings of the Torah. Observance of the Sabbath, in this conception, is no mere idiosyncrasy of an alien and self-segregated sect but a principle cherished in Hellenic song. Aristobulus thereby harnessed some of the most celebrated Greek thinkers and artists, real or legendary, to the antique traditions of the Jews.

In this venture Aristobulus was by no means alone. Jewish intellectuals ransacked the texts of Greek drama, chasing after verses that might suggest Hellenic borrowings from Hebraic ideas. And when they did not find appropriate lines, they simply manufactured them. Concepts with Jewish resonance were ascribed to the great fifth-century-B.C.E. tragedians Aeschylus, Sophocles, and Euripides, and to the comic poets Menander, Philemon, and Diphilus.[83]

Thunderous verses allegedly composed by Aeschylus exalt the authority of God. The eminent tragedian warns mortals to acknowledge his splendor and to recognize his presence in every manifestation of nature, an omnipotence that can shake the earth, the mountains, and the depths of the sea: "The glory of the highest god is all-powerful."[84] Such sentiments, whether authentic Aeschylus or not, would certainly play into Jewish hands. Sophocles too was ex-

---

82 Aristobulus, in Eus. *PE*, 13.12.13–15; Clement, *Strom.* 5.14.107.1–3. See the careful discussion in N. Walter, *Der Thoraausleger Aristobulos* (Berlin, 1964), 150–58, with reference to the relevant Homeric and Hesiodic lines; cf. Y. Gutman, *ha-Siprut ha-Yehudit-ha-Helenistit*, vol. 1 (Jerusalem, 1958) 210–12, and Holladay, *Fragments*, 3:234–37.

83 The fragments can be found in A.-M. Denis, *Fragmenta*, 161–74. A translation by H. Attridge is in J. Charlesworth, ed., *Old Testament Pseudepigrapha*, 2: 824–30. And see the valuable treatment by M. Goodman in Schürer, *History of the Jewish People*, vol. 3.1, 656–61, 667–71, with bibliographies.

84 The lines appear in Pseudo-Justin, *De Monarchia* 2; Clement, *Strom.* 5.14.131.2–3; Eus. *PE*, 13.13.60.

ploited, for similar purposes. He trumpeted the unity and uniqueness of the Lord, rebuking mortals who installed graven images of bronze, stone, gold, or ivory.[85] He even supplied an eschatological text that forecast the destruction of the universe in an all-consuming flame to issue in the salvation of the righteous.[86] Euripides also served to advance the cause. A passage attributed to him asserts that no dwelling fashioned by mortal hands can contain the spirit of God, and another characterizes God as one who sees all but who is himself invisible.[87] These concocted lines—and doubtless many others no longer extant—conscripted the Attic tragedians in the service of Hellenistic Judaism.

A similar process enlisted Greek comic poets. Passages ascribed to one or another of them disclose the objectives of those who preserved (or forged) them. They include admonitions to the wicked, assertions that God punishes the unjust, insistence that upright conduct is more important than sacrificial offerings, and exhortation to honor the one God who is Father for all time, the Inventor and Creator of every good.[88]

Hellenistic Jews were evidently tireless in rummaging through the Greek classics to find opinions and sentiments that evoked scriptural teachings. The assiduous efforts gave forceful reminders to their countrymen of Jewish priority in the thinking of great thoughts. More striking still, they imply that the Hellenic achievement, far from alien to the Hebraic, simply restated its principles.

A famous story, but not one usually cited in this connection, underscores the point. Paul's celebrated visit to Athens in the mid-first century C.E. can exemplify this form of appropriation. The tale is told in the Acts of the Apostles.[89] Paul proselytizes among the Jews and "God-fearers" in the synagogue—and with any person who passes by in the *agora* (central market place). This upsets certain Stoics and Epicureans, who haul him before the high tribunal of the Areopagus and question him about the new doctrine. Paul is quick to turn the situation to his own advantage—and in a most interesting way. He remarks to the Athenians that they are an uncommonly religious people. He has wandered through many of their shrines and has found one altar inscribed to an "unknown god." Of course, he is there to tell them precisely who that "unknown god" happens to be. Paul then speaks of the sole Divinity, Creator of the world and all that is

---

85 Ps. Justin, *De Monarch.* 2; Clement, *Strom.* 5.14.113.2; Eus. *PE,* 13.13.40.

86 Ps. Justin, *De Monarch.* 3; Clement, *Strom.* 5.14.121.4 – 122.1; Eus. *PE,* 13.13.48.

87 Clement, *Strom.* 5.11.75.1; *Protrepticus* 6.68.3; cf. Ps. Justin, *De Monarch.* 2.

88 Clement, *Strom.* 5.14.119.2, 5.14.121.1 – 3, 5.14.133.3; Eus. *PE,* 13.13.45 – 47, 13.13.62, 13.36.2; Ps. Justin, *De Monarch.* 2 – 5.

89 Acts 17:16 – 33.

in it, a God who dwells in no temples and can be captured in no images.[90] The description plainly applies to the God of the Hebrew Bible, with no Christian admixture. Paul, like other inventive Jews, quotes Greek poetry to underpin his claims. So, he remarks to the Athenians, "as some of your own poets have said, 'We too are His [God's] children.'"[91] The poet in question is, in fact, Aratus of Soli, no Athenian. But that detail can be comfortably ignored. The parallels with other texts cited above are quite striking. Paul deploys Greek poetic utterances as certification for Jewish precepts, and he cites a Greek dedicatory inscription as evidence for Hellenic worship of the right deity—even if the Greeks themselves do not know who he is.

This heartening construct of Hellenic dependence on Jewish precedents appears notably, and perhaps surprisingly, even in the work of Josephus. As we have seen, he took pains to underscore differences between the Jews and the Greeks, to stress the stability of Jewish institutions and the durability of faith as against the multiple inadequacies of Hellenic practices. Yet Josephus also follows the line that many Greeks have embraced Jewish laws—though some have been more consistent in maintaining them than others. Indeed, he acknowledges, Jews are more divided from Greeks by geography than by institutions.[92] Like Aristobulus and others, he finds Greek philosophers hewing closely to the concept of God that they obtained from acquaintance with the Books of Moses—noting in particular Pythagoras, Anaxagoras, Plato, and the Stoics.[93] And he makes still larger claims. Greek philosophers were only the first of those drawn to the laws of the Torah, adopting similar views about God, teaching abstinence from extravagance, and harmony with one another. The masses followed suit. Their zeal for Jewish religious piety has now spread around the world so that there is hardly a single community, whether Greek or barbarian, unaffected by observance of the Sabbath, various Jewish practices, and even dietary restrictions. Indeed, they labor to emulate the concord, philanthropy, industry, and undeviating steadfastness characteristic of the Jews.[94] The hyperbole is obviously excessive. But Josephus's insistence on the Greek quest to duplicate Jewish ethics, religion, institutions, and customs is noteworthy—and quite different from his drive elsewhere to underscore the distance that separated Jew from Greek.

An ostensible tension thus exists in Jewish perspectives on Hellas. A strong strain emphasized the differences in culture, and behavior between the peoples,

---

90 Acts 17:24–26.
91 Acts 17:28.
92 Jos., *C. Ap.*, 2:121–23.
93 Ibid., 2:168; cf. 1:162.
94 Ibid., 2:280–84.

categorized the Greeks as aliens, inferiors, even savage antagonists. Other voices, however, embraced and absorbed Hellenic teachings, reinterpreting them as shaped by acquaintance with the Hebraic tradition and as offshoots of the Torah. From that vantage point, the Hellenic character becomes, through emulation and imitation, molded to the model.

Is there an explanation for these discordant voices? The discrepancies that we discern or construct may not have had comparable significance in antiquity. It is especially striking that the supposedly different voices coexist in the same texts. The matter is obviously complex and involved.

The author of 2 Maccabees, as we have seen, writing in Greek and in the genre of Hellenistic historiography, reversed convention and labeled the Greeks themselves as *barbaroi*. That was ironic and pointed—but it did not set a style. Other Jewish writers adopted the very antithesis long current in the classical world, contrasting Greek with barbarian. It can be found, for instance, in the philosopher Philo of Alexandria, who boasts of the widespread attraction of Jewish customs, embraced in various parts of the world by both Greeks and barbarians.[95] Josephus employs the contrast regularly as a means of dividing the non-Jewish world.[96] It appears also in Paul, who proclaims his message to "Greeks and Barbarians, the wise and the ignorant"—no pagan could have said it better.[97] Philo, in fact, can even adopt the Hellenic perspective wholesale and count the Jews among the *barbaroi!*[98] Here is inversion indeed. Contrast between the nations need not betoken irreconcilability.

Nor, however, do the texts that signal cultural conjunction negate the force of pronouncements that differentiate the peoples. In various formulations, Greek poetic inspiration came from a Hebrew bard; Hellenic philosophers, dramatists, and poets who recognized the sole divinity, expressed lofty ethical precepts and honored the Sabbath took their cue from the Torah; and even the Athenians unwittingly paid homage to the god of the Scriptures. These fictive inventions hardly dissolved the distinctions between Hebrews and Hellenes. Instead, they elevated the best in Hellenism by providing it with Hebrew precedents. The rest, by definition, fell short.

The Jews' reconception of the Hellenic achievement turned it to their own benefit. They simultaneously differentiated their nation from that of the Greeks and justified their own immersion in a world of Hellenic civilization.

---

95 Philo, *Mos.* 2:18–20.
96 See, e.g., Josephus, *BJ*, 5:17; *A.J.*, 4:12; *C. Ap.*, 2:282.
97 Rom. 1:14.
98 Philo, *Mos.* 2:27; *Prob.* 73–75.

Inventive Tales for Populace and Elite

A critical question must now be addressed, a troubling but inescapable complication. To what degree do the Jewish texts that survive from this era give access
only to a small, elite segment of society? Do they seal us off from anything that
might be considered "popular culture"?

A difficult matter. Indeed, it raises further and even more formidable questions: how are these texts to be understood, to whom were they directed, by
whom were they composed, and what were their objectives?

The limitations under which we labor have to be acknowledged at once. We
normally do not know the author, the date, the place of composition, or the historical context of these works—let alone the motivations or intentions of the
composer. Much scholarly energy has been devoted to reconstructing (or, better,
to conjecturing and speculating about) when, where, and under what circumstances a text was produced. Much of it is an exercise in futility. More important,
however, the very questions of who, what, when, and why are not only often un-
answerable but are probably the wrong questions. It is crucial to remember that
we are dealing with texts that, for the most part, have gone through many versions, revisions, recasting, and redaction, and have passed through many
hands, indeed perhaps circulated orally over an extended period of time before
reaching the stage in which we finally possess them. Hence, to puzzle out the
historical circumstances of the original composition, the Ur-text, the audience
to which it was directed, and the society it reflects, even if we could do so,
might not be very helpful.

The texts as we have, them are the ones with which we must grapple. If they
appear to have different layers of meaning and more than one level of understanding, that should not surprise us. Indeed, it makes them all the more valuable—especially for the complex issue of elite vs. popular culture. That dichotomy
itself misleads and deceives. The texts can work on several planes, and they appeal to a diverse readership. The same stories ostensibly designed for "popular"
consumption, such as folktales, romances, and fantasies, and plainly enjoyed on
that level, can also carry deeper meaning and greater nuance directed to a sophisticated audience.

Joseph and Aseneth serves as an example. The entertainment value of the
novel is high. The dramatic transformation of the two chief figures from bristling
antagonists to a loving couple certainly has that quality. So does the adventure
story that has the "good" brothers of Joseph prevail over the wicked sons of Leah
and the nefarious plots of Pharaoh's son. The work can happily be read for diversion and amusement, and in that sense it is attractive to what is customarily considered a "popular" constituency.

But more serious, complex, and even baffling elements lurk within. As we have seen, the text raises pointed issues about Jewish/gentile relations in the circumstances of the Diaspora. Recurrent tension, animosity, and open conflict have as counterpoint union and harmony, reconciliation and communal concord. The meaning is not easy to ferret out. Further, the balance between royal authority and Joseph's extraordinary powers possesses political implications not readily explicable to readers content with the surface narrative.

Still more difficult matters confront interpreters of the text. Aseneth's adoption of Joseph's faith (nowhere identified as "Judaism" in the narrative) has stirred widespread discussion of what "conversion" might mean, whether the tract encourages missionary activity, what message is delivered about mixed marriages, and how gentile converts were viewed from a Jewish perspective.[99] All of this may be a red herring. An author engaged in missionary efforts would not likely feature a story in which the impulse to conversion came from sexual passion! But the ambiguities at least prompt deeper probing.

Even better examples occur in the Greek additions to the Book of Daniel. The author or authors, probably in the late second century B.C.E., fiddled freely with the received text, inserting folktales of independent provenance and applying some acid drollery to refashion the Jewish image. These include two quite amusing pieces of folklore: "Bel and the Dragon" and "Susanna."

"Bel and the Dragon" actually consists of two tales cobbled together and placed at the conclusion of what became the canonical text of Daniel. The first features Cyrus, king of Persia, as a devoted disciple of the Babylonian god Bel, on whom is lavished vast quantities of sheep, flour, and wine every day. Cyrus wonders why his chief adviser Daniel does not share his enthusiasm for this divinity. Daniel retorts that he worships only the God who created heaven and earth, not some fabricated idol, and offers to prove that Bel is the invention of conniving Babylonian priests. He devises a clever scheme whereby ashes are scattered around the floor of the sealed temple one night; after offerings are made to the idol. Telltale footprints the next morning showed that the priests and their families used a trapdoor to steal off with the provisions themselves. The somewhat dull-witted Cyrus now sees the light, orders the execution of the priests and their families, and turns the statue of Bel over to Daniel, who promptly destroys it and its temple.[100]

---

99 For a sampling of divergent views, see Philonenko, *Joseph et Aséneth*, 53–61; Chesnutt, *From Death to Life*, 153–84; and Barclay, *Jews in the Mediterranean Diaspora*, 204–16.
100 Dan. 14:1–22. On the texts that convey this tale, see C. A. Moore, *Daniel, Esther, and Jeremiah: The Additions* (Garden City, N.Y., 1977), 23–34. The date of composition, perhaps later

The narrator proceeds directly to the next legend, that of the dragon or the snake. Here the king, still looking for a tangible deity to revere, points to the large snake that the Babylonians worship and bids Daniel to pay it homage as well. The Jewish counselor, of course, remains faithful to his own God, and he offers to expose the snake's impotence by killing it without recourse to a weapon. Cyrus grants permission. Daniel then mixes a concoction of pitch, fat, and hair and feeds it to the snake, which bursts open on the spot, allowing Daniel to crow, "Now look at your object of worship!" The Babylonians strike back, pressuring the king to turn Daniel over to them and cast him into the lions' den. But Daniel is undeterred. The prophet Habbakuk, sent flying through the air by an angel who tugs him by the hair, brings food to Daniel that sustains him in the pit. And when the king finds him miraculously unharmed after seven days among the beasts, he heaps praise upon Daniel's god, rescues his counselor, and tosses his enemies to the lions.[101]

These tales amuse and instruct. Most readers would delight in the triumph of virtue over evil, of monotheism over the practitioners of idol worship, a dominant theme in biblical and post-biblical literature, an easy and obvious moral to grasp. But that does not exhaust the implications of the fables. In fact, theology hardly gets much emphasis in the narrative. Daniel makes only passing references to his God and says nothing about his beliefs. The emphasis throughout rests not on divine intervention but on Daniel's own sagacity and resourcefulness.

Different undercurrents would appeal to those, whether elite or common, who read more closely. Cyrus holds a high place in Jewish memory as the monarch responsible for the return of the Jews from the Babylonian Exile. But in these tales, the king, far from being a magnanimous benefactor of the humble Jews, is represented as something of a dullard, manipulated and even mocked by those around him—including the shrewd Jew. Daniel more than once laughs at Cyrus's folly. The Persian ruler is as gullible about the snake as about the idol, is brow-beaten and intimidated by his Babylonian subjects, and has little influence on the course of events. The narrator misses no chance to expose his naiveté and deride his vacillation. There is subtle irony here, not mere playfulness. If this is the ruler under whom the Jews returned to their homeland, one must infer that a Jew pulled the strings on this hapless puppet. The story has deeper meaning for a Diaspora existence. Daniel's people may have to live under the rule of alien kings, but the rewritten fables reassure them of how far they surpass those

---

second century B.C.E., remains uncertain; cf. M. J. Steussy, *Gardens in Babylon: Narrative and Faith in the Greek Legends of Daniel* (Atlanta, Ga., 1993), 28–32.
101 Dan. 14:23–42.

kings in mental agility and insight. The irony reflects a shared perspective of author and reader, a joint scorning of the inadequacies of the political authority. That element takes the stories out of the realm of mere diversion.

More revealing still is the celebrated tale of Susanna and the elders in the Greek text of Daniel. Is it "highbrow" or "lowbrow" literature? Is it a pleasant yarn conceived to amuse or does it have a deeper structure to provoke reflection upon Jewish conditions in the Diaspora? Is it aimed at a select group of intellectuals or the "common man"? Is it imaginative fiction or an authentic evocation of Jewish experience? In fact, one can argue, it is all of the above.

According to the narrative, Susanna, the beautiful and devout wife of a prominent Jew in Babylon, is lusted after by two elders of the people. They hide in the garden, spy upon her in the bath, and confront her with an intimidating proposition: either have intercourse with them or face (fraudulent) charges of adultery with a young man. Susanna, coerced into an unwelcome decision, chooses the latter. The lecherous elders then deliver their indictment before a gathering of the people and persuade the congregation to condemn Susanna to death. Young Daniel, however, emerges as God's answer to Susanna's prayer, roundly rebukes the people, and denounces them for exercising peremptory judgment even without interrogating the elders. He denies the validity of their statements and offers to grill them himself. Daniel wisely takes the precaution of separating the two men and questioning each independently. In this fashion, he brings to light discrepancies in their claims, exposes their perjury, and draws cheers from the congregation. The elders are executed, the virtuous Susanna is vindicated, and Daniel gains great esteem among the people from that day on.[102]

To what audience would such a work be addressed? It contains obvious folktale elements. The story of the wise youth outsmarting the wicked elders has many parallels. So does the motif of the innocent woman as victim but vindicated in the end. Analogous tales can be found in the *Arabian Nights*, Grimm's fairy tales, and a variety of Eastern and Near Eastern literary texts.[103] It has been widely popular across the ages and was doubtless popular in antiquity. The engaging character of the tale guarantees that. Daniel's outwitting of the two bungling, dirty old men and the confirmation of the matron's virtue would have wide appeal. For many readers or auditors, no more was needed: good yarn, happy ending, virtue rewarded, villains punished. It was also reassuring to have flawed

---

102 Dan. 13:1–64.
103 Cf. Moore, *Daniel, Esther, and Jeremiah*, 88–89, and L. M. Wills, *The Jew in the Court of the Foreign King: Ancient Jewish Court Legends* (Minneapolis, 1990), 76–79.

leaders exposed and flawed procedures denounced. Such might be a "popular" reading—and a perfectly legitimate and meaningful one.

It need not, however, be the only one. The tale takes place in Babylon; the Jews are presumably in exile or, at least, in an alien land. But they are represented as an autonomous community, with its own leaders, its own process of governance. The malefactors are Jews, not gentiles. And not only does the text depict the elders as corrupt and immoral, but it portrays the populace that rendered judgment as compliant, easily swayed—and not very bright. It requires a noble youth to bring them to their senses and rescue the maligned but blameless Susanna. Indeed, the noble youth himself is far from flawless. Daniel succeeds not as a devout adherent of the faith but as a crafty prosecuting attorney. He convicts the elders even before questioning them, and he declares the first to be a lascivious perjurer although his story has yet to be contradicted.[104] The lawyerly techniques hardly embody exemplary justice. A clear strain of Jewish self-criticism exists in this text. It offers a subtle reminder that Jews need to look to their own shortcomings, especially in a Diaspora setting. The legend, in short, carried import at more than one level and could have resonance with more than one stratum of society.

Does this narrative actually describe life in the Jewish community of Babylon at a particular point of history? That is more than dubious. The text mentions Babylon at the beginning, to supply an ostensible context, but the remainder of the work gives no concrete details about location. The story could take place anywhere; the setting is imaginary, and the events, of course, are fictitious. But the message is meaningful, more than mere entertainment. The exposure of arrogance in the leadership and gullibility in the rank and file delivered a pointed lesson to the nation. It recalled to mind basic principles of justice and morality that needed to be observed—especially in Jewish communities that governed their own activities but whose internal divisions could make them vulnerable to greater powers. The message did not apply to a particular geographic locale or to a specific time period. Indeed, the significance of the story is precisely that it transcends time and place. Nor does it speak only to an elite or only at a popular level. It holds a place in the cultural legacy for Jews across the generations, across geographical boundaries, and across intellectual strata.

An altogether different text can offer comparable conclusions. In 2 Maccabees one finds a peculiar and puzzling work that continues to intrigue scholars and students. It is a work of history, but one punctuated by miracles, marvels,

---

104 Dan. 13:49, 54–55.

and martyrologies. It celebrates the deliverance of Jerusalem, its Temple, and its inhabitants from the terrors wrought by a Hellenistic king, but it was composed, at least in its fuller form, by a Hellenized Diaspora Jew from Cyrene. It bears notice here for certain arresting stories that it preserves and that certainly cater to what is conventionally categorized as popular taste.

An engaging tale occurs near the beginning of the main narrative. Heliodorus, the agent of the Seleucid king, arrives in Jerusalem to check on reports that the Temple treasury possesses incalculable riches. When told by the high priest that there are indeed deposits held in trust for widows and orphans as well as the savings of a prominent and wealthy Jewish leader, Heliodorus insists that the monies belong to the king and should be handed over to him. He heads for the Temple to make an inventory, alarming the priests and people. Heliodorus, however, presses on. He is about to enter the Temple with his bodyguards when a fearsome rider on a mighty horse, splendidly attired, attacks him. Two strapping youths, magnificent in beauty and strength, then appear and pummel him further. The minister is carried off in a litter, now obliged to acknowledge the sovereignty of God. Indeed it looks as if he will not recover. But the merciful high priest Onias III sacrifices to God for Heliodorus's recovery, and he is spared. He goes back to the king and extols the power and majesty of the Jewish God.[105]

The popular appeal of such a story is obvious. The greedy minister of the king gets his comeuppance, the sacred Temple is spared, and divine intervention saves the day. But subtle thrusts exist in this text that go beyond the surface reading. The author has a wry sense of humor that seems aimed at a discriminating reader. One might note, for instance, the prayer uttered by the priests and the people when Heliodorus is about to violate the Temple treasury. It was not a plea to God to protect the sanctity of his house; rather, it calls upon the Lord Almighty to keep the deposits safe and secure for those who have placed their cash there![106] The author composed this with a wink and a nod. And Heliodorus receives no conventional punishment. He gets a double dose. It is not enough that a horse charges him and kicks him. There are also two powerful young men who beat him to a pulp.[107] That seems a bit of overkill—and another example of some whimsy on the author's part. The penchant for irony can hardly be missed in the finale of this episode. Heliodorus, though practically breathing his last, is spared by the high priest and returned to Antioch. When asked by his king who should next be sent to Jerusalem in order to recover the money, Helio-

---

105 2 Macc. 3:1–40.
106 Ibid. 3:15, 22.
107 Ibid. 3:25–27.

dorus replies, in effect, "If you want to send somebody, send your worst enemy; he will get thoroughly thrashed." And still another concealed barb can be discerned. Heliodorus remarks, "If you have an enemy or a plotter against the government, send him to Jerusalem."[108] As it happens, it was Heliodorus himself, not long thereafter, who plotted against the king and was responsible for his death. The anticipated audience here had to know its contemporary history— and to appreciate the irony.

In a different mode, it is instructive to look at the treatment in 2 Maccabees of the villainous Antiochus IV. The scene of his agonizing death is justly famous. The gory details, including the worms swarming about him and flesh rotting off, can be paralleled by various Greek texts. It appears to be a motif for the deaths of cruel tyrants. But the author of 2 Maccabees added an extra touch of his own when he had the persecutor repent in the end, declare Jerusalem a free city, grant prerogatives to the Jews, and promise to adorn the temple with lavish gifts and finance all its sacrifices.[109] The characterization of one of these promises is especially noteworthy. Antiochus vows that he will give privileges to the Jews equal to those enjoyed by the citizens of Athens. This would seem to be an allusion to the golden age of democratic Athens. Such an age, however, had long since passed—contemporary Athens was hardly a model of autonomy and privilege. The insertion here is yet another instance of the author's sardonic streak. Only a few select readers would detect that allusion.

The Book of Judith, composed perhaps in the early first century B.C.E., provides an edifying and uplifting tale. One need not have intellectual credentials to appreciate it. The setting (wholly imaginary) is a putative military campaign ordered by Nebuchadnezzar, here identified as an Assyrian monarch, against various peoples of the Near East, including those dwelling in Judaea and Samaria. The military man Holofernes is appointed commander-in-chief of the armies that sweep through the lands, looting, sacking, and destroying sacred shrines. When the forces threaten Judaea, the Israelites, their high priest, and their officials are terrified, block the mountain passes, put on sackcloth and ashes, and pray to the Lord for rescue. The Ammonite chieftain Achior, whose people have already surrendered to the invaders, warn Holofernes that the Israelites are invincible if their God favors them, but vulnerable if they have sinned against Him. Holofernes scorns the advice, mocks Achior, and delivers him to the Israelites themselves. The army then undertakes the siege of the (unlocatable) Israelite town of Bethulia. Its inhabitants swiftly become desperate, the people pressing their

---

108 Ibid. 3:37–38.
109 Ibid. 9:13–16.

leaders to surrender before they are annihilated. The city's most prominent figure, Uzziah, proposes a five-day wait, in hopes that God might intervene, but promises surrender if there is no sign of such intervention.[110]

At this point Judith enters the scene. A respected and wealthy widow, renowned for her piety and wisdom, Judith denounces the city's elders for giving a deadline to God and promises that she will take action to deliver Israel with the aid of the Lord. Uzziah and the magistrates give her free rein. Judith first prays to God, then takes matters into her own hands. A beautiful as well as wise woman, she bedecks herself alluringly and, with a single maidservant, goes straight to the camp of Holofernes. Judith dazzles the general not only with her beauty but also with beguiling and manipulative language, leading him to believe that, with her aid, he can subdue the Israelites without difficulty. A few days later comes the inevitable invitation to spend the night in Holofernes' tent. Judith arouses his desire, then plies him with wine. When the intoxicated Holofernes passes out, Judith, armed with prayer and a sword, lops off his head. She slips from the camp with the head in a sack and has the elders display it proudly on the battlements. The people are in awe of the deed, and Achior the Ammonite faints dead away. Upon recovery he praises Judith to the skies, has himself circumcised, and converts to the Israelite religion. The Assyrians, stunned and crestfallen, are easy prey for the Israelites. The city is saved, the enemy routed and despoiled. Judith, much lauded not only by the citizenry of Bethulia but also by the high priest and his council in Jerusalem, retires to her own estate, emancipates her loyal attendant, declines all offers of marriage, and lives out her days in serenity, dying at the age of 105.[111]

As a tale of Jewish success against heavy odds, this narrative has immense appeal. It was often retold over the ages and has been represented many times in European art. The image of Judith holding Holofernes' head can be found in museums throughout the world. Its hold on popular imagination is clear and readily comprehensible.

But, here again, currents of a less distinct and more subterranean character come into play. The tale upsets expectations, inverts the norm, and invites thoughtful interpretation.

Judith herself is an ambivalent, often surprising figure. Her story can be correspondingly perplexing. She is an adherent of law and ritual but has no hesitation in practicing deceit. She roundly rebukes Uzziah and the elders, but, far

---

110 Jdt. 1 – 7. See the valuable editions and commentaries in M. S. Enslin, *The Book of Judith* (Leiden, 1972), and C. A. Moore, *Judith* (Garden City, N.Y., 1985).
111 Jdt. 8 – 16.

from feeling aggrieved, they give her full authority. She exhibits greater devoutness than the males in her society but also exercises greater ruthlessness. She uses sexual wiles on Holofernes but remains a chaste widow to the end of her days. She plays the most central public role, and then retreats to an innocuous private life. She utters repeated prayers to the Lord but, in fact, accomplishes all through her own wits and guile.

Holofernes is a no less surprising, indeed implausible character. He rampages through most of the Near East and is then content with a long and leisurely siege of a small Judaean town. He swallows wholesale Judith's line about the Israelites and their God, although he has just rejected the same line when uttered by Achior. He waits patiently for four days before trying to seduce Judith—and then falls into a stupor when the opportunity arrives.

Minor personalities also behave in peculiar ways. Achior, gentile though he be, has a clearer vision of Jewish principles than Uzziah, the Judaean magistrate. Achior, warrior though he be, keels over at the sight of a severed head. And Uzziah, chief magistrate though he be, allows Judith to proceed with her plan—despite the fact that he has no idea what it is.

Reversals and surprises abound. Just what they signify cannot be determined with any certainty. But they subvert a simplistic reading. The text plays with chronology and geography, turns history into fantasy, casts doubt upon Jewish leaders' grasp of their own precepts and traditions, both asserts and questions religious values, and confuses gender roles. The Book of Judith blurs boundaries throughout. The straightforward triumph of pious Jews over gentile aggressors, exemplified by the image of Judith brandishing the head of Holofernes, dissolves upon closer scrutiny. Reception of the tale for its entertaining quality constitutes but one mode of understanding. Like all the works discussed here, the Book of Judith operates at several levels. Therein lies its strength and its enticement.

As is clear, these texts undermine any lowbrow/highbrow dichotomy. The idea that creations of this sort could only be appreciated either by a "popular" mentality, or by a sophisticated elite breaks down upon examination. Such a boundary eludes sharp definition. Folktales and romances are regularly transformed through retelling over time, with a range of readers or auditors. Populace and intelligentsia alike could take pleasure both in their narrative charm and in their subversive character. The richness of the texts signals a multitude of voices and the complex process of reshaping wrought by the interests and concerns of many generations.

Women in Fiction and Fact

The tale of Judith draws attention to yet another complication: the constructs of gender. Narrative texts that engaged Jews with gentiles or probed Jewish self-perception in a broader culture frequently centered upon the demeanor, actions, and place of women. The frequency of such constructs by (presumably) male authors betrays a need to confront the tensions produced in gender roles by the pressures of a wider society.

The subordinate position of Jewish women in this period (as in most others) is marked and clear. Hellenistic writers make no bones about it. A purveyor of proverbs, hymns, and doctrinal advice called Ben Sira, writing in the early second century B.C.E., deemed the birth of a daughter to be a major burden for her father, who would have to supervise her behavior and protect her chastity. Daughters are a constant source of anxiety, prone to be wayward, keeping fathers awake with concern lest they be unmarried or childless or, worse, unwed mothers. Given the slightest chance, they will leap into the embrace of strangers. Without surveillance, they are liable to humiliate their parents, bring disgrace on their families, and make their fathers a laughingstock to their foes and a disgrace in public. Not that wives are any better. Ben Sira claims that he would rather share a house with a lion or a snake than an evil woman. Husbands can expect nagging, tantrums, and misery. Indeed, he goes so far as to assert that a man's wickedness is preferable to a woman's goodness![112] Comparable statements can be found in other Jewish-Hellenistic texts.[113] The expressions are rhetorical and extreme. Ben Sira acknowledges that a virtuous woman can bring benefits. But the characterization of that virtue is still more revealing: a man can count himself happy in having a sensible and devoted wife.[114] That translates into a wife who is chaste and beautiful, honors her husband—and keeps quiet.[115]

Ben Sira's attitude corresponds, in no small measure, to the position of women in Second Temple society. They were expected to maintain a chaste and modest demeanor, remain for the most part at home, stay out of the sight of strangers, and hold as first priority the reputation of the household. Marriages, at least among the middle and upper classes, were arranged by parents. And wedlock was far from an equal partnership. Men had the option of polygamy; women did not. Adultery was punishable as a crime, but only for women;

---

112 Ben Sira 7:24, 22:3 – 5, 25:16 – 26, 26:6 – 12, 42:9 – 14. A useful translation and full commentary may be found in P. W. Skehan, *The Wisdom of Ben Sira* (New York, 1987).
113 See, e.g., T. Reu., 5:1 – 3, and Jos. *A.J.*, 5:294.
114 Ben Sira 25:8, 40:19.
115 Ibid. 26:13 – 26, 36:27 – 29.

men were exempt—unless they dallied with a married woman. A man could initiate a divorce at any time; a woman had no comparable privilege. Women were not even qualified to serve as witnesses in a legal proceeding. They could inherit, own, and bequeath property, but the instances of such activity are few in the era of the Second Temple. Insofar as they engaged in occupations and professions, these were largely confined to supporting their husbands and grew out of household tasks or areas appropriate to women such as weaving, spinning, cooking, baking, and midwifery.[116] In such circumstances, women could hardly expect to exercise leadership or achieve positions of authority.

Literature, however, seems to tell a different story. Women are conspicuous, active, and pivotal in the narratives. Memorable heroines stand out: Judith, Esther, Susanna, Aseneth. Did this represent a critique of gender hierarchy, a subversive treatment of societal norms? A closer reading of the texts may suggest more conformity than censure.

Judith is unquestionably the most potent female figure in Jewish-Hellenistic literature. She rescues a nation driven to despair and on the point of catastrophe. She rallies sagging spirits, seizes initiative from a languid leadership, devises a bold plan, and executes it remorselessly. Her resolute actions destroy the enemy and restore her nation to its glory. No male had been up to the task.

Yet even this dramatic narrative, with all its role reversal, does not challenge conventional social expectations. The dynamic and resourceful character of Judith serves primarily as a means to discredit the timid leaders of the community at a moment of crisis. The fact that Holofernes has to be dispatched by a woman, underscored more than once in the text, has less to do with female emancipation than with the acute humiliation of the men whose trust in the Lord has eroded.[117] Judith's rebuke of the elders is pointed and piercing.[118] Her own successes, even when achieved through guile and audacity, are always accompanied by prayers to Yahweh and humble obeisance to His presumed will, which is ultimately responsible for the outcome. Judith's piety is her most conspicuous characteristic.[119] And the outcome of her exploit is to restore an order and stability to the realm that allow it to settle back into its conformist mode. Appropriate gifts are offered to Yahweh, not only the customary sacrifices but also all the spoils from the camp of Holofernes. The Jews withdraw, each to

116 On all this, see the fine study of T. Ilan, *Jewish Women in Greco-Roman Palestine* (Tubingen, 1995), esp. 79–88, 122–47, 163–72, 184–90.
117 See Jdt. 13:15, 14:18, 16:5.
118 Jdt. 8:12–15.
119 Jdt. 8:6–8, 25, 9:1–14, 10:9, 12:8, 13:4–7, 14–16, 16:1–5, 13–17, 19.

his own inherited property, signifying the return of routine existence. Judith herself repairs to her estate, her public appearance brief and now concluded for good. She retired to private life and widowhood, a status she maintained, throughout the many decades that remained to her. Fittingly enough, she chose to be buried with her husband. Her spectacular deed has saved the nation. But, lest there be any anxiety over a reversal of social and gender hierarchy, Judith's withdrawal to quiet piety puts it to rest.[120]

The figure of Esther also upsets certain expectations—but reinforces most.[121] Her famous tale opens at the court of Ahasuerus, master of the Persian Empire, whose domain reaches from India to Ethiopia. The king hosts a lavish banquet for all the officialdom of the realm, thus to put his great wealth on display. The festivities are to be culminated by a visit from the ravishing Queen Vashti, summoned by the ruler to exhibit her beauty for his guests. Vashti, however, refuses, to parade herself before the assemblage. Ahasuerus swiftly consults his counselors and then banishes Vashti from his presence forever. He subsequently warns all women in his kingdom to be deferential to their husbands.

Ahasuerus decrees a competition—a beauty contest for the realm's young virgins—to find a new queen. Among those who answer the call is the beautiful Jewess Esther, an orphan raised by her cousin Mordekhai. After each of the maidens has undergone elaborate cosmetic treatments and spent a night with Ahasuerus, he selects Esther as his favorite (she had concealed her Jewish identity, on Mordekhai's advice) and sets the regal crown on her head. The event is celebrated by yet another extravagant banquet.

Ahasuerus's principal vizier is the ambitious Haman, promoted and honored by the king but ever grasping for more. The minister's demand for obeisance has been flouted by Mordekhai, who declined to bend a knee, thus prompting Haman to seek revenge on Mordekhai and the entire Jewish people. The compliant Ahasuerus authorizes the slaughter of Jews everywhere, man, woman, and child.

Mordekhai greets the news with sackcloth and ashes. But he also communicates with Esther, reminding her of her origins, and prodding her to intervene with the king. Esther overcomes her initial reluctance and takes the grave risk of an unsummoned appearance before Ahasuerus. Fortunately for Esther and

---

120 Jdt. 16:18–25. See the cogent comments of A.-J. Levine "Sacrifice and Salvation: Otherness and Domestication in the Book of Judith," in J. C. VanderKam, ed., *"No One Spoke Ill of Her": Essays on Judith* (Atlanta, Ga., 1992), 17–30.
121 Valuable analyses of the narrative may be found in S. B. Berg, *The Book of Esther: Motifs, Themes, and Structures* (Missoula, Mt.; 1979); M. V. Fox, *Character and Ideology in the Book of Esther* (Columbia, S.C., 1991); and J. Levenson, *Esther* (Louisville, Ky., 1997).

for the Jews, he is still smitten with his young consort, promising her anything, up to half his kingdom. Esther plays her cards carefully, inviting the king and Haman to dinner on two consecutive evenings, piquing the interest of the former and deftly misleading the latter.

Ahasuerus, in the meantime, learns that Mordekhai had once saved his life by warning him of an assassination plot. He therefore plans to honor the Jewish courtier. Haman, assuming at first that such favor will be his, learns with dismay of Mordekhai's elevation. The humiliations multiply. Not only must Haman humble himself before Mordekhai; he has to hear from his own wife that he cannot succeed against the Jew.

Esther's plan can now come to fruition. She unveils her request at last: a plea that she and her people be spared destruction. And she dramatically points to Haman as the villain who had plotted the genocide. Ahasuerus directs that his minister be hanged on the very gibbet he had prepared for Mordekhai.

The king's about-face is complete. He awards Haman's estate to Esther and gives carte blanche to Mordekhai and Esther to compose a decree that will be sent to every province of the empire, not only rescinding Haman's instructions but also authorizing the Jews to take up arms against their enemies, kill them all, and confiscate their property. The Jews implement those orders unhesitatingly and ruthlessly. Mordekhai took his place as the most trusted and powerful of the king's ministers as well as chief advocate for the welfare of Jews throughout the realm.

What implications does this story possess for the expectations and aspirations of women? The opening scene sets the conventions within which society operates. Vashti defies her husband and is banished. An imperial edict demands that wives respect the authority of their husbands and that men be masters in their own homes.[122] The setting, of course, is Persian, not Jewish, and the satiric quality of the account is transparent, but the restrictions on female behavior would not be altogether unfamiliar to a Jewish readership.

Esther is a complex and changing character, but she does not stray far beyond the boundaries. Mordekhai pushes her into the contest; Esther meekly complies. She continues to obey Mordekhai, who checks up on her daily.[123] When he learns of the palace plot to assassinate Ahasuerus, he directs Esther to disclose it, and she does.[124] When Mordekhai dons the garb of mourning, Esther, concerned but clueless, sends him some new clothes.[125] He has to instruct her on

---

122 Esth. 1:12 – 22.
123 Ibid. 2:5 – 20.
124 Ibid. 2:21 – 22.
125 Ibid. 4:1 – 4.

how to dissuade the king from the slaughter of the Jews. And his suggestion that she might have been made queen precisely to rescue her people gives her courage.[126]

Esther matures swiftly and suddenly. From this point on she acts with resolution and resourcefulness. She will face Ahasuerus no matter what the risk. Now it is she who gives Mordekhai instructions—which he obeys. She appears before the king, ensnares Haman, and persuades Ahasuerus to reverse his homicidal decree.[127]

Has Esther been transformed from obedient ward to formidable potentate, a model for subordinate Jewish women aspiring to burst the bonds of convention? Not exactly. Ahasuerus may be putty in her hands, but the lines of authority are not breached. The king awards Haman's estate to Esther, appropriately enough, for women could own property in the Persian system. Esther, however, immediately turns it over to Mordekhai. A magnanimous gesture by a queen? Perhaps. But more likely a dutiful gesture by a foster-daughter. This restores the proper gender relationship. Ahasuerus notably gives his signet ring—and with it the authority to issue decrees in the king's name—to Mordekhai. Esther gets her way, but only by falling at the feet of Ahasuerus, bursting into tears, and pleading with him to avert the calamity that Haman had planned for the Jewish people.[128] It is Mordekhai who, clad in royal purple and sporting a golden crown, wields power in the palace and directs the celebration of the festival of Purim.[129] The Book of Esther concludes with a reference to the royal chronicles, in which were inscribed the authority of the king and next to him, as second in-command, his grand vizier Mordekhai, most powerful of the Jews and spokesman for their welfare. No mention of Esther.[130]

As in the Book of Judith, the traditional order, in the end, is reinforced. Esther, demure and docile at the outset, placed in the palace through Mordekhai's machinations, spurred into action by his instructions, evolves into a clever and designing woman, even a vindictive one—but never usurps the role occupied by ascendant males.

The date of composition for the canonical Book of Esther cannot be fixed with precision. In all probability it came sometime in the late Persian or early Hellenistic period (between the mid-fifth and mid-third centuries B.C.E.). But

126 Ibid. 4:5–16.
127 Ibid. 4:17–5:8, 7:1–10.
128 Ibid. 8:1–6.
129 Ibid. 8:15 9:3–4, 20–23, 29–32.
130 Ibid. 10:2–3.

supplements were added in Greek, which must be Hellenistic in date, and these include a striking revision of the character of Esther.

Additions C and D, so labeled by scholars, were inserted in the story right after Mordekhai's appeal to Esther to intercede with Ahasuerus. The first invented prayers by both Mordekhai and Esther; the second supplied the actual encounter between Esther and the king. Esther's plea in Addition C is unlike anything in the Hebrew text. She strips off her splendid garments, covers herself with ashes and dung, and makes herself as unattractive as before she had been comely. She concedes that she slept with the uncircumcised king—but she hated every minute of it. Yes, she wears a crown, but only in public and only because she must. She twice proclaims her loathing of the crown and compares it to a polluted rag. She insists even that she never took food at Haman's table, thus to declare her adherence to dietary laws—though the canonical account betrays no concern on the matter.[131] The queen protests too much. The author of the addition, by stressing her strained denials, calls attention to her weaknesses.

Addition D buttresses this conclusion. It describes the audience of Esther before the king. Unlike the Hebrew text, she is here depicted as terrified. She has dressed herself once more in resplendent robes, she has summoned her God and savior, and she glows at the peak of her beauty, but inside she is racked with fear. When she sees the king, magnificent and awesome on his throne and flashing an angry glance at her, she passes out on the spot, not once but twice.[132] This is hardly the stuff of a heroine. The interpolator evidently augmented the tale at Esther's expense. Lest anyone think that Esther comes off too well in the Hebrew version, the Hellenistic Jewish author decided to fix that.

As for the striking figure of Aseneth: the chaste and haughty virgin who defies her parents and heaps scorn upon the noble Joseph, only to shift suddenly into reverse, shattering idols and abasing herself, cuts a memorable figure. With what meaning? One cannot argue that her saga, set in the milieu of the Egyptian elite in the legendary era of Jacob and Joseph, reflects in any significant way the ordinary lives of Hellenistic Jews. But it may well resonate with ideological presuppositions about women's appropriate role in Jewish society.[133]

Aseneth's arrogance, disdain, disobedience of her parents, and virginal superiority represent all that Jews (and not they alone) found threatening and repugnant in women. She even boasts of a bed in which she sleeps alone and

---

131 Add. Esth. C, 12 – 13, 26 – 28.

132 Add. Esth. D, 1 – 15.

133 See the provocative suggestions in R. S. Kraemer, *When Aseneth Met Joseph* (Oxford, 1998), 191 – 221.

which has never been sat upon by man or woman.[134] The fiery Aseneth breaches every convention, and her actions, for the author of the text, naturally go hand in hand with ignorance of the true God and reckless idolatry. Aseneth has few redeeming features.

With the arrival of Joseph, however, Aseneth's hard exterior, cockiness, and contemptuousness vanish. Once the embodiment of all that is undesirable in a woman, she is now submissive, subservient, and self-abasing. And her rescuer from the abyss of despair is, appropriately, a male, the angelic figure whose ministrations restore her former beauty and make her a fitting bride—though only after she has made a fool of herself yet again.[135] Aseneth humbly and gratefully welcomes her marriage, accepting her role as handmaiden to her bridegroom and insisting on washing his feet.[136] Her gratitude, expressed in a prayer to the Lord, consists of further self-denigration, confession of sins and offenses, and a declaration that her previous arrogance has been recast as humility.[137] Her former assertiveness could only be undone by degradation. *Joseph and Aseneth* reaffirms the suitable demeanor of women: deference to parents and submissiveness to husbands. Aseneth, who violates all the norms at the outset, spends much of the remainder of the tale reproaching herself, *ad nauseam.*

The story of Susanna sustains the theme. No need for remorse or transformation here: Susanna is virtue itself from the outset. The prim, modest, faithful matron was brought up properly by her parents: they instructed her in the Law of Moses. And she has been wed to a pillar of the Jewish community. Susanna epitomizes the figure of the pious and demure wife.[138] Her very innocence, however, renders her vulnerable to the wicked elders who present her with a grievous choice. The unhappy woman chooses the lesser evil: an unfair trial rather than the loss of her virtue. But her decision only underscores her helplessness. This is not so much steadfastness as resignation.

Susanna suffers further humiliation at the hearing: she is stripped naked (so the Septuagint version indicates), a prejudgment of her crime and public mortification. She does not utter a word in self-defense; only after being condemned does she release a plaintive wail, asking the Lord why an innocent victim must perish.[139] She is, of course, rescued and vindicated, but not through any actions of her own. Daniel materializes, as God's agent, to foil the elders' scheme.

---

134 *Jos. Asen.,* 2:8–9.
135 Ibid., 14–17; see, esp., 17:7–10.
136 Ibid., 19:4–5, 20:4–5.
137 Ibid., 21:11–21.
138 Dan. 13:1–4.
139 Dan. 13:32–35, 41–43.

The heroine of this tale, in short, is hardly heroic—an admirable, but a purely passive, figure. Susanna lacks the weight to resist the mighty and lets her fate
be decided by others. At the conclusion, her reputation restored, she returns
meekly to the household of her husband—who, so far as we can tell, had not
even been present at her trial. The public credit for this success goes to Daniel.[140]

Women, in sum, figure prominently in the fictional compositions of Hellenistic Jews. But these creations do not serve to challenge the conventions of society; they manage, in fact, to reinforce and confirm them. The uppity Aseneth becomes a penitent, and arrogance is turned into abject submissiveness. Esther's
position gives her access to power and a means to save her people, but she
needs to be prodded, gives way to stereotypically female faintheartedness, and
defers to male authority. The innocent and docile Susanna the ideal wife, is helpless in the face of injustice but is rescued by a male hero and restored to the
bosom of her presumed protectors. Even Judith, the respected widow, who bursts
from her privacy to eclipse inept male leadership, reverts to private life and public invisibility. The inventive constructs of fertile writers largely reasserted the
values of their society and the place of women within it.

Diaspora and Homeland

A firm sense of Jewish identity required more than the definition of a relationship with other cultures and peoples. A matter internal to the nation demanded
repeated reappraisal: the issue of Diaspora and the homeland.

The destruction of the Second Temple in 70 C.E. constitutes, in most analyses, a watershed event for the Jews of antiquity. The elimination of the center,
source of spiritual nourishment and preeminent symbol of the nation's identity,
compelled Jews to reinvent themselves, to find other means of religious sustenance, and to adjust their lives to an indefinite period of displacement. That trauma has pervasive and enduring resonance. But it tends to obscure a striking fact.
Jews faced a still more puzzling and problematic situation *prior* to the loss of the
Temple. Diaspora did not await the fall of Jerusalem. Very large numbers of Jews
dwelt outside Palestine in the roughly four centuries from the time of Alexander
the Great to that of Titus.[141] The era of the Second Temple in fact brought the
issue into sharp focus, inescapably so. The Temple still stood, a reminder of

140 Dan. 13:63–64; cf. 13:30.
141 For population estimates, see *Encyclopaedia Judaica*, 13: 866–903, and L. H. Feldman,
Jew and Gentile in the Ancient World (Princeton, 1993), 23, 468–69, 555–56.

the hallowed past, and a Jewish regime had authority in Palestine. Yet the Jews of the Diaspora, from Italy to Iran, far outnumbered those in the homeland. Although Jerusalem loomed large in their self-perception as a nation, only a few of them had seen it, and few were likely to. How then did Diaspora Jews conceive their association with Jerusalem, the emblem of ancient tradition?

A dark picture prevails. Diaspora appears as something to be *overcome*. Thunderous biblical pronouncements present it as the terrible penalty exacted by God for the sins of the Israelites. They will be scattered among the nations and pursued by divine wrath. Spread among the lands, they will worship false gods and idols and enjoy no repose from the anger of the Lord. If the children of Israel abandon the ancestral precepts, they will have to enter the servitude of foreign lords in foreign parts. They will be dispersed among peoples unknown to them or to their fathers and will suffer God's vengeance until their destruction.[142] Through much of the Scriptures, only a single goal keeps flickering hopes alive: the expectation, however distant, of returning from exile and regaining a place in the Promised Land. Obedience to the Lord and repentance for past errors will induce Him to regather the lost souls spread across the world and restore them to the land of their fathers. He will raise a banner among the nations and assemble the people of Judah from the four corners of the earth.[143] It should be no surprise that a negative verdict on Diaspora life and a correspondingly gloomy attitude are conventionally ascribed to the Jews of the Second Temple period.[144]

Yet that convention ignores a grave implausibility. It is not easy to imagine that millions of Jews in the Diaspora were obsessed with a longing for Jerusalem that had little chance of fulfillment. It seems only logical that they sought means whereby to legitimize the existence that most of them inherited from their parents and would bequeath to their descendants.[145] Large and thriving Jewish communities existed in numerous areas of the Mediterranean, with opportunities for economic advancement, social status, and even political responsibilities.[146]

---

142 Lev. 26:33; Deut. 4:26–28, 28:63–65; Jer. 5:19, 9:15.

143 Deut. 30:2–5; Isa. 11:12.

144 See, e. g., Y. F. Baer, *Galut* (New York, 1947), 9–13, and A. Eisen, *Galut* (Bloomington, Ind., 1986), 3–34. The most sweeping argument on melancholy Jewish attitudes toward the Diaspora in the Second Temple era is made in W. C. van Unnik, *Das Selbstverständnis der jüdischen Diaspora in der hellenistisch-römischen Zeit* (Leiden, 1993), *passim*. See also the very useful survey by W. D. Davies, *The Territorial Dimension of Judaism* (Berkeley, 1981), 28–34, 61–100.

145 See I. M. Gafni, *Land, Center, and Diaspora* (Sheffield, Engl., 1997), 19–40.

146 The classic study is J. Juster, *Les juifs dans l'empire romain,* 2 vols. (Paris, 1914). Among other treatments, see Schürer, *History of the Jewish People,* vol. 3.1, 1–176; Barclay, *Jews in*

Did their members, as some have claimed, take recourse in the thesis that the nation is defined by its texts rather than by its location?[147]

The dualism is deceptive. The Jews of antiquity, in fact, never developed a systematic theory or philosophy of Diaspora. The whole idea of valuing homeland over Diaspora or Diaspora, over homeland may be off the mark. Second Temple Jews need not have faced so stark a choice.

The characterization of Diaspora as exile occurs with some frequency in the works of Hellenistic Jewish writers. But close scrutiny discloses an important and neglected fact. The majority of these grim pronouncements refer to the *biblical* misfortunes of the Israelites: expulsion by Assyrians, the destruction of the Temple, and the Babylonian captivity. Were they all metaphors for the Hellenistic Diaspora? The inference would be hasty, and it begs the question.

Ben Sira, for instance, laments the sins of his forefathers and records the fierce retaliation of the Lord that uprooted them from their land and dispersed them into every other land.[148] The reference, however, is to the era of Elijah, and Elisha, to the ills of the Northern Kingdom, and to the Assyrian conquest that scattered the Israelites. It may have carried a warning to Ben Sira's contemporaries, whose shortcoming paralleled those of his ancestors—but it did not condemn the current Diaspora. The Book of Tobit tells a tale that ostensibly transpires in the Assyrian captivity as well. Tobit bewails his own fate, prompted by the sins of his forefathers, and the fate of his countrymen, an object of scorn and a vulnerable prey to those in the nations whence they have been dispersed.[149] But Tobit also forecasts the recovery of the Temple and portrays the outcome as the culmination of Israelite dreams, a happy ending to endure indefinitely.[150] This, hardly suggests that the Hellenistic Diaspora is a vale of tears.

One text, to be sure, with explicit reference to Hellenistic Jews, does suggest that they were in dire straits in the Diaspora. The inventive tale of 3 Maccabees, composed probably in the second or first century B.C.E., places the Jews of Egypt in the gravest peril. Thrice they are almost annihilated by the wicked schemes of the mad monarch Ptolemy IV. The fantasy implies a precarious existence at the

the *Mediterranean Diaspora*, 19–81, 231–319; and I. Levinskaya, *The Book of Acts in Its Diaspora Setting* (Grand Rapids, Mich., 1996), 127–93.
147 See, esp., G. Steiner, "Our Homeland, The Text," *Salmagundi* 66 (1985): 4–25. On the ambivalence of exile and homecoming in recent Jewish conceptions, see the comments of S. D. Ezrahi, "Our Homeland, the Text ... Our Text, the Homeland: Exile and Homecoming in the Modern Jewish Imagination," *Michigan Quarterly Review* 31 (1992): 463–97.
148 Ben Sira 48:15.
149 Tob. 3:3–4, 13:3–6, 14:4.
150 Tob. 13:10–11, 14:5–6.

mercy of their enemies. They are to perish unjustly, a foreign people in a foreign land.[151] But the dire foreboding does not come to pass. The Jews triumph, their enemies are thwarted, and their apostates are punished. More significantly, the victory will be celebrated by an annual festival—in Egypt.[152] The Diaspora existence can go on indefinitely and contentedly.

Satisfactory circumstances in the Diaspora, however, did not diminish the sanctity and centrality of Jerusalem. Its aura retained a hold on the consciousness of Hellenistic Jews, wherever they happened to reside. Jerusalem is referred to on several occasions as "the holy city." The Jews' devotion to their sacred "acropolis" is observed even by the pagan geographer Strabo.[153] Numerous other texts characterize Palestine as the "holy land." The designation appears in works as different as 2 Maccabees, the Wisdom of Solomon, the Testament of Job, the Sibylline Oracles, and Philo.[154] Most, if not all, of these texts stem from the Diaspora. They underscore the reverence with which Jews around the Mediterranean continued to regard Jerusalem and the land of their fathers. But the authors who speak of reverence do not demand the "Return."

How compelling was the notion of a "homeland" to Jews dwelling in Mediterranean communities? In principle, the concept held firm. Loyalty to one's native land was a deep commitment in the rhetoric of the Hellenistic world.[155] Philo more than once endorses the idea that adherence to one's *patris* has singular power. He speaks of the charms of kinsmen and homeland; trips abroad are good for widening one's horizons, but nothing better than coming home. Failure to worship God is put on a level with neglecting to honor parents, benefactors, and patris. Defending one's country is a prime virtue. And, as Philo has Agrippa say to Caligula, love of one's native land and compliance with its precepts is deeply ingrained in all men.[156] It does not follow, however, that Diaspora Jews set their hearts upon a return to the fatherland. Broad pronouncements about love of one's country accord with general Hellenistic attitudes and expressions. They do not require that those native environs be reinhabited for life to be complete.

Did Jewish settlement abroad carry a stigma? Jews in fact formed stable communities in the Diaspora, entered into the social, economic, and political life of

---

151 2 Macc. 6:3; cf. 6:10.
152 3 Macc. 6:36, 7:15, 19.
153 2 Macc. 1:12; Philo, *Legat.* 225, 281, 288, 299, 346; Strab., 16.2.37.
154 2 Macc. 1:7; Wis. 12:3; T. Job 33:5; 3 Sib. 267, 732–35; 5 Sib. 281; Philo, *Her.* 293; *In Flacc.* 46; *Legat.* 202, 205, 330. Cf. Zech. 2:16.
155 Cf. Plb. 1.14.4.
156 Philo, *Abr.* 63, 65, 197; *Mos.* 2:198; *Mut.* 40; *Cher.* 15; *Legat.* 277, 328.

the nations they joined, and aspired to and obtained civic privileges in the cities of the Hellenistic world. Josephus maintains that Jews have every right to call themselves Alexandrians, Antiochenes, or Ephesians. And Philo refers to his home as "our Alexandria."[157] That form of identification surfaces more poignantly in the petition of an Alexandrian Jew threatened with the loss of his privileges. He labels himself an "Alexandrian" at the head of the document, alluding to his father, also an Alexandrian, and the proper education he had received, and expresses his fear of being deprived of his patris.[158] Whatever legal meaning this terminology might have carried, it signals the petitioner's clear affirmation of his roots in the community. A comparable sentiment might be inferred from an inscription of the Phrygian city of Acmonia, alluding to fulfillment of a vow made to the "whole patris." A Jew or a group of Jews must have commissioned it, because a menorah appears beneath the text. Here again the "native city" is honored, presumably through a gift for civic purposes. The donor pronounces his local loyalty in a conspicuous public manner.[159] Philo confirms the sentiment in striking fashion: Jews consider the holy city as their "metropolis," but the states in which they were born and raised and which they acquired from their fathers, grandfathers, and distant forefathers they adjudge their *patrides*.[160] That fervent expression eradicates any idea of the "doctrine of return." Diaspora Jews, in Philo's formulation at least, held a fierce attachment to the adopted lands of their ancestors.

Commitment to one's local and regional community in no way diminished one's devotion to Jerusalem. That the two were mutually exclusive alternatives is plainly false. Reverence for Jerusalem was indeed publicly and conspicuously demonstrated every year by the payment of a tithe to the Temple by Jews all over the Mediterranean.[161] The ritualistic offering carried deep significance as a bonding device.

In the mid-sixties B.C.E., economic circumstances in Rome and abroad prompted a series of decrees forbidding the export of gold. In accord with this policy, the Roman governor of Asia, L. Valerius Flaccus, banned the sending of gold by the Jews of Asia Minor to Jerusalem. The action not only provoked resentment in Flaccus's province but also stirred a hornet's nest of opposition in Rome itself. Cicero, who conducted Flaccus's defense at his trial for extortion in 59,

---

157 Jos., *C. Ap.*, 2:38 – 39; Philo, *Legat.* 150.
158 *Corpus Papyrorum Iudaicarum*, II, #151.
159 *Corpus Inscriptionum Iudaicarum*, #771.
160 Philo, *Flacc.* 46.
161 See the useful summary of testimony and the discussion in S. Safrai and M. Stern, *The Jewish People in the First Century* (Philadelphia, 1974), 1:186 – 91.

comments bitterly about the horde of Jews crowding around the tribunal, exercising undue pressure upon the proceedings, and passionately exhibiting their "barbaric superstition."[162] The, account, of course, is partisan, rhetorical, and exaggerated—but Cicero conveys some precious information. First, he indicates the Jews' earnest commitment to provide funds annually to the Temple from Italy and, from all the provinces of the Roman empire. Next, his record of Flaccus's activities indicates that Jewish communities collected the tribute, city by city, wherever they possessed sufficient numbers in Asia Minor. And, most revealing, his speech, however embellished and overblown, shows that the plight of the Asian Jews who were prevented from making their contributions stirred the passions of their compatriots far off in Rome and generated impressively noisy demonstrations on their behalf.

References to the importance of the tithe abound. Josephus proudly observes that the donations came from Jews all over Asia and Europe, indeed from everywhere in the world, for countless years. And when local authorities interfered with that activity, the Jews would send up a howl to Rome.[163] The emperor Augustus himself, and Roman officials acting in his name, intervened to ensure the untroubled exercise of Jewish practices in the province of Asia and elsewhere.[164] And the Jews in areas beyond the reach of Roman power also tithed with rigor and consistency. Communities in Babylon and other satrapies under Parthian dominion sent representatives every year over difficult terrain and dangerous highways to deposit their contributions in the Temple.[165] The issue of paying homage to Jerusalem was paramount: Indeed the Romans, even after they destroyed the Temple, did not destroy that institution—an ironic acknowledgment of its power. They simply altered its recipient. The tithe would no longer go to the demolished shrine; it would metamorphose into a Roman tax. The money would now subsidize the cult of Jupiter Capitolinus.[166]

The stark symbolism of the tithe had a potent hold upon Jewish sentiment. That annual act of obeisance was a repeated reminder, or rather display, of affection and allegiance, visible evidence of the unbroken attachment of the Diaspora to the center. How to interpret its implications? Did the remittance imply that the Diaspora was only a temporary exile?

In fact, the reverse conclusion holds. The yearly contribution proclaimed that the Diaspora could endure indefinitely, and quite satisfactorily. The com-

---

162 Cicero, *Flacc.*, 66–68.
163 Jos. *A. J.*, 14:110, 16:28, 45–50; cf. 18:312–13; *BJ*, 7:45.
164 Philo, *Legat.* 291, 312; Jos. *A.J.*, 16:163, 166–71.
165 Philo, *Legat.* 216.
166 Jos., *B. J.*, 7:218; Dio Cassius, 66.7.2.

munities abroad were entrenched and successful, even mainstays of the center. Diaspora Jews did not and would not turn their backs on Jerusalem, which remained the principal emblem of their faith. Their fierce commitment to the tithe delivered that message unequivocally. But the gesture did not signify a desire for the "Return." It rendered the Return unnecessary.

A comparable phenomenon reinforces that proposition: the pilgrimage of Diaspora Jews to Jerusalem. Major festivals could attract them with some frequency and in quantity. According to Philo, myriads came from countless cities for every feast, over land and sea, from all points of the compass to enjoy the Temple as a serene refuge from the hurly-burly of everyday life abroad.[167] The most celebrated occasion occurred after the death of Jesus. The feast of Pentecost brought throngs of people into the city from far-flung and diverse locations: from Parthia, Media, and Elam, from Mesopotamia and Cappadocia, from Pontus and Asia, from Phrygia and Pamphylia, from Egypt and Cyrene, from Crete and Arabia, and, indeed, even from Rome, all witness to the miracle of the disciples speaking in tongues.[168] The women's court at the Temple was large enough to accommodate those who resided in the land and those who came from abroad—a clear sign that female pilgrims in some numbers were expected visitors.[169]

The holy city was a forceful magnet, but the demonstration of devotion did not entail a desire for migration. Pilgrimage, in fact, by its very nature, signified a temporary payment of respect. Jerusalem had an irresistible and undiminished claim on the emotions of Diaspora Jews; it was indeed a critical piece of their identity. But home was elsewhere.

The self-perception of Second Temple Jews projected a tight solidarity between Center and Diaspora. Images of exile and separation did not haunt them. What affected the dwellers in Jerusalem affected Jews everywhere. The theme of intertwined experience and identity is reiterated with impressive frequency and variety.

The *Letter of Aristeas*, for instance, makes an unequivocal connection between Jerusalemites and other Jews. King Ptolemy's letter to the high priest in Judaea asserts that his motive in having the Hebrew Bible rendered into Greek is to benefit not only the Jews of Egypt but all Jews throughout the world—even those not yet born. And it is fitting that, when the scholars from Jerusalem, complete their translation and it is read out to the Jews of Egypt, the large assemblage burst into applause, a dramatic expression of the unity of purpose.[170]

---

167 Philo, *Spec.* 1:69; cf. Safrai and Stern, *Jewish People,* 1:191–94.
168 Acts 2:1–11; cf. 6:9.
169 Jos., *B. J.,* 5:199.
170 *Let. Aris.,* 38, 307–11.

The narrative of 3 Maccabees depends on that same unity of purpose. It presupposes and never questions the proposition that the actions of Jerusalemites represent the sentiments of Jews anywhere in the Diaspora. When Ptolemy IV is thwarted in his design to enter the Holy of Holies in Jerusalem, he resolves to punish the Jews of Egypt. The king is determined to bring public shame, upon the *ethnos* of the Jews generally. Egyptian Jews are "fellow-tribesmen" of those who dwelled in Judaea.[171]

The affiliations emerge most dramatically and drastically in the grave crises that marked the reign of the emperor Caligula (37–41 C.E.). Harsh conflict erupted in Alexandria, bringing dislocation, persecution, and death upon the Jewish community. And a still worse menace loomed over Jerusalem when the erratic emperor proposed to have a statue of himself installed in the Temple. When Alexandrian Jews were attacked, says Philo, the word spread like wildfire. As the synagogues were destroyed in Alexandria, reports swept not only through all the districts of Egypt but from there to the nations of the east and from the borders of Libya to the lands of the west. Jews had settled all over Europe and Asia, and the news of a pogrom anywhere would race through the entire network.[172] Philo's claim of such speedy communications may stretch a point, but the concept of tight interrelationships among Jews of the Diaspora is plain and potent.

Philo himself headed the delegation to the emperor that would plead the cause of the Alexandrian Jews. Their objective, however, was swiftly eclipsed by word of Caligula's decision to install his statue in the Temple at Jerusalem. Philo's words are arresting: the most grievous calamity fell unexpectedly and brought peril not to one part of the Jewish people but to the entire nation at once.[173] The letter of Agrippa I, a friend of the emperor and recently awarded a kingdom among the Jews, urgently alerted Caligula to the gravity of the situation. Agrippa maintained that an affront to Jerusalem would have vast repercussions: the holy city was not merely metropolis of Judaea but of most nations in the world since Jewish colonies thrived all over the Near East, Asia Minor, Greece, Macedon, Africa, and the lands beyond the Euphrates.[174] The image of Jerusalem as binding together Jews everywhere in the world held a prominent place in the self-perception of the Diaspora.

A moving passage elsewhere in Philo encapsulates this theme. Although he thrived in the Diaspora, enjoyed its advantages, and broadcast its virtues, Philo nevertheless found even deeper meaning in the land of Israel. He interprets the

---

171 3 Macc. 2:21–27, 3:21.
172 Philo, *Flacc.* 45–46.
173 Philo, *Legat.* 184; cf. 178, 351, 373.
174 Philo, *Legat.* 277–83; cf. 330.

Shavuot festival as a celebration of the Jews' possession of their own land, a heritage now of long standing, and a means whereby they could cease their wandering.[175] Philo saw no inconsistency or contradiction. Diaspora Jews might find fulfillment and reward in their communities abroad, but they honored Judaea as a refuge for those who were once displaced and unsettled—and the prime legacy of all.

Josephus makes the point in a quite different context but with equal force. In his rewriting of Numbers, he places a sweeping prognostication in the mouth of the Midianite priest Balaam. The priest projects a glorious future for the Israelites: they will not only occupy and hold forever the land of Canaan, a chief signal of God's favor, but their multitudes will fill all the world, islands and continents, outnumbering even the stars in the heavens.[176] That is a notable declaration. Palestine, as ever, merits a special place. But the Diaspora, far from being a source of shame to be overcome, represents a resplendent achievement.

The respect and awe one paid to the Holy Land stood in full harmony with a commitment to the local community and allegiance to gentile governance. Diaspora Jews did not bewail their fate and pine away for the homeland. Nor, by contrast, did they shrug off the homeland and reckon the Book as surrogate for the Temple. The postulated alternatives are reductive and simplistic. Palestine mattered, and it mattered in a territorial sense—but not as a required residence. A gift to the temple and a pilgrimage to Jerusalem announced simultaneously one's devotion to the symbolic heart of Judaism and a singular pride in the accomplishments of the Diaspora.

The Jews forever refashioned their identity and adjusted their self-perception with an eye to the cultural milieu in which they found themselves. The age when Hellenic culture held sway in the Near East was no exception. Jews adopted a range of strategies that allowed them to negotiate their presence within that milieu. I have endeavored in this chapter to break down the usual dichotomies and question the customary boundaries. The image of confrontation, tension, and antagonism between Judaism and Hellenism needs to be reassessed. This was no zero sum game in which every move toward Hellenism meant a loss for Jewish tradition. A complex process of adjustment took place whereby Jews found expression for their own heritage in the language and conventions of the larger community. The process, to be sure, sometimes involved struggle, dissension,

---

175 Philo, *Spec.* 2:168.
176 Jos., *A. J.*, 4:115 – 16. Josephus departs here quite substantially from the corresponding text in Num. 23:6 – 10. Cf. also Jos., *A. J.*, 1:282, 2:213.

and occasional catastrophe, but it did not reduce itself to mere conflict between the cultures.

Jewish perspectives on the Greeks (or gentiles generally) in this era show variety, overlapping, and nuance, rather than the simplistic alternatives of sharp differentiation or a striving for accommodation. The internal boundaries were as fluid as the external ones. The divide between elite and popular Jewish culture is elided by the nature of our texts and their history. The process of transmission and rewriting over the course of many generations produced cultural artifacts that spoke in a variety of voices and at several levels of meaning across conventional social and intellectual barriers. Women were reconceived by Jewish fiction as figures of prominence and high visibility, in ostensible contradistinction to the realities of social life. Yet fiction and fact had more convergence than divergence: the imaginative tales largely endorsed the gender hierarchy. And even the familiar duality of homeland and exile requires reconsideration. Jews thoroughly embraced the Diaspora communities in which they could lead full and rewarding lives—without compromising their allegiance to the symbol of their faith in Jerusalem. They successfully negotiated their own place within the world of Greco-Roman society: they were appropriationists rather than assimilationists. And they shunned the melting pot.

Jewish Identity and Greco-Roman Culture

3. Fact and Fiction: Jewish Legends in a Hellenistic Context

The terms *Ioudaismos* and *Hellenismos* first appear in the text of II Maccabees.* That work provides the *locus classicus* for confrontation between the two cultures, a buttress for the idea that a clash or competition characterized the encounter. The coming of Hellenism to the land of the Jews, so it has been inferred, brought a threat to tradition and faith. Increasing Hellenization entailed erosion of ancestral Jewish practice or belief. And the Jews faced a choice of either assimilation or resistance to Hellenism.[1]

Various statements in II Maccabees ostensibly lend weight to the conclusion. New institutions introduced by the High Priest Jason in the 170's B.C.E., namely the gymnasium and the ephebate, were, according to that text, the "height of Hellenism."[2] He had the Jews conform to the "Greek style of life."[3] And in three separate passages, the author of II Maccabees refers to those who fought for Judas Maccabaeus and resisted the persecutor Antiochus Epiphanes as ad-

---

* This paper adheres closely to the lecture delivered in January 1993 at the Cambridge Ancient History Seminar honoring Frank Walbank—mentor, guide, and inspiration to all who have labored in the fields of Hellenistic studies for the past two generations. Footnotes have been added to supply essential citations, selective references to modern work, and some evaluation of the scholarship. The paper's principal purpose is to lay out ideas and research plans for *Heritage and Hellenism: The Reinvention of Jewish Tradition* Hellenistic Culture and Society (Berkeley: University of California Press, 1998).

1 The influential work of M. Hengel, *Judaism and Hellenism* (London, 1974) makes a strong case for the Hellenization of Judaea which, however, in his view, encountered vigorous Jewish resistance after the early 2nd century B.C.E. See the summary of his interpretation in *Judaism and Hellenism*, I, 247–54. The broad-ranging study of L. H. Feldman, *Jew and Gentile in the Ancient World: Attitudes and Interactions from Alexander to Justinian* (Princeton, N.J.: Princeton University Press, 1993), takes sharp issue with Hengel's findings on the spread of Hellenism among the Jews and attributes Jewish success to an internal strength and vitality that overcame the challenge of Greek culture; see, especially, 42–44, 416–22. Both scholars, however, operate from the premise that Jews who did not resist the blandishments of paganism ran the risk of succumbing to assimilation. A similar struggle is outlined by V. Tcherikover, *Hellenistic Civilization and the Jews*, 1st ed. (Philadelphia,: Jewish Publication Society of America, 1959), 152–74, 193–203; cf. C. Habicht, *JhrbHeidAkad* (1974) 97–110; A. Momigliano, *RivStorItal* 88 (1976) 425–43 = *Essays on Ancient and Modern Judaism* (Chicago, 1994) 10–28. For S. J. D. Cohen, the Maccabaean crisis stimulated the Jews to develop a sense of identity that would highlight their own distinctiveness and allow them to resist the forces of assimilation, in P. Bilde et al., *Religion and Religious Practice in the Seleucid Kingdom* (Aarhus, 1990) 204–23.

2 2 Macc. 4.13: ἀχμή τις Ἑλληνισμοῦ.

3 2 Macc. 4.10: πρὸς τὸν Ἑλληνιχὸν χαραχτῆρα; cf. 6.9, 11.24.

herents of *Ioudaismos*.[4] Hence it is not surprising that Hellenism and Judaism have regularly been reckoned as competing systems.

Yet a peculiar paradox lies here. The very work that employs those terms, its author a staunch advocate of the Maccabaean cause and fiercely hostile to the Seleucid invader, was composed in Greek and addressed to a readership conversant with the language. Outside that text, one would be hard pressed to find testimony to any conflict between Hellenism and Judaism in contemporary or near contemporary texts. No evidence for cultural strife appears in I Maccabees. It is absent also from the work of Ben Sira, written in the early second century. Ben Sira denounces those who fall away from righteousness, tyrannize the poor, and abandon fear of the Lord or the teachings of the law. But he nowhere contrasts Jews and Greeks or suggests a struggle for the conscience of his fellow-Jews being waged by Hellenizers and traditionalists.[5] Nor can one discern such a struggle in the Book of Daniel, composed at the very time of the Maccabaean revolt. The apocalyptic visions allude to contests among the Hellenistic powers and forecast delivery of the Jews from the foreign oppressor—but no cultural contest for the soul of Judaism.[6] In fact, not even II Maccabees juxtaposes the terms *Ioudaismos* and *Hellenismos* or expresses them as competing opposites. It is a mistake to imagine a zero-sum game, in which every gain for Hellenism was a loss for Judaism or vice-versa. That sort of analysis, as an increasing number of scholars now acknowledge, is simplistic and misleading.[7] Adaptation to Hellenic culture did not require compromise of Jewish precepts or conscience. When a Greek gymnasium was introduced into Jerusalem, it was installed by a Jewish High Priest. And other priests soon engaged in wrestling matches in the palaestra.[8] They plainly did not reckon such activities as undermining their priestly duties. The idea of an irremediable cultural conflict needs to be abandoned.

A different and more interesting line of inquiry warrants attention. How did Jewish intellectuals accommodate themselves to the larger cultural world of the Mediterranean—while at the same time reaffirming the character of their own traditions within it? The subject, of course, is massive and daunting. Only a select portion of it can be touched on here. This is not the place to pronounce on a

---

4 2 Macc. 2.21, 8.1, 14.38.
5 See the cogent remarks of J. Goldstein in E.P. Sanders, *Jewish and Christian Self-Definition* (Philadelphia, 1981) 70–81. *Contra:* Hengel, *Judaism and Hellenism*, I, 131–53; A. Momigliano, *Alien Wisdom* (Cambridge, 1975) 95.
6 Dan. 11.2–12.3. See Momigliano, *Alien Wisdom* 109–12.
7 Cf. E. Will and Cl. Orrieux, *Ioudaismos-Hellenismos* (Nancy, 1986) 120–36; G. Delling, *ANRW* II.20.1 (1987) 3–39; L. Grabbe, *Judaism from Cyrus to Hadrian* (Minneapolis, 1992) I, 169–70.
8 2 Macc. 4.12, 4.14.

number of matters that have been much discussed and defy treatment within a limited compass—such as how far Greek culture had penetrated Palestine in the Hellenistic period and how profound or superficial that penetration was, or to what degree Palestinian Judaism represented an entity distinct from "Hellenistic" Judaism of the Diaspora. Nor can one outline in brief the influence of Greek language, literature, philosophy, historiography, political theory, and art upon Judaism. Analyses along these lines, however learned and insightful, too often tend to presuppose passive receptivity on the part of Jewish thinkers to Hellenic culture, a one-way street. What this paper seeks to stress is a more dynamic relationship, an active engagement by Jews with the traditions of Hellas which they recast and refashioned for their own purposes. One form of such activity comes under investigation here, an especially intriguing one: the elaboration of legends, fictions, and inventions, by which the Jews both connected themselves with a Hellenic cultural legacy and simultaneously defined a distinctive cultural identity of their own.

The first and most revealing category of such stories involves putative kinship associations. The tracing of relationships between cities, states, or peoples through supposed genealogical links and imagined common ancestors regularly appears in Greek literary speculation—a familiar feature in Hellenic folklore and legend. It makes a more striking impression, however, to find tales of this sort attesting connections between Greeks and Jews.

A notable fiction stands in the forefront. Tradition had it that Jews and Spartans both descended from the line of Abraham. The web of tales requires only brief summary here. The subject has been treated more extensively elsewhere.[9] A diplomatic correspondence, consisting of three letters, recorded in I Maccabees and reproduced in a variant form by Josephus, constitutes the central testimony. The exchange began with a missive from King Areus to the Judaean High Priest Onias, ostensibly in the early third century B.C.E. Areus declared a blood tie between the two people, deriving from their common ancestor Abraham. He drew that information, so he claimed, from a written document in Sparta.[10] More than a century later, the Maccabaean leader Jonathan, successor of Judas, resumed relations with an embassy to Sparta, addressing the Lacedaemonians as ἀδελφοί and renewing the relations of friendship and alliance between the peoples.[11] The Spartans responded in kind. Some time later, when Simon had taken the reins

---

9 See E. S. Gruen, "The Purported Jewish-Spartan Affiliation," in R. W. Wallace and E. M. Harris, eds., *Transitions to Empire: Essays in Greco-Roman History, 360–146 B.C., in Honor of E. Badian* (Norman, Oklahoma, 1996) 254–69, also available in this volume.
10 1 Macc. 12.20–23; Jos. *A. J.* 12.225–27.
11 1 Macc. 6.12–18; Jos. *A. J.* 12.225–27, 13.164–70.

from the fallen Jonathan, envoys from their state reached Jerusalem, greeted the Jews as brothers, proclaimed their intent to renew friendship and alliance, and announced that the association would be preserved in written form in the Spartan archives.[12]

The authenticity of that correspondence has long engendered debate and controversy—with an increasing inclination toward belief. Some have proposed that King Areus' scribes managed to learn Aramaic and composed a letter in that language, or that the Spartans had read the Scriptures even before appearance of the Septuagint, or indeed that they had learned of the patriarch Abraham from reading Hecataeus of Abdera—of course, in some portion of his work that we no longer possess.[13] These exercises in imagination can be set aside. Areus, the enterprising and aggressive Spartan ruler of the early third century, had no need for the moral or substantive support of a remote dependency of the Ptolemaic empire. Nor would the Jews of the second century find any special political or diplomatic advantage in claiming connection with Sparta.

Two points only call for emphasis here. The kinship affiliation carried cultural, not political, implications. And it was an invention by the Jews. Abraham as ultimate progenitor makes the matter clear. Further, Areus is made to express himself in terms that sound suspiciously Biblical: "your cattle and goods are ours, and ours are yours."[14] And, equally revealing, the tone of Jonathan's letter to the Spartans conveys a distinctively Jewish orientation toward the relationship. Jonathan sets on record Jewish successes accomplished through divine grace and without aid of Spartans or others.

He reassures his Lacedaemonian allies that they can count on Jewish intercession through sacrifices and prayers, as is only proper for kinsmen.[15] The Jews, in other words, secured for Sparta the favor of the true god. The tone has a distinctly patronizing ring. Jonathan represents his people as indulgent benefactors.

Wherein lay the stimulus for this invention? Jewish intellectuals did not rush to attach themselves to a Hellenic heritage. The fictive forefather was Abraham, not Heracles. The Jews, to be sure, were claiming links with a Greek community.

---

12 1 Macc. 14.16–23; cf. Jos. *A. J.* 13.170.
13 For bibliography, see B. Cardauns, *Hermes* 95 (1967) 317–18, n. 1; R. Katzoff, *AJP* 106 (1985) 485, n. 1; Cl. Orrieux in R. Lonis, *L'étranger dans le monde grec: Actes du colloque organisé par l'Institut d'Études Anciennes* (Nancy, 1987) 187, n. 7; more recently, P. Cartledge and A. Spawforth, *Hellenistic and Roman Sparta* (London, 1989) 36–37, 239, n. 22. See, further, Gruen "The Purported Jewish-Spartan Affiliation".
14 1 Macc. 12.23.
15 1 Macc. 12.9–15.

But this fable represents a Jewish endeavor to fit Greeks into their own traditions rather than to seek assimilation to Hellenism.

The pattern repeats itself. An equally remarkable tradition derives from an obscure and untraceable writer named Cleodemus Malchus, cited by Alexander Polyhistor and preserved by Josephus and Eusebius.[16] Cleodemus, conventionally dated to the second century B.C.E., claims Moses as his authority, an ostensible reference to the book of Genesis. In his version, Abraham's children by Katoura included three sons named Assouri, Apher, and Aphran. Assouri became namesake of Assyria, the others of the city of Apher and the land of Africa respectively. The latter two made their way to Africa, there to participate in Heracles' successful crusade against the Libyan giant Antaeus. Heracles then proceeded to marry the daughter of Aphran, from whom the whole continent of Africa took its name.

The author Cleodemus Malchus escapes identification. A variety of modern conjectures have labeled him as either Jew, Samaritan, Syrian, Phoenician, Carthaginian, or some combination thereof.[17] No definitive solution is forthcoming, nor is one necessary. The scholarly debate operates on the assumption that if we could determine Cleodemus' nationality, we could discern the motives for the invention. But nothing shows that Cleodemus invented it anyway; we know only that Polyhistor found it in that source. The story itself could have originated earlier, elsewhere, and under any number of possible circumstances. What matters is not the origin of the legend but its meaning and implications. As with the Spartan-Jewish connection, the link between Abraham and Heracles represents an *interpretatio Judaica*, not *Graeca*. The line begins with the Hebrew patriarch, his grandson has the honor of a continent named after him, and Heracles' victory becomes by inference the outcome of Jewish intervention. The Greek hero gains stature by marrying into the house of Abraham. The fashioner of the narrative employed Hellenic tradition in the service of Jewish enhancement. What had been a Greek legend of Heracles bringing Hellenic civilization to barbarous Libya became transformed into one that implicitly gave that distinction to the line of Abraham.

---

16 Jos. *A. J.* 1.239–41; Eus. *PE* 9.20.2–4.

17 Important treatments by J. Freudenthal, *Alexander Polyhistor und die von ihm erhaltenen Reste judäischer und samaritanischer Geschichtswerke* (Breslau, 1875) 130–36, and N. Walter, *Jüdische Schriften aus hellenistisch-römischer Zeit*, I.2 (Gütersloh, 1973) 115–18. See the valuable text, commentary, notes and bibliography of C.R. Holladay, *Fragments from Hellenistic Jewish Authors*, vol. I: *Historians* (Chico, Calif., 1983) 245–59.

The process can be further illustrated. An interesting item surfaces in a decree of Pergamum, at least as conveyed by Josephus.[18] The historian dates it to the late second century and records it in a section of his work devoted to listing Roman edicts and pronouncements that had been issued in favor of the Jews over the centuries, thereby to indicate the high esteem in which his people were held.[19] The Pergamene decree was prompted by the Romans who sought to show backing for Jewish interests around the eastern Mediterranean. This supposed document, however, in addition to expressing the usual sentiments about friendship and benefactions, also makes reference to an ancient association between Pergamenes and Jews that dates back to the time of Abraham, "father of all Hebrews." One might observe further that the relationship is claimed on the basis of documents found in the public records of Pergamum.[20] That claim closely parallels the notice in the purported letter of Areus that he came upon knowledge of the Jewish-Spartan kinship through a Spartan document, a γραφή.[21] Neither text, of course, gives any reason to believe in the authenticity of the relationship or, for that matter, the documents. That Pergamenes would express themselves in this fashion in a public decree is most implausible. But the texts indicate a pattern whereby Jewish writers conjured up Greek records to substantiate connections between the two peoples. The Pergamene decree does not allude to συγγένεια, only to φιλία. As in the other instances, however, it gives primacy to the Jews. The inception of the relationship is dated by allusion to Abraham.

Diverse and diverting tales evidently circulated that certified kinship links and invented reasons for believing them. One sets the origins of the Jews in Crete, offering as testimony the resemblance of the name *Iudaei* to that of *Idaei*, the Cretan people who dwelled under Mt. Ida. Another pointed to the ostensible similarity between the names Hierosolyma (Jerusalem) and the Solymoi whom Homer lists among Lycian peoples, thus making the Jews derive from Asia Minor. Testimony on these postulated Jewish beginnings is preserved by Tacitus, his sources irrecoverable.[22] They may well stem from Greek speculation, the standard and familiar practice of ascribing Greek origins to alien peoples. But one can easily surmise that tales of this kind were picked up and developed by Hellenizing Jews who took pleasure in finding their ancestors linked with the epic

---

18 Jos. *A. J.* 14.247–55.
19 On the authenticity of these documents, a much disputed matter, see, most recently, M. Pucci Ben Zeev, *SCI* 13 (1994) 46–59, with bibliography.
20 Jos. *A. J.* 14.255: ἐν τοῖς δημοσίοις εὑρίσκομεν γράμμασιν.
21 1 Macc. 12.21: εὑρέθη ἐν γραφῇ.
22 Tac. *Hist.* 5.2.

traditions of Greece. They provided a convenient means whereby the Jews could reinvent themselves in a Hellenistic context.

We turn now to a second category of comforting fictions: the romantic tales that place Jews in confrontation or collaboration with rulers of the Hellenistic world. Most of those that survive, in one form or another, involve the Ptolemies, and were doubtless conceived or adapted by Alexandrian Jews. But the most celebrated narrative in this category stands outside the Ptolemaic context: the purported visit of Alexander the Great to Jerusalem.

The story, as preserved in Josephus, contains two or three separate strands awkwardly woven into one.[23] The central thread, however, has Alexander, at the head of his mighty host, march with hostile intent against the capital of the Jews. The High Priest Jaddus had declined to send him aid and had maintained his allegiance to Persia. Alexander would now wreak vengeance. Jaddus and his people were terrified, offered sacrifice to Jehovah, and prayed for deliverance from the Macedonian juggernaut. And Jehovah spoke to Jaddus in his dream, bidding him decorate the city with wreaths, have all the citizens dressed in white and himself decked out in priestly robes, and meet the Macedonian forces in person. This, of course, they did. When Alexander saw the white-clad Jewish populace, the High Priest in resplendent blue and gold, a mitre on his head with a gold plate on which was inscribed the name of Jehovah, the Macedonian monarch halted his invasion forthwith. Alexander the Great fell on his knees, performed *proskynesis* before the priest, and proclaimed that his god was the great god who had appeared to him also in a dream, clad in similar garb, and had promised him conquest of the Persian empire. The king then conducted his own sacrifices to Jehovah in the Temple and under the direction of the High Priest. A copy of the Book of Daniel was produced to authorize the prophecy that a Greek would dismantle the empire of the Persians. And Alexander proceeded to grant a variety of privileges not only to the Jews of Palestine but to those in Babylon and Media as well, a happy and satisfying conclusion.

The tale is outright fabrication. Alexander never approached Jerusalem. All the historical narratives of his march make it clear that he went straight to Egypt after the siege of Gaza and that, on his return trip, he went directly from Egypt to Tyre and from there to North Syria and Mesopotamia.[24] One need not pursue the

23 Jos. *A. J.* 11.317–39. Among modern treatments, see Momigliano, *Athenaeum* 57 (1979) 442–48; S. J. D. Cohen, *AJS Review* 78 (1982–1983) 41–68; D. Golan, *Berliner Theologische Zeitschrift* 8 (1991) 19–30.
24 Arr. *An.* 3.1.1, 3.6.1, 3.6.4, 3.7.1–3; Diod. 17.49.1, 17.52.6; Curt. 4.7.1–2, 4.8.9–16; Plut. *Alex.* 29.1, 31.1. Golan's effort to defend the substance of the tradition, *Berliner Theologische Zeitschrift* 8 (1991) 19–30, does not explain the silence of these narratives.

implausible details in the rest of the story—like the presentation of the Book of
Daniel a century and a half before it was composed! The fabrication itself is of
central importance. It does not, as one might have expected, present Alexander
as villain, have him humiliated by Jehovah and his priests, and bring the Jews to
triumph. Alexander's reputation, in fact, remains unscarred. The episode reaffirms his stature as great conqueror, indeed now furnishes a satisfactory Jewish
explanation for his successes. It is the Jewish god who guarantees him his conquest of Persia. The Macedonian turns from potential foe to actual friend.

The story, in short, implies a partnership between Jews and Greeks. Alexander will fulfill his promised destiny because Jehovah decrees it. The king correspondingly honors that deity and his chosen people with special prerogatives,
the right to live under their own laws and exemption from taxes every seventh
year. The Jewish state thereby becomes an integral part of the Macedonian empire, while holding a distinctive and privileged position at the behest of its ruler.
And the centerpiece of the narrative is a solemn vindication of the Jewish faith.
Those elements and implications make this fable an illuminating exemplar of
Jewish recreation of historical narrative to suit the larger world of power politics
while dramatizing their own centrality within it.

The text of III Maccabees furnishes another tale of this variety, though with
somewhat different import.[25] Ptolemy IV Philopator of Egypt appears as villain of
the piece. After the battle of Raphia in 217, Philopator decided to visit Jerusalem
and, impressed by its Temple, sought to enter the inner sanctuary. To the Jews, of
course, that would constitute sacrilege. They refused the request, but Ptolemy insisted upon access and endeavored to force his way in. The Jews turned in prayer
to Jehovah who paid heed to his people and struck Ptolemy down. The king then
abandoned his plan but returned to Alexandria determined to have his revenge.
This time he directed that all Jews in his realm be registered, branded with the
ivy leaf of Dionysus, and reduced to the status of servitude. When the Jews resisted, Philopator had them rounded up and herded into the hippodrome in Alexandria where they were to be trampled by five hundred crazed elephants, drugged
with huge quantities of frankincense and unmixed wine. The mass murder was
twice postponed when the Lord intervened to afflict Ptolemy with sleep or a temporary bout of amnesia. And when all was at last in readiness and the intoxicated pachyderms were loosed upon the multitude, Jehovah once again heeded the
call of his people. Two angels of the Lord arrived in the nick of time, interposing
themselves between the Jews and the inebriated beasts who then turned tail and

---

25 A useful discussion, with translation, notes, and bibliography by H. Anderson in J. H. Charlesworth, *The Old Testament Pseudepigrapha*, vol. 2 (New York, 1985) 509–29.

crushed the soldiers of the king. Ptolemy now saw the light, released the Jews, created a new festival in their honor, and instructed all his governors to assure their protection. The Jews thus emerged with greater authority and higher esteem.

Much of the discussion on this romantic narrative has concentrated on its date and on the historicity of its contents. Josephus supplies a suspiciously similar story about Ptolemy VIII Physcon who set intoxicated elephants upon the Jewish backers of his political rivals—only to have the beasts turn against his own supporters. Scholars divide on whether the true persecution belongs in Ptolemy VIII's reign, wrongly shifted by III Maccabees to Ptolemy IV, or vice-versa. Others find a historical basis in a much later time, either in the Augustan era or in the reign of Caligula, thus dating III Maccabees to the time of the Roman Empire.[26] No need to enter into that particular controversy here. It may well be fruitless to seek an appropriate occasion or period to which the narrative refers. A folk-tale of this sort could well serve more than one purpose. The historicity of the events, in any case, has less importance than the perception of the Jewish place in the larger world as reflected in the text. The story offers a valuable perspective on the manner in which Jews conceived their situation within a Hellenistic kingdom.

The narrative plainly has a sharper tone and delivers a more pointed blast at the excesses of Hellenistic rule than does the fictitious tale of Alexander and the Jews. That does not mean, however, as some commentators have suggested, that it is a piece of subversive literature or a document of Jewish resistance to Hellenic overlordship. In fact, the author more than once insists upon Jewish good will and loyalty to the crown, an allegiance to the monarchy that is unwavering—unless, of course, it conflicts with the demands of ancestral law.[27] And when Ptolemy relented, acknowledged the power of the Jewish god, and ordered his officials to secure Jewish rights, the cordial relationship between monarch and subjects resumed.[28] The king, however, remained in control.[29] So the message of III Maccabees is quite compatible with that of the Alexander narrative. Jewish

---

26 Among the more important discussions, see J. Moreau, *ChrEg* 31 (1941) 111–22; M. Hadas, *The Third and Fourth Books of Maccabees* (New York, 1953); J.J. Collins, *Between Athens and Jerusalem: Jewish Identity in the Hellenistic Diaspora* (New York, 1983) 104–11; E. Schürer, *The History of the Jewish People in the Age of Jesus Christ (175 B.C.–A.D. 135)*, rev. ed. by G. Vermes, F. Millar, and M. Goodman (Edinburgh, 1986) III.1, 537–42; A. Paul, *ANRW* II.20.1 (1987) 298–336; F. Parente, *Henoch* 10 (1988) 143–82.
27 3 Macc. 3.2–4, 7.7.
28 3 Macc. 6.36–41, 7.10–13.
29 Cf. 3 Macc. 7.20.

faith is once again vindicated, the Macedonian king mends his ways, recognizes the magnitude of the Jewish divinity, and becomes protector of the Jews themselves. Both of these stories concede by implication a subordinate status for the Jews in the political and military circumstances of the Hellenistic world. But in the fantasy of the fable, the rulers also pay special respect to that particular segment of their subjects.

In this connection, some comments on the famous "Letter of Aristeas" seem requisite.[30] The text, as is well known, concerns the supposed decision of Ptolemy II Philadelphus, on the advice of his librarian Demetrius of Phaleron, to have the Pentateuch translated into Greek and added to the Alexandrian library. The king, portrayed as a lover of learning and culture, and impressed by what he had heard about the Hebrew books of the law, sent to the High Priest in Jerusalem, respectfully requesting that he provide scholars of exemplary morality, knowledge of the law, and learned in Greek to translate the books of Moses. The High Priest duly selected six men who fit that description from each of the twelve tribes to bring their skills to Alexandria. Ptolemy then interrogated them in a long, drawn-out banquet that lasted seven days, putting a host of philosophical questions to them, mostly taken from Greek political theory on the nature of kingship, and seeking advice on the proper means of royal governance. The Jewish sages responded to each with answers derived from their own traditions, though expressed in Hellenic form and argument, stressing trust in god as the fundamental principle. The king and his assembled philosophers were mightily impressed by Jewish wisdom, filled with admiration for the intellectuals sent by the High Priest. Those seventy-two scholars proceeded to produce their translation in precisely seventy-two days. And when the new text was read, Ptolemy marveled at the genius of the Jewish lawgiver who had composed the Pentateuch. The king then sent back the translators with lavish gifts and his compliments to the High Priest in Jerusalem.

Yet another discussion of this much discussed text would be inappropriate. Debate continues on its date, purpose, and historical value. Some reckon it as a treatise designed to counteract the largely negative portrait of Ptolemaic kingship contained in III Maccabees by presenting a more favorable image and suggesting a harmonious relationship between Jews and Greeks—or, conversely, that the Letter of Aristeas came first, genuinely reflecting a happy period of collaboration in the early Ptolemaic era that later turned sour, thereby generating III Maccabees. Others propose that it defended the Septuagint as against a newer

---

30 A serviceable bibliography in Schürer, *History of the Jewish People*, rev. ed. by Vermes et al., III.1, 685–87.

translation perhaps deriving from the Jewish community in Leontopolis, or, on a different theory, that it promoted the Septuagint as a new translation against postulated earlier versions. In certain interpretations, it was directed generally to the Hellenic world, a broadcast of Jewish wisdom and religious superiority. Others view it, however, as a manifesto by Alexandrian Jews, with their openness toward Hellenism, in response to the more isolationist Jews of Palestine. And yet another analysis regards its audience as Alexandrian Jews themselves, thus to reconcile their ancestral faith with Greek culture. Comparable differences exist on the date. Efforts to elicit a suitable time have depended on postulating an occasion. On one view, composition came ca. 170 B.C.E., when Antiochus Epiphanes threatened the Jewish community in Jerusalem, thus inspiring the Jews of Alexandria to stress the ties that linked Jews and Greeks. On another, the letter of Aristeas belongs in the late second century B.C.E., reflecting the Hellenizing tendencies that characterized not only Alexandrian Jews but also the Hasmonean dynasty in Judaea.[31] All of this represents a mere sampling of the innumerable proposals and conjectures that have issued forth on the character and objectives of this text. For our purposes only a few central points need emphasis.

The letter of Aristeas expresses a deep unity between Palestinian and Diaspora Judaism. It has the Bible of Egyptian Judaism, the Septuagint, derive from the authority of the High Priest and scholars of Jerusalem. At the same time it gives voice to a genuine harmony between the Hellenistic ruler and the adherents of Judaism. As in the other texts treated here, the Greek monarch commands the political scene. The translation project is his decision, he summons the translators to Alexandria, he interrogates them, and he rewards them upon completion of their task.[32] The creation of the Septuagint, therefore, emerges as consequence of Ptolemy Philadelphus' cultural sensitivities and broad learning, a new addition to the holdings of the Ptolemaic monarchy. But, of course, the Letter of Aristeas also highlights the profound respect allegedly shown to Judaism by the pagan king. The author of the Letter has Ptolemy evince high regard for Jewish law and religious observances, makes him the grateful recipient of Jewish wisdom whose insistence on divine underpinnings for kingly

---

31 Diverse and conflicting opinions on these and other matters may be found, e. g., in S. Tracy, *YCS* 1 (1928) 241–52; Hadas, *HTR* 42 (1949) 175–84; Tcherikover, *HTR* 51 (1958) 59–85; Jellicoe, *NTS* 12 (1966) 144–50; O. Murray, *JTS* 18 (1967) 337–71; E. van't Dack, *Studia Hellenistica* 16 (1968) 263–78; G. E. Howard, *JTS* 22 (1971) 337–48; Schürer, *History of the Jewish People*, rev. ed. by Vermes et al., III.1, 677–87; L. Troiani in B. Virgilio, *Studi Ellenistici* 2 (1987) 31–61. And see now the acute comments by G. Boccaccini, *Middle Judaism: Jewish Thought, 300 B.C.E. to 200 C.E.* (Minneapolis, 1991) 163–85.
32 *Let. Aris,* 9–12, 38–40, 124, 173–75, 187–294 (the banquet), 317–21.

behavior eclipses the tenets of Greek philosophy—and even has him serve a kosher meal to his Jewish guests.[33] It is quite inadequate to characterize this and similar fictions as Jewish apologetic or Jewish propaganda. The saga constitutes more than rationalization for the Septuagint, justification for Diaspora Judaism, or a reactive pamphlet to III Maccabees. The positive and inventive features of the Letter of Aristeas merit greater stress. It has the *pagan* monarch initiate a project to bring *Jewish* sagacity into the service of a Hellenistic kingdom. In this way it both underscores the genuine power relationship—the Greek king calls the shots—and it also privileges Jewish tradition over Greek learning.

Space does not permit examination of further instances in this category of Jewish fictions. But mention might be made, in passing, of the tales of the Tobiads, recorded or embellished by Josephus.[34] The Tobiads constituted a family of financial officials in the employ of the Ptolemaic monarchy, having obtained royal favor through use of their wits and mental agility. The tales correspond very loosely to the Joseph story in the Book of Genesis, but tailored and elaborated to suit the Hellenistic context. They too are normally treated as propaganda vehicles either for heirs of the Tobiads or for their rivals the Oniads. But the motif itself has greater significance. Once again Jewish figures serve the Ptolemaic crown, in this case Jewish tax collectors and financiers. But these Jewish figures are the shrewd, clever, and successful manipulators who win the high regard of the Ptolemies.

One last example in this category. The Jew as trusted counselor of the pagan king appears in another purported letter. This one comes at the outset of II Maccabees, a communiqué from the people of Jerusalem to the Jews in Egypt. Its addressee is a certain Aristobulus, identified as of high priestly family and also as *didaskalos*, tutor, of Ptolemy.[35] Once again the Jew is servant of the king—but his intellectual and spiritual superior.

A third and final category of Jewish imaginative fabrication deserves attention: the tales that trace Hellenic culture itself to Jewish influence.

One may take as a revealing instance the romance composed by the Egyptian-Jewish writer Artapanus in the third or second century B.C.E. The lengthiest

---

33 *Let. Aris,* 124–25, 174–81, 293–94, 317.
34 Jos. *A. J.* 12.154–236. See especially the discussions of Tcherikover, *Hellenistic Civilization and the Jews,* 126–42; Hengel, *Judaism and Hellenism,* I, 267–77; Goldstein in J. Neusner, *Christianity, Judaism, and Other Greco-Roman Cults: Studies for Morton Smith at Sixty,* Part III (Leiden, 1975) 85–123; and D. Gera in A. Kasher, U. Rappaport, and G. Fuks, *Greece and Rome in Eretz Israel* (Jerusalem, 1990) 21–38.
35 2 Macc. 1.10.

and most substantial fragment from that work concerns Moses.[36] Artapanus' retelling of the Moses saga draws only in part on the Biblical version in the Book of
Exodus and depends largely on creative inspiration. Moses does not take on the
conventional role as the great lawgiver to the Israelites. Rather, he appears as author of most of the intellectual, religious, and cultural institutions among the
Egyptians. They include technological innovations, political structures, priestly
organization, philosophical learning, and even animal worship. And, for good
measure, Moses, after defeating the Ethiopians, taught them the practice of circumcision. But Moses did not neglect the Greeks. According to Artapanus, he
was much revered by that people, identified by them with the mythical Greek
poet Mousaios, an identification inspired by the similarity of names—a typical
Hellenic inference. In that guise he was reckoned as the teacher of Orpheus.
And, in a particularly syncretistic analysis, Artapanus has the Egyptians make
Moses equivalent to Hermes because of his skill in interpreting sacred texts.
This is the Hermes whom Egyptians identified with their god Thot and who, in
Greek mythology, appears as patron god of literature and the arts.[37] Moses
thus takes his place as culture hero *par excellence*, a source of inspiration to He-
brews, Egyptians, and Greeks alike.

How does one interpret the objective of Artapanus? The usual answer regards his work as a piece of apologetic propaganda, responding to antisemitic
critics of the Jews, an example of what has been called "competitive historiography." So, for instance, whereas tracts hostile to the Jews had accused Moses of
endeavoring to stamp out animal worship, Artapanus has him invent the institution himself.[38] If this is a response to critics, it is at least quite an imaginative

---

36 The fragments, conveyed by Alexander Polyhistor, are preserved by Eusebius and Clement of
Alexandria. For Artapanus' version of the Moses story, see Eus. *PE* 9.27.1–37; Clement
Strom. 1.154.2–3. A convenient text, with translation, commentary, notes, and bibliography,
in Holladay, *Fragments*, I, 189–243. Important treatments by Freudenthal, *Alexander Polyhistor*,
143–74, 215–18; D. L. Tiede, *The Charismatic Figure as Miracle Worker* (Missoula, 1972) 146–
77; Holladay, *THEIOS ANER in Hellenistic Judaism* (Missoula, 1977) 199–232; and G. E. Sterling,
Historiography and Self-Definition: Josephos, Luke-Acts, and Apologetic Historiography (Leiden,
1992) 167–86. See also the useful discussions by Collins in Charlesworth, *Old Testament Pseudepigrapha*, 2, 889–903 and Schürer, *History of the Jewish People*, rev. ed. by Vermes et al., III.1,
521–25, with additional bibliography.
37 Eus. *PE* 9.27.6. See G. Mussies in M. Heerma van Voss et al., *Studies in Egyptian Religion* (Leiden, 1982) 89–120.
38 So, e. g., P. M. Fraser, *Ptolemaic Alexandria* (Oxford, 1972) 705–706, 714; Collins, *Between
Athens and Jerusalem*, 33–35; Schürer, *History of the Jewish People*, rev. ed. by Vermes et al.,
III.1, 522–23; Sterling, *Historiography and Self-Definition*, 182–84. A modified version in Holladay, *THEIOS ANER*, 212–18. But see Tiede, *Charismatic Figure*, 175–76.

one. But Artapanus goes well beyond mere polemics. He was plainly very familiar with Egyptian institutions and religious traditions. His narrative appears aimed at demonstrating that the Jews, far from being aliens or outsiders in that culture, were its originators. They belong in Egypt as its most important denizens. Artapanus, of course, only ostensibly deals with Egypt of the Pharaohs. In fact, his eye is trained upon contemporary Hellenistic Egypt. Hence, Moses in the form of Mousaios or Hermes emerges also as cultural progenitor of Hellas itself.

Jewish contribution to Greek culture has a more central place in the work of the Alexandrian Jew Aristobulus. Only a few fragments of his writings survive, preserved primarily by Eusebius.[39] Aristobulus dedicated his book, we are told, to Ptolemy the king, a king whom Eusebius and Clement of Alexandria took to be Ptolemy VI Philometor.[40] If so, that would make our author the same Aristobulus whom II Maccabees describes as tutor to Ptolemy Philometor. Of course, a nice—and rare—coincidence of testimony along such lines immediately makes it suspect to some scholars. So, it has been argued, Eusebius and Clement simply inferred from the forged letter in II Maccabees that their Aristobulus was tutor of Philometor. Or the reverse can be postulated: the forger of the letter knew of Aristobulus' dedication of his book to a Ptolemy and conjectured that he was Philometor's tutor.[41] We do not need to decide the question. Nor is it vital to determine whether Aristobulus' allusion to the story of the Septuagint translation means that he knew the Letter of Aristeas, or vice-versa, or that both drew on a common source.[42] What matters is the content of the work, fascinating and revealing.

Aristobulus had read widely in the works of Greek authors—including some that they probably never wrote. And he regularly ascribes the wisdom and insights found therein to the Jewish lore with which he assumes their familiarity. So, Plato found the source for his *Laws* in the Pentateuch, Pythagorean philosophy was an adaptation of Hebraic doctrine, and all Greek philosophical ideas

---

39 Eus. *HE* 7.32.16–18; *PE* 8.9.38–8.10.17, 13.12.1–16. The major modern treatment by N. Walter, *Der Thoraausleger Aristobulus* (Berlin, 1964), with extensive bibliography. Additional titles and discussion in Schürer, *History of the Jewish People*, rev. ed. by Vermes et al., III.1, 579– 87. And see now C. R. Holladay, *Fragments from Hellenistic Jewish Authors*, vol. 3: *Aristobulus* (Atlanta, 1995).

40 Eus. *PE* 8.9.38; Clement, *Strom.* 1.150.1, 5.97.

41 See the arguments of Walter, *Thoraausleger*, 13–26; Hengel, *Judaism and Hellenism*, II, 106–107; Schürer, *History of the Jewish People*, rev. ed. by Vermes et al., III.1, 579–80; and Y. A. Collins in Charlesworth, *Old Testament Pseudepigrapha*, 832–33.

42 Eus. *PE* 13.12.1–2. Cf. Walter, *Thoraausleger*, 88–103; Fraser, *Ptolemaic Alexandria*, II, 964; Schürer, *History of the Jewish People*, rev. ed. by Vermes et al., III.1, 580–81.

with a monotheistic tinge derived from the Bible.[43] Aristobulus names in this connection not only Pythagoras, Socrates, and Plato, but even the Hellenistic writer Aratus, author of an astronomical poem, the *Phaenomena*, which he traces to Jewish influence.[44] Nor is that all. The Jewish reverence for the Sabbath, according to Aristobulus, found its way into the verses of Homer and Hesiod—of which he supplies a few examples, some of them spurious and possibly his own inventions.[45] And he reaches back to a mythological past: Orpheus imitated Moses in his verses on the Hieros Logos.[46] Of course, in the time of Homer and Hesiod, or even Socrates and Plato, the Septuagint had not yet been composed; the Hebrew Bible was still unavailable to Greek readers. Aristobulus recognized the problem—and then got around it. He simply postulated some earlier and superseded translation of the Pentateuch into Greek so as to make its doctrines accessible to early Hellenic poets and philosophers.[47]

Modern scholars commonly describe Aristobulus as a serious philosopher, well trained in Hellenic teachings. Perhaps so. But Aristobulus needs to be given his due in another realm: the most striking features of the fragments are the inventiveness and the imaginative reconstructions that amalgamate Jewish pronouncements with Greek philosophy and poetry. In this regard his mission parallels that of the other texts discussed above. And, equally important, the assimilation once more is not that of Judaism to Hellenism but the other way around.

The attribution of monotheistic sentiments to Greek poets became an increasingly stimulating activity for ingenious Jewish forgers. Their passion for ascribing to celebrated Hellenic literary artists attitudes toward the spirituality, unity, and transcendence of God that corresponded to Jewish belief has added considerably to our stock of spurious verses. Fictitious fragments or, at best, highly selective lines of this sort were assigned to Hesiod, Pythagoras, Aeschylus, Sophocles, Euripides, and comic writers like Epicharmus, Diphilus, Philemon, and Menander.[48] And that is not even to mention fictitious fragments of the fictitious poets Orpheus and Linus.[49] Jewish ingenuity here outdid itself. One noteworthy illustration might be offered. Among the verses attributed to the legendary Orpheus, recorded in the pages of Aristobulus, were noble senti-

---

43 Eus. *PE* 13.12.1, 13.12.4, 13.12.6.
44 Eus. *PE* 13.12.6 – 7.
45 Eus. *PE* 13.12.9 – 15.
46 Eus. *PE* 13.12.4.
47 Eus. *PE* 13.12.1 – 2.
48 Cf. Clement *Strom.* 5.112 – 14, 5.118 – 22, 5.127 – 31.
49 Eus. *PE* 13.12.4 – 5, 13.12.16; Clement *Strom.* 5.116.2, 5.123 – 26, 5.128.3.

ments about the transcendent glory of God that is invisible to mortals. Orpheus himself can make out only his traces and sees him as if engulfed in a cloud. But that is better than most mortals—with one exception. One man alone has seen God, says Orpheus: the man of the Chaldees, i.e., Abraham.[50] So, even the most noble of poets, the quintessential singer Orpheus who understands the nature of monotheism, has to give precedence to the Hebrew patriarch.

The reinterpretation of authentic sentiments and the inventions of bogus utterances give insight into the motives of Jews learned in Hellenic literature and lore. These works go beyond what is conventionally termed apologetic writing. They do not represent mere defensive, rear-guard action by a beleaguered minority in an alien world. What stands out is the aggressive inventiveness of the stories. The Jews, of course, were in no position to challenge the political supremacy of Hellenistic powers, whether in Palestine or in the Diaspora. And they did not do so. They accepted, even acknowledged their subordinate political status. But by selectively appropriating Hellenic culture, they could redefine it in their own terms, adopting categories and genres that would be familiar to a pagan readership but making more vivid the spiritual and intellectual precedence that the Jewish audience associated with their own traditions. Through creative fictions like kinship connections, tales of homage paid by Hellenic rulers to Jewish values, and the supposed Jewish roots of Greek culture, the Jews not only affirmed their place in the larger Hellenistic community. They also articulated their special identity in a form that bolstered self-esteem by accepting honestly their political subordination but asserting—perhaps not so honestly—their cultural ascendancy.

---

50 Eus. *PE* 13.12.4–5; Clement *Strom.* 5.123.

4. Kinship Relations and Jewish Identity

The special character of the Jews dominates the presentation of their self-identity. God singled them out from the beginning, bestowing divine favor—or indeed disfavor—upon them, whether as reward for fidelity or as punishment for disaffection. As Deuteronomy has it: "You are a people holy to the Lord your God: the Lord your God has chosen you to be a people for his own possession out of all the peoples that are on the face of the earth."[1] Or as the Lord says in Leviticus: "You shall be holy to me, for I the Lord am holy, and I have set you apart from other peoples to be mine."[2] Exclusivity and distinctiveness, it would seem, characterized the ancient Jews' self-perception.

This image pervades the Pentateuch, and additional biblical texts confirm the impression.[3] The Israelites stand alone, buttressed by God against a plethora of foes. The future of Israel depends upon a commitment to Yahweh, who alone can bring victory over nations who represent hostility, oppression, or temptation into evil. Jewish identity derives from distinguishing the clan from its neighbors and asserting its own special quality. To serve that end, it was useful to engage in "demonizing the "Other,"[4] as current academic parlance has it. Preeminent among hostile nations, of course, were the Canaanites who, from the outset, served as the quintessential "Other."[5] The memorable tale of Noah's three sons, Shem, Ham, and Japheth, exemplifies this. Ham observed his father naked, in a drunken sleep in his tent, but failed to cover his nakedness. As a consequence, Noah woke and learned what had happened, delivered a mighty curse

---

1 Deut. 7:6.

2 Lev. 20:26. Cf. Deut. 4:32–34, 14:2; Exod. 19:5–6.

3 E.g., Gen. 12:1–3; Exod. 6:7, 33:16; Num. 23:7–10; Deut. 10:15. Cf. A. Bertholet, *Die Stellung der Israeliten und der Juden zu den Fremden* (Freiburg: J. C. B. Mohr, 1896), 79–90. The motif could receive even more forceful expression in some post-biblical literature; cf. 2 Esdras 6:53–59; *Assumption of Moses* 1:12–13.

4 It would be quite impossible to catalogue the limitless bibliography on this topic. One might consult the incisive, though one-sided, recent monograph on the subject by E. Benbassa and J. C. Attias, *The Jew and the Other* (Ithaca: Cornell University Press, 2004). See also the articles collected in L. J. Silberstein and R. L. Cohn, *The Other in Jewish Thought and History: Constructions of Jewish Thought and Identity* (New York: New York University Press, 1994). Cf. the remarks of R. M. Schwartz, *The Curse of Cain: The Violent Legacy of Monotheism* (Chicago: University of Chicago Press, 1997), 120–42. For a more balanced statement, see F. A. Spina, *The Faith of the Outsider: Exclusion and Inclusion in the Biblical Story* (Grand Rapids, MI: Eerdmans, 2005), 1–13.

5 See R. L. Cohn, "Before Israel: The Canaanites as Other in Biblical Tradition," in Silberstein and Cohn, *The Other,* 74–90.

not upon Ham, as one might expect, but upon Ham's son Canaan: "Cursed be Canaan, the lowliest slave shall he be to his brothers."[6] Displacement of this curse upon the apparently innocent Canaan can have but one purpose: to fore-shadow and justify the eventual Israelite subjugation of the Canaanite land.

A comparable biblical pronouncement was directed against Moabites and Ammonites. The Book of Deuteronomy includes a ban on those nations, forbid-ding them from entering the congregation of the Lord. Edomites and Egyptians had a similar liability, but only to the third generation, while for Moabites and Ammonites the interdiction would hold forever.[7] An infamous legend in Genesis provided grounds for this prohibition—or was shaped to account for it. From the incest of Lot and his daughters came two sons, each given a name that alluded to the unlawful union, Moab and Ben-Ammi, the future progenitors of Moabites and Ammonites, respectively.[8] The legend itself does not condemn the acts. Lot was innocent and unaware, and the daughters sought to keep the family lineage alive in the only way that seemed left to them. But the names of the sons, an obvious accretion, plainly aimed to taint the peoples later branded as enemies of the Israelites.[9] Rejection of contact with those nations and the assertion of Israelite segregation emerge unmistakably.[10]

The shunning of exogamous marriages becomes a recurrent theme in bibli-cal and post-biblical literature. It surfaces most starkly in Ezra-Nehemiah. Ezra, an Israelite priest, representative of those restored to Judah after the Babylonian Exile, professed shock at the discovery of intermarriage between the former ex-iles and the daughters of various nations, notably the Canaanites, Ammonites, and Moabites. The distraught Ezra reacted with outrage and even hysteria. He tore his clothes, pulled hair from his head and beard, and sat in horror—shock-ing behavior by one of priestly rank.[11] He extracted a promise that the Israelites would segregate themselves from the locals of the land and from any alien women.[12] Nehemiah encountered the same problem: members of the community of former exiles had married women from Moab, Ammon, and Ashdod, and their

---

6 Gen. 9:18–27.
7 Deut. 23:4–9.
8 Gen. 19:30–38.
9 Cf. G. von Rad, *Genesis: A Commentary* (Philadelphia: Westminster, 1972), 218–19; C. West-ermann, *Genesis*, II: *12–36: A Commentary* (Minneapolis: Augsburg, 1985), 314–15.
10 They remain among the emblematic foes of Israel in, e.g., the War Scroll from Qumran; 1QM, 1.1–2: Edomites, Moabites, Ammonites, and Philistines.
11 Ezra 9:1–3. Cf. H. G. M. Williamson, *Ezra, Nehemiah,* Word Biblical Commentary 16 (Waco: Word Books, 1985), 129–33; J. Blenkinsopp, *Ezra-Nehemiah* (Philadelphia: Westminster, 1988), 174–78.
12 Ezra 10:1–12; Neh. 10:29–31.

children could no longer speak Hebrew. Nehemiah reinstituted the injunction in still stronger terms and purged the priesthood of all foreign elements.[13] The real conflicts at this time were complex and entangled, involving struggles between Israelites who had remained in the land during the Exile and those who had returned, among local and regional leaders, contests over land, property, legal rights, political ascendancy, and relationship to Persian suzerainty.[14] But the authors of Ezra-Nehemiah chose to underscore the conflict over intermarriage, to represent or misrepresent an indigenous population as Moabites, Ammonites, and other foreigners, and to take a firm line against assimilation.[15] The children of Israel in this construct had to maintain a separatist identity.

No need to belabor the point. Resistance to commingling and insistence upon separatism is a frequent refrain in Jewish texts. It appears in works as different as Jubilees, the Testament of Levi, the Testament of Job, Tobit, and Joseph and Aseneth. As a means to underscore a distinctive identity and to convey an ongoing attachment to unique traditions, it gave an internal assurance of a special character in an alien world. All this is well known, widely recognized, and no surprise.[16] Nor is it confined to Jewish texts. In the eyes of gentiles, Jews carried the reputation of preferring their own company to that of everyone else. They stuck to their own kind, they kept non-Jews at arm's length, and they maintained their own traditions unsullied by contacts with others. Pagan writers noticed this and made a point of remarking upon it.

The earliest Greek who wrote anything substantial about the Jews, Hecataeus of Abdera in the late fourth century B.C.E., observed that the laws of

---

13 Neh. 13:1–3, 23–30.
14 See M. Smith, *Palestinian Parties and Politics that Shaped the Old Testament* (New York: Columbia University Press, 1971), 75–112; L. Grabbe, *Ezra and Nehemiah* (London: Routledge, 1998), 123–97; D. L. Smith-Christopher, "The Mixed Marriage Crisis in Ezra 9–10 and Nehemiah 13: A Study of the Sociology of the Post-Exilic Judaean Community," in *Second Temple Studies*, II: *Temple Community in the Persian Period*, ed. T. C. Eskenazi and K. H. Richards (Sheffield: Sheffield Academic, 1994), 243–65; idem, *A Biblical Theology of Exile* (Minneapolis: Fortress, 2002), 150–62.
15 For M. Fishbane *Biblical Interpretation in Israel* (Oxford: Oxford University Press, 1985), 115–21, the authors employed an exegetical blend of Deut. 7:1–3 and Deut. 23:4–9, thereby to bring Moabites and Ammonites, contemporaries of the post-exilic community, under the same proscriptions that applied to Canaanites.
16 Examination of these texts is part of S. J. D. Cohen's *The Beginnings of Jewishness: Boundaries, Varieties, Uncertainties* (Berkeley: University of California Press, 1999), 241–62 argues that there was no general and sweeping prohibition of intermarriage, but acknowledges that there were bans against particular peoples and that circumstances after 587 B.C.E. changed practices in any case. He does not treat the texts discussed here.

Moses prescribed a rather anti-social and xenophobic lifestyle.[17] The comment came in an extended passage that also contained many positive reflections upon Jewish history and practices. Hecataeus did not engage in slander. But the Jewish image already had the taint of isolationism. Hecataeus' near contemporary, the Hellenized Egyptian intellectual Manetho (or perhaps Pseudo-Manetho), asserted that a Mosaic law forbade Jews from contact with anyone but their own co-religionists.[18] That perception persisted. The Greek rhetorician and intellectual of the first century B.C.E., Apollonius Molon, branded the Jews as atheists and misanthropes.[19] A little later, in a tale reported by the Sicilian historian Diodorus, the Jews were characterized as the only nation that shunned relationships with other peoples and regarded them all as their enemies.[20]

The characterization continued to hold in the Roman period. Pompeius Trogus, a Gallic intellectual writing in Latin, maintained that Jews held themselves apart from all gentiles—though he notes that this stemmed from the time when they were expelled from Egypt on the charge of carrying contagious diseases. It was a means to avoid further odium.[21] The Alexandrian writer Apion declared that Jews swear by their god to avoid cordiality with any non-Jews, especially Greeks.[22] That most formidable of historians, Tacitus, weighed in with a caustic comment: Jews show intense loyalty and compassion toward one another, but have fierce hostility toward all others; they won't eat with gentiles, they won't sleep with them—but there is no depravity that they won't commit with one another.[23] The satirist Juvenal went so far as to write that the Jews of Rome will not even give directions in the street to anyone who isn't circumcised![24] This may be comic exaggeration, but it testifies to the enduring reputation of separatism and misanthropy. One can readily cite numerous additional passages expressing similar sentiments.[25]

---

17 Hecataeus, in Diod. 40.3.4. See the discussion, with extensive bibliography, by K. Berthelot, *Philanthropia Judaica: Le débat autour de la "misanthropie" des lois juives dans l'Antiquité*, JSJSup 76 (Leiden: Brill, 2003), 80–94.

18 Manetho, in Jos. *C. Ap.* 1.239. Cf. Berthelot, *Philanthropia Judaica*, 94–101.

19 Apollonius, in Jos. *C. Ap.* 2.148, 258.

20 Diod. 34/35.1.1–4; cf. Jos. *A. J.* 13.245.

21 Trogus, in Justin, 36.2.15. Cf. R.S. Bloch, *Antike Vorstellungen vom Judentum: Der Judenexkurs des Tacitus im Rahmen der griechisch-römischen Ethnographie*, Historia. Einzelschriften 160 (Stuttgart: Steiner, 2002), 54–63; Berthelot, *Philanthropia Judaica*, 156–60.

22 Apion, in Jos. *C. Ap.* 2.121.

23 Tac. *Hist.* 5.5.1–2.

24 Juvenal 14.103–104.

25 See references in J. N. Sevenster, *The Roots of Pagan Anti-Semitism in the Ancient World*, Supplements to Novum Testamentum 41 (Leiden: Brill, 1975), 89–96; L.H. Feldman, *Jew and Gen-*

But another side to this story exists, one that does not get much notice yet offers a strikingly different vision. Jewish-identity did not require a commitment to exclusiveness, endogamy, and self-absorption; Jews had a more complex and nuanced sense of their relationship to the wider world. Indeed, they frequently connected themselves with, rather than severed themselves from, the broader community of nations. This feature merits attention. A notable element illustrates the connective threads most pointedly—fictive tales of kinship relations. The contexts, to be sure, are invented ones, but that makes the inventions all the more meaningful and significant as expressions of Jewish self-perception.

The engaging tale of Judah and Tamar comes immediately to mind. The narrative appears somewhat awkwardly in the midst of the Joseph story, whether as an intrusive insertion or as a subtle linkage of parts.[26] The Genesis account has Judah, fourth son of Jacob, wed a Canaanite woman who bore him three sons. As wife for his first-born, Judah found a certain Tamar, evidently also a Canaanite woman, clearly not an Israelite. Tamar's fortunes in marriage, however, as is well known, encountered difficulties. Her first husband offended God and was struck down by Him. Judah then arranged for Tamar to marry his second son, Onan, in expectation that he would do his proper duty, i.e., produce a son who would carry on his brother's line. But Onan would not go along with the plan. Irritated that any progeny of his would simply be proxy for his dead brother's stock, he decided to practice *coitus interruptus,* spilling his seed on the ground, as Genesis puts it. That angered God, who eradicated Onan as well. Judah was down to one son and was understandably nervous about *his* future. This youth, too, was promised to Tamar in order to keep the line intact, but Judah was in no hurry to implement the arrangement. Tamar waited for years, the boy grew up, but wedding plans failed to materialize.[27]

Tamar took matters into her own hands. Twice widowed but evidently determined to prolong the house of Judah, she set her sights on her father-in-law himself. She put on a disguise, sat at the entrance to the town, and awaited Judah's arrival. When he came by, he took her for a prostitute, as she had anticipated, and bargained for her sexual favors. A night of passion followed, and Tamar be-

---

tile in the Ancient World: Attitudes and Interactions from Alexander to Justinian (Princeton: Princeton University Press, 1993), 125–31; P. Schafer, *Judeophobia* (Cambridge, Mass.: Harvard University Press, 1997), 167–79; Berthelot, *Philanthropia Judaica,* 80–171.
26 For the latter view, against the bulk of scholarship, see R. Alter, *The Art of Biblical Narrative* (New York: Basic Books, 1981), 3–12.
27 Gen. 38:1–11.

came pregnant.[28] Further details are fascinating and familiar, but irrelevant for our purposes.

What matters is that Tamar gave birth to twins, the second scrambling over his brother in the womb to emerge first. He aptly received the name Perez (= breach).[29] The narrative ends there, but the knowledgeable reader would know what a pregnant event this indeed was. Perez turned out to be the direct ancestor of King David himself—and ultimately, according to the constructed genealogy, of none other than Jesus Christ.[30]

The repercussions of the story are telling. Maintenance of the line of Judah, with priority to the first-born, forms a central element of the yarn. Yet Tamar, not of that line, and not even an Israelite, showed herself more committed to keeping the tight household intact than did Judah himself. The Tamar story in Genesis shows not the slightest worry about ethnic mixture. Judah's marriage to a Canaanite passes without comment. And Tamar's genealogy, though evidently non-Israelite, causes no misgivings among the characters. Her accomplishment certainly earned the author's praise, praise that derived in no small part from Tamar's success in assuring continuity of the patriarchal clan—far more successful on that front than the patriarch himself.[31] The long-term consequences need to be underscored: Tamar's progeny, with non-Israelite blood, eventually issued in the house of David.

This startling story has significant echoes elsewhere. The book of Ruth develops the message in fruitful and fascinating ways. The endearing tale has long been a favorite, and justly so. Only a few highlights require emphasis here. The narrative is set in the days of the Judges, when a famine hit the land of Judah. Elimelech, his wife Naomi, and their two sons pulled up stakes from their home in Bethlehem and settled in Moab, where both sons married Moabite women. Our text describes the event without consternation or commentary, with no suggestion that Moab was dangerous territory or that law and custom forbade unions with Moabites.[32] The relocation, however, proved in the long run not to be propitious. Elimelech died, and a decade later both sons were dead as well. Naomi decided to return to her ancestral home, accompanied by her loyal Moabite daughter-in-law Ruth. Once again, we omit the familiar details.

An important development occurred when Ruth was befriended by the generous and wise Israelite landowner Boaz. Not fortuitously, he happened to be a

---

28 Gen. 38:12 – 19.
29 Gen. 38:20 – 30.
30 Ruth 4:12 – 22; 1 Chr. 2:4 – 15; Matt. 1:3 – 16.
31 For a similar analysis, see Spina, *Faith of the Outsider,* 35 – 51.
32 Ruth 1:1 – 4; cf. Spina, *Faith of the Outsider,* 120 – 21.

near of kin to Naomi, and he took on the responsibility of marrying Ruth to perpetuate the line and inheritance of her dead husband.[33] Witnesses gave their
blessings and expressed their favor toward the union. Indeed, they called
upon Yahweh to make it fruitful, on the model of Rachel and Leah, the wives
of Jacob who between them built the House of Israel. And they made explicit reference to the house of Perez, the first-born of Tamar and Judah—or at least the
one who pushed himself out of the womb first, shoving his brother back in so
that he, the first-born, would achieve priority.[34]

The connection gains further emphasis at the conclusion of the tale. Ruth, of
course, conceived and gave birth to a boy. The text closes with a revealing genealogy, a final link in the chain that goes back to Tamar and looks ahead to David.
That line began with Perez and produced in the tenth generation—as we learn for
the first time—none other than Boaz.[35] Through Boaz and Ruth, in just three
more generations, David would emerge. The significance of this lineage can
hardly be overstated. The text lists only the male members of Perez's line, but
the stories of Tamar and Ruth have already disclosed their pivotal and indispensable roles in providing the continuity of that line, the one probably a Canaanite
and the other a Moabite. The implications carry real importance.

For many, the book of Ruth represents a broadside against the advocates of
exclusionism, as represented by Ezra, Nehemiah, and their followers.[36] Their rigorous insistence upon endogamous marriages, part of the campaign to establish
ascendancy against rivals after the Exile, then provoked a reaction by the more
liberal-minded. The Ruth tale thus exemplifies the "universalist" trend as against
the narrow parochialism that prevailed. The dichotomy, however, is simplistic,
and the book of Ruth reads like anything but a polemical tract.[37] No villains appear in the piece, and the propriety of intermarriage is simply taken for granted.
The tale lacks any hint of a battleground.

---

33 Ruth 2–4.
34 Ruth 4:11–12.
35 Ruth 4:17–18. The lineage appears also in 1 Chr. 2:3–5, 9–15.
36 Cf. A. LaCocque, *The Feminine Unconventional: Four Subversive Figures in Israel's Tradition*
(Minneapolis: Fortress, 1990), 99–100; M. Goulder, "Ruth, a Homily on Deuteronomy 22–
25?" in *Of Prophets' Visions, and the Wisdom of Sages: Essays in Honour of R. Norman Whybray
on His Seventieth Birthday*, ed. H. A. McKay and D.J.A. Clines, JSOTSup 162 (Sheffield: JSOT,
1993), 307–19; Y. Zakovitch, *Das Buch Rut: Ein jüdischer Kommentar*, Stuttgarter Bibelstudien
177 (Stuttgart: Katholisches Bibelwerk, 1999), 38–41; C. Pressler, *Joshua, Judges, and Ruth*
(Louisville: Westminster John Knox, 2002), 266; A. LaCocque, *Ruth: A Continental Commentary*
(Minneapolis: Fortress, 2004), 2, 18–28.
37 So, rightly, E. F. Campbell, Jr., *Ruth*, AB 7 (New York: Doubleday, 1975), 26–27.

Is this a story of "assimilation"? Ruth the Moabite clung to Naomi. Most famously she vowed not only to make Naomi's home her own but also to make Naomi's god her own.[38] The novella, on this analysis, lauds not so much Israelite openness and broad-mindedness toward the "Other" as the decision of the Moabite woman to abandon her idols and embrace Yahweh. In short, it represents a conversion narrative.[39] That interpretation, too, however, misses the point. Ruth's pledge to Naomi was a personal one, not a religious decision. It is no accident that the text repeatedly refers to Ruth as a Moabite well after she had implemented her commitment to Naomi.[40] If this is a conversion story, it is rather weak stuff. Indeed, Yahweh barely has an impact in the narrative. He enters the picture only to make sure that Ruth will deliver a boy. Religion does not stand front and center, and the tale does not push for conversion. Ruth made an independent choice without theological overtones.[41]

The book of Ruth resolves itself neither into polemic against endogamy nor advocacy of conversion. The entrancing tale of personal fidelity, subtle seduction, legal contrivances, and clan continuity holds enduring appeal in its own right. But it also has a broader meaning. The legendary genealogy and the combination of the Tamar and Ruth stories call attention to what is often overlooked or underplayed: the strong strain in Jewish thinking that incorporates, rather than excludes, the foreigner—indeed, even acknowledges kinship relations with him.[42]

This strain, far from being marginal or minor, reappears with frequency and force in post-biblical writings. The motif of cross-cultural bloodlines surfaced in various forms. One striking story serves as illustration. It stems from an otherwise unknown writer named Cleodemus Malchus, but involves a mishmash of

---

38 Ruth 1:16–17.

39 C. Ozick, "Ruth," in *Reading Ruth: Contemporary Women Reclaim a Sacred Story,* ed. J. A. Kates and G. Twersky (New York: Ballantine, 1994), 211–32.

40 Ruth 1:4, 22, 2:2, 6, 21, 4:5, 10.

41 B. Honig "Ruth, the Model Emigrée: Mourning and the Symbolic Politics of Immigration," in *Ruth and Esther,* ed. A. Brenner, A Feminist Companion to the Bible. Second Series 3 (Sheffield: Sheffield Academic, 1999), 62–64, rightly has reservations about the idea of a conversion. But her proposal that Ruth's claim to embrace Naomi's god was simply a reassurance that she would be no trouble to her host at home trivializes the scene. A. Brenner in "Ruth as a Foreign Worker and the Politics of Exogamy," in Brenner, *Ruth and Esther,* 158–62, goes further still, comparing Ruth to a foreign worker who had no choice in the matter, performed a verbal contract to care for her patroness, received only the privileges that her employer accorded her, and had no right even to reclaim her baby who was taken by Naomi. This scenario departs wholesale from the text. For a more balanced view, see Campbell, *Ruth,* 80–82.

42 Cf. the remarks of Spina, *Faith of the Outsider,* 133–36.

biblical genealogy, Greek legend, and Jewish fiction. Genesis reports that Abraham married a second time, and his new wife Keturah bore him a number of sons who, in turn, produced a host of descendants.[43] Cleodemus reproduced this tradition in garbled form. He combined it with one of the countless legends of the Greek hero Herakles. In this particular one, Herakles entered Libya, wrestled the giant Antaeus into submission, and proceeded to a union with Antaeus' wife, thus spawning a new dynasty of rulers and bringing civilization to the barbarous land of Africa.[44] Cleodemus refashioned this Hellenic legend and produced a new concoction that brought Abraham into the story. In Cleodemus' fantasy, two sons of Abraham and Keturah—Apher and Aphran—fought side by side with Herakles in subduing Antaeus. Herakles' new bride, in this narrative, was not the wife of Antaeus but a daughter of Apher, granddaughter of Abraham, and through her derived the line of African rulers. Indeed, Abraham's progeny, according to Cleodemus, had an even more illustrious future: two of them were the forebears of Africa, and a third, Assouri, became the namesake of Assyria.[45]

Scholars have disputed the origins of the mysterious Cleodemus. But the fabrication of a tale that has Abraham's sons provide muscle for Herakles' victory and become the forefathers of nations must be an *interpretatio Judaica*, whether Cleodemus invented it or got it from elsewhere. The new narrative represents a usurpation of Hellenic legend to advance the patriarch's reputation. His sons had brought Herakles into the family, and his reach now extended to Africa and Assyria.[46]

The implications of the story need to be underscored. It does not constitute a Jewish effort at assimilation. Rather, the labors of Herakles and the African suc-

---

43 Gen. 25:1 – 4.
44 Apollod. *Bibl.* 2.5.11; Diod. 4.17.4 – 5; Plut. *Sert.* 9.3 – 5.
45 The sole extant fragment of Cleodemus that provides this reconstruction was transmitted by the first-century B.C.E. Greek scholar Alexander Polyhistor, preserved, in turn, by Jos. *A. J.* 1.239 – 41 and Eus. *PE*, 9.20.2 – 4. The best treatment of the literary background is that of Y. Gutman, *The Beginnings of Jewish-Hellenistic Literature* (Jerusalem: Bialik, 1963), II, 137 – 43 (Hebrew). See also J. Freudenthal, *Alexander Polyhistor und die von ihm erhaltenen Reste jüdischer und samaritanischer Geschichtswerke,* Hellenistische Studien 1 – 2 (Breslau: H. Skutsch, 1875), 130 – 36; C.R. Holladay, *Fragments from Hellenistic Jewish Authors,* I: *Historians,* Texts and Translations 20, Pseudepigraphia Series 10 (Chico: Scholars, 1983), 245 – 59; R. Doran, "Cleodemus Malchus," in *Old Testament Pseudepigrapha,* ed. J. H. Charlesworth (New York: Doubleday, 1985), II, 883 – 87; E. Schürer, *The History of the Jewish People in the Age of Jesus Christ,* III/1, rev. by G. Vermes, F. Millar, and M. Goodman (Edinburgh: T & T Clark, 1986), 526 – 29.
46 Cf. E. S. Gruen, *Heritage and Hellenism: The Reinvention of Jewish Tradition,* Hellenistic Culture and Society 30 (Berkeley: University of California Press, 1998), 151 – 53.

cession are brought into line on behalf of the heritage of Abraham. The fable doubtless circulated among Hellenistic Jews in the second or first century B.C.E.. It demonstrates an expropriation of Greek legend instead of an adaptation to it. Indeed, it has an even wider significance. The narrative that Cleodemus created or conveyed discloses a Jewish inclination to incorporate Hellenic tradition into its own national story. The outsider is brought inside. The new tale betokens a blend of nations that some Jews at least found perfectly compatible with their own sense of themselves.

Comparable kinship relations recur in another intriguing construct. Reports allude to communications that took place between the Judaean High Priest Onias and the Spartan king Areus, evidently in the early third century B.C.E.. The king wrote with considerable pleasure to announce that he had come upon a written text recording an ancient kinship between Spartans and Jews: both stemmed from the stock of Abraham.[47] Further exchanges occurred in the mid-second century. The Hasmonean High Priest Jonathan addressed the Spartans as "brothers," acknowledged Areus' letter of long ago, and asked for renewal of the friendship and alliance that held between the two peoples. The Spartan reply arrived after Jonathan's death, when his brother Simon had succeeded him. But it, too, contained warm greetings and an eagerness to keep the close relationship alive.[48] Spartans and Jews therefore not only collaborated in the Hellenistic age; they shared a common ancestor in Abraham and were thus bonded by blood.

A large corpus of scholarly literature has debated the genuineness of the letters, and a substantial number of commentators take them seriously. Indeed, they should, but hardly as history. That debate, however, need not be rehearsed here.[49] What matter are the character of the correspondence and the image of Jewish identity that it projects. There can be little doubt that the letters, as they have come down to us, are Jewish compositions. Abraham is the forefather in the fictive genealogy, not Herakles or some legendary Lacedaemonian figure. The idea of Spartans creating or accepting a lineage that traces their origin to a Hebrew patriarch would stretch the imagination. Whatever the validity of the diplomatic communication, the genealogical link between these two nations is

---

47 1 Macc. 12:20–23; Jos. *A. J.* 12.225–27.
48 1 Macc. 12:6–18, 14:16–23; Jos. *AJ.* 12.225–27, 13.164–70; cf. 2 Macc. 5:6–10.
49 See the skeptical treatment of E. S. Gruen, "The Purported Jewish-Spartan Affiliation," in *Transitions to Empire: Essays in Greco-Roman History, 300–146 B. C. in Honor of E. Badian,* ed. R. W. Wallace and E. M. Harris, Oklahoma Series in Classical Culture 21 (Norman: University of Oklahoma Press, 1996), 254–69, with extensive bibliography, also available in this volume. See also C. P. Jones. *Kinship Diplomacy in the Ancient World,* Revealing Antiquity 12 (Cambridge, Mass.: Harvard University Press, 1999), 75–79.

transparent fiction. What called it forth? Hellenistic Jews, or at least some of them, found the repute of Sparta appealing. The Spartan system had long been a source of admiration among Hellenes for its inculcation of military prowess, the premium it placed on rigorous training, and loyalty, its tolerance of suffering, its adherence to ancestral laws, and the endurance of its political institutions.[50] Josephus still used Spartans much later as the benchmark for judging the virtues and successes of other communities—although he made it clear that Jews had surpassed them in all matters in which they had once claimed superiority.[51] The value of an association with Sparta for Jewish self-esteem in a Greek world is plain enough.

The significance of this imaginary link, however, merits emphasis. Jews were not here attempting to fit themselves into a Hellenic social scene, adjusting their sights to some form of accommodation to the dominant culture—let alone hoping for political or diplomatic advantage. It was the other way around. The supposed connection underlines Jewish precedence: the Hebrew patriarch is progenitor of both clans. Jews could borrow some of the aura of the Spartan mystique, and set themselves in the pattern of a people renowned for authority, stability, self-sacrifice, and adherence to law (even if the reputation no longer matched reality in the Hellenistic period). But the constructed correspondence exhibits the superiority of Jewish institutions and faith. The fact that the linkage was conceived and broadcast, however, remains fundamental. Whether or not any Spartan ever acknowledged the concocted kinship, Jews had calculatingly fashioned an affiliation with a gentile people that enhanced their own self-image.

The cross-cultural connections extended beyond the Greek world. Jews could also bring Arabs into their extended family. The famed tale of Ishmael in Genesis stands at the foundation of this nexus.[52] A brief summary will suffice. Abram's wife Sarai could not conceive and generously offered to have her Egyptian slave-girl Hagar share her husband's bed in hopes of producing an heir.

---

50 Cf. F. Oilier, *Le mirage spartiate: étude sur l'idéalisation de Sparte dans l'antiquité grecque du début de l'école cynique jusqu'à la fin de la cité*, 2 vols., Annales de l'Université de Lyon. Troisième série, Lettres 13 (Paris: E. de Boccard, 1933–43); E.N. Tigerstedt, *The Legend of Sparta in Classical Antiquity*, 3 vols., Stockholm Studies in History of Literature 9, 15, 21 (Stockholm: Almqvist & Wiksell, 1965, 1974, 1978); N. M. Kennell, *The Gymnasium of Virtue: Education and Culture in Ancient Sparta* (Chapel Hill: University of North Carolina Press, 1995).
51 Jos. *C. Ap.* 2.225–35.
52 On the diverse strands and sources for this tale in Genesis, see the discussions in E. A. Knauf, *Ismael. Untersuchungen zur Geschichte Palästinas und Nordarabiens im 1 Jahrtausend v.Chr.* (Wiesbaden: Abhandlungen des deutschen Palästinavereins, 1985), 16–45, and J. Retsö, *The Arabs in Antiquity: Their History from the Assyrians to the Umayyads* (London: Routledge, 2003), 222–29.

Abram duly complied and Hagar became pregnant. Sarai's generosity, however, swiftly reached its limit and she had Hagar put to flight. The tale then took a sharp turn when Hagar, wandering in the wilderness, encountered a messenger of the Lord who directed her to return to Sarai but promised her the birth of a son, to be called Ishmael, a son who will be like a wild ass in a struggle against all, emblematic—it appears—of fierce independence and nomadic life. Hagar complied, returned to Abram and Sarai, and gave birth to Ishmael.[53] The previously barren Sarai (now Sarah) soon conceived and produced Isaac, a source of joy to Abram (now Abraham) but a potential strain on the household. Sarah once again insisted upon the expulsion of Hagar together with her son. The reluctant Abraham acceded to his wife's wishes, buoyed by the voice of God which promised that Abraham's seed would be perpetuated through Isaac—but adding that the house of Ishmael, too, will issue in a nation to carry on Abraham's heritage.[54] Hagar's second trip to the wilderness almost resulted in disaster when she could no longer nourish her son and gave him up to die. But God's messenger once again reassured the woman, provided sustenance for the child, and proclaimed that God would make him into a great nation.[55] Ishmael subsequently thrived, lived to a ripe old age, and produced twelve sons who would become chiefs of their tribes.[56]

Nothing in this narrative makes reference to Arabs. Nor are Arabs identified with the descendants of Ishmael anywhere in the Bible.[57] But later Jewish writers did indeed make the connection. The book of Jubilees, a rewriting of Genesis and part of Exodus, composed in Hebrew some time in the second century B.C.E., may be the earliest attestation of it.[58] The text supplies a deathbed scene for Abraham in which the patriarch summoned Ishmael and his twelve children, Isaac and his two sons, and Abraham's other children and grandchildren by his second wife Keturah. After delivering his final pronouncements, Abraham bestowed his possessions upon Isaac, but also gave gifts to Ishmael and his sons, and to the sons of Keturah, sending them away from the lands occupied by the

---

53 Gen. 16:1–16.
54 Gen. 21:8–13.
55 Gen. 21:14–21.
56 Gen. 25:12–17. Verse 18 seems to echo the initial prediction for Ishmael, that he would clash with his kinsmen (16:12), but its meaning is less than obvious; cf. E. A. Speiser, *Genesis*, AB 1 (New York: Doubleday, 1964), 188; Westermann, *Genesis*, 399.
57 See the discussion of I. Eph'al, "Ishmael and 'Arab(s)': A Transformation of Ethnological Terms," *JNES* 35 (1976), 225–31.
58 On the date of Jubilees, see J. C. VanderKam, *The Book of Jubilees* (Sheffield: Sheffield Academic, 2001), 47–21.

house of Isaac. Their families went to dwell in the territory that stretched from the entrance to Babylon all the way to Faramon, perhaps Pelusium in the north-eastern most part of the Nile Delta. The author concludes the segment, quite significantly, by stating that these people mingled with each other and were called Arabs and Ishmaelites.[59] By the second century B.C.E., in short, Jews (or some at least) associated Arabs with the descendants of Ishmael and thus with the house of Abraham.

That link appears, too, in the work of the Jewish-Hellenistic author Artapanus, writing in the second century B.C.E. as well. The few fragments of his work, quoted by Alexander Polyhistor and preserved by Eusebius, include a section on Joseph. Artapanus' version of the quarrel between Joseph and his brothers has him appeal to neighboring Arabs to convey him to Egypt. They proved willing to comply with Joseph's wishes, so reports Artapanus, because the kings of the Arabs were descendants of Ishmael, the son of Abraham and brother of Isaac.[60] The construct associating Arabs with Ishmaelites thus appears in second-century texts from both Palestine and the Diaspora. This connection, it seems, had gained acceptance well beyond the whims of idiosyncratic writers.

The fact is strikingly confirmed by reference to the tradition by a non-Jewish author, the first-century B.C.E. rhetorician Apollonius Molon of Rhodes. Molon, whose work on the Jews was not a sympathetic one, nonetheless transmits a version of the Ishmael story (without the name) that he must have picked up from a Jewish source or sources that had already modified the biblical narrative. In Molon's presentation, Abraham took two wives, one a kinswoman and neighbor, the other an Egyptian servant. He had twelve sons by the Egyptian woman who settled in Arabia and became the first kings of those who dwelled in the land. From that time on, the Arabs always have twelve kings whose names derive from them.[61] The confusion about who fathered the twelve sons (Abraham or Ishmael) is a minor matter. Molon's testimony demonstrates quite compellingly that the link between Ishmaelites and Arabs had become a widespread notion among Hellenistic Jews.

By the time Josephus composed his *Antiquities* a century and a half later, this was a well-established tradition. The biblical account formed the basis of his nar-

---

59 Jub. 20:1, 11–13. On the geography, see Retsö, *Arabs in Antiquity*, 338.
60 Eus. *PE* 9.23.1. The text itself reads: ἀπογόνους Ἰσραήλ, υἱοὺς τοῦ Αβραάμ, Ἰσαὰχ δὲ ἀδελφούς. The emendation, Ἰσμαήλ, υἱοῦ, readily suggests itself. See the apparatus in Holladay, *Fragments*, 206 and 228 n. 16—although he himself opts for the manuscript reading. Even without emendation, however, the connection between Arabs and the house of Abraham is clear, even if presented in confused form by Artapanus.
61 Eus. *PE* 9.19.1–2.

rative, but the Arab / Ishmaelite connection had now become a firm part of that expanded narrative.[62] Josephus repeats the Genesis listing of the sons of Ishmael in its Septuagintal version, and then adds that they occupied all the land that stretched from the Euphrates to the Red Sea, naming it Nabatene and giving their names to the nation of the Arabs and to the tribes that stemmed from them, thus signaling their own virtue and the distinction of Abraham.[63] As the Jewish historian has God later remind Amram, the father of Moses, Abraham bestowed Arabia upon Ishmael and his descendants.[64] Josephus explicitly identifies the traders to whom Joseph was sold by his brothers as "Arabs from the race of the Ishmaelites."[65] He affirms this continued connection in his own day with reference to circumcision: Jews circumcise their sons on the eighth day, as Abraham did for Isaac, and Arabs wait until the thirteenth year, when Abraham circumcised Ishmael.[66] Jewish writers had plainly planted their identity upon Arabs by making them offspring of the house of Abraham.

Did the identification of Arabs as Ishmaelites associate them with outsiders, the marginalized children of the marginalized Hagar, who was run out of Israel so as not to compete with the heritage of Isaac and the patriarchs? Genesis, as already noted, does indeed liken Ishmael to a wild ass acting in defiance of his kinsmen.[67] And Ishmaelites do appear in the Joseph story as nomadic tribes.[68] But this portrayal is not a negative one, even in Genesis.[69] Ishmael represents a different lifestyle, the hardy survivor of adverse circumstances, the brother who does not require the support of his kin to make a go of existing outside the conventional bounds of agricultural society. When Hagar and Ishmael were sent into the desert, God himself reassured Abraham that this son too would be the progenitor of a great nation.[70] And so, indeed, did he become in

---

62 See the valuable article of F. Millar "Hagar, Ishmael, Josephus, and the Origins of Islam," *JJS* 44 [1993], 23–45, who gives too much credit to Josephus for originality on this score.

63 Jos. *A. J.* 1.220–21: οἳ τὸ τῶν Ἀράβων ἔθνος καὶ τὰς φυλὰς ἀφ' αὐτῶν καλοῦσι διά τε τὴν ἀρτὴν αὐτῶν καὶ τὸ Ἀβράμου ἀξίωμα.

64 Ibid., 2.213; cf. 1.239.

65 Ibid., 2.32: ἐμπόρους ἰδὼν Ἄραβας τοῦ Ἰσμαηλιτῶν γένους. Cf. L. H. Feldman, *Flavius Josephus: Translation and Commentary*, III: *Judean Antiquities 1–4* (Leiden: Brill, 2000), 140.

66 Jos. *A. J.* 1.214; cf. 1.191–93.

67 Gen. 16:12; cf. 25:18. On the ambiguity of this phraseology, see C. Bakhos, *Ishmael on the Border: Rabbinic Portrayals of the First Arab* (Albany: State University of New York Press, 2006), 14–16.

68 Gen. 37:25. On other references to Ishmaelites in the Bible, see Knauf, *Ismael*, 10–16.

69 Of course, they do turn up occasionally among the enemies of the Israelites; e. g., Judg. 8:24; Ps. 83:4–8—but not identified as Arabs. Cf. Ephʿal, "Ishmael and Arab(s)," 225–26.

70 Gen. 21:13, 18. Cf. Jub. 15:20.

the Genesis narrative itself.[71] The post-biblical re-creations all present Ishmael in a positive light. Even the Genesis prognostication of a defiant life in the wilderness disappears in the later treatments.[72] Ishmael moves out of Canaan to become founder of a new race and to transmit the seed of Abraham to his progeny elsewhere. The literary appropriation of Arabs for Abraham's line in the Hellenistic period further illustrates that powerful propensity for incorporating the outsider by making him a kinsman.

The Israelites, it is worth recalling, were not an autochthonous people even in their own tradition. Abraham's family came from Ur of the Chaldees and then settled in Haran in Mesopotamia before moving to the land of Canaan.[73] Far from an embarrassment, this association with Chaldeans or Babylonians remained a source of pride. Philo does not hesitate to call Moses a Chaldean by race although born and raised in Egypt. Indeed he refers to the language of the Bible itself as Chaldean.[74] Josephus asserted unabashedly that the Chaldeans were the progenitors of the Jewish people and shared a blood relationship with them.[75] In a different version circulating in the Hellenistic period and picked up by Nicolaus of Damascus and Pompeius Trogus, Abraham ruled in Damascus, having come from the Chaldeans, thus giving rise to the idea that the Jews themselves had their origins in Damascus.[76] The idea very likely derived from Jewish sources. Pagans had no reason to make it up.

Other tales of Jewish origins made the rounds; Tacitus gathered no fewer than six of them. Most rest on flimsy conjectures or fabricated fiction, and we cannot be confident about which of them might have been welcomed or propagated by the Jews themselves. It is worth noting, however, that all connect the Jews from their beginnings with other peoples or places.

One speculation had it that the nation stemmed from Crete and then moved to the most distant parts of Libya when Jupiter had deposed Saturn—far into the mythical past.[77] Tacitus brands the tale as sheer conjecture. It was no more than an inference, he notes, drawn from the superficial similarity between the term *Iudaei* and the *Idaei,* who dwelled on Mt. Ida in Crete. Jews might not have drawn this inference, but they could well have bought into it. They would certainly have found it gratifying to be set in the remote antiquity of Greek mythol-

---

71 Gen. 25:12–18.
72 Cf. Jos. *A.J.* 1.189–90.
73 Gen. 11:27–12:1.
74 Philo, *Mos.* 2.31, 40; *Legat.* 4.
75 Jos. *C. Ap.* 1.71.
76 Jos. *A. J.* 1.159–160; Justin, 36.2.1.
77 Tac. *Hist.* 5.2.1.

ogy. Even better was the report that identified Jews with the Solymoi, an illustrious people who fought bravely in the Trojan War and were celebrated by Homer. This connection too had an etymological basis: the ostensible similarity of the name Hierosolyma, the city of the Solymoi, to Jerusalem.[78] Here, again, Jews were unlikely to have invented this link themselves. But they would not have been averse to spreading it.

Other hypotheses about Jewish beginnings transmitted by Tacitus have them as Ethiopians, Assyrians, or Egyptians.[79] They rest on surmise, hasty deduction, or simplistic fitting together of disparate testimonies. But they have an important feature in common—a consistent derivation of Jews from other peoples or an amalgamation with them. The stories, whatever their roots; presuppose that the nation is to be understood in terms of familiar entities in the Greek or Near Eastern worlds, that it does not exist in a vacuum, and that it constitutes no unique folk. Jews could thus fit into the matrix of Greek mythology, the legends of migration, and the interconnections of the Mediterranean world.

The claim on fictitious kinships was, in fact, a Mediterranean phenomenon. One finds it commonly among Greeks, Egyptians, Persians, Romans, and others.[80] That Jews also played this game is revealing and meaningful. It breaks that mold of exclusivity that is too readily associated with ancient Judaism.

To conclude: The subject treated here is not the overcoming of particularism by universalism, a dichotomy often noted by scholars.[81] One can, of course, as easily detect universalistic tones in Jewish tradition—whether in the covenant with Noah or the book of Isaiah, or through much of wisdom literature—as one can discern particularism in the frequent references to Jews as the Chosen People of Yahweh. Nor is the issue that of the openness of Jews to conversion or "God-fearers" and others who might be sympathetic to the tenets and practices of Judaism. A different feature captures attention here—neither universalism in which Yahweh embraces all people nor a call to conversion to bring as many as possible within the fold of Judaism. It is both less than this and more than this. Jews issued a claim on kinship relations between and among nations—or at least some nations. This carried no loss of distinctive identity. It involved a construction of family ties with other peoples of Palestine, the invention of common ancestry with Assyrians, Arabs, or Spartans, and an assertion of origins that

---

78 Tac. *Hist.* 5.2.3.

79 Tac. *Hist.* 5.2.1 – 5.3.1.

80 These are treated at length in my book, *Rethinking the Other in Antiquity* (Princeton: Princeton University Press, 2011).

81 See J. D. Levenson, "The Universal Horizon of Biblical Particularism," in *Ethnicity and the Bible*, ed. M. G. Brett, Biblical Interpretation Series 19 (Leiden: Brill, 1996), 143 – 69.

connected with Babylonian tradition or Greek mythology. Jewish identity did not reduce itself to a separatist singularity. Jews could also visualize themselves as part of a broader cultural heritage, discovering or fabricating links with other societies, and reckoning the intermingling of bloodlines not as a compromise but as an enrichment of their self-esteem.

5. Hellenism and Judaism: Fluid Boundaries

The dichotomy between "Hellenism" and "Judaism" has a long history. Tertullian framed it most famously in the third century C.E.: "What does Athens have to do with Jerusalem?"[1] The formulation gained extensive acknowledgment and influence through Matthew Arnold's familiar phraseology, "Hebraism and Hellenism," in 1869.[2] The resonance remains. Lee Levine's valuable and learned book *Judaism and Hellenism in Antiquity* retains the demarcation in his title. But he wisely complicates it in his text. Levine nuances the bifurcation by challenging the assumption "that Hellenism was a given phenomenon, to be either affirmed or denied." And he goes on to rob the idea of "Hellenization" of some of its Hellenic content. As Levine puts it, "indeed, the Hellenistic world was the scene of a veritable potpourri of cultural forces, a marketplace of ideas and fashions from which one could choose. ... Hellenization is not merely the impact of Greek culture on a non-Greek world, but rather the interplay of a wide range of cultural forces on an *oikoumene*."[3]

The reminder is a salutary one. Both "Hellenism" and "Judaism" are complex categories, not subject to reductionist characterizations. Jews spread themselves around the Mediterranean in increasing numbers, especially after Alexander's conquests vastly expanded the impact of Greek society and culture in the Near East. But the "Hellenism" they encountered encompassed a range of cultural phenomena in which Hellenic features intermingled with Egyptian, Phoenician, Mesopotamian, Anatolian, and indeed Roman elements. In Palestine itself, moreover, the Greek ingredient had become part of indigenous communities in Galilee, in Idumea, and even in Jerusalem.[4] Judaism, for that matter, resists a uniform definition, with a variety of manifestations ranging in diversity from the Qumran community to the Jews of Rome. Scholars in recent years have increasingly questioned the dichotomy and challenged the very notion of a

---

1 Tertullian, *De Prescriptione Haereticorum* vii
2 Y. Shavit, *Athens in Jerusalem* (London, 1997), p. 46 – 47; D.D. Stone "Matthew Arnold and the Pragmatics of Hebraism and Hellenism" *Poetics Today* 19:179 – 98 (1998); T. Rajak, *The Jewish Dialogue with Greece and Rome: Studies in Social and Cultural Interaction* (Leiden, 2001), 535 – 57.
3 L. Levine, *Judaism and Hellenism in Antiquity.* (Seattle, WA.1998), 16 – 19.
4 The classic study of Greek influences in Palestine remains M. Hengel, *Judaism and Hellenism: Studies in Their Encounter in Palestine during the Early Hellenistic Period.* 2 vols. (Philadelphia, 1974). For reflections on the subject, see M. Hengel, "Judaism and Hellenism Revisited" in *Hellenism in the Land of Israel.* edited by J. J. Collins and G. E. Sterling (Notre Dame, IN. 2001), 6 – 37 and J.J. Collins, "Cult and Culture: The Limits of Hellenization in Judea" p. 38 – 61 idem.

Kulturkampf.[5] But use of the terminology itself risks misunderstanding. The categorization of "Judaism" and "Hellenism" presupposes distinct entities that present the alternatives of confrontation or assimilation. But the concepts themselves may be inappropriate and anachronistic.

A significant fact needs to be stressed. The terms "Hellenism" and "Judaism" rarely surface in the ancient texts as modes of designation—let alone as competing concepts. That absence itself is noteworthy. The *locus classicus* occurs in the Second Book of Maccabees. "Hellenism" and "Judaism" appear there for the first time, in conjunction with the Maccabean upheaval as resistance to the policies of Antiochus IV.[6] But the relevant passages are highly exceptional rather than representative, and none of them actually counterposes the two terms as opposites.[7]

The Greeks did not come to the Near East to spread "Hellenism."[8] Nor is it obvious that use by (some) non-Greeks of the Greek language or adoption of Greek names or the importation of Greek artifacts or the adaptation of Greek institutions such as theaters and gymnasia amounts to "Hellenization." Greeks were no more interested in proselytizing than Jews were in converting (there being nothing to convert to).

Lee Levine, although he still employs the term "Hellenization," in the sense of an "ongoing process of cultural symbiosis," qualifies and expands it in fitting fashion: "Hellenization cannot be measured only by the extent to which the peoples and cultures of this region were drawn to the one regnant culture. What took place was as much a process of selection, adoption, and adaptation as it was of conquest and subjugation".[9]

A different form of conceptualization might be warranted. For the Jews of antiquity who grew up in the Greek-speaking world of the Mediterranean, especially those in the Diaspora (where the vast majority of Jews lived) and, to a significant degree, even those in Palestine, Hellenic culture was no alien entity to which adjustment was necessary but a significant part of their own lives. That culture need not represent a dilution of their traditions but could serve as a

---

5 In addition to Levine 1998: 3–32, see, e.g., E. Will and C. Orrieux, *Ioudiasmos-Hellenismos: Essai sur le judaisme judéen à l'époque hellénistique.* (Nancy, 1986), 120–36, 177–93; E. Gruen, *Heritage and Hellenism: The Reinvention of Jewish Tradition.* (Berkeley, CA, 1998), 1–40; J.K. Aitken, "Review Essay on Hengel" *Judaism and Hellenism. JBL* 123:331–41 (2004).
6 2 Macc 2:21; 4:10, 13, 15; 6:9; 8:1; 11:24; 14:38; cf. M. Himmelfarb, "Judaism and Hellenism in 2 Maccabees" *Poetics Today* 19:19–40 (1998).
7 Compare Rajak, *The Jewish Dialogue with Greece and Rome*, 61–80; Gruen, *Heritage and Hellenism*, 1–40.
8 This fact is now widely recognized; see, e.g., P. Green, *Alexander to Actium: The Historical Evolution of the Hellenistic Age* (Berkeley, 1990), xv–xvi.
9 Levine, *Judaism and Hellenism in Antiquity*, 18–19

mode whereby they expressed them. It is appropriate to question the idea of a tense and continuous struggle between competing societies or even an internal agonizing by Jews over how best to accommodate to adverse circumstances. Inherent overlapping rather than calculated interweaving may be a more suitable characterization.

A few literary texts can serve as examples at the level of the intelligentsia—then a larger number of epigraphic instances to illuminate the lives of ordinary Jews.

We begin with a celebrated passage from the so-called *Letter of Aristeas*. The narrator, a supposed Greek nobleman at the court of Ptolemy II in Alexandria, seeks to persuade the king to release the Jewish captives in his land. To this end, he employs the argument that the god whom Jews worship, the overseer and creator of all, is the same one worshiped by all, including "us" (Greeks), except that we call him Zeus and Dis.[10] The statement, put into the mouth of a Greek by a Jewish author, does not make a claim for syncretism or an amalgamation of the deities, nor does it breathe the spirit of some abstract universalism. The god in question here is certainly the Jewish god. "Aristeas" makes this clear in the preceding sentence that has God who gave laws to the Jews also serve as protector of Ptolemy himself.[11] In fact, the high priest Eleazar later insists on a sharp differentiation between Jewish religious practices and the practices of idolaters.[12] The passage has a different significance. It expresses a Jewish sense that their monotheistic faith can be ascribed without strain to Gentiles as well. The text makes no issue of this, and the matter does not surface again in the work. A congruence of belief in a single divinity could be taken for granted.

A text probably contemporary (or nearly so) with the *Letter of Aristeas* adds a relevant and intriguing report. The Jewish historian Eupolemus, of whose work, *On the Kings of Judaea*, only fragments survive, rewrote parts of the Bible, including a noteworthy recasting of Solomon's reign.[13] Among other things, Eupolemus embellishes the biblical tradition on Solomon's international connections by in-

---

10 *Let. Aris.* 16: τὸν γὰρ πάντων ἐπόπτην καὶ κτίστην θεὸν οὗτοι σέβονται, ὃν καὶ πάντες, ἡμεῖς δέ, Βασιλεῦ, προσονομάζοντες ἑτέρως Ζῆνα καὶ Δία.

11 *Let. Aris.* 15

12 *Let. Aris.* 134–42.

13 The fragments of Eupolemus are conveniently collected by C.R. Holladay, *Fragments from Hellenistic Jewish Authors*, vol. 1: *Historians* (Chico, CA,1983), 112–35. See the discussion by B. Z. Wacholder, *Eupolemus: A Study of Judaeo-Greek Literature* (Cincinnati, OH, 1974) passim, especially, on Solomon, pp. 151–201; G.E. Sterling, *Historiography and Self-Definition: Josephos, Luke—Acts and Apologetic Historiography* (Leiden, 1992), 207–22; with the cautionary comments of Gruen, *Heritage and Hellenism*, 143–46.

venting an exchange of correspondence between the Israelite king and the rulers of Phoenicia and Egypt. The former exchange concerns us here. It builds on the narrative in 1 Kings and 2 Chronicles that letters passed between Solomon and Hiram ("Souron" in Eupolemus's account), the king of Tyre, a friendly collaboration in the building of the Temple in Jerusalem.[14] Eupolemus has Souron not only as lord of Tyre but ruler of Sidon and all Phoenicia. His compliance with Solomon's requests for building materials and assistance in constructing the Temple thus adds to the Judean king's stature.[15] And Solomon was generous in return. Not only did he return the Phoenician craftsmen and laborers to their homeland with extensive pay for services, but he sent to Souron the king nothing less than a golden column which, according to Eupolemus, was set up in the Temple of Zeus at Tyre.[16]

The gift to honor a pagan shrine by Solomon who had just completed the Temple, a monumental act of piety to Yahweh, has brought modern commentators up short. How to account for such incongruity? It seemed necessary to explain away the passage or to postulate a later addition.[17] But the ancient author may not have felt any incongruity. Eupolemus presented Solomon both as dedicated servant of the Lord and as patron of a foreign prince who honored the cult of Zeus. Here again, application of the concept of syncretism would be inaccurate and misleading.[18] The Jewish historian describes something quite different from amalgamation of the deities. Souron's assistance made possible Solomon's great tribute to Yahweh, and Solomon's reciprocal act of generosity expressed itself as enhancing the shrine of the supreme pagan divinity.[19]

A third passage deserves notice. Josephus's *Against Apion* ostensibly devotes itself to refuting Greek criticisms of Jewish character, values, and attitudes. And it delivers a host of harsh judgments on Hellenic misperceptions and

---

14 1 Kgs 5:1 – 17; 2 Chr 2:1 – 18.
15 Eus. *PE* 9.33.1 – 9.34.3.
16 Eus. *PE* 9.34.18: τῷ δὲ Σούρωνι εἰς Τύρον πέμψαι τὸν χρυσοῦν κίονα, τὸν ἐν Τύρῳ ἀνακείμενον ἐν τῷ ἱερῷ τοῦ Διός.
17 see Wacholder, *Eupolemus*, 217.
18 as, e.g., Hengel *Judaism and Hellenism*, 1.94.
19 By contrast, 2 Macc 4:18 – 20 tells the tale of a delegation sent by Jason, the Hellenizing high priest, to Tyre with cash for sacrifices to Herakles (Melqart). The delegates, upon arrival, however, thought better of it and spent the money on triremes. This indicates some qualms on the part of the envoys. But they do not appear to have suffered for it. Different individuals drew their lines differently. Jason presumed, as did Solomon in Eupolemus's narrative, that a gift to finance reverence for the Phoenician god was compatible with the duties of a Jewish head of state.

misdemeanors.[20] Josephus on several occasions draws contrasts between the laws of the Jews and the practices of the Greeks.[21] Yet amidst these broadsides, he delivers a remarkable statement. In the course of his refutations of Apion, Josephus asserts that Jews stand apart from Greeks more by geography than by institutions.[22] This receives no elaboration, except to say that many Greeks have adopted the institutions of the Jews—a point that Josephus reiterates elsewhere in his text.[23] The historian was no innovator here. The claim of Jewish priority and Hellenic imitation goes back at least to the Jewish philosopher Aristobulus in the second century B.C.E.[24] Its reiteration by Josephus, however, in a tract otherwise sharply critical of Greeks, carries special meaning. To be sure, the statement serves a rhetorical purpose in this instance, as does so much of *Against Apion* in general. But this does not lessen its significance. It offers a telling reminder that readers of Josephus found the compatibility of Jewish and Greek institutions to be a perfectly plausible proposition.

These hints at interconnectedness between Jews and others are evocative— and they do not stand alone. A host of imaginative writings, whether the recasting of biblical stories, adaptation of Greek genres, or creation of historical novels attest to the Jewish construction of links to the non-Jewish world. We limit ourselves to just a small selection.

The most fascinating author under this heading is a relatively obscure figure named Artapanus. This at least is the name that has come down to us, a Persian name, perhaps a pseudonym, belonging to a writer known only from a few fragments quoted by Alexander Polyhistor and preserved for us by Eusebius. Of his life and times, we are ignorant, except to say that he lived sometime between the mid-third and early first centuries B.C.E., between the composition of the Septuagint and the *floruit* of Alexander Polyhistor.[25] He composed his work, *On the*

---

20 On this work, the excellent commentary by J.M.G. Barclay, *Flavius Josephus: Translation and Commentary*, vol. 10: *Against Apion* (Leiden, 2007) supersedes all previous studies. One may dispute whether Josephus reacted against serious allegations by Greek writers or engaged largely in a rhetorical exercise. A case for the latter is made by E. Gruen, "Greeks and Jews: Mutual Misperceptions in Josephus' *Contra Apionem*" in *Ancient Judaism in Its Hellenistic Context* edited by C. Bakhos (Leiden, 2005), 31–51.

21 e.g., Jos. *C. Ap.* 1.61, 68; 2.74–75, 163–67, 250–51; Barclay 2007: 232.

22 Jos. *C. Ap.* 2.123: τῶν Ἑλλήνων δὲ πλέον τοῖς τόποις ἢ τοῖς ἐπιτηδεύμασιν ἀφεστήκαμεν.

23 Jos. *C. Ap.* 2.168, 257, 280–82.

24 Eus. *PE* 8.10.4; 13.12.1–8; C.R. Holladay, *Fragments from Hellenistic Jewish Authors*, vol. 3: *Aristobulus* (Atlanta, 1995) passim.

25 A lengthy bibliography on Artapanus's dates and provenance existed already when summarized by C.R. Holladay, *Theios Aner in Hellenistic Judaism* (Missoula, MT, 1977), 199–204; subsequent references to the scholarship appear in Sterling 1992: 167–69; Gruen, *Heritage and*

Jews, in Greek and he was, almost certainly, a Jew.[26] The extant fragments consist of two short excerpts from his treatment of Abraham and Joseph and a somewhat lengthier treatment of Moses.[27] They exhibit an inventive mind and an idiosyncratic manipulation of his material. They also provide an arresting example of an intellectual's conception of interrelationships between Israelite traditions and other cultures of the ancient world. The name alone may be suggestive. "Artapanus" need not indicate actual Persian ancestry. Adoption of this name or pseudonym could signify the very outreach that his work embodies.

The figure of Abraham, even in the short fragment that we possess, exemplifies the approach.[28] Artapanus presents the patriarch as coming to Egypt with his entire household, there to instruct the Pharaoh in astrology. This particular notice both alludes to Abraham's Babylonian origins and makes him a contributor to Egyptian learning. And Artapanus adds another element. The same fragment includes a peculiar notice assigning the name "Hermiouth" to the Jews as a

---

Hellenism, 150–53; Collins *Between Athens and Jerusalem: Jewish Identity in the Hellenistic Diaspora.* 2nd ed. (Grand Rapids, MI., 2000), 38–39. Artapanus has drawn increased attention in recent years; see D. Flusser and S. Amorai-Stark, "The Goddess Thermuthis, Moses, and Artapanus" *JSQ* 1: 217–33 (1993–94); E. Koskenniemi, "Greeks, Egyptians, and Jews in the Fragments of Artapanus" *JSP* 13: 17–31 (2002); S.R Johnson *Historical Fictions and Hellenistic Jewish Identity: Third Maccabees in Its Cultural Context* (Berkeley, CA.2004), 95–108; R. Kugler, "Hearing the Story of Moses in Ptolemaic Egypt: Artapanus Accommodates the Tradition" in *The Wisdom of Egypt.* Edited by A. Hilhorst and G. H. van Kooten (Leiden, 2005), 67–80; H. Jacobson, "Artapanus Judaeus" *JJS* 57: 210–21 (2006). H. Zellentin "The End of Jewish Egypt: Artapanus and the Second Exodus" in *Antiquity in Antiquity.* Edited by G. Gardner and K. L. Osterloh. (Tübingen, 2008), 27–73 rightly points out that the assumption of Artapanus's dependence on the Septuagint is not water-tight—but it remains most plausible. Zellentin's efforts to find a more precise date for Artapanus by having his work respond directly to a Ptolemaic decree of 118 B.C.E. are ingenious but highly speculative. How many readers would have the knowledge and acuity to draw the inferences required by this theory?
26 The point was argued with force and cogency long ago by J. Freudenthal *Alexander Polyhistor.* 2 vols. (Breslau, 1874–75), 147–74, who added, more dubiously, the suggestion that Artapanus was masquerading as a pagan; rightly questioned by Sterling *Historiography and Self-Definition,* 167–68. A cautious doubt about Artapanus's Jewishness was injected by P.M. Fraser *Ptolemaic Alexandria.* 3 vols. (Oxford, 1972), 1.706; 2.985 and L. H. Feldman, *Jew and Gentile in the Ancient World.* (Princeton, 1993), 208 and has now been more seriously challenged by Jacobson, "Artapanus Judaeus". Jacobson is quite right that a favorable attitude toward the Hebrew patriarchs and Moses does not establish Artapanus as a Jew. But he obviously belonged to a circle that was thoroughly conversant with biblical traditions on these figures and in a position to discern the author's witty twists on and deviations from the standard version. A knowledgeable and discerning readership for such a work would include few Gentiles.
27 See Holladay *Fragments from Hellenistic Jewish Authors,* vol. 1 (1983), 204–25.
28 Eus. *PE* 9.18.1

Greek translation. Whatever this might mean, it hints at a connection with the Greek god Hermes, a name elsewhere employed by Artapanus as an alternative designation for Moses. Abraham thus does quadruple duty as forerunner of the Jews, conveyer of Chaldean traditions, mentor of Pharaoh, and a link to the Hellenic world.

In the fragment on Joseph, Artapanus molds the Genesis story to his own taste, leaving out most of it and shaping the rest as it suits him.[29] The biblical version has Joseph sold to the Ishmaelites, who took him to Egypt.[30] In Artapanus, they become "Arabs," a perfectly reasonable designation from a Hellenistic vantage point. However, they are no longer slave traders but neighboring peoples whom Joseph on his own initiative asked to bring him to Egypt—which, in friendly fashion, they did. Artapanus adds the explanation that the rulers of the Arabs, as sons of Abraham and brothers of Isaac, were descendants of "Israel." There is obvious confusion here, the name "Israel" perhaps garbled in transmission.[31] But Artapanus plainly evokes the tradition that has Arabs stemming from Ishmael, thus from the house of Abraham. Further, among the deeds of Joseph in Egypt singled out by our author (in addition to organizing the economy and introducing Egyptians to weights and measures) was his wedding to Aseneth, the daughter of a Heliopolite priest. The stress on ethnic interconnections can hardly be accidental.

Artapanus takes still greater liberties in rewriting the Moses story. He employs the book of Exodus as no more than a frame to construct his own adventure tales that make Moses a foiler of plots and assassinations, military hero, inventor, author of Egyptian institutions, and prime benefactor of humanity. And he made sure to associate Moses with a variety of cultures. In Artapanus's re-creation, Moses was named Mousaios by the Greeks and became the teacher of Orpheus, the legendary singer and father of Hellenic poetry.[32] The Egyptian priests for their part called him Hermes because he was able to interpret hieroglyphics.[33] In this they had more in mind than the Greek divinity; they associated Moses with the Egyptian version of Hermes, Thot, who, like Moses, possessed the skills of craftsmen and the capacity to interpret sacred writings.[34] By having Greeks

---

29 Eus. *PE* 9.23.1 – 4
30 Gen. 37:28
31 see Holladay v.1.228
32 Eus. *PE* 9.27.3 – 4
33 Eus. *PE* 9.27.6
34 See the valuable discussions of Y. Gutman *The Beginnings of Jewish-Hellenistic Literature.* 2 vols. (Jerusalem, 1958, 1963), 2.120 – 22 and G. Mussies "The Interpretatio Judaica of Thot-

and Egyptians make the identifications and the ascriptions, Artapanus gives Moses a central place in both cultures, the amalgam that was Ptolemaic Egypt.

The creativity of Artapanus is breathtaking. There was little in Egyptian society or experience that could not be traced to Moses. The Hebrew hero was responsible for inventing ships and weapons, for hydraulic and building devices, and for the introduction of philosophy. He divided the land into the nomes that became the basis of political organization, he set aside property for the priests, he apportioned divinities to each nome, and he even introduced animal worship to the people.[35] Nor was that all. When Moses buried his mother, Merris, he named the river and the site Meroe after her, thus establishing this designation for the greatest city of Ethiopia. He founded the city of Hermopolis, named after him (Hermes), and made the ibis sacred there. It was Moses also who introduced Ethiopians to the practice of circumcision. His magical rods so impressed the Egyptians that they installed rods in all their temples and associated them with the worship of Isis. And his advice on the best oxen to till the land turned out to inspire the consecration of the sacred bull Apis, a central element of Egyptian religion.[36]

The puckish quality of all this is plain. The idea that the Hebrew lawgiver actually brought Egyptian institutions into being (no mention is made of Moses giving laws to the Israelites) and endorsed, even introduced, animal worship could only invite amusement. But there is more than jocularity here. The theme, repeated in an ingenious variety of ways, of interconnections between the founder of the Israelite nation and other peoples and cultures pervades the text. Artapanus even brings Arabs into the mix. He alters the biblical narrative that has Moses wed the daughter of a Midianite priest, describing the union more broadly as marriage into the leading house of Arabia.[37] Egyptians saw him

---

Hermes" in *Studies in Egyptian Religion.* Edited by M. Voss (Leiden, 1982), 87 – 120, esp. 97 – 108.

35 Eus. *PE* 9.27.4 – 5: ἔτι δὲ τὴν πόλιν εἰς λϛ΄ νομοὺς διελεῖν καὶ ἑκάστῳ τῶν νομῶν ἀποτάξαι τὸν θεὸν σεφθήσεσθαι τά τε ἱερὰ γράμματα τοῖς ἱερεῦσιν, εἶναι δὲ καὶ αἰλούρους καὶ κύνας καὶ ἴβεις. For most scholars, Moses' responsibility for Egyptian religious institutions, especially animal worship, is hard to swallow, thus leading to the conclusion that Artapanus must have been a polytheist, a syncretist, a half-Jew, or a pagan—or a shrewd legislator who was patronizing inferior Egyptians without "buying into" their beliefs. See the summary of views by Koskenniemi, "Greeks, Egyptians, and Jews in the Fragments of Artapanus" 26 – 31, who adopts the last solution and Jacobson, "Artapanus Judaeus" 215 – 16, who reckons Artapanus a non-Jew. It does not help much to label Artapanus a "henotheist" or one who believes in "monolatry" rather than "monotheism." Almost all scholars overlook the playful and whimsical character of the text. See E. Gruen *Diaspora: Jews amidst Greeks and Romans.* (Cambridge, MA. 2002), 201 – 11.

36 Eus. *PE* 9.27.9 – 10, 12, 16, 32.

37 Eus. *PE* 9.27.19.

as Thot, Greeks as Mousaios; he brought hieroglyphics to Egypt and circumcision to Ethiopia; and his family could trace its bloodline to Arabia. The work qualifies as a prime document of cultural integration. Artapanus's capricious book exemplifies the self-perception of Jews who reckoned insight into other cultures as an enrichment of their own.

Artapanus was not alone in fitting figures of the biblical past into a cultural amalgam. An extended fragment attributed to a certain Eupolemus by Alexander Polyhistor and transmitted to us by Eusebius discloses a comparable design. The author rewrote parts of the Abraham story in Genesis and added elements that derived from both Babylonian and Greek legendary material. Polyhistor's attribution may or may not be accurate. Most moderns question it and have attached the label "Pseudo-Eupolemus" to the author. The case is far from definitive but matters little for our purposes. The text itself counts. And it shows remarkable similarity to the mind-set of Artapanus.[38]

The fragment uses a portion of Genesis as springboard but leaps well beyond it. The initial focus is on Babylon, first built by those who survived the Flood, according to "Pseudo-Eupolemus." He proceeds then to assign the building of the Tower of Babel to giants who were subsequently scattered over the earth after God destroyed the structure.[39] The report has echoes of Greek myths on the Gigantomachia, here imported into biblical exegesis. The author next introduces Abraham, the chief figure of the fragment, as discoverer of astrology and master of Chaldean craft. The phraseology recalls a line from the Babylonian historian Berossus, who wrote in Greek, thus suggesting that our author dabbled in Babylonian as well as Hellenic sources.[40]

Abraham not coincidentally imparts his Mesopotamian knowledge to other Near Eastern peoples. The patriarch, according to "Pseudo-Eupolemus," taught

---

38 The fragment is preserved by Eus. *PE* 9.27.19. See text and commentary in Holladay 1.170–75, 178–87. The case for the author of this fragment as a "Pseudo-Eupolemus" rather than the historian Eupolemus (usually identified with the like-named Maccabean supporter of the mid-second century) was made long ago by Freudenthal, *Alexander Polyhistor* (1875: 82–103) and followed by almost all scholars thereafter. See discussion and bibliography in Sterling *Historiography and Self-Definition*, 187–200; Collins *Between Athens and Jerusalem*, 47–51. But it is not definitive. See the arguments of R. Doran, "Pseudo-Eupolemus" in *Old Testament Pseudepigrapha*, vol. 2. Edited by J. H. Charlesworth. (Garden City, NY.1985), 873–78; cf. Gruen *Heritage and Hellenism*, 147–48. That the historian Eupolemus himself is identical with the Maccabean supporter should not be taken for granted—although almost no one has questioned it. See Gruen, idem 139–41.
39 Eus. *PE* 9.17.2–3.
40 Eus. *PE* 9.17.3. See, especially, Gutman, *The Beginnings of Jewish-Hellenistic Literature*, 1963: 97–99. The line of Berossus is preserved by Josephus (Ant. 1.158), who took it as a reference to Abraham.

the cycles of the sun and moon and much else besides to the Phoenicians (here perhaps equivalent to Canaanites), ingratiating himself with the Phoenician king. And later, when he moved to Egypt, Abraham became mentor to Egyptian priests, teaching them astrology and a range of other matters.[41] This cross-cultural mix becomes still more explicit in the author's gloss on Abraham's explanation to the Egyptians of the origins of astrology. The patriarch ascribed the discovery to Enoch. "Pseudo-Eupolemus" then went on to recount a mythical genealogy stemming from Kronos, also known as Belos (Baal) by the Babylonians, one of whose descendants, Canaan, became ancestor of the Phoenicians (Canaanites); another, Kush, the forefather of the Ethiopians; and still another, Mizraim, sired the Egyptians. The connection of all this with Enoch is quite unclear. But the author adds that Greeks acknowledge Enoch as the discoverer of astrology, although they call him Atlas. And through the line of Enoch, knowledge has come down through the ages to "us".[42]

The jumbled genealogy defies sorting out. But the author has clearly dug about in Babylonian, Israelite, and Greek lore and swept into its vortex Ethiopians and Egyptians as well, all of this connected, however awkwardly, with the narrative of Abraham. What did "Pseudo-Eupolemus" have in mind with this conglomerate? One need not read the purpose as verifying Jewish tradition by finding external confirmation, let alone as elevating that tradition against pagan or polytheistic versions. There is no hint of apologetics or polemics here. The author wove together diverse strands drawn from Hellenic and Near Eastern legends into the Jewish fabric to produce a new—though hardly seamless—tapestry. The Abraham narrative in Genesis became altogether transformed, the patriarch becoming associated with the legendary figure of Enoch, whose story had been inflated and embellished by Hellenistic Jews.[43] The Hebrew patriarch stands in the midst of this extraordinary intercultural web. He is both progenitor of Israelites and purveyor of culture to other peoples of the Mediterranean—both national hero and world historical figure. This imaginative network engineered by our anonymous author reinforces the idea of overlapping links and reciprocal advantages among the nations.

Such are some samples from the reflections of the intelligentsia. Constructs of the intersections between Jewish tradition and Hellenic legend, as expressed

---

41 Eus. *PE* 9.17.4, 8.
42 presumably the Jews; Eus. *PE* 9.17.8 – 9; see Gutman 1963: 100 – 101; B.Z. Wacholder, "Pseudo-Eupolemus' Two Greek Fragments on the Life of Abraham" *HUCA* 34: 83 – 113 (1963), esp. 89 – 99.
43 On the complex Enochic traditions, see G.W.E Nickelsburg, *1 Enoch 1*. (Minneapolis, MN. 2001) passim.

in learned speculation and inventive fiction, stem from the upper echelons of Jewish-Hellenistic society. How much can they tell us about the attitudes, behavior, and experience of everyday Jews or the routine existence within communities where the prevailing elements were Greek culture and Roman authority?

Not very much. But another avenue exists whereby to gain some glimpses of this level of existence: epigraphic evidence. For the most part, unfortunately, the testimony consists largely of fragments, usually lacking context and supplying minimal information. Space allows only for selective examples, but important clues can emerge from the limited material. Does one find a congruence of practices and institutions on the ground to provide tangible counterparts to the fancies of the intellectuals?

We begin with a subject that would seem least conducive to overlap: religion. But overlap there is. A surprisingly early inscription provides a remarkable instance. From Oropus on the Attic/Boeotian border, probably in the first half of the third century B.C.E., a certain Moschus, who identifies himself as a Jew, set up a stele at the altar of the god Amphiaraus. The offering commemorated Moschus's manumission by his former master Phrynidas, with a formula common to manumission documents known elsewhere in the Greek world, notably at Delphi. But Moschus went beyond the usual epigraphic conventions. He records a dream vouchsafed him by the god Amphiaraus and Hygieia (Health), presumably while he slept within the shrine. The divinities had instructed him to inscribe the manumission document on a stele and to install it by the altar.[44] It might seem natural to infer that Moschus was "thoroughly assimilated to his Greek environment" and was unlikely to have possessed "much communal Jewish feeling".[45] But the fact that he identifies himself as a Jew, thereby underscoring his ethnic affiliation, cannot be ignored. A "thoroughly assimilated" Jew would presumably have repressed his origins.[46] That Moschus can depict himself publicly and un-

---

44 D. Noy, A, Panayotov and H. Bloedhorn, *Inscriptiones Judaicae Orientis*, vol. 1: *Eastern Europe* (Tübingen, 2004) = *IJO* 1 (2004): Ach45, lines 11–15: Μόσχος Μοσχίωνος Ἰουδαῖος ἐνύπνιον ἰδὼν προστάξαντος τοῦ θεοῦ Ἀμφιαράου καὶ τῆς Ὑγιείας καθ᾽ ἃ συνέταξε ὁ Ἀμφιάραος καὶ ἡ Ὑγιεία ἐν στήλῃ γράψαντα ἀναθεῖναι πρὸς τῷ βωμῷ.
45 so Lewis 1957: 265–66.
46 Nor is there any reason to take Ἰουδαῖος here as a geographical designation. A strictly geographical allusion would more likely take the form of "Jerusalemite," "Tiberian," or "Sepphorite." See M.H. Williams, "The Meaning and Function of *Joudaios* in Graeco-Roman Inscriptions" *ZPE* 116: 249–62 (1997) esp. 251–52. S.J.D. Cohen *The Beginnings of Jewishness: Boundaries, Varieties, Uncertainties.* (Berkeley, 1999), 96–98 claims that the word should be translated 'Judean' here but acknowledges that the sense of "inhabitant of Judea" is nowhere attested and very unlikely for the Hellenistic period. For him, "Judean" has both ethnic and geographical significance.

abashedly as a Jew who is making a votive dedication to pagan divinities suggests that the act did not erase his Jewish identification. Moschus appealed to the protective agency of the shrine to guarantee the endurance of his new status as freedman—without abandoning his connection to Judaism.

The point is buttressed by two revealing inscriptions from the Temple of Pan at El-Kanais near Edfu in Egypt, probably of the Ptolemaic period. Each delivers praise to "god," the first, dedicated by "Theodotos the Jew" who had been saved from the sea, the second by "Ptolemy the Jew."[47] To be sure, the "god" is not specified. But the dedications inscribed on the rock face west of the Temple of Pan can leave little doubt as to their recipient. The first dedicator possesses a theophoric name, the second a common Greco-Egyptian name. But both unhesitatingly label themselves as Jews. Thanksgivings paid to Pan, a frequent practice among pagans, evidently did not compromise the men's Jewishness.

In yet another part of the Mediterranean, a quite different instance of Jewish engagement with Gentile religion deserves notice. From Iasos in Caria, we possess a list of donors who contributed to the Dionysiac festival in that city around the mid-second century B.C.E. Among the benefactors, the inscription lists two metics who supplied 100 drachmas each. One of them is designated Niketas, son of Jason, from Jerusalem.[48] No good reason exists to question Niketas's status as a Jew.[49] "Jason" serves frequently as a Jewish name in the Hellenistic era, and, although some non-Jews lived in Jerusalem, it would be a stretch to claim that Niketas's family had been among them. Jewish contributions to a pagan ceremony in a Greek city that included Jews among its inhabitants should cause no surprise. Nor should it prompt presumptions about apostasy or "conversion." The fluidity of the Hellenistic world allowed for a range of permutations and combinations.

This fluidity continued into the Roman period. Two epitaphs from different parts of the vast Roman world, both probably sometime in the second or third century C.E., can serve as illustration. In each case, the deceased, a woman, carries the ethnic marker of "Iudea," but the gravestone is headed by "D.M.," a stan-

47 William Horbury and David Noy, *Jewish Inscriptions of Graeco-Roman Egypt: With an Index of the Jewish Inscriptions of Egypt and Cyrenaica* (Cambridge; New York, NY, USA: Cambridge University Press, 1992) = *JIGRE* (1992): #121: θεοῦ εὐλογία. Θεύ[ο]δοτος Δωρίωνος Ἰουδαῖος σωθεὶς ἐκ πελ[άγ] ου'ς ; *JIGRE* (1992): #122: εὐλόγει τὸν θεόν. Πτολεμαῖος Διονυσίου Ἰουδαῖος. On the date, see Fraser 1972: 2.302 n. 353.
48 W. Ameling, *Inscriptiones Judaicae Orientis*, vol. 2: *Kleinasien* (Tübingen, 2004) = *IJO* 2 (2004): 21, lines 8 – 9: Νικήτας Ἰάσονος Ἱεροσολυμίτης, ἑκάτερος δ(αχμὰς).
49 as does E. Schürer, *The History of the Jewish People in the Age of Jesus Christ*, vol. 3/1. Revised by G. Vermes, F. Millar, and M. Goodman (Edinburgh, 1986), 25.

dard formula in pagan epitaphs denoting *Dis Manibus* (to the divine spirits of the dead).[50] The first comes from Pannonia, with a mother commemorating her daughter, dead at 18, who carried the name Septima Maria Judea. Efforts to explain away this ostensible anomaly by suggesting that "Judea" was simply a personal name or that the deceased was a convert whereas the mother was a pagan are quite unnecessary.[51] They operate on the assumption that no Jew would employ the formula *dis manibus*—which simply begs the question.

The second inscription comes from Cirta in Numidia, applying the same formula to a Julia Victoria Judea.[52] There is no more reason here than in the first document to see "Judea" as a personal name. A tripartite name, including Judea, which is virtually unknown as an onomastic, would be altogether extraordinary.[53] The appearance of *dis manibus*, to be sure, is rare in Jewish inscriptions, a wording that many perhaps were reluctant to embrace.[54] But plainly no prohibition prevented Jews from adopting a Gentile formula alluding to spirits of the dead and interpreting them in their own fashion.

That Jews could freely acknowledge pagan divinities (whatever they may have thought of them) can be exemplified in the manumission documents. At Delphi a certain *Ioudaios* emancipated his slave in conventional Hellenic fashion through fictitious sale to Pythian Apollo in the late second or early first century B.C.E.[55] *Ioudaios* here is obviously a personal name, but it is hardly likely to have been appropriated by a Gentile. He is plainly a Jew at home in this Hellenic institution. Adaptation to Greek practice seems quite comfortable and smooth and the recourse to Apollo perfectly natural. What bears special notice is the fact that the Jewish manumitter elected to liberate his slave in a pagan shrine under the aegis of a pagan deity.

---

50 *IJO* 1 (2004): Pan4: *DM Septimae Mariae Iudeae quae vixit annis XVIII Actia Sabinilla mater.*
51 see A. Scheiber, *Jewish Inscriptions in Hungary.* (Leiden, 1983), 42–45; R.S. Kraemer, "On the Meaning of the Term "Jew" in Greco-Roman Inscriptions" *HTR* 82: 35–53 (1989) esp. 41–42; Kraemer, "Jewish Tuna and Christian Fish: Identifying Religious Affilation in Epigraphic Sources" *HTR* 84: 141–62 (1991) esp. 156–57.
52 Y. Le Bohec, "Inscriptions Juives et Judaisantes de l'Afrique Romaine" *Antiquités Africaines* 17: 165–207 (1981) #71: *DM Iuliae Victoriae [Iu]deae.*
53 so, rightly, Williams "The Meaning and Function of *Joudaios*", 250–51, 253; D. Noy, A. Panayotov, and H. Bloedhorn, *Inscriptiones Judaicae Orientis*, vol. 1: *Eastern Europe* (Tübingen, 2004), 16.
54 compare P.W. van der Horst, *Ancient Jewish Epitaphs* (Kampen, 1991), 42–43; L.V. Rutgers, *The Jews in Late Ancient Rome: Evidence of Cultural Interaction in the Roman Diaspora* (Leiden, 1995), 269–72.
55 *IJO* 1 [2004] Ach44.

The manumission declarations from the Black Sea region show that Jews were fully at home with the forms and procedures familiar from Greek *paramone* documents.[56] The transactions themselves took place in Jewish synagogues, but the proceedings regularly followed Hellenic models. One record bears special attention. In an inscription from Gorgippia in the Bosporan kingdom on the Black Sea, dated explicitly to 41 C.E., the manumitter invokes "the god most high, all-powerful, blessed," and emancipates his slave in the synagogue (*proseuche*) in accordance with a vow that she be untouched and unmolested by every heir, under (the protection of) Zeus, Earth, and Sun.[57] The formula "god most high" appears commonly in Jewish inscriptions, as do "all-powerful" and "blessed," and reference to the "prayer-house" makes it nearly certain that this is a Jewish document.

However, placing the liberated slave under the pagan deities Zeus, Earth, and Sun has troubled commentators, some of whom have found the incongruity insurmountable and reckon the dedicator as less than a Jew, while others have concluded that the formula serves only as a meaningless formality.[58] Neither interpretation seems compelling. The Jewish features of the document, often paralleled, point powerfully to a Jewish inscriber. On the other hand, it seems less than plausible that a Jew would simply mouth empty phraseology in invoking major pagan divinities, when there was no need for him to do so. (The phrase does not normally occur in synagogue manumissions.) An easier inference is at hand. The dedicator found no strain or inconsistency between appealing to the Jewish god and calling upon the protection of Zeus, Earth, and Sun, a comfortable application of divine powers as understood by Gentiles. Religious differences, in short, need not represent insurmountable barriers for the Jews of the Diaspora.

Jews could also fit themselves conveniently and capably into the frame of other pagan institutions. A fascinating funerary text from Hierapolis in Phrygia, probably from the early third century C.E., supplies an instance. The author of the inscription, P. Aelius Glykon, declares the burial place to be reserved for his family and announces two endowments that he will supply for decorating

---

56 See the valuable collection of these texts, with extensive discussion, by E.L. Gibson, *The Jewish Manumission Inscriptions of the Bosporus Kingdom* (Tübingen, 1999). They are republished now, with additional commentary, in *IJO* 1 (2004): BS1–28.

57 *IJO* 1 (2004): BS20: θεῷ Ὑψίστῳ παντοκράτορι εὐλογητῷ ... ἀνέθηκεν [ἐν] τῇ προσευχῇ κατ᾽ εὐχὴν ... ὑπὸ Δία Γῆν Ἥλιο[ν].

58 for summaries of opinions, see Kraemer, "Jewish Tuna and Christian Fish", 146; Gibson, *The Jewish Manumission Inscriptions*, 119–21; Noy, Panayotov, and Bloedhorn *Inscriptiones Judaicae Orientis*, (2004) 1.307.

the gravesites on specified occasions annually. The first, a gift of 200 *denaria* to the guild of purple dyers to administer the ceremony each year at Passover, and the second a gift of 150 *denaria* to the association of carpet weavers to distribute the proceeds, half at the celebration of the Kalends and half at the festival of Pentecost.[59]

Recourse to associations as recipients of grants for maintaining gravesites and conducting annual or periodic ceremonies to honor them was not uncommon in pagan communities.[60] Glykon, who specified two Jewish holidays, Passover and Pentecost, as occasions for commemoration, plainly identified himself as a Jew or as an adherent of Jewish practices. Yet there is no reason to believe that the guilds of purple dyers and carpet weavers were Jewish associations. The purple dyers, at least, had been a prominent feature of Hierapolitan society for many generations.[61] And Glykon conspicuously included an endowment for decorating the gravesite at the festival of the Kalends, a pagan event that celebrated the Roman New Year. It is quite unnecessary to infer that Glykon was a partial convert to Judaism, a sympathizer or "god-fearer," who balanced his allegiances in this fashion, or to suppose that the guilds contained a mixed assemblage of Jews and non-Jews.[62] Postulates of this sort cannot be disproved, but they lack any attestation and are, in any case, superfluous. They depend on a presumption that Glykon's links to both Jewish and pagan festivals create a problem that requires explanation or justification.

Was there a problem? The rabbis may have been unhappy about participation in observance of the Kalends. But Glykon evidently saw no difficulty in it.

---

59 *IJO* 2 (2004): 196, lines 4–11: κατέλιψεν δὲ καὶ τῇ σεμνοτάτῃ προσεδρίᾳ τῶν πορπυρα-βάφων στεφανωτικο[ῦ] (δηνάρια) διακόσια πρὸς τὸ δίδοσθαι ἀπὸ τῶν τόκων … ἐν τῇ ἑορτῇ τῶν ἀζύμων. ὁμοίως κατέλιπεν καὶ τῷ συνεδρίῳ τῶν ἀκαιροδ[α]πιστῶν στεφανωτικοῦ (δηνάρια) ἑκατὸν πεντήκοντα … τὸ ἥμισυ ἐν τῇ ἑορτῇ τῶν καλανδῶν … καὶ τὸ ἥμισυ ἐν τῇ ἑορτῇ τῆς πεντηκοστῆς. See the revised publication of T. Ritti "Nuovi dati su una nota epigrafe sepolcrale con stefanotico da Hierapolis di Frigia" *Scienze dell' antichità storia archeologia antropologia* 6–7: 41–68 (1992–93); the remarks of E. Miranda, "La comunità giudaica di Hierapolis di Frigia" *Epigraphica Anatolica* 31: 109–55 (1999) esp. 140–45; the commentary in W. Ameling, *Inscriptiones Judaicae* Orientis, vol. 2: *Kleinasien* (2004), 413–22 and the valuable discussion in P.A. Harland, "Acculturation and Identity in the Diaspora: A Jewish Family and "Pagan" Guilds at Hierapolis" *JJS* 57: 222–42 (2006).
60 compare Harland "Acculturation and Identity", 234.
61 Strabo 13.4.14; Ameling *Inscriptiones Judaicae* Orientis, 2.417; Harland, "Acculturation and Identity:, 235–37.
62 compare Ritti, 1992–93: 61–68; Miranda 1999: 142–45; Ameling, 2.422; Harland 2006: 228–29, 236–39.

The burial prescriptions for this Jewish family adopted standard pagan practices such as the stipulation of a workers' association as tender of the gravesite and annual festivals as the time for commemoration. That one of the guilds would honor the site both on a Jewish holiday and on a civic holiday was, in this instance at least, perfectly acceptable and demanded no special explication. Glykon could operate within conventional pagan institutions by enlisting purple dyers and carpet weavers to commemorate the deceased of a Jewish family and could anticipate ready cooperation.

A comparable example bolsters this conclusion. At Akmoneia, also in Phrygia, a funerary inscription signals a different form of endowment for maintenance of a tomb in the early third century C.E. The owner of the site, on which his children had built a tomb to honor their parents, promised it and supplied implements to the "Neighborhood Association of the First Gate," with the proviso that they decorate the grave of his wife each year with roses.[63] The institution of the "Rosalia" had its origin in Italy and migrated through Roman influence to Greece and Asia Minor, becoming a standard mode of reviving the memory of a beloved deceased.[64] The inscriber here, almost certainly a Jew, embraced this institution, familiar to the Akmoneian community in which he resided, and added a formula indicative of Jews that, if they failed to carry out the annual Rosalia, they would answer to the justice of God.[65] Whether the "Neighborhood of the First Gate" was a Jewish association, a pagan one, or a mixed group cannot be determined and matters little. The practice of annual commemoration through the Rosalia represents yet another instance of Jews adapting without difficulty a pagan convention.

A pagan convention of a different sort illuminates further the ready adaptation of Hellenic practice by Jews. An inscription from Kyme or Phokaia in Ionia of uncertain date brings it to attention. The Jewish community in the city expresses its gratitude to Tation, a wealthy benefactress who had financed a major building and a surrounding enclosure out of her own private funds. As the inscription discloses, the congregants honored her with a golden crown and the *proedria*, a seat

63 *IJO* 2 (2004): 171, B, lines 1–10: ὑποσχόμενος τῇ [γ]ειτοσύνῃ τῶν πρ[ωτ]οπυλειτῶν ἄρμ[ε]-να, δικέ[λ]λας δύο κ[αὶ] ἀμὴν καὶ λ[ίστρο]ν ὀρυτόν ἔδωκεν, ἐφ' ᾧ κατὰ ἔτος ῥ[ο]δίσωσιν τὴν σύμβ[ι]όν μου Αὐρηλίαν.
64 discussion and bibliography in Trebilco 1991: 80–81; Ameling 2004: 360–61.
65 *IJO* 2 (2004): 171, C, lines 1–4: [ἐὰν δὲ μὴ ἐθέλωσιν] ῥοδίσαι κατὰ ἔτος, [ἔσ]ται αὐτοῖς πρὸ[ς τὴ]ν δικαιοσύ[νην] τοῦ θεοῦ. The expression appears in Phrygia only in Jewish and Christian inscriptions. But, since Jewish inscriptions are far more common in Akmoneia than Christian inscriptions, a strong presumption prevails that the author was a Jew. See L. Robert, *Hellenica.* Vols. 11–12 (Paris, 1960), 408–12; P. Trebilco, *Jewish Communities in Asia Minor* (Cambridge, 1991), 79–80; Ameling, *Inscriptiones Judaicae Orientis*, 2.360–61.

of honor.[66] Whether the woman was herself a Jewess or a pagan patron of the *synagoge* cannot be fully determined. But those who accorded the honors to Tation were certainly Jews acting on behalf of their community. And the nature of the honors warrants scrutiny. The golden crown and the privilege of a prominent seat follow closely the conventions of Greek cities recorded in innumerable documents as a means of acknowledging generous benefactions through civic distinctions.[67] The bestowal of such awards is still another sign that the Jewish collective worked smoothly within the traditional structures of the broader community.

There is hardly a more Hellenic establishment than the gymnasium and its attendant institution, the *ephebate*—the cadet corps of Greek youth in training for elite leadership in their communities. Jews may have had little desire for and limited access to the *ephebate* in most cities. Evidence for their participation is far from plentiful. Yet epigraphic testimony shows that they did gain admission to this exclusive club in certain locations, and perhaps in many more lost to us. Lists of *ephebes* in certain communities include persons with distinctly Jewish names. Two documents from Cyrene in the late first century B.C.E. and early first century C.E., for example, disclose names such as Jesus, Elazar, Judas, Theodotos, and Simon. The fact that one of these lists included an invocation to Hermes and Herakles evidently presented no stumbling block for the Jewish participants.[68] A comparable roster from Iasos in Caria from the early Roman period includes the names Judas, Theophilos, and Dositheos.[69] At Hypaepa in Lydia; an inscription probably from the late second century C.E. records what is apparently an association of "younger Jews," possibly a separate corps within the city's *ephebate*.[70]

Perhaps most notable, however, is a document from Hierapolis, only recently published, from the mid-second century C.E. It belongs to the sarcophagus of a certain Hikesios, "also named Judah," whose accomplishments deserved record. The inscription calls him "most famous victor in sacred contests"; indeed,

---

66 *IJO* 2 (2004): 36: Τατιον Στράτωνος τοῦ Ἐνπέδωνος τὸν οἶκον καὶ τὸν περίβολον τοῦ ὑπαίθρου κατασκευάσασα ἐκ τῶ[ν ... ἰδ]ίων ἐχαρίσατο τ[οῖς ... Ἰο]υδαίοις. ἡ συναγωγὴ ἐ[...τείμη]σεν τῶν Ἰουδαίων Τατιον Σ[...τράτ]ωνος τοῦ Ἐνπέδωνος χρυσῷ στεφάνῳ καὶ προεδρίᾳ.
67 see the valuable remarks of Trebilco *Jewish Communities in Asia Minor*, 110 – 11; and the commentary of Ameling, 2.162 – 67, with bibliography.
68 *CJZC*, #6 – 7.
69 *IJO* 2 [2004] 22.
70 *IJO* 2 (2004): 47: Ἰουδα[ί]ων νεωτέρων. Compare Trebilco, 177.

it adds "multiple victor."[71] Whether his triumphs came in athletic or musical contests is unspecified. But that a man who carried the name "Judah" could enter—and win—numerous "sacred contests" (that is, consecrated to pagan deities) holds real significance. Not only were gymnasial games open to Jews, but they advertised their participation proudly in these preeminently pagan competitions.

Jews could also move into positions of some authority within largely Gentile communities. A few texts will serve as illustrations. A third-century gravestone from Akmoneia identifies an individual, very likely a Jew, as member of the *boule* and archon in the community, plainly a man of considerable prominence.[72] Another Jewish councillor of the third century appears in Korykos in Cilicia.[73] The synagogue at Sardis records the vow of a Jew who held the rank of *comes*, probably in the fourth century C.E.[74] And one individual from Moesia, perhaps also in the fourth century, not only enjoyed the title *archisynagogos* among his own people but attained the rank of *principalis*, signifying either a military or a civil office in the larger society.[75] The sparse testimony allows for no sweeping conclusions. But in some cities, at least in Late Antiquity, Jews could rise to coveted civic positions and even combine them with lofty posts within the Jewish community.

We conclude with two recently published inscriptions. They provide examples of overlap and interchange that are quite striking. The first, a Phoenician epitaph from the fourth century B.C.E., gives the Hebrew name of a father and the Phoenician name of his son. Both of them possess theophoric names. The startling fact here is that one of the names alludes to Yahweh and the other to Astarte![76] This is a remarkable form of shared religious and ethnic identity.

The second document exhibits the other face of the adaptation that has been surveyed here. Pagans could appropriate from Jews, as Jews did from pagans. In

---

71 Miranda, "La comunità giudaica di Hierapolis di Frigia", 114–16; *IJO* 2 (2004): 189, lines 1–2: ἡ σορὸς καὶ τὸ ἡρῷον προγονικὸν Ἰκεσίου τοῦ [καὶ] Ἰούδα τοῦ Θέωνος [ἐνδ]ο[ξο]τάτου ἱερονίκου πλιστονίκου.
72 *IJO* 2 (2004): 172, line 6: βουλεύσας, ἄρξας. The document includes a warning to anyone who violates the tomb of "curses which are written" (lines 14–16). This clearly is shorthand for "curses written in Deuteronomy," as is explicit in *IJO* 2 (2004): 173, thus identifying the author of the inscription as a Jew.
73 *IJO* 2 (2004): 236, line 2. The sarcophagus on which the inscription was found also contains a menorah, thus making clear that its occupant was a Jew.
74 *IJO* 2 [2004] 64.
75 *IJO* 1 (2004): Moes.1. The name of the official, Joses, is plainly Jewish.
76 D. Noy and H. Bloedhorn, *Inscriptiones Judaicae Orientis*, vol. 3: *Syria and Cyprus* (Tübingen, 2004) = *IJO* 3 [2004]: Cyp7.

a text from Aspendos in Pamphylia, dating from the first or second century C.E., one can witness Jewish influence even upon a pagan dedication. The word is directed to a god who is infallible and is not made by hand.[77] The document is pagan, but the unusual expressions sound decidedly more Jewish than Gentile. The resonance could echo from either side.

None of this, of course, implies that Jews had submerged or subordinated their identity to a broader *oikoumene*. The large number of synagogues that existed far and wide in the Roman Empire both before and after the destruction of the Temple make this abundantly clear.[78] The epigraphic testimony confirms it. Not only do numerous inscriptions sport decorations with Jewish symbols such as the menorah, the shofar, the lulav, and the ethrog. We also, have several texts that put biblical quotations on display, including one long quotation from Deuteronomy, written in Hebrew, that comes from Palmyra.[79]

If the evidence assembled here can serve as a guide, it challenges the notion of a *Kulturkampf* or of insurmountable boundaries that rendered "Hellenism" and "Judaism" incompatible. At the same time, it discourages resort to the loaded terminology of "assimilation" or "integration." The Jews of Palestine and in scattered parts of the Mediterranean retained a powerful grasp on their distinctive traditions. But many of them participated actively in the social, cultural, and even religious realms of the Hellenic and Roman worlds. They were not forever adjusting to alien circumstances. They were part of a broader society in which they could articulate, reshape, and contribute their own heritage.

77 *IJO* 2 (2004): 218: θεῷ ἀψευ [δεῖ καὶ] ἀχειροποιήτῳ εὐχήν.
78 See the excellent and thorough survey by L. Levine, *The Ancient Synagogue: The First Thousand Years*(New Haven, CT. 2000). On Second Temple synagogues, see also D.D. Binder, *Into the Temple Courts: The Place of the Synagogues in the Second Temple Period* (Atlanta, 1999), and the briefer summary by E. Gruen *Diaspora*, 105–23.
79 *IJO* 2 (2004): Syr44 (possibly third century C.E.).

6. Jews and Greeks as Philosophers: A Challenge to Otherness

Identification of the Gentile as the Other has a long record in Jewish history. The biblical narrative reinforces the idea with regularity. Israelite identity goes hand in hand with demonizing the foe. Canaanites are stigmatized from the start in the tale of Noah's drunkenness and nakedness, culminating in a mighty curse upon his grandson Canaan (innocent though he be in the story) as one doomed to be the lowliest slave to his brothers.[1] Application of the curse plainly foreshadowed and legitimized the eventual Israelite conquest of Canaanite land, rendering its people the quintessential Other.[2] Moabites and Ammonites suffered similar stigma. Deuteronomy forbids those nations from entering the congregation of the Lord forever. Edomites and Egyptians are slightly better off. Their ban extends only to the third generation.[3] The blemish, however, endured. The *War Scroll* from Qumran brands the Edomites, Moabites, Ammonites, and Philistines as enemies of Israel.[4] One need hardly mention the condemnation of exogamous marriages with Canaanites, Ammonites, Moabites, and others in Ezra-Nehemiah.[5] Resistance to commingling with the alien appears repeatedly in Second Temple texts like *Jubilees*, the *Testament of Levi*, the *Testament of Job*, Tobit, and *Joseph and Aseneth*. It constitutes a standard motif.[6] And it became enshrined in the celebrated prayer of thanksgiving in the Mishnah: "Thank you, O Lord, for not making me a slave, for not making me a woman—and for not making me a goy!"

That is not, however, the whole story. The Hellenistic period witnessed a far more complex and ambivalent relationship between Jews and Gentiles (first and

---

1 Gen. 9:18–27.
2 On Canaanites as the Other, see R. L. Cohn, "Before Israel: The Canaanites as Other in Biblical Tradition," in *The Other in Jewish Thought and History,* ed. L. Silberstein and R. L. Cohn (New York: New York University Press, 1994), 74–90. See also the essay by Katell Berthelot, "The Original Sin of the Canaanites" in D. Harlow, K.M. Hogan, M. Goff, and J.S. Kaminsky, *The "Other" in Second Temple Judaism* (Grand Rapids, 2011).
3 Deut. 23:4–9.
4 1QM 1:1–2.
5 Ezra 10:1–2; Neh. 10:29–31; 13:1–3, 23–30.
6 See, e.g., the articles collected in Silberstein and Cohn, *The Other in Jewish Thought and History: Constructions of Jewish Culture and Identity* (New York: New York University Press, 1994). Also E. Benbessa and J.-C. Attias, *The Jew and the Other* (Ithaca, N.Y.: Cornell University Press, 2004); cf. R. M. Schwartz, *The Curse of Cain* (Chicago: Chicago University Press, 1997), 120–42. A more balanced statement can be found in F. Spina, *The Faith of the Outsider: Exclusion and Inclusion in the Biblical Story* (Grand Rapids: Eerdmans, 2005), 1–13.

foremost, Greeks) than conventional dualities would suggest. Scholarship in the past generation has moved beyond the simplistic bifurcation of "Judaism" and "Hellenism," recognizing that, while distinctions still mattered, they were fuzzier and more tangled than previously assumed. Scholars have in recent years increasingly questioned the dichotomy and challenged the very notion of a *Kulturkampf.* John Collins, of course, has been a central figure in this scholarly shift.[7] The idea that Jews could have regarded Greeks as the Other at a time when they were enmeshed in Hellenic culture and part of the society of Hellenisitic cities seems singularly off the mark.

Jews and Greeks did indeed view each other through their own peculiar lenses. But they did not do so with the presupposition that the object of their gaze was an alien people whose idiosyncratic characteristics served only to set off and underscore the distinctiveness of the superior culture. Quite the contrary. A noteworthy and fascinating instance of this deserves exploration: the interest that both peoples exhibited in the concept of philosophy. The issue here is not that of the influence of Greek philosophy upon Jewish thinking. That subject has had extensive treatment and, at least along broad lines, is uncontroversial. That Hellenic philosophical tenets made their way into Jewish writings from Qohelet to Philo does not need to be argued here. A rather different topic claims attention: the reciprocal set of perceptions (or constructs) in which Greeks understood Jews as philosophers and Jews viewed Greek philosophers as dependent on Jewish lore. This double lens, however distorted its refractions, seriously complicates the concept of Otherness.

I. Greek Authors on Jews as Philosophers

Theophrastus

A fragment of Theophrastus, the most celebrated pupil of Aristotle and his successor as head of the Peripatetics, demands notice in this connection. Writing as he did in the late fourth and early third century, Theophrastus belongs to the very beginning of the Hellenistic period and is thus unlikely to have had much (if any) acquaintance with Jews, their customs, or their principles. And

---

7 See especially John J. Collins, *Between Athens and Jerusalem: Jewish Identity in the Hellenistic Diaspora,* 2d ed. (Grand Rapids: Eerdmans, 2000); idem, *Jewish Cult and Hellenistic Culture: Essays on the Jewish Encounter with Hellenism and Roman Rule* (Leiden: Brill, 2005). See also the review of scholarship, stemming from the classic work of Hengel, by J. K. Aitken, "Review Essay on Hengel, *Judaism and Hellenism,*" *JBL* 123 (2004): 331–41.

his comments on Jewish sacrificial practices reflect that lack of comprehension. The fragment comes from Theophrastus's *Peri Eusebeias*, as transmitted by Porphyry, and reflects his hostility to the institution of animal sacrifice. Jews are mentioned in this connection as a people among the Syrians who sacrifice animals in a way repellent to Greeks, for they do not eat the victims but burn them whole, pouring honey and wine upon them so that the deed is finished quickly and at night lest this terrible thing be witnessed under the sun. And they proceed to fast on intervening days. Theophrastus goes on to claim that Jews were the first to conduct human as well as animal sacrifices.[8]

A puzzling passage. Just what it was that Theophrastus found objectionable in nighttime holocausts remains obscure. Holocausts were not uncommon in antiquity and were often done at night. References to honey, wine, refraining from meat, and fasting evidently derive from erroneous or confused information. As for human sacrifice, Theophrastus is more concerned to excuse than to condemn: the Jews did this, according to him, out of compulsion rather than zeal. Nor does he suggest even that they maintain this practice in his own day.

The segment has given rise to tortured and ingenious interpretations. Most of them focus on the question of whether Theophrastus had a positive or a negative impression of Jews.[9] That issue has occupied too much scholarly energy. It is not likely to be resolved, it appears irrelevant to Theophrastus's objectives, and it bears only marginally on our purpose. The passage demonstrates little more than that the author retailed misinformation, had only marginal familiarity with Judaism, and was prepared to embrace unreliable reports. Ignorance rather than ideology seems paramount.

More to the point are Theophrastus's remarks elsewhere in that fragment. He calls the Jews "a nation of philosophers" who converse with one another about God, gaze at the stars and speculate about them, and summon the divinity through their prayers.[10] Here again Theophrastus's knowledge of the Jews has distinct limitations. The description as star-gazers appears to equate them with

---

8 Porphyry, *Abst.*, 2.26 = M. Stern, *Greek and Latin Authors on Jews and Judaism*, vol. 1 (Jerusalem: Israel Academy of Sciences & Humanities, 1974), 10.
9 E.g., Stern, *Greek and Latin Authors*, 1:8; J. Mélèze-Modrzejewski, "L'Image du Juif dans la pensée grecque vers 300 avant notre ère," in *Greece and Rome in Eretz Israel*, ed. A. Kasher et al. (Jerusalem: Yad Izhak Ben-Zvi, 1996), 107 – 10; L. H. Feldman, *Jew and Gentile in the Ancient World* (Princeton: Princeton University Press, 1993), 7 – 8, 203 – 4; B. Bar-Kochva, *The Image of the Jews in Greek Literature: The Hellenistic Period* (Berkeley: University of California Press, 2009).
10 Porphyry, *Abst.*, 2.26 = Stern, *Greek and Latin Authors*, 1:10: ἅτε φιλόσοφοι τὸ γένος ὄντες, περὶ τοῦ θείου μὲν ἀλλήλοις λαλοῦσι, τῆς δὲ νυκτὸς τῶν ἄστρων ποιοῦνται τὴν θεωρίαν, βλέποντες εἰς αὐτὰ καὶ διὰ τῶν εὐχῶν θεοκλυτοῦντες.

astrologers, an attribution that he would not have drawn from a knowledgeable source. That they discuss God among themselves and call upon him with prayers suggests priestly responsibilities, as if all Jews were priests, a characterization that could hardly be based on serious research. Theophrastus relied on surmise and inference rather than trustworthy authorities (or perhaps any authorities).

That does not, however, render the surmise any less significant. How did Theophrastus reach the conclusion that Jews were a nation of philosophers? A number of possibilities have been proposed, none of them exclusive of the others. Perhaps Theophrastus knew of Jews as monotheists and inferred that those who speculated about a solitary divinity must be philosophers by nature.[11] Or he was impressed by Jewish aniconism, which he associated with a strong Greek philosophical tradition rejecting anthropomorphic representations of the divinity.[12] Or he reckoned Jews as a philosophic caste within the Syrians.[13] Or he confused the priestly class in Judea with the people as a whole.[14] Embrace of any of these propositions has to come with considerable caution. Nothing in the passage alludes to monotheism or aniconism. The denotation of the Jews as a people of the Syrians refers to their sacrificial customs, not to their philosophic character.[15] And the conclusion that Theophrastus might have conflated Jewish priests with Jews as a whole, turning them into philosophers as well, is hardly an obvious one. The root of Theophrastus's tangled description cannot be recovered. On any reckoning, however, he regarded Jews as a nation of philosophers, a people whose conception of divinity involved them in rational discussions among themselves, thus plainly seeing them in the light of Greek philosophical tradition. It is pointless and immaterial to argue about whether this puts Theophrastus into the camp of those who viewed Jews positively.[16]

---

11 W. Jaeger, "Greeks and Jews: The First Greek Records of Jewish Religion and Civilization," *Journal of Religion* 18 (1938): 131–34; Stern, *Greek and Latin Authors*, 1:11; E. Gabba, "The Growth of Anti-Judaism or the Greek Attitude Towards the Jews," in *The Cambridge History of Judaism*, vol. 2, *The Hellenistic Age*, ed. W. D. Davies and L. Finkelstein (Cambridge: Cambridge University Press, 1989), 619; Meleze-Modrzejewski, "L'Image du Juif," 107–8.

12 M. L. Satlow, "Theophrastus's Jewish Philosophers," *JJS* 59 (2008): 15–19.

13 So J. Bernays, *Theophrastos' Schrift über Frömmigkeit* (Berlin, 1866), 111, in the classic work on Theophrastus. Similarly Stern, *Greek and Latin Authors*, 1:10; Feldman, *Jew and Gentile*, 525; Bar-Kochva, *Image of the Jews*, who prefers the term "community" to "caste."

14 Satlow, "Theophrastus's Jewish Philosophers," 13–14.

15 Bar-Kochva, *Image of the Jews*, combines these and has Theophrastus regard the Jews as a community of philosopher-priests among the Syrians.

16 Bar-Kochva, *Image of the Jews*, maintains that the identification of Jews as philosophers does not outweigh the critical character of his comments on their sacrificial practices. Satlow, "Theo-

In all probability, he, like his younger contemporaries Clearchus and Megasthenes (see below), viewed them as among Eastern nations whose wise men
presided over practices and beliefs that seemed akin to Greek philosophical inquiry. Later Hellenic writers regularly cast legendary or semi-legendary religious
figures of the East together in comparative schemata. Moses thus found his place
with Orpheus, Musaeus, Amphiarius, the Magi in Persia, and the gymnosophists
in India.[17] Theophrastus may have been among the first to set Jews on a plane
with other Eastern nations to whom Greek writers imputed an "oriental wisdom"
that they found to resonate with Greek philosophy.

Clearchus of Soli

A fragment from yet another pupil of Aristotle belongs in this category.
Clearchus, from the Cyprian city of Soli, produced a work (now lost) entitled
On Sleep, from which Josephus quoted a choice item.[18] The Jewish historian utilizes the passage as part of his lengthy argument that Greek writers knew of Jews
from an early period and found much to admire. Clearchus's text (or Josephus's
extract from it) served this purpose very conveniently.[19] Clearchus described a
chance encounter in Asia Minor between his master Aristotle and an unnamed
Jew from Coele-Syria. He puts the narrative into the mouth of Aristotle, although
the tale itself may have been a concoction of the pupil.[20] Whether fictitious or
not, it offers a striking instance of a Greek intellectual's depiction of a learned
Jew. According to the anecdote, the man mightily impressed Aristotle. He admired in particular the man's remarkable endurance and self-restraint. He de-

---

phrastus's Jewish Philosophers," 1–2, rightly questions the value of categorizing Greek thinkers
in terms of their supposedly positive or negative opinions of Jews.
17 See, e.g., Strabo, 16.2.39; cf. 16.1.68, 16.1.70. Cf. H. Lewy, "Aristotle and the Jewish Sage
According to Clearchus of Soli," *HTR* 31 (1938): 216–21; A. Momigliano, *Alien Wisdom: The
Limits of Hellenization* (Cambridge: Cambridge University Press, 1975), 85–86; Gabba, "Growth
of Anti-Judaism," 618–24; Feldman, *Jew and Gentile,* 7–9. In the view of Satlow, "Theophrastus's Jewish Philosophers," 10–11, Greeks blurred the line between Eastern philosophers and
ritual experts.
18 On Clearchus's work and career, the evidence is assembled by F. Wehrli, *Die Schule des Aristoteles,* Vol. III: *Klearchos* (Basel: Schwabe, 1948). See also the discussions by Lewy, "Aristotle
and the Jewish Sage," 205–35, and Bar-Kochva, *Image of the Jews.*
19 Jos. C. *Ap.* 1.176–83; cf. Clement, *Strom.* 1.15.70.2.
20 Whether the anecdote is historical has properly been doubted by Jaeger, "Greeks and Jews,"
130–31; Bar-Kochva, *Image of the Jews.*

scribes him as a Jew τὸ γένος from Coele-Syria.[21] The Jews, evidently unfamiliar to Clearchus's presumed readership, then receive a fuller description. They are descendants of philosophers in India, men called Calanoi by the Indians but Jews by the Syrians. This particular individual, so notes Clearchus in the voice of Aristotle, was a frequent guest among many Greeks in Asia on his visits from the highlands to the coastal places, for he was Greek not only in his speech but in his very soul.[22] When he encountered Aristotle and other scholars in Asia, he tested their wisdom and, in view of his having dwelled with many people of παιδεία, he was rather able to impart something of his own.[23] "Aristotle" went on to recount in detail the Jew's great and astounding endurance and the self-restraint he exhibited in the conduct of his life, but Josephus chose not to repeat all of that, encouraging his readers to look up Clearchus's book themselves.[24] Such is the account.

Here again, the question of whether Clearchus sought to deliver a favorable assessment of Jews misses the point. He had his own agenda. And his portrait plainly imposes an *interpretatio Graeca*. For Clearchus, the skills of the cultivated Jew came not from being steeped in biblical texts but from his time spent in the company of numerous learned Greeks, the men of παιδεία. The esteem felt for him expresses itself as praise for his Greekness. The ability to hold his own in philosophical dialogue exhibited the Hellenic soul. The "Greek" qualities serve

---

21 Jos. C. *Ap.* 1.179. The term τὸ γένος, employed twice by Clearchus and also by Theophrastus in reference to Jews as philosophers τὸ γένος, does not readily lend itself to precise translation. Here it appears to mean something like "by origin." So Bar-Kochva, *Image of the Jews;* J. M. G. Barclay, *Flavius Josephus: Translation and Commentary,* vol. 10: *Against Apion* (Leiden: Brill, 2007), 104, prefers "by ancestry" or "by descent." But since Clearchus proceeds to speak of Jews as descendants of Indian philosophers, this seems inappropriate. Satlow, "Theophrastus's Jewish Philosophers," 13 – 14, chooses "race" for Clearchus but leans toward "caste" for Theophrastus, which would be a highly unusual rendering.
22 Jos. C. *Ap.* 1.180: Ἑλληνικὸς ἦν οὐ τῇ διαλέκτῳ μόνον, ἀλλὰ καὶ τῇ ψυχῇ.
23 Jos. C. *Ap.* 1.181: ἐντυγχάνει ἡμῖν τε καί τισιν ἑτέροις τῶν σχολαστικῶν πειρώμενος αὐτῶν τῆς σοφίας. ὡς δὲ πολλοῖς τῶν ἐν παιδείᾳ συνῳκείωτο, παρεδίδου τι μᾶλλον ὧν εἶχεν. On the meaning of μᾶλλον here, not "more" but "rather," see Barclay, *Against Apion,* 105; Bar-Kochva, *Image of the Jews.*
24 Just why Josephus elected to omit the rest has been the subject of much fruitless speculation. For Stern (*Greek and Latin Authors,* 1:52) Josephus did not have access to Clearchus's text but only a later compilation that included parts of it. Bar-Kochva, *Image of the Jews,* suggests that, by ascribing the virtues of καρτερία and σωφροσύνη to the Jews, he really transferred to them characteristics of the Indian gymnosophists, the principal focus of his attention, and Josephus omitted the details because he recognized them as inapplicable to Jews. The idea is ingenious but implausible. Josephus was not averse to ascribing καρτερία and σωφροσύνη to Jews; Jos. C. *Ap.* 2.146, 2.170; see Barclay, *Against Apion,* 106.

as the measuring rod. Nevertheless, characterization of the Jew in those terms is a telling fact. Clearchus elevates him by making him a philosopher.[25]

But more than "Greekness" is involved here. Clearchus has Aristotle bring in Indian wise men. And not incidentally. He introduces Jews themselves as a people descended from philosophers in India. Indeed they are philosophers in their own right, called Jews among Syrians on a par with those called Calanoi among Indians.[26] Clearchus evidently reckons Jews as a philosophic sect. They hold that place among Syrians, as Calanoi do among Indians. Confusion, as well as invention, permeates this text. Calanoi, as such, do not exist. Clearchus has simply and erroneously extrapolated from the figure of Calanus, the celebrated Indian gymnosophist noted for his sparring with Alexander the Great.[27] But the connections he evokes are significant. Clearchus elsewhere in his corpus claims that Indian gymnosophists descended from Persian *magi*. And others conjectured that Jews themselves had *magi* as ancestors.[28] As the philosophic elite of Persia, *magi* stood with Chaldeans in Babylon, and gymnosophists in India.[29] Clearchus placed the Jews in that category. These speculative fantasies, however remote from reality, offer insight into what passed as plausible perceptions of Jews in the early Hellenistic period. They belonged to the wise men of the East. Characterization as philosophers allowed them to combine Eastern wisdom with Hellenic παιδεία. The associations counted for more than any Otherness.

Megasthenes

The notion of Jews as philosophers certainly went beyond the school of Aristotle. The erudite Megasthenes served as envoy of Seleucus I at the court of the Indian ruler Chandragupta on one or more occasions and dwelled in India for a number of years, whether on several visits or an extended one. At some point, perhaps in the 290's, he composed a major study of that land and its people, the *Indica*, cited and quoted by several later Greek and Roman writers, evidently a classic work on the subject. Only one preserved fragment refers to the Jews, but it is

---

25 Nothing in the text supports the interpretation of Bar-Kochva, *Image of the Jews*, that praise for the Jew signified only surprise that a member of a "barbarian" nation had managed to acquire Greek speech and learning.
26 Jos. C. *Ap.* 1:179: οὗτοι δ' εἰσιν ἀπόγονοι τῶν ἐν Ἰνδοῖς φιλοσόφων, καλοῦνται δέ, ὥς φασιν, οἱ φιλόσοφοι παρὰ μὲν Ἰνδοῖς Καλανοί, παρὰ δὲ Σύροις Ἰουδαῖοι.
27 On Calanus, see Arrian, *An.* 7.2 – 3; Strab., 15.1.61 – 68; Plutarch, *Alexander* 65, 69.
28 Diogenes Laertius 1.9.
29 Diogenes Laertius 1.1; Clement, *Strom.* 1.15.71.4.

a most intriguing one, particularly in light of the comments of Theophrastus and Clearchus, his slightly earlier but near contemporaries. The passage appears in the *Stromateis* of Clement of Alexandria who was eager to find parallels between Greek philosophy and Eastern learning, and thereby to establish that Hellenic precepts were derivative from the older wisdom of the east. To that end Clement quotes Megasthenes as witness to the antiquity of Jewish philosophy, its priority to and influence over the Greeks. In the segment quoted, Megasthenes asserted that everything said about nature by the ancient Greeks can also be found among those outside Greece who philosophize, some of the views held by the Brahmans in India, some by those called Jews in Syria.[30]

The passage is often misconstrued. It does not show that Megasthenes himself gave priority to Jewish learning (or to Indian learning) over that of the Greeks —even though Clement used it to that purpose. Megasthenes seems in fact to employ Greek views as the touchstone of the argument, with the others seen by comparison with it. Strabo quotes Megasthenes at greater length on the Brahmans and the parallels he found with Hellenic opinions about nature. The quotation significantly contains Megasthenes' remark that some of the Brahmans' ideas rest on myths and suffer from simplicity because Brahmans are better at deeds than words. That would hardly qualify them as sages from whom Greeks drew their philosophy.[31] The approach once again suggests an *interpretatio Graeca*. The Hellenic vantage point is paramount. How far Megasthenes may have researched or written about Jewish beliefs is beyond our knowledge. What parallels he discerned, if any, with the Brahmans also elude conjecture. The sole surviving passage implies that Jewish and Brahman beliefs, at least in some respects, diverged.[32] More importantly, however, both overlapped with Greek ideas and both engaged in philosophizing, the central point of Megasthenes' text. He refrains from making a genealogical connection, as does Clearchus. But Jews are once again bracketed with Indian wise men and their opinions associated with Greek philosophers. The juxtaposition carries meaning. Hellenic thinkers seemed quite comfortable in ascribing to Jews conceptualizations that coincided with their own and reckoning them as part of Greek philosophical tradition.

---

30 Clement, *Strom.* 1.15.72.5 = Stern, *Greek and Latin Authors*, 1:46: ἅπαντα μέντοι τὰ περὶ φύσεως εἰρημένα παρὰ τοῖς ἀρχαίοις λέγεται καὶ παρὰ τοῖς ἔξω τῆς Ἑλλάδος φιλοσοφοῦσι, τὰ μὲν παρ' Ἰνδοῖς ὑπὸ τῶν Βραχμάνων, τὰ δὲ ἐν τῇ Συρίᾳ ὑπὸ τῶν καλουμένων Ἰουδαίων.
31 Strab., 15.1.59. See the valuable discussion of Bar-Kochva, *Image of the Jews*.
32 So, rightly, Bar-Kochva, *Image of the Jews*. See Clement, *Strom.* 1.15.72.5 = Stern, *Greek and Latin Authors*, 1:46: τὰ μὲν ...ὑπὸ τῶν Βραχμάνων... τὰ δὲ... ὑπὸ τῶν καλουμένων Ἰουδαίων.

II. Jewish Authors on Greek Philosophy

Letter of Aristeas

This was not, however, a one-sided proposition. Hellenistic Jews who had drunk deep (or even shallow) at the springs of Greek philosophy could turn the relationship around to their own advantage. The celebrated *Letter of Aristeas*, a Jewish composition, is a striking case at point. The work purports to tell of the translation of the Hebrew Bible into Greek. But it contains much more than that. The narrative has significant implications for the place of Jewish intellectuals in the culture of Hellenism.

Familiarity with Greek philosophy pervades the text. The Jewish author has Demetrius of Phaleron, Athenian philosopher and statesman, now counselor to Ptolemy II of Egypt, advise the king to commission the translation. In doing so, Demetrius commends the legislation contained in the Scriptures for its particularly philosophical character.[33] Hellenic virtues like justice, piety, self-restraint, and philanthropy gain repeated mention as Jewish qualities.[34] The high priest in Jerusalem, in recounting the significance of Jewish dietary prescriptions, explains them in good Greek style either as having a rational basis or as requiring allegorical interpretation.[35] Jewish legislation on food and drink, as he puts it, is an expression of "right reason."[36]

The central exhibit on this score is the extended symposium recorded by the *Letter of Aristeas*. In this scenario the king interrogates each of the seventy-two Jewish sages who had come from Jerusalem to Alexandria for the task of rendering the Bible into Greek.[37] The episode occupies fully one third of the whole work, something to which the author evidently sought to call attention.[38] The banquet with intellectual exchange is a quintessentially Greek institution, familiar from Plato's *Symposium,* and the format of a king asking questions of sages appears in Plutarch's *Symposium of the Seven Wise Men.* Ptolemy, over a period

---

33 *Let. Aris.* 31: φιλοσοφωτέραν.

34 E.g., *Let. Aris.* 2, 131, 147, 189, 208, 209, 237, 292.

35 *Let. Aris.* 128–71.

36 *Let. Aris.* 161. See also *Let. Aris.* 244.

37 On the banquet scene, see O. Murray, "Aristeas and Ptolemaic Kingship," *JTS* 18 (1967): 344–61; P. M. Fraser, *Ptolemaic Alexandria,* vol. 1 (Oxford: Clarendon, 1972), 701–3; F. Parente, "La lettera di Aristea come fonte per la storia del Giudaismo Alessandrino durante la prima meta del 1 secolo a.C," *Annali della Scuola Normale Superiore de Pisa, Classe di Lettere e Filosofa.* 2.1–2 (1972): 549–63.

38 *Let. Aris.* 184–296.

of a week, asks each of the Jewish elders in turn a question, receives a reply, and (without fail) praises the speaker. A large proportion of the questions involve the proper means for a monarch to govern his realm, thus putting this segment in a genre similar to that of Hellenistic treatises on kingship. And a substantial number of the responses stem from Greek philosophy or political theory, each one, however, punctuated by reference to God as ultimate authority. But the divinity often appears in mechanical, even irrelevant, fashion. The context is strictly philosophical rather than theological. To the question of what constitutes the strongest form of rule, for instance, the Jewish interlocutor replies "to control oneself and not be carried away by passions"—standard Stoic ideology.[39] Ptolemy's queries to the Jews included the Socratic one of whether wisdom can be taught, though the term τὸ φρονεῖν refers to practical wisdom rather than theoretical wisdom. The response looks like a clever side-step: if the soul's receptivity to all that is good is guided by divine power, this would hardly amount to being taught.[40] To one guest Ptolemy actually poses the direct question of "What is philosophy?"—indicating that the answer would best come from a Jew. The response was little different from those delivered several times in various forms by the guests: to deliberate with reason and resist passions, a perfectly good Stoic formulation in the mouth of the Jew.[41]

The relationship with Greek philosophy, however, takes a more complex and ambiguous turn. The author of the *Letter of Aristeas* has a mischievous side. Greek philosophers appear directly in the narrative, appointees of the king and members of the court, playing a supportive role that sets off the wisdom of the Jews by comparison and contrast. When Ptolemy completed his first round of questioning and hailed each of the Jewish scholars for the acuity of their answers, he turned to his own sages asking for confirmation of his opinion. Their spokesman Menedemus of Eretria, who gained repute as a significant thinker in the early third century B.C.E., responded appropriately, endorsing the king's assessment and praising the Jewish guests for their focus upon God.[42] Menedemus's approbation of the Jews, solicited by Ptolemy, and Ptolemy's immediate assent to his remarks in turn imply a staged event, an implication that the author perhaps offers with a wink and a nod. At the conclusion of

---

39 *Let. Aris.* 222; cf. 211.
40 *Let. Aris.* 236.
41 *Let. Aris.* 256.
42 *Let. Aris.* 200 – 201. Menedemus served at the court of Antigonus Gonatas; Diogenes Laertius 2.125 – 44. Both his dates and his service with the Macedonian kingmake it improbable that he would become a confidant of Ptolemy II in Alexandria. "Aristeas" may have imported him into the text simply as a philosopher whose name might be known to his readership.

the next day's interrogation, the king, having once more commended every answer, however banal or commonplace, looked again to his entourage for assent. All responded on cue and joined in the approbation—especially the philosophers.[43] The author surely did not inject this item fortuitously. His portrait of Greek intellectuals, prompted by the king, acknowledging their own inferiority through what were doubtless clenched teeth, has to be deliberate whimsy. And he underscores the point by adding in his own voice that the Jewish wise men, in their conduct and speech, far outpaced the philosophers.[44] At the end of the seven-day banquet, "Aristeas" gives high marks to the Jewish scholars who had supplied such prompt, careful, and acute answers to difficult questions that should have required lengthy deliberation. He concludes the section by reiterating his earlier message: everyone admired the Jews' replies, especially the philosophers.[45] The repetition here gives a satiric edge to the author's treatment. Jewish sages, though fresh from Jerusalem, had fully absorbed the tenets of Greek philosophy, better than the Greek professionals themselves. The playful character of the exchange is hard to miss.[46] The oblique mockery does not represent a challenge to the caliber of Hellenic learning. But it reminds the readership that Jewish thinkers had assimilated it, shaped it to their own purposes, and even improved upon it. Once again, and this time from the Jewish side, the links take precedence over any sense of alienation.

Aristobulus

Other Hellenistic Jews took the matter further and on a different track. They made Greek philosophers dependent upon Jewish text and tradition. First and foremost among perpetrators of that endeavor was the gifted and inventive intellectual Aristobulus, probably an Alexandrian of the second century B.C.E.[47] Like

---

43 *Let. Aris.* 235: μάλιστα δὲ τῶν φιλοσόφων.
44 *Let. Aris.* 235: ταῖς ἀγωγαῖς καὶ τῷ λόγῳ πολὺ προέχοντες αὐτῶν ἦσαν.
45 *Let. Aris.* 295–96.
46 For this interpretation of the *Letter of Aristeas* more generally, see E. S. Gruen, *Heritage and Hellenism: The Reinvention of Jewish Tradition* (Berkeley: University of California Press, 1998), 206–22; idem, "The Letter of Aristeas and the Cultural Context of the Septuagint," in *Die Septuaginta—Texte, Kontexte, Lebenswelten,* ed. M. Karrer and W. Krdus (Tubingen: Mohr-Siebeck; 2008), 134–56 also available in this volume.
47 Specific provenance and date remain somewhat disputed. But few will challenge the conclusion that Aristobulus was a Jewish intellectual of the mid-Hellenistic period. The most important study remains that of N. Walter, *Der Thoraausleger Aristobulos* (Berlin: Akademie, 1964), 13– 123. On the lengthy debate, see the valuable summary of C. R. Holladay, *Fragments from Hellen-*

the author of the *Letter of Aristeas,* a treatise perhaps contemporary or nearly so, Aristobulus offered an engagingly imaginative presentation of Jewish involvement with Greek philosophy.[48] He had or at least was purported to have had philosophical credentials. Clement of Alexandria and Eusebius, who preserve the extant fragments of his work, designate him a Peripatetic.[49] The characterization need not, strictly speaking, mean that he was a follower of the Aristotelian school. It signifies more general philosophical interests or even wider intellectual leanings. He certainly had a familiarity with a range of Greek philosophical traditions.[50] Aristobulus, purportedly a tutor to Ptolemy VI of Egypt, produced an extensive composition, either a commentary on or a substantial exegesis of the Torah, of which only a few fragments survive.[51] They suffice, however, to disclose a notable agenda. Aristobulus undertook the task of establishing that the Hebrew Bible lay behind some of the best of Greek philosophical thought.

The author reached back to a famed and fabled figure: Pythagoras of Samos, the sixth-century philosopher, scientist, and religious thinker around whom legends collected and a pseudonymous literature accumulated. In Aristobulus's formulation, Pythagoras borrowed heavily from the books of Moses and incorporated them into his own doctrines.[52] Whether he had actually read any Pythagoras may be doubted. But the aura of Pythagoras's mystique invited a fictive association—especially one in which Jews got the credit. Aristobulus pressed the point with regard to an even more celebrated figure, Plato, who, in his view, followed the precepts of the Jewish lawgiver and worked assiduously through every detail of the laws.[53] He added Socrates, too, to that lineup, alluding to his famous "divine voice" and putting him in the company of Pythagoras and Plato, who claimed that they heard the voice of God when they observed the form of the universe

istic *Jewish Authors,* vol. 3: *Aristobulus* (Atlanta: Scholars Press, 1995), 49–75. Further bibliography in E. S. Gruen, *Diaspora: Jews Amidst Greeks and Romans* (Cambridge, Mass.: Harvard University Press, 2002), 337, n. 55. See also the essay by Patricia D. Ahearne-Kroll, "Constructing Jewish Identity in Ptolemaic Egypt: The Case of Artapanus" in D. Harlow, K.M. Hogan, M. Goff, and J.S. Kaminsky, *The "Other" in Second Temple Judaism* (Grand Rapids, 2011).
48 The relative dates of Aristobulus and the *Letter of Aristeas* and the question of who influenced whom have long been debated, with no consensus; see, e.g., Walter, *Aristobulos,* 88–103; Holladay, *Aristobulus,* 64–65, 86, n. 90, with bibliography. Each could easily have drawn on the same tradition.
49 Clement, *Strom.* 1.15.72.4; Eus. *PE* 9.6.6; 13.11.3.
50 See Walter, *Aristobulos,* 10–13.
51 Eus. *PE* 7.13.7; 7.32.16; *Chronicle* 151; Clement, *Strom.* 5.14.97.7; cf. Holladay, *Aristobulus,* 74, 92–94.
52 Clement, *Strom.* 1.22.150.3; Eus. *PE* 9.6.8; 13.12.1.
53 Clement, *Strom.* 1.22.150.1; Eus. *PE* 13.12.1.

so meticulously created and sustained by him and used Moses' words to affirm the fact.[54] Nor did Aristobulus stop with the ancient philosophers. He saw fit also to cite the Hellenistic poet Aratus of Soli, who had studied with the Stoic master Zeno and whose astronomical poem, the *Phaenomena*, suffused with Stoicism, served his purposes nicely. Aristobulus seized upon the opening lines of the poem in which Aratus offered a pantheistic vision of God not only as father of all but as permeating every corner of the universe. By the simple device of altering Aratus's terminology from Δὶς or Ζεύς to θεός, he underlined the debt owed by the Stoic poet to Jewish ideas.[55] In case anyone missed the point, Aristobulus added a still more sweeping statement that a consensus holds among all (Greek) philosophers about the necessity of maintaining reverent attitudes toward God. And that conviction, he notes, is most prominently promoted in the Jewish school of philosophy.[56] Indeed, Mosaic law enshrines the principles of piety, justice (righteousness), self restraint, and all other qualities that are genuinely good.[57] It is hardly an accident that Aristobulus cites those virtues that became standard traits in Greek philosophical thought. The creative writer had no hesitation in framing Hellenic philosophy as an expression of Jewish tradition.

Indeed, he needed to be creative. Pythagoras, Socrates, and Plato lived long before the composition of the Septuagint. Unless they miraculously gained a command of Hebrew, they could hardly have had access to the laws of Moses. Aristobulus did not resort to conjuring up miracles, but he did the next best thing. He got around the problem by compounding the fiction: Greek translations of at least parts of the Bible, he claimed, had been available some centuries before the compiling of the Septuagint. So Pythagoras, Plato, and others could have studied the Scriptures in an accessible language to their heart's content.[58] The idea, of course, is preposterous. How many people might actually have believed it can be left to the imagination. One might indeed suggest that Aristobulus concocted the idea with tongue largely in cheek. A certain playfulness exists in his whole contrived scenario not only of Greek philosophers poring over biblical texts but also of numerous Greek poets and dramatists reproducing the les-

---

54 Clement, *Strom.* 5.14.99.3; Eus. *PE* 13.12.4. Cf. Y. Gutman, *The Beginnings of Jewish-Hellenistic Literature,* vol. 1 (Jerusalem: Bialik, 1958, in Hebrew), 192–94, who sees the proposition as a plausible one.
55 Clement, *Strom.* 5.14.101.4b; Eus. *PE* 13.12.6–7; Gutman, *Beginnings of Jewish-Hellenistic Literature,* 195–96.
56 Eus. *PE* 13.12.8: ὃ μάλιστα παρακελεύεται καλῶς ἡ καθ᾿ ἡμᾶς αἵρεσις. Use of αἵρεσις here is noteworthy, for the term regularly denotes a Greek philosophical school.
57 Eus. *PE* 13.12.8.
58 Clement, *Strom.* 1.22.150.2; Eus. *PE* 13.12.1.

sons of the Bible.[59] But whether serious or not, Aristobulus's imaginative fabrications set Greek philosophy into the framework of the Jewish intellectual and religious achievement—the reverse of "othering."

Philo of Alexandria

Aristobulus's work heralded a long tradition of Jewish claims to the priority of their teachings and the indebtedness of Hellenic philosophers. This edifying inference found its way into the works of the great Jewish philosopher and exegete Philo of Alexandria, where it appears in various forms and in numerous scattered places of his vast corpus. Philo, like Aristobulus, traced the effects of Jewish learning back to the pre-Socratics. Greeks had claimed that Heraclitus first hatched the idea that only the contemplation of opposites leads to understanding of the whole. Philo dismissed that claim: Moses had propounded the notion long before Heraclitus.[60] Even Heraclitus's famous statement regarding the soul's death as entombment in the body and its release to life when the body dies merely follows the teaching of Moses.[61] Philo duly acknowledges the persuasiveness of Plato's cosmology that sees the world as created and indestructible. But, although some ascribe the origin of this view to Hesiod, Philo asserts that one can find it already in Genesis, thus to the credit of Moses.[62] The Jewish philosopher also paraphrases with approbation Plato's famous dictum that states can only reach their potential if kings become philosophers or philosophers become kings. But he points out that Moses had long since blended both kingship and philosophy in his own person—not to mention his roles as lawgiver, priest, and prophet.[63] So, the Scriptures again supplied precedent for Plato.

Hellenistic philosophy, for Philo, owes a similarly heavy debt to the teachings of the Scriptures. He cites with high praise the thesis of Zeno the Stoic

---

59 For this interpretation, see Gruen, *Heritage and Hellenism*, 246–51; idem, *Diaspora*, 221–24. Other scholars take Aristobulus's endeavor as an altogether serious enterprise. E. g., Gutman, *Beginnings of Jewish-Hellenistic Literature*, 186–220; Walter, *Aristobulos*; M. Hengel, *Judaism and Hellenism*, vol. 1 (London: SPCK, 1974), 163–69; E. Schürer, *The History of the Jewish People in the Age of Jesus Christ*, vol. 3, rev. ed., ed. G. Vermes, F. Millar, and M. Goodman (Edinburgh: Clark, 1986), 579–87; J. M. G. Barclay, *Jews in the Mediterranean Diaspora: From Alexander to Trajan (323 BCE–17 CE)* (Edinburgh: T. & T. Clark, 1996), 150–58; Collins, *Between Athens and Jerusalem*, 186–90.
60 Philo, *Her.* 207–14.
61 Philo, *Leg. All.* 1.105–8.
62 Philo, *Aet.* 13–19.
63 Philo, *Mos.* 2; cf. Plat. *Rep.* 5.473D.

with regard to the necessity of subjecting the intemperate to the wise, but adds
the conjecture that he must have got this idea from Isaac's command in Genesis
that Esau serve his brother Jacob.[64] Stoic doctrine held that the wise man alone,
no matter his material circumstances, is true ruler and king and that virtue has
unassailable authority. Philo, however, finds this principle already enshrined in
a passage of Genesis wherein the Hittites (Canaanites) hail Abraham as a Prince
of God among them.[65] Philo elsewhere allows himself a rather gratuitous bit of
one-upmanship. He notes that Greek philosophers regarded those who first applied names to things as sages. But Moses had the better of them on that, for he
had the distinction of naming Adam![66] Philo rarely shows flashes of humor. But
this just might be an instance of it. And one can perhaps find another in his arresting claim that Socrates' thoughts about God's fashioning of body parts that
perform excretory functions drew on Moses![67] Philo's powers of invention were
not negligible. In re-creating the education of Moses, he performs a neat and surprising twist on the interpenetration of Greek and Jewish learning. Philo has
Moses not only learn arithmetic, geometry, music, and hieroglyphics from erudite Egyptians, but progress through the rest of the curriculum, presumably rhetoric, literature, and philosophy, with Greek teachers.[68] Just where Moses might
have found itinerant Greek schoolmasters in late Bronze Age Egypt Philo leaves
to the imagination. This, too, may have been no more than a half-serious flight of
fancy. But it attests to a continuing by-play of *interpretationes Graecae* and *interpretationes Iudaicae.*

Josephus

A generation after Philo, the idea that Greek philosophers hewed closely to the
concept of God obtained from acquaintance with the Books of Moses still made
the rounds. The Jewish historian Josephus retailed the notion in his last—and
most contrived—treatise, the *Contra Apionem.*[69] Josephus interestingly forbears,
as he puts it, to make the case that the wisest of the Greeks learned their doc-

---

64 Philo, *Prob.* 53 – 57; cf. Gen. 27:40.
65 Philo, *Mut.* 152; *Som.* 2.244; cf. Gen. 23:6.
66 Philo, *Leg. All.* 2.15.
67 Philo, *QG* 2.6.
68 Philo, *Mos.* 1.23.
69 On the contrived character of the work, see E. S. Gruen, "Greeks and Jews: Mutual Misperceptions in Josephus' Contra Apionem," in *Ancient Judaism in Its Hellenistic Context,* ed. C. Bakhos (Leiden: Brill, 2005), 31 – 51 also available in this volume.

trines about God from the formulations of Moses. The idea could by that time be taken for granted. He affirms indeed that Greek philosophers have long since testified to the excellence and suitability of Jewish formulations with regard to the nature and glory of God. He cites Pythagoras, Anaxagoras, Plato, and the Stoics as witnesses to the fact. But why stop there? Josephus extends the point to encompass nearly all philosophers, since they hold similar views about the nature of God. And he gives the advantage to Moses on more than just priority. The Greeks philosophized to a small circle; Moses spoke with both actions and words not only to his contemporaries but to all future generations.[70] The historian makes a similar point elsewhere: the first imitators of Mosaic laws were Greek philosophers who, although ostensibly observing the practices of their native lands, actually in their deeds and their philosophizing followed the, precepts of Moses.[71] Josephus can also become more specific. He cites two principles of Plato, that citizens should study their laws assiduously with precision and that they restrict the introduction of foreigners so as to limit the state to those who adhere to its laws. On both those counts, he maintains, Plato took his cue from Moses.[72] For the Jewish readership of Josephus, like that of Philo, such claims were evidently uncontroversial. They had been around a long time.

For how long? As we have seen, Greek writers had already made connection between Jewish sages and Greek philosophy in the late fourth century B.C.E. The assertion that Greeks owed philosophical doctrines to the Jews, on the other hand, appears, as one might expect, in Jewish texts, stemming at least from Aristobulus in the mid-second century B.C.E. This bifurcation, however, is crossed by a fascinating passage from a Hellenic author with no obvious Jewish axes to grind, one who precedes any extant Jewish texts on the matter. Hermippus of Smyrna, a pupil of Callimachus in Alexandria, composed a wide range of works, including a biography of Pythagoras, some time in the late third or early second century B.C.E.[73] This puts him approximately a half century earlier than Aristobulus. Yet Hermippus included the arresting statement that Pythagoras imitated and adapted the views of Jews and Thracians. Coming from a Greek at so early a date, this striking remark demands attention.

---

70 Jos. *C. Ap.* 2.168–69. Josephus refers to Pythagoras's knowledge of Jewish matters also at *Ag. Ap.* 1.162.
71 Jos. *C. Ap.* 2.281: πρῶτοι μὲν γὰρ οἱ παρὰ τοῖς Ἕλλησι φιλοσοφήσαντες τῷ μὲν δοκεῖν τὰ πάτρια διεφύλαττον, ἐν δὲ τοῖς πράγμασι καὶ τῷ φιλοσοφεῖν ἐκείνῳ κατηκολούθησαν; cf. 1.175.
72 Jos. *C. Ap.* 2.257: Πλάτων μεμίμηται τὸν ἡμέτερον νομοθέτην.
73 On the life and works of Hermippus, see the discussion, with testimony and bibliography, by J. Bollansée, *Hermippos of Smyrna and His Biographical Writings: A Reappraisal* (Leuven: Peeters, 1999), 1–20; also Bar-Kochva, *Image of the Jews*.

The quotation comes from Josephus's *Contra Apionem,* which has as one of its chief aims a demonstration that Jews were held in esteem by eminent Greeks familiar with their writings. Josephus indeed has an axe to grind. But that does not itself cast suspicion upon the accuracy of Hermippus's remarks that he conveys. A curious story about Pythagoras appeared in the first book of Hermippus's biography, as reported by Josephus. The philosopher spoke about the death of one of his followers, Calliphon of Croton, whose soul then accompanied him day and night. He urged that one ought not to cross a spot where an ass sank to its knees, to avoid any thirst-producing water, and to refrain from all blasphemy.[74] An odd combination of precepts. To this point, Josephus appears to be paraphrasing Hermippus. He then quotes him directly as saying that Pythagoras acted upon and spoke about such matters by imitating and adapting to himself the views of Jews and Thracians.[75] And in his own voice Josephus adds that Pythagoras is rightly said to have brought into his philosophy many of the precepts found among the Jews.[76]

The passage is noteworthy. One will not be surprised to learn that some scholars have seized upon this information to argue that Hermippus falls into the category of those Greek intellectuals who had a positive appreciation of the Jews and that he embraced the idea of a Jewish influence upon Greek philosophy even before the Jews did.[77] But, as usual, the matter is not so simple. Hermippus's writings gained popularity—enough to warrant epitomes of them for a wider readership already in the second century B.C.E. by Heraclides Lembus.[78] But the popularity did not arise from sober, scholarly monographs. Hermippus earned the reputation of a lively storyteller, noted for parody, fantasy, and rather caustic comments on the subjects of his works.[79] His depiction of Pythagoras falls into that category. It was no laudatory one. Fragments of the biography suggest sarcasm, innuendo, and mockery.[80] Nor was Hermippus the first. Pythagoras was a controversial figure who drew considerable criticism from philoso-

---

74 Jos. *C. Ap.* 1.164. Whether the advice comes from Pythagoras or from the soul of Calliphon is ambiguous in the text. See Bar-Kochva, *Image of the Jews.* A decision is not required for our purposes.

75 Jos. *C. Ap.* 1.165: ταῦτα δὲ ἔραττε καὶ ἔλεγε τὰς Ἰουδαίων καὶ Θρακῶν δόξας μιμούμενος καὶ μεταφέρων εἰς ἑαυτόν.

76 Jos. *C. Ap.* 2.165. See below.

77 E.g., Gabba, "Growth of Anti-Judaism," 623–24; Feldman, *Jew and Gentile,* 201–2.

78 On the subsequent reputation of Hermippus, see Bollansée, *Hermippos of Smyrna,* 104–16.

79 See Bollansée, *Hermippos of Smyrna,* 118–53; Bar-Kochva, *Image of the Jews.*

80 Examples in Bar-Kochva, *Image of the Jews.* See, e.g., Diogenes Laertius 8.41. Cf. Bollansée, *Hermippos of Smyrna,* 44–52, who, however, takes far too generous a view of Hermippus's bias.

phers and others.[81] That puts a very different slant on the passage conveyed by Josephus.

The particulars ascribed to Pythagoras appear, under this lens, to border on the ludicrous. The story of Calliphon's spirit dwelling night and day with the philosopher looks like an ironic comment on his doctrine of the immortality of the soul.[82] And the three prohibitions that he prescribed hardly suggest earnest guidance to his followers. Avoidance of a spot where an ass sank to his knees and refraining from salty or sugary water recall a host of Pythagorean pronouncements that few outside his sect (or perhaps even within) would take seriously.[83] The ban on blasphemy looks more solemn. But it is one so widely shared among creeds and sects that it might have been included for its banality rather than its solemnity.[84] Hermippus was having some fun with the superstitions and ritual taboos associated with Pythagoreanism.

What then are we to make of Hermippus's statement (here in a direct quote by Josephus) that Pythagoras both asserted and practiced these precepts in imitation of Jewish and Thracian doctrines? It certainly constituted no compliment to Jews or Thracians. A search for Jewish parallels for the three prohibitions leads nowhere, let alone guesswork as to which may have been Thracian and which Jewish.[85] On the other hand, it does not follow that Hermippus was denigrating Jews and Thracians together with Pythagoras. The philosopher was said to have been conversant with and influenced by various Eastern traditions, including those of Egyptians, Chaldeans, and *magi*.[86] It would be logical enough to add Jews to that company. As for Thracians, a people usually regarded as on the periphery of civilization, one might be tempted to infer that Hermippus inserted them as yet another sardonic jab at Pythagoras. He did not, however, invent the connection. Biographical references to the sage include one that has his slave bring Pythagorean teachings to the Thracians.[87] More important

---

81 E.g., Diogenes Laertius 5.1, 8.7, 8.36, 9.1, with the discussion of Bar-Kochva, *Image of the Jews.*

82 Cf. Diogenes Laertius 8.32; Barclay, *Against Apion,* 96; Bar-Kochva, *Image of the Jews.*

83 H. Jacobson, "Hermippus, Pythagoras, and the Jews," *REJ* 135 (1976): 145–49, makes a laudable but ultimately unsuccessful attempt to find biblical prescriptions behind Hermippus's statements. Similarly, P. Gorman, "Pythagoras Palestinus," *Philologus* 127 (1983): 33–36. See the criticisms of Bar-Kochva, *Image of the Jews.*

84 Bar-Kochva, *Image of the Jews,* goes further to argue that Greeks did not worry about blasphemy anyway except at a sacred shrine—an extreme position.

85 So, rightly, Barclay, *Against Apion,* 97–98; Bar-Kochva, *Image of the Jews.*

86 Diogenes Laertius 8.3; Porphyry, *Vita Pythagorae* 6, 11–12.

87 Herodotus 4.95; Strabo 7.3.5; Iamblichus, *Vita Pythagorae* 14–15.

perhaps is the association of Pythagoras with Orphism.[88] Since legend has Orpheus, the father of Hellenic song and poetry, as a Thracian, the suggestion of influence from Thrace upon Pythagoras need not itself be a hostile one. But it is easy enough to imagine that Hermippus might have turned the relationship to his own purpose in comic fashion.

Josephus's own comments go well beyond what might be inferred from the Hermippus fragment. The historian introduces the subject by stating that Pythagoras, a figure of great antiquity, preeminent among philosophers in wisdom and piety, not only knew about Jewish matters but was a most eager emulator of them.[89] And he closes the segment by affirming that Pythagoras is correctly said to have imported many Jewish precepts into his own philosophy.[90] This plainly embellishes and enhances the information in Hermippus. It is picked up and further amplified by Origen, who cites Hermippus for the view that Pythagoras transferred his own philosophy from Jews to Greeks.[91] Those sweeping assertions have more to do with the objectives of Josephus and Origen than with the more cynical intent of Hermippus.

This does not, however, obviate the main point. There is no reason to doubt that the association of Pythagoras with Jewish ideas and traditions was already current in the time of Hermippus. Even if he alluded to the presumed connection only in order to mock Pythagoras, he attests to its existence. It matters not whether Josephus had access to Hermippus's text, to an epitome of it, or even a reference to it in a Jewish author. Hermippus's affirmation that Pythagoras was influenced by Jewish beliefs can hardly be sheer invention.[92] It reflects

---

88 Cf. Iamblichus, *Vita Pythagorae* 146; Barclay, *Against Apion*, 97.

89 Jos. *C. Ap.* 1.162: σοφίᾳ δὲ καὶ τῇ περὶ τὸ θεῖον εὐσεβείᾳ πάντων ὑπειλημμένος διενεγκεῖν, τῶν φιλοσοφησάντων, οὐ μόνον ἐγνωκὼς τὰ παρ' ἡμῖν δῆλός ἐστιν, ἀλλὰ καὶ ζηλωτὴς αὐτῶν ἐκ πλείστου γεγενημένος.

90 Jos. *C. Ap.* 1.165: λέγεται γὰρ ὡς ἀληθῶς ὁ ἀνὴρ ἐκεῖνος πολλὰ τῶν παρὰ Ἰουδαίοις νομίμων εἰς τὴν αὑτοῦ μετενεγκεῖν φιλοσοφίαν.

91 Origen, *Contra Celsum*, 1.15.334. Cf. also Porphyry, *Vita Pythagorae* 11.

92 Bar-Kochva, *Image of the Jews*, whose dissection of the text is decidedly superior to other treatments, nevertheless takes a minimalist approach. His conclusion that Hermippus made no allusion to Jews except for the three precepts actually recorded by Josephus is implausible. A similar view is in Schürer, *History of the Jewish People*, 3:696. Gorman ("Pythagoras Palestinus," 32 – 33), Barclay (*Against Apion*, 98), and Bar-Kochva (*Image of the Jew*) propose that Josephus based his broader statement about Jewish influence upon Pythagoras strictly or largely on Aristobulus (Eusebius, *Praep. Evang.* 13.12.1). The language is indeed similar (though not identical). But many Jewish writers, now lost, may have conveyed parallel information. Josephus nowhere cites Aristobulus. To infer that he simply adopted Aristobulus's formulation about Jewish impact upon Pythagoras and ascribed it to Hermippus without any basis except the three precepts is highly questionable. Bar-Kochva's view that Origen's statement is a mere paraphrase

both the Hellenic conceptualization that links Eastern wisdom with Greek philosophy and the Jewish construct that has Greek philosophers derive their ideas from Jewish learning. The overlap and interconnection leave a deep impression.[93]

III. Conclusion

The reciprocation has a long history. Two striking passages provide a coda to underscore it. Philo in the mid—first-century C.E. comments that the world contains multitudes of rich, eminent, and pleasure-seeking individuals, but very few who are wise, just, and virtuous. He then specifies important examples of the latter category: the seven sages of Greece, the Persian *magi*, the Indian gymnosophists, and the Jewish Essenes.[94] The Jewish philosopher, therefore, echoes a linkage between Hellenic savants and Eastern wise men (including Jews) that goes back more than three centuries to Greek thinkers like Megasthenes, Clearchus, and Hermippus.[95] And as late as the second half of the second century C.E., the Platonist philosopher Numenius of Apamea (whom some referred to as a Pythagorean) reiterated the affinities of Plato and Pythagoras with the teachings of Brahmans, Egyptians, *magi*, and Jews.[96] Numenius has the signal distinction of uttering the most celebrated remark on this entire subject: "For what is Plato, but Moses speaking in good Attic Greek?"[97] As Philo the Jew mirrors the constructed interconnections first formulated by Greeks, so Numenius the Greek mirrors the conceit of Jewish origins for Greek philosophy first formulated by Jews. The mutual regard stands out. There is no sign of Otherness here.

---

of Josephus also stands on shaky ground. Whereas Josephus cites *Hermippus's Life of Pythagoras*, Origen drew his information from Hermippus's work *On Lawgivers; Contra Celsum*, 1.15.334. Bar-Kochva's conclusion that the information simply passed from Aristobulus to Josephus to Origen, denying any role to Hermippus, is unpersuasive.

93 Note also the comment of Josephus that Essenes borrowed their way of life from Pythagoras! Jos. *A. J.* 15.371.

94 Philo, *Prob.* 72–75.

95 The presumed parallels were still very much alive among Greek thinkers in the time of Strabo; see 16.1.39.

96 Eus. *PE* 9.7.1.

97 Eus. *PE* 9.6.9: τί γάρ ἐστι Πλάτων ἢ Μωσῆς ἀττικίζων. Other references in Stern, *Greek and Latin Authors*, 2:210.

7. The Purported Jewish-Spartan Affiliation

Spartans and Jews might seem, on the face of it, to be the most unlikely partners. Yet a remarkable tale affirms not only political and diplomatic association but a blood tie: both peoples claimed Abraham as an ancestor. Putative kinship associations among peoples and nations who derived from a common progenitor, usually a god, hero, or renowned figure of legend, constituted a staple item in Hellenic folklore. This particular tall tale, however, does not occur in epic, drama, or a work of romantic fiction but appeals to ostensible documents and diplomatic correspondence.

The story piques the imagination and lends itself to creative speculation. A voluminous scholarly literature attests to it. Clever conjectures have proposed occasions that called forth this connection and circumstances that rendered it advantageous. The quest, however, has almost invariably concentrated on presumed political motivation, specific conditions, and objectives that prompted Spartans or Jews to initiate the association—or forgers to invent it.

A different approach may be more productive. The reputed kinship has broader cultural ramifications. The advent of Macedonian imperialism in the Near East had profound consequences for the Jews. Collapse of Persian authority restructured power relationships and reshaped the political geography of the region. Alexander the Great had no time to spare for Judaea, but the struggles of the Diadochoi and their outcome left enduring marks. Palestine in general fell under the aegis of the Ptolemies for over a century after the death of Alexander and, when power shifted at the end of the third century B.C.E., was swept under the suzerainty of the Seleucids for another half century. Greek *poleis* began to spring up on the Levantine coast and at certain inland sites. The experience of Palestinian Jews encompassed a growing familiarity with Greek practices, institutions, and traditions.[1] And, equally important, the Jews of the Diaspora located themselves in increasing numbers in Hellenistic cities like Alexandria, Antioch, and the communities of Asia Minor. Isolation from the expanding culture of the Mediterranean was hardly possible and, for many, not desirable. Jewish intellec-

---

1 How profound was the penetration of Hellenism into Palestine is a matter of considerable debate and cannot be pursued here. The strongest case for Hellenic influence among the Jews of Palestine in the pre-Maccabean period was made by M. Hengel's learned but controversial *Judaism and Hellenism: Studies in Their Encounter in Palestine during the Early Hellenistic Period* (Philadelphia, 1974). But see the criticisms by L. Feldman, "Hengel's *Judaism and Hellenism* in Retrospect," *JBL 96* (1977): 371–82, and F. Millar, "The Background to the Maccabean Revolution: Reflections on Martin Hengel's 'Judaism and Hellenism,'" *Journal of Jewish Studies* 22 (1978): 1–21.

tuals faced the challenge of coming to terms with that expanding culture, a challenge that provoked them to look beyond mere resistance or assimilation. The Jews undertook to redefine and even to enhance their own identity in the new circumstances of a Hellenic world. That provides the appropriate cultural setting for the creation of the Jewish-Spartan kinship.

The supposed relationship will repay close inspection. Three letters represent the principal testimony, recorded in 1 Maccabees and reproduced in a variant form by Josephus. The exchange began with a missive from King Areus of Sparta to the Judaean High Priest Onias. The individuals are historical and the ostensible time of the communication can be approximated. Only two Spartan kings carried the name Areus, the second of whom died as a small boy. Hence the presumed author of the letter must be Areus I whose regnal years fell between 309 and 265 B.C.E. and whose active role occupied the last decade and a half of that period.[2] The alleged recipient is either Onias I, who became High Priest in the late fourth century, or Onias II, who held the office in the reign of Ptolemy III Euergetes (246–221). The king's letter, therefore, if authentic, came in the early third century.[3] Areus offered friendly greeting, announcing that he had discovered the kinship of the two peoples in a written text: Jews and Spartans are brothers, both from the stock of Abraham. He hopes for a reply with news of the Jews' current circumstances and affirms that their goods and property are joint possessions.[4]

The affiliation was reaffirmed more than a century later when Jonathan, successor to Judas Maccabaeus as leader of the Jews, sent an embassy to Sparta ca. 144, with the consent of the Jewish Council of Elders. His message addressed the Lakedaimonians as ἀδελφοί, acknowledged Areus's letter of long ago, and enclosed a copy. Jonathan adds reference to friendship and alliance between

---

2 On Areus, see G. Marasco, *Sparta agli inizi dell'età ellenistica: Il regno di Areo I* (Florence, 1980).

3 For Onias I, see Jos. *A. J.* 11.347; for Onias *II*, Jos. *A. J.* 12.157–167. Given the dates, most commentators opt for Onias I as the probable correspondent. But Areus's chief exploits came in the later years of his reign; see below. And Onias II was evidently of advanced age in the reign of Ptolemy III: Joseph. *AJ* 12.158–163. Hence the story may well allude to the later Onias. See the discussions of V. Tcherikover, *Hellenistic Civilization and the Jews* (New York, 1959), 128–29; J. A. Goldstein, "The Tales of the Tobiads," in J. Neusner, *Christianity, Judaism, and Other Greco-Roman Cults: Studies for Morton Smith at Sixty* III (Leiden, 1975), 94–95; J. A. Goldstein, *I Maccabees* (New York, 1976), 455–56. Jos. *A. J.* 12.225–27, wrongly considers the recipient to be Onias III. The latter, who was High Priest in the early second century, could hardly have received a letter from Areus.

4 1 Macc. 12.20–23; Joseph. *AJ* 12.225–27. Josephus's close paraphrase makes it nearly certain that he used 1 Maccabees. But he evidently had additional information as well; see 12.227.

the nations, now overdue for renewal since so many years had passed without direct communication. But he observes that his countrymen over the years regularly mentioned Spartans in their prayers and sacrifices and rejoiced at their fame. Further, the letter reports Jewish successes against all the enemies in their vicinity, successes attained without the assistance of allies. They supplied the occasion for envoys sent with this announcement to Rome and to Sparta, in the latter place to renew the bonds of brotherhood. The letter concludes with a polite request for a reply.[5]

The Lakedaimonian reply arrived only after Jonathan's death, addressed in our text to his successor, Simon, perhaps in the year 142. Spartan envoys conveyed their government's desire to renew the friendship and alliance. The letter they brought greeted the Jews as brothers, reporting the warm welcome with which Jewish delegates had been received in Sparta and the decision to inscribe their speeches for preservation in the Spartan archives.[6]

One other piece of evidence alludes to the kinship association. In 168 B.C., according to 2 Maccabees, Jason, the former Jewish High Priest, failed in his violent efforts to reclaim the office and was driven out of Judaea. Hunted down by his enemies, the fugitive sought refuge among the Nabataean Arabs, then in Egypt, and finally headed for Sparta, hoping to find safety in view of their συγγένεια, but he perished instead.[7]

So much for the testimony. To what extent does it warrant confidence? The extraordinary diplomatic exchange has engendered a lengthy and still lengthening list of scholarly publications. The authenticity of the letters has often been impugned in whole or in part; questions have been raised about one, two, or all three of the missives. But a growing number of commentators now incline to accept the correspondence as genuine.[8] Ingenuity of a high order has been expended in defense of Areus's letter. Perhaps the Spartan king took note of a Jewish community in his midst and sought to establish relations with Judaea, now a

---

5 1 Macc. 12.6–18. On use of the term ἀδελφοί rather than συγγενεῖς, perhaps an inaccurate rendering of the Hebrew original, see O. Curty, "A propos de la parenté entre juifs et spartiates," *Historia* 41 (1992): 246–48. The letter of Areus in this narrative is supplied by Jonathan's envoys to remind Sparta that the kinship had been initially acknowledged by one of their monarchs. Jos., *A. J.* 12.225–27, records the letter independently of Jonathan's mission, but adverts to it again in the latter context: Jos. *A. J.* 13.164–70.

6 1 Macc. 14.16–23; cf. Joseph. *AJ* 13.170.

7 2 Macc. 5.6–10.

8 Bibliographical summaries can be found in B. Cardauns, "Juden und Spartaner," *Hermes* 95 (1967): 317–18 n. 1; R. Katzoff, "Jonathan and Late Sparta," *AJPh* 106 (1985): 485 n. 1; Cl. Orrieux, "La 'parenté' entre juifs et spartiates," in R. Lonis, *L'Etranger dans le monde grec: Actes du colloque organisé par l'Institut d'Études Anciennes* (Nancy, 1987), 187 n. 7.

Ptolemaic dependency, to strengthen ties with the rulers of Egypt.[9] A link with the Jews, reinforcing the Ptolemaic connection, might bolster Spartan resistance to encroachment of the Peloponnese by the Antigonids of Macedon.[10] Recruitment of Jewish mercenaries could even help fill up the depleted ranks of the Spartiatai![11] Other motives, too, have been hypothesized. The Spartan overture, so one interpreter proposes, represents an offer to establish commercial relations in joint business activities.[12] The Spartans may have actually read the Scriptures (before composition of the Septuagint!), learned of Abraham, and embraced the idea of kinship.[13] And, it has been suggested, they employed scribes literate in Aramaic to communicate their zeal for the Jewish connection.[14]

The ingenuity is misplaced. That Areus in the early third century would have sought either military or moral support from a tiny, distant, and impotent dependency of the Ptolemaic empire surely strains imagination. The Spartans did indeed enjoy an alliance with Ptolemy II Philadelphos, concluded at some time prior to the Chremonidean War in the 260's.[15] That, if anything, makes it even less likely that they would engage in independent relations with a principality under Ptolemaic authority. As for Macedonian aggression, Sparta could hardly hope to buttress resistance by courting a Jewish connection. The Peloponnese was no more than a sidelight for Antigonid ambitions anyway.[16] The notion that Areus contracted with Jews to supply soldiers for the Lakedaimonian forces or to enter into cooperative business ventures does not warrant refutation. Even if the king had such unattested objectives, he did not need to invent a mythology to attain them. Where indeed would the Spartans have ever encountered legends of the patriarchal age in Israel? That Areus's contemporaries had

---

9 M. S. Ginsburg, "Sparta and Judaea," *CP* 29 (1934): 117–22; V. Ehrenberg, "Sparta," *RE* IIIA.2 (1929): 1425, 1445; H. Michell, *Sparta* (Cambridge, 1952), 92; P. Oliva, *Sparta and Her Social Problems* (Amsterdam, 1971), 207. That the Egyptian connection might account for Areus's interest in the Jews is allowed as a possibility by P. Cartledge and A. Spawforth, *Hellenistic and Roman Sparta* (London, 1989), 36–37.
10 S. Schüller, "Some Problems Connected with the Supposed Common Ancestry of Jews and Spartans and Their Relations during the Last Three Centuries B.C.," *JSemStud* 1 (1956): 259.
11 Goldstein, *I Maccabees* (above, n. 3), 457; Orrieux, "La 'parente'" (above, n. 8), 174.
12 W. Wirgin, "Judah Maccabee's Embassy to Rome and the Jewish-Roman Treaty," *PalEQ* 101 (1969): 15–17.
13 Wirgin, "Judah Maccabee's Embassy" (above, n. 12), 15.
14 Goldstein, *I Maccabees* (above, n. 3), 456–57. Josephus's enigmatic remark, *AJ* 12.227, about the Spartan missive conveyed in "square writings" hardly proves that it was composed in Aramaic. What reason would Josephus or an archivist have for expressing the fact in such circuitous language?
15 The alliance is attested by the Chremonidean decree; *Syll.*³ 434/5.
16 See Cartledge and Spawforth, *Hellenistic and Roman Sparta* (above, n. 9), 29–31.

access to a Greek translation of the Scriptures (or a part thereof) prior to the commissioning of the Septuagint is a fanciful idea altogether devoid of testimony or plausibility.[17] Perhaps, then, Spartan intellectuals, including King Areus himself, had learned of Abraham through reading the work of Hekataios of Abdera?[18] If so, it must have been in some portion of Hekataios that subsequently vanished. The extant fragments make no mention of Abraham.[19] Belief in genuineness requires credulity.

Jonathan's letter has a comparably shaky claim on historicity. What reason would Jews have to enter into diplomatic negotiations with Sparta in the midsecond century B.C.E.? Some scholars have manufactured motives. A connection with Sparta, it is claimed, would put the Jews in touch with the one Peloponnesian state that retained some independence.[20] Or Sparta might serve as an avenue to a greater power. An approach to the Lakedaimonians in the late 140's can be seen as a means to curry favor with Rome. The western power had smashed Achaea in 146, leaving political devastation in its wake. But Sparta had been spared, indeed protected by Rome, its position strengthened by Rome's forceful intervention in the Peloponnesos. Hence assertion of an ancestral bond with Sparta offered the Jews an indirect route to Rome.[21]

The speculation carries little conviction. That Jews courted the patronage of Rome by linking themselves to a Roman ally simply will not do. The Romans had their own reasons for assaulting the Achaean League in 146, reasons that did not stem from closeness to Sparta. Nor did the Lakedaimonians receive any conspicuous favors in the aftermath of the Achaean War.[22] If Jonathan sought out Sparta as an intermediary with Rome, it is most peculiar that the Jewish embassy, ac-

---

17 Reference by Aristoboulos to translations earlier than the Septuagint is plainly invented to account for his assertion that Plato and even Pythagoras imitated the legal codes of the Hebrews: Eus., *PE* 13.12.1. The *Letter of Aristeas*, 30, notes the existence of early Hebrew scrolls in the Alexandrian library—by no means a clear allusion to Greek translations. No one can take seriously its tale of divine intervention to prevent Theopompos from quoting Greek passages in the Scriptures: *Letter of Aristeas*, 312–15.
18 So Goldstein, *I Maccabees* (above, n. 3), 450, 458–59.
19 The alleged work of Hekataios on Abraham (Joseph. *AJ* 1.159; Clem. Al. *Strom.* 5.113; Eus. *PE* 13.13.40) is spurious; cf. M. Stern, *Greek and Latin Authors on Jews and Judaism* I (Jerusalem, 1976), 22.
20 Schüller, "Some Problems" (above, n. 10), 266; A. Momigliano, *Prime linee di storia della tradizione maccabaica*[2] (Amsterdam, 1968) 143–44.
21 Goldstein, *I Maccabees* (above, n. 3), 448; L. Feldman, *Jew and Gentile in the Ancient World* (Princeton, 1993), 143.
22 E. S. Gruen, *The Hellenistic World and the Coming of Rome* (Berkeley and Los Angeles, 1984), 520–27.

cording to 1 Maccabees, went to Rome first and only stopped in at Sparta on the way home.[23] In fact, the Jews already had a treaty of alliance with Rome, one that had been in force since 161 and which Jonathan's envoys now took the occasion to renew. They plainly had no need of Spartans as intermediaries.[24] Little practical advantage would accrue from connection with a relatively weak Hellenic state that might embroil the Jews in distant affairs. Certainly they could expect no Spartan assistance in the Near East! Efforts to find political motives underlying the putative συγγένεια seem doomed to failure.[25]

No need to dwell on the ostensible third letter, the purported response of Sparta to Jonathan's overtures. Its historicity is bound up with the embassy that called it forth. And the text of 1 Maccabees appears to muddle the missions. The Spartan message refers to Jonathan's delegates but makes response to Simon.[26] The confusion gives little reason for confidence. No subsequent sign of the partnership surfaces in the testimony. In fact, after Simon sent his own embassy to Rome to confirm his alliance with that state, the Romans dispatched messages to a wide array of cities and kings requesting them to refrain from any hostilities toward the Jews—among them, the Spartans. The passage obviously evinces no knowledge of any special relationship between Lakedaimonians and Jews.[27]

Jason's supposed flight or attempted flight to Sparta adds little weight to the case. The former High Priest allegedly expected sanctuary because of συγγένεια

---

23 The sequence is clear in 1 Macc. 12.1 – 5, and Joseph. *AJ* 13.163 – 64.

24 On the treaty of 161, see 1 Macc. 8; Joseph *AJ*, 12.414 – 19; cf. *BJ* 1.38. To be sure, not all scholars accept the treaty as genuine, but no good reasons, exist for falsification or invention. The bibliography on the subject is enormous. See summaries of the literature in E. Schürer, *The History of the Jewish People in the Age of Jesus Christ (175 B.C. – A.D. 135)* I, rev. ed. by G. Vermes and F. Millar (Edinburgh, 1973), 171 – 72 n. 33; J.-D. Gauger, *Beiträge zur jüdischen Apologetik* (Cologne and Bonn, 1977), 156 – 61. A recent case for authenticity is given in Gruen, *Hellenistic World* (above. n. 22), 42 – 46, with additional bibliography. On the renewal, see 1 Macc. 12.1 – 4, 12.16; Joseph. *AJ* 13.163 – 65, 13.169.

25 At a different level of interpretation, Katzoff suggests that Jonathan saw in Sparta a kindred spirit, a society honored by other Greeks but one whose institutions stood outside the Hellenic mainstream: "Jonathan" (above, n. 8), 488 – 89. The texts, however, point in a quite different direction. Sparta serves to exemplify the best that Greeks had to offer, not a deviant from Hellenism. See below.

26 1 Macc. 14.16 – 23. Goldstein's suggestion, *I Maccabees* (above, n. 3), 492, that a private Jewish traveler reported the, news of Jonathan's death while the latter's envoys were still in Sparta is quite implausible,

27 1 Macc. 14.24, 15.15 – 24. The point is noted by Cardauns, "Juden und Spartaner" (above, n. 8), 321.

between the peoples.[28] But the report of Jason's movements, even if true, has him flee from city to city before finally hoping for haven in Sparta—and then in vain.[29] The ascription of motive can hardly count as independent testimony. It means only that the tale of the συγγένεια was known to the author of 2 Maccabees or to Jason of Cyrene whose work he abridged.

The quest for authenticity runs into a blind alley. It has, in any case, commanded excessive scholarly energies. The correspondence is best reckoned as an invention. And inventions often have more to reveal than genuine documents. They can speak to deeper cultural objectives.

The invention in this case is clearly a Jewish one. The idea of joint descent from Abraham can have no other meaning. The language of Areus's letter should suffice to make the point. As conveyed in 1 Maccabees, it includes the striking phrase, with Biblical overtones, "your cattle and goods are ours, and ours are yours."[30] No Spartan would have expressed himself in that manner. More telling still is the tone of Jonathan's missive, which has not received adequate emphasis in modern scholarship. Far from petitioning for Spartan aid, the letter underscores Jewish primacy. Jonathan asserts that the Jews have at every opportunity remembered Sparta in their sacrifices and their prayers during festivals and other suitable occasions.[31] The Jews, in short, are the benefactors, not the beneficiaries.

This prompts a further query. If Jews conceived the Hellenic connection, why fasten on the Spartans in particular? Spartans would hardly seem the most logical Greeks with whom to claim a kinship that had religious and cultural reverberations. The problem has inspired considerable conjecture. Some discern in Hekataios of Abdera's narrative of migrations from Egypt to Judaea and Greece the roots of the affiliation. Hekataios records the banishment of aliens from Egypt, some of whom, led by Danaos and Kadmos, reached Hellenic shores; the majority, however, settled in Judaea, taken there by Moses.[32] The tale brings to mind the legend of the Danaids, settlers in the Peloponnesos and progenitors

---

28 2 Macc. 5.9.
29 2 Macc. 5.7 – 9.
30 1 Macc. 12.23: τὰ κτήνη ὑμῶν καὶ ἡ ὕπαρξις ὑμῶν ἡμῖν ἐστι, καὶ τὰ ἡμῶν ὑμῖν ἐστιν. Cf. 1 Kings 22.4; 2 Kings 3.7. Josephus modifies the text to supply a more Hellenic flavor; *AJ* 12.227: τά τε ὑμέτερα ἴδια νομιοῦμεν καὶ τὰ αὐτῶν κοινὰ πρὸς ὑμᾶς ἕξομεν.
31 1 Macc. 12.11: ἡμεῖς οὖν ἐν παντὶ καιρῷ ἀδιαλείπτως ἔν τε ταῖς ἑορταῖς καὶ ταῖς λοιπαῖς καθηκούσαις ἡμέραις μιμνησκόμεθα ὑμῶν, ἐφ' ὧν προσφέρομεν θυσιῶν, καὶ ἐν ταῖς προσευχαῖς; Joseph. *AJ* 13.168.
32 *FGH* IIIA, 264 Fr. 6 = Diod. 40.3.2. Cf. Ginsburg, "Sparta and Judaea" (above, n. 9), 120 – 21; Schüller, "Some Problems" (above, n. 10), 262 – 63; Hengel, *Judaism and Hellenism* (above, n. 1), II: 50 – 51 n. 124; L. J. Piper, *Spartan Twilight* (New Rochelle, 1986), 148 – 49.

of the Spartan royal dynasties.[33] But this is still quite some distance from suggesting a link between Spartans and Jews. Readers of Hekataios would not readily extract that association from his text. The hypothesis has had further extension. In the formulation of the obscure early Imperial writer Claudius Iolaus, one of the "Spartoi" sown by Kadmos as ancestors of the Thebans was a certain "Oudaios" from whose name derives the appellation Judaea.[34] To reckon this tradition as lurking behind the Spartan-Jewish affiliation, however, is, on the most generous assessment, far-fetched. The tale of Kadmos and the "Spartoi" concerns the origins of Thebes, not Sparta. And the conjecture of Claudius Iolaus, based on nothing more than a similarity of sound and preserved only in Stephanos of Byzantium, carries little weight.[35] It would be reaching indeed to consider such remote associations as prompting the fabricated correspondence in 1 Maccabees.[36]

Strained surmises can be left aside. Certain features of the Spartan character —or at least the Spartan image—would have appealed to Hellenistic Jews. For those knowledgeable about Spartan traditions and public posture, parallels might well have suggested themselves. Hekataios of Abdera had already left an account of Moses that set him in the mold of a recognizable Hellenic lawgiver. Moses, in Hekataios's conception, not only ordered civic and religious institutions for his people but also provided for physical training and martial prowess. His legislation aimed at inculcating the military arts through a compulsory program for Jewish youth that prepared them for manly virtue, endurance, and tolerance of every form of suffering.[37] The model of the Spartan ἀγωγή appears to lurk in the background here. And Hekataios's further description puts the matter beyond doubt. He has Moses follow up his military victories and territorial ac-

---

33 The Egyptian-Spartan connection is known to Herodotus: 2.91, 6.53.2; cf. 2.80, 6.55.

34 *FGH* IIIC, 788 Fr. 4 = Stern, *Greek and Latin Authors* (above, n. 19), I, no. 249.

35 The hypothesis has marginal support from the fact that a cult of Kadmos existed at Sparta: Paus. 3.15.8. But it requires quite a leap from that to a kinship connection between Spartans and Jews.

36 Still more indirect is the association inferred from Kleodemos Malchos's story of a marriage alliance between Herakles and the house of Abraham: Joseph. *AJ* 1.239–41; Eus. *PE* 9.20.2–4. The legend has been cited in this connection on the grounds that Herakles was a putative ancestor of Sparta; so, e.g., Momigliano, *Prime linee* (above, n. 20), 144–45; Goldstein, *I Maccabees* (above, n. 3), 458; Hengel, *Judaism and Hellenism* (above, n. 1), II: 50–51 n. 124; Feldman, *Jew and Gentile* (above, n. 21), 143. But the tale itself has nothing to do with Sparta and could hardly justify the συγγένεια of Lakedaimonians and Jews.

37 *FGH* IIIA, 264 Fr. 6 = Diod. 40.3.6: ἐποιήσατο δ' ὁ νομοθέτης τῶν τε πολεμικῶν ἔργων πολλὴν πρόνοιαν καὶ τοὺς νέους ἠνάγκαζεν ἀσκεῖν ἀνδρείαν τε καὶ καρτερίαν καὶ τὸ σύνολον ὑπομονὴν πάσης κακοπαθείας.

quisitions with an apportioning of land in equal lots and a requirement that those lots be inalienable. Such legislation would prevent the greedy from acquiring the land, squeezing the poor, and causing a decline in manpower.[38] The parallel, both in measures and in motives, to Spartan traditions associated with the legendary lawgiver Lykourgos seems quite incontestable. In the Spartans' conception of their system's origin, Lykourgos too allocated land to fellow citizens in equal κλῆροι to break down the vast discrepancies in wealth and power that plagued Spartan society. And he firmly discouraged the alienation of land in order to preserve that equality.[39]

The analogy becomes more explicit in Josephus. He names Lykourgos himself as exemplary in Greek eyes, and the Spartan system as a source of admiration among Hellenes, for its citizens adhered for the longest time to the precepts of their lawgiver. The *politeia* of Lykourgos thereby became the benchmark whereby to judge the virtues and success of all commonwealths. The Jews, however, in Josephus's formulation, had exceeded Spartan achievements. Their faithfulness to ancestral laws remained unshaken long after the Lakedaimonian system collapsed. And the hardships endured by the Jews, the tests put to their courage, far outstrip the Hellenic model, obedience to the law the clearest demonstration of Jewish nobility of spirit.[40]

The appeal of a Spartan affiliation is intelligible. The Jews could associate themselves with a society reckoned as a yardstick for Hellenic excellence and achievement. But why select Areus as the Spartan who first authenticated the kinship? He was far from the most celebrated of Lakedaimonian leaders, hardly an obvious choice to affirm a fictitious bond between the peoples. That troublesome fact has served to strengthen the hand of those who argue for the genuineness of an exchange between Spartans and Jews in the third century: no forger would have dug up Areus for the purpose.[41]

The conclusion is hasty and unwarranted. Areus's repute stood much higher in the Hellenistic era than it does today. The absence of a biography by Plutarch constitutes an unjust liability. Few contemporary observers on the international scene would, for instance, have ranked the "reformer" king Agis IV on a level

---

38 *FGH* IIIA, 264 Fr. 6 = Diod. 40.3.7: καὶ πολλὴν κατακτησάμενος χώραν κατεκληρούχησε, τοῖς μὲν ἰδιώταις ἴσους ποιήσας κλήρους... οὐκ ἐξῆν δὲ τοῖς ἰδιώταις τοὺς ἰδίους κλήρους πωλεῖν, ὅπως μὴ τινες διὰ πλεονεξίαν ἀγοράζοντες τοὺς κλήρους ἐκθλίβωσι τοὺς ἀπορωτέρους καὶ κατασκευάζωσιν ὀλιγανδρίαν.

39 Plut. *Lyc.* 8; *Agis*, 5.1; Plb. 645.3, 6.48.2 – 3; Arist., *Pol.* 2.6.10; Herakleides Lembos 373.12 Dilts.

40 Jos. *C. Ap.*, 2.225 – 35.

41 Cf. Goldstein, *I Maccabees* (above, n. 3), 456.

with Areus. The latter had a dramatic career, pushing himself and his state into major events of Hellenistic politics and diplomacy. A coalition of Greek states, so we are told, chose Areus as leader in an assault on the Aitolian League, an indirect thrust against the power of Macedon in Hellas in 280. Although the venture ended in failure, it attests to the stature and reputation of Areus.[42] He expanded his connections in subsequent years on the island of Crete, not only a source of mercenaries but its cities soon linked in alliance with Sparta.[43] Greater notoriety came from the incursions of Pyrrhos into the Peloponnesos in the late 270s. The Epirote invasion of Lakonia occurred during Areus's absence in Crete. A valiant Spartan resistance thwarted Pyrrhos, Macedonian mercenaries entered the fray, and then Areus returned with a force from Crete. Pyrrhos withdrew and turned his attention to Argos.[44] Areus now took a prominent part in the contest, first harassing Pyrrhos's route, then commanding Spartan and Cretan troops against him in battle, leading to the death of the redoubtable Epirote prince.[45] Areus's renown rapidly spread. Indeed, he promoted it actively through the minting of Sparta's first silver coinage, tetradrachms inscribed with his own name and displaying an image modeled on the types of Alexander the Great. Areus plainly projected himself as in the line of the Diadochoi, a major figure on the international stage.[46]

The resurgence of Spartan power can be read without ambiguity in the famed Chremonidean Decree from Athens in 268. The measure sets forth a string of Spartan allies, the fruit of Areus's policy: Elis, Achaea, Tegeia, Mantineia, Orchomenos, Phigaleia, and Kaphuai. Sparta had reaffirmed ascendancy in the Peloponnesos. Its network, in fact, went beyond Greece proper. The decree records Sparta's formal links with the Cretans and, as a capstone, the alliance with Ptolemy II of Egypt.[47] Areus's prominence gains explicit acknowledgment in the document: the king is singled out as an individual in addition to the Lakedaimonians as a whole five different times.[48] There seems little doubt that Areus was the pivotal figure in assembling the grand anti-Macedonian coalition reflect-

---

42 Just. 24.1.1 – 7; cf. Plb. 2.41.11 – 12; Marasco, *Il regno di Areo I* (above, n. 2), 63 – 73.
43 Cf. *Syll.*[3] 434/5, lines 25 – 26, 39 – 41; see Marasco, *Il regno di Areo I* (above, n. 2), 84 – 90.
44 Plut. *Pyrrh.* 26.7 – 30.1.
45 Plut. *Pyrrh.* 30.2 – 34.2; Marasco, *Il regno di Areo I* (above, n. 2), 100 – 14.
46 On the coins, see A. R. Bellinger, *Essays on the Coinage of Alexander the Great* (New York, 1963), 89 – 90; S. Grunauer-von Hoerschelmann, *Die Munzprägung der Lakedaimonier* (Berlin, 1978), 1 – 4, 112 – 13, Tafel 1. Cf. Marasco, *Il regno di Areo I* (above, n. 2), 124 – 27; Cartledge and Spawforth, *Hellenistic and Roman Sparta* (above, n. 9), 34 – 35.
47 *Syll.*[3] 434 – 35, lines 21 – 26, 35 – 41.
48 *Syll.*[3] 434 – 35, lines 26, 29, 40, 50, 55. See, e. g., lines 25 – 26: ὅσοι εἰσὶν ἐν τεῖ συμμ[αχίαι τ]εῖ Λακεδαιμονίων καὶ Ἀρέως καὶ τῶν ἄλλων συμμάχω[ν].

ed in the decree of Chremonides.[49] Statues of him were dedicated by Orchomenos, by the Eleians and others at Olympia, by Polyrrhenia in Crete, and, most strikingly, by Ptolemy Philadelphos himself, also at Olympia.[50] Areus had a high profile in the world of Hellenistic politics. It should not, therefore, cause surprise that attestation of the genealogical tie between Spartans and Jews was ascribed to Areus, a figure who would lend stature to the connection.[51] It certainly does not vouch for its authenticity.

Jewish initiative and Jewish inventiveness created this fictive συγγένεια. Scrutiny of the text in 1 Maccabees puts the matter beyond question. Jonathan's purported letter asks nothing of the Spartans, asserting instead the special position of the Jews, the senior partner in the association. After alluding to Areus's missive that attested the kinship and to the warm reception of Sparta's envoy by Onias, who hailed the message of friendship and alliance, Jonathan sets it all in perspective. The Jews, so his letter asserts, have no need of these bonds for they have in their hands the holy books as encouragement.[52] They seek to renew the fraternity and friendship only in order not to have the long absence of contact weaken the relationship.[53] The tone borders on patronizing, Jonathan insists that Jewish success owes nothing to alliance or partnership with other states. His people fended off attacks from neighboring kings and hostile powers without requesting the aid of Spartans or other allies. The assistance of heaven suffices to rescue the Jews from their enemies and to lay those enemies low.[54] Jonathan de-

---

49 Cf. H. Heinen, *Untersuchungen zur hellenistischen Geschichte des 3. Jahrhunderts v. Chr. Zur Geschichte der Zeit des Ptolemaios Keraunos und zum chremonideischen Krieg* (Wiesbaden, 1972), 126–32; Marasco, *Il regno di Areo I* (above, n. 2), 131–35.

50 Orchomenos: L. Moretti, *Iscrizioni storiche ellenistiche* I (Florence 1967), no. 54 (also noting Areus's connection with Ptolemy); statuary at Olympia: Paus. 6.12.5, 6.15.9; Polyrrhenia: *IC* II, xxiii, 12; Ptolemy: *Syll.*³ 433.

51 The reputation of Areus is recognized by Momigliano, *Prime linee* (above, n. 20), 146, and Marasco, *Il regno di Areo I* (above n. 2), 161–65.

52 I Macc. 12.8–9: καὶ ἡμεῖς οὖν ἀπροσδεεῖς τούτων ὄντες παράκλησιν ἔχοντες τὰ βιβλία τὰ ἅγια τὰ ἐν ταῖς χερσὶν ἡμῶν. Josephus's paraphrase alters the meaning quite substantially. In his version Jonathan declares that the Jews did not need Spartan proof of the kinship for which they could trust in their own sacred writings; *AJ* 13.167: περὶ τῆς ὑπαρχούσης ἡμῖν πρὸς ὑμᾶς συγγενείας... οὐ δεόμενοι τῆς τοιαύτης ἀποδείξεως διὰ τὸ ἐκ τῶν ἱερῶν ἡμῶν πεπιστεῦσθαι γραμμάτων. This makes for a more polite reply, perhaps a deliberate effort on Josephus's part to supply suitable diplomatic language. But it undercuts the real thrust of the remarks in 1 Maccabees.

53 1 Macc. 12.10; cf. Joseph. *AJ* 13.168.

54 I Macc. 12.13–15: οὐκ ἠβουλόμεθα οὖν παρενοχλεῖν ὑμῖν καὶ τοῖς λοιποῖς συμμάχοις καὶ φίλοις ἡμῶν ἐν τοῖς πολέμοις τούτοις; ἔχομεν γὰρ τὴν ἐξ οὐρανοῦ βοήθειαν βοηθοῦσαν ἡμῖν καὶ ἐρρύσθημεν ἀπὸ τῶν ἐχθρῶν ἡμῶν, καὶ ἐταπεινώθησαν οἱ ἐχθροὶ ἡμῶν; Joseph. *AJ* 13.169.

livers a clear message of Jewish ascendancy in this relationship. The Spartans, in their reply that reached Jerusalem after the death of Jonathan, acknowledged the ambassadorial speeches that declared Jewish fame and prestige and noted that copies of them had been deposited in their own public records.[55]

The Judeocentric quality of all this is unmistakable. The fact that Abraham, the Hebrew patriarch, appears as ultimate ancestor of both Spartans and Jews makes the point without ambiguity. In this regard it parallels the legend recounted by a certain Kleodemos Malchos that the sons of Abraham joined with Herakles in his war on the Libyan giant Antaios and that the Greek hero married the daughter of one of those sons who became the eponymous forebear of Africa.[56]

The fiction of Spartan-Jewish affiliation, like that which brings Herakles into the family of Abraham, puts the prestige of the Jews on display. When will such a tale have gained currency? Any attempt to pinpoint its emergence with precision brings frustration. Indeed, efforts along these lines have plagued scholarship by prompting a fruitless search for specific historical occasions that provoked the invention. That approach is best abandoned. The most that can be said with confidence is that the kinship story surfaced prior to the composition of 1 Maccabees, probably at the end of the second century B.C.E.[57] It was known also to Jason of

---

55 1 Macc. 14.20–23: οἱ πρεσβευταὶ οἱ ἀποσταλέντες πρὸς τὸν δῆμον ἡμῶν ἀπήγγειλαν ἡμῖν περὶ τῆς δόξης ὑμῶν καὶ τιμῆς. The preceding lines, 1 Macc. 14.16–19, appear to refer to a Roman rather than a Spartan response to the Jews; cf. F.-M. Abel, *Les livres des Maccabées* (Paris, 1949), 252–53. The efforts of Goldstein, *I Maccabees* (above, n. 3), 494, to excise references to Rome and to a treaty with Judas as interpolations are tempting but beyond proof.
56 Joseph. *AJ* 1.239–41; Eus. *PE* 9.20.2–4.
57 The date of composition has attained at least a broad consensus. The laudatory remarks on Rome rule out a time of writing after Pompey's conquest of Jerusalem in 63 B.C.: 1 Macc. 8.1–16; cf. 14.40, 15.15–24. At 1 Macc. 13.30, the author refers to a mausoleum Constructed at the time of Simon ca. 142 as still standing in his own day—thus implying the perspective of at least a generation later. And, more telling, the work closes with a citation of the "book of days" of John Hyrkanos's high priesthood, a Biblical phrase that indicates a date after Hyrkanos's death in 104: 1 Macc. 16.23–24; cf. 1 Kings 14.29, 16.27; 2 Kings 20.20. It is, of course, possible to argue that the two passages were later additions or interpolations, but that constitutes special pleading. For discussions, see Abel, *Les livres des Maccabées* (above, n. 55), xxviii—ix; J. C. Dancy, *I Maccabees: A Commentary* (Oxford, 1954), 8–9; Goldstein, *I Maccabees* (above, n. 3), 62–63; H. W. Attridge, in *Jewish Writings of the Second Temple Period*, ed. M. Stone (Assen and Philadelphia, 1984), 171; Schürer, *The History of the Jewish People in the Age of Jesus Christ* III.1, rev. ed. by G. Vermes, F. Millar, and M. Goodman (Edinburgh, 1986), 181; J. Sievers, *The Hasmoneans and Their Supporters* (Atlanta, 1990), 3. The recent attempt by B. Bar-Kochva, *Judas Maccabaeus* (Cambridge, 1989), 151–70, to put the book early in Hyrkanos's reign on grounds of the vividness of the battle narratives is unconvincing. Even if such vividness did imply eyewitness testimony, Bar-Kochva too hastily discounts the possibility that the author of 1 Maccabees made use of an early account.

Cyrene or his epitomator, the author of 2 Maccabees, who included the notice that Jason the Oniad fled to Sparta because of the affiliation. The complexities and uncertainties in attempting to date this work, however, are so formidable that no hypothesis is likely to win much assent. Relationship between 1 and 2 Maccabees remains highly controversial, not to mention disputes over possible common sources, different levels of composition, and the problems involved in detecting what material derives from Jason of Cyrene and what from his abridger.[58] A conservative guess would place Jason some time in the later second century B.C.E. and the abridgment of his history no later than the early first century B.C.E.[59] The tale of a Spartan-Jewish kinship, therefore, circulated among Jewish intellectuals around the turn of the second century.

What objectives did those who created or disseminated the legend have in view? Inquirers, as already noted, have generally applied too narrow a focus to the question. Proposed answers tend to concentrate on political advantage and special circumstances—like an indirect Spartan overture to the Ptolemies or an indirect Jewish overture to Rome—that amount to reductionism. A recent study offers a mishmash of motives, each of similarly circumscribed scope. Perhaps the story represents Hasmonean propaganda to justify control of the high priesthood by having a neutral state like Sparta acknowledge their legitimacy? Or anti-Oniad polemic by the supporters of Jonathan and Simon? Or a ruse by the renegade Jason to pave the way for his exile in Sparta? Or a product of the Hellenizing party in Jerusalem prior to the Maccabean revolt.[60] One will not make much headway in this fashion.

---

58 It is certainly unwarranted to take the notice of Jason the Oniad's flight as giving a *terminus ante quem* of 168 for the kinship tale, as do, e. g., Hengel, *Judaism and Hellenism* (above, n. 1), 1: 72, and A. Momigliano, *Alien Wisdom* (Cambridge, 1975), 113 – 14.

59 The assertion at 2 Macc. 15.37 that Jerusalem was still in the hands of the Hebrews suggests a date before 63 B.C., as do the friendly references to Rome: 2 Macc. 4.11, 11.34 – 38. One of the letters attached at the beginning of the text is dated to 124 B.C.: 2 Macc. 1.10. Whether this offers a clue to the date of Jason or of the summarizer or of yet a third editor remains altogether uncertain. Among many treatments, see Abel, *Les livres des Maccabées* (above, n. 55), xlii—xliii; J. G. Bunge, *Untersuchungen zum zweiten Makkabäerbuch* (Bonn, 1971); Momigliano, "The Second Book of Maccabees," *CP* 70 (1975): 81 – 88; C. Habicht, *2 Makkabäerbuch* (Gütersloh, 1976), 169 – 77; Goldstein, *I Maccabees* (above, n. 3), 62 – 89; and *II Maccabees* (New York, 1983), 28 – 83; Attridge, *in Jewish Writings of the Second Temple Period* (above, n. 57), 176 – 78. A valuable bibliography of recent works is in Schürer, *History of the Jewish People* (above, n. 57), III.1, 536 – 37. See now the sensible and sober remarks by Bar-Kochva, *Judas Maccabaeus* (above, n. 57), 182 – 85, and Sievers, *The Hasmoneans* (above, n. 57), 4 – 7.

60 These and other possibilities are canvassed by Orrieux, "La 'parenté'" (above, n. 8), 176 – 86.

The course of the second century B.C.E. brought the Jews into increasing contact with Hellenic literature, legends, and traditions, both in Palestine and in the Diaspora. For cultivated Jews who learned Greek and absorbed Greek culture, this was the real residue of Macedonian imperialism in the Near East. They faced squarely the burden of articulating their own people's place within the broader cultural community. The process is too often reckoned as apologia or assimilation. So, a scholar characterized the Jews' embrace of the Spartan συγγένεια as "a ticket of admission to the Hellenic club."[61] For that purpose, however, the purported ancestor of both peoples should be a Greek hero or legendary figure, hardly a Jewish patriarch. Identification of Abraham as the common forefather delivers the appropriate message. The Jews attempted to assimilate Greeks into their own traditions rather than subordinate themselves to Hellenism. The distinction is a critical one.

Jews are no mere passive recipients of a tradition here. Nor did they promote a connection for political, military, or economic advantage. The cultural character of this association holds pride of place, a means whereby to declare Jewish identity in a Hellenistic context. Sparta served as an eminently suitable vehicle. In the fragmented and turbulent scene of the post-Alexander era, the image of Sparta still glowed brightly, at least in the impression of intellectuals. Perception, as so often, counted for more than reality. Sparta continued to stand for martial virtue, voluntary sacrifice, order, stability, and the rule of law.[62] The Spartan model, evoking respect and admiration, would be an ideal one—especially when shaped to Jewish advantage. The invention of the συγγένεια did more than to assert bonds between the Jewish and Hellenic worlds. It constituted a Jewish expropriation and transformation of the Spartan mystique in order to declare the primacy of the Jews.[63]

---

61 E. Bickerman, *The Jews in the Greek Age* (Cambridge, Mass., 1988), 184.

62 Note for example, the claim by the people of Selge in Pisidia to a συγγένεια with the Lakedaimonians; Plb. 5.76.11. For the persistence of the Spartan image, see P. Ollier, *Le mirage spartiate*, 2 vols. (Paris, 1933–43); E. N. Tigerstedt, *The Legend of Sparta in Classical Antiquity*, 3 vols. (Stockholm, 1965, 1974, 1978); E. Rawson, *The Spartan Tradition in European Thought* (Oxford, 1969).

63 This essay profited substantially from the sage suggestions of C. P. Jones and the editors of *Transitions to Empire: Essays in Greco-Roman History, 360–146 B.C., in Honor of E. Badian* (Norman: University of Oklahoma Press, 1996).

Reciprocal Perspectives

8. Jewish Perspectives on Greek Culture and Ethnicity

The encounter of Jew and Greek in antiquity continues to exercise a hold on scholarly attention and public imagination. The conquests of Alexander the Great spread Greek language and institutions all over the lands of the Near East, from Asia Minor to Iran where Jews were settled—including Palestine itself. The convergence of cultures was inescapable. Not only does it represent a historical confrontation of high significance, but the very terms "Hellenism" and "Judaism" have served as metaphors for a tension between reason and religion, between rationality and spirituality, through the ages.

The subject has, of course, attracted extensive scholarly treatment, with increased interest in recent years. But inquiry has proceeded largely on three fronts: (1) the influence of Hellenic language, literature, philosophy, historiography, and even religion upon the Jewish experience,[1] (2) the attitude of Greeks (or pagans more generally) toward Jews,[2] (3) the changing self-image of the Jews in the circumstances of a Hellenic world.[3] By contrast, little scrutiny has been applied to a related but quite distinct issue: the Jewish perception of Greeks.[4] Did the Jews have a clear and consistent sense of Greeks as an ethnic entity?

The very notion of "the Jews" carries its own perils. It would be illusory to imagine a monolithic group with a unitary viewpoint. The analysis here centers

---

1 The most detailed and comprehensive study is still that of M. Hengel, *Judaism and Hellenism* (2 vols.; Philadelphia: Fortress, 1974). His conclusions on the extensive and early spread of Hellenism among the Jews, however, are challenged by L. Feldman, *Jew and Gentile in the Ancient World* (Princeton: Princeton University Press, 1993), especially 42–44, 416–22, and bibliographical references.
2 Enormous literature exists on this subject. The relevant texts are conveniently collected by M. Stern, *Greek and Latin Authors on Jews and Judaism* (2 vols.; Jerusalem: Israel Academy of Sciences, 1976). Among recent works, with references to earlier scholarship, see especially J. G. Gager, *The Origins of Anti-Semitism* (Oxford: Oxford University Press, 1985); Z. Yavetz, "Judeophobia in Classical Antiquity," *JJS* 44 (1993) 1–22; P. Schäfer, *Judeophobia: Attitudes toward the Jews in the Ancient World* (Cambridge, Mass.: Harvard University Press, 1997).
3 The classic study is that of Y. Gutman, *The Beginnings of Jewish-Hellenistic Literature* (2 vols.; Jerusalem: Bialik, 1958, 1963 [Hebrew]). Cf. also J. J. Collins, *Between Athens and Jerusalem: Jewish Identity in the Hellenistic Diaspora* (New York: Crossroad, 1983; revised ed. Grand Rapids, Mich.: Eerdmans, 2000). A good general discussion may be found in D. Mendels, *The Rise and Fall of Jewish Nationalism* (New York: Doubleday, 1992). And see now E. Gruen, *Heritage and Hellenism* (Berkeley: University of California Press, 1998), with further bibliography.
4 The treatment by C. Sirat, "The Jews," in K. Dover, ed., *Perceptions of the Ancient Greeks* (Oxford: Blackwell, 1992) 54–78, is too broad and selective.

upon that segment of the Jews (no small one) for whom coming to grips with Hellenism was a matter of critical importance. As is well known, many Jews were thoroughly familiar with the Greek language, with Hellenic myths, traditions, religion, and institutions. They engaged in a protracted effort to redefine themselves within the terms of an ascendant Mediterranean culture that was largely Greek. How did they conceive of Greeks as a people, nation, or society and what relation did their concept or concepts have on the shaping of the Jews' own self-perception?

Daunting questions. Relevant texts do not exist in abundance. A substantial number of Greek authors concerned themselves with Jewish customs, traits, and practices, their works cited by later authors or occasionally extant in fragments. But nothing comparable issued from the pens of Jewish authors about Greeks. Perspectives need to be pieced together from stray remarks, inferences, and implications. And they add up to no neat and tidy picture. The results, however, offer some intriguing insights into the mentality of Hellenistic Jews and their sense of interconnectedness with the dominant *ethnos* of the Mediterranean cultural world.

The Jews, on the face of it, might provide a useful "external" view of *Hellenismos*. In fact, however, they are, in an important sense, both "external" and "internal" witnesses. They represent a different culture, background, tradition, and history. Yet in the Hellenistic era, and indeed in the Greek East of the Roman period, the Jews were part and parcel of a Greek cultural community. That very fact, of course, was central to their grappling with a new sense of identity which they sought to articulate through the genres and the media familiar to Greeks while expressing the distinctiveness of their own character and achievement. Hence, Jews needed both to establish their own secure place within a Hellenistic framework and also to make it clear that they were not swallowed up by that prevailing cultural environment. The construct of Jewish identity in the Hellenistic world, therefore, an ongoing, complex, and shifting process, was tightly bound up with the construct of Greek ethnicity, i. e., the character, values, and beliefs of the Greek *ethnos* in Jewish eyes.

That these were constructs is inescapable. Although Jewish intellectuals could draw distinctions among Greek peoples, communities, and conventions, they frequently lapsed into broad characterizations and stereotypes. For obvious reasons. They had a definite agenda. In some form or other, Jews had to confront —or to formulate—those Hellenic traits from which they wished to disassociate themselves and, at the same time, to account for those characteristics which they had themselves embraced.

The texts discussed here, for the most part, were directed inward. Jews spoke largely to their own compatriots, striving to fashion a self-consciousness that could negotiate a cultural realm of alien origin. If Greeks read these works, so much the better. But few were likely to. The texts contributed to the articulation of Jewish identity by and for Jews.

Greeks regularly reckoned other *ethnē* as *barbaroi*, a familiar cliché of this subject. Jews suffered that disability, in Hellenic eyes, like everyone else. But they could also turn the tables. A striking text serves as suitable entrance into the inquiry. The author of the Second Book of Maccabees was a Hellenized Jew of the late second century B.C.E. who composed his work in Greek, a writer thoroughly steeped in the traditions of Greek historiography.[5] His topic, however, was the background, circumstances, and consequences of the brutal persecution of Jews by the Hellenistic monarch Antiochus IV Epiphanes. The Jews resisted and retaliated under Judas Maccabeus. According to 2 Maccabees, they fought nobly on behalf of Judaism and, though few in number, ravaged the entire land and drove out the "barbarian hordes."[6] So the composer of this work, well-versed in the conventions of the genre, employed the standard Hellenic designation for the alien—but applied it to the Hellenes themselves. And it was not the only such occasion.[7] The pejorative contexts in which the term appears in 2 Maccabees make it clear that it signifies a good deal more than mere "speakers of a foreign tongue."

Biblical precedents, to be sure, could be drawn upon. The Canaanites carried a comparable stigma of barbaric backwardness, a necessary construct in order to justify their dispossession by the Hebrews. And the Philistines, fiercest of the Israelite foes, received a similar portrayal as savage idolators, thus to legitimize the triumph of Yahweh.[8] But the dire circumstances of the Maccabean era brought the Greeks sharply into focus. The cultivated author of 2 Maccabees expropriated the Hellenic characterization of "the Other" to his own purposes. The Greek *ethnos* itself could now be cast in that role.

---

5 The work is itself an epitome of the now lost five-volume history of the Maccabees by Jason of Cyrene, plainly also a Hellenized Jew; 2 Macc 2:19–31. For a register of scholarship on 2 Maccabees, see E. Schürer, *The History of the Jewish People in the Age of Jesus Christ* 3.1 (rev. and ed. G. Vermes, F. Millar and M. Goodman; Edinburgh: Clark, 1986) 536–37.

6 2 Macc 2:21: τοῖς ὑπὲρ τοῦ Ἰουδαϊσμοῦ φιλοτίμως ἀνδραγαθήσασιν, ὥστε τὴν ὅλην χώραν ὀλίγους ὄντας λεηλατεῖν καὶ τὰ βάρβαρα πλήθη διώκειν.

7 Cf. 2 Macc 4:25; 5:22; 10:4.

8 See the discussions of T. Dothan and R. Cohn, "The Philistine as Other: Biblical Rhetoric and Archaeological Reality," in *The Other in Jewish Thought and History* (ed. L. Silberstein and R. Cohn; New York: New York University Press, 1994) 61–73; and Cohn, "Before Israel: The Canaanites as Other in Biblical Tradition," in ibid., 74–90.

A range of texts underscores the drive of Hellenistic Jews to brand the Greeks as villainous or ignorant aliens—or both. This would, of course, distinguish all the more conspicuously the advantages of being a Jew.

Apocalyptic literature served this purpose. The visions of Daniel received their current shape in the very era of the persecutions. And they speak in cryptic but unmistakable tones of the catastrophic evils brought by the rule of the Hellenic kingdom. The terrifying dream that paraded four huge beasts in succession represented the sequence of empires, the fourth most fearsome of all, a dreadful monster with iron teeth and bronze claws that devoured and trampled all in its path. That portent signified the coming of the Greeks, to culminate in the tenth and most horrific prince, plainly the figure of Antiochus Epiphanes, responsible for the abomination of desolation. The forecasts vouchsafed for Daniel, however, would end in triumph over the wicked, a divine intervention to sweep aside the brutal Hellenic Empire and bring about an eternal kingdom under the sovereignty of the Most High.[9] The Greeks here emblematize the mightiest of empires—and the one targeted for the mightiest fall.

That theme is picked up in the prophecies of the *Third Sibylline Oracle*. The Sibyl had venerable roots in pagan antiquity, but the surviving collection of pronouncements stems from Jewish and Christian compilers who recast them for their own ends. The contents of the *Third Sibyl* represent the earliest portion, almost entirely the product of Jewish invention, and some parts at least dating to the era of the Maccabees.[10] One group of verses echoes Daniel directly, employing some of the same imagery, with reference to the Macedonian kingdoms which impose an evil yoke and deliver much affliction upon Asia but whose race (*genos*) will be destroyed by the very race it seeks to destroy.[11] The text also repeats in different form the sequence of empires, including the Greeks as arrogant and impious and the Macedonians as bearing a fearful cloud of war upon mortals. Internal rot will follow, extending from impiety to homosexuality and afflicting many lands—but none so much as Macedon.[12] Elsewhere the Sibyl condemns Greeks for overbearing behavior, the fostering of tyrannies, and moral failings.

---

9 Daniel 2:31–45; 7:1–27; 8.1–26; 11:21–45; 12:1–3. This, of course, is not the place to explore these visions and their interpretations in detail. Among commentaries, see L. Hartman and A. Di Lella, *The Book of Daniel* (Garden City, N.Y.: Doubleday, 1978); J. J. Collins, *Daniel* (Hermeneia; Minneapolis: Fortress, 1993).

10 The chronology is complex and contested. A valuable treatment may be found in J. Barclay, *The Jews in the Mediterranean Diaspora* (Edinburgh: Clark, 1996) 216–25. The matter is taken up afresh in Gruen, *Heritage and Hellenism*, 271–83.

11 *Sib. Or.* 3: 381–400.

12 *Sib. Or.* 3: 166–90.

She predicts that their cities in Asia Minor and the Near East will be crushed by a terrible divine wrath; Greece itself will be ravaged and its inhabitants dissolved in strife for gain.[13] In this bitter and wrathful composition, the Jewish author brands the people of Hellas as insolent, sacrilegious, and brutal, doomed to suffer the vengeance of the Lord.

The portrait is hardly less severe in the First Book of Maccabees. That work appeared first in Hebrew, the product of a strong supporter of the Hasmonean dynasty, composed probably late in the second century B.C.E.[14] The book opens with a harsh assessment of Alexander the Great, an arrogant conqueror whose campaigns brought slaughter and devastation in their wake. And his successors over the years delivered multiple miseries upon the earth.[15] The wickedness reached its peak, of course, with the arrival of Antiochus IV, symbol not only of evil but of the alien. The author of 1 Maccabees stigmatizes his measures as introducing the practices of the foreigner to the land of Judea.[16]

The stark contrast between Jew and Greek receives dramatic elaboration in the martyrologies recorded in 2 Maccabees. The elderly sage Eleazer resisted to the death any compromise of Jewish practice by spurning the cruel edicts of Antiochus Epiphanes, calmly accepting his agonizing torture. The same courage was exhibited by the devout mother who witnessed proudly the savage slaying of her seven steadfast sons and joined them herself in death, memorable testimony to Jewish faith and Hellenic barbarity.[17] The stories were retold many generations later, at a time when the fierce emotions of the Maccabean era were a distant memory. The torments inflicted upon Eleazer and the mother with her seven sons were elaborated in exquisite detail in a text preserved in some manuscripts of the Septuagint under the title of 4 Maccabees. The work was composed in Greek, probably in the first century C.E. by a Jew trained not in history but in Greek philosophy. He employed the martyrologies to illustrate Stoic doctrines of the command of reason over the passions. The author, therefore, ironically appropriated the Hellenic medium to convey Jewish commitment to the Torah by contrast with the irrationality and atrocities of the Greeks themselves.[18]

---

13 *Sib. Or.* 3: 202–04, 341–49, 545–55, 638–45.
14 On the date, see F.-M. Abel, *Les livres des Maccabées* (Paris: Lecoffre, 1949) xxviii–xxix; J. Goldstein, *1 Maccabees* (Garden City, N.Y.: Doubleday, 1976) 62–63; Schürer, *The History*, 3.1:181; J. Sievers, *The Hasmoneans and their Supporters* (Atlanta: Scholars Press, 1990) 3.
15 1 Macc 1:9: ἔτη πολλὰ καὶ ἐπλήθυναν κακὰ τῇ γῇ.
16 1 Macc 1:43–44: πορευθῆναι ὀπίσω νομίμων ἀλλοτρίων τῆς γῆς.
17 2 Macc 6:18–7:41.
18 4 Macc 4–18. For discussions of the text, with bibliography, see H. Anderson, "4 Maccabees," in *The Old Testament Pseudepigrapha* (ed. J. H. Charlesworth; Garden City, N.Y.: Double-

The abhorrence of philosophically minded Jews for the excesses of the Greeks surfaces almost inadvertently in another treatise roughly contemporary with 4 Maccabees. The so-called Wisdom of Solomon falls within the tradition of Jewish wisdom literature but comes from the hand of a Hellenized Jew thoroughly familiar with Greek philosophy.[19] Although the setting itself is strictly biblical, an interesting remark of the author bears notice for our purposes. He ascribes to the unspeakable Canaanites every form of loathsome practice, including orgiastic mystery rites, human sacrifice, and cannibalism. And he describes them in terms characteristic of participants in a Dionysiac *thiasos*.[20] The notorious Hellenic ritual thereby serves to epitomize barbaric behavior.

Jewish imagination went further still on this score. A full-scale story, almost entirely fictitious, depicted the lunatic crusade of a Hellenistic king against the nation of the Jews. And this time the villain was not Antiochus Epiphanes. The text appears in some of the manuscripts of the Septuagint, misleadingly entitled 3 Maccabees for it has nothing whatever to do with the history or legend of the Maccabees.[21] It depicts the mad monarch, Ptolemy IV, determined to eradicate the Jews of Egypt because their compatriots had denied him access to the Holy of Holies in the temple at Jerusalem. A frenzy of hatred drove Ptolemy to his scheme of genocide. He ordered subordinates to round up all the Jews in the land, confine them in the hippodrome outside Alexandria, and have them trampled *en masse* by a herd of crazed elephants drugged with huge quantities of frankincense and unmixed wine. But a happy ending concluded the tale. Ptolemy's dastardly plot was thrice thwarted, the final time when God's messengers turned around the great beasts to crush the minions of the king. The Jews ended in honor and triumph. But they had suffered a fearsome travail. The nar-

---

day, 1985) 2.531–43; Schürer, *The History*, 3.1: 588–93; J. W. van Henten, *The Maccabean Martyrs as Saviours of the Jewish People: A Study of 2 and 4 Maccabees* (Leiden: Brill, 1997) 58–82; D. deSilva, *4 Maccabees* (Sheffield: Sheffield Academic Press, 1998) 11–142.

19 See the excellent treatment by D. Winston, *The Wisdom of Solomon* (Garden City, N.Y.: Doubleday, 1979).

20 Wisdom of Solomon 12:3–5: καὶ σπλαγχνοφάγον ἀνθρωπίνων σαρκῶν θοῖναν καὶ αἵματος ἐκ μέσου μύστας θιάσου. Cf. Winston, *The Wisdom of Solomon*, 238–40, with references.

21 A valuable summary of scholarship on this text may be found in F. Parente, "The Third Book of Maccabees as Ideological Document and Historical Source," *Henoch* 10 (1988) 150–68. See also J. Mélèze-Modrzejewski, *The Jews of Egypt* (Philadelphia: The Jewish Publication Society, 1995) 141–53; Barclay, *The Jews in the Mediterranean Diaspora*, 192–203; and the excellent dissertation of S. Johnson "Mirror-Mirror: Third Maccabees, Historical Fictions and Jewish Self-Fashioning in the Hellenistic Period," Ph.D. diss., University of California, Berkeley, 1996 later revised and published see *Historical Fictions and Hellenistic Jewish Identity: Third Maccabees in Its Cultural Context* (Berkeley, CA. 2004)

row escape only highlighted the hostility of those committed to the elimination of the Jews. Ptolemy's enmity did not stand alone. A group of friends, advisers, and soldiers urged the destruction of that *genos* which refused to conform to the ways of other nations.[22] And a far wider populace rejoiced at the prospect of Jewish demise, their festering hatred now given free rein in open exultation.[23] More significant, the Hellenized Jewish author of this work designates the Greeks themselves as "the aliens": ἀλλόφυλοι. And the exaltation of the Jews in the end elevates them to a position of authority, esteem, and respect among their "enemies."[24]

An incidental notice regarding one of the Jews' most notorious fictional antagonists warrants mention here. Haman, the grand vizier of the Persian king in the Book of Esther, endeavored to institute a policy of genocide against the Jewish nation. In the Greek additions to the Hebrew original, composed in the Hellenistic era, the wicked Haman, notably and significantly, is transformed into a Macedonian![25] The schema that pits Jews against Greeks, their opponents who stand outside the bounds of morality and humane behavior, persists in all these texts.

A comparable contrast appears in a far more unexpected place. The *Letter of Aristeas* narrates the celebrated legend of the translation of the Pentateuch into Greek. The job was done, so the story has it, at the directive of the cultivated King Ptolemy II, in collaboration with the Jewish high priest, and through the efforts of Jewish sages, experts in both languages—and in Greek philosophy besides— who were warmly welcomed and lavishly hosted by the Hellenistic monarch. No text seems better calculated to convey harmony and common objectives between the *ethnē*.[26] Yet all is not sweetness and light even here. In the warm glow of cultural cooperation that bathes most of the text, it is easy to forget the pointed words of Eleazer, the high priest, when he responded to queries by Greeks about the peculiar habits of the Jews. He affirmed in no uncertain terms that

---

22 3 Macc 3:2; 3:6 – 7; 5:3; 6:23 – 24; 7:3.
23 3 Macc 4:1: δημοτελὴς συνίστατο τοῖς ἔθνεσιν εὐωχία μετὰ ἀλαλαγμῶν καὶ χαρᾶς ὡς ἂν τῆς προκατεσκιρωμένης αὐτοῖς πάλαι κατὰ διάνοιαν μετὰ παρρησίας νῦν ἐκφαινομένης ἀπεχθείας. This attitude did not prevail, however, among all the Greeks in Alexandria itself; 3 Macc 3:8 – 10.
24 3 Macc 3:6 – 7; 3:21.
25 Esther, Addition E, 10 – 14.
26 This work, of course, has generated a lengthening stream of publications. Among the serviceable commentaries, see R. Tramontano, *La lettera di Aristea a Filocrate* (Naples: Ufficio succursale della civiltà cattolica, 1931); M. Hadas, *Aristeas to Philocrates* (New York: Harper, 1951); A. Pelletier, *Lettre d'Aristée à Philocrate* (Paris: Cerf, 1962); N. Meisner, "Aristeasbrief," *JSHRZ* 2.1 (1973) 35 – 87. Additional works cited in Schürer, *The History,* 3.1: 685 – 87.

Jews alone held to monotheistic beliefs and that those who worship many gods engage in foolishness and self-deception. Idolators who revere images of wood and stone, he observed, are more powerful than the very gods to whom they pay homage, since they were themselves responsible for their creation. And he became quite explicit about those who manufactured myths and concocted stories: they were adjudged the wisest of the Greeks![27] It is hard to miss the irony there. Eleazer proceeded to declare that Moses, in his wisdom, fenced the Jews off with unbreakable barriers and iron walls to prevent any mingling with other *ethnē*, to keep them pure in body and soul, and to rid them of empty beliefs.[28] So, even the veritable document of intercultural concord, the *Letter of Aristeas,* contains a pivotal pronouncement by the chief spokesman for Judaism, who sets his creed decisively apart from the ignorant and misguided beliefs of the Greek *ethnos*.[29]

The contrast is elaborated at some length by Josephus. The historian distinguishes unequivocally between the virtues of the Jews and the deficiencies of the Greeks, a harsh critique of Hellenic behavior and institutions. The fact merits special notice. For Josephus notes at one juncture in the *Antiquities* that he addresses his work to Greeks, in the hope of persuading them that Jewish customs had been held in high esteem, protected by a series of Roman decrees.[30] But he records repeated interference by Greeks with the ancestral practices of the Jews and outright atrocities in Cyrenaica, Asia Minor, Alexandria, Damascus, Caesarea, and other cities of Palestine.[31] Josephus pulls no punches: the disposition of the Greeks is labeled as "inhumanity."[32]

In the *Contra Apionem* he developed the contrast at greater extent and on a different level. Josephus took aim even at Greek achievements in philosophy and

---

27 *Let. Aris.* 137: καὶ νομίζουσιν οἱ ταῦτα διαπλάσαντες καὶ μυθοποιήσαντες τῶν Ἑλλήνων οἱ σοφώτατοι καθεστάναι.

28 *Let. Aris.* 139: ὁ νομοθέτης, ὑπὸ θεοῦ κατεσκευασμένος εἰς ἐπίγνωσιν τῶν ἀπάντων, περιέφραξεν ἡμᾶς ἀδιασκόποις χάραξι καὶ σιδηροῖς τείχεσιν, ὅπως μηθενὶ τῶν ἄλλων ἐθνῶν ἐπιμισγώμεθα κατὰ μηδέν, ἁγνοὶ καθεστῶτες κατὰ σῶμα καὶ κατὰ ψυχὴν ἀπολελυμένοι ματαίων δοξῶν.

29 The same point about the folly of those whose objects of worship were fashioned by their own hands is made by *Wisdom of Solomon* 14–17, and Philo, *De Decalogo* 69.

30 Jos. *A. J.* 16.174–75. Cf. C. Stanley, "'Neither Jew nor Greek': Ethnic Conflict in Graeco-Roman Society," *JSOT* 64(1996) 106–108.

31 See, e.g., Jos. *A. J.* 16.160–61, 18.257–60, 19.300–12, 20.173–84. For additional references and discussion, especially on the outbursts against Jews by Greeks during the Great Revolt, see A. Kasher, *Jews and Hellenistic Cities in Eretz-Israel* (Tübingen: Mohr Siebeck, 1990) 245–87; Feldman, *Jew and Gentile,* 113–22.

32 Jos. *A. J.* 16.161: τῆς τῶν Ἑλλήνων ἀπανθρωπίας.

law. He singles out Moses as most venerable of lawgivers, and speaks with scorn of Greeks who take pride in such figures as Lycurgus, Solon, and Zaleucus. They were Moses' juniors by several centuries. Indeed, Homer himself had no concept of law, an idea incomprehensible to the Greeks of his day.[33] Josephus proceeds later in the treatise to disparage Hellenic philosophy and education. The philosophers, he maintains, directed their precepts only to the elite, withholding them from the masses, whereby Moses' teaching encompassed all. Moses did not list piety as simply one among several virtues but subsumed all the virtues under piety, thus rendering them accessible to everyone. Whereas some Greek educational systems rest on verbal articulation of principles and others on practical training in morals, the Hebrew lawgiver alone blended both. Jews therefore escaped the imperfections and one-sidedness of both the Spartan and Athenian systems.[34] Josephus subsequently provides an extended excursus that brings the superiority of Jewish character, morality, and national qualities over the Greek into sharper focus. He places particular weight upon the Jews' faithful and consistent adherence to their own laws. To the Greeks such unswerving fidelity can hardly be imagined. Their history is riddled with inversions and deviations. Plato might have constructed a Utopian scheme to which readers could aspire, but those engaged in Greek public affairs themselves found his model laughably unrealistic. And it was not nearly as demanding as that which the Jews actually abide by![35]

For most Greeks, in fact, the semilegendary Spartan lawgiver Lycurgus and the sociopolitical structure that he installed in Sparta represented the exemplar to be imitated. The longevity of its system drew high praise throughout the Hellenic world. That record, however, prompted only scorn from Josephus. The endurance of the Lacedaemonian system was a mere trifle, not comparable to the two thousand years that had elapsed since the time of Moses—whose laws were still in operation. The Spartans themselves only held to their constitution while fortune smiled upon them, abandoning it when matters turned for the worse, whereas Jews remained steadfast throughout their vicissitudes and calamities.[36] The historian adverts to the record of martyrdom for the faith and the heroic resistance of the Jews to any effort to force them into betraying their traditions, even in the face of torture and execution. His rhetoric here spins out of control,

---

33 Jos. *C. Ap.* 2.154–56.
34 Jos. *C. Ap.* 2.168–74.
35 Jos. *C. Ap.* 2.220–24.
36 Jos. *C. Ap.* 2.225–31, 2.279.

denying that a single Jew had ever turned his back on the laws.[37] The subject evidently encouraged hyperbole.

Josephus exploited Hellenic writings themselves to drive home his point. Plato and other authors who censured their own poets and statesmen served his purposes nicely. They had already castigated the makers of public opinion for spreading preposterous conceptions of the gods. The myths multiplied deities without number, portrayed them in a variety of human forms, and had them engage in every type of licentiousness, misdemeanor, folly, and internecine warfare with one another. And, as if that were not enough, the Greeks grew weary of their traditional divinities and imported foreign gods by the score, stimulating poets and painters to invent new and even more bizarre images of worship.[38] No wonder Plato declared the precincts of his ideal state as off limits to all poets![39] Josephus reiterates once again the core of his thesis: Jews hold tenaciously to their laws and traditions, allowing neither fear of the powerful nor envy of the practices honored by others to shake their constancy.[40] There could be no stronger contrast with the inconstancy of the Greek character.

The celebrated lines of the apostle Paul allude directly to the antithesis between the *ethnē:* "There is neither Jew nor Greek, slave nor free, male nor female, for you are all one in Jesus Christ."[41] The string of contraries makes it clear that the two *ethnē* represented conventionally opposite poles. The same phraseology appears in another Pauline text: "We have all been baptized into one body and in one spirit, whether Jews or Greeks, slaves or free."[42] The distinctions held firm in Jewish circles. Paul had an uphill battle to surmount them.

So far the evidence seems clear and consistent. Jewish compositions constructed the Hellenes as foils, as aliens, as the "Other," thereby the better to set off the virtues and qualities of their own *ethnos*. One may note that this characterization crosses genre boundaries, appearing in apocalyptic texts, histories,

---

37 Jos. *C. Ap.* 2.232–35, ἆρ᾽ οὖν καὶ παρ᾽ ἡμῖν, οὐ λέγω τοσούτους, ἀλλὰ δύο ἢ τρεῖς ἔγνω τις προδότας γενομένους τῶν νόμων ἢ θάνατον φοβηθέντας.

38 Jos. *C. Ap.* 2.239–54.

39 Jos. *C. Ap.* 2.256.

40 Jos. *C. Ap.* 2.271: καὶ τούτων ἡμᾶς τῶν νόμων ἀπαγαγεῖν οὔτεφόβος ἴσχυσε τῶν κρατησάντων οὔτε ζῆλος τῶν παρὰ τοῖς ἄλλοις τετιμημένων.

41 Gal 3:28: οὐκ ἔνι Ἰουδαῖος οὐδὲ Ἕλλην, οὐκ ἔνι δοῦλος οὐδὲ ἐλεύθερος, οὐκ ἔνι ἄρσεν καὶ θῆλυ. πάντες γὰρ ὑμεῖς εἷς ἐστε ἐν Χριστῷ Ἰησοῦ. See the expanded and more complex version in Col 3:11.

42 1 Cor 12:13: καὶ γὰρ ἐν ἑνὶ πνεύματι ἡμεῖς πάντες εἰς ἓν σῶμα ἐβαπτίσθημεν, εἴτε Ἰουδαῖοι εἴτε Ἕλληνες εἴτε δοῦλοι εἴτε ἐλεύθεροι. Cf. also 1 Cor 10:32; Rom 1:16; 2:9–10; 3:9; 10:12; Acts 19:10; 19:17; 20:21; Stanley, "'Neither Jew nor Greek,'" 123. The Greeks are themselves made equivalent to τὰ ἔθνη; 1 Cor 1:22–24.

apologetic treatises, and imaginative fiction. The diverse formulations range
from the relatively mild strictures in the *Letter of Aristeas,* castigating Greeks
for foolish and delusive idolatry, and Josephus' derisive blast at their irresolu-
tion, instability, and ludicrous concoctions of the divine, to the fierce portrayals
of Hellenic character in texts like 1 Maccabees, in the apocalypic visions of Daniel and the *Third Sibyl,* in the martyrologies contained in 2 and 4 Maccabees, and
in the fictive tale of 3 Maccabees, branding Greeks as barbaric, irrational, and
murderous. All seems relatively straightforward and aggressively hostile.

But those constructs do not tell the whole story. Jewish perceptions (or at
least expressed perceptions) of the Greeks were more complex, varied, and subtle. One might note, for instance, that Jewish writers did not frequently resort to
the term *barbaroi* in referring to gentiles. The most commonly used phrase is a
less offensive one: *ta ethnē*—"the nations." This occurs with regularity in
1 and 2 Maccabees, a phrase that can encompass Greeks but is by no means confined to them.[43] It can, of course, be employed pejoratively depending on context, as it frequently is in the Books of the Maccabees. But even there the term
carries no inherently negative connotation. Indeed 1 Maccabees employs *to ethnos* repeatedly to refer to the Jewish nation itself, usually in circumstances of
diplomatic correspondence between Jews and Hellenistic dynasts or Romans.[44]
And, as is well known, Paul uses the phrase *ta ethnē* again and again, sometimes
synonymously with "Greeks," usually with a broader denotation. But the term
signifies no more than "those who are not Jews."[45] The construct is plainly malleable, not necessarily a vehicle of opprobrium.

Furthermore, in various Jewish authors and texts, Greek character and culture acquire a notably more positive aspect. But they do so because they are conceived as owing those qualities to the Jews themselves.

The approach can be illustrated through diverse examples. A fragment of the
Hellenistic—Jewish historian Eupolemus has relevance here. His date and provenance are not quite secure—unless he is identical, as most assume, with the Eupolemus who was a member of Judas Maccabeus' entourage. That would place

---

43 See, e.g., 1 Macc 1:11; 1:13; 1:14; 2:68; 3:10; 3:45; 3:48; 2 Macc 8:5; 12:13; 14:14 – 15.
44 See, e.g., 1 Macc 8:23; 10:25; 11:30; 12:3; 13:36; 14:28; 15:1 – 2; also 2 Macc 11:27. Note
further the letter of Antiochus III, recorded or recast by Josephus, in which Judaea is an *ethnos*
among other *ethnē;* Jos. *A. J.* 2.141 – 42: τῆς Ἰουδαίας καὶ ἐκ τῶν ἄλλων ἐθνῶν.
45 So, e.g., Rom 3:29: ἢ Ἰουδαίων ὁ θεὸς μόνον οὐχὶ καὶ ἐθνῶν; similarly, Rom 9:24; 11:11 –
12; 11:25; 2 Cor 11:26; Gal 2:14 – 15. Cf. also Acts 4:27; 13:45 – 46; 14:5; 21:21. For the identification of Greeks with *ta ethnē,* see 1 Cor 1:22 – 24; Acts 14:1 – 2.

him in Palestine in the mid-second century B.C.E.[46] Whether the identification be accepted or not, Eupolemus' work certainly belongs in the circles of cultivated Jews writing in Greek in the Hellenistic period. Ancients accorded it the title of *On the Kings in Judaea*. But the coverage was wider. The pertinent fragment, in any case, concerns Moses. Eupolemus has him hand down the knowledge of the alphabet first to the Jews, from whom the Phoenicians acquired it, and they, in turn, passed it on to the Greeks.[47] The brevity of that passage does not justify lengthy exegesis. For our purposes, suffice it to say that it makes the Greeks indirect beneficiaries of the Hebrews rather than their antagonists. And this theme has resonance elsewhere.

The imaginative writer Artapanus, a Hellenized Jew from Egypt in the second or first century B.C.E., offers an interesting parallel.[48] His inventive re-creation of biblical stories includes an elaborate account of Moses' exploits that goes well beyond any scriptural basis. Apart from ascribing to Moses the inception of a host of Egyptian institutions and technologies, he also adds a Greek connection. The name Moses, Artapanus claims, induced Greeks to identify him with Musaeus, the legendary poet and prophet from Attica, son or pupil of Orpheus who stands at the dawn of Hellenic song and wisdom. Artapanus, however, gave a slight but significant twist to the legend. He has Musaeus as mentor of Orpheus, rather than the other way round.[49] Moses therefore becomes the father of Greek poetic and prophetic traditions. In striking contrast to the message de-

---

46 The fragments may be conveniently consulted in C. Holladay, *Fragments from Hellenistic Jewish Authors*. Volume 1: *The Historians* (Chico, Calif.: Scholars Press, 1983) 93–156, with notes and commentary. Among the important treatments of Eupolemus, see especially J. Freudenthal, *Alexander Polyhistor* (Breslau: Skutsch, 1875) 105–30; Gutman, *The Beginnings*, 73–94 (Hebrew); B. Z. Wacholder, *Eupolemus, A Study of Judaeo-Greek Literature* (Cincinnati: Hebrew Union College, 1974); D. Mendels, *The Land of Israel as a Political Concept in Hasmonean Literature* (Tübingen: Mohr, 1987) 29–46; G. Sterling, *Historiography and Self-Definition: Josephos, Luke-Acts and Apologetic Historiography* (Leiden: Brill, 1992) 207–22, with valuable bibliography. Some doubts on Eupolemus' origins and date are expressed by Gruen, *Heritage and Hellenism*, 139–41.

47 Eupolemus *apud* Eus. *PE* 26.1: γράμματα παραδοῦναι τοῖς Ἰουδαίοις πρῶτον, παρὰ δὲ Ἰουδαίων Φοίνικας παραλαβεῖν, Ἕλληνας δὲ παρὰ Φοινίκων.

48 Fragments collected and commented upon by Holladay, *Fragments*, 1. 189–243. See the discussions of Freudenthal, *Alexander Polyhistor*, 143–74; Gutman, *The Beginnings*, 109–35 (Hebrew); C. Holladay, *Theios Aner in Hellenistic Judaism* (Missoula: Scholars Press, 1977) 199–232; Sterling, *Historiography and Self-Definition*, 167–86; Barclay, *Jews in the Mediterranean Diaspora*, 127–32.

49 Artapanus *apud* Eus. *PE* 9.27.3–4: ὑπὸ δὲ τῶν Ἑλλήνων αὐτὸν ἀνδρωθέντα Μουσαῖον προσαγορευθῆναι. γενέσθαι δὲ τὸν Μωϋσον τοῦτον Ὀρφέως διδάσκαλον. Cf. Holladay, *Theios Aner*, 224.

livered in Josephus' *Contra Apionem,* Artapanus does not disparage or reject those traditions but counts them as part of a Hebrew heritage.

A more obscure allusion in Artapanus has Moses receive the designation of Hermes by the Egyptian priests who honored him as interpreter of hieroglyphics.[50] The Hellenic aspect is not here in the forefront. Artapanus makes reference to the Egyptian version of Hermes, an equivalent to Thot, the mythical progenitor of much of Egyptian culture.[51] But his creative reconstruction clearly amalgamates the cultural strands. Artapanus writes ostensibly about Pharaonic Egypt but looks, in fact, to contemporary Ptolemaic Egypt. His Moses absorbs both Musaeus and Hermes and becomes the fount of Greek culture in the Hellenistic era.

Further fragments from another Jewish intellectual expand the perspective. Aristobulus, a man of wide philosophical and literary interests (though the depth of his mastery might be questioned), wrote an extensive work, evidently a form of commentary on the Torah, at an uncertain date in the Hellenistic period.[52] Only a meager portion of that work now survives, but enough to indicate a direction and objective: Aristobulus, among other things, sought to establish the Bible as foundation for much of the Greek intellectual and artistic achievement. Moses, for Aristobulus as for Eupolemus and Artapanus, emerges as a culture hero, precursor and inspiration for Hellenic philosophical and poetic traditions. But Aristobulus' Moses, unlike the figure concocted by Eupolemus and Artapanus, does not transmit the alphabet, interpret hieroglyphics, or invent technology. His accomplishment is the Torah, the Israelite law code. And from that creation, so Aristobulus imagines, a host of Hellenic attainments drew their impetus. Foremost among Greek philosophers, Plato was a devoted reader of the Scriptures, poring over every detail, and faithfully followed its precepts.[53]

---

50 Artapanus *apud* Eus. *PE* 9.27.6: ὑπὸ τῶν ἱερέων... προσαγορευθῆναι Ἑρμῆν, διὰ τὴν τῶν ἱερῶν γραμμάτων ἑρμενείαν.

51 On Artapanus' manipulation of the Hermes/Thot characteristics, see Gutman, *The Beginnings*, 120–22 (Hebrew); G. Mussies, "The Interpretatio Judaica of Thoth-Hermes," in *Studies in Egyptian Religion* (ed. M. Voss; Leiden: Brill, 1982) 97–108.

52 The fullest treatment of Aristobulus may be found in N. Walter, *Der Thoraausleger Aristobulus* (Berlin: Akademie, 1964). Among other worthy contributions, see Gutman, *The Beginnings*, 186–220 (Hebrew); Hengel, *Judaism and Hellenism*, 1.163–69; 2.105–10; N. Walter, "Aristobulos," *JSHRZ* 3.2: 261–79; Barclay, *Jews in the Mediterranean Diaspora*, 150–58. The whole subject has now been placed on a firmer footing by the excellent new edition of the fragments, with translation, notes, and bibliography by C. Holladay, *Fragments from Hellenistic Jewish Authors*. Volume 3: *Aristobulus* (Atlanta: Scholars Press, 1995).

53 Aristobulus *apud* Eus. *PE* 13.12.1: φανερὸν ὅτι κατηκολούθησεν ὁ Πλάτων τῇ καθ᾽ ἡμᾶς νομοθεσίᾳ καὶ φανερός ἐστι περιειργασμένος ἕκαστα τῶν ἐν αὐτῇ.

And not only he. A century and a half earlier, Pythagoras borrowed much from the books of Moses and inserted it into his own teachings.[54] Never mind that the Torah had not yet been translated into Greek by the time of Plato—let alone that of Pythagoras. Aristobulus had a way around that problem. He simply proposed that prior translations of the Bible circulated long before the commissioned enterprise of Ptolemy II, before the coming of Alexander, even before Persian rule in Palestine.[55] That, of course, is transparent fiction, compounding his concoction in order to save the thesis. But it was all in a good cause. It made Moses responsible for the best in Greek philosophy.

Other philosophers, too, came under the sway of the Torah. So at least Aristobulus surmised. The "divine voice" to which Socrates paid homage owed its origin to the words of Moses.[56] And Aristobulus made a still broader generalization. He found concurrence among all philosophers in the need to maintain reverent attitudes toward God, a doctrine best expressed, of course, in the Hebrew Scriptures which preceded (and presumably determined) the Greek precepts. Indeed, all of Jewish law was constructed so as to underscore piety, justice, self-control and the other qualities that represent true virtues—i.e., the very qualities subsequently embraced and propagated by the Greeks.[57] Aristobulus thereby brought the whole tradition of Greek philosophizing under the Jewish umbrella.

That was just a part of the project. Aristobulus not only traced philosophic precepts to the Torah. He found its echoes in Greek poetry from earliest times to his own day. The Sabbath, for instance, a vital part of Jewish tradition stemming from Genesis, was reckoned by Aristobulus as a preeminent principle widely adopted and signaled by the mystical quality ascribed to the number seven.[58] And he discovered proof in the verses of Homer and Hesiod. This required some fancy footwork. Aristobulus cavalierly interpreted a Hesiodic reference to the seventh day of the month as the seventh day of the week. And he (or his source) emended a line of Homer from the "fourth day" to the "seventh day." He quoted other lines of those poets to similar effect—lines that do not corre-

---

54 Aristobulus *apud* Eus. *PE* 13.12.1: καθὼς καὶ Πυθαγόρας πολλὰ τῶν παρ' ἡμῖν μετενέγκας εἰς τὴν ἑαυτοῦ δογματοποιίαν κατεχώρισεν.
55 Aristobulus *apud* Eus. *PE* 13.12.1.
56 Aristobulus *apud* Eus. *PE* 13.12.3 – 4.
57 Aristobulus *apud* Eus. *PE* 13.12.8. See Gutman, *The Beginnings*, 192 – 99 (Hebrew).
58 Aristobulus *apud* Eus. *PE* 13.12.12. See, on this, Gutman, *The Beginnings*, 203 – 10 (Hebrew); Walter, *Der Thoraausleger*, 68 – 81; Holladay, *Fragments*, Volume 3, 230 – 32.

spond to anything in our extant texts of Homer and Hesiod. It would not be too bold to suspect manipulation or fabrication.[59]

The creative Aristobulus also enlisted in his cause poets who worked in the distant mists of antiquity, namely the mythical singers Linus and Orpheus. Linus, an elusive figure variously identified as the son of Apollo or the music master of Heracles, conveniently left verses that celebrated the number seven as representing perfection itself, associating it with the heavenly bodies, with an auspicious day of birth, and as the day when all is made complete.[60] The connection with the biblical origin of the Sabbath is strikingly close—and too good to be true. Aristobulus summoned up still greater inventiveness in adapting or improvising a wholesale monotheistic poem assigned to Orpheus himself. The composition delivers sage advice from the mythical singer to his son or pupil Musaeus (here in proper sequence of generations), counseling him to adhere to the divine word and describing God as complete in himself while completing all things, the sole divinity with no rivals, hidden to the human eye but accessible to the mind, a source of good and not evil, seated on a golden throne in heaven, commanding the earth, its oceans and mountains, and in control of all.[61] The poem, whether or not it derives from Aristobulus' pen, belongs to the realm of Hellenistic Judaism. It represents a Jewish commandeering of Orpheus, emblematic of Greek poetic art, into the ranks of those proclaiming the message of biblical monotheism.

Aristobulus did not confine himself to legendary or distant poets. He made bold to interpret contemporary verses in ways suitable to his ends. One sample survives. Aristobulus quoted from the astronomical poem, the *Phaenomena*, of the Hellenistic writer Aratus of Soli. Its opening lines proved serviceable. By substituting "God" for "Zeus," Aristobulus turned Aratus' invocation into a hymn for the Jewish deity.[62] Brazenness and ingenuity mark the enterprise of Aristobulus.

---

59 Aristobulus *apud* Eus. *PE* 13.12.13 – 15; Clement, *Strom.* 5.14.107.1 – 3. See the careful discussion of Walter, *Der Thoraausleger*, 1964: 150 – 58, with reference to the relevant Homeric and Hesiodic lines; cf. Gutman, *The Beginnings*, 210 – 12 (Hebrew); Holladay, *Fragments*, Volume 3, 234 – 37.
60 Aristobulus *apud* Eus. *PE* 13.12.16: ἑβδομάτη δ'ἠοῖ τετελεσμένα πάντα τέτυκται. See Walter, *Der Thoraausleger*, 158 – 66; Hengel, *Judaism and Hellenism*, 1.166 – 67; Holladay, *Fragments*, Volume 3, 237 – 240.
61 Aristobulus *apud* Eus. *PE* 13.12.4 – 5. Various versions of the poem are preserved by Christian authors in addition to Eusebius, and scholarly disputes over its transmission and over what counts as authentic Aristobulus remain unsettled. The subject now claims a whole new volume to itself: C. Holladay, *Fragments from Hellenistic Jewish Authors*. Volume 4: *Orphica* (Atlanta: Scholars Press, 1996).
62 Aristobulus *apud* Eus. *PE* 13.6 – 7; cf. Clement, *Strom.* 5.14.101.4b.

One can only imagine what inventive creations existed in those portions of his work that no longer survive. The campaign to convert Hellenic writings into footnotes on the Torah was in full swing.

In that endeavor Aristobulus had much company. Resourceful Jewish writers searched through the scripts of Attic dramatists, both tragic and comic, for passages whose content suggested acquaintance with Hebrew texts or ideas. And where they did not exist, alterations or fabrications could readily be inserted. Verses with a strikingly Jewish flavor were ascribed to Aeschylus, Sophocles, and Euripides, and others to the comic playwrights Menander, Diphilus, and Philemon, again a combination of classical and Hellenistic authors. The fragments are preserved only in Church Fathers and the names of transmitters are lost to us. But the milieu of Jewish-Hellenistic intellectuals is unmistakable.[63] Verses from Aeschylus emphasized the majesty of God, his omnipotence and omnipresence, the terror he can wreak, and his resistance to representation or understanding in human terms.[64] Sophocles insisted upon the oneness of the Lord who fashioned heaven and earth, the waters and the winds; he railed against idolatry; he supplied an eschatological vision to encourage the just and frighten the wicked; and he spoke of Zeus' disguises and philandering—doubtless to contrast delusive myths with authentic divinity.[65] Euripides, too, could serve the purpose. Researchers found lines affirming that God's presence cannot be contained within structures created by mortals and that he sees all, but is himself invisible.[66] Attribution of comparable verses to comic poets is more confused in the tradition, as Christian sources provide conflicting notices on which dramatist said what. But the recorded writers, Menander, Philemon, and Diphilus, supplied usefully manipulable material. One or another spoke of an all-seeing divinity who will deliver vengeance upon the unjust and wicked, who lives forever as Lord of all, who apportions justice according to deserts, who scorns offerings and votives but exalts the righteous at heart.[67]

All of this attests to feverish activity on the part of Hellenistic Jews. Which of these texts are authentic but taken out of context and which were manufactured

---

63 The fragments are collected by A.-M. Denis, *Fragmenta pseudepigraphorum graeca* (Leiden: Brill, 1970) 161–74. See the valuable discussion by Goodman in Schürer, *The History*, 3.1: 667–71, with bibliographies.

64 Pseudo Justin, *De Monarchia* 2; Clement, *Strom.* 5.14.131.2–3; Eus. *PE* 13.13.60.

65 Pseudo Justin, *De Monarchia* 2–3; Clement, *Strom.* 5.14.111.4–6, 5.14.113.2, 5.14.121.4–122.1; Eus. *PE* 13.13.38, 13.13.40, 13.13.48.

66 Clement, *Strom.* 5.11.75.1; *Protrepticus* 6.68.3. The second passage is attributed by Pseudo Justin, *De Monarchia* 2, to the comic poet Philemon.

67 Clement, *Strom.* 5.14.119.2, 5.14.121.1–3, 5.14.133.3; Eus. *PE* 13.13.45–47, 13.13.62; Pseudo Justin, *De Monarchia* 2–5

for the occasion can no longer be determined with confidence. No matter. The energy directed itself to discernible goals. Jewish writers appropriated, manipulated, reinterpreted, and fabricated the words of classical and contemporary Greek authors to demonstrate dependency on the doctrines of the Torah. These comforting fancies, of course, promoted the priority and superiority of the Jewish tradition. But, more interesting, they imply that the Hellenic achievement, far from alien to the Hebraic, simply restated its principles. The finest of Greek philosophers from Pythagoras to Plato, poets from Homer to Aratus, and even the legendary singers Orpheus and Linus were swept into the wake of the Jews.

A familiar story, but not one usually cited in this connection, underscores the point. Paul's celebrated visit to Athens can exemplify this genre of appropriation. The tale is told in the Acts of the Apostles.[68] Paul proselytized among the Jews and "God-fearers" in the synagogue—and with any person who happened to pass by in the *agora*. This upset certain Stoics and Epicureans who hauled him before the high tribunal of the Areopagus and questioned him about the new doctrine he was peddling.[69] Paul was quick to turn the situation to his own advantage—and in a most interesting way. He remarked to the Athenians that they were an uncommonly religious people. He had wandered through many of their shrines and had found one altar inscribed to an "unknown god."[70] Of course, he was there to tell them precisely who that "unknown god" happened to be. Paul proceeded to speak of the sole divinity, creator of the world and all that is in it, a god who dwells in no temples and can be captured in no images.[71] The description plainly applies to the god of the Hebrew Bible, with no Christian admixture. Paul, like other inventive Jews, quoted Greek poetry to underpin his claims. So, he remarked to the Athenians, "as some of your own poets have said, 'We too are his [God's] children.'"[72] The poet in question happened to be Aratus of Soli, no Athenian. But that detail can be comfortably ignored. The parallels with other texts cited above are unmistakable. Paul deployed Greek poetic utterances as certification for Jewish precepts. And he cited a Greek dedicatory inscription as evidence for Hellenic worship of the right deity—even if the Athenians themselves did not know who he was.

---

68 Acts 17:16–33.
69 The author of Acts adds the snide remark that Athenians have nothing better to do with their time than to talk or hear about the latest fad; Acts 17:21.
70 Acts 17:23: Ἀγνώστῳ θεῷ.
71 Acts 17:24–26.
72 Acts 17:28: ὡς καί τινες τῶν καθ᾽ ὑμᾶς ποιητῶν εἰρήκασιν: τοῦ γὰρ καὶ γένος ἐσμέν.

This heartening construct of Hellenic dependence on Jewish precedents took hold over the generations. It did not await the Church Fathers for resurrection. Notably, and perhaps surprisingly, it appears in the work of Josephus. The Jewish historian, as we have seen, took pains to underscore differences between Jews and Greeks, to stress the stability of Jewish institutions and the durability of faith as against the multiple inadequacies of Hellenic practices. Yet Josephus also follows the line that many Greeks have embraced Jewish laws—though some have been more consistent in maintaining them than others. Indeed, he acknowledges, Jews are more divided from Greeks by geography than by institutions.[73] Like Aristobulus and others, he finds Greek philosophers hewing closely to the concept of God which they obtained from acquaintance with the Books of Moses—noting in particular Pythagoras, Anaxagoras, Plato, and the Stoics.[74] The prescriptions in Plato's *Republic* obliging citizens to study closely all the laws of their state and prohibiting social intercourse with foreigners in order to keep the polity pure for those who abide by its regulations came, according to Josephus, in direct imitation of Moses.[75] Toward the end of his treatise, *Contra Apionem,* Josephus makes even larger claims. Greek philosophers were only the first of those drawn to the laws of the Torah, adopting similar views about God, teaching abstinence from extravagance and harmony with one another. The masses followed suit. Their zeal for Jewish religious piety has now spread around the world so that there is hardly a single *polis* or *ethnos,* whether Greek or barbarian, unaffected by observance of the Sabbath, various Jewish practices, and even dietary restrictions. Indeed, they labor to emulate the concord, philanthropy, industry, and undeviating steadfastness characteristic of the Jews.[76] One may set aside the hyperbole. But Josephus' insistence on the Greek quest to duplicate Jewish ethics, religion, institutions, and customs is quite notable. And it seems poles apart from his drive elsewhere to underscore the distinctions between the *ethnē.*

At the very least, a tension, if not an inner contradiction, exists in Jewish perspectives on the people of Hellas. A strong strain emphasized the differences in culture and behavior between the peoples, categorized the Greeks as aliens, inferiors, barbarians, even savage antagonists. Other voices, however, embraced and absorbed Hellenic teachings, reinterpreting them as shaped by acquaintance with the Hebraic tradition and as offshoots of the Torah. From that vantage

---

73 Jos. *C. Ap.*2.123: τῶν Ἑλλήνων δὲ πλέον τοῖς τόποις ἢ τοῖς ἐπιτηδεύμασιν ἀφεστήκαμεν.
74 Jos. *C. Ap.* 2.168; cf. 1.162.
75 Jos. *C. Ap.* 2.257: μάλιστα δὲ Πλάτων μεμίμηται τὸν ἡμέτερον νομοθέτην.
76 Jos. *C. Ap.* 2.280–84.

point, the Hellenic character becomes, through emulation and imitation, molded to the model.

For some Jewish intellectuals that was not enough. They postulated a still closer attachment, one that would give a common basis to the *ethnē*—a kinship connection. The postulate was imaginary but imaginative. Among Greeks, such a construct was standard fare. Hellenic cities and nations frequently cemented relations by tracing origins to a legendary ancestor from whom each derived.[77] A nice idea—and one the Jews were happy to pick up. Here, as elsewhere, they took a leaf from the Greek book.

This extraordinary link crops up more than once in the testimony. The most striking instance involves some unlikely partners: Spartans and Jews. Both peoples claimed Abraham as their forefather—so, at least, one tradition affirms. The claim appears in 1 Maccabees, asserted by King Areus of Sparta, evidently in the early third century B.C.E. He corresponded with the Jewish high priest and announced the happy discovery of a document that showed their people's common descent from the Hebrew patriarch. Areus conveyed his warmest wishes and employed language with biblical resonance: "Your cattle and possessions are ours, and ours are yours."[78] A century later, we are told, the Hasmonean Jonathan, who succeeded his brother Judas Maccabeus as leader of the Jews, renewed contact with the Spartans, sending them a copy of Areus' letter. Jonathan called attention to the long-standing alliance between the two peoples, an alliance unneeded from a military point of view (for the Jews rely on the support of heaven to help them humble their foes) but emblematic of the kinship bonds between them. The message simply reasserted those bonds and noted that Jews never fail to remember the Spartans in their sacrifices and prayers. Jonathan asked nothing in return except resumption of contact and renewal of their brotherhood.[79] The Spartans graciously obliged with a missive that reached Jerusalem after Jonathan had been succeeded by his brother Simon c. 142 B.C.E. The letter hailed the Jews as brothers, sent warm greetings, expressed great pleasure at the revival of relations, and announced that the alliance and even the speeches by Jewish envoys had been inscribed on bronze tablets and deposited in the Lacedaemonian archives.[80]

---

77 An extensive collection of the epigraphic evidence on fictitious kinship connections between Greek states is now available in O. Curty, *Les parentés legéndaires entre cités grecques* (Geneva: Droz, 1995).

78 1 Macc 12:23: τὰ κτήνη ὑμῶν καὶ ἡ ὕπαρξις ὑμῶν ἡμῖν ἐστιν καὶ τὰ ἡμῶν ὑμῖν ἐστιν.

79 1 Macc 12:6 – 18.

80 1 Macc 14:16 – 23. One other reference to the kinship exists, an allusion to the former high priest Jason, later an exile, who sought refuge in Sparta in reliance on the *suggeneia* between the

What does it all mean? The subject has been treated at some length elsewhere and requires only a summary of the main issues.[81] Debate continues on the authenticity of Jonathan's correspondence. That matter can be set aside. Few will now deny the invention of Areus' letter—let alone the kinship ties between Jews and Spartans. The invention is plainly a Jewish one. The postulate of Abraham as ultimate forebear of both nations makes that clear enough. A Spartan might have opted for Heracles. Nor is Areus likely to have adopted biblical language in expressing the reciprocity of the relationship. And Jonathan, in transmitting a copy of Areus' letter, reestablishes contact by patronizing the Spartans: he assures them that the Jews have consistently sacrificed and prayed on their behalf—as is appropriate for brothers.[82] The Jews have the upper hand in this association, the benefactors rather than the beneficiaries.

An undeniable fact emerges. Jewish intellectuals conceived a kinship bond with Sparta. Ethnic differentiation evaporated. Abraham had sired both peoples. The traditions of Sparta—or, more properly, the image of Sparta—had obvious appeal in Judaea. The Lacedaemonians stood for martial virtue, voluntary sacrifice, order, stability, and the rule of law.[83] A Greek historian, Hecataeus of Abdera, had already described the measures of Moses in terms that his readers would recognize as resembling the acts of Lycurgus and the statutes of Sparta.[84] Josephus, in turn, acknowledges that Lycurgus as lawgiver and Lacedaemon as a model polity draw universal praise—although he is at pains to show, as we have

nations; 2 Macc 5:9. Areus' letter and the exchange with Jonathan is given also by Josephus, following 1 Maccabees, with some additions and changes of wording; *Ant.* 12.225–27, 13.164–70.

81 See Gruen, "The Purported Jewish-Spartan Affiliation," in *Transitions to Empire: Essays in Greco-Roman History, 300–146 BC in Honor of E. Badian* (Norman: University of Oklahoma Press, 1996) 254–69, with references to earlier literature. This article is available in this volume. Previous bibliographical summaries may be found in B. Cardauns, "Juden und Spartaner," *Hermes* 95 (1967) 317–18, n. 1; R. Katzoff, "Jonathan and Late Sparta," *American Journal of Philology* 106 (1985) 485, n. 1; C. Orrieux, "la 'parenté' entre Juifs et Spartiates," in *L'étranger dans le monde grec* (ed. R. Lonis; Nancy: Presses Universitaires de Nancy, 1987) 187, n. 7.

82 1 Macc 12:11: ἡμεῖς οὖν ἐν παντὶ καίρῳ ἀδιαλείπτως ἔν τε ταῖς ἑορταῖς καὶ ταῖς λοιπαῖς καθηκούσαις ἡμέραις μιμνησκόμεθα ὑμῶν ἐφ' ὧν προσφέρομεν θυσιῶν καὶ ἐν ταῖς προσευχαῖς ὡς δέον ἐστὶν καὶ πρέπον μνημονεύειν ἀδέλφων.

83 On the Spartan image, see F. Oilier, *La mirage spartiate* (2 vols.; Paris: de Boccard, 1933–1943); E. Tigerstedt, *The Legend of Sparta in Classical Antiquity* (3 vols.; Stockholm: Almqvist & Wiksell, 1965, 1974, 1978); E. Rawson, *The Spartan Tradition in European Thought* (Oxford: Oxford University Press, 1969); N. Kennell, *The Gymnasium of Virtue* (Chapel Hill: University of North Carolina Press, 1995).

84 Hecataeus in Diodorus Siculus 40.3.6–7. Cf. Gruen, "The Purported Jewish-Spartan Affiliation," 260.

seen, that Jewish stability and endurance have outstripped that model.[85] Those who invented the purported kinship affiliation plainly had the Spartan mystique in mind. Jews could now partake of it. Indeed, better than partake of it, they could take credit for it. Abraham was ultimately responsible.

Such a construct, of course, elided ethnic distinctions and denied discord between Hellenic and Hebrew cultures. The virtues ascribed to Spartan society reflected principles enshrined in the Bible. And the Hebrew patriarch symbolized the blending of the peoples from their origins.

Another tradition utilizes the figure of Abraham as progenitor to fuse the *ethnē* and the cultures on a still broader level. A Greek legend furnished the basis for it. Among the adventures of Heracles was one in which he grappled with the Libyan giant Antaeus and overcame him, a victory that emblematized the bringing of Hellenic civilization to barbarous Africa. An elaboration of the tale has Heracles wed the wife of Antaeus, a union from which descended a lineage through Sophax and Diodorus to the rulers of North Africa.[86] Jewish writers later fiddled with the story and transformed it—in an intriguing and illuminating way. The book of Genesis supplies a brief genealogy stemming from Abraham's marriage to Keturah. In the Hellenistic period that record was exploited and amalgamated with the legend of Heracles and Antaeus. In the new version, two of Abraham's sons by Keturah, Apher and Aphran, fought side by side with Heracles in subduing Antaeus. Heracles then married Aphran's daughter, producing a son, Diodorus, who later provided a grandson, Sophon, whence derived the name of a barbarian people, the Sophanes. The exploits of Apher and Aphran had still greater ramifications. The city of Aphra was named after the one, the whole continent of Africa after the other. And a third brother, Assouri, became the namesake of Assyria. This wonderfully imaginative construct is ascribed to an otherwise unknown writer Cleodemus Malchus.[87]

The identity of Cleodemus has generated substantial discussion which can be happily passed by here.[88] Only the text matters. Here again the tale has re-

---

85 Jos. *C. Ap.* 2.225–35.
86 On the various versions of the Greek tale, see Diodorus Siculus 1.17.21, 1.17.24, 4.17.4; Plutarch, *Sertorius* 9. Cf. N. Walter, "Kleodemos Malchas," *JSHRZ* 1.2 (1976) 116; R. Doran, "Cleodemus Malchus," in *OTP* 2. 884–85. The best analysis, exploring both classical and Jewish texts on North Africa, is that of Gutman, *The Beginnings* 2 (1963) 137–43 (Hebrew).
87 The text is preserved in Jos. *A.J.* 1.239–41 and Eus. *PE* 9.20.2–4, with some variations in the names. The biblical genealogy occurs in Gen 25.1–6.
88 Among the more important treatments, see Freudenthal, *Alexander Polyhistor*, 1875: 130–36; Gutman, *The Beginnings*, 2.136–37 (Hebrew); Walter, "Kleodemos Malchas," 115–18; Holladay, *Fragments*, 1.245–59; Doran, "Cleodemus Malchus," 883–87; Goodman, in Schürer, *The History*, 3.1: 526–29.

ceived an *interpretatio Judaica,* not an *interpretatio Graeca.* The line begins with
Abraham, his son has the honor of a continent named after him, and Heracles'
victory over the giant was made possible by the collaboration of Hebrew figures.
The invention in this case is especially notable. Not only does the Greek legend
of Heracles bringing civilization to a barbarous land metamorphose into one in
which Abraham's progeny took part in the endeavor and bestowed their names
upon national entities, but also the manipulated narrative now implies a kinship
affiliation between Hebrews and Hellenes at the dawn of history. The greatest of
Greek heroes marries into the patriarch's family. And together they are responsible for the ruling dynasty of North Africa—*barbaroi* though they be. Here is ethnic mixture indeed. The Jewish version absorbs the Heracles legend, links the nations, and even encompasses the *barbaroi.* This seems at the farthest remove
from those texts in which the distinctions are vital and the Hellene as alien
serves to highlight the superior values of the Jew.

A quite different variety of tale but one with comparable import warrants notice here: speculation on Jewish origins. Two versions supply a direct connection
with the Greek world, one with the island of Crete, the other with a people of
Asia Minor. Both survive amidst a list of hypotheses recorded by Tacitus—
who, however, supplies neither sources nor significance.

In the view of some, says the Roman historian, the Jews were refugees from
Crete who settled in distant parts of Libya at the time when Saturn had been driv-
en from his realm by Jupiter. Tacitus notes the grounds for this conjecture, essentially etymological. Mt. Ida in Crete gave the name "Idaei" to its inhabitants, a
name later barbarized into "Iudaei."[89] Whence derived this notion and how
widespread it was we cannot know. It may well have stemmed from speculation
by Greeks, a typical tendency to associate foreign peoples with Hellenic
origins.[90] Jewish researchers may not have embraced the identification but
would welcome the inferences that their people date to the earliest era of
Greek mythology, that they share a heritage with the Hellenes, and even that
they had an ancient foothold in Africa.[91]

---

89 Tacitus, *Histories* 5.2.1: *Iudaeos Creta insula profugos novissima Libyae insedisse memorant,
qua tempestate Saturnus vi Iovis pulsus cesserit regnis. Argumentum e nomine petitur: inclutum in
Creta Idam montem, accolas Idaeos aucto in barbarum cognomento Iudaeos vocitari.*
90 Cf. E. Bickerman, "Origenes Gentium," *Classical Philology* 47 (1952) 65–81.
91 The learned might also recall that tradition had Zeus himself born in Crete; Hesiod, *Theogony* 470–80. And the age of Saturn would have the resonance of a golden era of stability. Cf.
L. Feldman, "Pro-Jewish Intimations in Tacitus' Account of Jewish Origins," *Revue des Études
Juives* 159 (1991) 339–46.

The other tale was still more agreeable. It ascribed especially illustrious beginnings to the Jews: they were identified with the Solymoi, a Lycian people celebrated in the epics of Homer, whose name is reflected in the city they founded,
Hierosolyma (Jerusalem).[92] The etymological assumption again accounts for the
conclusion. A pagan source here, too, probably conceived the coincidence, standard fare for finding links between contemporary folk and Greek legend. It is unlikely that a Jew invented the idea that his ancestors' roots were in Asia Minor.
But association with a Homeric people, particularly one described in the *Iliad* as
"glorious" and as having given the Greek hero Bellerophon his toughest fight,
would be congenial to the Jews—at least to those who regarded an ethnic amalgamation with nations honored in classical myths as an enhancement of their
own cultural identity.[93]

Do we here reach an impasse? The texts seem to suggest inconsistency and
ambivalence, if not outright self-contradiction, in Jewish perspectives on the
people of Hellas. A strong strain in Jewish literature emphasized the differences
in culture and behavior between the two peoples, categorizing the Greeks as aliens, inferiors, even savage antagonists and barbarians. Other voices, however,
embraced and absorbed Hellenic institutions, finding them entirely compatible
with Hebraic teachings. And still other traditions, invented or propagated by
Jewish writers, far from stressing the contrast, brought the nations together
with a blending of the races and the fiction of a common ancestor.

Is there an explanation for these discordant voices? Should one postulate a
change over time in Jewish attitudes toward the Hellenes and Hellenic culture?
Or was there perhaps a division within Jewish communities between those committed to the purity of the tradition, thus drawing a firm distinction between the

---

92 Tacitus, *Histories* 5.2.3: *Clara alii Iudaeorum initia: Solymos, carminibus Homeri celebratam
gentem, conditae urbi Hierosolyma nomen e suo fecisse.*
93 The relevant Homeric passage is *Iliad* 6.184–85. In *Odyssey* 5.283, the bard mentions the
"Solymian hills." The reference is picked up by the fifth century BCE poet Choerilus, who includes those dwelling in the Solymian hills among the Asian nations who marched with Xerxes
against Greece. That passage is preserved by Josephus, a noteworthy point, for he interprets it
(whatever Choerilus may have intended) as an allusion to the Jews and employs it as evidence
for early Hellenic acquaintance with his people; Jos. *C. Ap.* 1.172–75. The process neatly illustrates the adaptation of a Greek text for Jewish purposes. And it suggests that the tale of Jews as
Solymoi could well have found its way into Jewish texts. The claim that a Jewish exegete made
the initial identification is improbable; so I. Lévy, "Tacite et l'origine du peuple juif," *Latomus* 5
(1946) 334–39; M. Stern, *Greek and Latin Authors on Jews and Judaism* (2 vols.; Jerusalem: Israel Academy of Sciences, 1974) 2. 5–6. See Feldman, "Pro-Jewish Intimations," 351–54;
1993: 192, 520–22, who, however, goes too far in implying that Jews would have found the
story unacceptable.

cultures, and those inclined toward assimilation and accommodation? Neither explanation will do. In fact, supposedly different voices coexist in the same texts. So, the *Letter of Aristeas* proclaims a harmonious relationship between cultivated Greeks and learned Jews, a fruitful collaboration in the translation of the Pentateuch into *koine* Greek, but also presents a forceful reminder that idolatry still grips the Hellenes and that their childish beliefs distance them immeasurably from the genuine piety of the Jews.[94] Similarly, the dire forecasts of the Third Sibylline Oracle predict vengeance to be wreaked upon the aggressive and brutal Hellenic conquerors, repayment for their inner malevolence as well as their external aggrandizement. But the same work contains lines that indicate a reaching out by Jews to those Greeks who will repent and reform, a promise of divine favor in return for righteousness and piety, the expectation that Greeks will share with Jews in the glories of the eschaton.[95] And Josephus himself, as we have seen, not only draws the sharpest contrast between Hellenic deficiencies and Jewish virtues but also embraces the view that the noblest expressions of Greek philosophy cohere with the teachings of Moses.[96]

The matter is plainly more complex and more involved. The discrepancies and inconsistencies that we discern (or construct) may not have been so perceived by the ancients who viewed them with multiple visions. Could they both associate and contrast Jews and Greeks? Why not? The texts that betoken cultural conjunction in no way negate or compromise Jewish distinctiveness. On the contrary. They serve to underscore, rather than to undermine, Jewish superiority. In various formulations, the Greek alphabet arrived through a Jewish intermediary; poetic inspiration came from a Hebrew bard; the most sublime Greek thought derived from the teachings of the Pentateuch; Hellenic philosophers, dramatists, and poets who recognized the sole divinity, expressed lofty ethical precepts, and honored the Sabbath took their cue from the Torah; and even the Athenians unwittingly paid homage to the god of the Scriptures. These fictive inventions hardly dissolved the distinctions between Hebrews and Hellenes. Instead, they elevated the best in Hellenism by providing it with Hebrew precedents. The rest, by definition, fell short. All of this, and more, reflects energetic and often ingenious efforts to commandeer Hellenic achievements for Jewish purposes.

Nor is there any dilution of ethnic singularity in the tales that made kinsmen of Jews and Spartans or linked Heracles with biblical figures. Inventive Jewish

---

94 See above pp. 176–8.
95 *Sib. Or.* 3:545–72, 625–56, 732–61.
96 See above pp. 187–9.

writers exploited the Hellenic practice of signaling consanguinity among the nations by positing a common ancestor. But the Jews did it their own way: the mythical forefather was to be the Hebrew patriarch. That established the proper priority. The admirable qualities and the storied exploits of the Hellenes were enlisted to demonstrate the special eminence that attached to the *ethnos* of the Jews. This was no blend of the cultures. It was Jewish appropriation.

The strategy is neatly exemplified by an anecdote derived from the Mishnah. As the tale has it, Rabbi Gamaliel went to Acco, a largely gentile city on the coast of Palestine. There he took a bath in the bathhouse dedicated to Aphrodite and adorned by a statue of the goddess—no doubt in her most provocative pose. The rabbi was then asked by an astonished witness whether he was violating Jewish law by entering the sacred space of a pagan shrine and one marked by a statue of Aphrodite. Gamaliel had an answer: "The bathhouse was not built as an ornament for the statue, but the statue for the bathhouse; hence I did not come into Aphrodite's domain, she came into mine!"[97] The rabbi's reasoning may be a bit sophistical, but it was quite characteristic. Jews engaged in clever cultural aggrandizement.

The process, however, was not all one-sided. Greek writers did some appropriating of their own. As is well known, Greeks frequently traced the origins of some of their institutions and practices to peoples of the Near East, most particularly the Egyptians. Herodotus, of course, spoke with great respect of Egypt's ancient traditions and institutions to which Hellas owes a large debt.[98] Tales circulated later of Homer's birth in Egypt, of visits to Egyptian priests by Orpheus and Musaeus, by Lycurgus and Solon, by Pythagoras and Plato, all to take intellectual nourishment from that ancient land.[99]

Would the Greeks be willing to articulate a comparable debt to the Jews? A harder proposition. Few Greeks had any familiarity with Jewish history, literature, and traditions. Yet stereotypes and impressions existed. And, in fact, there are traces of a reciprocal recognition and of Hellenic concession to Jewish characteristics that could resonate with their own. Hecataeus of Abdera, writing in the late fourth century B.C.E., has an excursus on the Jews. Among other things, he makes some admiring remarks about Moses as law-giver, agricultural reformer, and initiator of a military system.[100] Hecataeus, to be sure, makes no

---

97 M. Avodah Zarah, 3.4. See discussion by S. Schwartz, in P. Schäfer, *The Talmud Yerushalmi and Graeco-Roman Culture, 1* (Tübingen: Mohr Siebeck, 1998), 203–17.
98 Cf. Herodotus 2.4, 2.43, 2.49–58, 2.82, 2.123, 2.167.
99 See, e.g., Isocrates, *Busiris* 28–29; Diodorus Siculus 1.68.2–4, 1.76.5–6, 96.1–3, 98.1–4; Plutarch, *Solon* 26.1.
100 Hecataeus, *apud* Diodorus Siculus 40.3.3–8.

claim that the Greeks learned anything from him. Nevertheless, the description of Moses as a proto-Lycurgus is striking. Of course, the version is an *interpretatio Graeca*, but it suggests at least a willingness to express an indirect affiliation.

In the perspective of several early Hellenistic authors, the Jews were a nation of philosophers.[101] That perception emerges most memorably in a story told of Aristotle by one of his pupils, Clearchus of Soli. According to the anecdote, Aristotle, while in Asia Minor, ran into a Jew from Coele-Syria whom he much admired for his learning and his impeccable character. Jews in general are known as philosophers, he said. And this particular one was especially notable. For he was *Hellenikos* not only in his speech, but in his very soul.[102] So the Jewish concept that the best in Greek philosophy derives from biblical roots is here mirrored by a Greek tale that has the Jew as quintessential philosopher. But the anecdote is given a Hellenic spin: the Jew has the soul of a Greek.

A two-way process existed, a mutual manipulation of cross-cultural interchange, a double mirror. Hence it comes as no surprise to find in other Greek writers reverberations of, or parallels to, the thesis expressed by Aristobulus and Josephus. The late third century B.C.E. historian and biographer of philosophers Hermippus of Smyrna remarked that Pythagoras imitated and made use of Jewish and Thracian doctrines and that he introduced many principles from the Jews into his philosophy.[103]

By the second century C.E., Numenius of Apamea, a Neo-Pythagorean philosopher, could declare quite baldly: "What is Plato but Moses speaking in Attic Greek?"[104]

While Greeks acknowledged Moses' influence on Hellenic philosophy, however, the Jewish philosopher Philo turned that idea on its head. He has Moses himself not only learn arithmetic, geometry, music, and hieroglyphics from erudite Egyptians, but progress through the rest of his curriculum, presumably rhet-

---

101 Cf. Theophrastus, *apud* Porphyry, *De Abstinentia* 2.26; Megasthenes, *apud* Clement, *Stromateis* 1.15.72.5; Clearchus, *apud* Jos. *C. Ap.* 1.176–83. The texts may be readily consulted in Stern, *Greek and Latin Authors*, vol. 1, numbers 4, 14, 15.
102 Clearchus, *apud* Jos. *C. Ap.* 1.176–83: Ἑλληνικὸς ἦν οὐ τῇ διαλέκτῳ μόνον, ἀλλὰ καὶ τῇ ψυχῇ.
103 Hermippus, *apud* Jos. *C. Ap.* 1.165: λέγεται γὰρ ὡς ἀληθῶς ὁ ἀνὴρ ἐκεῖνος πολλὰ τῶν παρὰ Ἰουδαίοις νομίμων εἰς τὴν αὐτου μετενεγκεῖν φιλοσοφίαν. Cf. Origen, *Contra Celsum*, 1.15.334. See H. Jacobson, "Hermippus, Pythagoras, and the Jews," *Revue des Études Juives* 135 (1976) 145–49, who suggests, somewhat speculatively, that Hermippus or his source got the information from a Jewish text in Greek that cited biblical passages. Cf. also Feldman, *Jew and Gentile*, 201–2.
104 Numenius, *apud* Clement, *Stromateis* 1.22.150.4: τί γὰρ ἐστι Πλάτων ἢ Μωυσῆς ἀττικίζων. The line is quoted in several other texts; see Stern, *Greek and Latin Authors* 2, no. 363a-e.

oric, literature, and philosophy, with Greek teachers.[105] What itinerant Greek schoolmasters there might have been in Egypt in the late Bronze Age can be left to the imagination. In any event, there was a lively traffic in stories, whether filtered through *interpretationes Graecae* or *interpretationes Judaicae,* whereby the two *ethnē* reflected themselves in one another's culture.

Comparable inversions occur with respect to the slippery term *barbaros.* The Jewish author of 2 Maccabees, as we have seen, writing in Greek and in the genre of Hellenistic historiography, turned the tables on conventional practice and labeled the Greeks themselves as *barbaroi.*[106] That was ironic and pointed—but it did not become a dominant mode. Other Jewish writers embraced the long-established Hellenic antithesis that divided the world into Greeks and barbarians. It can be found, for instance, in Philo of Alexandria, who boasts of the widespread attraction of Jewish customs, applied in various parts of the world by both Greeks and barbarians—who reject the institutions of others within their own category.[107] Josephus employs the contrast regularly as a means of categorizing the non-Jewish world.[108] It appears also in Paul, who proclaims his message to "Greeks and Barbarians, the wise and the ignorant"—no pagan could have said it better.[109] Philo, in fact, can even adopt the Hellenic perspective wholesale and count the Jews among the *barbaroi!*[110] And while the Jewish philosopher in Egypt brackets Jews with barbarians, the Greek tax collector in Ptolemaic Egypt places Jews in the category of *Hellenes.*[111] Here is inversion upon inversion. And we have noticed already the unusual variant in Cleodemus Malchus' story about intermarriage between the houses of Abraham and Heracles: one of the descendants of that union gave his name to the "barbarian" Sophanes of Africa.[112] That is ethnic mixture indeed: not only linkage of Greek and Jew, but even a joint embrace of *barbaroi.*

The counterpoint and transposition complicate matters considerably. But they also show with accuracy just how entangled was the reciprocity of the cultures. Jewish intellectuals, it appears, negotiated an intricate balance in their depiction of Greek ethnicity and culture. They simultaneously differentiated their

---

105 Philo, *Mos.* 1.23.
106 See above p. 173.
107 Philo, *Mos.* 2.18–20: τῶν κατὰ τὴν Ἑλλάδα καὶ βάρβαρον.
108 See, e.g., Jos. *B. J.* 5.17: Ἕλλησι πᾶσι καὶ βαρβάροις; Jos. *A. J.* 4.12: οὔτε παρ' Ἕλλησιν οὔτε παρὰ βαρβάροις; *Jos. C. Ap.* 2.282: οὐ πόλις Ἑλλήνων ... οὐδὲ βάρβαρος.
109 Rom. 1:14: Ἕλλησίν τε καὶ βαρβάροις σοφοῖς τε καὶ ἀνοήτοις ὀφειλέτης εἰμί.
110 Philo, *Mos.* 2.27; Philo, *Prob.* 73–75.
111 *Corpus Papyrorum Raineri,* XIII, 4.109–201.
112 Cleodemus Malchus *apud* Eus., *PE* 9.20.4.

nation from that of the Greeks and justified their own immersion in a world of Hellenic civilization. The differentiation, sharp though it might be, did not preclude imaginary kinship associations. And, on the other side of the coin, the thorough engagement with Greek culture did not mean compromise with the principles and practices of Judaism.

Jewish perspectives predominate in the texts here examined. But their discourse was not altogether lost on the Greeks themselves. The latter, who sought to enhance their stature by proclaiming a link with the venerable teachings of Egypt, also gave a nod in the direction of the Jews. It added yet another dimension to Hellenic self-perception to have Pythagoras and Plato acquainted with the Pentateuch, as they were with Egyptian learning. And even Aristotle could comfortably benefit from the erudition of a cultivated Jew—so long as he possessed the soul of a Greek. The double mirror captured the *ethnē*.

9. The Use and Abuse of the Exodus Story

The Exodus was a defining moment, perhaps *the* defining moment in ancient Israelite tradition. As the legend has it, the Israelites' escape from Egypt under the leadership of Moses shook off the yoke of Egyptian oppression and gave them the impetus for articulating principles and values, surmounting an arduous journey through the wilderness, and shaping their identity as a people and a culture. The day of their release from the tyranny of Pharaonic Egypt, so the Lord declared in the Book of Exodus, would thereafter be commemorated in an annual festival, among the most sacred on the calendar, the ceremony of Passover.[1] The Exodus generated high drama, an unforgettable tale in the Bible, perhaps the single most familiar one to Jew and Gentile alike. As inspiration to subsequent generations of Jews and their admirers, its power is manifest.

But what of the villains of the piece? They, or rather their presumed descendants, would not have found this story very entertaining. Indeed, we might imagine, they would have reason to feel maligned and defamed. The heartless Pharaohs, the hostile Egyptian populace, and the royal army as an agent of evil hardly supplied models for imitation. And the tale could bring little satisfaction to the indigenous dwellers in the land of the Nile.

The spread of the story should only have aggravated matters. Jewish soldiers and Jewish settlers in Egypt occasionally appear on record in the centuries that followed the supposed time of the Exodus, most notably in the garrison at Elephantine.[2] But the principal wave of Jewish reentry into Egypt appears to have come at the end of the Persian period and in the early years of the Hellenistic age.[3] The Exodus story could have seeped into Egyptian consciousness in the course of this era, thus to stir reaction and response. Indeed, echoes of a very different variety of the tale emerge in the literature produced by pagan au-

---

1 Exodus, 12.14–20, 12.25–27.
2 See B. Porten, *Archives from Elephantine: The Life of a Jewish Military Colony* (Berkeley, 1968), 3–61. There were, of course, Jews in Egypt prior to the Elephantine garrison; cf. Jeremiah, 41–44; *Let. Aris.* 13, 35; J. Mélèze-Modrzejewski, *The Jews of Egypt: From Rameses II to Emperor Hadrian* (Philadelphia, 1995), 21–26.
3 *Let. Aris.* 12–27; Jos. *A. J.* 12.5–9, 12, 17. 12.28–33. The tale itself of the deportation of 100,000 Jews by Ptolemy I and their release by Ptolemy II is questionable. Nor can one place implicit faith in the more agreeable version ascribed to Hecataeus of Abdera by Jos. *C. Ap.* 1.186–194, that has numerous Jews follow Ptolemy I voluntarily from Palestine to settle in Egypt. See also B. Bar Kochva, *Pseudo-Hecataeus "On the Jews"* (Berkeley, 1996), 71–82. But the congruence of testimony does at least suggest that a significant movement of Jews to Egypt occurred at the beginning of the Hellenistic period.

thors in Egypt. In assorted versions, Jews appear as villains rather than victims, oppressors rather than oppressed, the perpetrators of sacrilege rather than the upholders of the faith, and ultimately the defeated rather than the triumphant. Scholars have drawn what seems to be a logical conclusion: the conflicting versions represent a form of competing historiography; pagans produced a "counter-history" to negate or reverse the effects of the Jewish legend; a polemical contest ensued, a war of propaganda between Jews and Egyptians over the nature of the biblical Exodus.[4]

Josephus, vehicle for much of the variant tradition, buttresses the interpretation. His treatise, the *Contra Apionem,* devotes itself in large part to refuting anti-Jewish tracts by Alexandrian writers and others perceived as hostile to the Jews. Diverse treatments of the Exodus constitute a substantial portion of the work, drawing Josephus' fire and prompting elaborate counteractions to undermine the negative portrayals by Manetho, Lysimachus, Apion, and Chaeremon.[5] Josephus' apologia has set the terms for modern discussion. Perhaps misleadingly so. That the Exodus narrative became transformed and manipulated seems obvious enough. But the manipulators and their motives are not quite so obvious. Complexity and ambiguity adhere to the several versions, undermining trust in the stark and simplistic approach of Josephus.

Modern scholarship, taking its cue from Josephus, discerns a basic dichotomy. In general, pagan writings on the Jews are assessed along a spectrum with a clear division in the center: they were either favorably inclined, admiring of Jewish character and practices, with positive judgments on their traditions and institutions, or they were virulently antisemitic, hostile to Jewish customs, distort-

---

4 See, e. g., the formulations of A. Funkenstein, "Anti-Jewish Propaganda: Pagan, Christian, and Modern," *The Jerusalem Quarterly* 19 (1981), 59; idem, *Perceptions of Jewish History* (Berkeley, 1993), 36–40; A. Kasher, *The Jews in Hellenistic and Roman Egypt* (Tübingen, 1985), 327–334; C. Aziza, "L'utilisation polémique du récit de l'Exode chez les écrivains alexandrins," *Aufstieg und Niedergang der römishchen Welt,* II.20.1 (1987), 53–63; E. Gabba, "The Growth of Anti-Judaism or the Greek Attitude towards Jews," in W. D. Davies and L. Finkelstein, *The Cambridge History of Judaism* (Cambridge, 1989), vol. 2, 653–655; M. Pucci ben Zeev, "The Reliability of Josephus Flavius: The Case of Hecataeus' and Manetho's Accounts of Jews and Judaism," *Journal for the Study of Judaism,* 24 (1993): 233–234; Z. Yavetz, "Judeophobia in Classical Antiquity: A Different Approach," *Journal of Jewish Studies* 44 (1993): 21; P. Schäfer, "The Exodus Tradition in Pagan Greco-Roman Literature," in I. M. Gafni, A. Oppenheimer, and D. R. Schwartz (eds.), *The Jews in the Hellenistic-Roman World: Studies in Memory of Menahem Stern* (Jerusalem, 1996), 12, 16–17.
5 See especially Jos. *C. Ap.* 1.223–319, 2.8.32, 2.121–122. On Josephus' apologetics and polemics, see A. Kasher, "Polemic and Apologetic," in L. H. Feldman and J. R. Levinson (eds.), *Josephus' Contra Apionem: Studies in its Character and Context with a Latin Concordance to the Portion Missing in Greek* (Leiden, 1996), 143–186.

ing their history and slandering their values. They might, to be sure, combine aspects of both. But analyses consistently apply the categories of "pro or anti-Jewish." Researchers differ on where the balance lies. For some, the negative prevails: the attitude of most pagans was sharply antagonistic.[6] Others take a quite different line: pagans on the whole either looked upon Jews with favor or merely indulged in scorn and mockery, but showed no race hatred against them.[7] One can refine this division further by resorting to statistics. An eminent scholar recently reviewed the texts and tabulated the results, calculating that 18 percent of pagan assessments were favorable, 23 percent unfavorable, and 59 percent neutral.[8] Hence, a judicious selectivity can provide support for any line that one seeks to argue on this matter. But the whole approach is conceptually flawed. No numbers game will determine the issue, no reckoning of sums or statistical tables can elucidate pagan attitudes toward the Jews. Even to characterize a majority of Gentile remarks as "neutral" may misconceive the situation. It begs a critical question by assuming the existence of a war of words, a polemical setting in which all pagan appraisals of Jews can be placed. But that is the very proposition that needs reevaluation.

The story of the Exodus supplies a central exhibit. As the common reconstruction has it, that drama served as vehicle either for enhancing the Jewish image or for maliciously undermining it, depending on how the tale was told. A different perspective is offered here.

Two starkly contrasting versions of the Exodus can set the matter in a bold light. Their sharp differences make the two presentations, those of Strabo and Lysimachus, particularly useful and revealing. On the face of it, they seem to confirm definitively the notion that rival interpretations of the tale stemmed

---

6 See, e.g., J. L. Daniel, "Anti-Semitism in the Hellenistic-Roman World," *Journal of Biblical Literature* 98 (1979), 46: "Jews in the Hellenistic-Roman literature... were almost universally disliked or at least viewed with an amused contempt;" M. Goodman, in E. Schürer (ed.), *The History of the Jewish People in the Age of Jesus Christ* (rev. and ed. by G. Vermes, F. Millar, and M. Goodman, Cambridge, 1986), III.1, 607: "Most pagan authors who spoke about the Jews at all after c. 300 B.C. did so in a polemical sense. Hostility was almost universal after the first century B.C."
7 See, e.g., J. Isaac, *Genèse de l'antisémitisme* (Vanves, 1956), 49 – 126; R. Ruether, *Faith and Fratricide: The Theological Roots of Antisemitism* (Minneapolis, 1974), 23 – 28; M. Simon, *Verus Israel* (Oxford, 1986), 202 – 207.
8 L. H. Feldman, "Anti-Semitism in the Ancient World," in D. Berger (ed.), *History and Hate: The Dimensions of Anti-Semitism* (Philadelphia, 1986), 30; idem, "Pro-Jewish Intimations in Anti-Jewish Remarks Cited in Josephus' *Against Apion*," *Jewish Quarterly Review* 78 (1988): 190 – 191; idem, *Jew and Gentile in the Ancient World* (Princeton, 1993), 124.

from polarized attitudes toward the Jews. Careful scrutiny might suggest otherwise.

Strabo, an indefatigable researcher, traveler, historian, and geographer from Pontus, produced most of his work, in Greek, during the age of Augustus. In the course of his monumental geographic treatise, Strabo describes the terrain, topography, and economies of Syria, Phoenicia, and Judaea. And he takes the occasion to append notes on the historical background and traditions of the region. That treatment includes a striking rendition of the Exodus events and their central figure, Moses. For Strabo, the most reliable report about the ancestors of contemporary Jews has them as Egyptians by origin. Moses indeed was an Egyptian priest who became disgruntled with the religious observances of his own people, rejecting their representations of divinity in the form of animals and even taking a side-swipe at Greeks for depicting gods in human shape.[9] In Strabo's account Moses proclaimed that God was all-encompassing, that he cannot be conceived or worshipped through images, and that he responds only to those who live temperately and through righteousness.[10] With such statements, Moses won over a substantial number of right-thinking persons who followed him out of Egypt to the site of Jerusalem. There he installed a just and pious religion where God could be properly worshipped and where Moses himself won widespread admiration.[11] Such, in brief, is the substance of Strabo's recreation of the Exodus—a very far cry from the biblical narrative. It does, however, deliver a highly flattering portrait of Moses and of those who accompanied him out of Egypt into the Promised Land. Moses did not, in this version, rescue an oppressed people. He and his followers left their native land for the best of religious motives: to pay proper homage to the supreme deity, unsullied by perverse images. Moses thus stands out as an esteemed religious leader and molder of his people, in a category with the most venerated Greek lawgivers like Lycurgus and Minos and a host of sage prophets.[12] Strabo consequently and for obvious reasons has been counted among those pagan writers who held the Jews and their principles in high regard.[13]

---

9 Strabo, 16.2.34–35. Cf. Jos. *A. J.* 14.118. What Greek art Moses might be expected to have seen remains a mystery. The idea of Moses inspecting Bronze Age figurines that turned up in Egypt requires a feat of imagination.
10 Strabo, 16.2.35.
11 Ibid., 16.2.36.
12 Ibid., 16.2.38–39.
13 It is not pertinent here, even if it were possible, to determine the sources of Strabo on this matter, how far he was influenced by Hecataeus, how much he paraphrased from Posidonius, and what proportion stemmed from his own researches. See the discussions by J. G. Gager, *Moses in Greco-Roman Paganism* (Nashville, 1972), 44–47; M. Stern, *Greek and Latin Authors*

At the opposite end of the spectrum stands the Graeco-Egyptian writer Lysimachus. Of the man and his time we know virtually nothing, apart from the fact that Josephus considered him as fiercely hostile to the Jews. A chronological clue lies in Josephus' remark that Apion provided the same invented figure for the number of Jews who fled Egypt as did Lysimachus. That would date Lysimachus somewhat prior to Apion who lived in the early and middle first century CE, and possibly make him a near contemporary of Strabo.[14] It would be imprudent to claim greater precision or certainty. Lysimachus' presentation of the Exodus, in any case, puts him at very sharp odds with Strabo. According to Lysimachus, Jews in the reign of Pharaoh Bocchoris suffered from leprosy, scurvy, and other afflictions and, in seeking to alleviate their ailments, took refuge in the temples and resorted to begging for sustenance. A famine then struck the land, prompting the king to seek counsel with the oracle of Ammon. On the god's advice, Bocchoris expelled the suppliants from the holy places, drowning the victims of scurvy and leprosy and leaving the rest to perish in the desert. He then cleaned the temples, now rid of their impure and impious occupants.[15] The survivors managed to make their way through the desert, instructed by Moses to exhibit no kindness to anyone, to give wicked counsel, and to overturn all temples and altars they happen to come across. Still worse, after they reached inhabited land, the Jews treated the indigenous population with disdain, looted and burned their shrines, and built their own city of Jerusalem from which they could exercise power.[16] Not a very pretty picture. It is hardly surprising that Lysimachus conventionally ranks among the arch antisemites of antiquity.[17]

---

on Jews and Judaism (Jerusalem, 1976) I, 264–267; B. Bar-Kochva, The Image of the Jews in Greek Literature: The Hellenistic Period (Berkeley: UC Berkeley Press, 2010), with bibliography.
14 Jos. C. Ap. 2.20: τὸν δὲ ἀριθμὸν τῶν ἐλασθέντων τὸν αὐτὸν Λυσιμάχῳ σχεδιάσας. Whether he is identical with "Lysimachus the Alexandrian," a writer on marvels and myths, need not be decided; see A. Gudeman, "Lysimachos," Real-Encyclopädie der klassischen Altertumswissenschaft, vol. 14 (1928): 32–39; P. M. Fraser, Ptolemaic Alexandria (Oxford, 1972), vol. 2, 1092–1093, n. 475. For Josephus' characterization of Lysimachus' animus, see Jos. C. Ap. 1.304, 1.319, 2.145, 2.236. Bar-Kochva, The Image of the Jews in Greek Literature, places him at the end of the second century BCE. But the evidence is indirect and indecisive.
15 Jos. C. Ap. 1.305–307.
16 Ibid., 1.310–311.
17 So, e.g., Feldman, Jew and Gentile, 163: "anti-Jewish bigot;" 192: "arch Jew-baiter;" 171: "arch anti-Jewish bigot;" Aziza, 56: "inspirée par des sentiments antijuifs." Ibid., 56–57, who dates Lysimachus to the mid-second century B.C.E., speculates that his animosity was provoked by the Jewish settlement at Leontopolis and that his depiction of atrocities inflicted upon the land had in mind Jewish mercenaries employed by the second-century Ptolemies—a tissue of unsupported conjectures.

The two narratives, in short, move in drastically different directions. For Strabo, the Jews left Egypt on their own initiative and of their own accord, in order to promote a purer form of worship, devoid of Gentile idolatry. For Lysimachus, the Jews themselves were the impure, polluting the temples with their presence, had to be expelled from the country, and then compounded their sacrilege with further desecration. Such presentations undergird the idea of bipolar pagan approaches to Judaism.

The matter is not so simple. A closer look at the texts of Strabo and Lysimachus breaks down the bold antithesis. How far does Strabo present an authentic pro-Jewish line and Lysimachus an antisemitic one? Strabo, in fact, while expressing a high opinion of Moses and ascribing noble motives to those who exited from Egypt, also finds progressive deterioration in the character and behavior of Jews in subsequent generations. Moses' initial successors held to his model of righteousness and piety, but later priests fell into superstition and aggressive behavior, promoting abhorrent dietary laws and circumcision. The rulers of Judaea engaged in plunder and seizure of land not only in their own country but in neighboring territories, even subjugating much of Syria and Phoenicia.[18] Strabo plainly found offensive the actions of the later Hasmonaeans, the transformation of priestly leadership into kingly rule, and the aggressive expansionism that marked Judaean policy from the later second century B.C.E. to the intervention of Pompey.[19] The idea of falling away from a golden age of admirable leaders to that of unworthy successors is, of course, a commonplace in classical literature and philosophy. Nor was Strabo the first to apply that schema to the history of the Jews.[20] The topos carries little weight as history. But it supplies a critical clue on Strabo's attitude toward Jews closer to his own day. The Greek geographer plainly did not convey his laudatory version of the Exodus in order to celebrate the qualities of contemporary Jews. To judge this account as motivated by pro-Jewish sympathies misses the point.

A comparable assessment can be made on the other side, with regard to Lysimachus. His Exodus narrative delivers a severe verdict on Jewish behavior, ostensibly reflecting retaliation by Egyptian intellectuals for the defamatory version in the Bible. Yet even Lysimachus' treatment betrays some grudging

---

18 Strab., 16.2.37: ἔπειτῷ ἐφισταμένων ἐπὶ τὴν ἱερωσύνην τὸ μὲν πρῶτον δεισιδαιμόνων, ἔπειτα τυραννικῶν ἀνθρώπων...οἱ μὲν γὰρ ἀφιστάμενοι τὴν χώραω ἐκάκουν καὶ αὐτὴν καὶ τὴν γειτνιῶσαν, οἱ δὲ συμπράττοντες τοῖς ἄρχουσι καθήρπαζον τὰ ἀλλότρια καὶ τῆς Συρίας κατεστρέφοντο καὶ τῆς Φοινίκης πολλήν.
19 Strab., 16.2.40. The formulation of Schäfer ("Exodus Tradition"), 23, that "Strabo becomes a bit less pro-Jewish" misconceives the matter.
20 One can find a parallel interpretation in Diod. 40.3.8.

admiration. He reports that the Jews survived hardship and near death in the desert, were rallied by Moses to run the risk of pressing on, and eventually exercised power and sovereignty in Judaea.[21] Here too, therefore, the notion that this work conveys pure spleen against the Jews overstates and distorts the case. It would be wise to apply some skepticism to the thesis that these variants of the Exodus drama represent either simple denunciation of or apologia for the Jews.

Another text serves to underscore the point. Pompeius Trogus, a Romanized Gaul, writing in Latin in the age of Augustus, composed a wide-ranging and massive history of Greek and Near Eastern affairs, concentrating upon the Hellenistic kingdoms, a work preserved only in a summary version by the much later compiler Justin. Trogus was, therefore, a contemporary of Strabo, and possibly of Lysimachus.[22] In the course of his discussion of Seleucid history in Syria in the later second century B.C.E., Trogus offers an excursus on early Jewish history.

Unlike most Graeco-Roman writers, Trogus knows that the Hebrews had a history prior to Moses—or, at least, the tradition about a history. He has heard about a patriarchal period, he locates Jewish origins in Damascus, he speaks of early Jewish rulers who included Abraham and Israhel, evidently Jacob, and he transmits a highly condensed account of Joseph's experiences in Egypt.[23] More to the point, Trogus supplies a noteworthy rendition of the Exodus. In his view, Moses was the son of Joseph, an error of course but not an especially egregious one. In the Book of Exodus, the Moses story follows almost directly upon that of Joseph—although the text does insert a sentence about much fruitful multiplying in between.[24] Trogus proceeds to describe Moses not only as having inherited Joseph's knowledge but as possessing a most handsome countenance. The Exodus story then follows in abbreviated form, a version with some familiar and some unfamiliar features. The Egyptians, in Trogus' variant, afflicted with leprosy and other skin diseases, took oracular advice and expelled Moses and others suffering from ailments, lest the pestilence spread further. Moses then assumed leadership of the exiles and took them out of Egypt—making off with a number of Egyptian sacred objects as they went. The Jews headed

---

21 Jos. *C. Ap* . 1.308–311: Μωυσῆν τινα συμβουλεῦσαι αὐτοῖς παραβαλλομένους μίαν ὁδὸν τέμνειν ἄχρις ἂν ὅτου ἔλθωσιν εἰς τόπους οἰκουμένους... ἱκανῶς δὲ ὀχληθέντας ἐλθεῖν εἰς τὴν οἰκουμένην χῶραν... ὕστερον δ᾽αὐτοὺς ἐπικρατήσαντας. Elsewhere Lysimachus passed harsh judgment on Moses as lawgiver; Jos. *C. Ap*. 2.145.
22 A translation of Justin's epitome by J. C. Yardley includes useful introductory material by R. Develin, *Justin: Epitome of the Philippic History of Pompeius Trogus* (Atlanta, 1994), 1–10.
23 Justin, 36.2.1–10.
24 Justin, 36.2.11; Exodus, 1.6–7.

for Damascus, stopping at Mt. Sinai on the way, and creating the Sabbath to commemorate the end of their hunger in the Arabian desert. They began the practice of keeping themselves apart from other peoples, recalling that their expulsion had been due to Egyptian fear of contamination by plague.[25]

A detailed critique of Trogus' text would here serve little purpose.[26] But an interesting element in his digression deserves special note. The expulsion of the Jews from Egypt as consequence of leprosy and other diseases, normally considered to be a quintessentially antisemitic ingredient, is presented by Pompeius Trogus in a purely matter of fact fashion, with no polemical overtones. Indeed, the remarks follow directly upon Trogus' praise of Moses not only for his brains but even for his good looks. To be sure, he noted the Jews' theft of Egyptian objects of worship on their way out of the country. But that says no more than the Scriptures themselves, which have the Jews trick their Egyptian neighbors out of some precious articles before making their escape from the land.[27] And Trogus adds an epilogue, observing that the Jewish practice of combining kingship with high-priesthood gave them a blend of justice and religion that led to incredible power.[28]

The labels of philosemitic or antisemitic plainly have no applicability to Pompeius Trogus. The whole conceptual approach needs revision. The categorization of pagan texts that treat the Exodus as standing on one side or another of a hostile exchange is off the mark. The episode of the Exodus held a central place in Jewish consciousness and the self-perception of Jews. But only for them. Writers of the Graeco-Roman world had no comparable stake in the matter. To Gentiles who took notice of it at all, the Exodus constituted little more than a colorful sidelight or the obligatory *origo* in an ethnographic study. And one can go further. Those Hellenic intellectuals in Egypt who happened to know the tale would surely have felt no urge to refute it. Why rehabilitate the villains who represented a regime that the Greeks themselves had eventually supplanted? Egyptians, to be sure, might have had grounds for annoyance—if they were aware of the story. But how far is it likely to have spread outside the synagogues? Would Jews have propagated a narrative that highlighted their flight from Egypt at a time when they sought to establish their credentials as residents? And how ur-

---

25 Justin, 36.2.12 – 15.
26 See the sensible discussion of Gager, *Moses*, 48 – 56. Cf. Schäfer, 24 – 26.
27 Exod. 3.21 – 22, 11.2 – 3, 12.35 – 36.
28 Justin, 36.2.16: "semperque exinde hic mos apud Iudaeos fuit, ut eosdem reges et sacerdotes haberent, quorum iustitia religione permixta incredible quantum coaluere." Trogus or his source evidently assumed here that the political and religious arrangements that held in the later Hasmonaean period could be traced all the way back to the generation after Moses.

gent was it for Greeks and Egyptians to refute a Jewish legend that could safely be ignored or dismissed? It is time to abandon the image of a mudslinging campaign between those sympathetic and those antipathetic to Jews. A fresh approach may be more productive.

For that purpose, we go back to the beginning, i.e. the beginning of pagan interest in the Jewish Exodus from Egypt. The first extant writer to exhibit such interest is readily identifiable: Hecataeus of Abdera, a contemporary of Alexander the Great and Ptolemy I, thus active in the late fourth century B.C.E. Available information on his career and writings is frustratingly sparse, thereby producing a voluminous scholarly literature that dwarfs the ancient testimony. As pupil of the Skeptic Pyrrho, Hecataeus evidently had philosophic as well as historical interests. He traveled and lived for a time in Egypt, an intellectual who profited from the patronage of the court in the age of Ptolemy son of Lagus. Among his works, one at least was composed there, a major study of Egyptian history, culture, and traditions. From that work, in all probability, comes a lengthy extract concerning the Jews that includes a version of the Exodus.[29]

The fragment that survives comes at third hand. Diodorus quoted it, and his text, in turn, is preserved by Photius. How much condensation has taken place and how far the extant material has been pieced together rather than belonging together in the original remain beyond proof. Nonetheless, the transmitted text can be taken as a generally reliable indicator of the author's attitude. Hecataeus records a plague that afflicted the land of Egypt. Its severity drove the populace to interpret it as divine wrath. They concluded that ancestral religious practices

---

29 See Diod 1.46.8; Jos. *C. Ap.* 1.183. Josephus' claim that Hecataeus wrote a book entirely devoted to the Jews has generated a long and probably undying controversy. This is not the place to explore it, nor is it relevant to the subject at hand, for the fragments quoted by Josephus do not bear on the Exodus. A powerful argument against authenticity is delivered by Bar-Kochva, *Pseudo-Hecataeus*, 54–121. For a summary of recent scholarship on the topic, see Pucci ben Zeev, 217–224. On Hecataeus himself, the literature is immense. See, among the more important works, F. Jacoby, "Hekataios," *Real-encyclopädie der klassischen Altertumswissenschaft,* vol. 7 (1912), 2750–2769; W. Jaeger, *Diokles von Karystos* (Berlin, 1938), 134–153: O. Murray, "Hecataeus of Abdera and Pharaonic Kingship," *Journal of Egyptian Archaeology* 56 (1970): 141–171; Fraser, *Ptolemaic Alexandria,* vol. 7, 496–505; Gager, *Moses,* 26–37; B. Z. Wacholder, *Eupolemus* (Cincinnati, 1974), 85–96; F. H. Diamond, "Hecataeus of Abdera and the Mosaic Constitution," in S. M. Burstein and L. A. Okin (eds.), *Panhellenica: Essays in Ancient History and Historiography in Honor of Truesdell S. Brown* (Lawrence, Kansas, 1980), 77–95; J.-D. Gauger, "Zitate in der jüdischen Apologetik und die Authentizität der Hekataios-Passagen bei Flavius Josephus und im Ps. Aristeas-Brief," *Journal for the Study of Judaism,* 13 (1982): 6–46; E. Will and C. Orrieux, *Ioudaismos-Hellènismos: essai sur le judaisme judéen à l'epoque hellénistique* (Nancy, 1986), 83–93; Gabba (n. 4), 624–630; G. E. Sterling, *Historiography and Self-Definition: Josephus, Luke-Acts, and Apologetic Historiography* (Leiden, 1992), 59–91.

were no longer being consistently observed, for there were too many foreigners in the land engaged in alien rites and rituals. Hence they called for removal of the strangers in their midst.[30] The non-Egyptians were forthwith expelled from the country, the most eminent and energetic among them landing in Greece and certain other places, under the leadership of Danaus and Cadmus. But the larger number of exiles were driven to an uninhabited land later called Judaea. Moses brought them there, a man of exemplary wisdom and courage, and responsible both for the founding of Jerusalem and for the installation of the Temple.[31] Hecataeus proceeds to ascribe to Moses a host of admirable political, religious, social, and economic institutions, including division of the people into twelve tribes, enforcement of aniconic worship, appointment of distinguished persons who would serve both as priests and heads of state, assignment of land to settlers, establishment of marriage and burial practices, and promotion of military training.[32]

The laudatory character of that presentation appears to prevail. And Hecataeus of Abdera has been reckoned by many scholars as the fountainhead for the favorable pagan tradition on the Jews. His gloss on the Exodus story and his admiration for Moses' achievement would seem to qualify as the paradigmatic positive assessment by Gentiles of Jewish principles and traditions.[33] Hecataeus' acquaintance with the tale apparently indicates serious interest in the history of the Jews and the origins of their teachings. It has even been claimed that he includes in his discussion a phrase that was lifted from the Pentateuch: "a postscript to the laws at their conclusion stated that Moses declared these measures to the Jews, having heard them from God."[34]

Focus upon Hecataeus' sympathies, however, diverts attention from the larger implications of his text. Hecataeus did not write to advance a brief for the Jews. His treatment of them comes only as a digression in a broader study devoted to Egyptian culture. And his attitude toward Judaism is by no means unrelievedly appreciative. In a much discussed passage, Hecataeus describes the Jewish way of life as somewhat antisocial and hostile to others—albeit as consequence

---

30 Diod. 40.3.2 – 3.
31 Ibid., 40.3.2 – 3.
32 Ibid., 40.3.3 – 8.
33 So, e. g., Jaeger, *Diokles*, 144 – 153; idem, "Greeks and Jews," *Journal of Relligion* 18 (1938): 139 – 143; Will-Orrieux, *Ioudaismos-Hellènismos*, 90 – 93; Gabba (n.4), 624 – 630; Sterling, *Historiography and Self-Definition*, 78 – 80; Feldman, *Jew and Gentile*, 234 – 236.
34 Diod. 40.3.6: προσγέγραπται δὲ καὶ τοῖς νόμοις ἐπὶ τελευτῆς ὅτι. Μωσῆς ἀκούσας τοῦ θεοῦ τάδε λέγει τοῖς Ἰουδαίοις. Cf. Lev. 26 – 46, 27.34; Num. 26.13; Deut. 29.1. The parallel is not close enough to be decisive.

of their own experience of banishment. However one interprets the phraseology, it amounts to rather less than a ringing endorsement.[35] Further, Hecataeus' description of emigration from Egypt identifies those who went to Greece as the most eminent and most vigorous, whereas those who headed for Judaea were simply "the vast majority."[36] This too hardly adds luster to the Jewish experience. And most telling is a passage which has received surprisingly little attention. Hecataeus notes that when the High Priest announces directives from God in political assemblies or other gatherings, the Jews are so submissive that they immediately fall to the ground when he interprets those directives for them. Hecataeus' use of the word προσκυνεῖν particularly warrants notice. For Greeks, the act of προσκύνησις before a man was a mark of barbaric servility.[37] None of this implies animosity on Hecataeus' part, let alone antisemitism.[38] To label Hecataeus in terms of his attitude towards the Jews is simply beside the point.

A more marked characteristic stands out in Hecataeus' account: the sheer volume of misinformation therein. The segment on the Jews contains numerous errors, inaccuracies, and misconceptions. To list only the most egregious ones: that the Jews occupied an uninhabited land; that Moses founded Jerusalem and erected the Temple; that he conceived God as a globe-encircling heaven which ruled the universe; that the Jews were never governed by kings; that the

---

35 Diod. 40.3.4: διὰ γὰρ τὴν ἰδίαν ξενηλασίαν ἀπάνθρωπόν τινα καὶ μισόξενον βίον εἰσηγήσατο (Moses). A most generous appraisal of the passage by Gabba, 629. Note also Jaeger, *Diokles*, 148–149; Diamond, *Panhellenica*, 85–86; Will-Orrieux, *Ioudaismos-Hellènismos*, 92–93. A more negative interpretation by J. N. Sevenster, *The Roots of Pagan Anti-Semitism in the Ancient World* (Leiden, 1975), 188–190; cf. V. Tcherikover, *Hellenistic Civilization and the Jews* (New York, 1959), 360–361; J. Mélèze-Modrzejewski, "L'image du Juif dans la pensée grecque vers 300 avant notre ère," in A. Kasher et al. (eds.), *Greece and Rome in Eretz Israel* (Jerusalem, 1990), 111; Feldman, *Jew and Gentile*, 126; Schäfer, 11–12. A balanced treatment by Bar-Kochva, *Pseudo-Hecataeus*, 39–40, with extensive bibliography.
36 Diod. 40.3.2: οἱ μὲν ἐπιφανέστατοι καὶ δραστικώτατοι... ὁ δὲ πολὺς λέως.
37 Ibid., 40.3.6: τοῦτον δὲ κατὰ τὰς ἐκκλησίας καὶ τὰς ἄλλας συνόδους φησὶν ἐκφέρειν τὰ παραγγελλόμενα, καὶ πρὸς τοῦτο τὸ μέρος οὕτως εὐπιθεῖς γίνεσθαι τοὺς Ἰουδαίους ὥστε παραχρῆμα πίπτοντας ἐπὶ τὴν γῆν προσκυνεῖν τὸν τούτοις ἑρμηνεύοντα ἀρχιερέα. Controversy over attempted introduction of the Persian practice of proskynesis plagued the expedition of Alexander the Great, a contemporary of Hecataeus; see, especially, Arrian, 4.10.5–4.12.5; Curt. Ruf. 8.5.5–24, 8.7.13; Plut. *Alex.* 54–55, 74.1–2.
38 The concluding lines of the excerpt report that many of the Jews' ancestral practices were upset through their mingling with other nations in the time of the Persian and then the Macedonian overlordship; Diod. 40.3.8. But this is almost certainly Diodorus, not Hecataeus, speaking. The latter, writing in the late fourth century, would be in no position to assess the effects of Macedonian rule.

High Priest was chosen for his superiority in virtue and wisdom.[39] And, most central for our purposes, vast discrepancies exist between the Biblical narrative of the Exodus and the version conveyed by Hecataeus. They have remarkably little in common.

Wherein lies the basis for Hecataeus' adaptation? As has long been recognized, the form and structure of the presentation owe much to standard Greek folk-tales about colonization, the founding of settlements abroad, and the establishment of institutions to govern the lives of the settlers. Moses therefore fits the pattern of the οἰκιστής or κτίστης. Hecataeus, in fact, employs the language characteristically applied to the leading out of a colony and the foundation of cities.[40] The schema makes it easy to see why Hecataeus would assume that the man who brought the Israelites out of Egypt would also have been responsible for founding Jerusalem and the Temple. The *interpretatio Graeca* pervades the presentation. Moses' measures on allocation of land and inalienability of the lots, the training of youth for military service, even the exhortation to Jews to keep themselves apart and their practices distinct from other peoples strongly recall the image of the Spartan system. Other elements, such as the equation of an encircling heaven with the deity, an elitist priesthood with special privileges that governed the land, and a broad-gauged set of laws that regulated public and religious practices, all suggest the influence of Greek philosophy and political theory.[41] The juxtaposition of Jewish migration and the legendary voyages of Danaus and Cadmus to Greece thus underscores the Hellenic character of the narrative. Jewish traditions have at best a marginal role.

The Greek shape of the narrative, however, does not account for everything. Hecataeus relied heavily upon Egyptian informants for the work as a whole, a study of the history, traditions, and culture of the land which stressed above

---

39 Diod. 40.3.3 – 5. The efforts of Bar-Kochva, *Pseudo-Hecataeus*, 25 – 33, to explain away all these inaccuracies as mere errors in dating and sequence of institutions and events are unconvincing.

40 Diod. 40.3.3: ἡγεῖτο δὲ τῆς ἀποικίας ὁ προσαγορευόμενος Μωσῆς... ἄλλας τε πόλεις ἔκτισε καὶ τὴν νῦν οὖσαν ἐπιφανεστάτην, ὀνομαζομένην Ἱεροσόλυμα. Diodorus himself, in introducing the Hecataean fragment, refers to the establishment of the nation from its beginnings as κτίσις; 40.3.1. Cf. the discussion of Bar-Kochva, *Pseudo-Hecataeus*, 25 – 33.

41 The Hellenic influence in Hecataeus' formulation has been widely and variously noticed. See Jaeger, *Diokles*, 144 – 153; idem, "Greeks and Jews," 40 – 43; Murray, "Hecataeus of Abdera", 158; M. Hengel, *Judaism and Hellenism* (London, 1974), 255 – 256; Gager, *Moses*, 31 – 34; E. Bickerman, *The Jews in the Greek Age* (Cambridge, Mass., 1988), 16 – 18; Gabba, 627 – 629; Bar-Kochva, *Pseudo-Hecataeus*, 29 – 39. Numerous parallels between Greek and Israelite foundation stories have been discerned by M. Weinfeld, *The Promise of the Land* (Berkeley, 1993), 1 – 51, but none directly applicable to the Hecataeus narrative.

all its place as fountainhead for civilizations all over the Mediterranean and the Near East.[42] An Egyptian substratum certainly underlies the digression on the Jews. In fact, it incorporates two separate strands, both rooted in national pride. On the one hand, the notion of foreign rites and customs diminishing respect for Egypt's religious traditions, bringing a plague from the gods, and requiring removal of aliens reflects common Egyptian attitudes: the land needs to be purged of foreign pollution in order to appease divine wrath.[43] On the other, dispatch of Cadmus and Danaus to Greece and Moses to Judaea also reinforced the idea that those cultures owed their ultimate derivation to Egypt. The impetus for the story therefore came from Hecataeus' Egyptian informants, not from the Book of Exodus.

But there is more to be said. Hecataeus was not innocent of contact with Jews. Neither the Hellenic echoes nor the Egyptian conceptualization can explain the data on the Jews, however garbled and confused, which Hecataeus transmitted. These include the Jewish sojourn in Egypt, Moses as leader and lawgiver, the division of the people into twelve tribes, the prohibition on images of the deity, the central role of the High Priest, and perhaps even a paraphrase from the Scriptures. All of these items must have been obtained through oral communication with Egyptian Jews. The deduction is incontrovertible, and generally acknowledged.[44] But it creates a dilemma. If Hecataeus drew much of his data from knowledgeable Jews, why are there such sharp discrepancies between Jewish traditions, practices, and belief on the one hand and their representation by Hecataeus on the other—not to mention the contrast between his account and that in the Book of Exodus? It will not do to ascribe to Jewish informants only those details in Hecataeus' text that are accurate, while assigning the rest to ma-

---

42 See Sterling, *Historiography and Self-Definition*, 64 – 75.

43 Cf. Jaeger, *Diokles*, 144; J. Yoyotte, "L'Égypte ancienne et les origines de l'antijudaisme," *Revue de l'Histoire des Religions*, 103 (1963): 140; D. B. Redford, *Pharaonic King-Lists, Annals, and Day Books* (Mississauga, Ontario, 1986), 276 – 281; Will-Orrieux, *Ioudaismos-Hellenismos*, 83.

44 See, e. g., Jaeger, *Diokles*, 146; F. Jacoby, *Die Fragmente der griechischen Historiker* (Leiden, 1943), IIIa, 264, 50 – 51; Gager, *Moses*, 37. Wacholder, *Eupolemus*, 91 – 92, even speculates that Hecataeus visited Jews in Palestine. For Diamond, *Panhellenica* 81, 87, all of Hecataeus' information came from a "reliable Jewish source." But she does not specify how or in what form. That the Greek historian had any direct knowledge of the Bible is highly unlikely, the Septuagint did not yet exist. Aristobulus, to be sure, claims that earlier translations of the Hebrew had circulated; Eusebius, *PE*, 13.12.1. But Aristobulus had a special axe to grind: the postulate of earlier translations was required to support his thesis that Jewish writings influenced Greek thinkers like Pythagoras and Plato. The allusions to prior Greek renditions of the Bible in the *Letter of Aristeas*, 314 – 316, are mere fables.

licious Egyptians, Hellenic formulas, or Hecataeus' own errors. That is too easy. And it should now be abundantly clear that the question of whether the Greek historian was favorable or unfavorable to the Jews is quite irrelevant and devoid of meaning.

A very different proposition needs to be considered. The Diaspora Jews themselves may have had a hand in molding even the non-traditional parts of the story, thereby to have a better fit with the cultural milieu in which they found themselves. It would be a gross error to assume that Jewish intellectuals adhered rigidly to the Exodus tale as it appears in the Bible and that departures from it represent manipulation by Gentiles. Variants on the story may in fact owe more to Jewish ingenuity than we customarily allow.[45] The portrayal of Moses' leadership as based on φρόνησις and ἀνδρεία, the selection of the governing class for their outstanding merit and ability, and the Exodus as issuing in the establishment of a religious and political center as well as a Temple could well be adaptation of the scriptural narrative by Hellenized Jews themselves. The concepts would strike familiar chords to those of the Diaspora brought up in an atmosphere pervaded by Greek culture. It is time to question the idea that pagans were primarily responsible for reshaping or misshaping the Biblical Exodus for polemical purposes. On the contrary. Few of them would have had the occasion, interest or motivation to do so.[46] The Jews played a large part in the refashioning of their own past.[47]

---

45 D. Mendels, "Hecataeus of Abdera and a Jewish *patris politeia* of the Persian Period (Diodorus Siculus XL, 3)," *Zeitschrift für die Alttestamentliche Wissenschaf* 95 (1983): 96–110, offers the inventive and intriguing suggestion that Hecataeus' material came from Jewish priestly circles in the late fourth century who represent the ideology of the Persian period as reflected in the books of Ezra and Nehemiah. Mendels finds a number of provocative parallels. But the argument too often rests on strained conjectures. It is not easy to believe, for instance, that Jewish priests in the Persian period promulgated the idea of Moses as founder of Jerusalem and the Temple in order to diminish the stature of the Davidic kingdom. Nor can one readily concur with the idea that a downplaying of David's line translated itself into a denial that the Jews ever had a king. Still less probable is the notion that Moses' supposed measures on military training and land distribution reflect the actual policies of Nehemiah with a mere overlay of *interpretatio Graeca*. Mendels properly recognizes that Jews played a part in revamping the tradition that appears in the Bible. But he fails to explain how priestly opinions in Judaea would have reached Hecataeus in Egypt.

46 On Greek attitudes to foreigners' accounts of their own origins generally, see E. J. Bickerman, "Origines Gentium," *Classical Philology,* 47 (1952): 68–73.

47 D. R. Schwartz, "Diodorus Siculus 40.3—Hecataeus or Pseudo-Hecataeus?" in A. Oppenheimer and M. Mor, Jews and Gentiles in the Holy Land in the Days of the Second Temple, the Mishnah, and the Talmud (Jerusalem, 2003) 181–198, maintains that the entire fragment actually derives from a Jewish "Pseudo-Hecataeus" of the late Hasmonaean period. This is not the place

The hypothesis can be pursued through a different avenue. The Egyptian priest Manetho (first half of the third century) sketches a portrait of the Exodus that diverges widely from that of Hecataeus. The Jews possess a rather positive image in Hecataeus' narrative, although, as we have seen, that does not explain the author's objective. Manetho, by contrast, supplies an account that earned him the label of the first of the pagan antisemites, source of the Egyptian counter-history of the Exodus. It will pay dividends to examine how the legend fares in the hands of Manetho—or, more properly, what form it takes in a text which has been ascribed, on disputed authority, to Manetho.

A welter of textual, biographical, source-critical, and historical problems confront any researcher who treads on this slippery terrain. We focus mercifully upon those elements of Manetho's work that bear on the Exodus and its variants. Little enough is known of his life, and not all of that fully reliable. A Hellenized Egyptian intellectual, he attained priestly rank in the reign of Ptolemy I Soter or Ptolemy II Philadelphus, probably at Heliopolis, and took part in establishing or developing the cult of Sarapis in Alexandria. Most important, he authored influential works in Greek, notably his *Aigyptiaka,* addressed to Philadelphus, a political and religious history of his native land from its beginnings down to the eve of the Hellenistic period.[48] Two long extracts in Josephus purportedly derive from that work and appear to relate versions that connect to the Exodus of Hebrews from Egypt. Both are mired in controversies that cannot here be settled. Nor is it necessary to settle them in order to discern the texts' value in illuminating perceptions of the Exodus story.

The first extract, from Josephus, can in fact be disposed of briefly. Manetho recounts an assault on Egypt by invaders of obscure origin from the east who conquered the land without a blow. They overcame the rulers of the country, burned cities ruthlessly, destroyed temples, oppressed the natives, installed garrisons, and exacted tribute. Their king Salitis established a capital at Avaris, fortifying it to protect the frontier. The invaders ruled through six generations of kings, their race known as Hyksos, which connotes some form of shepherds,

---

to review his incisive and attractive but ultimately unpersuasive arguments. If he is right, of course, this would only strengthen the case made here.

48 A reliable summary of what is known or conjectured about Manetho's life and career in W. G. Waddell's Loeb edition, *Manetho* (Cambridge, Mass., 1940), vii-xxvii. See also R. Laqueur, "Manetho," *Real-encyclopädie der klassischen Altertumswissenschaft,* vol. 14 (1928), 1060–1101; Fraser, *Ptolemaic Alexandria,* vol. 1, 505–510; Sterling, *Historiography and Self-Definition,* 117–135. Scholarship is usefully summarized by Pucci ben Zeev, 224–234. See also the interesting thesis by D. Mendels, "The Polemical Character of Manetho's *Aegyptiaca,*" *Studia Hellenistica* 30 (1990): 91–110.

and their aim was to stamp out the Egyptian stock. The "shepherds" held sway for more than five centuries, until the Egyptians rose up to overthrow their oppressors, drive them to confinement in Avaris, and eventually arrange their departure from Egypt through a negotiated treaty. The shepherds then migrated *en masse,* 240,000 strong, and crossed the desert to Syria, where they built the city of Jerusalem in Judaea.[49]

Whether this narrative has anything whatever to do with the Biblical Exodus is questionable. In essence, Manetho simply retails the Hyksos' invasion and occupation of Egypt, a central feature of his nation's history. Josephus, not Manetho, makes the connection with the Jews. And Josephus has a special axe to grind. He proposes to dispel Greek doubts about the antiquity of the Jews by pointing to Egyptian and Phoenician writings that attest to his people in the remote past. Manetho serves as prime exhibit for Josephus' partisan purposes.[50] Manetho himself, it bears repeating, makes no explicit identification of Hyksos with Jews in the quoted fragment. That is left to Josephus. The reference to Jerusalem does, to be sure, evoke an association with Jews.[51] But even if it belongs in Manetho's original text (a disputed proposition), this hardly affects the principal issue. His story of Hyksos departing for Judaea under a negotiated truce carries not the faintest resemblance to the Book of Exodus. For our purposes, it can safely be set aside.[52]

Manetho's second excerpt has greater relevance and higher significance. The narrative is drawn, according to Josephus, not from priestly records but from invented stories and rumors.[53] The Jewish historian introduces this segment by as-

---

49 Jos. *C. Ap.* 1.75 – 90.

50 Ibid., 1.69 – 74, 1.103 – 104, 1.228.

51 Ibid., 1.90, 1.94, cf. 1.228.

52 Josephus could plausibly seize upon the term "shepherds" for his objectives, since the Hebrews in the time of Joseph's migration to Egypt were shepherds; cf. Genesis, 46 – 34, 47.3. And it is possible that the name of the Hyksos' first ruler, Salitis, reflects the title of *shalit* that Joseph took as governor of Egypt; Genesis, 42.6. But the absence of any mention of Jews by Manetho in this passage remains the central fact. It takes a real stretch to find contact with the Exodus tale. A valuable review of earlier scholarship appears in L. Troiani, "Sui frammenti di Manetone," *Studi classici e orientali* 24 (1975): 98 – 100, n. 3. Some of the more recent literature is cited by Pucci ben Zeev, 225 – 226. The case for a connection between Manetho's Hyksos and the Hebrews is made, among others, by Tcherikover, *Hellenistic Civilization and the Jews,* 362 – 363; Stern, *Greek and Latin Authors,* vol. 1, 62 – 63; Sevenster, *Roots of Pagan Anti-Semitism,* 186 – 188; Kasher, *Jews in Hellenistic and Roman Egypt,* 328 – 330; Pucci ben Zeev, 225 – 230; Bar-Kochva, *Image of the Jews.* The skeptics include Laqueur, 1066 – 1070; A. Momigliano, "Intorno al *Contro Apione,*" *Rivista di Filologia,* 9 (1931): 497 – 502; Jacoby, *Fragmente* III C, 609, 84; Troiani, 103 – 110; Gabba, 631 – 632; Aziza, 49 – 50.

53 Jos. *C. Ap.* 1.229: τὰ μυθευόμενα καὶ λεγόμενα; cf. 1.105.

serting that Manetho maliciously amalgamated Jews with the mob of Egyptian lepers and those with other afflictions who were banished from Egypt. He then proceeds to reproduce a substantial text ascribed to Manetho. The text has the Egyptian Pharaoh Amenophis, of uncertain date and place in the sequence of kings, manifest a desire to witness the gods themselves directly. That feat would be possible, a wise counselor advised him, only if he purged Egypt of all lepers and other polluted persons. The king thereupon gathered the afflicted people, 80,000 of them, set them to work in the stone quarries where they would not contaminate the rest of the population, then later allowed them to occupy the abandoned city of Avaris, sacred to the pernicious god Typhon, enemy of Osiris. The impure then appointed as their leader a certain Osarsiph, one of the priests of Heliopolis, who bound his people by oath and promulgated legislation forbidding them to worship Egyptian gods and indeed enjoining them to sacrifice and feast upon all animals sacred to the Egyptians. The aggressive enactments issued in even greater aggressive action. Osarsiph prepared his followers for rebellion and war, summoning to their aid the shepherd people, 20,000 strong, former occupants of Avaris and now dwelling in Jerusalem. Together the rebels and the shepherds forced Amenophis onto the defensive. The king, fearful because of a prophet's prediction, declined battle and withdrew his army, his family, as many sacred animals as he could collect, and a multitude of Egyptians across the border to Ethiopia where they dwelled in exile for thirteen years. In the meanwhile, the polluted Egyptians and their allies from Jerusalem went on a rampage, plundering the land, burning cities and villages, robbing temples, defacing images of the gods, persecuting priests and prophets, and using the sanctuaries themselves to roast the sacred animals of the Egyptians. Osarsiph, the Heliopolitan priest who had taken his name from Osiris and who authored a constitution and laws, chose to adopt the new appellation of Moses. And Manetho concludes the tale with a postscript, adding that at a later time Amenophis with his now grown son returned from Ethiopia with large forces, defeated the shepherds and their polluted comrades, driving them out of Egypt to the borders of Syria.[54]

Such is the gist of Manetho's—or perhaps pseudo-Manetho's—presentation. How should one interpret or characterize it? For many scholars, it represents an exemplar of Egyptian anti-semitism, a hostile twist on the Exodus tale, a reversal of that story, an upside-down Exodus in which the Jews serve as the powers of evil and the Egyptians as the innocent and victimized, Moses the tyrant who tramples upon tradition and terrorizes the land of Egypt until he and his villain-

---

54 Ibid., 1.230–251.

ous compatriots are driven out by the resurgent and ultimately triumphant Egyptians. Manetho's text thus delivered a stinging reply to the Book of Exodus and generated the counter-tradition that flowed into tracts like those of Lysimachus, Chaeremon, and Apion.[55] That thesis, widely adopted and influential, is less than compelling. A reconsideration is warranted.

Authorship of the second fragment itself has stimulated controversy, a long-standing dispute. Is it genuine Manetho or pseudo-Manetho?[56] The debate can be happily avoided. Decision on the question does not affect the main issue. Does the extract, in fact, constitute an inverted Exodus, an antisemitic response to the Biblical tale? A closer look raises doubts. The Jews as such do not appear in the narrative. The polluted persons are Egyptians, placed in the quarries to segregate them from other Egyptians; indeed some of the lepers were Egyptian priests.[57] Manetho's reference to the Σολυμῖται need mean no more than the inhabitants of Jerusalem; the text refrains from indicting Jews as a nation.[58] Explicit association of the Jews with lepers and the impure is attributed to Manetho by Josephus but does not surface in the quoted text.[59] Manetho indeed explicitly distinguishes the polluted persons who are Egyptians from the Jerusalemites who come to their aid.[60] The equation of Osarsiph with Moses might seem decisive for Manetho's attitude. But the equation itself is a jarring intrusion in the narra-

---

55 So, e.g., Tcherikover, *Hellenistic Civilization and the Jews,* 361 – 364; Stern, *Greek and Latin Authors,* 64; Sevenster, *Roots of Pagan Anti-Semitism,* 186 – 188; Kasher, "The Propaganda Goals of Manetho's Accusations in the Matter of the Low Origins of the Jews," in B. Oded et al. (eds.), *Studies in the History of the Jewish People and the Land of Israel* (Haifa, 1974), vol. 3, 69 – 84 (Hebrew); idem, *Jews in Hellenistic and Roman Egypt,* 327 – 332; Funkenstein (n.4), 59; idem, *Perceptions of Jewish History,* 36 – 40; Aziza, 54 – 55; Mendels, "Creative History in the Hellenistic Near East in the Third and Second Centuries BCE: The Jewish Case," *Journal for the Study of the Pseudepigrapha,* 2 (1988): 16; idem, "Polemical Character," 103 – 109; Pucci ben Zeev, 233; Bar-Kochva, *Image of the Jews.* A somewhat peculiar twist on this theory occurs in A. Catastini, "Le testimonianze di Manetone e la 'storia di Giuseppe' (Genesis 37 – 50)," *Henoch* 17 (1995), 279 – 300, who has Manetho respond to the Exodus story but then sees the Joseph tale in Genesis as a counter-retort in the polemic.
56 Doubts about authenticity have been expressed, e.g., by E. Meyer, *Aegyptische Chronologie* (Berlin, 1904), 71; Laqueur, 1070 – 1080; Momigliano, 490 – 495; Gabba, 632 – 633; Bickerman, *Jews in the Greek Age,* 224 – 225.
57 Jos. *C. Ap.* 1.233 – 235: τῶν ἄλλων Αἰγυπτίων εἶεν κεχωρισμένοι. εἶναι δέ τινας ἐν αὐτοῖς καὶ τῶν λογίων ἱερέων φησὶ λέπρᾳ συνεχομένους.
58 Ibid., 1.248: οἱ δὲ Σολυμῖται κατελθόντες σὺν τοῖς μιαροῖς τῶν Αἰμυπτίων; cf. 1.241: ποιμένας εἰς πόλιν τὴν καλουμένην Ἱεροσόλυμα.
59 Ibid., 1.228 – 229: ἀναμῖξαι βουλόμενος ἡμῖν πλῆρθος Αἰγυπτίων λεπρῶν καὶ ἐπὶ ἄλλοις ἀρρωστήμασιν.
60 Ibid., 1.233 – 234, 1.241.

tive, a glaring anomaly that surely did not belong in the original. Manetho had already introduced Osarsiph earlier in the story as priest of Heliopolis and lawgiver. The second introduction with a change of name is mere repetition, unnecessary, and out of place.[61]

The very concept of antisemitism as applied to Manetho grossly oversimplifies the matter. Even Josephus, who goes to great lengths to refute Manetho's narrative, pointing out its inconsistencies, chronological blunders, and self-contradictions, stops short of branding him with anti-Jewish prejudice. He takes Manetho to task for that part of his narrative that abandoned written records and relied on fictitious stories and rumors, thus inducing him to confuse the Israelites with Egyptian lepers and the generally polluted. Manetho did not miss truth by much, according to Josephus, when he relied on the ancient chronicles, but when he turned his attention to inauthentic legends, he either framed implausible tales or trusted those motivated by bias.[62] This does not amount to animus against the Jews, even in Josephus' eyes.[63] Nor is it likely that a work addressed to Ptolemy II would set out an assault on Jews. The reign of that king has come down, at least in Jewish tradition, as one most generous and favorable to the Chosen People.[64]

The point can be driven home even more sharply. Does Manetho's yarn constitute a retort to the biblical Exodus at all? In fact it shares little or nothing with the Scriptures. Only a committed prejudgment could read Manetho as a counterblast to the Jewish tradition. Departure of the "Shepherds" from Egypt in the first fragment came under a negotiated treaty, not as flight or escape. And the second excerpt has the Jerusalemites return to Egypt rather than seek release from it.

---

61 Ibid., 1.238–240: ἡγεμόνα αὐτῶν λεγόμενόν τινα τῶν Ἡλιοπολιτῶν ἱερέων Ὀσάρσιφον ἐστήσαντο...τοιαῦτα δὲ νομοθετήσας; 1.250: λέγεται δὲ ὅτι <ὁ> τὴν πολιτείαν καὶ τοὺς νόμους αὐτοῖς καταβαλόμενος ἱερεὺς τὸ γένος Ἡλιοπολίτης ὄνομα Ὀσαρσὶφ... μετετέθη τοὔνομαι καὶ προσηγορεύθη Μωυσῆς. Cf. Gager, Moses, 117; Schäfer, 15; A. J. Droge, "Josephus between Greeks and Barbarians," in L. H. Feldman and J. R. Levinson (eds.), Josephus' Contra Apionem: Studies in its Character and Context with a Latin Concordance to the Portion Missing in Greek (Leiden, 1996), 134–136; contra: Troiani, 126. The insertion of <ὁ> in the above text might make the idea of an interpolation a little less likely. But that insertion is itself more than questionable. The fact that Osarsiph has to be identified again not only as lawgiver but as Heliopolitan priest points almost inescapably to interpolation. Whether "Osarsiph" is actually a form of "Joseph" need not here be investigated. See Gager, 115, n. 5; Troiani, 113–118; Catastini, 287–288.
62 Jos. C. Ap. 1.228–229, 1.287: Μανέθως ἕως μὲν ἠκολούθει ταῖς ἀρχαίαις ἀναγραφαῖς, οὐ πολὺ τῆς ἀληθείας διημάρτανεν, ἐπὶ δὲ τοὺς ἀδεσπότους μύθους τραπόμενος ἢ συνέθηκεν αὐτοὺς ἀπιθάνως ἢ τισι τῶν πρὸς ἀπέχθειαν εἰρηκότων ἐπίστευσεν.
63 Contrast Josephus' more explicit blast against Lysimachus; Jos. C. Ap. 1.304: συντεθεικὼς κατὰ πολλὴν ἀπέχθειαν. Noted also by Troiani, 111.
64 Let. Aris., passim; Jos. A. J. 12.11–118.

Their eventual expulsion, together with the leprous and diseased Egyptians, appears as an afterthought and epilogue to the story, not at the heart of it. As a twist or parody of the Hebrew Exodus it would fall flat.

One may go further still. An Egyptian rejoinder to the biblical version presumes circulation of the latter in Gentile circles. Yet the Septuagint, even if trust be placed in the legend conveyed by the *Letter of Aristeas,* dates no earlier than the time of Ptolemy II himself. Its effect upon Egyptian intellectuals literate in Greek, if ever it had any, could hardly have been so swift and powerful as to require a refutation by Manetho. One can, of course, postulate earlier versions or oral propagation of portions of the Pentateuch—perhaps even noisy celebrations of the Passover. But such conjectures border on circular reasoning and do not advance matters. The Jews of Egypt had no motivation for disseminating the tale in Gentile circles—nor indeed to emphasize their escape from a land in which they now resided. The version as we have it in Josephus' second extract either belongs to a later time, foisted upon Manetho in order to give it greater authority or, if it is authentic Manetho, has no relation to the Book of Exodus.

In fact, Manetho's narrative fits within an established Egyptian tradition. A potent strain in Egyptian literature fastens blame for evils suffered by the populace upon the impure and the diseased, carriers of pollution. The gathering of the impure in a city devoted to the rival god Typhon or Seth, enemy of Osiris, reinforces the contrast between the good and the wicked. The ravaging of land, pillaging of temples, and sacrilegious sacrificing of the animal deities represent the malevolent enemy in characteristic fashion. The subsequent expulsion of the foreigner gives final victory and vindication to the native forces. Similar sentiments received expression in Middle Kingdom Egypt, and the echoes resonate in Hellenistic texts like the Demotic Chronicle, the Potter's Oracle, and the Prophecy of the Lamb. The traditions had special relevance in the late Egyptian period when inhabitants of the country had suffered a comparable form of religious oppression at the hands of the Persians. Nationalist overtones ring out clearly.[65] The Manethonian tale does not derive from the Exodus or some garbled form of it. In its essentials, it has nothing whatever to do with Jews.

---

65 The Egyptian background to Manetho's story and others similar to it is well brought out by Yoyotte (n. 43), 133–143, and Redford, *Pharaonic King-Lists,* 276–283. But Yoyotte retains the notion that Jews were cast into this villainous role. So also, J.-W. Van Henten and R. Abusch, "The Jews as Typhonlans and Josephus' Strategy of Refutation in *Contra Apionem,*" in Feldman and Levison (eds.), *Josephus' Contra Apionem,* 271–309. For discussions of these texts and others, see C. C. McCown, "Hebrew and Egyptian Apocalyptic Literature," *Harvard Theological Review* 18 (1925): 357–411; S. K. Eddy, *The King is Dead* (Lincoln, 1961), 257–294; J. G. Griffiths, "Apocalyptic in the Hellenistic Era," in D. Hellholm, *Apocalypticism in the Mediterranean World*

How then did Jews enter this tangle of stories? Why should Osarsiph, otherwise a renegade Heliopolitan priest, become identified with Moses? Why should the polluted prisoners at Avaris have received assistance from persons dwelling in Jerusalem? Even those scholars who take the line that direct or indirect allusions to Jews in the narrative are accretions or interpolations, tacked on at a later time, nevertheless agree that the additions stem from antisemitic Egyptians or Greeks eager to set Jews in the guise of the conventional polluter, oppressor, and purveyor of impiety.[66] But what would prompt Graeco-Egyptian writers to cast Jews in this particular mold? Why would they care?

Jewish mercenaries in the army of the Persians have been reckoned as the culprits. But the suggestion that they provoked a hostile misrepresentation has little plausibility. It would not easily explain the longevity of the portrait.[67] The Elephantine garrison, to be sure, could be a source of trouble. Friction arose between the Egyptian priests of the ram-god Khnum and the Jews of Elephantine, resulting in the destruction of the Jewish temple in 410 B.C.E.[68] Did the celebration of the Passover and an emphasis on the Exodus generate this reaction? So it might be surmised.[69] But Passover had certainly been celebrated for some time before the end of the fifth century.[70] And no other evidence exists for strife of this sort during the two or more centuries of the Jewish community at Elephantine. The conflict in 410 may indeed have been connected with an Egyptian revolt against Persian authority.[71]

A different argument traces the negative characterization to friction between Jews and Greeks over citizenship privileges in Alexandria.[72] Even if the friction is real, however, it hardly accounts for a fable that equates Jews with invaders who

---

and the Near East (Tübingen, 1983), 273–293, with useful bibliography; D. Frankfurter, Elijah in Upper Egypt (Minneapolis, 1993), 174–183. On Seth as god of foreigners and emblematic of the enemies of Egypt, at least since Assyrian times, see H. te Velde, Seth. God of Confusion (Leiden, 1967), 109–151. On Persian oppression in Egypt, exaggerated by Greek sources but by no means negligible and punctuated by Egyptian uprisings, see E. Bresciani, "The Persian Occupation of Egypt," in I. Gershevitsh, (ed.), The Cambridge History of Iran (Cambridge, 1985), vol. 2, 502–512, 522–527.

66 So, e.g., Laqueur, 1071–1074; Gager, Moses, 116–118; Gabba, 633.

67 The suggestion is that of Yoyotte, 142–143.

68 A. Crowley, Aramaic Papyri of the Fifth Century BC (Oxford, 1923), #21, 27, 30–33, 37–38.

69 Cf. Porten, Archives from Elephantine, 279–293; idem, in W. D. Davies and L. Finkelstein, The Cambridge History of Judaism (Cambridge, 1984), vol. 1, 388–390; Mélèze-Modrzejewski, The Jews of Egypt, 37–43.

70 See Porten, Archives from Elephantine, 128–133.

71 See Crowley, Aramaic Papyri, #27. The reconstruction of Porten, Archives from Elephantine, 279–281, is highly speculative.

72 Cf. Bickerman, Jews in the Greek Age, 224–225.

devastated the land, terrorized the populace, and assaulted the venerated gods of Egypt. If a quarrel over citizen rights produced so elaborate a scenario, it was surely over-kill. Indeed, the Alexandrian Greeks are most unlikely perpetrators of the portrait. They would have had little incentive to champion the legacy of a native people whom they did not even permit to share their own privileges and prerogatives.[73]

The idea that Egyptians themselves felt resentment over the hostile representation of their ancestors contained in the Book of Exodus might seem to make more sense. But not upon scrutiny. How many of them ever had occasion to read the Book of Exodus? No intelligible version circulated in the time of Manetho. And it helps little to resort to a later "pseudo-Manetho." The Septuagint did not have any discernible impact outside the Jewish communities—let alone among the indigenous inhabitants of Egypt.[74] Moreover, as noted above, Jews had no obvious reason for spreading to Gentile communities a legend that glorified their evacuation of Egypt—a land in which they now sought to establish roots. The idea that the story in the Scriptures roused patriotic passions or ethnic retaliation lacks any sound basis.

An alternative possibility demands a hearing: that introduction of the Jews into Manetho's narrative, as into Hecataeus', came from Jewish sources themselves. A paradoxical idea on the face of it, even altogether implausible one might assume. Would Jews really represent themselves in so ruthlessly negative a fashion? Presumably not. But further probing alters the picture. We need to bear in mind that the story went through at least two or three versions before it reached its present form. We see Manetho's text only as it came to Josephus and through the latter's eyes. That point must be stressed. From the Jewish historian's perspective, Manetho's work was the first of several Egyptian tracts that set out to slander the Jews, distorting the truth both about the Israelites' entrance into Egypt and their evacuation of it.[75] In fact, however, Josephus' specific criticisms of Manetho's version confine themselves to pointing out internal in-

---

73 Cf. Jos. *C. Ap.* 2.29–32.

74 See V. Tcherikover, "Jewish Apologetic Literature Reconsidered," *Eos* 48 (1956), 169–193; cf. A. D. Nock, *Conversion: The Old and the New in Religion from Alexander the Great to Augustine of Hippo* (Oxford, 1933), 79; A. Momigliano, *Alien Wisdom: The Limits of Hellenization* (Cambridge, 1975), 91.

75 Jos. *C. Ap.* 1.223: τῶν δ'εἰς ἡμᾶς βλασφημιῶν ἤρξαντο μὲν Αἰγύπτιοι. Βουλόμενοι δ'ἐκείνοις τινὲς χαρίζεσθαι παρατρέπειν ἐπεχείρησαν τὴν ἀλήθειαν. Οὔτε τὴν εἰς Αἴγυπτον ἄφιξιν ὡς ἐγένετο τῶν ἡμετέρων προγόνων ὁμολογοῦντες, οὔτε τὴν ἔξοδον ἀληθεύοντες.

consistencies, implausibilities, and absurdities. None of them has anything to do with entrance into or exit from Egypt.[76]

Still more significant are Josephus' subsequent remarks. He proceeds to excogitate the motives of those authors whom he seeks to refute: jealousy and hatred of his ancestors because they had ruled Egypt and because they then prospered after return to their own land.[77] These are striking remarks rarely noted or commented upon. Josephus in short accepts the tradition that Jews had taken control of the country of Egypt! That tradition, set in a negative light by the text of Manetho which Josephus sought to ridicule, also has a fundamentally positive side which the Jewish historian found quite acceptable.[78]

To put the matter more pointedly. One can envision an earlier layer slanted to the benefit of the Jews. The coalition of shepherds and rebels overthrew Egyptian rule, drove the Pharaoh and his minions across the border, and held ascendancy for an extended period in that land, a significant military success in which the Jerusalemites could take pride. The most likely fashioners of such a tale are surely Jews themselves. The story, it is true, has the victors plunder and ravage the land, actions painted in lurid colors by Manetho or pseudo-Manetho. But that would not preclude a Jewish origin for the narrative. The destructive deeds inflicted humiliation upon the Egyptians, a demonstration of the conquerors' power. Jewish writers would find satisfaction in recounting or embellishing those elements of the tale. According to the Book of Exodus itself, after all, God authorized the Hebrews to despoil the Egyptians before departing from the land —which they proceeded to do.[79] Desecration of the temples and slaughter of the animals worshipped by Egyptians would also announce the triumph of the Chosen People and their faith. Taking action against rival cults and abhorrent practices had a long tradition among Jews, a sign of supremacy, not a source of shame. One need cite only the imperatives of Deuteronomy, enjoining the Israelites to drive out their foes, destroy them utterly, smash their altars and sacred objects,

---

76 Ibid., 1.254–278.

77 Ibid., 1.224: αἰτίας δὲ πολλὰς ἔλαβον τοῦ μισεῖν καὶ φθονεῖν, τὸ μὲν ἐξ ἀρχῆς ὅτι κατὰ τὴν χώραν αὐτῶν ἐδυνάστευσαν ἡμῶν οἱ πρόγονοι κἀκεῖθεν ἀπαλλαγέντες ἐπὶ τὴν οἰκείαν πάλιν εὐδαιμόνησαν.

78 Cf. ibid., 1.252: δέδωκε γὰρ οὗτος [Manetho] ἡμῖν καὶ ὡμολόγηκεν ἐξ ἀρχῆς τὸ μὴ εἶναι τὸ γένος Αἰγυπτίους, ἀλλ'αὐτοὺς ἔξωθεν ἐπελθόντας κρατῆσαι τῆς Αἰγύπτου καὶ πάλιν ἐξ αὐτῆς ἀπελθεῖν.

79 Exodus, 3.22, 12.36. Only much later did apologetic Jewish writers like Philo and Josephus feel the need to justify or deny the plundering; Philo, *Moses*, 1.140–142; Josephus, *Ant.* 2.314. Cf. I. Lévi, "La dispute entre les Égyptiens et les Juifs," *Revue des Études Juives* 63 (1912), 211–213.

and burn their idols.[80] Such commands were duly fulfilled by Joshua who left a trail of total destruction wherever he went.[81] And the later prophecies of Isaiah included the forecast that the land of Judah would bring terror to the Egyptians themselves.[82] On this reconstruction, therefore, the identification of Osarsiph with Moses and the introduction of Jerusalemites into the story, far from injecting antisemitic elements, represent Jewish expropriation of an Egyptian tradition, thus to establish the claims of Jews to a place of eminence in the history of Egypt.[83]

The rendition, as we have it, must be a composite. At least two quite independent strands are here interwoven: first, a tale of lepers and contaminated persons herded and confined to the city of Seth; and, second, a narrative of Jerusalemites who invaded, conquered, and pillaged the land of Egypt. Who put them together, and when, remains beyond our grasp. But the second strand could easily derive from a Jewish construct.

A form of the story seems to have found its way even among the traditions of Jewish origins reported by Tacitus. One of the tales ascribed by the Roman historian to unidentified sources has the Jews as Assyrian refugees whose paltry land-holdings induced them to leave their country. They migrated to Egypt where they achieved dominance in part of that land.[84]

The idea of an assault by Israelites upon Egypt can, in fact, be found in a Jewish-Hellenistic source. A fragment of Artapanus, little known or commented upon, provides some startling information. The author, a Hellenized Jew from Egypt, writing probably in the second century B.C.E., was quite uninhibited in his recreation of biblical tales—and he was by no means alone.[85] In Artapanus'

---

80 Deut. 7.1–5, 7.25, 12.1–3.

81 E.g. Joshua, 8.24–29, 10.28–40, 11.10–22.

82 Isaiah, 19.16–17.

83 A similar view was proffered long ago by Momigliano, 485–503, and largely ignored in subsequent literature. Momigliano, however, indulges in excessive speculation when seeking to identify separate strands deriving from Egyptians, Jewish interpolators, anti-semites, and philo-semitic refutations. Just which particulars can be assigned to Jewish writers remains unknowable, especially as the surviving versions have come through so many hands. Presumably, however, Jews did not designedly associate themselves with lepers, the diseased, or the adherents of Seth. It is noteworthy, as we have seen, that even Manetho clearly disassociates the lepers from the people of Jerusalem; Jos. *C. Ap.* 1.233–234, 1.241.

84 Tacitus, *Hist.* 5.2.3: "sunt qui tradant Assyrios convenas, indigum agrorum populum, parte Aegypti potitos."

85 On Artapanus, his date, and provenance, see J. Freudenthal, *Alexander Polyhistor* (Breslau, 1875), 143–175; C. Holladay, *Theios Aner in Hellenistic Judaism* (Missoula, 1977), 199–232; Sterling, *Historiography and Self-Definition*, 167–186.

version, the voice from the burning bush instructed Moses to lead an army against Egypt. Moses took heart from this command and determined to assemble a force and make war on the Egyptians.[86] The fragment breaks off shortly thereafter and the outcome is unreported.[87] But it provides direct testimony for a Jewish tradition on mobilization against Egypt.

Hellenistic testimony exists also for the razing of alien temples and altars by Jews. The smashing of pagan shrines, indeed pre-Greek shrines, by the Maccabees is amply attested.[88] Further, a preserved text refers to similar actions in the Persian period evidently in Palestine, and the author explicitly expresses admiration.[89] There can be little doubt that a Jew composed that tale, wrongly ascribed by Josephus to Hecataeus.[90] And, whatever its historicity, it demonstrates a favorable Jewish tradition on the destruction of foreign shrines, an action still worthy of praise in the Hellenistic era.[91] One might recall also that the literature of the Jews in that era did not shrink from recording and applauding what we might regard as Jewish atrocities. In the Book of Esther, Mordecai received permission from the Persian king for his countrymen to slaughter all the people hostile to them in his domains, including women and children, and to plunder their property. The Jews proceeded to cities in various satrapies of the empire and massacred 75,000 people—although they did refrain from the plunder. The event prompted inauguration of a commemorative celebration.[92] In a closely parallel case, III Maccabees portrays triumphant

---

86 Eus. *PE*, 9.27.21 – 22: φωνὴν δ'αὐτῷ θείαν εἰπεῖν στρατεύειν ἐπ'Αἴγυπτον... τὸν δὲ θαρρήσαντα δύναμιν πολεμίαν ἐπάγειν διαγνῶναι τοῖς Αἰγυπτίοις. Cf. also Jos. *A. J.* 2.268: καὶ θαρροῦντα ἐκέλευεν εἰς τὴν Αἴγυπτον ἀπιέναι στρατηγὸν καὶ ἡγεμόνα τῆς Ἑβραίων πληθύος ἐσόμενον.

87 Artapanus has Moses go directly to meet Aaron after the burning bush episode. And the scene then shifts abruptly to the summoning of Moses by Pharaoh; Eus. *PE*, 9.27.22. A break in the text is rightly noted by N. Walter, *Jüdische Schriften aus hellenistisch-römischer Zeit* (Gütersloh, 1.2, 1976), 133, n. 22a.

88 See, e.g., 1 Macc. 5.44, 5.68, 10.83 – 84; 2 Macc. 12.26.

89 Jos. *C. Ap.* 1.193: ἔτι γε μὴν τῶν εἰς τὴν χώραν, φησί, πρὸς αὐτοὺς ἀφικνουμένων νεὼς καὶ βωμοὺς κατασκευασάντων ἅπαντα ταῦτα κατέσκαπτον... ὅτι δίκαιον ἐπὶ τούτοις αὐτοὺς ἐστι θαυμάζειν.

90 See Bar-Kochva, *Pseudo-Hecataeus*, 97 – 101, with bibliography.

91 Note also the Jewish destruction of a pagan altar at Jamnia in 39 CE; Philo, *Leg. ad Gaium*, 200 – 202.

92 Esth., 8.9 – 12, 9.1 – 19. Not that Hellenistic Jews abstained from plunder when they had the opportunity. Even the author of 2 Maccabees revels in the fact that Judas Maccabaeus' forces ravaged the whole country and put barbarian hordes to flight; 2 Macc. 2.21: τὴν ὅλην χώραν... λεηλατεῖν καὶ τὰ βάρβαρα πλήθη διώκειν. And he does not hesitate to record other Jewish savaging of the Gentiles; cf. II Macc. 8.6, 12 – 16, 12.26 – 28.

Jews in the time of Ptolemy IV petitioning and obtaining from the king the right
to execute all the apostates from within their own ranks. They murdered more
than 300 wayward Jews in a single day, exulting in the punishment and establishing the day as an annual festival.[93] As is clear, Jewish writers of the Hellenistic age quite comfortably recorded (or invented) sanguinary attacks on their
foes, destruction of shrines and holy places, and brutal assertion of their own
religious supremacy.

These examples help to set the various versions of the Exodus legend in
proper perspective. The violent and aggressive features of the tale indeed occupied its central segment. So integral had they become that they demanded incorporation in the Egyptian version of Manetho or pseudo-Manetho. The Egyptian
author, in fact, had to supply an addendum that brought Amenophis and his
supporters back into power after Egypt had long been at the mercy of its conquerors.

Of course, once those elements entered the tradition, they could be reshaped
and twisted to different purposes. As we have seen, in the hands of Lysimachus,
the lepers and other diseased folk were themselves Jews, the very persons who
polluted the country and had to be expelled from it. That hostile version circulated already by the mid first century B.C.E., for it appears in a tale reported
by Diodorus Siculus.[94] Even in Lysimachus' text, however, the strength of their
conviction and the potent leadership of Moses allowed the Israelites not only
to survive but to plunder the lands which they traversed. That central aspect adhered to the tradition. And it did not originate with antisemites.

If this be so, one might ask, why are there so few traces of the tale in Jewish
writings themselves? A fair question. But where would we expect to find them?
Extant Jewish-Hellenistic writings on this subject, it must be emphasized, are
very fragmentary prior to the Roman period. And by that time the story of Israelite occupation of Egypt had been reinterpreted by antagonistic authors as a slan-
derous drama of evil and diseased villains who conducted sacrilegious rapine.
Philo and Josephus denied by implication that Jews could have committed
such acts. They suppressed the Deuteronomic prescriptions and even claimed
that Mosaic law prohibited blasphemy of other gods or plundering of alien
temples.[95] To that end they could claim scriptural authority—or rather that of
the Septuagint. Exodus, 22.28, simply forbids the reviling of God. The Septuagint
version of that text, however, renders Elohim as the plural θεούς, perhaps as a

---

93 3 Macc. 7.10 – 15.
94 Diod. 34/5.1.1 – 2. Cf. Schäfer, 19 – 21. The source for Diodorus' tale is much disputed. See
discussion and bibliography in Bar-Kochva, *The Image of the Jews*.
95 Philo, *Moses*, 2.205; *Spec. Leg.* 1.53; Jos. *C. Ap.* 2.237; Jos. *A. J.* 4.207.

gesture toward Gentiles, perhaps as defense against Gentile criticism.[96] Philo and Josephus, in adapting the passage, certainly had the latter motive. Other Jewish writers took a more militant line, magnifying the misdeeds of Egyptians and emphasizing the vengeance of the Lord.[97] One need not be surprised that few signs of the earlier story survive.

Subsequent instances of the hostile version can be treated with brevity. The Graeco-Egyptian writer Apion had a clear grievance with the Jews. A grammarian, Homeric scholar, and author of a five-volume work on Egyptian history, Apion obtained citizen privileges in Alexandria and served as representative of the city on an embassy to the emperor Caligula. There he firmly opposed the claims of Jewish envoys who complained of their mistreatment at the hands of Alexandrians. Apion included some harsh comments about Jewish history and traditional customs in his *Aigyptiaka,* thus providing a stimulus for Josephus' lengthy counter-treatise, the *Contra Apionem.*[98] Apion himself, oddly enough, receives relatively little attention in Josephus' tract, with few quotations and even less on his recreation of the Exodus. What survives, however, indicates that his version has affinities with those already discussed. Apion cites the elders of Egypt for the report that Moses was a Heliopolitan who evidently took great liberties with ancestral practices, building outdoor synagogues, erecting columns instead of obelisks, and installing the image of a boat to serve as a sundial.[99] The significance of all this is unclear, but the identification of Moses as a Heliopolitan connects with Manetho's version. More significantly, Apion has Moses lead the lepers, the blind, and the lame out of the country.[100] That statement parallels the presentation of Lysimachus. The Jews themselves were the lepers and the handicapped who successfully departed from the land. The tale, Egyptian in origin but modified and transformed by Jews, had been refashioned again by Egyptian intellectuals to suit their own ends. Apion, it appears, had access to

---

96 Cf. G. Hata, "The Story of Moses Interpreted within the Context of Anti-Semitism," in L. H. Feldman and G. Hata (eds.), *Josephus, Judaism, and Christianity* (Detroit, 1987), 192–193; P. W. van der Horst, "'Thou Shalt Not Revile the Gods': The LXX Translation of Exod. 22:28," *Studia Philonica Annual* 5 (1993): 1–4.

97 Wis. Sol. 10.15, 19–20: 11.6–16; 12.23–27; 15.14–19; 16.1–9; 17.1–21; 18.5–25; 19.13–21; Sib. Or. 3.29–45, 314–318, 596–600, 611–623.

98 On Apion, see Gager, *Moses,* 122–124; Stern, *Greek and Latin Authors,* I, 389–390; Goodman, 604–607; Aziza, 61–63. The hostile comments on Jews to which Josephus responds all derive from the Αἰγυπτιακά. Clement of Alexandria claimed that Apion wrote an entire work κατὰ Ἰουδαίων, *Strom.* 1.21.101.3–4. But that may be no more than an erroneous inference from Josephus.

99 Jos. *C. Ap.* 2.10–11.

100 Ibid., 2.15: φησι τὸν Μωσῆν ἐξαγαγεῖν τοὺς λεπρῶντας καὶ τυφλοὺς καὶ τὰς βάσεις.

more than just Egyptian traditions. He knew of Moses on Mt. Sinai and a sojourn of forty days before he descended with the laws.[101] The Septuagint, of course, was now available, but there is nothing to suggest that Apion read it. Pompeius Trogus, doubtless among others, had already placed Moses on Mt. Sinai. Apion could get his information elsewhere than in the Scriptures. But he clearly wove the tales into his narrative. And, whatever his animus, Jewish sources indirectly provided many of the ingredients for his reconstruction.[102]

A contemporary of Apion, the Hellenized Egyptian priest and Stoic intellectual Chaeremon, offers a variant on the story in Manetho but one intermingled with still additional Jewish elements. Chaeremon, who wrote on Egyptian history and mythology, combined the training of a Greek philosopher with a deep engagement in native religious traditions. Later report has it that he was a teacher of Nero and, if he is the Chaeremon who appeared on an embassy to Claudius, he may well have shared Apion's animosity toward Alexandrian Jews.[103] Josephus, in any case, brackets him with Manetho, Lysimachus, and Apion as Egyptian writers whose representations of the Jews he is determined to controvert. Chaeremon's version, however, or at least those fragments of it that Josephus had access to and chose to transmit, disclose more confusion than hostility. He has king Amenophis provoked by the goddess Isis in his sleep and then advised by a sacred scribe to purge the land of its contaminated populace. Amenophis thereupon gathered and banished 250,000 infected persons who were led by two scribes named Moses and Joseph, each of whom also had an Egyptian name—perhaps implying a change of appellation, as with the purported Osarsiph-Moses. The exiles left for Pelusium, where they joined 380,000 would-be immigrants whose entrance had been blocked by Amenophis. Their combined

---

101 Ibid., 2.25; cf. Exodus, 24.15–18.

102 For Trogus on Moses and Mt. Sinai, see Justin, 36.2.14. A curious tale repeated by three later and obscure writers, Nicharchus, Ptolemy Chennus, and Helladius, all preserved by Photius, maintains that Moses was called "Alpha" by the Jews because he had many leprous spots, *alphoi*, on his body; text in Stern, *Greek and Latin Authors*, vol. 1, 533; vol 2, 149, 491. The report is generally connected with the negative Alexandrian tradition that associates Jews with lepers as part of the Exodus story; Gager, *Moses*, 129–133; Feldman, *Jew and Gentile*, 240–241; but see Aziza, 63–65. That would not, however, explain why Moses received the name from the Jews. One might recall the famous passage in Exodus 4.6 regarding Moses' leprous hand. Cf. also the story of Miriam, Aaron's wife, as leper; Num. 12. The tale of Moses as "Alpha" may indeed have come through a Jewish rather than an anti-Jewish route.

103 On Chaeremon and the meager sources related to his career, see H. R. Schwyzer, *Chairemon* (Leipzig, 1932), 9–16; Gager, *Moses*, 120–122; Stern, *Greek and Latin Authors*, I, 417–418; Goodman, 601–604, with bibliography; P. W. van der Horst, *Chaeremon: Egyptian Priest and Stoic Philosopher* (Leiden, 1984), ix–xiv, 2–7; Aziza, 60–61.

forces allowed them to invade the land, drive Amenophis into Ethiopia, and evidently hold the country for many years until Amenophis' son, born in exile,
reached maturity, chased the Jews to Syria, and restored his father.[104] The narrative has obvious similarities with that of Manetho's second extract, but also
marked differences. There is little convergence with Lysimachus' account, and
still less with what is known of Apion's. In Chaeremon's fragment, it is not
even clear with whom the Jews are to be identified: the exiles, the blocked migrants, or some combination thereof. Josephus exploits the confusion to discredit the account.[105] But Chaeremon's presentation doubtless had a fuller tapestry
than the fragment reveals—and perhaps than Josephus himself saw. The divergences in any case indicate that even in the early Empire the tradition was splintered and subject to repeated variations.[106] The Egyptian substratum, however,
remains evident. And the Jewish accretions, represented here by both Moses
and Joseph, as well as by Jews enjoying conquest and dominance, still held central place.

The foregoing analysis sets other pagan versions of the Exodus in a new
light. It is no longer surprising that an author like Pompeius Trogus could report
that Jews were evicted from Egypt as lepers and diseased persons, who purloined
sacred objects as they left, while at the same time characterizing their leader
Moses as a man of consummate wisdom and great beauty. Indeed the form of
the story even as it came down to Tacitus, usually regarded as the chief of
pagan antisemites, shared these mixed elements. He supplies a tale on which,
he claims, most authorities agree. A plague had struck Egypt, ravaging the bodies of its inhabitants and inducing the Pharaoh Bocchoris, on recommendation
of the Oracle of Ammon, to purge his kingdom by banishing the Jews, reckoned
as hateful to the gods. The exiles, abandoned in the desert, nearly gave way to
despair but were rallied by Moses who exhorted them to courage and self-reliance and led them to safety, culminating in their seizure of new lands, expulsion

---

104 Jos. *C. Ap.* 1.288–292.
105 Ibid., 1.293–303.
106 Chaeremon's version seems alluded to in a third century C.E. papyrus that speaks of the
anger of Isis, an attack on Jews (?), and the expulsion of the "lawless" from Egypt; *CPJ*, III,
no. 520; see the commentary *ad loc.*; also M. Stern, "A Fragment of Greco-Egyptian Prophecy
and the Tradition of the Jews' Expulsion from Egypt in Chaeremon's History," *Zion* 28 (1963),
223–227 (Hebrew); *Greek and Latin Authors,* vol. 1, 420. n. 289. See discussion with bibliography by D. Frankfurter, "Lest Egypt's City be Deserted: Religion and ideology in the Egyptian Response to the Jewish Revolt, 116–117 CE," *Journal of Jewish Studies,* 43 (1992): 208–212.
G. Bohak, "CPJ III, 520: The Egyptian Reaction to Onias' Temple," *Journal for the Study of Judaism,* 26 (1995): 32–41, speculatively associates the papyrus with an Egyptian reaction to Onias'
second-century BCE temple in Heliopolis.

of the conquered, and establishment of a city and temple.[107] The ingredients here can be found, each with a different mix, in one or more of the Egyptian writers already discussed. Eviction of the foreigner to relieve Egypt of divine wrath reflects the indigenous legend, overlaid by Jewish supplements that celebrate an admired leader and his triumphant people. Tacitus does not stumble into inconsistency or incoherence. He transmits a tradition that had itself been repeatedly manipulated, modified, and refashioned.

A summation would be salutary. The distorting lens of Josephus has slanted our vision for too long. The Jewish historian relished the task of combating Graeco-Egyptian writers like Manetho, Lysimachus, Apion, and Chaeremon whose works he saw as malicious and mendacious. That angle of sight helps to account for most subsequent interpretations of the texts as antisemitic perversions of the Exodus tale. But Josephus shows little sensitivity to the complexities imbedded in the narratives he attacks. And he fails to see the combination of Egyptian legend and Jewish infiltration that lift those narratives outside the category of simplistic antisemitism.

The Book of Exodus held profound meaning for Jewish identity and memory. But those Jews scattered in the Diaspora and particularly those dwelling in Egypt had strong incentive to reshape the tale. To them the reasons for escape from Egypt were less important than the justification for their return. The self-esteem of Hellenistic Jews in Egypt could be bolstered by an enhancement of their ancestors' history in that land. Their new cultural milieu presented Jews with a genre of Egyptian legends that depicted the foreigner as an alien presence who polluted the land, trampled upon native religion and traditions, and was eventually expelled. Such narratives, taking diverse forms as framed by writers like Hecataeus and Manetho, did not originate as responses to the Book of Exodus, nor were they initially directed against Jews. Instead, Jewish writers and thinkers themselves grafted their people's presence onto those stories, found analogues to Moses, set up their forefathers as conquerors, and took credit for the overthrow of false Egyptian idols. The Jews could reckon themselves as former rulers of the land—an edifying and comforting past. Such a twist on the Egyptian legends gave them a proud presence on the Nile in its remote antiquity.

Pagans did not invert the Biblical story to construct a counter-history and advance the antisemitic cause.[108] Few would have any familiarity with the biblical

---

107 Tacitus, *Hist.* 5.3.1 – 2.
108 Droge (n. 61), 136 – 137, who had access to an earlier version of this paper, agrees that the hostile pagan stories did not take an "anti-Exodus" form. But he oddly sees them as attacking Hecataeus' representation of the Jews.

story, even after composition of the Septuagint.[109] And oral transmission would have provided very different variants. Egyptian lore about contests with the foreign oppressor or the polluted alien is quite independent of the Scriptures. To put it boldly, the extant narratives do not derive from Egyptian distortion of the Jewish legend, but exactly the reverse. Jewish inventiveness expropriated Egyptian myth in order to insert their own heroes, their religious superiority, and even their military triumphs.

Later Alexandrian writers like Lysimachus, Apion, and Chaeremon did have anti-Jewish axes to grind. But they found themselves saddled with stories that made Moses an effective leader and the Jews successful warriors, undetachable elements that adhered to their own versions.[110] Josephus, in contending with them, saw only their animus and strained to undermine their credibility. He missed the traces of Jewish intrusion that held fast through all the variations. Hence he overlooked what may have been a pivotal step in the shaping of the tradition. The Jews freely adapted the Exodus legend and infiltrated native fables in order to elevate their own part in the history of their adopted land.[111]

---

109 Tcherikover, "Jewish Apologetic Literature Reconsidered," 169–193, argues forcefully for the absence of Gentile interest in or acquaintance with Jewish-Hellenistic literature. That would certainly seem to be the case with regard to the Septuagint which has left little mark on the pagan scene. But Tcherikover somewhat overstates the case in general, relying largely on an *argumentum e silentio*; see the criticisms of Feldman, "Pro-Jewish Intimations," 230–241. Variants fashioned by Jewish intellectuals on familiar Egyptian folk-tales could readily have circulated among Hellenized Egyptians.

110 A similar idea, that traditions favorable to the Jews could be retained even in hostile accounts, is expressed (with regard to different matters) by Feldman, "Pro-Jewish Intimations," 249; idem, "Reading Between the Lines: Appreciation of Judaism in Anti-Jewish Writers," in Feldman and Levison, *Josephus' Contra Apionem*, 269.

111 *Author's note:* This article appears in a closely parallel version as a chapter in my book, *Heritage and Hellenism: The Reinvention of Jewish Tradition* (University of California Press, Berkeley 1998).

10. Persia Through the Jewish Looking-Glass

Persia holds a special place in Jewish tradition. Whereas the Bible's cast of villains and oppressive states is a long one, the Persian kingdom stands out as a shining exception. The victories of Cyrus toppled the Babylonian empire, the king released the Israelites from their bondage, ordered the restoration of their sacred objects, and authorized their return to the homeland—even encouraged and helped to finance it.

Cyrus, not surprisingly, receives a very good press in Jewish sources. And so, by extension, does the Persian realm under whose aegis the Jews dwelled quite contentedly (as far as the record goes) for two centuries thereafter. Cyrus enjoys extraordinarily high esteem from the author whom we conventionally label as Second Isaiah and in the books of Ezra-Nehemiah. Second Isaiah heaps praise upon him, proclaiming his triumphs over all foes, prophesying his victory over Babylon, his liberation of the exiles, and his instructions to rebuild Jerusalem and its temple, as the arm of the Lord.[1] The Book of Ezra on two separate occasions records a decree (or two decrees) in which Cyrus officially authorizes the construction of the Temple, the restoration of the sacred articles, and provisions for paying the costs.[2] And allusion to his role in the creation of a new temple resurfaces in the Sibylline Oracles.[3]

Nor is this rosy portrait of Cyrus a purely Jewish construct. He gets high marks in Herodotus and in Aeschylus' play the *Persae*. Xenophon made him the subject of a laudatory fictional biography. Alexander the Great paid signal homage to the tomb of Cyrus in Pasargadae, ordering its repair, renovation, and enhancement. It was a point of pride for the Macedonian king.

The Jews certainly had reason to express gratitude. Cyrus' successful supplanting of Babylonian rule made possible the Israelite return from exile and legitimized the reconstruction of the Temple, according to tradition. The portrait, however, is too good to be true. Cyrus, as we know, did not always act as the gentle and generous conqueror.[4]

But that raises a fundamental question. Whatever the truth of the matter, why should the Jewish composers of Deutero-Isaiah and of Ezra-Nehemiah have presented a picture that underscored Jewish debt to a gentile ruler and dependence upon a foreign power? Grateful Jews huddling under the protection of

---

1 Isa., 41.2, 41.25, 44.28 – 45.1, 45.13 – 14, 48.14 – 15.

2 Ezra, 1.2 – 4, 6.3 – 5.

3 3 *Sib.Or.*, 286 – 294.

4 See J. Wiesehöfer, *Ancient Persia* (London, 1996), 49 – 51, with references.

the powerful prince is not the most uplifting image. Would this not simply reinforce the idea of the helpless subordinate nation suffering under oppressive despots and prospering under benevolent autocrats? Such a construct of Persia would do little to bolster the self-esteem of the Jews.

I want to reexamine the representation of Persian rulership in a whole range of Jewish texts. And I want to suggest that the portrait is not quite so flattering as we customarily think. Jewish writers who fashioned the representation had more devious ends in view than mere gratitude toward or reassurance from the mighty monarch. The projected idea of Persia allowed them to reconceive their own society within a larger Mediterranean empire.

The prophecies of Second Isaiah herald the victories and benefactions of Cyrus the Great. On the face of it, the prophet shows remarkable prescience. A consensus sets the author in the early years of Cyrus' reign, prior to the fall of Babylon in 539, and thus a genuine anticipator of events.[5] The proposition is implausible. A sharp prognosticator, informed of Cyrus' taking of Ecbatana in 550 and of Sardis in 546, might have forecast that Babylon was next on the agenda. But it would take considerable clairvoyance to envisage Cyrus' decree to liberate the exiles, rebuild Jerusalem, and restore the Temple.[6] And greater foresight still would be required to record in advance the re-peopling of Judah and the construction of the walls of Jerusalem.[7] This reads very much like the clarity of hindsight.[8]

---

5 See, for instance, C.R. North, *The Second Isaiah* (Oxford, 1964), 3–4; C. Westermann, *Isaiah 40–66: A Commentary* (Philadelphia, 1969), 3–5; P.R. Ackroyd, *Israel under Babylon and Persia* (Oxford, 1970), 105–106; J. Blenkinsopp, *Isaiah 40–55* (New York, 2000), 93. Doubts, however, have appeared in A. Kuhrt, "Nabonidus and the Babylonian Priesthood," *Pagan Priests: Religion and Power in the Ancient World*, ed. M. Beard and J. North, (Ithaca, 1990), 117–155, esp. 145; K. Baltzer, *Deutero-Isaiah* (Minneapolis, 2001), 30–32; J. Goldstein, *Peoples of an Almighty God* (New York, 2002), 158–160.

6 Isa., 44.26–28, 45.13.

7 Isa., 49.16, 49.19, 54.11–12.

8 To be sure, the prophet speaks of the devastation of Babylon and the humiliation of its gods; Isa., 46.1–2, 47.1–15. Cyrus, in fact, proved to be a gentle conqueror in Babylon, honored its deities, and spared the city; see the "Cyrus cylinder", A, Kuhrt, "The Cyrus Cylinder and Achaemenid Imperial Policy," *JSOT*, 25 1983, 83–97; J.B. Pritchard, *The Ancient Near East: An Anthology of Texts and Pictures* (Princeton, 1958), 206–208, 315–316. The discrepancy has often been pointed out; e.g. C.E. Simcox, "The Role of Cyrus in Deutero-Isaiah," *JAOS* 57, 1937, 158–171. But the language of Second Isaiah is metaphorical here, the conventional thunder of prophets. The lines certainly do not require that the author live before Cyrus' triumph in Babylon; so, rightly, Goldstein, *Peoples of an Almighty God,* 159–160. They represent, in fact, a Jewish spin on Cyrus' deeds. The discrepancy causes no surprise.

The role of Cyrus in the conception of Second Isaiah is clear and consistent—and not necessarily to the credit of the king. Cyrus serves as the instrument of God. The author does not ascribe any sterling qualities or lofty aims to the ruler of Persia. It is God who summons Cyrus to his service, delivers up nations to him, and subjects kings to his power.[9] Cyrus is the shepherd of the Lord, even his "anointed one," whom God leads by the hand to do his will, i.e. to subdue nations and strip monarchs of their weapons.[10] Even the title and authority of Cyrus derive from divine election.[11] The Lord alone instructs his shepherd to announce the rebuilding of Jerusalem and its temple and to restore the exiles.[12] God calls his agent to carry out predetermined duties and to fulfill the word of the Lord.[13] In short, Cyrus' success against Babylon amounts to little more than the discharge of divine commands.[14] Deutero-Isaiah has, in effect, claimed for Yahweh the imperial accomplishments of the Persian king. That work constitutes not so much celebration or admiration as usurpation. Cyrus' victories came at the behest of God and for the benefit of the Jews.[15] Deutero-Isaiah assumed prophetic garb to place a Jewish stamp upon Cyrus' achievements.

Josephus, in his rewriting of the story, got the message right. Where did Cyrus get the idea of liberating the Israelites and ordering the reconstruction of the Temple? He got it from reading the Book of Isaiah![16]

A strikingly similar idea may be found in the famous fiction of Alexander the Great at the gates of Jerusalem. The invincible Macedonian monarch, according to the tale, marched upon the Holy City, intent upon taking it, but was stopped dead in his tracks. The High Priest appeared before Alexander, dressed like a vision that Alexander had once had and that promised him conquest of the Persian empire. Alexander performed *proskynesis* and acknowledged the power of Yahweh. Jewish priests duly displayed the Book of Daniel to him—never mind that it had not yet been written—and it prophesied the fall of Persia at the hands of a Greek. That was all that Alexander needed. The story, as is clear, ap-

---

9 Isa., 41.2, 41.25.
10 Isa., 44.28–45.1.
11 Isa., 45.3–5.
12 Isa., 44.28, 45.13.
13 Isa., 46.11.
14 Isa., 48.14–15.
15 Indeed the future belongs to the people of Israel who will be a "light unto the nations;" Isa., 42.1, 42.6, 49.6, 51.4. The covenant has now devolved from the house of David to the Israelites as a collective; Isa., 55.3–5; cf. Blenkinsopp, *Isa. 40–55*, 370; Baltzer, *Deut. -Isa.*, 470. Whether this implies a rejection of monarchy generally on the part of Deut.-Isa., as is suggested by R. Albertz, *Die Exilzeit, 6. Jahrhundert v.Chr.* (Stuttgart, 2001), 329–330, is more questionable.
16 Jos. *A. J.* 11.1–7.

propriates for Jewish ends the future conquests of Alexander the Great. They had all been foretold and guaranteed by Yahweh himself.[17] The parallel with Cyrus in Second Isaiah is close. Yahweh gave Cyrus the means to create the Persian empire—and gave Alexander the means to destroy it. In both cases the Jews were beneficiaries. Their god could claim credit for the imperial successes of the mightiest of conquerors. The stories have less to do with history than with appropriation.

The conception by Second Isaiah gains reinforcement from the Book of Ezra. That text supplies two versions of a purported decree by Cyrus, one in Hebrew, the other in Aramaic, authorizing the rebuilding of the Temple in Jerusalem. The authenticity of those documents is disputed and dubious. But they reveal much about the *Tendenz* of the author.

The book of Ezra begins with Yahweh stirring up the spirit of Cyrus to issue an empire-wide proclamation. The edict asserts that Yahweh has accorded him all the kingdoms of the earth and has appointed him to see to the building of the Temple in Jerusalem. The king then exhorts all of God's people to move to Jerusalem and assist in the construction of the Temple to the Lord, god of Israel whose dwelling place is Jerusalem. Those who remain, he adds, should support the project with their wealth, resources, and voluntary donations.[18] It is not easy to swallow this text as the genuine article. An open declaration to the entire realm that the Jewish god had promised Cyrus all the kingdoms of the world can hardly be imagined.[19] Royal homage to the gods of others, of course, causes no surprise. It was wise to accumulate protective deities and to encourage the backing of their worshippers. But a declaration to the world that Yahweh alone had accorded Cyrus his empire has altogether different resonance. The hand of the Jewish composer is unmistakable here. The text, with its stress on Yahweh's responsibility for Persian successes and Yahweh's stimulus for the Persian edict to rebuild the Temple and reinstate the exiles, fits perfectly with the forecasts of Deutero-Isaiah.

---

17 Jos. *A. J.* 11.304 – 345. See the analysis in E. Gruen, *Heritage and Hellenism: The Reinvention of Jewish Tradition* (Berkeley, 1998), 189 – 198, with references to earlier literature.

18 Ezra, 1.1 – 4. This is not the place to argue about who is meant by "the remnant." But it is most unlikely that Cyrus directed gentiles all over his empire to provide financial assistance to the Jews. Cf. E. Bickerman, "The Edict of Cyrus in Ezra 1," *JBL*, 65, 249 – 275 1946, esp. 258 – 260; H.G.M. Williamson, *Ezra Nehemiah* (Waco, 1985), 14.

19 A case for authenticity was made, with characteristic acumen and learning, by Bickerman, "The Edict of Cyrus in Ezra 1," 253 – 268. But it has not managed to shake off all doubts. See L. Grabbe, *Ezra-Nehemiah* (London, 1998), 126 – 128; P.R. Bedford, *Temple Restoration in Early Achaemenid Judah* (Leiden, 2001), 114 – 129.

No temple construction, in fact, took place in the years of Cyrus. The endeavor resumed (or began) in the second year of the reign of Darius I, according to the narrative of Ezra.[20] The Jews who undertook it, with the leadership of Zerubbabel, claimed authorization from Cyrus' original decree and persuaded the Persian satrap to seek proof in the royal archives of the empire. In this context the author of Ezra records Cyrus' decree a second time. It is followed immediately by a purported edict of Darius. The king instructs his satrap to give the Jews free rein in erecting their temple, to make sure that they receive payment for their expenses from the royal revenues, to supply them *daily* with all the livestock needed for their sacrifices, as well as wine, oil, salt, and wheat, and to execute and destroy the property of anyone who obstructs the orders! Darius concludes with a flourish, exhorting the god of the Jews to topple any king or people who attempt to undermine the decree and destroy the Temple.[21]

The tendentiousness here cannot be missed. Would the king single out Jews for such magnanimous treatment, put the taxes of the province at their disposal, supply all their needs on a daily basis, take vigorous and violent action against anyone who obstructs their cause, and invoke the god of the Jews to overthrow kings and peoples who violate his edict? One might notice in particular the rather graphic detail in which the text describes the penalty to be inflicted upon any offender: he would be impaled upon a beam torn from his own house before it is reduced to rubble![22] Darius may have sanctioned the rebuilding of the Temple and even dug out the sacred vessels once plundered by Nebuchadnezzar and now in Persian possession (why had Cyrus not done so?), but the whole narrative is so encased in Jewish partiality that it must be considered more construct than history.

An important motif stands out in Ezra-Nehemiah. And this merits notice. The author consistently and repeatedly insists upon the close association of Judaean fortunes—and indeed the people's own laws—with the rulers of Achaemenid Persia. The decrees of Cyrus and Darius, of course, exemplify this. But the theme runs throughout the work. Zerubbabel, for instance, claimed exclusive rights to building a house for the god of Israel and asserted that those rights derive directly from the king of Persia.[23] This establishes unequivocally the linkage between Achaemenid authority and the worship of Yahweh. The Temple was duly constructed and completed, so we are told, in the sixth year of Darius. The text suitably adds that this accomplishment came in accord with the com-

20 Ezra, 4.24.
21 Ezra, 6.6–12.
22 Ezra, 6.11.
23 Ezra, 4.3.

mand of God and with the decrees of Cyrus, Darius, and Artaxerxes.[24] The two sources of authority seem inseparable.

The tight association emerges again in the mission of Ezra to Judaea. Artaxerxes' letter of appointment to Ezra concludes with the notable pronouncement that punishment be swiftly applied to those who do not comply with the law of "your god"—and the law of the king.[25] The two are firmly conjoined. The mission of Nehemiah received similar sanction.[26] Again and again the text reiterates its message. Worshippers of Yahweh enjoy the grace of the Achaemenid court, indeed require it to reinstall and enhance their own national traditions. The law of God and the law of the king are mutually reinforcing.

But this prompts the same question raised with regard to Second Isaiah. Does this message not underline the dependency of the Jews upon the great power? Why should Jewish writers belabor that point? Not an easy question. There may be more subtlety and sub-texts than meet the eye. The Persian empire provides security and advantage for the Jews, so the tradition indicates. But a closer reading of the text suggests that the Achaemenid rulers were less than paragons of wisdom and virtue. The author, in clever fashion, could give his readers a sense of superiority over their overlords.

A few examples can make the point. The discrepancy between Cyrus' pronouncements on the one hand and his failure to implement them on the other stands out starkly. The king's pious pronouncements about building the Temple, exhorting subjects to supply the means for construction, and restoring the sacred objects once pilfered by Nebuchadnezzar proved to be quite empty. When Darius came to the throne nearly two decades later, no Temple existed.[27] This does not redound to the credit of Cyrus.

If the author of Ezra be believed, construction efforts resumed in the time of "Artaxerxes." The reign is misplaced chronologically and the whole narrative has little claim on historicity. But the portrayal of the ruler matters. Opponents of the building program in Jerusalem wrote to Artaxerxes, warning that restoration of the city and erection of its walls would lead to rebellion against the crown. The king bought the whole story, ordered his researchers to dig up the

---

24 Ezra, 6.14.

25 Ezra, 7.26.

26 Neh., 2.1–9, 13.6–7.

27 To be sure, the narrative in Ezra, 2.68–4.5 indicates that money was collected, work begun, and the foundations laid, but resistance within the homeland halted matters. Even if true, this shows that Cyrus was too indifferent to see to the execution of his plans. But it is unlikely to be true. The prophets Haggai and Zechariah, contemporaries of the actual rebuilding under Darius, know nothing of any earlier efforts—let alone any decrees by Cyrus.

records, and discovered that Jerusalem indeed had a rebellious history and that its monarchs had once ruled over all of Trans-Euphrates! Artaxerxes thus ordered an end to any construction.[28] Whatever one makes of this bizarre episode, it shines no positive light upon the king. He (and presumably his satraps) knew nothing of what was happening in Jerusalem. It took a tendentious report to prod him into checking the records—where he got a still more tendentious report. Yet Artaxerxes swallowed it all, acted on misinformation and terminated the building program. Not a flattering portrait.

Cyrus' decree, still unimplemented, had to be sought out again in the reign of Darius. Indeed there was some scurrying about to find it. Darius directed the researchers to look for it in Babylon, only to have it turn up in Ecbatana.[29] Evidently neither the king nor anyone else knew where it was! A reflection perhaps upon both Cyrus and Darius. The very fact that the decree (albeit in much altered form) had to be read out once more, thirty years after its issue, only reminded the audience of how valueless it had been.

Darius' own edict, after recovery of Cyrus' decree, borders on excessive generosity. The Persian monarch showers livestock and resources upon the Jews, even giving the priests carte blanche to make daily requests of anything they wish and detailing the gruesome execution of anyone who fails to comply—hardly a dignified posture for the ruler of the world.[30]

Artaxerxes goes him one better in outfitting the mission of Ezra. The king provided him with an expense account of lavish proportions, more gold and silver than could imaginably be transported, hundreds of gallons of wine and oil, hundreds of bushels of wheat—and a limitless supply of salt.[31] Perhaps the king sought to flaunt his wealth. But the portrait of a reckless spendthrift hardly adds to his stature.

To be sure, the principal impression remains that of a Persian kingdom committed to the support and welfare of the Jews. But the hints about flawed rulers, fruitless actions, and heedless extravagance add a dimension that diminishes their stature. The careful reader would find reason to question the esteem of the empire.

The mildly mocking elements in Ezra-Nehemiah may have triggered the incorporation of an altogether new tale into this tradition. A Greek version appears

---

28 Ezra, 4.7 – 23.
29 Ezra, 5.17 – 6.1.
30 Ezra, 6.8 – 11.
31 Ezra, 7.15 – 22, 8.24 – 30. Grabbe, *Ezra-Nehemiah*, 138 – 141, rightly notes the excesses here, and points to the absurdity of such a caravan of wealth allowed to travel without even a bodyguard.

in the Septuagint, commonly referred to as I Esdras, not a direct translation but a hodgepodge of material somewhat rearranged and recast. One story, however, thrust into the narrative, appears nowhere else and stands out as a centerpiece of I Esdras.

The story takes place in the court of Darius, an amusing folk-tale or fable of three young bodyguards of the king. They made a wager among themselves, arranging that each would choose what he considered to be "the most powerful thing," defend his choice before the king, and the winner would be rewarded with rich gifts and prizes, elevating him to a position close to the throne.[32]

The first young man made a case for wine as the most powerful element in the universe, the second claimed the king as strongest, and the third, the only one given a name in the story, Zerubbabel, put forth his choice: women. But, having argued for his point, Zerubbabel suddenly shifted gears and offered a better alternative: truth. It represents justice and righteousness and it abides forever.[33]

Zerubbabel's second thoughts won the day. Darius immediately pronounced Zerubbabel the wisest, promoted him to the status of kinsman, and offered to grant any wish he might have. Of course, Zerubbabel asked the king to carry out the vow he had already made to rebuild Jerusalem and to restore the sacred vessels that Cyrus had confiscated from the Babylonians. Darius instantly acceded to the request. He arranged for the safe conduct of Zerubbabel through his dominions, authorized substantial funds for erecting the Temple, restored the sacred objects, and carried out all that Cyrus had once decreed. Zerubbabel, overjoyed, informed his fellow-Jews in Babylon, and touched off a week-long festival. Darius then gave the Jews a splendid send-off, with an armed escort—and a marching band![34]

Such is the tale, a surprising and independent insert into a narrative otherwise drawn, however raggedly, from the canonical tradition. The motive for its insertion remains disputed. But I focus here on the significance of the story as a Jewish portrayal of the Achaemenid monarch and the Persian court.[35]

The whimsicality of the episode needs to be underscored. The arguments made by each of the bodyguards for his favored definition convey more jocularity than sincerity. And they show very little respect for the monarch who sits in their audience and whose favor they supposedly seek to win. The first speaker touts wine as the most powerful of entities, noting that it meddles with the minds

---

32 I Esd., 3.10–17.
33 I Esd., 3.18–4.40.
34 I Esd., 4.41–5.3.
35 For what follows, see also the analysis in Gruen, *Heritage and Hellenism*, 166–167.

of king and commoner alike and that its imbibers pay no heed to the ruler or his satraps.[36] The double reference to the monarch, in his presence, first as placed on a plane with all others, then as subject to slights, can hardly be innocent.

The second speaker was no more delicate or diplomatic. Although he took the line that the king's power exceeded all, the manner in which he chose to illustrate this was far from flattering. He referred to the king's autocratic authority, his power of life and death, the compulsion he exercises, and the servility of his attendants.[37] This hyperbolic speech plainly conveys the stereotypical image of the despot, hardly a characterization designed to elicit the king's approval. Either the youthful speaker took a reckless and dangerous line, careening toward self-destruction, or the whole speech was composed with tongue in cheek.

Zerubbabel's initial choice, namely that of women as the universe's most powerful agents, also came with barbs at the ruler. He unblushingly observes that, while Darius holds sway in an empire that overawes all nations, he is a mere plaything in the hands of his own concubine. On one occasion, says Zerubbabel, she even removed Darius' diadem, set it on her own head, and gave the king a slap for good measure. Nor was that an isolated instance. Darius, according to Zerubbabel, catered to her every whim, rejoiced in her good moods, and did all in his power to assuage her anger in a bad mood.[38] And even when Zerubbabel abandoned his frivolous advocacy of female power and substituted "truth" as his candidate for most potent of entities, he did not omit a jab at the king. Zerubbabel elevated truth to the highest pinnacle on the grounds that it embodies justice. This he contrasts notably with the injustice that lurks in wine, women, men—and kings.[39]

The notion that such speeches could be delivered before a sitting king is, of course, preposterous. The fictitious scene, however, would be a source of self-satisfied amusement for a Jewish audience. Darius, despite this parade of indignities, took no offense, indeed heaped upon Zerubbabel all and more than he could ask to assure the rebuilding of Jerusalem. Discerning readers could only come away with the impression that Darius was a dunce. In this version of the return from exile and the creation of the Second Temple, the Persian ruler is not so much a magnanimous benefactor as a witless agent manipulated by the shrewd Jew.

The Book of Daniel supplies only a blurred image of Persia. The diverse tales in the first half are set mostly in Babylon. Cyrus appears but three times as a

---

36 I Esd., 3.17–20.
37 I Esd., 4.4–11.
38 I Esd., 4.13–31.
39 I Esd., 4.34–40.

chronological marker (Daniel supposedly survived into his reign).[40] But the portrayal of "Darius the Mede," almost certainly a fictitious character, in the story of Daniel in the lions' den does demand attention.[41] It possesses some noteworthy similarities to the depiction of Persian royalty that we have witnessed in other Jewish texts.

The king is decidedly sympathetic to the Jewish god and his prophet, promoting Daniel to high office, rejoicing in his rescue, and declaring his own allegiance to Daniel's god who carries such authority. Daniel, according to the tale, was one of the king's favorites, appointed by him as one of his three chief ministers and even considered to be in line for the top post in the Achaemenid administration. His position roused jealousy within the officialdom and engendered a conspiracy among his enemies to discredit him with the king. Darius was induced to sign a document that outlawed prayers to anyone but himself for a period of thirty days, any violators to be hurled into a pit of lions. As the conspirators knew, Daniel prayed regularly to Yahweh, and he continued to do so in the period of the ban. He was easily discovered and reported to the king as a criminal offender who had transgressed the prohibition. Darius heard the news with great distress and cast about for means to save Daniel from this cruel fate. But his own decree put him in a strait-jacket. As Darius' evil counselors reminded him, no law of the Medes and Persians, once signed by the king, can be revoked.[42] The reluctant monarch had to go along with the plot and ordered Daniel to be thrown to the lions—though not without offering him the hope that his god will come to his rescue. Not that Darius was all that confident. He spent a sleepless night in fasting and anxiety, refusing even the company of concubines. At first light of dawn, the king nervously approached the sealed lions' den, calling out Daniel's name with an anguished cry. Much to his relief and joy, Daniel answered back with the news that his prayers to God had clamped the jaws of the lions, and he was safe and sound. Darius immediately reversed the whole process, releasing Daniel from the pit and tossing his accusers in instead, together with their wives and children, where no prayers sufficed to

---

40 Dan., 1.21, 6.29, 10.1.

41 Little progress has been made in identifying "Darius the Mede" with any particular Achaemenid monarch since the efforts of H.H. Rowley, *Darius the Mede and the Four World Empires in the Book of Daniel* (2nd ed.), (Cardiff, 1959). A large bibliography attests to the fruitlessness of the quest. For some references, see J.J. Collins, *Daniel* (Minneapolis, 1993), 30–32.

42 Dan., 6.2–16. On the inviolability of the king's decrees, see Esther, 1.19, 8.8; Diod. Sic. 17.30. But the notion is questionable in view of Herodotus, 3.31. See the discussion in Collins, *Daniel*, 267–268. In fact, Ahasuerus' edict on behalf of the Jews in Esther, 8.8 was itself a reversal of his own previous legislation.

save them.[43] The story concludes with a magnanimous gesture on the part of Darius. The king issued a declaration throughout his realm, to every nation, people, and language group dwelling within it. The decree eulogized Daniel's god, his sway to endure forever, his power to work wonders exemplified by the rescue of Daniel, and his kingdom never to be destroyed. And it commands all of Darius' subjects to fear and revere the god of Daniel.[44]

The portrayal of "Darius the Mede" in the Book of Daniel has some notable similarities to the depictions of Persian royalty in the texts discussed earlier. The king is decidedly sympathetic to the Jewish god and to his prophet, promoting Daniel to high office, rejoicing in his rescue, and declaring his own allegiance to the divinity who carries such authority. The association of the Achaemenid crown with the Jewish cult goes hand in hand with the alliance between the two in Second Isaiah, Ezra-Nehemiah and I Esdras. And here again the king, despite the awesome extent of his power, does not call the tune. "Darius" is meekly misled and deceived by his advisers, condemns Daniel when they force him into a corner, awaits helplessly the fate of his favorite, and nearly collapses in relief when his fears prove unfounded. This is no "take-charge guy." "Darius the Mede" was as much a pushover as his counterpart in I Esdras. Jewish readers could gain yet a firmer sense of their own superiority.

The relatively mild mockery of a Persian king that appears in the canonical text of Daniel becomes more pointed parody in the Greek additions to that text. The additions include two brief tales commonly termed "Bel and the Dragon," welded together, which reflect a sharper and more sardonic commentary on the foibles of Persian monarchs.

The first fable depicts Daniel at the court of Cyrus, founder of the Achaemenid empire who was mentioned but not developed in the biblical Daniel. Cyrus, who had become overlord of Babylon, adopted its principal deity, here termed Bel, in whom he had implicit faith. The king asked Daniel, whom he considered the wisest of his counselors, also to pay homage to this divinity. After all, Bel demonstrated his existence daily by devouring vast quantities of food and wine that were deposited in his shrine. Daniel, of course, loyal to the god of his own people, scorned idols, and indeed expressed amusement at the king's gullibility in believing that an object of clay and bronze could consume anything at all. Cyrus, now confused, turned to his priestly advisers and demanded proof that the god actually ate the stores provided for him every day. The priests proposed an experiment wherein the food would be left as usual but the door of

---

43 Dan., 6.17–25.
44 Dan., 6.26–28.

Bel's temple be locked and sealed to be sure that none but the god would have access to it. They were secure in the knowledge of a secret underground passageway, unknown to the naive king, through which the priests and their entire families passed each night and carried off all the provisions. But Daniel managed to foil this dastardly scheme. He had the floor of the shrine sprinkled with ashes, a tell-tale device which, in the morning, showed the incriminating footsteps of the conniving priests. Cyrus himself nearly upset the plan, having forgotten about the ashes and almost barged into the shrine where he would have inadvertently scattered the evidence. Daniel, once again laughing at the king's guilelessness, had to restrain him physically. Once the prophet pointed out the distinctive footprints on the floor, Cyrus at last got the message. He ordered the execution of the priests and their families and gave Daniel free rein to destroy the statue and the temple of Bel.[45]

The implications of the tale stand out starkly. Cyrus, lord of Babylon and sovereign of the Persian empire, depends on the wits and skill of his Jewish adviser. The king himself lacks both acuity and common sense, credulous and deceived by his priests. Indeed the author makes sport of the benighted Cyrus by having Daniel twice break up in laughter over his naiveté and actually block his path lest he destroy the testimony that he had himself agreed to have set in place just the night before. The thrusts that were somewhat subtle and indirect in Ezra-Nehemiah, I Esdras, and canonical Daniel are here unmistakable. The master of the universe is a bit of a buffoon.

The connected tale conveys a comparable portrait. The thick-headed Cyrus did not learn lessons quickly. Having given up on Bel, he turned to another Babylonian object of worship, a great serpent or dragon. This one he proudly displayed to Daniel as a creature of flesh and blood, no bronze idol. So, why not worship him? Daniel handled this one even more swiftly and effectively. He told the king that he could kill this purported divinity without even the use of a sword or a club. And he proceeded to do so by feeding the snake a concoction of pitch, hair, and fat that caused the hapless creature to burst its insides and blow apart. The rest of the story is a variant on the lions' den tale. The Babylonian priests intimidated the king into ordering Daniel to be tossed into the pit of lions. But of course Daniel survived. And the priests were tossed into the pit, to be instantly devoured by lions. Cyrus now publicly proclaimed the supremacy of Daniel's god.[46]

---

45 Dan., 14.1 – 2.
46 Dan., 14.23 – 42.

Here again virtue triumphs and evildoers are crushed, the Lord through his agent has trumped idols and idolators. Cyrus retains his throne, and the empire is intact. But the monarch hardly cuts an admirable figure. He had put his faith in an absurd creature who was blown to bits by an unappetizing meal, he allowed himself to be overawed by his own subordinates, and he switched as swiftly to Daniel's god as he had from Bel to the dragon. Weakness, vacillation, and fatuity emerge as his principal characteristics. The lesson is clear enough. If Jews successfully negotiated their position within the Achaemenid realm, it must have come through their own resourcefulness and talents—not through the attention of clownish Persian princes.[47]

One last text can make the point in fuller fashion: the Book of Esther. The entire work is devoted to a narrative of Jews dwelling in the Persian empire. Its composition dates to the Persian period itself, or perhaps a bit later. The story is familiar and need not be summarized in detail. Our focus remains on the depiction of the sovereign and his relations with the Jews.[48]

The narrative takes place in the reign of Ahasuerus (evidently Xerxes) who hosts a spectacular six month banquet enjoyed by all the officials, satraps, governors, and military commanders throughout his realm. This alone should prompt readers to wonder about a king who tied up his entire political and military officialdom for half a year in the palace—while leaving the empire untended. Ahasuerus then, after his wife Vashti refused to appear before his guests and to be ogled by them, not only dismissed her from the palace but sent a proclamation throughout his realm declaring that all women were obliged to follow the wishes of their husbands.[49] Such a decree, of course, only advertised to the world that he could not even control his own wife!

As is well known, Ahasuerus arranged (again on the advice of a counselor) a contest to select a new bride, a contest won by the Jewess Esther. But matters soon took a turn for the worse for Jews. A conflict ensued between the king's chief vizier Haman and Esther's cousin Mordecai, Haman took grave offense

---

47 The treatment here adapts in part the discussion in Gruen, *Heritage and Hellenism*, 168–172. For somewhat different interpretations, see, e. g., M.J. Steussy, *Gardens in Babylon: Narrative and Faith in the Greek Legends of Daniel* (Atlanta, 1993), 69–99; Collins, *Between Athens and Jerusalem: Jewish Identity in the Hellenistic Diaspora*. Rev.ed. (Grand Rapids, 1999), 335–345; L.M. Wills, *The Jewish Novel in the Ancient World* (Ithaca, 1995), 60–65.

48 The analysis here relies on the version preserved in the Masoretic text. For discussion of the different extant versions, see K. Jobes, *The Alpha-Text of Esther: Its Character and Relationship to the Masoretic Text* (Atlanta, 1996); C.V. Dorothy, *The Books of Esther: Structure, Genre, and Textual Integrity* (Sheffield, 1997); R. Kossmann, *Die Esthernovelle vom Erzählten zur Erzählung* (Leiden, 2000).

49 Esth., 1.1–22.

at a slight perpetrated by Mordecai and decided to avenge himself upon Mordecai's people. The vizier persuaded the compliant Ahasuerus to decree the annihilation of all Jews within his kingdom and confiscate their property. Ahasuerus
himself had no cause for complaint against Jews, but went along mindlessly with
Haman.[50] Unanticipated events, however (without any divine intervention), suddenly reversed matters. Ahasuerus, suffering from insomnia, had his aides read
to him the most soporific of texts, the royal chronicles. Therein he discovered
that Mordecai had once saved the king's life by warning of an assassination attempt. Ahasuerus had evidently not even remembered the occasion—even
though he had personally ordered its insertion into the chronicles. But he
would make up for it. Ahasuerus now arranged for special honors to be paid
to Mordecai, much to the chagrin of Haman.[51] And worse was to come for the
vizier. Esther the queen invited both Ahasuerus and Haman to a banquet and
there pleaded with the king not to carry out the planned destruction of the
Jews. The baffled sovereign wondered who would have ordered such a wicked
deed, completely oblivious to the fact that his fellow-guest Haman had put the
whole idea in his head and that he had himself signed the order![52] Ahasuerus,
suddenly enlightened and indignant, briefly took the air in the garden, then returned to find Haman in a compromising position. The vizier had been pleading
with Esther for his life, sprawled across the couch as an abject petitioner. Ahasuerus, however, interpreted the scene as an attempted rape, thus sealing the
doom of Haman.[53] In other words, the reversal of fortune for the Jews came
not as an act of rationality but as an absurd misconception on the part of the
moronic monarch.

Ahasuerus swiftly became putty in the hands of Esther and Mordecai, much
as he had been manipulated in Haman's hands. They requested a written order
that would reverse the previous decree on the Jews. This one would give Jews authority to engage in the very slaughter and plunder of their enemies that had
been planned for them. Ahasuerus not only readily complied, but gave Esther
and Mordecai full authority to draw up any edict that they wished in his
name and he would sign it.[54] This is clearly not a monarch who was paying
much heed to the affairs of his empire. And when word came that Jews, embold-
ened by the new edict, had felled five hundred men in the citadel at Susa, Aha-

---

50 Esth., 3.8–14.
51 Esth., 2.21–23, 6.1–13.
52 Esth., 7.1–6.
53 Esth., 7.7–10.
54 Esth., 8.3–12.

suerus reported the matter to Esther with great glee.[55] The clueless king evidently overlooked the fact that the victims were his own Persians!

It should now be obvious that the doltish Ahasuerus bears a close resemblance to the inept and occasionally ridiculous Achaemenids who people the pages of Ezra-Nehemiah, I Esdras, Daniel 6, and the Greek additions to Daniel.

To summarize. Creative Jewish writers did not deny the fact that their people recovered the homeland and rebuilt the Temple with Persian permission. Nor did they conceal the fact that Jews dwelled for two centuries under Persian overlordship rather than as an autonomous entity. But their literary constructs reconceived the situation in ways most comfortable and pleasurable for their own self-image. The triumphs of Cyrus became the awards of Yahweh, Achaemenid monarchs lavished excessive gifts upon Jews and made implausible public protestations on their behalf, Jewish prophets and leaders manipulated dim-witted Persian princes to further their ends, and one hapless monarch even gave Jews the green light to massacre his own population. The texts resonate with disparagement rather than deference.

These works have little to do with history. But they carry vital meaning for the reflective understanding of Jews who dwelled (or whose ancestors dwelled) within the confines of the Persian empire. Common impression today still has it that Persia was friend and ally of the Jews, benefactor and protector of their interests, responsible for their restoration and champion of their well-being. Cyrus and Darius, in particular, stand on the side of the virtuous, shining images to set against the dark visages of a Nebuchadnezzar or an Antiochus Epiphanes. Yet the Jews did not quite present it in that fashion. The texts, on closer scrutiny, show a more cynical and subversive stance. Framers and audience of these tales, whether living in the Persian era or looking back on it in the Hellenistic age, cultivated a self-perception that minimized gratitude for benefaction and down-played dependence on the greater power. Instead, they claimed Cyrus' victories as exhibiting the power of Yahweh, they tied Persian policy to the laws of Moses, they represented royal actions as reliant upon Jewish initiative, and they held kings up to mockery. The Achaemenids might rule an empire, but they borrowed their moral and intellectual authority from the Jews. Persian power in this cultural construct is simultaneously enhanced and diminished. It comes packaged as a Jewish appropriation.[56]

---

55 Esth., 9.11–12.

56 Comments and criticism by Peter Bedford and Josef Wiesehöfer have been of high value for the paper and have earned the gratitude of the author. For additional resources on the issues discussed in this article see the following: P.-R. Berger, "Der Zyroszylinder mit dem Zusatzfragment BIN II, 32 und die akkadischen Personennamen im Danielbuch," *Zeitschrift für Assyriolo-*

gie, 64 1975, 192–234; J. Blenkinsopp, *Ezra-Nehemiah: A Commentary* (Philadelphia, 1988); P. Briant, "Histoire impériale et histoire régionale à propos de l'histoire de Juda dans l'empire achéménide," *Congress Volume Oslo 1998: Suppl. to Vetus Testamentum,* 80, ed. A. Lemaire and M. Saebo (Leiden, 2000), 235–245; J. Briend, "L'édit de Cyrus et sa valeur historique," *Transeu,* 11 1996, 33–44; J.J. Collins, "'The King has become a Jew.' The Perspective on the Gentile World in Bel and the Snake," *Diaspora Jews and Judaism,* ed. J.A. Overman and R.S. MacLennan (Atlanta, 1992), 335–345; M. Delcor, *Le livre de Daniel* (Paris, 1971); R. De Vaux, *The Bible and the Ancient Near East* (Garden City, 1971); P. Frei, "Die persische Reichsautorisation," *Zeitschrift für altorientalische und biblische Rechtsgeschichte,* (1995) 1, 1–35; A.E. Gardner, "The Purpose and Date of I Esdras," *JJS,* 37 1986, 18–27; E.S. Gruen, *Diaspora: Jews amidst Greeks and Romans* (Cambridge, Mass, 2002); J. Harmatta, "The Literary Pattern of the Babylonian Edict of Cyrus," *Acta Antiqua,* 19 (1971), 217–249; L.F. Hartman and D.F. Di lella, *The Book of Daniel* (Garden City, 1978); C.A. Moore, *Daniel, Esther, and Jeremiah: The Additions* (Garden City, 1977); J.M. Myers, *I and II Esdras* (Garden City, 1974); R. H. Pfeiffer, *History of New Testament Times* (New York, 1949); K.F. Pohlmann, *Studien zum dritten Ezra* (Göttingen, 1970); U. Rütterswörden, "Die persische Reichsautorisation der Thora: Fact or Fiction?" *Zeitschrift für altorientalische und biblische Rechtsgeschichte,* (1995) 1, 47–61; H. Schaudig, *Die Inschriften von Nabonids Babylon und Kyros' des Grossen* (Münster, 2001); J. Schüpphaus, "Das Verhältnis von LXX- und Theodotion-Text in den apokryphen Zusätzen zum Danielbuch," *ZAW,* 83 (1971), 49–72; E. Schürer, *A History of the Jewish People in the Time of Jesus Christ,* III.2 rev. ed. by G. Vermes, F. Millar, and M. Goodman (Edinburgh, 1987); Z. Talschir, *I Esdras: From Origin to Translation* (Atlanta, 1999) and *I Esras: A Text Critical Commentary* (Atlanta, 2001); C.C. Torrey, *Ezra Studies* (Chicago, 1910); J.W. Watts, *Persia and Torah: The Theory of Imperial Authorization of the Pentateuch* (Atlanta, 2001); J. Wiesehöfer, "'Reichsgesetz' oder 'Einzelfallgerechtigkeit'? Bemerkungen zu P. Freis These von der Achämenidischen 'Reichsautorisation,'" *Zeitschrift für altorientalische und biblische Rechtsgeschichte,* (1995) 1, 36–46 and "The Medes and the Idea of the Succession of Empires in Antiquity," *Continuity of Empire: Assyria, Media, and Persia,* ed. G. Lanfranchi and R. Rollinger (Padova, 2003); Y.M. Yerushalmi, *Diener von Königen und nicht Diener von Dienern* (Munich, 1995).

11. Greeks and Jews: Mutual Misperceptions in Josephus' *Contra Apionem*

The confrontation of Athens and Jerusalem remains a powerful symbol. The two iconic emblems of Hellenic culture and Jewish tradition have long seemed to define the study of Jewish experience in the world of classical antiquity. A cultural clash between Greek and Jew continues to be the prevailing image.

The *Contra Apionem* of Josephus may not be his best known or his most widely read work. But the text contains considerable material that has helped to shape the view of a collision between the cultures. It was Josephus' last *opus*, composed probably in the late 90s C.E., evidently a reflection upon the place of Judaism in the intellectual and social context of Greco-Roman antiquity—and particularly its place vis-à-vis the Greeks.[1] It merits close scrutiny.

The title, *Contra Apionem* (Against Apion), was probably not the one applied by Josephus himself. Apion plays considerably less than a predominant role in the treatise. One ancient author, the Neo-Platonic philosopher Porphyry, referred to the tract as "Against the Greeks."[2] That may or may not have been Josephus' own tide, but it is a perfectly reasonable description. The bulk of the work consists of Josephus' rejoinders to a host of criticisms, calumnies, and slanders by Greek intellectuals or those writing in Greek against Jews and Jewish practices. Hence, this text *prima facie* constitutes a vital repository of information on the attitudes of articulate Hellenes toward the Jews. It also represents a most valuable example of the rhetorical devices employed (with mixed success) by an articulate Jew but drawn from the classical armory in order to respond to and to refute the accusations leveled.[3]

---

1 References to *Contra Apionem* will be noted within the text. On the date, see C. Gerber, *Ein Bild des Judentums für Nichtjuden von Flavius Josephus: Untersuchungen zu seiner Schrift Contra Apionem* (Leiden, 1997), 65–66; M. Goodman, "Josephus' Treatise *Against Apion*," in M. Edwards, M. Goodman, and S. Price, *Apologetics in the Roman Empire* (Oxford, 1999), 50. It certainly came after publication of the *Antiquities* in 93/4; Jos. *C. Ap.* 1.1, 1.54, 1.127, 2.136, 2.287.

2 Porphyry, *De Abstinent.* 4.11.

3 On the rhetoric of the *Contra Apionem*, see D. Balch, "Two Apologetic Encomia: Dionysius on Rome and Josephus on the Jews," *JSJ* 13 (1982) 102–122; A. Kasher, "Polemic and Apologetic Methods of Writing in *Contra Apionem*," in Feldman and Levison (1996) 143–186; R.G. Hall "Josephus' *Contra Apionem* and Historical Inquiry in the Roman Rhetorical Schools," in L.H. Feldman and J. R. Levison, *Josephus' Contra Apionem: Studies in its Character and Context* (Leiden, 1996), 231–249; J.-W. van Henten and R. Abusch, "The Jews as Typhonians and Josephus' Strategy of Refutation in *Contra Apionem*," in Feldman and Levison (1996), 296–308;

What accusations did Greeks bring against the Jews? First and foremost, according to Josephus, they insist that Jews are a relatively new phenomenon in the Mediterranean world. Jews do not go back to distant antiquity, so they need not be taken seriously. After all, Greek historians—the only ones who count—almost never mention the Jews. That is proof positive that Jews merit no attention. Josephus addresses this charge vigorously right at the outset of his treatise (1.1–5).[4] And he proceeds to devote a substantial portion of Book One to that subject, the first half of the treatise. No wonder that some later writers gave the title of the work as "On the Antiquity of the Jews."[5]

In fact, however, Josephus jousts against a plethora of criticisms. The opening round merely sets the stage for repeated bouts against Hellenic censures. As a choice example, Josephus cites Agatharchides, a second century B.C.E. historian and geographer from Cnidus,[6] who mocked the Jewish practice of observing the Sabbath. For Agatharchides, this constituted colossal folly. Jews refuse to take up arms on the Sabbath, and, as a consequence, they were routed by the armies of Ptolemy I and fell helplessly under harsh Egyptian rule (1.205–212).

More significantly, and perhaps more far-reaching, an entire body of literature existed in Greek, stemming from Egypt, primarily from Alexandria, that offered versions of the ancient Hebrews' experiences in Egypt very different from what one would find in the Book of Exodus. Josephus takes them on as a major challenge. The bewildering variety of tales stems ultimately from Manetho, no Greek but an Egyptian writing in Greek in the early third century B.C.E.[7] Manetho himself may not have been referring to the Hebrews at all but to Hyksos, the hostile invaders of Egypt who were eventually expelled by indigenous Egyptians. Later variations, however, amalgamated Hyksos with Hebrews and turned the ex-

---

J.M.G. Barclay, "Josephus v. Apion," in S. Mason, *Understanding Josephus: Seven Perspectives* (Sheffield, 1998) 194–221.

4 Barclay's commentary on the *Contra Apionem* (Brill, 2007) leaves open the possibility that Josephus refers to Romans who give credence to Greek historians. But the allusions in 1.6 and, especially, 1.15, make it clear that Greeks are his targets.

5 Origen, *Contra Celsum*, 1.16, 4.11; Eus. *HE*, 3.9.4.

6 On Agatharchides and his geographical work, see P.M. Fraser, *Ptolemaic Alexandria* (Oxford, 1972), 516–517, 539–553; S.M. Burstein, *Agatharchides of Cnidus: On the Erythraean Sea* (London, 1989).

7 On Manetho, see the review of scholarship in M. Pucci ben Zeev, "The Reliability of Josephus Flavius: The Case of Hecataeus' and Manetho's Accounts of Jews and Judaism," *JSJ* 24 (1993), 224–234, and Barclay *Contra Apionem*. Josephus introduces this segment by stressing that Egyptians inaugurated the calumnies against Jews (1.223). But this does not dilute the impression that criticism by contemporary Greeks fueled Josephus' response.

pulsion into something that looks like an upside-down and fiercely negative version of the Exodus.

That angle of the tale appeared in a work that Josephus tackles directly. Its author was Chaeremon, cited by Josephus as having written a history of Egypt, a man probably identical with the Chaeremon who was both a Stoic philosopher and an Egyptian priest, active in the mid 1st century C.E. (1.288–293).[8] Chaeremon retailed a story that has the goddess Isis appear in a dream to the Egyptian Pharaoh and tell him to expel from the land the polluted peoples who are contaminating the country with their afflictions. The identity of those polluted peoples is no mystery, for Chaeremon names their leaders: Joseph and Moses (1.290).

A more virulent version surfaces in the work of another Greco-Egyptian writer, the mysterious Lysimachus. His date and identity remain uncertain.[9] But it may be not far from that of Chaeremon. Lysimachus has the Jews as afflicted with leprosy, scurvy, and a variety of disgusting diseases, some of them driven out of Egypt into the wilderness and others packed into sheets of lead and drowned in the sea. Those who did leave the country made sure to burn, loot, and ravage on their way out, until they reached Judaea and built Jerusalem (1.304–311). Not a pretty picture of the Jews in Lysimachus' conception.

Then there was Apion.[10] Josephus faced a range of inventive, creative, and diabolical anecdotes or narratives transmitted by the Alexandrian grammarian, historian, and Homeric scholar from whom the *Contra Apionem* derives its name. Apion too retailed a pseudo-Exodus story in his history of Egypt. He makes Moses an Egyptian from Heliopolis (2.8–9). And he has Moses lead the lepers, the blind, and the lame—evidently as undesirable polluters (2.15). As if that

---

8 For Chaeremon, one should consult the full scale study, including commentary on the fragments, by P.W. van der Horst, *Chaeremon: Egyptian Priest and Stoic Philosopher* (Leiden, 1984).
9 See the thorough treatment of Lysimachus by B. Bar-Kochva, "Lysimachus of Alexandria and the Hostile Traditions Concerning the Exodus," *Tarbiz* 69 (1999–2000b), 471–506 (Hebrew)— although his conjecture on the date (late 2nd century B.C.E.) is speculative.
10 On Apion, the old study of A.G. Sperling, *Apion der Grammatiker und sein Verhältnis zum Judentum* (Dresden, 1886) remains useful. See also A. von Gutschmid, *Kleine Schriften*, vol. 4 (Leipzig, 1893), 356–371; E. Schürer, *The History of the Jewish People in the Age of Jesus Christ*, vol. III.1, rev. and ed. by G. Vermes, F. Millar, and M. Goodman (Edinburgh, 1986), 604–607; P.W. van der Horst, "Who was Apion?" in P. W. van der Horst, *Japheth in the Tents of Shem* (Leuven, 2002), 207–221. K.R. Jones offers a thorough reassessment of Apion as presented in the *Contra Apionem* in "The Figure of Apion in Josephus" *Journal for the Study of Judaism* 36, no. 3 (2005): 278–315. For Josephus, Apion was born an Egyptian, only subsequently obtaining Alexandrian citizenship; 2.28–29, 2.41, 2.65–67, 2.81, 2.85, 2.137–138. Whatever the truth of that, it is clear that Apion wrote from a decidedly Hellenic vantage-point; cf. 2.30–32, 2.73–74, 2.79, 2.89–102, 2.121, 2.135.

were not bad enough, Apion's narrative claims that the Hebrews contracted tumors in their groins, causing them to rest on the seventh day, and thus giving it the name Sabbath because of the Egyptian word *sabbo* which means disease of the groin (2.20–21). That sounds rather nasty.

Apion had other mud to sling as well. He had it in for the Jews of Alexandria in particular. He disputed their claims to Alexandrian citizenship and denied that they had a right to call themselves Alexandrians (2.32, 2.38). He posed the pointed question that if Jews are citizens of Alexandria, why do they not worship the same gods as the Alexandrians (2.65)? And there is more. Apion branded the Jews as sowers of sedition (2.68). He ridiculed the practice of circumcision (2.137). He censured them for slaughtering animals as sacrificial offerings and then rebuked them for not eating pork (2.137). And, having named a number of Greek thinkers with awesome intellectual attainments, Apion maintained that he could not think of any distinguished Jews in the arts, the sciences, or the life of the mind generally (2.135). On that score he echoed the view of Apollonius Molon of Rhodes, the famous rhetorician and man of letters in the 1st century B.C.E. Apollonius called the Jews the dullest of barbarians and the only ones who had contributed no discovery to benefit our lives (2.148).[11] Apollonius and Lysimachus both got a dig in at Moses, characterizing him as a sorcerer and deceiver, and branded Mosaic law as instruction not in virtue but in vice (2.145).

The insults could get worse. A certain Mnaseas, possibly identical with Mnaseas of Patera, a pupil of the great scholar Eratosthenes in the late third century B.C.E., retails a strange story to illustrate the credulity of the Jews (2.112–114).[12] According to Mnaseas, they were taken in by a ruse concocted by an Idumaean in the course of a war between Jews and Idumaeans. This clever fellow promised the Jews that if they ceased to attack his city, he would deliver to them the god Apollo himself, the city's protector. The Jews readily agreed, and the Idumaean proceeded to dress himself in a bizarre attire that, to the untrained eye, would resemble Apollo. The dumfounded and gullible Jews meekly withdrew and kept their distance from this apparition. As a result, the cool Idumaean took the occasion to slip into the Jewish Temple and steal off with a precious object, nothing less than the golden head of an ass (2.112–114). Clearly the Jews do not emerge with much credit in this eccentric tale.

The idea of an ass's image in the Temple in Jerusalem received an embellished version from the indefatigable Apion. He added that Jews not only kept a

---

11 On Apollonius and the Jews, see now B. Bar-Kochva, "The Anti-Jewish Treatise of Apollonius Molon," *Tarbiz* 69 (1999/2000a), 5–58 (Hebrew).
12 For Mnaseas, see M. Stern, *Greek and Latin Authors on Jews and Judaism*, vol. I (Jerusalem, 1974), I, 97–101.

golden ass's head which turned up when Antiochus Epiphanes plundered the Temple, but that they actually worshipped the animal (2.80). And the story of what Antiochus found in the Temple when he entered it reached its wildest and most malicious form in another tale spun by unknown authors and repeated by Apion. That is the notorious blood-libel fiction. In this fable, Antiochus entered the Temple and there encountered a Greek captive who recounted his tale of woe. Jews had kidnapped him, so the Greek alleged, locked him in isolation in the Temple, fattened him up with lavish feasts, and prepared him for a sacrificial ritual. Indeed, he had learned that Jews did this annually. They would kidnap some innocent and unsuspecting Greek, balloon him into obesity for a whole year, and then feast on his flesh while they swore a mighty oath to maintain hostility against Greeks. This particular Greek, however, managed to escape his fate when Antiochus arrived in the nick of time, just a few days before the prospective victim's time was up (2.89–96).

As a body, this constitutes quite a chilling array of defamatory yarns. The defamations range from censure of Sabbath worship to the slander of ritual murder. Josephus apparently had his work cut out for him in trying to meet the challenge of this smorgasbord of smears. Greek and Greek speaking intellectuals, it seems, had marshaled an arsenal of verbal assaults against the nation of the Jews.

Josephus, as he presents himself, took up the cudgels as standard-bearer for Judaism. The *Contra Apionem* contains an assemblage of counter-attacks. The historian hones his rhetorical stratagems and his polemical weapons, and sallies out to battle.

Josephus fixes his eye on the initial target: the Greek denial that Jews go back to remote antiquity. He dwells on the matter at considerable length. Greeks claimed as proof that their own historians make almost no mention of Jews in their treatment of the distant past. Josephus turns the charge on its head. What do the Greeks know about antiquity? They are mere Johnnys-come-lately. They have not been on the planet long enough to make any such claims. When they write history, it is just modern history, hardly better than journalism; they do not go back much further than yesterday or the day before (1.6–7). Indeed, they did not learn the alphabet until it was taught to them by the Phoenicians (1.10). Homer is their earliest authority—and he could not even write (1.13). Why should anyone pay attention to Greek historians? They cannot agree among themselves. They constantly snipe at one another. They accuse their rivals of inaccuracy, sloppiness, and mendacity. Even Thucydides faced the charge of falsification. And nobody believes Herodotus (1.15–18). How could anyone trust them? The Greeks do not keep records, so their historians have to make things up. Even the Athenians, renowned for their supposed learning, retain no archives to speak of. The earliest laws they can cite only go back to Draco, in the late 7th century. The Arcadians, allegedly the most ancient of Greek folk, did not even become literate until late in Greek history (1.19–22). In all these matters, the Hellenes lagged well behind the Egyptians, Babylonians, and Phoenicians—not to mention the Hebrews (1.28–36).

As for the claim that Greek writers never mention the Jews, Josephus has a barrage of answers. First of all, they only write about people whom they happened to have encountered on the Mediterranean coasts. They know nothing about nations that dwell inland. They never even heard of the Romans until late in their own history (1.60–68). Secondly, some Greek historians, like Hieronymus of Cardia, who composed the most influential history of the Successors of Alexander in the third century B.C.E., though he lived very close to the Jews, wrote nothing about them out of sheer malice (1.213–214).[13] So the absence of Jews from the books of Greek historians stems either from ignorance or from malevolence. But who needs them? The antiquity of the Jews, as Josephus recounts at excessive length, has authentication by much earlier and far more trustworthy sources: Egyptians, Phoenicians, and Babylonians (1.70–160). Josephus revels in his refutations of Greeks ignorant of the great antiquity of the Jews.

The historian then turns to the calumnies and slanders by hostile intellectuals. Chaeremon's tale of the expulsion of Jews from Egypt is, according to Josephus, riddled with errors, inconsistencies, and sheer fabrications. Chaeremon even made Joseph and Moses contemporaries! He did not know enough to be aware that there were four generations between them (1.293–303). Next on the agenda was Lysimachus' version that has victims of leprosy and scurvy driven into the desert or drowned in sheets of lead. Josephus subjects this narrative to withering scorn. Were Jews the only people who contracted such diseases, all others escaping the epidemic? And, if they were either drowned or tossed helplessly into the wilderness, how did so many of them not only survive but cross the desert, subdue the promised land, found the city of Jerusalem, and build a celebrated temple (1.312–319)?

Josephus hits his stride in taking on Mnaseas' outlandish tale. The notion of an Idumaean who dressed up like some comic Apollo to deceive the credulous Jews is too ridiculous, in Josephus' eyes, to merit much refutation. Did Jews really take this imposter walking about in a costume ringed with an array of lamps on his body to be the god Apollo? Did they leave the gates of the Temple's inner sanctuary unlocked and wide open, so that he could just walk in and make off

---

13 On Hieronymus, see the valuable study of Jane Hornblower, *Hieronymus of Cardia* (Oxford, 1981).

with the head of an ass? And did he later bring it back so that it would be in the Temple again for Antiochus Epiphanes to find (2.113–120)? Josephus leaves the story in a shambles.

There remained the unspeakable Apion. No need to dwell at any length on Josephus' numerous rebuttals. Apion's chronology for the Exodus was off by several hundred years (2.15–19). Apion had claimed that Jewish wanderers in the wilderness were afflicted by disease of the groin. What, all one hundred and ten thousand of them? And yet they marched through the desert to Judaea in just six days without a problem? Where did the ailments go (2.20–27)? And what about Apion's challenge to Jewish claims on Alexandrian citizenship? Josephus tosses the charge right back at him. Apion himself was born in rural Egypt and only later became a naturalized Alexandrian (2.29–32, 2.40–41). And he is too dumb to know that Jews are not only Alexandrians in Alexandria but Antiochenes in Antioch, Ephesians in Ephesus, and so on (2.38–39). In fact, Jews enjoy civic privileges in Alexandria, so Josephus insists, that were guaranteed to them from the time of Alexander the Great and Ptolemy I (2.42–47, 2.72). He also hurls the charge of sedition back at Apion. Are not the Egyptians, especially those dwelling in Alexandria, the most unruly and violent people in the world (2.68–70)?

Apion even had the gall to blame Jews for not erecting images of the Roman emperor. Does he not know that the Romans themselves exempted Jews from this practice and respected their ancestral prohibition of images? The historian then adds a little twist of the knife. Of course, Greeks do not mind setting up statues to the emperor. They make statues for everyone in sight: parents, wives, children, even their favorite slaves (2.73–78).

Apion knows nothing of Jewish aniconism anyway. Did he not spread the stupid story that Jews house an ass's head made of gold in their temple? Josephus has a field day with that one. He notes a whole series of foreign conquerors, including Roman generals, who entered the Jerusalem Temple—and found nothing therein. But Apion is ignorant of all that, says Josephus. Unsurprisingly so. After all, he has the brains of an ass, as well as the impudence of a dog—an animal which his countrymen, the Egyptians, worship as divine, along with crocodiles, asps, and vipers (2.79–88).

Josephus delivers scathing criticism of the allegation that a captured Greek was fattened up for a year and then chopped up to be eaten. No one with even a minimal knowledge of the rigid restrictions surrounding the practices of the Temple could entertain such an idea for an instant. For Josephus, this is a gratuitous lie perpetrating a gross impiety that could only be conveyed by someone who does not have the smallest regard for the truth (2.97–111).

And that was not all. Apion had the impudence to claim that Jews had produced no men preeminent in wisdom or science, naming among Greeks who earned that distinction Socrates, Zeno, Cleanthes—and Apion himself. Josephus has only to cite his own *Jewish Antiquities* for a gallery of Jewish geniuses. Apion's inclusion of himself among Hellenic sages decisively discredits the idea (2.135–136). Further, his criticism of Jews for sacrificing domestic animals, refraining from pork, and practicing circumcision results in even greater absurdity. Is Apion not aware that all people, including Greeks and Macedonians, slaughter animals for sacrifice? Or that his own Egyptians abstain from pork and carry out circumcision (2.137–142)? The man's ignorance, if we believe Josephus, is simply astounding.

Josephus does not spend much time refuting other Greek indictments. It sufficed, for example, to dismiss Apollonius Molon by pointing out that in different parts of his work he accused the Jews both of cowardice and of temerity. The two traits hardly go together—so much the worse for Apollonius (2.148).

Josephus' more serious and sustained rejoinder to Greek detractors took the form of a lengthy encomium to Jewish laws, customs, and beliefs.[14] In the course of it, he hails Moses as decidedly superior to the much praised but undeserving Greek lawgivers like Solon, Lycurgus, and Zaleucus (2.154, 2.161). Spartans and Athenians fall short. The laws of the former are too pragmatic, those of the latter too abstract. Only Moses struck the proper balance (2.172–173). And only Jews really adhere to their laws (2.176–178, 2.182–183, 2.232–235, 2.272). The measures conceived by Plato are reckoned by his fellow Greeks as too utopian to expect compliance. Yet, for Josephus, they are much easier to comply with than the rigorous Jewish code—with which Jews do in fact comply (2.223–224). Greek tradition holds up the Spartans as the most faithful observers of law. But, so Josephus notes, they do so only when fortune smiles upon them. When things go bad, they swiftly forget almost all their conventions (2.225–231).

A common Greek complaint, voiced, among others, by Apollonius Molon, held that Jews were exclusionists. They scorned foreigners, and they were dismissive of all those who did not share their customs. To this Josephus had a sharp rebuttal. He pointed out that Greeks are by no means immune from this attitude. Spartans, in particular, expel aliens from their midst and try to prevent

---

14 On this aspect of the work, see Y. Amir, "Θεοκρατία as a Concept of Political Philosophy: Josephus' Presentation of Moses' *Politeia*," *SCI* 8–9 (1985–8), 89–105; T. Rajak, "The *Against Apion* and the Continuities in Josephus' Political Thought," in T. Rajak, *The Jewish Dialogue with Greece and Rome: Studies in Social and Cultural Interaction* (Leiden, 2001), 195–217, and the full scale treatment by C. Gerber, *Ein Bild des Judentums für Nichtjuden von Flavius Josephus: Untersuchungen zu seiner Schrift Contra Apionem* (Leiden, 1997), *passim*; esp. 133–208.

their own citizens from going abroad lest they become corrupted by others' practices. And even the supposedly liberal Athenians executed Socrates and persecuted other philosophers when they propounded ideas that did not cohere with traditional Athenian beliefs (2.258–268). Finally, Josephus, in condemning Greek infringements of their own laws, cites sodomy, incest, and indulgence in every imaginable unnatural and disgusting pleasure (2.275). That is the flourish he employs to conclude his denunciation of the Hellenes.

The message of the treatise seems to ring out loud and clear. A fierce antagonism held between the cultures, at least at the level of savage verbal exchange. As is plain, the *Contra Apionem* ranks as a prime document for that antagonism. Josephus composed a vigorous apologia for Jews under attack.[15] And it contains a substantial proportion of the evidence for a split between Athens and Jerusalem.

Yet the matter is not so simple. A closer examination of the text suggests more ambiguity and complexity than meets the eye. And a number of the accusations leveled at Jews by Greeks seem on inspection surprisingly peculiar and paradoxical.

Consider the opening charge to which Josephus devotes a substantial amount of text: i.e. the Greek denial that Jews date back to early antiquity. Josephus takes great pains to refute that allegation. A noteworthy fact, however, needs to be stressed here. Josephus does not attach the accusation to any particular author or authors. This contrasts with most of the rest of the text where he regularly cites and addresses specific writers. The view that Jews are recent arrivals in the Mediterranean has only vague and unidentified perpetrators. That causes some misgivings right away.

Further, there is something particularly odd about this alleged Greek complaint. Greeks did not normally find it necessary to debunk other nations or

---

15 This is the standard interpretation. See, e.g., T. Reinach, *Flavius Josèphe, Contre Apion* (Paris, 1930), xv–xx; Balch "Two Apologetic Encomia", 114–122; C. Schäublin, "Josephus und die Griechen" *Hermes* 110 (1982), 316–340; P. Bilde, *Flavius Josephus between Jerusalem and Rome* (Sheffield, 1988), 118–120; idem "Contra Apionem 1.28–56: Josephus' View of his own Work in the Context of the Jewish Canon," in Feldman and Levison (1996) 94–114; Kasher, "Polemic and Apologetic Methods of Writing in *Contra Apionem*," 150–157; J.M.G. Barclay *Jews in the Mediterranean Diaspora* (Edinburgh, 1996), 362–363; Gerber, *Ein Bild des Judentums für Nichtjuden von Flavius Josephus*, 78–88; Rajak, "The *Against Apion* and the Continuities in Josephus' Political Thought" 197; Barclay, "The Politics of Contempt: Judaeans and Egyptians in Josephus's *Against Apion*," in J. M. G. Barclay, *Negotiating Diaspora: Jewish Strategies in the Roman Empire* (London, 2004), 109–111. Goodman "Josephus' Treatise *Against Apion*" 45–58, doubts that there was a tradition of Jewish apologetic, but acknowledges such an objective in this work.

other ethnic groups for their relative youth in the history of the world. Quite the contrary. Hellenes readily acknowledged, in admiring fashion, the great antiquity of Egypt. Herodotus had no difficulty in recording a range of Greek borrowings from Egyptian culture, including the worship of Dionysus, the belief in transmigration of souls, and various philosophical and religious precepts.[16] Aristotle conceded that Egypt is the oldest of nations, the first to create political institutions, and the first to discover the mathematical arts.[17] Isocrates noted that the Spartans adopted their social and political system in imitation of Egypt.[18] Nor did Greek writers like Herodotus hesitate to recognize that Greeks owed their very literacy to the teachings of the Phoenicians.[19] Numerous other instances of these acknowledged borrowings can readily be cited. The famous anecdote of the Egyptian priest who told Solon that, by comparison with Egypt, all Greeks are children, comes to us from a Greek, Plato, with no hint of embarrassment.[20]

The fact needs stress. It seems quite unlikely that Greek writers would see the lack of a long chronological pedigree as a reason for reproach. And it is even less likely that they would fasten this label upon the Jews for whom it was manifestly specious. No wonder that Josephus failed to provide a single name for any Greek author who held such a view. One cannot avoid the strong suspicion that he has concocted a confrontation on this issue. It certainly allowed Josephus to discredit the idea quite easily and unequivocally. A neat set-up.[21]

One can say much the same about Josephus' sniping at Greek historians as untrustworthy on the grounds that they disagreed with one another (1.15–18). That is a cheap shot.[22] Of course, historians quarrel with one another—to this very day. That does not itself diminish their credibility. Josephus was hardly im-

---

16 Herodotus, 2.49, 2.123.

17 Aristotle, *Pol.* 7.1329b.20–34; *Met.* 1.1.981b.

18 Isocrates, *Busiris*, 17–18.

19 Herodotus, 5.57–59.

20 Plato, *Tim.* 22b.

21 Goodman "Josephus' Treatise *Against Apion*," 52–53, rightly raises the suspicion that some of the arguments against which Josephus tilts were artificial creations. That possibility is noted also by A.J. Droge "Josephus between Greeks and Barbarians," in Feldman and Levison (1996), 117–118. Neither pursues the matter.

22 S.J.D. Cohen, "History and Historiography in the *Against Apion* of Josephus," in A. Rapoport-Albert, *Essays in Jewish Historiography* (*History and Theory*, Beiheft 27, 1988), 3–9, recognizes the weakness, even absurdity, of Josephus' position here, but nevertheless takes this as an authentic historiographical debate and polemic. See also Schaublin, "Josephus und die Griechen," 320–321; Bilde "*Contra Apionem* 1.28–56", 98–101; Barclay, *Contra Apionem*.

mune. He came under heavy criticisms from other historians as well (1.2, 1.46 –
47, 1.53, 1.56). This begins to look more and more like an artificial construct.

In fact, Josephus, in his more sober moments, draws heavily on Greek historians himself—even when he does not cite them. He gives as reason for the antiquity and accuracy of Jewish records the fact that their archives record an unbroken succession of High Priests who go back for two thousand years (1.36). That is
a variant on the closely comparable tale told by Herodotus who has the Egyptians tell the naive Greek historian Hecataeus of Miletus that they can trace an
unbroken succession of high priests and kings who go back for three hundred
and forty one generations, or about 11,340 years.[23] And when Josephus responds
to the critics of his own historical writing—again without naming any names—he
pilfers the thought and language directly from Thucydides and Polybius. He
stresses his own commitment to personal, eyewitness testimony, and rejects
those who treat his work like a schoolboy's submission for a prize essay
(1.53 – 56). That comes straight out of Thucydides and Polybius.[24]

More significantly, Josephus is not averse to citing Greek authors, whether
apparently discredited historians or other writers, so long as they advance his
own agenda—even if he has to press their statements into service. When useful
for his purpose, they suddenly become credible and reliable. He even quotes Herodotus as speaking of the Syrians in Palestine who practice circumcision and
concludes that he must be referring to Jews (1.168 – 171). In all likelihood Herodotus, who never mentions Jews, alluded to the Philistines.[25] Josephus would
not inquire further. He sought out Greek sources who acknowledged (even indirectly) the existence of the Jews. He cites a certain Choerilus who recorded a people from the Solyman hills among the troops accompanying Xerxes on the Persian expedition to Greece. Josephus takes this to be an allusion to
Hierosolyma and thus a reference to Jews from Jerusalem (1.172 – 175).[26] A bit
of a stretch. He has still better material from Clearchus, a pupil of Aristotle. Josephus found a useful anecdote in Clearchus who reports that his teacher encountered a learned Jew in Asia Minor and was much impressed by his erudition.

---

23 Herodotus, 2.142 – 143.
24 Thucydides, 1.22.4; Polybius, 3.31.12 – 13.
25 Gutschmid *Kleine Schriften*, 565 – 567; Reinach *Flavius Josèphe, Contre Apion*, 33; Stern
Greek and Latin Authors on Jews and Judaism, 2 – 4; Barclay *Contra Apionem*.
26 See the discussions of Gutschmid *Kleine Schriften*, 567 – 578; Reinach *Flavius Josèphe, Contre Apion*, 35; Barclay, *Contra Apionem*.

Clearchus added the tidbit that this (unnamed) Jew was not only Hellenic in language but in his very soul (1.176 – 182).[27]

Most suitable for Josephus' ends was the early 3rd century historian Hecataeus of Abdera. He quotes or paraphrases at great length from excerpts attributed to Hecataeus—or, at least to someone whom he took to be or presented as the Greek historian Hecataeus. The extended snippets disclose Hecataeus' great admiration for Jewish adherence to their laws, the splendor of their temple, their military skills, and the high esteem in which they were held by Hellenistic kings (1.183 – 204). Josephus further cites a number of Greek authors who attest to the antiquity of the Jews, even if they do not have all the facts straight (1.216 – 217). And he notes three in particular who are demonstrably accurate and trustworthy: Demetrius of Phalerum, Philo the Elder, and Eupolemus (1.218). Here, misconception or deceit cannot be gainsaid. We may be confident that each of these writers was, in fact, a Jew, writing under a Greek pseudonym. That is surely true of Hecataeus and almost as surely of Philo, Demetrius, and Eupolemus. Josephus ought to have known this—and probably did.[28] But whether he deliberately passed them off as Greeks or was himself deceived matters little for our purposes. More to the point, he was perfectly happy, even proud, to parade Greek authors, or what he took to be Greek authors, as confirming the favorable impressions and the prestige that Jews enjoyed among the intelligentsia of the Mediterranean world.

So, what happened to the chasm between Jew and Greek? Where did the animosity disappear to? Josephus in fact lets slip a telling phrase: he says that Jews are more distant from Greeks in geography than in their way of life (2.123). Indeed he goes further still. He singles out certain Greek intellectuals for high praise, notably Plato. Josephus particularly likes Plato's criticism of Hellenic myths and his rebuke of those naive persons who believe in them, for they represent gods as men and women with all the faults and vices that attach to mortals—only more so (2.239 – 256). In Josephus' conception, Plato is here more akin

---

27 On the passage from Clearchus, see now Bar-Kochva, "Aristotle, the Learned Jew, and the Indian Kalanoi," *Tarbiz* 67 (1997/8), 435 – 481 (Hebrew); Barclay, *Contra Apionem*.

28 That "Hecataeus" was a Jewish author has been firmly established by Bar-Kochva, *Pseudo-Hecataeus on the Jews: Legitimizing the Jewish Diaspora* (Berkeley, 1996a), 54 – 121, 143 – 181. An extensive commentary on these fragments will appear in Barclay, *Contra Apionem*. For the fragments of Philo, Demetrius, and Eupolemus, Jewish writers whom Josephus misidentified, see C.R. Holladay, *Fragments from Hellenistic Jewish Authors, Vol. I: Historians* (Chico, 1983), 51 – 156; *Fragments from Hellenistic Jewish Authors, Vol. II: Poets* (Atlanta, 1989), 205 – 299. For B.Z. Wacholder, *Eupolemus: A Study of Judeo-Greek Literature* (Cincinnati, 1974), 2 – 3, Josephus knew the truth but was deliberately ambiguous.

to Moses, indeed follows Moses on this and other matters (2.257). The idea that the Greek intelligentsia got much of its best ideas from Jewish thinkers and the books of Moses had already been voiced by other Jewish writers. Josephus readily picks up the theme. He proclaims that Hellenic philosophers, whether they knew it or not, were really following the precepts of Moses (2.281). And he is able to cite the Greek biographer Hermippus of Smyrna who wrote a life of Pythagoras in the 3rd century B.C.E. to show that some Greeks bought this idea as well. Hermippus affirmed that the great Pythagoras adopted many aspects of Jewish law into his own teaching (1.162–165). Whatever the truth of these claims—and there is good reason to be skeptical—what matters is that Josephus retailed them and presented them as authentic.[29] The same man who composed the *Contra Apionem* to underscore the divide between Jews and their detractors also finds the Greeks as intellectual heirs to the Jews and as reproducers of Jewish doctrines.[30]

What is going on here? The more one reads, the more one wonders how real is this confrontation. How should we interpret the verbal assaults by Greek writers and the rhetorical rejoinders by Josephus? It is hard to escape an increasing sense of mendacity and manipulation. An important point requires notice—one that is obvious enough but all too easily forgotten. What we possess of these ostensibly hostile writers are simply excerpts—excerpts carefully chosen for us by Josephus. It would be foolish indeed to infer that what survives through that medium is representative or characteristic of the authors and works as a whole. Very far from it.

One example can serve as pointed illustration. Agatharchides, as noted earlier, criticized Jews who observed the Sabbath, declined to take up arms, and thus got smashed by Ptolemy I. This passage, however, did not derive from an anti-semitic work. Nor is there reason to believe that Agatharchides even censured the observance of the Sabbath. He simply offered instances of human folly driven by superstition. The prime exhibit indeed involved a Hellenistic princess who perished because she delayed escape when stopped by a dream. The Jewish failure served him only as a parallel (1.205–212).[31] That is not the impression one would get, however, from Josephus' presentation of the excerpt. He represents it tendentiously as anti-Jewish.

---

29 Hermippus' own comments may have been mocking ones. But Josephus' selective excerpt evidently omitted that feature. So, rightly, Barclay *Contra Apionem*.

30 Some of the internal tensions in Josephus' treatment are noted by Barclay *Jews in the Mediterranean Diaspora*, 364–366.

31 Cf. the remarks of Barclay *Contra Apionem*, who sees a sharper critique of the Jews here.

Another instance delivers a similar lesson: Mnaseas' narrative of the Idumaean who put on a fancy get-up, posing as Apollo, and completely hoodwinking the Jews (2.111–114). The story makes no sense as it stands, and we have no idea of the context. The brief selection that Josephus provides seems deliberately designed to make it preposterous and thus to allow him to shoot it down with ease.

The pseudo-Exodus stories packaged under the names of Chaeremon and Lysimachus neatly serve as set-ups for demolition by Josephus (1.288–293, 1.304–311). It warrants mention that the quoted or paraphrased excerpts are a good deal shorter than Josephus' refutation of them. Once again, they seem chosen, indeed manipulated, to highlight their inconsistencies, chronological blunders, exaggerated numbers, ignorance of Jewish tradition, and inexplicable omissions. Another point needs stress. Neither of these authors wrote about the Jews *per se*. They composed histories of Egypt in which the Jews just briefly came into play—and probably in passing. Even the excerpts do not make much of the Jews themselves. They focus on the Pharaoh's efforts to rid the land of pollution. Lysimachus indeed seems to admire Moses for rallying his people in the wilderness (1.309). And both authors, in pointing to successful Jewish assaults on Egypt, may actually be drawing on Jewish sources for whom this was a point of pride.[32] Josephus' packaging bears the principal responsibility for saddling these authors with anti-Jewish motivation, thereby to make them easier for the historian to knock over.

Even the arch-villain Apion may not be quite so evil as he seems.[33] He too almost certainly did not write a history of the Jews. He did produce a work on Egypt in which the Jews naturally cropped up (2.10).[34] It is entirely possible that almost everything Apion had to say about Jews appears in the selections supplied by Josephus—unless, of course, he had anything favorable to say. What Apion reports about Moses is at least not obviously hostile. He observes that Moses set up open-air prayer houses in each district of his home town Heliopolis, that he erected pillars instead of obelisks, created the relief of a boat

---

32 See the arguments of E.S. Gruen, *Heritage and Hellenism: The Reinvention of Jewish Tradition* (Berkeley, 1998), 55–70. Cf. the treatment of Droge "Josephus between Greeks and Barbarians," 134–141.

33 For a comparable approach, see Jones, "The Figure of Apion in Josephus".

34 See Gellius, 5.14.4, 6.8.4, 10.10.2; Tatian, *Orat. Ad Graec.* 38; Eus. *PE*, 10.11.13. Reference to a work on the Jews appears in Julius Africanus, *apud* Eus. *PE*, 10.10.16, and Clement, *Strom.* 1.21.101.3. But these probably depend on inference from Josephus. See the convincing arguments of Jones "The Figure of Apion in Josephus". Cf. also Schürer, *The History of the Jewish People in the Age of Jesus Christ*, 606–607; *contra:* B. Motzo, "Il κατὰ Ἰουδαίων di Apione," *Atti della R. Accademia delle scienze di Torino* 48 (1912–13), 459–464.

and perhaps a statue that cast a shadow paralleling the course of the sun (2.10 – 11). Josephus makes mincemeat of this, interpreting it as a graven image which Moses would never have dreamed of (2.12 – 14). What Apion actually had in mind seems impossible to fathom. But he would surely not have pilloried Moses for erecting graven images. This small selection contains nothing of an anti-Jewish character.

Apion merits a closer look. The majority of blasts leveled at him by Josephus in the treatise direct themselves against errors, ignorance, and stupidity rather than prejudice. This holds, for example, in Josephus' mockery of Apion for listing the most eminent Greek sages and including himself among them (2.135 – 136). Josephus skewers him for that boast. Apion doubtless included no Jews in that select company of wise men. But he may very well have excluded all others besides Greeks as well. It is Josephus who puts the spotlight on the Jews. He also lambasts Apion for his version of the Exodus story, making hash of his etymological connection between Sabbath and the Egyptian *sabbo* that signified disease of the groin (2.20 – 27).[35] The connection may indeed be specious, and the joke sardonic, but the purpose need not have been malicious—except in Josephus' formulation.

Much the same can be said about Apion's questioning of Jewish rights to civic privileges in Alexandria (2.33 – 42). One might consider the possibility that Apion, who acquired Alexandrian citizenship rather than possessing it by birth, could have reason to question that privilege for a whole range of immigrants—not just Jews as Jews (2.32). It was Josephus who converted this position into a glorious opportunity to wax eloquent about the generous privileges bestowed upon Jews from the time of Alexander the Great through the Ptolemies and to the Romans (2.42 – 50, 2.61 – 64, 2.71 – 72). Insofar as Apion did have occasion to assail the Jews in particular we know the context: he served as spokesman for the Alexandrians in 40 C.E. at a hearing before the emperor Caligula, where he sought to blame the Jews for the recent upheaval in that city.[36] There he confronted a rival Jewish delegation, and the rhetorical exchange must have been a heated one. It is in that setting that Apion most probably delivered accusations of sedition and failure to set up statues of the emperor (2.68, 2.73).[37] But a notable fact needs to be registered. Although Josephus reports Apion's role

---

35 Cf. M. Scheller "σάββω und σαββάτωσις," *Glotta* 34 (1955), 298 – 300. See J. Dillery, "Putting him Back Together Again: Apion Historian, Apion *Grammatikos*," *CP* 98 (2003), 387 – 389, who sees Josephus' assault as, in part, an attack on Apion's repute as a *grammatikos*.
36 Jos. *A.J.* 18.257 – 259.
37 It does not follow that all or most of Apion's remarks on the Jews in his written work stemmed from that political hearing, as is claimed by Motzo "Il κατὰ Ἰουδαίων di Apione," 461 – 463.

as Alexandrian envoy to Rome in his *Jewish Antiquities,* he makes no mention of it in the *Contra Apionem.* Why? An answer can be surmised. It would spoil his picture. In the latter treatise the historian seeks to suppress specific circumstances and postulate a wider Hellenic hostility to Judaism. The broader scene furthers his design of presenting himself as champion of Jewish principles and traditions.

The misrepresentations multiply. Apion's story of the golden ass's head in the Temple, whatever its origin, would not, from a pagan point of view, constitute an attack on erecting graven images (2.80 – 88).[38] But it served Josephus' purpose to make his point about the purity of Jewish piety. As for the blood-libel tale, the annual ritual murder of a Greek, Josephus evidently plucked out that slander precisely because it was preposterous (2.89 – 96). Few Greeks could have believed it. The libel appears almost nowhere else in all the Greco-Roman literature of antiquity. And, of course, we do not know in what context Apion made reference to it.[39] For Josephus who dug it out, however, it provided the useful occa-

---

38 The belief or purported belief that Jews paid homage to an ass in the Temple circulated in different versions, whether as ass's head, statue of an ass, or Moses seated on an ass; Diod. 34/35.1.3; Tac. *Hist.* 5.4.2; Plut. *Quaest. Conviv.* 4.5.2; Jos. *CAp.* 2.112 – 114. For efforts to sort out the entangled tales, see, esp., E. Bickermann, "Ritualmord und Eselkult: Ein Beitrag zur Geschichte antiker Publizistik," in E. Bickermann, *Studies in Jewish and Christian History,* vol. 2 (Leiden, 1980), 245 – 255; Bar-Kochva "An Ass in the Jerusalem Temple—The Origins and Development of the Slander," in Feldman and Levison (1996b), 310 – 326. The stories may have originated in Egypt, later incorporated into the narrative of Antiochus IV's assault on Jerusalem. That the Jewish nation is here being assimilated in hostile fashion to Seth-Typhon, the enemy of Osiris in Egyptian tradition and the god whose sacred animal was an ass, is now a scholarly consensus; e. g. van Henten and Abusch, "The Jews as Typhonians and Josephus' Strategy of Refutation in *Contra Apionem*", 284 – 289; P. Schafer, *Judeophobia* (Cambridge, Mass., 1997), 55 – 62; Bar-Kochva "An Ass in the Jerusalem Temple", 318 – 325. If so, however, it is remarkable that that connection is nowhere explicitly made. The nearest to it is Plutarch, *De Iside et Osiride,* 31, who, in fact, questions it. Cf. Bickermann "Ritualmord und Eselkult," 246. Whatever its origins, the claim that Jews revered an ass hardly represents a major pagan critique of Judaism that Josephus felt obliged to refute. Schafer *Judeophobia*, 60 – 61, regards it as an invention of Apion. L.H. Feldman, "Pro Jewish Intimations in Anti-Jewish Remarks Cited in Josephus' *Against Apion,*" *JQR* 78 (1988), 212 – 215; "Reading Between the Lines: Appreciation of Judaism in Anti-Jewish Writers Cited in *Contra Apionem,*" in Feldman and Levison (1996), 257 – 258, even considers association with the ass as having positive features.
39 It appears elsewhere only in the Suda, ascribed to a certain Damocritus; see Stern *Greek and Latin Authors on Jews and Judaism,* 530 – 531. And this may well derive from Apion's own report. The tale had more than one formulation, pieced together in the source employed by Apion; Bickermann "Ritualmord und Eselkult," 225 – 245; Bar-Kochva, "The Hellenistic Blood-Libel—Content, Origins, and Transformations," *Tarbiz* 65 (1995/6), 347 – 374 (Hebrew). Like the ass stories, it too may have originated in Egypt and was subsequently blended into the narrative on

sion for a tirade against Apion's stupidity and an encomium of the Temple and its rituals (2.97–111).

The calculated selectivity of snippets and the deliberate repression of context mark the *Contra Apionem* throughout. The labors of modern scholars who assembled the fragments of Greek writers from this treatise and constructed an epidemic of anti-Judaism that had to be resisted and refuted show just how effectively Josephus has shepherded his readership. The *Contra Apionem* is not a genuine antidote to a wave of Hellenic hostility toward Judaism. Josephus ransacked his texts to find the most outrageous claims that he could most readily rebut with zest and panache, a collection of straw men to be knocked over. And he massaged his material to simulate a confrontation in which he could take up the banner for his countrymen. This was not an authentic crusade but a rhetorical showpiece.

Why do it? Some have suggested that it supplied a means to encourage Jewish proselytism.[40] If so, then Josephus has been exceedingly subtle and the message is muted. To be sure, the work contains references to an openness to converts, a welcome to those who wish to share Jewish principles and practices, indeed a pride in the fact that many have already chosen to do so (2.123, 2.209–210, 2.261, 2.282–286). But it is hard to conceive of anyone rushing to conversion as a consequence of reading this tract. Another suggestion proposes that Josephus responded to anti-Jewish propaganda circulating in Flavian Rome where he was writing, in the wake of the Jewish rebellion.[41] If that be the case, however, it is most peculiar that the criticisms that appear most commonly in Roman writers, namely those regarding observance of the Sabbath, dietary laws, and circumcision, barely play any role at all in the *Contra Apionem*. Even in the circles in which Josephus might have moved in Rome, he would

---

Antiochus IV. But Josephus' claim (2.90–91), that Antiochus' propagandists fashioned it to justify his assault upon the Jews, widely accepted by moderns, has little to recommend it. Cf. Schafer, *Judeophobia* (1997), 65. Why should the partisans of Antiochus worry about producing an apologia to defend his actions against Jews? And to what audiences? Insofar as any retrospective explanations were needed for Antiochus' attack, they cited Jewish misanthropy and practices contrary to custom, not ritual murder; see Diod. 34/5.1.3–4. In any event, there is no indication that this "blood-libel" had much circulation and demanded a response from Josephus.

40 Bilde *Flavius Josephus between Jerusalem and Rome*, 120–121; S. Mason, "The *Contra Apionem* in Social and Literary Context: An Invitation to Judean Philosophy," in Feldman and Levison (1996), 208–224.

41 Goodman "Josephus' Treatise *Against Apion*," 55–57.

hardly have picked up conversations about Agatharchides, Chaeremon, or Apion![42]

A more personal motive may play a role. Josephus himself had come under censure for his previously published works. The issue surfaces right at the beginning of the *Contra Apionem,* precisely with regard to the antiquity of the Jews (1.2–3). As we have seen, this could hardly have been a matter of widespread concern to Greeks. But it evidently did stimulate some critics who charged Josephus with exaggeration on that score. Others, according to Josephus, had written rival histories of the Jewish war, challenging his version (1.46–47). And, as has already been noted, some described his work as a schoolboy's exercise, questioning its reliability and its veracity (1.53, 1.56; cf. 1.127, 2.136, 2.287). Josephus elected not to respond to his critics with a personal apologia or polemic. Rather, he chose a different and more elevated cause. In essence, Josephus wrapped himself in the mantle of Judaism as a whole. The reply to his critics transmogrified into a retort to attacks on Jewish values and Jewish character generally.

The attacks themselves, to be sure, did not all stem from Josephus' fertile imagination. Jewish traditions and practices had often been a subject of amusement or derision. But the historian, in numerous instances, applied exaggeration, embellishment, and contrivance. He selected, condensed, trimmed, and paraphrased in order to make the judgments easier targets for his own rejoinders. Josephus, in brief, presents himself not as acting from personal pique but as defending the integrity of his own people everywhere.

The audience for such a treatise remains a matter of conjecture. None can proclaim a definitive answer (though some have approached such a proclamation). A growing number of scholars now concur that Josephus had Gentiles as his target readership, whether Romans among whom he dwelled when composing his work or wider circles in the Greco-Roman world who might have been sympathetic to Jews. For those who conjecture a missionary purpose, such a readership needs to be postulated.[43] But that purpose is itself questionable.[44]

---

42 A study by Barclay, "The Politics of Contempt: Judaeans and Egyptians in Josephus's *Against Apion.*" 111–121, suggests that Josephus sought to undermine the widespread belief, in Rome and elsewhere, that associated Jews with Egyptians. But there is no evidence that the Romans held this putative association (insofar as they took it seriously) against the Jews. It is difficult to believe that Josephus felt impelled to slander Egyptians in order to reassure Romans that Jews were quite distinct from them.

43 See Bilde *Flavius Josephus between Jerusalem and Rome*, 120; Mason "The *Contra Apionem* in Social and Literary Context," 223; cf. Feldman "Pro Jewish Intimations in Anti-Jewish Remarks Cited in Josephus' *Against Apion,*" 230–243; but see Gerber *Ein Bild des Judentums für Nichtjuden von Flavius Josephus*, 374–379.

44 See above.

Others imagine an array of readers across the spectrum, ranging from hostile libelers of Jews who were being answered, those influenced by the slanders who needed to be convinced, those either ignorant of Jews or interested in Judaism, those close to the administration in Rome or governing circles in the Roman empire, and educated Jews who needed an arsenal to use against their opponents.[45] If this is what Josephus had in mind, he would have required the mechanisms and marketing of a modern publishing house. One might observe that some of the description of Jewish practices and customs would seem too basic for a Jewish audience, thus suggesting Gentile targets (2.180–219).[46] But this means no more than that non-Jews may have been a purported audience for the purpose of the rhetoric, not that they were an intended one. Certainly one can rule out the idea that Josephus expected Greeks to welcome this tract. They could only have read it with fury, disdain, or incredulity. And how many Romans would take an interest in Josephus' sniping at obscure Greek and Egyptian writers, quarreling about Jewish antiquity, and claiming the superiority of Judaism over Hellenic institutions? Josephus needed to make a case to his fellow-Jews.[47]

The *Contra Apionem* is a shrewd and effective treatise. But it should not be taken as a genuine deposit of Hellenic thrusts against the Jews nor as a selfless championship of Judaism against its enemies. Josephus' own agenda prevails. The *Contra Apionem* may, in some ways be his cleverest work. But it is not authentic reflection of a war between Athens and Jerusalem.

---

45 Kasher "Polemic and Apologetic Methods of Writing in *Contra Apionem*," 150–157 proposes this motley assemblage. Barclay "The Politics of Contempt," 111, 121–126, puts principal stress on a putative Roman or "Romanized" readership.
46 So Goodman "Josephus' Treatise *Against Apion*", 50–51.
47 Rajak "The *Against Apion* and the Continuities in Josephus' Political Thought," 197, recognizes Jews as the audience, but sees the purpose as supplying them with an armory for their defense.

12. Tacitus and the Defamation of the Jews

Jews do not fare very well at the hands of Cornelius Tacitus. The great consular historian devoted thirteen chapters to them at the beginning of Book V of his Histories, chapters constituting a digression from his main text, but a remarkably extensive one. Tacitus sets them at the point where he intends to embark on the narrative of the Roman siege of Jerusalem in 70 CE. The reason, as he puts it, is that, since he is about to relate the demise of a famous city, he thought it appropriate to say something about its origins.[1] The opening sends its own signal. Tacitus employs the phrase *famosa urbs*, a characteristically Tacitean touch, i. e. "infamous" or "notorious" city, rather than "renowned" or "celebrated". And matters seem to go downhill from that point on.

This excursus is the longest extant discussion of the Jews by any Greek or Latin author—or rather by any pagan author. Hence it merits a spotlight for the treatment of ancient attitudes toward Jews. And it does so on more than one count. The digression arguably contains some of the most hostile comments on record regarding that people.[2] Among other remarks, Tacitus brands the Jews as a race of men hated by the gods.[3] They regard as profane everything that we (Romans) hold as sacred—and vice versa.[4] Their practices are base and wicked, and prevail through their own depravity.[5] They are a people most especially inclined to lust. Although they won't sleep with gentiles, among themselves there is nothing they won't do (*nihil inlicitum*). Those who cross over to their ways scorn the gods, abandon their own nation, and hold their parents, siblings, and children cheap.[6] Jewish rites are sordid and ridiculous.[7] Jews throughout their history were the most despised of subject peoples and the basest of nations.[8]

---

1 Tac. Hist. 5.2.1: *sed quoniam famosae urbis supremum diem tradituri sumus congruens videtur primordia eius aperire.*
2 On the harsh and unusual language employed, see K. Rosen "Der Historiker als Prophet: Tacitus und die Juden", *Gymnasium*, 103 (1996), 107–108; R.S. Bloch *Antike Vorstellungen vom Judentum: Der Judenexkurs des Tacitus im Rahmen der griechisch-römischen Ethnographie* (Stuttgart, 2002), 75–79.
3 Tac. *Hist.* 5.3.1.
4 Tac. *Hist.* 5.4.1.
5 Tac. *Hist.* 5.5.1.
6 Tac. *Hist.* 5.5.2. Cf. Juv. *Sat.* 14.96–106.
7 Tac. *Hist.* 5.5.5.
8 Tac. *Hist.* 5.8.2.

That is pretty strong stuff. One should hardly be surprised that Tacitus has been reckoned as the quintessential pagan anti-Semite, the Jew-baiter, a representative of fierce Roman animosity toward Jews, indeed of its most virulent strain. That view prevails almost without dissent.[9] Even those who have found some favorable allusions to Jews in this dark text ascribe them to Tacitus' sources rather than to Tacitus himself.[10] An odd conclusion. If so, did Tacitus transmit those favorable views inadvertently? This historian almost never did anything inadvertently. Modern scholars have without exception taken the digression on the Jews as an authentic reflection of Tacitean animosity.[11]

An immediate question arises. Just why should Tacitus have expressed such offensive opinions about the Jews? The question has important bearing upon our understanding of the historian himself. Although his remarks have often been taken as exemplifying Roman reactions in general and hence a window on broader attitudes toward alien religions, they do not, in fact, fit neatly into such a picture.

---

9 So, e. g., I. Levy "Tacite et l'origine du people juif", *Latomus*, 5 (1946), 339 – 340; B. Wardy "Jewish Religion in Pagan Literature during the Late Republic and Early Empire", *ANRW*, II.19.1 (1979), 613, 633 – 635; J.G. Gager *The Origins of Anti-Semitism: Attitudes toward Judaism in Pagan and Christian Antiquity* (Oxford, 1985), 63 – 64, 83; Y. Lewy "Tacitus on the Jews", in J. Dan, *Binah*, vol. 1: *Studies in Jewish History* (New York, 1989), 15 – 46; L.H. Feldman "Pro-Jewish Intimations in Tacitus' Account of Jewish Origins", *REJ*, 150 (1991), 336 – 339; R. Mellor *Tacitus* (London, 1993), 38, 49, 109; Z. Yavetz "Judeophobia in Classical Antiquity: A Different Approach", *JJS*, 44 (1993), 17; "Latin Authors on Jews and Dacians", *Historia*, 47 (1998), 90 – 98; K. Rosen "Der Historiker als Prophet," 108 – 126; J.M.G. Barclay *Jews in the Mediterranean Diaspora* (Edinburgh, 1996), 314 – 315, 362 – 363; P. Schäfer *Judeophobia: Attitudes toward the Jews in the Ancient World* (Cambridge, Mass., 1997), 31 – 33, 74 – 75. See the valuable review of scholarship by Bloch *Antike Vorstellungen vom Judentum*, 17 – 26. Although he shares the view that Tacitus' portrait is a hostile one, Bloch offers a more nuanced and complex analysis that sets the author apart from simplistic anti-Semites; op. cit. 159 – 176.

10 Feldman "Pro-Jewish Intimations in Tacitus' Account of Jewish Origins", 336 – 339, 359 – 360; (1993), 192 – 194. See also D. Rokeah "Tacitus and Ancient Antisemitism", *REJ*, 154 (1995), 293 – 295, for whom Tacitus embraced earlier Greek denunciations of the Jews, but transmitted some favorable traditions as well. Yavetz "Latin Authors on Jews and Dacians," 83, acknowledges only hostile Greek sources. None gives much credit to Tacitus' own shaping of the portrait

11 The greatest of Tacitean scholars, Sir Ronald Syme, surprisingly evinced almost no interest in the matter. The more than 800 pages of his magisterial two-volume work on the historian devote only a few lines to the subject of Tacitus on the Jews. The opinion expressed, however, takes the standard line: "Tacitus appears to nourish in hypertrophy all the prejudices of an imperial race. His anger bears most heavily upon the Greeks and the Jews". Jews are "beyond the pale"; R. Syme *Tacitus*, 2 vols. (Oxford, 1958), 530.

The vast majority of preserved comments about Jews by Roman writers and intellectuals in the early and high Empire deliver a rather different impression.[12] Such writers were not, of course, great advocates or admirers of Jews. But their comments, on the whole, do not fall into the category of intense antipathy. They were generally dismissive or scornful rather than malicious. They puzzled over the observance of the Sabbath, they found monotheism foolish, they wondered why anyone would exclude pork from his diet, and they regarded circumcision as mutilation of the genitals. So, for instance, Seneca made the crack that, by observing the Sabbath, Jews use up one seventh of their lives in idleness.[13] Pliny the Elder indeed claims to know of a river in Judaea that dries up every Sabbath. One should presumably infer that even Jewish rivers take one day a week off.[14]

Abstention from pork struck the Romans as especially bizarre. Petronius concluded that since Jews don't touch pork, they must worship a pig-god (*porcinum numen*).[15] Juvenal observed that Judaea is the one place in the world where pigs must be happiest, for they can live to a ripe old age.[16] Plutarch went to the lengths of inventing a full-scale dialogue in which the interlocutors debated whether Jews shrank from pork out of reverence for the hog or abhorrence of that creature. It is not easy to take the arguments on either side as entirely serious. The spokesman who maintained that Jews honored the animal suggested that pigs first dug up the soil with their projecting snouts, thereby prompting men to conceive the idea of inventing the plow from which Jews learned to farm the soil. And the interlocutor on the other side offered as one explanation for Jewish distaste for pork that pigs' eyes are so twisted and pointed downward that they can never see anything above them unless they are carried upside down.[17] That hardly seems a compelling reason for refraining from swine's flesh. One may well suspect that Plutarch was having his own little joke in this fictitious after-dinner debate.

Circumcision provoked a similar combination of perplexity, misinformation, and amused disdain. Petronius remarks about a talented Jewish slave who pos-

---

12 For a fuller discussion, see E.S. Gruen "Roman Perspectives on the Jews in the Age of the Great Revolt", in A.M. Berlin and J.A. Overman, *The First Jewish Revolt: Archaeology, History, and Ideology* (London, 2002), 27 – 42; *Diaspora: Jews Amidst Greeks and Romans* (Cambridge, Mass., 2002a), 41 – 52.

13 Seneca *apud* Augustine, *CD*, 6.11.

14 Pliny, *NH*, 31.24.

15 Petronius, fr. 37.

16 Juv. *Sat.* 6.159 – 160; cf. 14.98 – 99.

17 Plut. *Quaest. Conv.* 4.4 – 5.

sesses many skills that he has but two faults: he is circumcised and he snores,— never mind that he is also cross-eyed.[18] And Juvenal observes that Jews are so exclusive in keeping their own company that they decline even to give directions in the street to those who are not circumcised—quite a feat since men were not in the habit of going about unclothed.[19]

In short, most Romans writing in the early Empire who deigned to take notice of this alien people contented themselves with superficial appearances and impressions. As a consequence, they retailed shallow, half-baked, and misinformed opinions. They were either indifferent to Jews or derided them with mockery.

Why should Tacitus be any different? Did he carry a bitterness and anger that set him apart? Some scholars have indeed detected a deep-seated antagonism and proposed reasons for it. A number of explanations have made the rounds. Tacitus sought, so it is claimed, to justify Rome's destruction of the Temple in Jerusalem and thus felt a pressing need to blacken Jews, their beliefs, and their practices as forcefully as possible.[20] On a different view, Jewish proselytism enraged Tacitus. The historian was furious that this defeated people should still be in Rome and elsewhere converting good gentiles to their wicked creed and undermining Roman morals.[21] Or else his intense aversion represented anxiety about this rebellious folk who continued to multiply, rejected Roman deities, grew in strength, and threatened Roman values.[22] The digression has elsewhere simply been dismissed as the product of anti-Semitism, ignorance, and silliness.[23]

None of these suggestions compels assent. The idea that the Jewish nation, so devastatingly crushed in the failed revolt of 66–73 CE, represented any sort of threat to Rome or was even perceived to do so stretches the imagination. Tacitus composed his *Histories* in the period from roughly 105 to 110 CE, long after the

---

18 Petr. 68.8; cf. 102.14.

19 *Juv. Sat.* 14.104.

20 Lewy "Tacitus on the Jews," 28–34; Yavetz "Latin Authors on Jews and Dacians," 94; S.J.D. Cohen *From the Maccabees to the Mishnah*, 2nd ed. (Louisville, 2006), 49. Rightly questioned by Bloch *Antike Vorstellungen vom Judentum*, 167–168.

21 Yavetz "Judeophobia in Classical Antiquity," 17; *Judenfeindschaft in der Antike* (Munich, 1997), 47–48; "Latin Authors on Jews and Dacians," 97–98; Barclay *Jews in the Mediterranean Diaspora* , 315, 409–410.

22 Wardy "Jewish Religion in Pagan Literature," 633–635; Gager *The Origins of Anti-Semitism*, 63–64; Lewy "Tacitus on the Jews," 31–42; Rosen "Der Historiker als Prophet," 110–111; Schäfer *Judeophobia*, 185–192. For Bloch *Antike Vorstellungen vom Judentum*, 102–107, Tacitus emphasizes the rebelliousness of the Jews.

23 G.E.F. Chilver *A Historical Commentary on Tacitus' Histories IV and V* (Oxford, 1985), 90.

Jewish revolt and in a period of Jewish quiescence. To be sure, new outbreaks of rebellion would occur near the end of Trajan's reign, several years after publication of the *Histories*. But unless we confer upon Tacitus the mantel of a prophet, he can have had no inkling of that.[24] The Jews of Rome itself, it is worth noting, did not participate in either uprising. Their circumstances, so far as we can tell, were no different in Tacitus' time than they had been before. If they engaged in any vigorous proselytism, for which there is in fact little or no evidence, they seem to have carried it on without interference—and without any concern on the part of Roman authorities.

What of the purported need to justify the destruction of the Temple? No hint exists that Tacitus or any other Roman felt the urgency to manufacture an apologia by ascribing moral failings or religious perniciousness to the Jews. The practices of the Jews had been familiar to dwellers in Rome for at least two centuries. They may have found them bizarre, but hardly menacing. Nothing in monotheism gave cause for anxiety, and Romans had long tolerated Jewish unwillingness to participate in the imperial cult. Destruction of the Temple followed a lengthy and tenacious rebellion. The Jews, as the conqueror and future emperor Titus put it in the account of Josephus, had been ingrates, turned against their Roman benefactors, and bit the hand that fed them.[25] Romans required no further justification.

How then does one account for Tacitus' rage and bitterness? To begin, it is important to note that the historian's excursus on the Jews by no means constitutes a consistently anti-Jewish tract. A number of remarks imply a rather positive assessment, even admiration of Jewish character or actions. So, for example, among the stories that Tacitus retails regarding the origin of the Jews is one that identifies them with the Solymoi, celebrated in the Homeric poems, whence they got the name Hierosolyma (Jerusalem) for their central city—a most distinguished lineage, says Tacitus.[26] In recounting a version of the Israelite exodus from Egypt, Tacitus ascribes to Moses a speech affirming self-reliance and determina-

---

24 Rosen "Der Historiker als Prophet," 119–126, actually attributes foresight of this sort to Tacitus on the grounds of Jewish apocalyptic literature of which he might have had at least indirect knowledge—a far-fetched hypothesis. Bloch *Antike Vorstellungen vom Judentum*, 132, is rightly skeptical. References to scholarly discussions in H. Heubner and W. Fauth *P. Cornelius Tacitus: Die Historien Band V: Fünftes Buch* (Heidelberg, 1982), 151–155. Some even find source material for Tacitus in the Dead Sea Scrolls; J.G. Griffiths "Tacitus, *Hist.* 5.13.2 and the Dead Sea Scrolls", *RhM*, 113 (1970), 363–378; "Tacitus and the *Hodayot* in the Dead Sea Scrolls", *RhM*, 122 (1979), 99–100; D.S. Barrett "Tacitus, *Hist.* 5.13.2 and the Dead Sea Scrolls Again", *RhM*, 119 (1976), 366.
25 Jos. *BJ*, 6.333–336.
26 Tac. *Hist.* 5.2.2.

tion in his people.[27] The historian, in his own voice, pays a comparable compliment, asserting that the inhabitants of Judaea were men of healthy constitution and capable of enduring fatigue.[28] Indeed, they proved themselves durable in other ways. Tacitus elsewhere affirms that the Jews patiently suffered the oppression of Roman procurators until the arrival of Gessius Florus when they could not take it any longer.[29] Jews then readied themselves for the onslaught of Roman power. They had, according to Tacitus, made every provision well in advance for a lengthy siege.[30] When the assault came, everyone who could take up arms did so, indeed more than their numbers would ever have suggested.[31] Men and women exhibited tenacious resolve, reckoning death preferable to loss of their country.[32] This was unmistakably admirable behavior. And not for the first time. Tacitus reports that when Gaius Caligula proposed to set up his image in the Temple in Jerusalem, the Jews preferred to take up arms rather than to acquiesce.[33] Further, Tacitus notes, Jews may not be eager to mix with gentiles, but among themselves they show a fierce loyalty and a ready compassion.[34] They regard it as evil to slay any late-born child, they consider all souls lost in battle or by execution to be immortal, and they thus have no fear of death.[35] In all these statements Tacitus takes a decidedly admiring line on Jewish traits, values, and behavior.

What do we make of this paradox? Is this schizophrenia on the part of Tacitus? One does not readily discern such a characteristic in that crafty and calculating historian. Did he get the favorable bits from his sources and transmit them, even though inconsistent with his own assessment? If so, this can only be by design, not through inattention. Did he underscore Jewish courage and determination in order to alert Romans to the possible menace that Jews represented? Hardly a plausible scenario for a people whose rebellion, for all its dogged-

---

27 Tac. *Hist.* 5.3.1. See the notes on this passage by Heubner and Fauth *P. Cornelius Tacitus*, 33 – 38.

28 Tac. *Hist.* 5.6.1.

29 Tac. *Hist.* 5.10.1. Bloch *Antike Vorstellungen vom Judentum*, 106 – 107, unjustifiably puts a negative interpretation upon this.

30 Tac. *Hist.* 5.12.2; cf. *Hist.* 2.4.3.

31 Tac. *Hist.* 5.13.3: *arma cunctis, qui ferre possent, et plures quam pro numero audebant.*

32 Tac. *Hist.* 5.13.3: *obstinatio viris feminisque par; ac si transferre sedis cogerentur, maior vitae metus quam mortis.* Bloch *Antike Vorstellungen vom Judentum*, 112, 150 – 157, here too sees this as an unfavorable verdict.

33 Tac. *Hist.* 5.9.2.

34 Tac. *Hist.* 5.5.1.

35 Tac. *Hist.* 5.5.3. See the commentary of Heubner and Fauth *P. Cornelius Tacitus*, 74 – 76.

ness, had ended in abject failure. Have we then reached a dead end? Should one regard the Tacitean account a mere muddle, a mass of confusion? Few will take that route.

A different approach may be salutary. Whatever else may be said about Tacitus, one aspect of his work holds primacy. Tacitus is the consummate ironist. None questions the fact, which is obvious on almost every page of the historian's work.[36] Paradox and inconsistency abound, juxtaposed statements and explanations undermine one another, suggestions are put forward, then turned upside down, plausible versions emerge only to be compromised by subtle hints, bitter jibes, or cynical analysis. None of this is innocent, none of it is inadvertent. The wit is sharp, and the humor is dark. One thinks immediately, of course, of the barbs aimed at the Julio-Claudians in the *Annals*. But Tacitus' caustic wit was already there in the *Histories*. None can forget the concentrated contempt in his assessment of Galba: *capax imperii—nisi imperasset*[37] Equally devastating is the historian's remark on the exchange of letters between Otho and Vitellius, each accusing the other of shamelessness and felonies: they were both right (*neuter falso*).[38]

A fresh look at the excursus on the Jews in this light offers provocative possibilities. Previous interpretations have tended to play it straight. They have taken the anti-Jewish statements as read, a symptom of Tacitean prejudices and animosity, even of a broader Roman malice. The ostensibly favorable comments are then explained away as conveying the opinions of others, not Tacitus' own, or as a means of alerting Romans to the dangers of Jewish strengths and accomplishments. All of this misses the irony and black humor for which Tacitus is otherwise justly renowned.[39]

Perhaps the most conspicuous paradox occurs in relation to a matter that speaks directly to Jewish religious sensibilities: images in the Temple. Tacitus as-

---

36 See P. Robin *L'Ironie chez Tacite* (Paris, 1973), 1 – 24, 245 – 323, and *passim;* E. O'Gorman *Irony and Misreading in the Annals of Tacitus* (Cambridge, 2000), 10 – 22, 176 – 183, and *passim.*
37 Tac. *Hist*, 1.49.
38 Tac. *Hist*. 1.74.
39 Bloch *Antike Vorstellungen vom Judentum*, the best study of the excursus, does recognize ironic elements in it, 174 – 176, but sees them in the service of Tacitus' broader purpose, a dark portrait of the Jews. The fine treatment of Tacitean irony by O'Gorman *Irony and Misreading in the Annals of Tacitus* confines itself to the *Annales*. Robin *L'Ironie chez Tacite*, takes a much broader sweep. But the excursus on the Jews receives only one brief paragraph in his extensive work; op. cit. 303. P. Plass's useful monograph *Wit and the Writing of History: The Rhetoric of Historiography in Imperial Rome* (Madison, 1988) has much of value to say about wit, parody, and incongruity in Tacitus, but also gives less than a paragraph to the Jewish excursus; op. cit. 55.

serts flatly, without ascribing the report to other authors, gossip, or rumor, that the Jews dedicated an image of an ass in the inner sanctum of their sacred shrine. That animal, he had earlier noted, this time on the authority of other writers, had directed Israelites wandering in the wilderness to a watering hole, thus preventing them from perishing of thirst.[40] The image of an ass in the Temple? Is this evidence for anti-Semitic propaganda retailed by our historian? That would be a hasty inference. In a subsequent paragraph, Tacitus, without referring to his previous statement, refutes it unequivocally. He asserts that the Jewish conception of the deity is a purely mental construct, and that Jews condemn as profane those who set up images of gods in the form of men.[41] Moreover, he adds, they erect no statues in their cities, let alone in their temples.[42] Tacitus reinforces this affirmation a bit later in the text when he records the entrance into the Temple of the conquering Pompey who found the shrine empty, devoid of any representation of the gods.[43]

Where did the statue go? Interpreters have scrambled to explain away this starkly discordant note.[44] Perhaps Tacitus only transmitted other writers' accounts of the ass story? Not very likely. He alludes to no other authors here. Does the image, *effigies*, refer only to a dedication, not a sacred object, i.e. an *anathema* rather than an *agalma?* In the context of his statement which involves a direct contrast of Jewish and Egyptian *worship* of divinities, that is a most implausible interpretation. Was Tacitus simply nodding the first time, then corrected himself, without having the mettle to admit the earlier mistake? That too has been suggested. In such an event, however, the historian could simply have erased the offending lines. And it is always hazardous to ascribe inattention to the ever vigilant Tacitus.

Leaving the two inconsistent assertions in place and unreconciled must be deliberate. The story of Jewish adherence to a cult of the ass had made the rounds. In one form or another, it had appeared in Diodorus, in Apion, and in

---

40 Tac. *Hist.* 5.4.2: *effigiem animalis, quo monstrante errorem sitimque depulerant, penetrali sacravere;* cf. 5.3.2: *grex asinorum.*
41 Tac. *Hist.* 5.5.4: *Iudaei mente sola unumque numen intellegunt; profanes qui deum imagines mortalibus materiis in species hominum effingant.*
42 Tac. *Hist.* 5.5.4: *igitur nulla simulacra urbibus suis, nedum templis sistunt.*
43 Tac. *Hist.* 5.9.1.
44 These and other efforts to wriggle out of the inconsistency are conveniently assembled by Bloch *Antike Vorstellungen vom Judentum*, 66. See also J.N. Sevenster *The Roots of Anti-Semitism in the Ancient World* (Leiden, 1975), 120–121. They point to the paradox but provide no real resolution. Bloch's view that Tacitus did not worry about inconsistencies so long as they left his general picture unaffected is unsatisfactory; op. cit. 65–67, 159–160.

Josephus (who, of course, rejected it).[45] Without explicitly refuting it, a heavy-handedness that would not accord with Tacitus' style, he presents it in a matter-of-fact fashion—and then, in similar fashion, reports Jewish aniconism as well-known and long-established. The implication was subtle and suggestive: no need for argument, let alone for reconciling contradiction. The irony exposed the fatuousness of those who imagined an *Eselkult* among a people who scorned both images and animals.

A comparable example emerges from close scrutiny of another item in the text. Tacitus ostensibly reacts with *ira* and *studium* against the converts to Judaism: they despise the gods, turn their backs on their *patria,* and hold their own parents, children, and siblings in contempt.[46] The language is harsh, suspiciously so, perhaps consciously hyperbolic. Tacitus' outburst here, unsurprisingly, has caused many to infer that Jewish proselytism had deeply infiltrated Roman society and undermined Roman values.[47] Commentators, however, have overlooked a rather intriguing incongruity in the Tacitean presentation on this point. Only a few lines earlier, he had depicted in sardonic fashion the Jews' observance of the Sabbath. The Jews, in his account, adopted the practice of taking leisure every seventh day because, so they say (*ferunt*), it represents an end to their labors.[48] This, of course, had been observed by a number of Latin writers such as Seneca who, as we saw, derided the Jews for wasting one seventh of their lives in idleness.[49] But Tacitus went him one better, adding that they enjoyed the delights of indolence so much that they created the sabbatical year in order to prolong their sloth.[50] That delivers a characteristically Tacitean insinuation. But a more interesting implication lies therein. A proclivity to idleness is hardly compatible with a policy of energetic proselytism. Once again, this surely represents no innocent conjunction by Tacitus. In the directly preceding passage, which contains his remarks about converts to Judaism who were indoctrinated to de-

---

45 On the "ass-libel", see B. Bar-Kochva "An Ass in the Jerusalem Temple: The Origins and Development of the Slander", in L.H. Feldman and J. Levison, *Josephus' Contra Apionem: Studies in its Character and Context with a Latin Concordance to the Portion Missing in Greek* (Leiden, 1996), 310–326.

46 Tac. *Hist.* 5.5.2: *transgressi in morem eorum idem usurpant, nec quicquam prius imbuuntur quam contemnere deos, exuere patriam, parentes liberos fratres vilia habere.*

47 See the works cited by Heubner and Fauth *P. Cornelius Tacitus,* 70–73. Add also Feldman *Jew and Gentile in the Ancient World* (Princeton, N.J., 1993), 300; Barclay *Jews in the Mediterranean Diaspora,* 315, 410; Schäfer *Judeophobia,* 32.

48 Tac. *Hist.* 5.4.3: *septimo die otium placuisse ferunt, quia is finem laborum tulerit.*

49 Seneca, *apud* Augustine, CD, 6.11. Other references in Heubner and Fauth *P. Cornelius Tacitus,* 54–57.

50 Tac. *Hist.* 5.4.3: *dein blandiente inertia septimum quoque annum ignaviae datum.*

spise their own gods, country, and families, Tacitus provided a noteworthy account of Jewish practices. The Jews, he claims, keep themselves apart from all other peoples, even exhibit an undeviating detestation of them. They emphasized their distinction from all gentiles.[51] The paradox is stark. How does one gain converts among gentiles while insisting upon dissimilitude and distance from them? The juxtaposition of two incompatible ideas, once more, is unlikely to be an accident. The historian deftly discloses the incongruity of holding both those opinions simultaneously. This is less a statement of Tacitus' own attitude toward Jews than a sardonic comment on simplistic stereotypes.

At the outset of his Jewish excursus, Tacitus lists no fewer than six different —and largely incompatible—versions of where the Jews came from. They have received much discussion.[52] For our purposes it is unnecessary to dwell on them at length. Most of the debate has centered upon the issue of which of these versions Tacitus actually believed—or wanted his readers to believe. That may be precisely the wrong question to ask. Scholars have pored over the different tales, finding some favorable, some neutral, and at least one downright hostile. General agreement has it that Tacitus opted for the last, the most negative portrait, one drawn from Egyptian sources that conveyed a dark tale of the Exodus as an expulsion of Jews for having brought a plague upon the land.[53] On the face of it, that appears to make sense. Tacitus saves the story for the end, he ascribes to it a consensus of most authorities, and he devotes more space to it than all the other versions combined. Presumably, then, this is what he wanted his readers to remember, without having committed himself to it—a familiar Tacitean technique. One need mention only the famous account of Augustus' character and motivations as perceived by two opposing groups of interpreters at his funeral in the beginning of the *Annals*.[54] The debunking interpretation comes last, has greater length, and is more memorable. On that analogy, Tacitus here too opts for the most hostile tale, further evidence for his animosity toward the Jews.

---

51 Tac. *Hist.* 5.5.1 – 2: *adversus omnis alios hostile odium; separati epulis, discreti cubilibus... circumcidere genitalia instituerunt ut diversitate noscantur.*
52 See, e.g., Levy "Tacite et l'origine du people juif," 331 – 340; Feldman "Pro-Jewish Intimations in Tacitus' Account of Jewish Origins," 339 – 360; *Jew and Gentile in the Ancient World*, 184 – 196; Yavetz "Latin Authors on Jews and Dacians," 91 – 94; Bloch *Antike Vorstellungen vom Judentum*, 84 – 90. See also the valuable assemblage of references in Heubner and Fauth *P. Cornelius Tacitus*, 20 – 43.
53 Tac. *Hist.* 5.3.1; Heubner and Fauth *P. Cornelius Tacitus*, 30; Rosen "Der Historiker als Prophet," 111 – 112; Schäfer *Judeophobia*, 31; Yavetz "Latin Authors on Jews and Dacians," 91 – 94.
54 Tac. *Ann.* 1.9 – 10; cf. Yavetz "Latin Authors on Jews and Dacians," 93.

The conclusion seems obvious. But the obvious solution is not always the correct one. Strong reasons call for reconsideration. First, the allegedly negative narrative, saved for the end and given at some length, is not all that negative. The story identifies the Jews as stemming from Egypt, blamed for a plague that infected the country, and expelled by the king on the advice of the oracle of Ammon.[55] Hence began the Exodus, a wandering in the wilderness under the leadership of Moses, the discovery of an oasis through the arrival of a herd of wild asses, a march of six days, and, on the seventh, they seized the promised land, drove out the inhabitants, and founded a city in which they dedicated their Temple.[56] Comparable stories, with variants, can be found in several earlier authors, from the time of Manetho in the early 3rd century BCE. Tacitus did not invent the material, but he did put his own spin on it. The earlier narratives, from Manetho to Apion, contained far harsher assessments of the Hebrews as lepers and villains. Tacitus omits most of that, and even holds Moses in some esteem for his leadership in bringing his people to eventual triumph.[57] To be sure, he calls them "a race of men hateful to the gods" (*genus hominum invisum deis*). But it is essential to stress that Tacitus does not here deliver his own judgment. He conveys the characterization applied to Jews by the Egyptian king, and the gods in question are the Egyptian gods—a vital distinction. These are not divinities whom Tacitus embraced (the Egyptians, after all, worshipped animals). And the last part of the passage is particularly noteworthy. The Hebrews wandered for just six days and accomplished their purpose on the seventh. The figure of six days for the time spent in the wilderness plainly served others as an aetiological explanation for the Sabbath.[58] But Tacitus takes it to a whole new level. He has them not only arrive in the Promised Land on the seventh day but expel all the indigenous dwellers and occupy the whole country, founding Jerusalem and building the Temple![59] To debate the degree to which this account is favorable or unfavorable seems singularly irrelevant. Its main characteristic is absurdity. And one would be hard pressed to imagine that Tacitus expected anyone to believe it. As a vehicle for blackening Jews, this would hardly do the job.

---

55 Tac. *Hist.* 5.3.1.

56 Tac. *Hist.* 5.3.1–2.

57 Cf. Heubner and Fauth *P. Cornelius Tacitus*, 30–33; Feldman "Pro-Jewish Intimations in Tacitus' Account of Jewish Origins," 354–357; *Jew and Gentile in the Ancient World*, 192–194.

58 Justin, 36.2.14; Apion apud Jos. *CAp.* 2.21; Plut. *Isis and Osiris*, 31.

59 Tac. *Hist.* 5.3.2: *et continuum sex dierum iter emensi septimo pulsis cultoribus obtinuere terras, in quis urbs et templum dicata.* The phraseology, probably intentional, leaves the impression that the city and temple were founded in Moses' lifetime. Cf. Heubner and Fauth *P. Cornelius Tacitus*, 42.

Furthermore, the other stories of Jewish origins that Tacitus retails more briefly and ascribes to unnamed sources claim no greater credibility. Some of them assigned Jewish beginnings to the island of Crete at the time when Saturn lost his throne to Jupiter. The explanation for this theory, according to Tacitus, lay in the existence of Mt. Ida in Crete which led some to identify the Idaei of Mt. Ida with the Iudaei of Judaea.[60] Such a notion stands neither to the advantage nor to the disadvantage of the Jews.[61] Rather it serves to discredit the story. The alternative versions reach similar levels of implausibility. One has the Jews migrate from Egypt at the time of Isis, also in the distant mists of legendary antiquity.[62] Another has them stem from Ethiopia, driven by fear and hatred to seek new lands in the reign of king Cepheus, father of Andromeda, once more shrouded in myth and beyond chronology.[63] Still another makes them Assyrian by origin, a striking contrast with the biblical narrative in which Assyrians are the fiercest foes of the Israelites. In Tacitus' account they lacked sufficient land in Assyria, packed their bags, conquered part of Egypt, and planted their own cities in the Hebrew country adjoining Syria.[64] Further, he records the apparently flattering tale that identifies Jews with the Solymoi, a Lycian people renowned in the Homeric epics for their toughness as fighters. But flattery is not Tacitus' prime objective. The root of this fiction counts for more. The name of Jerusalem, Hierosolyma, suggested to some a connection with the Solymoi, thereby generating the conjecture.[65] Once again the issue of whether or not the yarn compliments the Jews misses the point. Tacitus in this entire segment simply plays with a farrago of legends that foolish authors have transmitted and credulous readers have bought. We hear the voice of the sardonic historian, not the Jew-baiter.

---

60 Tac. *Hist.* 5.2.1. See Feldman "Pro-Jewish Intimations in Tacitus' Account of Jewish Origins," 339–346; *Jew and Gentile in the Ancient World*, 184–188, for whom this represents a most positive assessment of Jews.

61 The claim of Bloch *Antike Vorstellungen vom Judentum*, 84–86, that Tacitus here delivers a negative judgment, presenting the Jews as a *Randvolk*, is implausible.

62 Tac. *Hist.* 5.2.2; cf. Plut. *Isis*, 31. Bloch *Antike Vorstellungen vom Judentum*, 86–87, sees this as a hostile report.

63 Tac. *Hist.* 5.2.2. On this legend, see the discussions of Levy (1946), 332–334; Heubner and Fauth *P. Cornelius Tacitus*, 25–26.

64 Tac. *Hist.* 5.2.3.

65 Tac. *Hist.* 5.2.3; cf. Jos. *Ant.* 7.67; *CAp.* 1.172–174. See Levy "Tacite et l'origine du people juif," 334–339; Feldman "Pro-Jewish Intimations in Tacitus," 351–354; *Jew and Gentile in the Ancient World*, 190–192.

The digression reinforces this analysis at several junctures. Comments frequently serve Tacitus' purpose less as reflections on the Jews than as indirect jabs against others. So, for instance, he refers to Jewish sacrifices of rams and oxen. Why make this seemingly innocuous point? Tacitus leaves his readers in little doubt. Jews sacrifice the ram, he explains, as if to deliver a deliberate insult to Egyptian reverence for the ram-god Ammon. And they slay the ox as a further affront to the Egyptians, worshippers of the Apis bull.[66] Tacitus, we may venture to assume, knew full well that the ancient Israelites led a variety of animals to the sacrifice—as did the Greeks and the Romans. That he should single out these particular motives for sacrificing the ram and the ox and cast them as derisive of Egyptian religion suggests recourse to some black humor. The remarks serve more as a snide commentary on Egyptian homage to animals than on the customs of the Jews.

Nor does Tacitus miss a chance to take an indirect swipe at the Caesars. The Jews, he says, refuse to set up images in their cities or temples. They pay no such flattery to their kings, nor such honor to the emperors.[67] Some have taken this as a Tacitean criticism of the Jews for failing to pay due allegiance to Rome.[68] Not very likely. Tacitus had little enthusiasm for emperor worship himself. One might recall his nasty remark about Augustus' aggressive push to have his own priests and flamens, and to promote reverence of his sacred images in temples. The historian adds that there would be nothing left by which to honor the gods.[69] A similarly caustic comment surfaces when Tacitus reports a proposal to build a temple to the divine Nero. Some interpreted it, so he notes with relish, as a sign of Nero's impending death.[70] One may be quite confident that when the historian narrates the Jews' refusal to accept a statue of Caligula in their Temple, he was holding no brief for Caligula.[71] In short, the mention of Jewish aversion, to divine honors for the Caesars constitutes a sneer at the imperial cult, rather than at the Jews. Tacitus further takes a gratuitous slap at Claudius in this excursus. He speaks of the Jews as having bought the privilege of constructing walls in peacetime as if they were going to war, thus availing themselves of Roman avar-

---

66 Tac. *Hist.* 5.4.2: *caeso ariete velut in contumelidm Hammonis; bos quoque immolatur, quoniam Aegyptii Apin colunt.* On Egyptian practices here, see the scholarship cited by Heubner and Fauth *P. Cornelius Tacitus*, 48–51.
67 Tac. *Hist.* 5.5.4: *nulla simulacra urbibus suis, nedum templis sistunt; non regibus haec adulatio, non Caesaribus honor.*
68 Bloch *Antike Vorstellungen vom Judentum*, 95–96.
69 Tac. *Ann.* 1.10.
70 Tac. *Ann.* 15.74.
71 Tac. *Hist.* 5.9.2.

ice in the age of Claudius.[72] Even one of Tacitus' supposedly favorite *principes* comes in for a cutting put-down. Titus preferred to assault Jerusalem rather than wait for its surrender. Why? Tacitus offers his own elucidation: Titus already envisioned the wealth and pleasures he could enjoy in Rome, and, unless Jerusalem fell swiftly, he would have to delay his delights.[73] The cynical historian injects a characteristic analysis—and he has the Roman leader, not the Jews, as his victim.

Jewish history also afforded Tacitus an opportunity to skewer one of his favorite targets: the imperial freedman. He maintains that Claudius converted Judaea into a Roman province and entrusted it to *equites* or to freedmen. That happens to be inaccurate, but no matter. Tacitus' objective was to heap further abuse upon Antonius Felix. That individual was, in fact, the only *libertus* to serve as procurator of Judaea, an appointee of Claudius, a man who had insinuated himself into the imperial household and family, and one who behaved with monarchical savagery and licentiousness in his procuratorial capacity.[74] Tacitus' strictures, of course, did not arise out of compassion for the Jews but from malevolence toward ex-slaves appointed to the imperial service. The digression on the Jews served a variety of purposes for the acerbic historian.

Finally, the matter of religion. The excursus concludes with a chapter on prodigies that flared up at the time of the Jewish rebellion against Rome. Armies were spotted contending in battle in the skies, the fiery gleam of arms flashed, and suddenly the Temple itself lit up with a flame from the clouds.[75] Tacitus remarks that the Jews misconceived and fatally misunderstood those omens. As a people inclined to *superstitio* and hostile to *religio*, they rejected as improper any expiation of prodigies by sacrifice or vows.[76] Instead, they relied on their own messianic prophecies that promised world rule by men who set forth from Judaea. The Jewish commons, blinded by ambition, insisted upon interpreting those predictions in their own favor and refusing, even in adversity, to see the truth. For the truth was, according to Tacitus, that the ambiguous prophecy pointed to the future universal power of Vespasian and Titus, not to any supremacy of Jews.[77]

---

72 Tac. *Hist.* 5.12.2: *per avaritiam Claudianorum temporum.*
73 Tac. *Hist.* 5.11.2: *ipsi Tito Roma et opes voluptatesque ante oculos; ac ni Hierosolyma conciderent, morari videbantur.*
74 Tac. *Hist.* 5.9.3.
75 Tac. *Hist.* 5.13.1.
76 Tac. *Hist.* 5.13.1: *evenerant prodigia, quae neque hostiis neque votis piare fas habet gens superstitioni obnoxia, religionibus adversa.*
77 Tac. *Hist.* 5.13.2.

On the face of it, that interpretation appears to be a decisive rebuke of Jewish belief, practice, and trust in the divine. And so it is always read. Yet one might well ask just how much faith Tacitus himself put in prodigies—*quindecemvir sacris faciundis* though he was.[78] The historian, of course, rarely wears his heart on his sleeve on such, or indeed any, matters. In this connection, however, it is worth considering his comment at the beginning of the *Histories*. Tacitus takes note of warning prodigies in heaven and on earth, whether equivocal or obvious (*ambigua manifesta*). He then adds that the gods do not trouble themselves about our well-being, only about our punishment.[79] Even more telling, later in the *Histories*, he records a whole series of bizarre omens, almost in the style of Livy, that spread terror at the time of Otho's preparations against Vitellius. The canny Tacitus does not commit himself to their authenticity. Men took as omen or prodigy, he says, what actually came by chance or nature.[80] The historian was even more direct in recording a torrent of portents that followed the assassination of Agrippina the Younger. They came with frequency, he observes— and without meaning (*prodigia crebra et inrita*). Indeed they exhibited only the indifference of the gods (*sine cura deum*).[81]

In view of these passages, the vigilant reader could put into perspective Tacitus' sneer about the Jews' proclivity to read omens to their own advantage. Romans were as prone to misinterpret prodigies as the Jews—or anyone else. As Tacitus notes, it was a general human inclination (*mos humanae cupidinis*). In fact, as he put it elsewhere, the gods treat instances of virtue and vice with perfect impartiality.[82] In short, at the close of the excursus we still hear the caustic tone of the master of irony.

Tacitus is not quite finished on this subject. He includes one other striking omen among those forecasting the doom of the Jewish rebellion. He remarks that the doors of the Temple suddenly flew open, and a superhuman voice was heard to exclaim that the gods were exiting the sacred shrine.[83] That sort of portent, i.e. divine abandonment of a city or shrine thereby signaling its imminent demise, is a common convention, a means of reassuring the besiegers or justifying their victory. But why "gods" in the plural? The Jews had only one deity who could abandon them, as he had done so many times in the past. Was this a slip by Tacitus,

---

78 On his priesthood, see Tac. *Ann.* 11.11.
79 Tac. *Hist.* 1.3: *non esse curae deis securitatem nostram, esse ultionem.*
80 Tac. *Hist.* 1.86: *a fortuitis vel naturalibus causis.*
81 Tac. *Ann.* 14.12.
82 Tac. *Ann.* 16.33: *aequitate deum erga bona malaque documenta.*
83 Tac. *Hist.* 5.13.1: *apertae repente delubri fores et audita maior humana vox, excedere deos.*

an unconscious use of customary language, or an *interpretatio Romana?*[84] Not a likely solution. The historian had made a point of underscoring Jewish monotheism, contrasting Jews here not with Romans, interestingly enough, but with the Egyptians who worship a multitude of bestial and composite divinities.[85] Tacitus once again, it would be reasonable to infer, plays with paradox, testing his readers. Are they alert? Do they recognize the dissonance? What will they make of it? The narrative teases as much as it informs.

A summary is in order. This investigation does not propose that Tacitus was a friend of the Jews. They were hardly his favorite people. The text contains a number of offensive statements that cannot easily be dismissed or explained away. Tacitus undoubtedly shared the preconceptions and misgivings of many Romans before, during, and after his time toward the practices of alien peoples which they found outlandish and did not bother to understand properly. But he did not compose the excursus on the Jews to effect a denunciation and intellectual demolition of that people. Tacitus acts here neither as polemicist nor as advocate. This segment of the *Histories* has for too long been taken too straightforwardly. It is no mere ethnographical diversion.[86] What we find instead is the familiar Tacitus, the historian fond of paradox and antinomies, prone to irony and incongruity, who challenges his readers, forces them to pick apart the opinions and images set before them, offering solutions and then snatching them away, forever eluding their grasp. The digression on the Jews served to put on display the skills of the cunning and cynical writer who professed to inform his readers but in fact teased and toyed with them.

---

84 Bloch *Antike Vorstellungen vom Judentum*, 111–112, presumes that Tacitus thinks purely in Roman terms, offering Verg. *Aen.* 2.351–352 as parallel. Similarly, Heubner and Fauth *P. Cornelius Tacitus*, 150. But Josephus, *BJ* 6.300 also uses the plural here, presumably not as an *interpretatio Romana*. Whether this indicates that Josephus and Tacitus drew on the same source is a question that can be left aside. We may, in any case, be confident that Tacitus did not mindlessly adopt a phraseology inconsistent with assertions about Jewish monotheism.
85 Tac. *Hist.* 5.5.4.
86 Bloch *Antike Vorstellungen vom Judentum*, 143–166, usefully compares the excursus with Tacitus' treatments of Germans and Britons, finding both parallels and illuminating differences that give the discussion of the Jews a special character. His stress on the negative side of the Jewish excursus is somewhat unbalanced. But he rightly observes that none of the excursuses is pure ethnography for its own sake. Cf. also Bloch "Geography without Territory: Tacitus' Digression on the Jews and its Ethnographic Context", in J.U. Kalms, *Internationales Josephus-Kolloquium* (Münster, 2000), 38–54.

Jewish Experience in a Pagan World

13. Diaspora and Homeland

Diaspora lies deeply rooted in Jewish consciousness. It existed in one form or another almost from the start, and it persists as an integral part of the Jews' experience of history. The status of absence from the center has demanded time and again that Jews confront and, in some fashion, come to terms with a seemingly inescapable concomitant of their being.[1] The images of uprootedness, dispersal, and wandering haunt Jewish identity throughout. Jews have written about it incessantly, lamented it or justified it, dismissed it or grappled with it, embraced it or deplored it.

At a theoretical level, that experience has been deconstructed from two quite divergent angles. The gloomy approach holds primacy. On this view, diaspora dissolves into *galut*, exile, a bitter and doleful image, offering a bleak vision that issues either in despair or in a remote reverie of restoration. The negative image dominates modern interpretations of the Jewish psyche. Realization of the people's destiny rests in achieving the "return," the acquisition of a real or mythical homeland.[2] The alternative approach takes a very different route. It seeks refuge in a comforting concept: that Jews require no territorial sanctuary or legitimation. They are "the people of the Book." Their homeland resides in the text—not just the canonical Scriptures but an array of Jewish writings that help to

---

1 See the stimulating discussion by A. Eisen, *Galut* (Bloomington, 1986). Eisen recapitulates his thesis in A. A. Cohen and P. Mendes-Flohr, eds., *Contemporary Jewish Religious Thought* (New York, 1987), 219–25.

2 See, in general, the important works of Y. F. Baer, *Galut* (New York, 1947); Y. Kaufmann, *Exile and Estrangement* (in Hebrew), 2 vols. (Tel Aviv, 1962); Eisen, *Galut*. See also D. Vital, *The Origins of Zionism* (Oxford, 1975), 1–10; E. Levine, "The Jews in Time and Space," in E. Levine, ed., *Diaspora: Exile and the Jewish Condition* (New York, 1983), 1–11. For the notion of exile and return as a construct invented by the composers of the Pentateuch, dominating Jewish self-definition ever thereafter, see J. Neusner, "Exile and Return as the History of Judaism," in J. M. Scott, ed., *Exile: Old Testament, Jewish, and Christian Conceptions* (Leiden, 1997), 221–37, summarizing his lengthier presentation in *Self-Fulfilling Prophecy: Exile and Return in the History of Judaism* (Boston, 1987). In a similar vein, with specific reference to the Assyrian and Babylonian "exiles," see R. P. Carroll, "Exile! What Exile? Deportation and the Discourses of Diaspora," in L. Grabbe, ed., *Leading Captivity Captive: "The Exile" as History and Ideology* (Sheffield, 1998), 62–79; T. L. Thompson, "The Exile in History and Myth: A Response to Hans Barstad," in Grabbe, ed., *Leading Captivity Captive*, 101–18; P. R. Davies, "Exile? What Exile? Whose Exile?" in Grabbe, ed., *Leading Captivity Captive*, 128–38. This concept of the Jewish experience has become a paradigm for the diaspora mentality everywhere. Cf. W. Safran, "Diasporas in Modern Societies," *Diaspora* 1 (1991): 83–99. The use of such an ideal type is rightly criticized in the acute discussion of J. Clifford, *Routes: Travel and Translation in the Late Twentieth Century* (Cambridge, Mass., 1997), 244–77.

define the nation and give voice to its sense of identity. Their "portable Temple" serves the purpose. A geographical restoration is therefore superfluous, even subversive. To aspire to it deflects focus from what really counts, the embrace of the text, its ongoing commentary, and its continuous reinterpretation.[3] Diaspora, in short, is no burden; indeed, it is a virtue in the spread of the word. This justifies a primary attachment to the land of one's residence, rather than the home of the fathers.

The destruction of the Temple in 70 C.E., of course, constitutes a principal watershed for the Jews of antiquity. Both of the above analyses apply primarily as constructs to comprehend Jewish mentality in the generations, even centuries, after that cataclysmic event. The elimination of the center, source of spiritual nourishment and preeminent symbol of the nation's identity, compelled Jews to reinvent themselves, to find other means of religious sustenance, and to adjust their lives to an indefinite period of displacement. That story has been told many times and in many ways.[4]

But another story demands closer attention. Jews faced a more puzzling and problematic situation prior to the loss of the Temple. Diaspora did not await the fall of Jerusalem to Roman power and destructiveness. The scattering of Jews had begun long before—occasionally through forced expulsion, much more frequently through voluntary migration. The major push came with the arrival of the Greeks, the Hellenistic period. Alexander the Great's conquests stimulated wholesale settlements of Greek veterans, merchants, travelers, and adventurers in the lands of the eastern Mediterranean and the former subject areas of the Persian empire. That development proved to be an irresistible magnet. Jews migrated to the new settlements and expanded communities in substantial numbers. A Greek diaspora, in short, brought the Jewish one in its wake. Perhaps three to five million Jews dwelled outside Palestine in the roughly four centuries that stretched from Alexander to Titus.[5] The era of the Second Temple brought the

3 See especially G. Steiner, "Our Homeland, the Text," *Salmagundi* 66 (1985): 4–25. On the ambivalence of exile and homecoming in recent Jewish conceptions, see the comments of S. D. Ezrahi, "Our Homeland, the Text ... Our Text, the Homeland," *Michigan Quarterly Review* 31 (1992): 463–97.
4 The article by C. Milikowsky, "Notions of Exile, Subjugation, and Return in Rabbinic Literature," in Scott, ed., *Exile*, 265–81, argues, most interestingly, that early midrashic texts do not single out the Roman conquest as a pivotal turning point, but conceive a more continuous period of exile and subjugation, stretching through the Second Temple era and beyond. The notion of the Temple's fall as a caesura emerges only in later rabbinic writings,
5 Cf. Strabo, *apud* Jos. *A. J.* 14.115. For population estimates, see S. Baron, *Encyclopedia Judaica*, 13 (Jerusalem, 1971), 866–903; L. H. Feldman, *Jew and Gentile in the Ancient World* (Princeton, 1993), 23, 468–69, 555–56. Much uncertainty remains.

issue into sharp focus, inescapably so. The Temple still stood, a reminder of the hallowed past, and, through most of the era, a Jewish regime existed in Palestine. Yet the Jews of the diaspora, from Italy to Iran, far outnumbered those in the homeland. Although Jerusalem loomed large in their self-perception as a nation, few of them had seen it, and few were likely to. How then did diaspora Jews of the Second Temple conceive their association with Jerusalem, the emblem of ancient tradition?

In modern interpretations a dark picture prevails. Diaspora is something to be *overcome*.[6] Thunderous biblical pronouncements had presented it as the terrible penalty exacted by God for the sins of the Israelites. They will be scattered among the nations and pursued by divine wrath.[7] Spread among the lands, they will worship false gods and idols and enjoy no repose from the anger of the Lord.[8] Abandonment of ancestral precepts means that the children of Israel will have to enter the servitude of foreign lords in foreign parts.[9] They will be dispersed among peoples unknown to them or to their fathers and will suffer God's vengeance until their destruction.[10] Failure to heed the divine commandments or the warnings of prophets produces the scattering of Israel at the hands of the Lord.[11] The dismal character of exile seems reinforced by the words of the learned Hellenistic Jew Philo in the first century C.E. For him, banishment far exceeds death as the most feared penalty. Death at least puts an end to one's misery; exile perpetuates it, the equivalent of a thousand deaths.[12] No solace lies in adjustment. There seems nothing worth adjusting to. Only a single goal can keep flickering hopes alive: the expectation, however distant, of returning from exile and regaining a place in the Promised Land. The Bible offers that possibility. Obedience to the Lord and eradication of past errors will induce him to regather the lost souls spread across the world and restore them to the land of

---

6 A doleful portrait of diaspora for Hellenistic Jews is drawn most forcefully by W. C. van Unnik, *Das Selbstverständnis der jüdischen Diaspora in der hellenistisch-römischen Zeit* (Leiden, 1993), a posthumous publication of papers actually delivered in 1967. Van Unnik shows that the term "diaspora"—or more usually its verbal form—is almost always employed with a negative connotation in the Septuagint (which uses it to render various Hebrew words); *op. cit.*, 89 – 107. It has a negative meaning also in the large majority of its appearances in Hellenistic Jewish writers; *op. cit.*, 108 – 47.

7 Lev. 26.33.

8 Deut. 4.26 – 28, 28.63 – 65.

9 Jeremiah, 5.19.

10 Jeremiah, 9.15.

11 Dan., 9.4 – 7.

12 Philo, *Abr.* 64.; cf. *Conf. Ling.* 120 – 21, 196.

their fathers.[13] He will raise a banner among the nations and assemble the people of Judah from the four corners of the Earth.[14] Given such a tradition, it causes no surprise that the grim sense of diaspora and a correspondingly gloomy attitude are conventionally ascribed to Jews of the Second Temple.[15]

Yet that convention ignores a grave implausibility. It is not easy to imagine that millions of ancient Jews dwelled in foreign parts for generations mired in misery and obsessed with a longing for Jerusalem that had little chance of fulfillment. Many of them lived hundreds, even thousands, of miles away from Jerusalem, in Memphis, or Babylon, or Susa, or Athens, or Rome. To imagine that they repeatedly lamented their fate and pinned their hopes on recovery of the homeland is quite preposterous. Signs of a shift in scholarly attitudes are now discernible. Some recent works tip the balance away from the center to the periphery. It seems only logical that Jews sought out means whereby to legitimize a diaspora existence that most of them had inherited from their parents and would bequeath to their descendants.[16] As is well known, large and thriving Jewish communities existed in numerous areas of the Mediterranean with opportunities for

---

13 Deut. 30.2 – 5; cf. 1 Kgs., 8.33 – 34, 8.46 – 51; 2 Chron. 6.24 – 25, 6.36 – 39; Jeremiah, 29.10 – 14.

14 Isaiah, 11.12.

15 Baer, *Galut,* 9 – 13; Eisen, *Galut,* 3 – 34. As noted above, the most sweeping argument on melancholy Jewish attitudes toward the diaspora in the Second Temple era is made by van Unnik, *Das Selbstverständnis.* See also the useful survey by W. D. Davies, *The Territorial Dimension of Judaism* (Berkeley, 1982), 28 – 34, 61 – 100.

16 Davies, *Territorial Dimension,* 116 – 26, endeavors to resolve the "contradiction" between commitment to the Land at the center and the realities of life on the periphery, concluding that, although the pull of the Land is personal and powerful, it is not territorial. In the view of A. T. Kraabel, "Unity and Diversity among Diaspora Synagogues," in L. Levine, ed., *The Synagogue in Late Antiquity* (Philadelphia, 1987), 56 – 58, Jews shifted from an "Exile theology" to a "Diaspora theology," although he appears to believe that this really took hold only after the destruction of the Temple. The trenchant review article of J. Price rightly stresses the diversity of diaspora communities and the successes enjoyed by Jews therein; "The Jewish Diaspora of the Graeco-Roman Period," *SCI* 13 (1994): 170 – 79. But he plays down too much the power still wielded by the concept of the Holy Land. J. M. G. Barclay, *Jews in the Mediterranean Diaspora* (Edinburgh, 1996), 418 – 24, offers a sensible and balanced statement, arguing that attachment to the "motherland" could coexist with rootedness in regions abroad, although he regards the degree of attachment as dependent on circumstances. The fine study of I. M. Gafni, *Land, Center, and Diaspora* (Sheffield, 1997), 19 – 40, explores various strategies whereby diaspora Jews sought to account for or legitimize their situation. He places perhaps too much emphasis, however, upon the apologetic character in Hellenistic Jewish representations of local patriotism; *op. cit.,* 42 – 52.

economic advancement, social status, and even political responsibilities.[17] The essential facts are not in dispute.[18] Does it follow then that the displaced and dispersed had recourse to the thesis that mobility takes preference over territoriality, that the nation is defined by its texts rather than its location?

The dichotomy is deceptive. Hellenistic Jews did not have to face the eradication of the Temple. It was there—but they were not. Yet they nowhere developed a theory or philosophy of diaspora. The whole idea of privileging homeland over diaspora, or diaspora over homeland, derives from a modern, rather than an ancient, obsession. The issue is too readily conceived in terms of mutually exclusive alternatives: either the Jews reckoned their identity as unrealizable in exile, and the achievement of their destiny as dependent upon reentry into Judaea; or they clung to their heritage abroad, shifting attention to local and regional loyalties and cultivating a permanent attachment to the diaspora. Those alternatives, of course, have continuing contemporary resonance.[19] But Second Temple Jews did not confront so stark a choice.

Hellenistic texts, upon initial examination, would appear to support a solemn conclusion: life in foreign parts came as consequence of divine disfavor, a banishment from the homeland. The characterization of diaspora as exile occurs with some frequency in the works of Hellenistic Jewish writers.[20] And this

---

17 The classic study is J. Juster, *Les Juifs dans l'empire romain,* 2 vols. (Paris, 1914). Among treatments, see M. Stern, "The Jewish Diaspora," in S. Safrai and M. Stern, eds., *The Jewish People in the First Century* (Philadelphia, 1974), vol. 1, 117 – 83; E. Schürer, *The History of the Jewish People in the Age of Jesus Christ (175 B.C. – A.D. 135),* rev. ed. by G. Vermes, F. Millar, and M. Goodman (Edinburgh, 1986), vol. 3, part 1, 1 – 176; Barclay, *Jews in the Mediterranean Diaspora,* 19 – 81, 231 – 319; I. Levinskaya, *The Book of Acts in its Diaspora Setting* (Grand Rapids, 1996), 127 – 93.

18 On the variety of motives and circumstances that induced Jews to settle in various parts of the Mediterranean, see the evidence assembled and the discussion by A. Kasher, "Jewish Emigration and Settlement in Diaspora in the Hellenistic-Roman Period" (in Hebrew), in A. Shinan, ed., *Emigration and Settlement in Jewish and General History* (Jerusalem, 1982), 65 – 91.

19 See the contrasting views expressed by E. E. Urbach, "Center and Periphery in Jewish Historical Consciousness: Contemporary Implications," in M. Davis, ed., *World Jewry and the State of Israel* (New York, 1977), 217 – 35, and J. J. Petuchowski, "Diaspora Judaism—An Abnormality," *Judaism* 9 (1960): 17 – 28. Davies, *Territorial Dimension,* 91 – 100, usefully summarizes the positions.

20 Not that the two terms were reckoned as equivalent in antiquity. Indeed *galut* or *golah* is never translated as *diaspora* in Greek. The Septuagint employs a variety of Greek words, including ἀποικία [colony], μετοικεσία [change of abode], παροικία [residence abroad], and αἰχμαλοσία [captivity]. See van Unnik, *Das Selbstverständnis,* 80 – 85. Van Unnik, *op. cit.,* 150 – 52, even argues, paradoxically and implausibly, that diaspora was a grimmer concept for Jews than exile.

has prompted what seems to be a natural assumption: that the gloom represents Jewish attitudes in the contemplation of their current fate. But that assumption is shaky and vulnerable. A caveat has to be issued from the start. The majority of these grim pronouncements refer to the biblical misfortunes of the Israelites, expulsion by Assyrians, the destruction of the Temple, and the Babylonian Captivity. Were they all metaphors for the Hellenistic diaspora? The inference would be hasty, and it begs the question.[21]

Ben Sira laments the sins of his forefathers and records the fierce retaliation of the Lord that brought uprooting from their land and dispersal into every other land.[22] The reference, however, is to the era of Elijah and Elisha, to the ills of the Northern Kingdom, and to the Assyrian conquest that scattered the Israelites. It may, indeed, have contained a warning to Ben Sira's contemporaries, whose shortcomings paralleled those of his ancestors—but it did not condemn the current diaspora. The Book of Tobit tells a tale that ostensibly takes place in the Assyrian Captivity as well. Tobit bewails his own fate, prompted by the sins of his forefathers, and the fate of his countrymen, now an object of scorn and a vulnerable prey to those in the nations whither they have been dispersed.[23] A later prayer by Tobit once again labels the diaspora as a penalty for Israel's abandonment of tradition, but looks ahead to divine mercy and redemption.[24] And a final prediction anticipates another calamity, the loss of the Temple, the desolation of the land, and yet another dispersal abroad.[25] To suppose that the author of Tobit sees in all this a reflection of his present circumstances is a simplistic leap. Tobit also forecasts the recovery of the Temple and portrays the outcome as the culmination of Israelite dreams, a happy ending to endure indefinitely.[26] That hardly suggests that the Hellenistic diaspora is a vale of tears.

See the just criticisms by J. M. Scott, "Exile and the Self-Understanding of Diaspora Jews," in Scott, ed., *Exile,* 180–84.

21 Scott, in Scott, ed., *Exile,* 185–87, notes certain passages in the Septuagint on the expulsion of the Jews to which the translators added phrases such as "until this day"; Deut. 29.28; 2 Kgs., 17.23; 2 Chron. 29.9. It hardly follows that these were intended to apply to the Hellenistic era.

22 Ben Sira, 48.15: ἕως ἐπρονομεύθησαν ἀπὸ γῆς αὐτῶν / καὶ διεσκορπίσθησαν ἐν πάσῃ τῇ γῇ. Elsewhere he offers up a prayer for divine deliverance in an ostensibly contemporary context, including a plea for gathering all the tribes of Jacob and restoring their inheritance as from the beginning; 36.10. But Ben Sira here echoes biblical language and by no means implies a longing for return felt in the diaspora.

23 Tobit, 3.3–4.

24 Tobit, 13.3–6, 13.10–11.

25 Tobit, 14.4.

26 Tobit, 13.10–11, 14.5–7.

The same can be found in the Book of Judith. Achior, the Ammonite leader, briefly sketches the highlights of Israelite history to Holofernes and includes the deportation to Babylon and the scattering of Jews as a devastating penalty for waywardness. But the penalty was canceled with the return from exile and the rebuilding of the Temple.[27] Nothing in Judith suggests that subsequent dispersion, when the Temple remained intact, derived from sin and punishment.

The dire predictions that occur in the Testaments of the Twelve Patriarchs include the calamity of dispersal to the four corners of the Earth, wrought by the wrath of God, the equivalent of captivity among the nations. Here too the sons of Jacob foresaw the capture of the Temple and the grief of their people in Babylon—but also the renewal of divine compassion and eventual restoration.[28] This makes no direct, and probably no indirect, allusion to diaspora Jews of the Greco-Roman era.[29] Similar conclusions apply to various other statements in Second Temple texts. Jubilees reports the afflictions suffered by Israelites who succumbed to idolatry and were scattered by God into captivity amidst the nations.[30] The Psalms of Solomon include a hymn praising the righteousness of the Lord in expelling Israel's neglectful inhabitants from their land and sending them into exile around the world.[31] The Greek additions to Jeremiah, incorporated as I Baruch in the Septuagint, echo the self-reproach for misdeeds that produced the Lord's dispersal of the Israelites and landed them in an accursed exile.[32] And the thunderous forecasts of the Third Sibylline Oracle contain a segment on abandonment of the Temple, enslavement by Assyrians, desolation of the land, and distribution of the despised throughout Earth and sea.[33] This repeated theme runs through the texts, extending over a lengthy stretch of time. The biblical allusions are stern and severe, reminders of past punishments and warnings against future apostasy.[34] Diaspora dwellers in the Greco-Roman

---

27 Judith, 5.18 – 19.

28 Test. Levi, 10.3 – 4, 15.1 – 2, 16.5; Test. Judah, 23.3 – 5; Test. Iss. 6.1 – 4; Test. Zeb. 9.6 – 8; Test. Dan, 5.8 – 13; Test. Asher, 7.2 – 6.

29 The Testament of Naphtali, 4.1 – 5, speaks of two separate calamities inflicted by God, an exile and a scattering, after each of which he restores his favor to the children of Israel. For van Unnik, *Das Selbstverständnis*, 119 – 20, the second actually refers to the Hellenistic diaspora. But it may well allude to the aftermath of the destruction in 70 C.E.; so M. de Jonge, *The Testaments of the Twelve Patriarchs* (Leiden, 1978), 85.

30 Jubilees, 1.9 – 13.

31 Ps. Solomon, 9.1 – 2.

32 I Baruch, 3.8.

33 3 Sib.Or., 266 – 79.

34 Even Josephus, who rarely indulges in this form of outburst, expands on Deuteronomy and has Moses warn his people of dispersal and servitude everywhere in the inhabited world as con-world are put on notice, lest they lapse again. But a notable fact needs emphasis. The texts do not make the current scattering itself a target of reproach or a source of discontent.[35]

Our sources do, it can be conceded, make reference to Jews in Ptolemaic Egypt who did not arrive there of their own free will. Convoluted and controversial evidence applies to the transfer of Jews to Egypt in the wake of Ptolemy I's campaigns in Palestine. The *Letter of Aristeas* reports that some Jews migrated south after being removed from Jerusalem by the Persians and a far greater number, more than one hundred thousand, came as prisoners of war after Ptolemy I's invasion.[36] Josephus, however, preserves a different version, ostensibly drawn from Hecataeus of Abdera, but almost certainly composed by a Jewish writer cloaking himself in the persona of Hecataeus. In this happy account, the Jews accompanied Ptolemy voluntarily and enthusiastically, impressed by his gentleness and magnanimity, making a contented home for themselves in his country.[37] The truth of the matter may be indeterminable. It is, in any case, irrelevant for our purposes. Even the harsh version in the *Letter of Aristeas* is immediately softened. Ptolemy I employed the newly arrived Jews in his army, paid them handsomely, and set them up in garrisons.[38] His son went much further. Ptolemy II excused his father's severe actions as necessary to appease his troops and then proceeded not only to liberate all Jewish captives in Egypt, but to enroll many in the forces and even to promote the more trustworthy leaders to official positions in the realm.[39] The reality or unreality of this rosy picture makes no difference. This was the image conveyed by Egyptian Jews. They did not portray themselves as laboring under the yoke. Josephus, extrapolating from the narrative of "Pseudo-Hecataeus," pointedly contrasts the forcible expulsion of the

---

sequence of their rebellion; *Ant.* 4.189–91. In the view of B. Halpern-Amaru, "Land Theology in Josephus' *Jewish Antiquities*," *JQR* 71 (1980/81): 219–21, Josephus here obliquely alludes to the Jewish revolt of 66–70 C.E. So also van Unnik, *Das Selbstverständnis*, 141–42.

35 As is assumed, e.g., by Price, *SCI* 13 (1994): 172.

36 *Let. Aris.* 12: τοὺς μὲν μετῴκιζεν, οὓς δὲ ἠχμαλώτιζε; 35: ἀνασπάστους ... ὑπὸ Περσῶν ... αἰχμαλώτους.. Similarly, Jos. *A. J.* 12.7.

37 Jos. *C. Ap.* 1.186; cf. Jos. *A. J.* 12.9. That this is the work of a Jewish "Pseudo-Hecataeus" is cogently argued by B. Bar-Kochva, *Pseudo-Hecataeus "On the Jews": Legitimizing the Jewish Diaspora* (Berkeley, 1996), 71–82.

38 *Let. Aris.* 13–14, 36. Josephus even adds that he bestowed citizen privileges equivalent to those of the Macedonians; Jos. *A. J.* 12.8.

39 *Let. Aris.* 19–27, 36–37.

Jews to Babylon by the "Persians" with their migration to Egypt and Phoenicia after the death of Alexander the Great.[40]

The inventive tale of III Maccabees places the Jews of Egypt in the gravest peril. Thrice they were almost annihilated by the wicked schemes of the mad monarch Ptolemy IV The text alludes to a precarious existence at the mercy of their enemies. They were to perish unjustly, a foreign people in a foreign land.[41] But the dire forecast did not come to pass. The Jews triumphed in the tale, their enemies thwarted and their apostates punished. More significantly, their vindication would be celebrated by an annual festival—in Egypt.[42] The diaspora existence, in III Maccabees as in the *Letter of Aristeas,* could go on indefinitely and contentedly.

What of restoration to the homeland, the presumed sole remedy for the anguish of exiles? Such a promise derives from the Pentateuch: the Lord who issued the banishment will eventually return the children of Israel from the most remote regions to the land of their fathers.[43] That happy ending recurs in the same Hellenistic writers who bemoan the transgressions that brought about dispersal in the first place. Tobit affirms that God's fury will be followed by his mercy, thus to produce an ingathering of the exiles and even conversion of the Gentiles.[44] Achior, in the Book of Judith, informs the Assyrian general that the Israelites have regained their city and their temple. To be sure, they might lose them again if they go astray—but that anticipates perilous times in Palestine, not the drawbacks of diaspora existence.[45] The prophecy in Asher's testament foresees the same reinstatement of the scattered faithful through the benevolence of God.[46] Similar sentiments are expressed in the Psalms of Solomon.[47] And God himself makes the identical promise to Moses in the text of Jubilees: after consigning his people to captivity among their foreign enemies,

---

40 Jos. *C. Ap.* 1. 194: ἀνασπάστους εἰς Βαβυλῶνα Πέρσαι πρότερον ἐποίησαν μυριάδας, οὐκ ὀλίγαι δὲ καὶ μετὰ τὸν Ἀλεξάνδρου θάνατον εἰς Αἴγυπτον καὶ Φοινίκην μετέστησαν. On the truth of these matters, see the discussion by Bar-Kochva, *Pseudo-Hecataeus,* 101–5, 143–44.
41 3 Macc. 6.3: λαὸν ἐν ξένῃ γῇ ξένον ἀδίκως ἀπολλύμενον. Cf. 6.10: κατὰ τὴν ἀποικίαν; 6.15: ἐν τῇ γῇ τῶν ἐχθρῶν αὐτῶν.
42 3 Macc. 6.36, 7.15, 7.19.
43 Deut. 30.1–5; cf. Jeremiah, 23.8; Ezek. 11.16–17. Philo's reference, *Praem. et Poen.* 115, to the change from a "spiritual diaspora" to wisdom and virtue, allegorizes the prophecy in Deuteronomy but does not refer to Hellenistic expectations or desire for return to Judaea. Nor does his gloss on Deut. 30.4 at *Conf. Ling.* 197.
44 Tobit, 13.5, 13.10–11, 13.13, 14.5–7.
45 Judith, 5.19.
46 Test. Asher, 7.7.
47 Ps. Solomon, 8.28.

he will reassemble them once more in the place of their origins to revere their newly rebuilt sanctuary.[48] But in each instance the termination of exile and return to the homeland is connected to the reconstruction of the Temple. Its demolition as symbol of the faith had rendered foreign enslavement—or its representation—especially wrenching. A comparable condition, however, did not hold in the Hellenistic diaspora.[49] The Temple stood again in Jerusalem, and few Jews abroad were held there by constraint.[50]

Just one text takes up this theme and applies it to the ingathering of exiles in the Hellenistic age. The preamble of II Maccabees contains a letter purportedly sent by Judah Maccabee, the council of elders, and the people of Jerusalem and Judaea to the Jews of Egypt. The vexed questions of whether or not the letter is authentic, whether Judah ever sent it, whether it was composed by the author of II Maccabees or attached later, and what parts are original and what parts interpolated can all here be set aside.[51] It is, on any reckoning, a Hellenistic com-

---

48 Jubilees, 1.15 – 17. Cf. the analysis of B. Halpern-Amaru, "Exile and Return in Jubilees," in Scott, ed., *Exile*, 139 – 41. See also I Baruch, 2.29 – 35.

49 The arguments of Scott, in Scott, ed., *Exile*, 209 – 13, for a continuing hope of return through the Greco-Roman period lack foundation in the evidence. The texts cited do not derive from the diaspora.

50 Philo, in a puzzling passage, does make reference to Jews in Greek and barbarian islands and continents, enslaved to those who had taken them captive, and ultimately to strive for the one appointed land; *Praem. et Poen.* 164 – 65. He draws here on the texts of Lev. 26.40 – 45 and Deut. 30.1 – 10. But the language must be metaphorical and the sense is allegorical, with messianic overtones, as the Jews will be conducted by a divine and superhuman vision; 165: ξεναγούμενοι πρός τινος θειοτέρας ἢ κατὰ φύσιν ἀνθρωπίνην ὄψεως. Cf. van Unnik, *Das Selbstverstandis*, 132 – 36. It is unjustified to see here a concrete concept of the return, as does J. M. Scott, "Philo and the Restoration of Israel," *SBL Seminar Papers* (1995), 567, or a belief in the eventual disappearance of the diaspora, as proposed by J. J. Collins, *Between Athens and Jerusalem*, 2d ed. (Grand Rapids, 2000), 134 – 35. The passage is best understood as a symbolic voyage to God or true wisdom. Philo expresses a closely comparable idea in *Conf. Ling.* 81. In any case, Philo's references to the ingathering of the exiles, even in an obscure fashion, occur almost exclusively in the *De Praemiis et Poenis*. Cf. the treatment by B. Halpern-Amaru, "Land Theology in Philo and Josephus," in L. A. Hoffmann, ed., *The Land of Israel: Jewish Perspectives* (Notre Dame, 1986), 83 – 85. On Philo's messianic ideas, see the valuable discussions with surveys of earlier opinions by R. D. Hecht, "Philo and Messiah," in J. Neusner, W. S. Green, and E. Frerichs, eds., *Judaisms and their Messiahs at the Time of the Christian Era* (Cambridge, Eng., 1987), 139 – 68, and P. Borgen, "'There Shall Come Forth a Man': Reflections on Messianic Ideas in Philo," in J. H. Charlesworth, ed., *The Messiah* (Minneapolis, 1992), 341 – 61.

51 2 Macc. 1.10 – 2.18. See, e.g., E. Bickermann, "Ein jüdischer Festbrief vom Jahre 124 v.Chr.," *ZNW* 32 (1933): 234 – 35; J. Bunge, *Untersuchungen zum zweiten Mackabäerbuch* (Bonn, 1971), 32 – 94; C. Habicht, *2 Makkabäerbuch*, Jüdische Schriften aus hellenistisch-römischer Zeit, vol. 1, part 3 (Gütersloh, 1976), 201 – 2; B. Z. Wacholder, "The Letter from

position. The missive concludes with the hope that God, who has now delivered Jews from great evils (the persecutions by Antiochus IV) and has purified the sanctuary, will show compassion and reassemble Jews from all regions of the world to the holy place.[52] Do we have here then a reflection of a continued wish for dissolving the diaspora and repopulating Judaea with those languishing abroad?

The inference is far from inevitable. This concocted letter, whatever its genuineness, represents a Maccabaean line. Judah deliberately and pointedly echoes the biblical theme.[53] The final lines of the epistle follow closely the wording in Deuteronomy 30.3 – 5. And they are not the only allusion to this motif of regathering the dispersed. Earlier in the letter Judah cites Nehemiah, recently returned to Jerusalem, issuing a prayer after the erection of the Second Temple that God liberate the enslaved among the nations and reassemble those in the diaspora.[54] Later he adverts to Jeremiah at the time of the exile and the prophet's promise that God will show pity and bring his people together again.[55] The latter two passages are inventions by the composer, without authority in the Scriptures. The purpose plainly is to link Judah's achievement in the purification of the Temple to grand moments of the Israelite past. The letter alludes not only to the rebuilding of the Temple in the time of Nehemiah but to its initial construction by King Solomon himself and even to divine signs vouchsafed to Moses.[56] Judah is set in the line of the grand figures of biblical antiquity. That context accounts for the phraseology of regathering the exiles, a dramatic plea with scriptural resonance, not a mirror of contemporary longings by diaspora Jews.

The point can be strengthened. Judah's epistle directed itself to the Jews of Egypt. Its principal objective was to declare the celebration of Hanukkah (or its original version as a Feast of Tabernacles) and to encourage the Judaeans' Egyptian compatriots to celebrate it as well.[57] The message contemplates no dissolution of that diaspora community, but rather presupposes its continued existence.

Judah Maccabee to Aristobulus," *HUCA* 49 (1978): 89 – 133; J. A. Goldstein, *II Maccabees* (Garden City, 1983), 154 – 88.

52 2 Macc. 2.18: ἐλπίζομεν γὰρ ἐπὶ τῷ θεῷ ὅτι ταχέως ἡμᾶς ἐλεήσει καὶ ἐπισυνάξει ἐκ τῆς ὑπὸ τὸν οὐρανὸν εἰς τὸν ἅγιον τόπον. ἐξείλετο γὰρ ἡμᾶς ἐκ μεγάλων κακῶν καὶ τὸν τόπον ἐκαθάρισεν.

53 See, most recently, T. A. Bergren, "Nehemiah in 2 Maccabees, 1:10 – 2:18," *JSJ* 28 (1997): 249 – 70.

54 2 Macc. 1.27: ἐπισυνάγαγε τὴν διασπορὰν ἡμῶν, ἐλευθέρωσον τοὺς δουλεύοντας ἐν τοῖς ἔθνεσιν.

55 2 Macc. 2.7: ἕως ἂν συναγάγῃ ὁ θεὸς ἐπισυναγωγὴν τοῦ λαοῦ καὶ ἵλεως γένηται.

56 2 Macc. 8 – 12.

57 2 Macc. 1.9, 1.18, 2.16.

A consistency holds amidst these texts. Dismal memories of misery and exile recall the biblical era, sufferings under Assyrians and Babylonians. But redemption came, the promise of a new Temple was kept. The lamentations do not apply to current conditions. Hellenistic constructs have Jews thrive in Egypt, overcome their enemies, and enjoy festivities that celebrate triumphs won in Palestine and the diaspora alike.

How compelling was the notion of a "homeland" to Jews dwelling in distant and dispersed communities of the Mediterranean?[58] In principle, the concept held firm. The sanctity of Jerusalem retained a central place in the consciousness of Hellenistic Jews, wherever they happened to reside. They had not wrapped themselves in the text as the real meaning of their identity, embracing their location in the diaspora and indifferent to their territorial roots. Judah Maccabee labels Jerusalem as the "Holy City" in his epistle to the Egyptian Jews, as one might expect.[59] The phrase also appears several times in the work of the Alexandrian Jew Philo, who never doubts the primacy of Jerusalem.[60] And the Jewish devotion to their sacred "acropolis" is observed even by the pagan geographer Strabo.[61] Numerous other texts characterize Palestine as the "holy land." That designation occurs in II Maccabees, the Wisdom of Solomon, the Testament of Job, the Sibylline Oracles, and Philo.[62] Most, if not all, of these works stem from the diaspora. They underscore the reverence with which Jews around the Mediterranean continued to regard Jerusalem and the land of their fathers.[63]

---

58 This, of course, is not the place to examine the concept of the "Land of Israel" in Jewish thought generally, a vast topic. See the succinct and valuable study by Davies, *Territorial Dimension*.

59 2 Macc. 1.12: ἐν τῇ ἁγίᾳ πόλει.

60 Philo, *Legat.* 225: κατὰ τὴν ἱερόπολιν; 281, 288, 299, 346; *Somn.* 2.246. See also his emphasis upon the centrality of the Temple in Jewish practice and allegiance; Philo, *Spec.* 1.66–68. Cf. A. Kasher, "Jerusalem as 'Metropolis' in Philo's National Consciousness" (in Hebrew), *Cathedra* 11 (1979): 48–49.

61 Strabo, 16.2.37.

62 2 Macc. 1.7; Wisdom, 12.3; Test. Job, 33.5: ἐν τῇ ἁγίᾳ γῇ; 3 Sib. 267: πέδον ἁγνὸν; 732–35; 5 Sib. 281; Philo, *Heres*, 293; *Somn.* 2.75; Philo, *Spec.* 4.215; *Flacc.* 46; Philo, *Legat.* 202: τῆς ἱερᾶς χώρας; 205, 330. Cf. Zech. 2.16. On Philo and the "Holy Land," see B. Schaller, "Philon von Alexandreia und das 'Heilige Land,'" in G. Strecker, ed., *Das Land Israel in biblischer Zeit* (Gottingen, 1983), 175–82, who finds the philosopher's appeal to this concept largely determined by the particular circumstances in which he was writing—most of the references coming when Judaea was under threat. Cf. R. L. Wilken, *The Land Called Holy* (New Haven, 1992), 34–37; G. Delling, *Die Bewaltigung der Diasporasituation durch das hellenistische Judentum* (Gottingen, 1987), 37–39.

63 Philo, in fact, indicates that even the migration of Abraham to Canaan was more like a return to his native land than a movement to foreign parts, thus associating the Jews with Pales-

Loyalty to one's native land was a deep commitment in the rhetoric of the Hellenistic world.[64] A striking passage in the *Letter of Aristeas* pronounces that precept in unequivocal fashion. Amidst the myriad questions put to his Jewish guests by Ptolemy II at his week-long symposium was one that asked "how to be a lover of one's country." The respondent made as strong a contrast as can be imagined between a native land and residence abroad, between *patris* and *xenia*. It is a noble thing, he said, to live and die in one's own country; by contrast, *xenia* brings contempt to the poor and shame to the rich—as if they had been expelled for criminal behavior.[65] The statement, surprisingly enough, has received almost no comment from commentators.[66] Prima facie, it looks like a *locus classicus* for Jewish belief that life in Palestine alone is worth living and that diaspora existence is mere despair and disgrace.

Philo more than once endorses the idea that adherence to one's *patris* has compelling power. He speaks of the charms of kinsmen and homeland; trips abroad are good for widening one's horizons, but nothing better than coming home.[67] Failure to worship God is put on a level with neglecting to honor parents, benefactors, and *patris*.[68] Defending one's country is a prime virtue.[69] And, as Philo has Agrippa say to Caligula, love of one's native land and compliance with its precepts is deeply ingrained in all men.[70]

Palestine as the *patris* appears as a recurrent theme. The diaspora author of II Maccabees brands the Jewish villains of his piece, Simon, Jason, and Mene-

tine from the dawn of history; *Abr.* 62: καθάπερ ἀπὸ τῆς ξένης εἰς τὴν οἰκείαν ἐπανιὼν ἀλλ᾽ οὐκ ἀπὸ τῆς οἰκείας εἰς τὴν ξένην. Cf. Artapanus, *apud* Euseb. *PE*, 9.18.1; Wisdom, 12.2–7; Jos. *A. J.* 1.159–60.

64 Cf. Polybius, 1.14.4: καὶ γὰρ φιλόπιλον εἶναι δεῖ τὸν ἀγαθὸν ἄνδρα καὶ φιλόπατριν.
65 *Let. Aris.* 249: ὅτι καλὸν ἐν ἰδίᾳ καὶ ζῆν καὶ τελευτᾶν. ἡ δὲ χενία τοῖς μὲν πένησι καταφρόνησιν ἐργάζεται, τοῖς δὲ πλουσίοις ὄνειδος, ὡς διὰ κακίαν ἐκπεπτωκόσιν.
66 Cf., e. g., the standard commentaries, R. Tramontano, *La lettera di Aristea a Filocrate* (Naples, 1931), 211–12; H. G. Meecham, *The Letter of Aristeas* (Manchester, 1935), 290–91; M. Hadas, *Aristeas to Philocrates* (New York, 1951), 197; A. Pelletier, *Lettre d'Aristée à Philocrate* (Paris, 1962), 212, 250.
67 Philo, *Abr.* 63, 65.
68 Philo, *Mos.* 2.198; *Mut.* 40; cf. Philo, *Spec.* 1.68; *Plant.* 146; *Ebr.* 17; *Fug.* 29; *Deus Imm.* 17.
69 Philo, *Cher.* 15; *Abr.* 197; *Leg.* 328.
70 Philo, *Legat.* 277: πᾶσιν ἀνθρώποις αὐτοκράτορ, ἐμπέφυκεν ἔρως μὲν τῆς πατρίδος, τῶν δὲ οἰκείων νόμων ἀποδοχή. Cf. *Migr. Abr.* 217; Philo, *Spec.* 1.68, 4.16–17. Philo's references to πάτρις in the metaphorical sense, as abandonment of the territorial homeland for the true πάτρις, are not, of course, relevant to this point. See, e. g., Philo, *Spec.* 1.51–53; *Conf. Ling.* 78, 81. Other references in S. Pearce, "Belonging and Not Belonging: Local Perspectives in Philo of Alexandria," in S. Jones and S. Pearce, eds., *Jewish Local Patriotism and Self Identification in the Graeco-Roman Period* (Sheffield, 1998), 100.

laus, as betrayers of their homeland.[71] Judah Maccabee, on the other hand, is a preeminent champion of his *patris* and its laws.[72] The Hebrews, according to Philo, had migrated to Egypt as if it were a second fatherland, but eventually they conceived a longing for the real thing, their ancient and native land.[73] A comparable formulation can be found in Artapanus' recreation of the Exodus,[74] and in the Greek drama on that theme composed by Ezekiel.[75] That the term *patris* is no mere shorthand expression for traditions, practices, the site of their faith, or even Jerusalem is clear from an unambiguous assertion in II Maccabees. Judah Maccabee called upon his troops to fight nobly and to the death for their laws, their temple, their city, their *patris,* and their way of life.[76] *Patris* is not synonymous with any of the rest. The native land is Palestine.

So, Jerusalem as concept and reality remained a powerful emblem of Jewish identity—not supplanted by the Book or disavowed by those who dwelled afar. How then to interpret this tenacious devotion? Do these pronouncements entail a widespread desire to pull up stakes and return to the fatherland? It might seem logical, even inevitable, to conclude that diaspora Jews set their hearts upon such a return. Fulfillment could come only with a reconnection to the *patris.*[77]

Logical perhaps, but not inevitable. Broad pronouncements about love of one's country accord with general Hellenistic attitudes and expressions.[78] They do not require that residence abroad be abandoned and native environs reinhabited lest life remain incomplete. References to the Hebrews' migration to Egypt from the fatherland and subsequent recovery of that fatherland are perfectly reasonable and acceptable—without imposing upon them the burden of masquerading for aspirations by Hellenistic Jews. It is noteworthy that the texts that speak of reverence for the *patris* do not speak of the "return."

The bold and forceful statement in the *Letter of Aristeas,* noted above, offers an ostensibly formidable obstacle. The Jewish spokesman, in a Hellenistic composition and a Hellenistic setting, draws a stark contrast between the nobility of living and dying in one's *patris* and the ignominy of dwelling abroad.[79] Is the ref-

---

71 2 Macc. 4.1, 5.8–9, 5.15, 13.3.
72 2 Macc. 8.21, 13.10.
73 Philo, *Mos.* 1.36; *Hyp.* 6.1.
74 Artapanus, *apud* Eus. *PE,* 9.27.21.
75 Ezekiel, *Exagoge, apud* Eus. *PE,* 9.28.12.
76 2 Macc. 13.14: παρακαλέσας τοὺς σὺν αὐτῷ γενναίως ἀγωνίσασθαι μέχρι θανάτου περὶ νόμων, ἱεροῦ, πόλεως, πατρίδος, πολιτείας.
77 So, e.g., Kasher, *Cathedra* 11 (1979): 52–56.
78 Cf. I. Heinemann, "The Relationships between the Jewish People and Its Land in Jewish-Hellenistic Literature" (in Hebrew), *Zion* 13–14 (1948): 3–6; Kasher, *Cathedra* 11 (1979): 45–50.
79 *Let. Aris.* 249. See above, n. 65.

erence here to Palestine? Not an obvious conclusion. In the context of the whole work, a disparagement of Egypt as residence for Jews would be absurd. The main message of the *Letter* directs itself to Egyptian Jews for whom the Hebrew Scriptures are rendered into Greek, an accomplishment they greet with fervid gratitude. Indeed, they insist that not a word be changed in the translation, so that it remain forever inviolable.[80] The entire tale rests on the premise that diaspora Jews will now have direct access to the tenets of their faith and a solid foundation for enduring communities abroad. Why then this statement in the symposium? It is well to remember that each question posed by Ptolemy II seeks advice from a Jewish sage on some aspect of how to govern his kingdom or how to lead a good life. In this instance, the king asks how he might be a genuine lover of his country.[81] The first part of the answer, that which contrasts native land and foreign residence, seems curiously irrelevant. And the last part, which advises Ptolemy to bestow benefits on all, just as he regularly does, and thus to be reckoned a real patriot, presupposes (if it carries any substantive meaning) the continued and contented community of resident aliens. Like so many of the swift and brief retorts by Jewish sages at the banquet, this one is bland and unsatisfying, containing statements that barely pertain to the king's query. The passage, whatever its significance, can hardly serve as a touchstone for the thesis that diaspora Jews were consumed with a desire to forsake their surroundings.

Did Jewish settlements abroad carry a stigma? A term sometimes employed to characterize them might, at first sight, seem to suggest it. They were reckoned as *apoikiai* [colonies]. That designation presented them as offshoots from the metropolis, secondary to the original. But the term in customary Greek usage lacked pejorative overtones and, as employed by Jewish writers, its implications were, in fact, decidedly positive.

The Jews hounded and herded in Alexandria faced nearly certain death in the fantasy depicted in III Maccabees. A final prayer reached God from the elderly and respected priest Eleazer. Among his pleas Eleazer included a reference to possible impieties committed by Jews in their *apoikia*.[82] But the sins, not the location, provide the grounds for potential destruction. And the happy ending vindicates and perpetuates the colony. The new festival instituted by the Egyptian Jews to celebrate their rescue and triumph would hold for generations to

---

80 *Let. Aris.* 308–11.
81 *Let. Aris.* 249: πῶς ἂν φιλόπατρις εἴη.
82 3 Macc. 6.10: εἰ δὲ ἀσεβείαις κατὰ τὴν ἀποικίαν ὁ βίος ἡμῶν ἐνέσχηται.

come and throughout the time of their settlement abroad—here designated as *paroikia*.[83]

Philo uses the word *apoikia* with reference to Moses leading the Hebrews out of their abode in Egypt. No negative overtones characterize that statement. The same phraseology in the same context was employed three and a half centuries earlier by the Greek writer Hecataeus of Abdera.[84] Indeed, Philo elsewhere makes clear his very positive assessment of Jewish "colonies" abroad. God reassured Moses that Jews dwelling abroad in future generations would be on the same footing as Jews in Palestine with regard to fulfilling sacred rites. The diaspora Jews, he affirms explicitly, live at a distance through no transgression, but through the need of an overpopulated nation to send out *apoikiai*.[85] The philosopher reiterates that statement in fuller form in Agrippa's letter to Caligula, proudly detailing the colonies that had been sent out from Judaea over the years to places all over the Mediterranean and the Near East.[86] Josephus echoes Philo in asserting that Jewish participation in colonies sent abroad by other nations gave them an honored presence in those settlements from the start.[87] In a most revealing passage, Philo, in fact, asserts that in the case of those sent to a colony, by contrast to those simply away from home, the *apoikia,* rather than the *metropolis,* becomes the *patris*.[88] Jerusalem was indeed the mother city.[89] But, as

---

83 3 Macc. 6.36: ἐπὶ πᾶσαν τὴν παροικίαν αὐτῶν εἰς γενεάς; 7.19: ταύτας ἄγειν τὰς ἡμέρας ἐπὶ τὸν τῆς παροικίας αὐτῶν χρόνον εὐφροσύνους. The latter may be a doublet of the former. These passages do not imply that the author emphasized the temporary character of the sojourn in Egypt and looked ahead with enthusiasm to the "ingathering of the exiles," *pace* Heinemann, *Zion* 13 – 14 (1948): 7; Scott, in Scott, ed., *Exile*, 192.

84 Philo, *Mos.* 1.71: ἡγεμόνα τῆς ἐνθένδε ἀποικίας; Hecataeus, *apud* Diod. 40.3.3: ἡγεῖτο δὲ τῆς ἀποικίας.

85 Philo, *Mos.* 2.232. On this passage, see Gafni, *Land*, 58 – 59. Cf. Josephus' reference to the same principles that apply to priestly practices both in Judaea and wherever there is a community of Jews; *Cap.* 1.32, employing the term σύστημα.

86 Philo, *Legat.* 281 – 82. Y. Amir, "Philo's Version of the Pilgrimage to Jerusalem" (in Hebrew), in A. Oppenheimer, U. Rappaport, and M. Stern, *eds., Jerusalem in the Second Temple Period* (Jerusalem, 1980), 154 – 57, presses the analogy with Greek colonization a little too far.

87 Philo, *Flacc.* 46; Jos. *C. Ap.* 2.38. The view of Kasher, *Cathedra*, 11 (1979), 49 – 53, that this sets "colonies" in a lower or dependent status with regard to the metropolis, misplaces the emphasis.

88 Philo, *Conf. Ling.* 78: τοῖς μὲν γὰρ ἀποικίαν στειλαμένοις ἀντὶ τῆς μητροπόλεως ἡ ὑποδεξαμένη δήπου πατρίς, ἡ δ' ἐκπέμψασα μένει τοῖς ἀποδεδημηκόσιν, εἰς ἣν καὶ ποθοῦσιν ἐπανέρχεσθαι. Scott, *SBL Seminar Papers* (1995), 562 – 63, misses the contrast between the μέν and the δέ clauses and wrongly sees the passage as a negative comment on the contemporary diaspora.

89 Cf. Jos. *B. J.,* 7.375; Jos. *A. J.* 3.245.

is clear, the expression "colony" had a ring of pride and accomplishment, signaling the spread of the faith and its adherents, not a fall from grace.[90]

Jews formed stable communities in the diaspora, entered into the social, economic, and political life of the nations they joined, aspired to and often obtained citizen privileges in the cities of the Hellenistic world. Adequate evidence attests a Jewish striving for full and acknowledged membership and a genuine sense of belonging. Philo expresses the principle of the matter clearly enough. He declares that *xenoi* should be reckoned as residents and friends eager to enjoy privileges equal to those of citizens and, indeed, as being hardly any different from the indigenous people themselves.[91] Josephus maintains that Jews have every right to designate themselves as Alexandrians, Antiochenes, Ephesians, or whatever name belongs to the city in which they have settled.[92] Further, in discussing elsewhere the Jews of Ionia who sought redress from Rome against their opponents in the time of Augustus, he claims that they established their status as "natives."[93] Philo, indeed, referred to his city as "our Alexandria."[94] That form of identification emerges more poignantly in the petition of an Alexandrian Jew threatened with loss of his privileges. He labels himself an "Alexandrian" at the head of the document, alluding to his father, also an Alexandrian, and the proper education he had received, and expresses his fear of being deprived of his *patris*. The petitioner or the scribe who composed the letter in its final form then altered the term "Alexandrian" to "a Jew from Alexandria."[95] Whatever legal

---

90 Cf. Philo's use of the term in a very different context; Philo, *Spec.* 4.178. J. Mélèze-Modrzejewski, "How to Be a Greek and Yet a Jew in Hellenistic Alexandria," in S. J. D. Cohen and E. Frerichs, eds., *Diasporas in Antiquity* (Atlanta, 1993), 66–70, rightly points out that the Septuagint often translates *galut* [exile] or *golah* [the collective exiled] with *apoikia*, thus, in effect, offering an *interpretatio Graeca*. His further assertion, however, that Jews, unlike Greeks, invariably expected a return to the land of their fathers, is questionable. Scott, in Scott, ed., *Exile*, 189–93, unconvincingly takes the connotation of ἀποικία in a negative sense.

91 Philo, *Mos.* 1.35.

92 Jos. *C. Ap.* 2. 38–39.

93 Jos. *A. J.* 16.59: οἱ δὲ ἐγγενεῖς τε αὐτοὺς ἐδείκνυσαν.

94 Philo, *Legat.* 150: τὴν ἡμετέραν Ἀλεχάνδρειαν. Cf. *Leg. All.* 2.85. On Philo's attitude toward Alexandria, see, most recently, Pearce, in Jones and Pearce, eds., *Jewish Local Patriotism*, 97–104. He was, of course, fiercely hostile to Egyptians, their practices, institutions, and beliefs. This served him well in distinguishing the superior qualities of the Jews and their association with Greco-Roman culture. Cf. K. Goudriaan, "Ethnical Strategies in Graeco-Roman Egypt," in P. Bilde, ed., *Ethnicity in Hellenistic Egypt* (Aarhus, 1992), 81–85; Pearce, *op. cit.*, 83–97. But that would not compromise his affection for Alexandria; it might indeed reinforce it.

95 *Corpus Papyrorum Iudaicarum (CPJ)*, II, #151. Just what this change signified has been much debated and need not be explored here. See, e. g., V. A. Tcherikover, *CPJ, ad loc.* The discussion of Kasher, *Cathedra* 11 (1979): 53, concentrates only on the political aspect.

meaning this terminology might have carried, it signals the petitioner's clear affirmation of his roots in the community.[96] A comparable sentiment might be inferred from an inscription of the Phrygian city Acmonia, alluding to fulfillment of a vow made to the "whole *patris*." A Jew or a group of Jews must have commissioned it, for a menorah appears beneath the text. Here again the "native city" is honored, presumably through a gift for civic purposes. The donor pronounces his local loyalty in a conspicuous public manner.[97]

The most telling statement comes in Philo's *In Flaccum*. The passage is often cited for its reference to the impressive span of the Jewish diaspora, the spread of Jews to many places in Europe and Asia, including the most prosperous, whether on islands or on the mainland. But Philo proceeds to offer a striking depiction of Jewish attitudes both toward Jerusalem and toward the lands where they (and previous generations) had made their home. As Philo puts it, they considered the Holy City as their "metropolis," but the states in which they were born and raised and which they acquired from their fathers, grandfathers, and distant forefathers they adjudged their *patrides*.[98] That fervent expression eradicates any idea of the "doctrine of return." Diaspora Jews, in Philo's formulation at least, held a fierce attachment to the adopted lands of their ancestors.

Jews around the Mediterranean appear unapologetic and unembarrassed by their situation. They did not describe themselves as part of a diaspora. They did not suggest that they were cut off from the center, leading a separate, fragmented, and unfulfilled existence. They could eschew justification, rationalization, or tortured explanation for their choice of residence. They felt no need to construct a theory of diaspora.

Commitment to the community and devotion to Jerusalem were entirely compatible. That devotion had a public and conspicuous demonstration every year:

---

96 Cf. also the epitaph of a young woman from Leontopolis, so evidently a Jewess, which refers to her "homeland and father"; *CPJ*, III, #1530 = W. Horbury and D. Noy, *Jewish Inscriptions of Graeco-Roman Egypt* (Cambridge, Eng., 1992), #38, line 2: πάτραν καὶ γενέτην. To be sure, the *patris* here is the land of Onias, a Jewish enclave in Egypt, but the inscription discloses an unequivocal local allegiance. Cf. Gafni, *Land*, 48.

97 *Corpus Inscriptionum Iudaicarum (CIJ)*, #771: ὑπὲρ εὐχῆ[ς] πάσῃ τῇ πατρίδι. The *patris* here almost certainly refers to the city of Acmonia, not to the Jewish community; see P. Trebilco, *Jewish Communities in Asia Minor* (Cambridge, Eng., 1991), 81–82. Gafni, *Land*, 49–50, questions the degree to which conventional formulations of this sort disclose any genuine feelings of local patriotism.

98 Philo, *Flacc.* 46: μητρόπολιν μὲν τὴν ἱερόπολιν ἡγούμενοι... ἃς δ' ἔλαχον ἐκ πατέρων καὶ πάππων καὶ προπάππων καὶ τῶν ἔτι ἄνω προγόνων οἰκεῖν ἕκαστοι πατρίδας νομίζοντες, ἐν αἷς ἐγεννήθησαν καὶ ἐτράφησαν. Cf. Schaller, in Strecker, ed., *Das Land Israel*, 174–75.

the payment of a tithe to the Temple from Jews all over the Mediterranean.[99] The ritualistic offering carried deep significance as a bonding device. Its origins are obscure and require no investigation here. That it rests on a biblical prescription, the half-shekel imposed by the Lord upon Israelites counted in a census in the wilderness, may be questioned.[100] A more direct link perhaps comes with Nehemiah's establishment of a one-third shekel tax to help finance maintenance of the new Temple's operations.[101] When such a contribution was first expected of Jews in the diaspora can only be guessed at. The Seleucid overlords of Palestine had subsidized the financial needs of the Temple in the early second century B.C.E., as the Ptolemies may have done before them, and the Persian kings before them.[102] At some time after installation of Hasmonaean rule, support for the Temple came in from abroad, soon a matter of established practice and an accepted obligation of the faithful.[103]

The fact impressed itself notably among the Romans. Events of the mid 60s B.C.E. brought it to their attention in a forceful fashion. Economic circumstances in Rome and abroad had prompted a series of decrees forbidding the export of gold. The Roman governor of Asia, L. Valerius Flaccus, enforced the policy in various ways, including a ban on the sending of gold by the Jews of Asia Minor to Jerusalem.[104] The action not only prompted resentment among the Jews in Flaccus' province but stirred a hornet's nest of opposition among the Jews in Rome itself. Cicero, who conducted Flaccus' defense at his trial for extortion in 59, comments bitterly about the horde of Jews crowding around the tribunal, exercising undue pressure upon the proceedings and passionately exhibiting their "barbaric superstition."[105] The account, of course, is partisan, rhetorical, and exaggerated, but it also conveys some precious information. First, Cicero indicates the earnest commitment of Jews to provide funds annually to the Temple from Italy and from all the provinces of the Roman empire.[106] Next, his record of Flaccus' activ-

99 See the useful summary of testimony and the discussion by S. Safrai, "Relations between the Diaspora and the Land of Israel," in Safrai and Stern, eds., *The Jewish People*, vol. 1, 186–91.
100 Exodus, 30.11–16; cf. Philo, *Heres*, 186; *Spec. Leg.* 1.77–78.
101 Nehemiah, 10.32–34.
102 For the Seleucids, see 3 Macc. 3.3; Jos. *A. J.* 12.138–44; cf. 2 Macc. 9.16; Jos. *A. J.* 11.16. For the Ptolemies, see Jos. *A. J.* 12.40–41. For the Persian kings, see Ezra, 6.8–10, 7.18–21.
103 It was certainly well entrenched by the early first century B.C.E.; Jos. *A. J.* 14.110–13; Cic. *Pro Flacco*, 67.
104 On possible reasons for Roman policy here, see A. J. Marshall, "Flaccus and the Jews of Asia (Cicero, *Pro Flacco* 28.67–69)," *Phoenix* 29 (1975): 139–54.
105 Cic. *Pro Flacco*, 66–68.
106 Cic. *Pro Flacco*, 67: cum aurum Iudaeorum nomine quotannis ex Italia et ex omnibus nostris provinciis Hierosolymam exportari soleret.

ities indicates that tribute for the Temple was collected by Jewish communities, city by city, wherever they possessed sufficient numbers in Asia Minor.[107] And, most revealingly, Cicero's speech, however embellished and overblown, shows that the plight of Asian Jews who were prevented from making their wonted contributions to the Temple stirred the passions of their compatriots far off in Rome and provoked impressively noisy demonstrations on their behalf. Cicero remarks both on the pressure and size of the Jewish assemblage and on its community of interests—features, he claims, well known in Rome.[108] The whole episode exhibits the solidarity of sentiments among diaspora Jews from Italy to the Near East in the matter of expressing their allegiance to Jerusalem.[109]

The centrality of Jewish commitment to the tithe is demonstrated again and again. Philo reinforces the testimony of Cicero. His comment on the large Jewish community in Rome at the time of Augustus once again associates it with zeal for gathering the sacred tithes for Jerusalem—a fact with which the *princeps* was well acquainted.[110] The size of contributions over the years had brought substantial wealth to the Temple. Josephus proudly observes that the donations had come from Jews all over Asia and Europe, indeed from everywhere in the world, for a huge number of years.[111] When that activity was interfered with by local authorities, Jews would send up a howl to Rome. So, for instance, when M. Agrippa, overseeing the eastern provinces for Augustus, appeared in Ionia, Jews from various Ionian communities complained loudly of Greek interference with their prerogatives, naming first and foremost the seizure of cash destined as contributions to Jerusalem.[112] If Josephus' collection of Roman decrees be trusted, the emperor Augustus himself intervened to assure the untroubled exercise of Jewish practices in the province of Asia. In promulgating an edict to put Roman muscle behind the protection of Jewish privileges, Augustus placed at the head of the list the inviolability of sacred monies sent to Jerusalem

---

107 The Ciceronian speech singles out Apamea, Laodicea, Adramyttium, and Pergamum; *Pro Flacco*, 68. Cf. Philo, *Spec. Leg.* 1.78.

108 Cic. *Pro Flacco*, 66: scis quanta sit manus, quanta concordia, quantum valeat in contionibus.

109 Modern discussions of Cicero's attitude toward the Jews pay little attention to the implications of his statements on this score. So, e. g., Y. Levi, "Cicero on the Jews," *Zion* 7 (1942): 109 – 34; B. Wardy, "Jewish Religion in Pagan Literature during the Late Republic and Early Empire," *ANRW* 2.19.1 (1979): 596 – 613.

110 Philo, *Leg.* 155 – 56.

111 Jos. *A. J.* 14.110; cf. 18.312 – 13; *BJ*, 7.45.

112 Jos. *A. J.* 16.28, 16.45.

and designated for the treasury officials of the Temple.[113] That prerogative and that alone is noted in the emperor's letter to the proconsul of Asia.[114] Agrippa followed it up with directives to officials in Ephesus and Cyrene, as did the Roman governor in a message to Sardis.[115] The active support by Augustus and Agrippa for Jewish interests on this matter is attested also by Philo, a close contemporary.[116] Monies collected for Jerusalem form the centerpiece in each of the Roman pronouncements. That emphasis must come from Jews pressing their claims upon the imperial government. Indeed, areas beyond the reach of Roman power also contained Jews who pursued the same practice with rigor and consistency. Communities in Babylon and other satrapies under Parthian dominion sent representatives every year over difficult terrain and dangerous highways to deposit their contributions in the Temple.[117] Even if the documents are not genuine, they reflect the order of priorities expressed by the Jewish sources of Philo and Josephus. The issue of paying homage to Jerusalem was paramount.[118]

Proof, if proof be needed, is provided by a hostile witness with no axe to grind on this score. Tacitus, in a list of depraved and deplorable Jewish habits, sets in first place the institution of collecting tribute and donations to increase the resources of the Jews.[119] And there is ironic significance in the fact that when the Romans destroyed the Temple they refrained from destroying this institution; rather, they altered its recipient. The annual tithe would no longer go to the nonexistent sacred shrine; it would metamorphose into a Roman tax. The cash would now serve to subsidize the cult of Jupiter Capitolinus.[120]

The stark symbolism of the tithe had a potent hold upon Jewish sentiment. That annual act of obeisance was a repeated reminder, or rather display, of affec-

113 Jos. A. J. 16.163: τά τε ἱερὰ εἶναι ἐν ἀσυλίᾳ καὶ ἀναπέμπεσθαι εἰς Ἱεροσόλυμα καὶ ἀποδίδοσθαι τοῖς ἀποδοχεῦσιν Ἱεροσολυμιτῶν. Cf. further a ruling by Julius Caesar that also appears to guarantee the Temple tithe; Jos. Ant. 14.202: ἔστησε κατ' ἐνιαυτὸν ὅπως τελῶσιν ὑπὲρ τῆς Ἱεροσολυμιτῶν πόλεως.
114 Jos. A. J. 16.166.
115 Jos. A. J. 16.167–71. Another similar letter by the governor of Asia to Ephesus is preserved by Philo, Leg. 315.
116 Philo, Leg. 291, 312.
117 Philo, Leg. 216.
118 Cf. Philo, Spec. Leg. 1.76–77. In addition to the annual contributions felt as an obligation by all Jews, there were more substantial gifts by wealthy diaspora donors to express their reverence; Jos. B. J., 4.567, 5.5, 5.201–5; Jos. A. J. 18.82, 20.51–53.
119 Tacitus, Hist. 5.5.1: cetera instituta, sinistra foeda, pravitate valuere; nam pessimus quisque spretis religionibus patriis tributa et stipes illuc congerebant, unde auctae Iudaeorum res.
120 Jos. B. J., 7.218; Dio Cassius, 66.7.2.

tion and allegiance. Jerusalem cast the most compelling image and gripped the imaginations of Jews everywhere in the Mediterranean and the Near East. The repeated, ritualistic contributions emblematized the unbroken attachment of the diaspora to the center. Even the Romans recognized the symbolic power of the payment. Its transformation into a subsidy for the preeminent deity of the empire would serve as dramatic signifier of a new loyalty.

What implications does the tithe possess for our question? Did the outpouring of cash for the Temple by Jews from Italy to Iran imply that the diaspora was reckoned as fleeting and temporary, an interim exile or refuge, an affliction to be endured until restoration to the Holy City? In fact, the reverse conclusion holds. The continuing pledge of allegiance proclaimed that the diaspora could endure indefinitely and quite satisfactorily. The communities abroad were entrenched and successful, even mainstays of the center. Diaspora Jews did not and would not turn their backs on Jerusalem, the principal emblem of their faith. Their fierce commitment to the tithe delivered that message unequivocally. But the gesture did not signify a desire for the return. On the contrary, it signaled that the return was unnecessary.

A comparable phenomenon demands attention: the pilgrimage of diaspora Jews to Jerusalem. How often and in what numbers is unclear.[121] Major festivals could attract them with some frequency and in quantity. If Philo be believed, myriads came from countless cities for every feast, over land and sea, from all points of the compass, to enjoy the Temple as a serene refuge from the hurly-burly of everyday life abroad.[122] The most celebrated occasion occurred after the death of Jesus. The feast of Pentecost had brought numerous persons into the city from far-flung and diverse locations: peoples from Parthia, Media, and Elam, from Mesopotamia and Cappadocia, from Pontus and Asia, from Phrygia and Pamphylia, from Egypt and Cyrene, from Crete and Arabia, and, indeed, even from Rome, all witness to the miracle of the disciples speaking in the whole array of diverse tongues.[123] When the Roman governor of Syria visited Jerusalem at the time of Passover in the mid 60s C.E. he encountered crowds of in-

---

121 The biblical prescription indicates three times a year; Exodus, 23.17; cf. Jos. *A. J.* 4.203. But actual practice varied widely; cf. Safrai, in Safrai and Stern, eds., *Jewish People,* vol. 1, 191 – 94; A. Kerkeslager, "Jewish Pilgrimage and Jewish Identity in Hellenistic and Early Roman Egypt," in D. Frankfurter, ed., *Pilgrimage and Holy Space in Late Antique Egypt* (Leiden, 1998), 106 – 7.
122 Philo, *Spec. Leg.* 1.69: μυρίοι γὰρ ἀπὸ μυρίων ὅσων πόλεων… καθ' ἑκάστην ἑορτὴν εἰς τὸ ἱερόν.
123 Acts, 2.1 – 11; cf. 6.9.

calculable numbers.[124] Even the Great Revolt did not discourage pilgrims from coming at Passover. A large number found themselves trapped in the city and perished in the Roman siege.[125] Huge crowds from abroad, including Gentiles, at Passover were evidently common.[126] The women's court at the Temple was large enough to accommodate those who resided in the land and those who came from abroad – a clear sign that female pilgrims in some numbers were expected.[127]

The delivery of the annual tithe itself brought diaspora Jews to Jerusalem on a regular basis, a ritual performance analogous to, even identical with, a pilgrimage. Philo attests to the sacred messengers who not only deposit the monies but perform the sacrifices.[128] And they might be accompanied by many others, especially when arduous and perilous journeys required numbers for protection.[129] The adherents of Paul who went with him to Jerusalem from Greece, Macedon, and Asia may also have been performing a pilgrimage.[130] The Holy City exercised tremendous force as a magnet. Josephus' romantic tale about the conversion to Judaism by the royal family in far-off Adiabene, whatever its authenticity, illustrates the point nicely. The queen mother, Helena, an ardent proselyte, felt that confirmation of her new status required a visit to the sacred site and worship in the Temple. Helena proceeded to shower Jerusalem with gifts, a gesture duplicated by her son Izates, the king of Adiabene. Izates sent his five young sons to Palestine to receive training in Hebrew language and culture. And both mother and son were buried not in Adiabene but outside Jerusalem in monuments whose construction Helena herself had directed.[131] The experience of the royal house,

---

124 Jos. *BJ*, 2.280. Josephus' figure of "no less than three million" is, of course, preposterous. Cf. also Jos. *BJ*, 6.422 – 25.

125 Jos. *B. J.*, 6.420 – 21.

126 Jos. *B. J.*, 6.426 – 27. Cf. Jos. *A. J.* 17.214. On the numbers, see J. Jeremias, *Jerusalem in the Time of Jesus* (Phildelphia, 1969), 77 – 84.

127 Jos. *B. J.*, 5.199.

128 Philo, *Leg.* 156: χρήματα συνάγοντας ἀπὸ τῶν ἀπαρχῶν ἱερὰ καὶ πέμποντας εἰς Ἱεροσόλυμα διὰ τῶν τὰς θυσίας ἀναξόντων. So also 216, 312; *Spec. Leg.* 1.78. Philo could also, of course, employ the concept of pilgrimage in an allegorical sense; cf. Amir, in Oppenheimer et al., eds., *Jerusalem in the Second Temple Period*, 158 – 65.

129 See Jos. *A. J.* 18.312 – 13; cf. 17.26.

130 Acts, 20.4, 21.29.

131 The tale of the royal house of Adiabene and its conversion is told in a long excursus by Josephus, Jos. *A. J.* 20.17 – 96. For the attachment to Jerusalem, see 20.49 – 53, 20.71, 20.95; cf. *BJ*, 5.55, 5.119, 5.147. The desire to be buried in Jerusalem is attested also by epitaphs recording the transferral of bones to the Holy City. See, e. g., J. A. Fitzmyer and D. Harrington, *A Manual of Palestinian Aramaic Texts* (Rome, 1978), #68 (first century B.C.E. or first century C.E.). Cf. I. M. Gafni, "Reinternment in the Land of Israel," *The Jerusalem Cathedra*, 1 (1981): 96 – 104.

at least as represented in the tale, recapitulates the behavior of diaspora Jews, which they had, in effect, become.[132] The visits to Jerusalem and gifts to the Temple followed the appropriate mode of expressing homage, but that demonstration of devotion did not entail a desire for migration. Pilgrimage, in fact, by its very nature, signified a temporary payment of respect. The Holy City had an irresistible and undiminished claim on the emotions of diaspora Jews. It was indeed a critical piece of their identity. But home was elsewhere.

The self-perception of Second Temple Jews projected a tight solidarity between center and diaspora. The images of exile and separation did not haunt them. They were not compelled to choose between restoration to Eretz Israel and recourse to the Word as their "portable homeland." What affected the dwellers in Jerusalem affected Jews everywhere. The theme of intertwined experience and interdependent identity is reiterated with impressive frequency and variety.

Many of the texts already noticed, and a good number of others besides, fortify this conclusion. The author of II Maccabees—or at least of the letters attached to the beginning of that work—gives pointed expression to the idea. The Jews of Jerusalem take for granted the intimate relationship that exists with their brethren in Egypt. The preamble of the first letter greets them as "brothers" to "brothers" and alludes to their common heritage, God's covenant with Abraham, Isaac, and Jacob.[133] The central message of both missives is that the Egyptian Jews should celebrate the new festival honoring the recovery and purification of the Temple after the desecration by Antiochus IV[134] The concluding lines of the second letter make reference to the desired reunion of all Jews in the holy site. As argued above, that is not a call for an end to the diaspora. It represents

---

132 For additional evidence, including rabbinic texts, and discussion of diaspora pilgrimages to Jerusalem, see S. Safrai, *Die Wallfahrl im Zeitalter des Zweiten Tempels* (Neukirchen, 1981), 65 – 97. A condensed version is in Safrai and Stern, eds., *The Jewish People,* vol. 1, 191 – 204. Cf. Delling, *Die Bewältigung,* 36 – 37. On visitors to Jerusalem generally, see the testimony and discussion by Jeremias, *Jerusalem,* 58 – 77. The speculation of M. Goodman, "The Pilgrimage Economy of Jerusalem in the Second Temple Period," in L. I. Levine, ed., *Jerusalem: Its Sanctity and Centrality to Judaism, Christianity, and Islam* (New York, 1999), 69 – 76, that large-scale pilgrimage began only in the reign of Herod, encouraged by the king for economic reasons, rests on little more than an argument from silence.

133 2 Macc. 1.1 – 2: τοῖς ἀδελφοῖς τοῖς κατ᾽ Αἴγυπτον Ἰουδαίοις χαίρειν οἱ ἀδελφοὶ οἱ ἐν Ἱεροσολύμοις Ἰουδαῖοι... εἰρήν ην ἀγαθήν.

134 2 Macc. 1.9, 1.18, 2.16 – 17. A similar promotion of a festival advocated by Jerusalemites for diaspora Jews occurs with regard to Purim. See the Greek supplements to Esther, Addition, F, 11.

the party line of the Maccabaeans.[135] But even if pressed, it signifies no more than a summons to a festival—and thus a reaffirmation of solidarity among Jews everywhere. It reflects the practice of pilgrimage rather than a program to dissolve the dispersal.

The *Letter of Aristeas* makes the connection between Jerusalemites and other Jews still more forcefully and unequivocally. King Ptolemy's letter to the High Priest in Judaea asserts that his motive in having the Hebrew Bible rendered into Greek was to benefit not only the Jews of Egypt but all Jews throughout the world—even those not yet born.[136] And it is fitting that, when the scholars from Jerusalem completed their translation and it was read out to the Jews of Egypt, the large assemblage burst into applause, a dramatic expression of the unity of purpose.[137]

The narrative of III Maccabees depends on that same unity of purpose. It presupposes and never questions the proposition that the actions of Jerusalemites represent the sentiments of Jews anywhere in the diaspora. After Ptolemy IV was thwarted in his design to enter the Holy of Holies in Jerusalem, his immediate reaction upon his return to Egypt was to inflict punishment upon the Jews in Egypt. The king had determined to bring public shame upon the *ethnos* of the Jews generally.[138] A few were prepared to yield to his offer of civic privileges in Alexandria in return for apostasy. But most of them held firm, reckoning the apostates as enemies of the nation and refusing them any part in communal life and mutual services.[139] Whatever Ptolemy IV may in fact have thought, the author of III Maccabees certainly presumed a commonality of interests within the Jewish *ethnos* as a whole. Egyptian Jews were "fellow-tribesmen" of those who dwelled in Judaea.[140]

The Book of Tobit offers a parallel episode. A principal theme of that work concerns proper burial rites. Tobit, dwelling in exile at Nineveh, felt it incumbent

---

135 2 Macc. 2.18. See above. It does not follow that the letter represents Hasmonaean policy to claim ascendancy over diaspora Jews, as is argued by U. Rappaport, "Relations between the Jews of Eretz-Yisrael and the Jewish Diaspora in the Hellenistic and Hasmonaean Period" (in Hebrew), in B. Isaac and A. Oppenheimer, eds., *Te'uda* 12 (Tel Aviv, 1996–97), 3–4.
136 *Let. Aris.* 38: βουλομένων δ' ἡμῶν καὶ τούτοις χαρίζεσθαι καὶ πᾶσι τοῖς κατὰ τὴν οἰκουμένην Ἰουδαίοις καὶ τοῖς μετέπειτα.
137 *Let. Aris.* 307–11.
138 3 Macc. 2.21–27: προέθετο δημοσίᾳ κατὰ τοῦ ἔθνους διαδοῦναι ψόγον.
139 3 Macc. 2.28–33: … ὡς πολεμίους τοῦ ἔθνους ἔκρινον καὶ τῆς κοινῆς συναναστροφῆς καὶ εὐχρηστίας ἐστέρουν.
140 3 Macc. 3.21: τοὺς ὁμοφύλους.

upon himself, despite the dangers and difficulties involved, to bury the bodies of all Jews executed on the orders of the Assyrian king Sennacherib. Like the wicked Ptolemy of III Maccabees, Sennacherib wreaked vengeance upon Israelites in Assyria because of a rout he had suffered at the hands of their compatriots in Israel.[141] Once again, the assumption of solidarity among Jews in the center and those abroad underpins the narrative.

Apart from the pagans of fiction, real ones found Jewish solidarity as well. The notorious passage of Cicero, treated earlier, offers a vivid example. When a Roman governor sought to prevent export of gold from Asia for the Temple in Jerusalem, a large crowd of Jews in Rome protested vociferously and exerted heavy pressure on the public proceedings.[142]

In the perception of Philo and Josephus, no breach existed, no discernible difference even, between the practices of Palestinian Jews and of those abroad. The priestly classes in the diaspora maintain the same rigid adherence to genealogical purity as do those in the homeland. Moreover, the scrupulous records of the family lines are regularly sent to Jerusalem as a token of esteem and a sign of solidarity. Josephus here employs the term διςσπαρμένοι [scattered]—and plainly without any derogatory undertone.[143] Philo asserts the equivalence of diaspora Jews, with regard to the ritual of honoring the dead, in still more forceful terms: those who settle abroad have committed no wrongs and cannot be denied equal privileges. The nation has simply spilled over its borders and can no longer be confined to a single land.[144]

The community of interests could have direct effect on the events of Jewish history. In the late second century B.C.E., Cleopatra III, the queen of Egypt, gained the upper hand in a war against her son Ptolemy Lathyrus and was urged by some of her advisers to seize the opportunity for an invasion of Judaea. The plan never materialized because better advice came from another quarter. The Jewish military man Ananias, a loyal and effective general in Cleopatra's army, dissuaded her with a compelling argument. He counted the High Priest in Judaea, Alexander Jannaeus, as his own kinsman. And any attack on the High Priest, so he claimed, would make enemies of all the Jews in Egypt. Cleo-

---

141 Tobit, 1.18: καὶ εἴ τινα ἀπέκτεινεν Σενναχηριμ, ὅτε ἀπῆλθεν φεύγων ἐκ τῆς Ἰουδαίας,... ἔθαψα. The subject of ἀπῆλθεν is certainly Sennacherib, as observed by C. A. Moore, *Tobit* (New York, 1996), 120. Cf. 2 Kgs., 19.35.
142 Cic. *Pro Flacco,* 66–67, 69.
143 Jos. *C. A.* 1.32–33.
144 Philo, *Mos.* 2.232: μὴ χωρούσης διὰ πολυανθρωπίαν τὸ ἔθνος μιᾶς χώρας.

patra reconsidered the matter, dropped plans for an invasion, and instead concluded an alliance with Jannaeus.[145]

A half century later, the close ties of Judaean and Egyptian Jews and the prestige of the High Priest once more had a telling effect on the course of historical events. At the height of the Roman civil war, Julius Caesar found himself besieged in Alexandria in 48/7 B.C.E. A troop of three thousand Jewish soldiers marched to his rescue under their general, Antipater, who had rounded up additional support from Arabia, Syria, and Lebanon. But their path was blocked by Egyptian Jews who dwelled in the Oniad district, that is, in the enclave of Leontopolis, the site of a long-standing Jewish community. Antipater, however, overcame any resistance by appealing to their common nationality and, indeed, their loyalty to the High Priest Hyrcanus. Antipater wielded a letter from Hyrcanus requesting that Egyptian Jews support the cause of Caesar. No further persuasion was necessary. The Jews both of Leontopolis and of Memphis declared themselves for Caesar and helped to turn the tide of the war.[146] The sense of Jewish solidarity and the respect for the High Priest's authority in Jerusalem had an impressive impact. No sign of an "exilic" mentality here. Leontopolis itself endured as an autonomous center of Judaism with its own temple for well over two hundred years, until its destruction by the Romans in the wake of the Great Revolt. But, as this episode indicates, there was no schismatic separatism here. The Jews of Leontopolis continued to acknowledge the ascendancy of Jerusalem.[147]

One might note also the active involvement of Roman Jews in pressing Augustus to put an end to Herodian rule in Judaea after the death of Herod the Great. Fifty envoys came from Judaea for this purpose and eight thousand Jews resident in Rome joined in their lobbying efforts.[148] When a pretender to

145 Jos. *A. J.* 13.352–55: ὅτι τὸ πρὸς τοῦτον ἄδικον ἐχθροὺς ἅπαντας ἡμᾶς σοι τοὺς Ἰουδαίους καταστήσει. Cf. M. Stern, "Relations between the Hasmoneans and Ptolemaic Egypt in Light of the International Relations of the Second and First Centuries" (in Hebrew), *Zion* 50 (1985): 101–2.

146 Jos. *A. J.* 14.127–37. See, especially, 14.131: πείθει δὲ καὶ τούτους τὰ αὐτῶν φρονῆσαι κατὰ τὸ ὁμόφυλον Ἀντίπατρος, καὶ μάλιστα ἐπιδείξας αὐτοῖς τὰς Ὑρκανοῦ τοῦ ἀρχιερέως ἐπιστολάς. Cf. also Jos. *BJ*, 1.190.

147 For this interpretation of Lentopolis, see E. S. Gruen, "The Origins and Objectives of Onias' Temple," *SCI* 16 (1997): 47–70, with bibliography, also available in this volume. For a different view, see D. R. Schwartz, "The Jews of Egypt between Onias' Temple, the Jerusalem Temple, and the Heavens" (in Hebrew), *Zion* 62 (1997): 5–22. The authority of the High Priest in diaspora communities is attested also by the request of Saul (Paul) for letters from the High Priest to the synagogues in Damascus, authorizing him to arrest Christians in their midst and bring them back to Jerusalem; Acts, 9.1–2.

148 Jos. *A. J.* 17.300–301.

the throne emerged, claiming to be a reincarnation of one of Herod's sons, he found widespread support from Jews in Crete, in Melos, and in Rome itself.[149] These events provide a revealing window upon the lively interest and occasionally energetic engagement of diaspora Jews in the affairs of Palestine.

The affiliations and interconnections emerge perhaps most dramatically in the grave crises that marked the reign of the emperor Caligula. Harsh conflict erupted in Alexandria, bringing dislocation, persecution, and death upon large numbers in the Jewish community of that city. Philo's accounts of these events contain their own bias and agenda, but they do convey the reflections of an eyewitness and participant and they afford an insight into the attitudes of articulate Jews in the diaspora. The attacks upon the Alexandrian Jewish community came under the authority of the Roman prefect of Egypt, A. Flaccus. And when they came, so Philo maintains, the word spread like wildfire. Once synagogues were destroyed in Alexandria, reports would swiftly sweep not only through all the districts of Egypt but from there to the nations of the East and from the borders of Libya to the lands of the West. Jews had settled all over Europe and Asia, and the news of a pogrom anywhere would race through the entire network.[150] So Philo says. And, although his claim of such speedy communications might stretch a point, the concept of tight interrelationships among Jews of the diaspora can hardly be gainsaid. Flaccus, of course, eventually perished for his misdeeds, an appropriate ending to the morality tale. And Philo makes sure to emphasize that this was no peculiar Alexandrian affair: Flaccus is described as the "common enemy of the Jewish nation."[151]

Philo himself headed the delegation to the emperor that would plead the cause of the Jewish community in Alexandria. The timing of their arrival in Rome only heightened the drama. Word soon arrived of the larger crisis: Caligula's decision to install his statue in the Temple at Jerusalem. The initial motive for the embassy now seemed paltry by comparison. Philo's words are arresting: this most grievous calamity fell unexpectedly and brought peril not to one part of the Jewish people but to the entire nation at once.[152] Indeed, Philo berates himself for even thinking about parochial Alexandrian matters when a much greater catastrophe threatened the very existence of the Jewish polity and the name common to the nation as a whole.[153] The magnitude of Caligula's decision had al-

---

149 Jos. *A. J.* 17.321–38.
150 Philo, *Flacc.* 45–46.
151 Philo, *Flacc.* 124: κοινὸν ἐχθρὸν τοῦ ἔθνους. Cf. 1, 117.
152 Philo, *Leg.* 184: ἕτερον κατασκήπτει βαρύτατον ἐξαπιναίως ἀπροσδόκητον κακόν, οὐχ ἑνὶ μέρει τοῦ Ἰουδαϊκοῦ τὸν κίνδυνον ἐπάγον, ἀλλὰ συλλήβδην ἅπαντι τῷ ἔθνει. Cf. 178, 351, 373.
153 Philo, *Leg.* 193–94.

ready occurred to P. Petronius, the legate of Syria, whose task it was to oversee the erection of the statue. Petronius dragged his feet and reached for excuses to postpone the job. For he knew (or so Philo reconstructs his thoughts) that such an act would outrage Jews everywhere and provoke resistance not only in Judaea, where their ranks were especially strong, but from the large number of Jews dwelling across the Euphrates in Babylon and all the provinces of the Parthian empire, indeed almost throughout the world.[154] The letter of Agrippa I, a friend of the emperor who had recently been accorded a kingdom among the Jews, urgently alerted Caligula to the severe gravity of the situation. Agrippa's plea to the Roman ruler maintained, among other things, that an affront to Jerusalem would have vast repercussions: the Holy City was the metropolis not only of Judaea but of most nations in the world, since Jewish colonies thrived all over the Near East, Asia Minor, Greece, Macedon, Africa, and the lands beyond the Euphrates.[155] No matter how self-serving Agrippa's statement—or indeed the account of Philo in which it is embedded—the image of Jerusalem as binding together Jews everywhere in the *oikoumene* surely held a prominent place in the self-perception of the diaspora. And, in Philo's account at least, that perception is not confined to Jews. If Gentiles in any city received authorization to attack Jews, their counterparts in all cities would take it as a green light to conduct their own terrorist activities.[156]

The consistency of this portrait leaves a potent impression. Philo articulated an unbroken bond among diaspora Jews and between them and Jerusalem. No trauma in one community would go unfelt in the rest. And the ripples from any threat to Jerusalem would quickly extend throughout the Jewish world.

A moving passage elsewhere in Philo's corpus neatly encapsulates the theme of this essay. It stands outside the context of crisis and turmoil, outside the fears of pogrom in Alexandria or the megalomania of a Roman monarch. Philo, who thrived in the diaspora, enjoyed its advantages and broadcast its virtues, nevertheless found even deeper meaning in the land of Israel. In his discussion of Jewish festivals, he interprets the Shavuot Festival as a celebration of the Jews' possession of their own land, a heritage of long standing and a means whereby they could cease their wandering over continents and islands and their existence as

---

154 Philo, *Leg.* 213–17: ὀλίγου δέω φάναι πᾶσα ἡ οἰκουμένη.
155 Philo, *Leg.* 277–83. Cf. 330: οὐ μόνον τοῖς τὴν ἱερὰν χώραν κατοικοῦσιν ἀλλὰ καὶ τοῖς πανταχοῦ τῆς οἰκουμένης Ἰουδαίοις.
156 Philo, *Leg.* 371; cf. 159–61.

foreigners and vagabonds dwelling in the countries of others.[157] Philo saw no inconsistency or contradiction. Diaspora Jews might find fulfillment and reward in their communities abroad, but they honored Judaea as refuge for the formerly displaced and unsettled, and the prime legacy of all.

Josephus makes the point in a quite different context but with equal force. In his rewriting of Numbers, he places a sweeping prognostication in the mouth of the Midianite priest Balaam. To the consternation of the king of Moab, who had expected a dark oracle for the Israelites, Balaam projected a glorious future. They will not only occupy and hold forever the land of Canaan, a chief signal of God's favor, but their multitudes will fill all the world, islands and continents, outnumbering even the stars in the heavens.[158] That is a notable declaration. Palestine, as ever, merits a special place. But the diaspora, far from being a source of shame to be overcome, represents a resplendent achievement.

The respect and awe paid to the Holy Land stood in full harmony with commitment to local community and allegiance to Gentile governance. Diaspora Jews did not bewail their fate and pine away for the homeland. Nor, by contrast, did they ignore the homeland and reckon the Book as surrogate for the Temple. The postulated alternatives are severe and simplistic. Palestine mattered, and it mattered in a territorial sense, but not as a required residence. Gifts to the Temple and pilgrimages to Jerusalem announced simultaneously a devotion to the symbolic heart of Judaism and a singular pride in the accomplishments of the diaspora. Jewish Hellenistic writers took the concurrence for granted. They were not driven to apologia. Nor did they feel obliged to reconcile the contradiction. There was none.

---

157 Philo, *Spec. Leg.* 2.168. Cf. Schaller, in Strecker, ed., *Das Land Israel,* 176 – 78. Van Unnik, *Das Selbstverständis,* 127 – 37, who finds no optimistic assessment of the diaspora in Philo, notably omits this passage.

158 Jos. *A. J.* 4.115 – 16: τὴν δ᾽ οἰκουμένην οἰκητήριον δι᾽ αἰῶνος ἴστε προκειμένην ὑμῖν, καὶ τὸ πλῆθος ὑμῶν ἔν τε νήσοις καὶ κατ᾽ ἤπειρον βιοτεύσετε ὅσον ἐστὶν οὐδ᾽ ἀστέρων ἀριθμὸς ἐν οὐρανῷ. Josephus departs quite substantially here from the corresponding text in Numbers, 23.6 – 10. See the good discussion by Halpern-Amaru, *JQR* 71 (1980/81): 225 – 29; *eadem,* in Hoffmann, *Land of Israel,* 81 – 82; cf. also Price, *SCI* 13 (1994): 171. For comparable statements in Josephus, see Jos. *A. J.* 1.282: οἷς ἐγὼ τὸ ταύτης κράτος τῆς γῆς δίδωμι καὶ παισὶ τοῖς αὐτῶν, ὃ πληρώσουσιν ὅσην ἥλιος ὁρᾷ καὶ γῆν καὶ θάλασσαν; 2.213; 14.115; *BJ,* 7.43. On Josephus' generally positive attitude toward diaspora, see L. Feldman, "The Concept of Exile in Josephus," in Scott, ed., *Exile,* 145 – 72.

14. Was There Judeophobia in Classical Antiquity?

Pagan attitudes and behavior toward the Jews present us with a puzzling paradox. Greeks and Romans have a relatively good track record in their treatment of alien peoples, foreign cults, and exotic customs. They normally welcomed—or at least put up with—other cultures, ethnic groups, and strange modes of worship. They had good reason to do so. Many Greek cities and, of course, Rome itself traced their own origins to peoples from abroad, postulated a racial mixture within their own composition, and acknowledged the salutary influences that they had absorbed from other cultures.[1] Even on matters of religion, Romans in particular adapted practices that stemmed from elsewhere, and rarely suppressed or resisted foreign cults that might enrich their own civilization.[2]

Yet the experience of the Jews would appear to be a real blot on the record. Some unsettling, disturbing, indeed horrific, events marked that experience in the Greco-Roman period. Probably the most dramatic and notorious episode occurred in Alexandria, the so-called "pogrom" of 38 C.E. Certain Greek troublemakers in that city, so we are told in the account of Philo, a contemporary and possibly an eye-witness, provoked the Roman prefect of Egypt at the time of the emperor Caligula into curtailing the privileges of Jews in the city. This tapped into some deep-seated hatred of Jews among the Egyptians. There followed an escalating series of attacks, arising out of political, religious, or social discontents, or some combination thereof. As a consequence, Jews were confined to a ghetto, where mobs indulged in beatings, torture, humiliation, and murder. In addition, Jewish women were arrested and compelled to eat swine's flesh or suffer intolerable torments.[3]

---

1 See E.S. Gruen *Rethinking the Other* (Princeton, 2011), 223–249.
2 See E.M. Orlin *Foreign Cults in Rome* (Oxford, 2010), *passim*.
3 Principal evidence in Philo, *Flacc.* 16–96. The bibliography on the riots in Alexandria is huge. Unnecessary to register it here. See the references and discussion in E.S. Gruen *Diaspora: Jews amidst Greeks and Romans* (Cambridge, Mass., 2002), 54–68, 277–282; add also P.W. van der Horst *Philo's Flaccus: The First Pogrom* (Leiden, 2003); A. Kerkeslager "The Absence of Dionysios, Lampo, and Isidoros from the Violence in Alexandria in 38 C.E." *Studia Philonica Annual*, 17 (2005), 49–94; J.E. Atkinson "Ethnic Cleansing in Roman Alexandria in 38," *Acta Classica*, 49 (2006), 31–54; A. Harker *Loyalty and Dissidence in Roman Egypt: The Case of the Acta Alexandrinorum* (Cambridge, 2008), 212–220; A. Avidov *Not Reckoned among Nations* (Tübingen, 2009), 171–176; and, especially, the fine study of S. Gambetti *The Alexandrian Riots of 38 C.E. and the Persecution of the Jews: A Historical Reconstruction* (Leiden, 2009)., with full ref-

The Alexandrian riot may have been the best documented case of this sort. But it was by no means alone. The citizens of Babylon, Josephus reports, had long harbored hostility to Jews dwelling in their midst because of the incompatibility of their laws. Hence the Jews in 40 C.E. pulled up stakes and moved to Seleuceia on the Tigris. Their arrival, however, complicated tensions between Syrians and Greeks, then galvanized these two groups into combined action, leading to the victimization of the Jews. More than 50,000, according to Josephus, were killed; others fled to neighboring cities in Mesopotamia.[4] At Caesarea around 59 C.E., quarrels erupted over competing civic privileges in the city between Jews and Syrians. The two groups engaged in physical assaults on one another, thus prompting the intervention of the Roman prefect—who then turned his fire power primarily on the Jews.[5] Those hostilities escalated in lethal fashion during the Jewish rebellion against Rome. The residents of Caesarea rose once more and slaughtered, so we are told, 20,000 Jews, emptying the city altogether of its Jewish population.[6] The event sparked reprisals by Jews and counter-attacks by their enemies in city after city of the Decapolis and greater Syria. Josephus paints a lurid picture of massacres and pillaging, piles of corpses, no sparing of the elderly, women, and infants, a host of unspeakable atrocities.[7] These are chilling episodes.

How does one square this information with the general forbearance and *laissez-faire* attitudes of pagan antiquity toward foreign peoples and beliefs? Are the Jews a special case? Does the targeting of that people count as anti-semitism, a form of racism or proto-racism?

As is well known, "anti-semitism" is a modern expression, not an ancient one. It first surfaces in 19th century Germany.[8] No equivalent of this phrase occurs

---

erences to the literature. See further B. Ritter *Judeans in the Greek Cities of the Roman Empire: Rights, Citizenship and Civil Discord* (Leiden, 2015).

4 Jos. *A. J.* 18.371–379.

5 Jos. *B. J.*, 2.266–270; Jos. *A. J.* 20.173–178. See the valuable notes of S. Mason *Flavius Josephus, Translation and Commentary*, vol. 1b, *The Judean War 2* (Leiden, 2008), 215–221.

6 Jos. *B. J.*, 2.457.

7 Jos. *B. J.*, 2.458–468, with the commentary of S. Mason *Flavius Josephus*, 337–344.

8 Earlier scholarship on "anti-semitism" in antiquity is conveniently summarized by J.G. Gager *The Origins of Anti-Semitism* (New York, 1983), 11–34. See further N. de Lange "The Origins of Anti-Semitism: Ancient Evidence and Modern Interpretations," in S.L. Gilman and S.T. Katz, *Anti-Semitism in Times of Crisis* (New York, 1991), 21–37; Z. Yavetz "Judeophobia in Classical Antiquity: A Different Approach," *JJS*, 44 (1993), 1–13; P. Schäfer *Judeophobia: Attitudes toward the Jews in the Ancient World* (Cambridge, Mass., 1997), 1–6, 197–211; B. Isaac *The Invention of Racism in Classical Antiquity* (Princeton, 2004), 442–446; V. Herholt *Antisemitismus*

in Greek or in Latin. Indeed, "anti-semitism" as a formulation is misleading on any count. Semitic peoples encompass more than just Jews. Babylonians were Semites too—as indeed are Arabs. Some have substituted "anti-Judaism" for "anti-semitism." But this does not help much.[9] If the former signifies animosity toward the religion rather than toward race or ethnicity, that seems inapplicable to the ancient situation. Religion as such, whatever that might mean (a matter of considerable dispute), was not suppressed, persecuted, or eradicated. Judaism was not the target—Jews were.

Another phrase has gained some currency: "Judeophobia." The term was advocated independently by two distinguished scholars in the 1990s and retains force.[10] It merits scrutiny. Are we to believe that there was widespread *fear* of Jews in pagan circles or pagan communities? Does some form of anxiety lie at the root of hostility to Jews, one that could even issue in a pogrom?

Jews were noticed by some Greek and Roman writers, intellectuals, and framers of opinion. We possess a fair number of remarks and observations from a range of pagan authors who had occasion to comment on the Jews.[11] It is easy enough to find passages in which Jews are stigmatized for one failing or another.

So, for instance, the celebrated rhetorician Apollonius Molon, who taught on the island of Rhodes in the 1st century B.C.E., characterized Jews as atheists and misanthropes. He went further to accuse them of both recklessness on the one hand and cowardice on the other. The traits of recklessness and cowardice do

---

in der Antike (Mörlenbach, 2009), 19–30. The survey by D. Nirenberg *Anti-Judaism: The Western Tradition* (New York, 2013), 13–47, focuses exclusively on Egypt and Alexandria.

9 Cf. J.N. Sevenster *The Roots of Pagan Anti-Semitism in the Ancient World* (Leiden, 1975), 1–8; Yavetz "Judeophobia in Classical Antiquity," 18–19; *idem, Judenfeindschaft in der Antike* (Munich, 1997), 49–53.

10 Yavetz "Judeophobia in Classical Antiquity"; Schäfer *Judeophobia*. It is interesting that Yavetz's lectures in German were entitled, *Judenfeindschaft*, which is rather different from "Judeophobia"; Yavetz (1997). *Judenfurcht*, however, does not seem to surface in the scholarly literature. See the remarks on this formulation by M.H. Williams "Review of Yavetz, *Judenfeindschaft* and Schäfer, *Judeophobia*," *JRS*, 89 (1999), 213; Isaac (2004), 443–444.

11 The indispensable collection, of course, is that of M. Stern *Greek and Latin Authors on Jews and Judaism*, 3 vols. (Jerusalem, 1974, 1980, 1984). Space allows treatment only of a small selection. For a discussion of the rival Exodus stories by Jewish and gentile authors, often taken as exemplary of mutual antagonism, see the paper by E.S. Gruen "The Use and Abuse of the Exodus Story," *Jewish History*, 12 (1998) 93–122 [available in this volume] and the responses to it by L.H. Feldman "Did Jews Reshape the Tale of the Exodus?" *Jewish History*, 12 (1998), 123–127; J.G. Gager "Some Thoughts on Greco-Roman Versions of the Exodus Story," *Jewish History*, 12 (1998), 129–132; and J.M. Mélèze Modrzejewski, "The Exodus Traditions: Parody or Parallel Version?" *Jewish History*, 12 (1998), 133–136.

not normally coincide. But Apollonius seems unconcerned about inconsistency— if Josephus' paraphrase is accurate. He adds that Jews were the least talented of all barbarians (i.e. non-Greeks) and the only ones who had made no creative contribution to civilization.[12] A century later, the caustic Alexandrian writer Apion showered invective upon the Jews. Among other things, he denounced them for worshipping the wrong gods, for promoting sedition, and for swearing an oath to be nasty to all gentiles, especially Greeks.[13] Apion supplies a host of other slanders, even adding gratuitously his own etymology for the word "Sabbath": it comes from an Egyptian root meaning disease of the groin.[14] Latin writers too carried on this disparagement. One need cite only Tacitus, who delivered the most sweeping condemnation. For the Roman historian, the Jews were a people hateful to the gods, their practices of worship contrary to those of all other mortals, and they show animosity toward all people except themselves.[15] This, of course, is a mere sample. One could readily cite other passages and other authors. The Jews, it appears, lent themselves to varied, colorful, and inventive abuse by Greek and Latin writers.

That does not, however, answer our question. The hostile comments can, if one wishes, be balanced by numerous admiring assessments of Jews delivered by pagan intellectuals. So, for example, Varro, the Roman polymath writing at the end of the Republic, praised Jewish aniconism, claiming that the early Romans followed the same practice but abandoned it to their detriment.[16] The author of *On the Sublime*, usually labeled as Pseudo-Longinus, in the 1st century C.E., quoted and praised the beginning of Genesis, accepting the Jewish ascription of it to Moses.[17] The Neoplatonic philosopher Numenius of Apamea in the 2nd century C.E. quoted from Jewish prophets and remarked in a famous phrase:

---

12 Apollonius Molon in Jos. *C. Ap.* 2.148. See now the full study of Apollonius on the Jews by B. Bar-Kochva *The Image of the Jews in Greek Literature: The Hellenistic Period* (Berkeley, 2010), 469–516.

13 Apion, in Jos. *C. Ap.* 2.65, 2.68, 2.79, 2.121.

14 Apion, in Jos. *C. Ap.* 2.20–21. A large portion of the ostensibly hostile remarks about Jews in Greek writers derive from Josephus' final work, the *Contra Apionem*. But it needs to be borne in mind that that treatise is riddled with rhetoric and misrepresentations, with Greek intellectuals as a collection of straw men to be knocked down by the Jewish historian. For this interpretation, see E.S. Gruen "Greeks and Jews: Mutual Misperceptions in Josephus' Contra Apionem," in *Ancient Judaism in Its Hellenistic Context*, ed. C. Bakhos (Leiden: Brill, 2005), 31–51 [available in this volume].

15 Tac. *Hist.* 5.3.1, 5.5.1–5.

16 Varro, in Aug. *CivDei*, 4.31.

17 *De Subl.* 9.9.

"What is Plato but Moses speaking in good Attic Greek?"[18] Even Tacitus himself, no champion of the Jews, paid tribute to their determination and courage in the resistance to Rome.[19] One could, of course, continue in this vein, recording a variety of comments reflecting a positive evaluation of Jewish achievements or values.[20]

Some indeed have gone further. It is possible to draw up a ledger of favorable and unfavorable comments by pagan authors about Jews. One scholar actually did that very thing a number of years ago. He tabulated the results and announced that 18% of pagan assessments were favorable, 23% were unfavorable, and 59% were neutral.[21] Few, however, would regard that as settling the matter. The comments that have survived constitute only a fraction of what might have been said. The contexts of the statements also vary enormously, thus giving rise to their diverse tenor and significance. And a decision on what constitutes favorable or unfavorable depends very much on the eye of the beholder. The problem will not be solved by calculating sums and producing a table of results. This is no numbers game. Even to characterize the majority of pagan remarks as "neutral" misconceives the situation. The notion of "neutrality" implies that some sort of war of words was taking place. In fact, however, it is quite striking to observe that very few of the pagan statements occur in a polemical context at all. That point requires emphasis.

What stands out in many of these writings is neither admiration of the Jews nor hostility toward them. Instead, a considerable number leave the impression of a remarkable ignorance. This displays itself as much in the works that cast a positive light as in those that deliver criticism. Take, for example, the Greek historian Hecataeus of Abdera, writing in the late 4th century B.C.E., who had some approving remarks to make about Moses but also some reservations about Mosaic laws and the mode of life that subsequent Jews embraced as a consequence.[22]

---

18 Numenius, in Clement, *Strom.* 1.22.150.4; Origen, *CCelsum*, 1.15.

19 Tac. *Hist.* 5.13.3. Tacitus' excursus on the Jews in his *Histories* is much more complex and ironic than the usual interpretation placed upon it as a virulently hostile text. The case for this understanding of Tacitus' attitude cannot be developed here. It is argued in Gruen *Rethinking the Other*, 179–196; *idem* "Tacitus and the Defamation of the Jews," in J. Geiger, H. Cotton and G. Stiebel, *Israel's Land:Papers Presented to Israel Shatzman on his Jubilee.* (Jerusalem, 2009), 77–96 [available in this volume]. A different interpretation in R.S. Bloch *Antike Vorstellungen vom Judentum: Der Judenexkurs des Tacitus im Rahmen der griechisch-romischen Ethnographie* (Stuttgart, 2002).

20 See Gager *The Origins of Anti-Semitism*, 67–88.

21 L.H. Feldman *Jew and Gentile in the Ancient World* (Princeton, 1993), 124.

22 On Hecataeus, see now the treatment by Bar–Kochva *The Image of the Jews in Greek Literature*, 90–135.

He was evidently not engaged in polemic. And he got some important facts wrong. Hecataeus reports that the Jews never had a king, that they chose their High Priest for his virtue and his wisdom, and that Moses founded the city of Jerusalem where he installed the Temple.[23] In fact, of course, the ancient Israelites had many kings, their High Priesthood was a hereditary office, and Moses never made it to the Holy Land. Hecataeus, at least in part, drew on erroneous information and may not have had much first-hand experience. Roman writers were hardly more reliable in their depiction of Jewish practices, even though many Jews lived in their midst. The Sabbath, for example, was regarded by many as a day of fasting.[24] Others connected it with the god Saturn.[25] Plutarch, the biographer and collector of arcane information, even compared the Sabbath to a Dionysiac feast.[26] The speculations in short ran from fast day to feast day. As is clear, pagans entertained a number of misconceptions, confusions, and inaccuracies. These need not reflect animus nor deliberate distortion. Instead, they suggest a lack of serious inquiry, a superficial curiosity, and a general indifference. It appears that most of the authors did not care enough to get their facts straight.

Indeed a substantial proportion of pagan references to Jews and Judaism fall into a single category. They constitute allusions to peculiar Jewish traits, practices, and customs. Greeks and Romans, as already noted, could live comfortably with religious and cultural activities practiced by a wide variety of ethnic groups. The Jews, however, struck them as being particularly weird. Hence their strange habits turn up rather frequently in pagan texts. Romans who had the opportunity to observe Jews in their midst remarked often on their peculiarities. A few instances will suffice. Some Romans regarded the keeping of the Sabbath as a colossal folly. Seneca quipped that by observing the Sabbath Jews waste 1/7 of their lives in idleness.[27] Tacitus speculated that the charms of laziness not only induced Jews to while away every seventh day but even prompted them to devote every seventh year to lolling about.[28] The abstention from pork provoked similar cracks. As Augustus famously put it, in speaking about the intrigues and murders that took place in the family and court of Herod, "I would feel safer as Herod's pig than as his son."[29] Petronius mocked the Jews as worshipping a pig-

---

23 Hecataeus, in Diod. Sic. 40.3.3 – 5.
24 Strabo, 16.2.40; Trogus, *apud* Justin, 36.2.14; Suet. *Aug.* 76.2; Petronius, fr. 37, Ernout; Martial, 4.4.7.
25 Tibullus, 1.13.8; Frontinus, *Stratagems*, 2.1.17; Tac. *Hist.* 5.4.4.
26 Plut. *Quaest. Conviv.* 4.6.2.
27 Seneca, in Aug. *CivDei*, 6.11.
28 Tac. *Hist.* 5.4.3.
29 Macrob. *Sat.* 2.4.11.

god.[30] And Juvenal observed that Judaea is the one place where pigs can live to a ripe old age.[31] Circumcision, of course, drew similar jibes and mockery. Not only did Roman satirists like Petronius, Juvenal, and Martial find it a source of amusement, but the Jewish philosopher Philo acknowledged that it prompted ridicule and laughter among many.[32]

Remarks of this kind might be droll and parodic, but they hardly constituted deep animosity. The derogatory comments qualify more as amused disdain than as a campaign of vilification. Nor were Jews the sole objects of scorn. Much is made of Cicero's notorious statement that Jews and Syrians are born to be slaves.[33] But, when circumstances called for it, in other speeches, the orator could spout comparable vitriol at Gauls and Sardinians, at Phrygians, Mysians, Lydians, and Carians—all of whom come off no better than Jews.[34] Tacitus, sometimes labeled as the arch anti-semite, certainly did not reserve his fire for Jews alone. He can be quite indiscriminate in his assault. He blasts Britons and Germans too, he is contemptuous of Egyptian religion, and he despises Christianity.[35] One need not belabor the point with regard to satirists. For Juvenal, easterners of every stripe are offensive. He expresses his contempt infamously in the lines about the Orontes river pouring its refuse into the Tiber. And he blasts the Egyptians without mercy.[36] Some of this may well be tongue-in-cheek. But Juvenal does not single out Jews for opprobrium.

Jews, in short, had no monopoly as victims of invective. Pagans frequently poked fun at those who did not share their customs, their gods, their institutions, their garb, or their language. That gave ample scope for mockery, wisecracks, and caricature. The jibes were aimed at those who were different. But they fall well short of outrage or animus, let alone oppression. Most of the disparaging remarks made by pagans derive from Greco-Roman cultural snobbery and a disdain for alien customs, especially the more eccentric ones. The sneers, jokes, and put-downs marked no path to persecution. To regard this collection of sarcastic and dismissive utterances as building a picture of Jews that prompted pog-

---

30 Petronius, fr. 37, Ernout.

31 Juv. 6.160.

32 Philo. *Spec.* 1.1 – 2: ἄρξομαι δ' ἀπὸ τοῦ γελωμένου παρὰ τοῖς πολλοῖς. Γελᾶται δὲ ἡ τῶν γεννητικῶν περιτομή. For satiric lampoons of circumcision, see, e.g., Petronius, 68.3 – 4; Juv. 14.103 – 104; Martial, 7.30.5, 7.82, 11.94

33 Cic. *Prov. Cons.* 10.

34 See E.S. Gruen "Cicero and the Alien," in D. Lateiner, B.K. Gold, and J. Perkins, *Roman Literature, Gender and Reception* (New York, 2013), 13 – 27.

35 See Tac. *Germ.* 4.1, 14.2 – 3, 22.1, 39.1, 45.4; *Agr.* 11 – 12; *Hist.* 1.11.1, 5.5; *Ann.* 15.44.3 – 5.

36 Juv. 3.62 – 65, 15.1 – 11.

roms would be well off the mark.[37] The perpetrators of outright brutality against the Jews in Alexandria, Caesarea, and elsewhere did not study at the feet of Apollonius Molon, learn philosophy from Seneca, or take their cue from the pungent witticisms of Petronius and the wry ironies of Tacitus.

Was there, in fact, Judeophobia in classical antiquity? What did Greeks or Romans have to fear from Jews? It is worth looking at those passages often cited to suggest concern about Jewish influence, impact, and infiltration into pagan society.

Cicero's powerful speech on behalf of Flaccus, the Roman governor of Asia, in 59 B.C.E. provides a striking picture of the weight that Jews could bring to bear in public deliberations at Rome. They objected sharply to Flaccus' actions in preventing the shipment of gold from Jews in the cities of Asia Minor to the Temple in Jerusalem. Cicero lamented that the Jews of Rome constituted a pressure group, that they rounded up a substantial crowd, and that they exercised considerable authority in *contiones*, the political assemblies that gathered to discuss public issues and consider legislative enactments.[38] Those lines certainly attest to a thriving community of Jews in Rome, one that could work in unison when a matter affected them directly and could engage in public demonstrations if the occasion called for it. But one must exercise caution here. The forensic context, as so often, generated Ciceronian rhetoric that thrives on exaggeration and overstatement. It is hardly likely that Jews would customarily show up in force to attend *contiones* and throw their weight around. Moreover, Cicero's fulminations include no suggestion that Romans felt nervous about the authority wielded by Jews.

The text of Pompeius Trogus, historian of the Hellenistic kingdoms, writing around the end of the 1st century B.C.E. or the beginning of the 1st century C.E., as transmitted by Justin, contains an intriguing statement. Trogus offered an ill-researched and muddled digest of early Israelite history, including the assertion that Moses was son of Joseph, and that Moses' son became both priest and king of his people. He adds that this elevation became the model for all subse-

---

37 See Gruen *Diaspora*, 41–52; cf. M. Goodman *Rome and Jerusalem: The Clash of Ancient Civilizations* (New York, 2007), 366–376. They are taken much more seriously by Feldman *Jew and Gentile in the Ancient World*, 123–176; Schäfer *Judeophobia*, 180–195; B. Rochette "Juifs et Romains: Y a-t-il eu un antijudaisme romain?" *REJ*, 160 (2001), 18–31. Cf. also Isaac *The Invention of Racism in Classical Antiquity*, 463–477, *idem* "The Ancient Mediterranean and the pre-Christian Era," in A.S. Lindemann and R.S. Levy, *Antisemitism: A History* (Oxford, 2010), 37–44.
38 Cic. *Flacc.* 66–67: *illa turba quaesita est; scis quanta sit manus, quanta concordia, quantum valeat in contionibus. . . . multitudinem Iudaeorum flagrantem non numquam in contionibus.*

quent Jewish rulers who combined high priesthood with kingship. And he marvels that the combination of justice and religion has made the Jews incredibly powerful.[39] Trogus, in this hash of Jewish history, is plainly thinking about the combination of political and sacred offices that did not occur until the 2nd century B.C.E. under the Hasmoneans. The statement has been taken as a reflection of pagan awe at Jewish power in the early years of the Roman Empire.[40] That is surely over-interpretation. Judaea had become more conspicuous on the international scene under the Herodian dynasty, probably the time when Trogus composed his history. But, quite apart from the fact that monarchy was no longer combined with High Priesthood in that period, Judaea was very much in thrall to and under the shadow of Rome in the Herodian years. Whatever Trogus intended to convey in his jumbled history, it could hardly represent serious Roman worry about Jewish power—nor does Trogus himself (whose account is rather positive on the Jews) suggest any such worry.

Of greater account, at least in modern interpretations, are references to conversion to Judaism, the growing numbers of Jews, and the alarm expressed by pagan authors at the apostasy of their compatriots. Tacitus' denunciation of those who entered the Jewish fold is virulent and memorable. He deplores the fact that they agreed to undergo circumcision, and he castigates them for despising their own gods, for rejecting their native tradition, and for holding their parents, children, and siblings cheap.[41] Juvenal expresses comparable displeasure with gentiles who embraced Judaism. He upbraids them for observing the Sabbath, abstaining from pork, yielding to circumcision, and worshipping no gods but the clouds and some divinity of the sky. Even worse, they accustomed themselves to scorning Roman laws, and, instead, study, observe, and revere Judaic justice, which Moses handed down in a secret volume.[42] Seneca goes still further. He claims that the ways of this most criminal nation prevail so extensively that they are accepted in all lands, to the point that the vanquished now give laws to the victors.[43]

---

39 Trogus, in Justin, 36.2.1–16, esp. 36.2.16: *ut eosdem reges et sacerdotes haberent, quorum iustitia religione permixta incredibile quantum coaluere.*

40 Cf. Feldman *Jew and Gentile in the Ancient World*, 174.

41 Tac. *Hist.* 5.5.2: *transgressi in morem eorum idem usurpant, nec quicquam prius imbuuntur quam contemnere deos, exuere patriam, parentes liberos fratres vilia habere.*

42 Juv. 14.96–102: *Romanas autem soliti contemnere leges/ Iudaicum ediscunt et servant ac metuunt ius/ tradidit arcano quodcumque volumine Moyses..*

43 Seneca, in Aug. *CivDei,* 6.11: *cum interim usque eo sceleratissimae gentis consuetudo convaluit, ut per omnes iam terras recepta sit; victi victoribus leges dederunt.*

Does this combination of texts establish that Judeophobia gripped the Romans, that the proliferation of the Jews frightened pagans, that Jewish proselytizing panicked the officialdom and the populace?[44] The testimony can hardly sustain that inference.

The Tacitean passage signals no widespread alarm. The historian directs his vitriol against proselytes who turn their backs on their own gods, nation, and families. So much the worse for them. But he does not infer that their conversion represents a menace to pagan society as a whole. Tacitus does follow that statement with the report that Jews take care to increase their own numbers. But it is quite clear that this has nothing to do with encouraging converts. Tacitus speaks here explicitly of Jewish prohibition on the slaying of any late-born child and their commitment to increasing progeny.[45]

Juvenal's caustic lines should not be taken as serious anxiety about a Jewish threat to pagan well-being. Apart from the satirist's grumbling about converts adopting bizarre Jewish habits, his principal complaint is leveled at their study of, adherence to, and reverence for the Mosaic code and their contempt for Roman laws. There is patent exaggeration here. We have no record of Jews, let alone proselytes, violating Roman laws or of being charged with such actions. Even if one were to take the satirical caricature seriously, Juvenal says nothing about hordes of pagans abandoning their traditions and yielding to Jewish blandishments. No hint surfaces in this text about an epidemic of conversions that might prompt Roman dread.

The only alarming notice comes from Seneca. His remark that Jewish practice is received throughout the world and that the conquered now dictate laws to the conqueror would seem to imply that Jews have spread everywhere and have the upper hand wherever they are. The latter claim is surely preposterous. How much credence should be given to the former?

It is noteworthy that Seneca's near contemporary, the Jewish historian Josephus, made a comparable claim, in his case a boast with a positive spin. He maintained that there was not a city or a people, whether Greek or barbarian, to which Jewish observance of the Sabbath, fasts, lighting of lamps, and dietary

---

44 So, e.g., J.L. Daniel "Anti-Semitism in the Hellenistic-Roman World," *JBL*, 98 (1979), 62–64; Gager *The Origins of Anti-Semitism*, 59–61; K. Rosen "Der Historiker als Prophet: Tacitus und die Juden," *Gymnasium*, 103 (1996), 116, 121; Schäfer *Judeophobia*, 183–192.

45 Tac. *Hist.* 5.5.3: *augendae tamen multidudini consulitur; nam et necare quemquam ex agnatis nefas . . . hinc generandi amor.* The statement is not an elaboration on what Tacitus had just said about proselytes. Note the *tamen*.

regulations has not spread.[46] A closely similar assertion had been made by Philo a generation or so earlier. He affirms that the Sabbath and Yom Kippur are honored by Greeks and barbarians, by those who dwell on the continents or on islands, by east and west, Europe and Asia, indeed the whole world from one end to the other.[47] These statements too are rhetorical outbursts, not be taken literally (or even close) by ancient or by modern readers. In combination with Seneca's tirade, however, they do confirm (what we otherwise know from epigraphic, archaeological, and additional literary evidence) that Jews had indeed found their way to numerous sites in the Mediterranean world, that they had established communities widely, and that an extensive diaspora had taken hold well before the time of Seneca, Philo, and Josephus.[48] Nor would it be at all surprising that many gentiles in those communities had emulated or adopted various Jewish practices.[49]

Was this perceived as a threat? Only Seneca betrays any hint of it. And one needs to bear in mind that his overblown statement comes not in any extant text of Seneca but only in a quotation (paraphrase?) by St. Augustine four centuries later. We do not know the context of the original. Further, it is noteworthy that Seneca's surviving work (a substantial corpus) nowhere makes direct mention of Jews. They were hardly an obsession for him. If there was pervasive fear of Jewish numbers or of the growing predominance of Jewish practices, the lone passage of Seneca would certainly not prove it. His allegation that the conquered imposed their laws upon the conqueror need mean no more than that the observance of the Sabbath and other customs associated with the Jews had gained wide welcome in the Roman world. Seneca may not have been happy about that. But even he (if the quotation is accurate) does not say that pagans panicked over the increase of Jewish numbers and influence.

---

46 Jos. *C. Ap.* 2.282; cf. *BJ*, 7.43. See the valuable commentary by J.M.G. Barclay *Flavius Josephus, Translation and Commentary*, vol. 10, *Against Apion* (Leiden, 2007), 327–328.

47 Philo, *Mos.* 2.20–21.

48 See the discussion in Gruen *Diaspora*, 105–132, with references.

49 Suetonius, *Dom.* 12.2, reports that those who sought to evade the *fiscus Iudaicus* under Domitian consisted both of those who live a Jewish life without professing themselves to be Jews and those who concealed their origins in order to avoid paying the tax. Whether the first category (or even both) included proselytes cannot be determined from the text, although it is often assumed. Cf. L.A. Thompson "Domitian and the Jewish Tax," *Historia* , 31 (1983), 329–342; M.H. Williams "Domitian, the Jews, and the 'Judaizers'—A Simple Matter of Cupiditas and Maiestas?" *Historia*, 39 (1990), 196–211; Schäfer *Judeophobia*, 113–116. But they were certainly persons who shared Jewish practices and ways of life.

The whole issue has been tied by modern scholars to the fraught question of Jewish proselytism.[50] Did the Jews engage in missionary activity to solicit converts and enhance their prominence? This is not the place to engage in an extended discussion of that much debated subject. But it may be worth noting that the evidence for proselytizing by Jews is vanishingly small. The texts already discussed, while they attest to converts and the spread of Jewish customs to the gentiles, say nothing about aggressive proselytizing.

Nor should it be inferred from other passages sometimes cited in that cause. Some notorious lines of Horace have offered ostensible support. He states that "if you are unwilling to yield to this, the large band of poets would come and be of assistance to me, for we are much larger in number and we, like the Jews, will force you to yield to this throng."[51] The phraseology has suggested to some that Horace implies aggressive proselytizing.[52] But the inference is unwarranted. The text says nothing of conversion to Judaism. It refers to the band of poets who will compel assent, just as Jews do. And compulsion was nowhere a Jewish means of winning proselytes for their clan.[53]

Where does one find any traces of proselytizing activity? The argument has made use of episodes in which Jews were expelled from Rome. For some the expulsions stemmed from Jewish efforts to win converts, thus generating alarm and prompting removal of the missionaries. That position is dubious at best, and ultimately unsustainable. First of all, we know of only three examples of such banishments, and they are widely spaced in time. The first came in 139 B.C.E., the second in 19 C.E., and the third in 49 C.E. Did the Jews do no proselytizing in the interim periods? Or did no one notice or care?

---

50 See, e. g., Sevenster *The Roots of Pagan Anti-Semitism in the Ancient World*, 191 – 218; Daniel "Anti-Semitism in the Hellenistic-Roman World," 62 – 64; Gager *The Origins of Anti-Semitism*, 59 – 66; Feldman *Jew and Gentile in the Ancient World*, 288 – 341, with the criticisms by L.V. Rutgers "Attitudes to Judaism in the Greco-Roman Period: Reflections on Feldman's *Jew and Gentile in the Ancient World*, " *JQR*, 85 (1995), 361 – 395; Isaac *The Invention of Racism in Classical Antiquity*, 453 – 463; *idem* "The Ancient Mediterranean and the pre-Christian Era," 39 – 42.
51 Horace, *Serm.* 1.4.140 – 143: *cui si concedere nolis/ multa poetarum veniat manus, auxilio quae/ sit mihi; nam multo plures sumus, ac veluti te Iudaei cogemus in hanc concedere turbam.*
52 Stern *Greek and Latin Authors on Jews and Judaism* (1974), 323; Sevenster *The Roots of Pagan Anti-Semitism in the Ancient World*, 203; Feldman *Jew and Gentile in the Ancient World*, 299.
53 See J. Nolland "Proselytism or Politics in Horace, *Satires*, I,4,143?" *Vigiliae Christianae*, 33 (1979), 347 – 355; J.M.G. Barclay *Jews in the Mediterranean Diaspora from Alexander to Trajan (323 BCE – 117 CE)* (Edinburgh, 1996), 295 – 296; Schäfer *Judeophobia*, 107 – 108. It is true that efforts to bring about conversion by force occurred under the Hasmoneans. But this involved large-scale compulsion of peoples after military victory, not proselytizing activity; Jos. *A. J.* 13.257 – 258, 13.319. And Horace was surely not thinking about the Hasmoneans.

A noteworthy fact needs emphasis. In each instance, the exiled Jews did not stay away very long. A large Jewish community thrived in Rome in the 1ˢᵗ century B.C.E., as Cicero happens to attest in 59.[54] They had surely not just arrived. So, the expulsion in 139 was far from permanent or sweeping, more a demonstration than a full-scale eviction. Further, Jews were not the sole targets. The Roman praetor's decrees ordered the exile of both Chaldeans (astrologers) and Jews. And there is nothing to suggest astrological proselytizing. The evidence itself is exceedingly thin and confused. It derives from Valerius Maximus, writing in the reign of Tiberius, more than a century and a half later. Moreover, his text itself is transmitted in two versions through epitomes by two separate Byzantine exceptors. The ground is at best shaky. One version alleges that Jews had attempted to pass their sacred rites to the Romans, the other that they wished to infiltrate Roman mores with the cult of Jupiter Sabazius.[55] No need to dwell on this muddle. If any proselytism took place, it may just as likely have come from adherents of Jupiter Sabazius as from Jews.[56] And the prime victims may well have been astrologers rather than Jews (they were the first to be expelled). The whole episode represents an effort to trumpet official concern for reaffirming traditional Roman values.[57] If Jews actually left in any numbers, they were soon back. Proselytism, insofar as there was any, did not unduly trouble the authorities.

The much discussed expulsion of 19 C.E. under the emperor Tiberius requires no lengthy treatment here. It has already received extensive scrutiny.[58] One need note only that our main sources on the episode, Josephus, Tacitus, and Suetonius, give no hint that proselytizing triggered the government action. One source alone, Dio Cassius, writing almost two centuries later, mentions such activity. His brief text states simply that when many Jews gathered in Rome and were turning the inhabitants to their ways of life, Tiberius banished most of them.[59] And the text was transmitted by the 7th century Christian author

---

54 Cic. *Flacc.* 66–68.
55 Val. Max. 1.3.3 (Nepotianus): *Iudaeos quoque, qui Romanis tradere sacra sua conati errant.* Val Max. 1.3.3 (Paris): *idem Iudaeos, qui Sabazi Iovis cultu Romanos inficere mores conati erant.*
56 See the discussions of E.N. Lane "Sabazius and the Jews in Valerius Maximus: A Re-examination," *JRS*, 69 (1979), 35–38; P. Trebilco *Jewish Communities in Asia Minor* (Cambridge, 1991), 140–142; H.D. Slingerland *Claudian Policymaking and the Early Imperial Repression of Judaism at Rome* (Atlanta, 1997), 41–42.
57 This interpretation receives fuller treatment in Gruen *Diaspora*, 15–19.
58 See the analysis, with full bibliographic references, in Gruen *Diaspora*, 29–36. Add Goodman *Rome and Jerusalem*, 369.
59 Dio, 57.18.5a: Τῶν τε Ἰουδαίων πολλῶν ἐς τὴν Ῥώμην συνελθόντων καὶ συχνοὺς τῶν ἐπιχωρίων ἐς τὰ σφέτερα ἔθη μεθιστάντων, τοὺς πλείονας ἐξήλασεν.

John of Antioch. The fragment lacks all context, and it coincides with nothing else in the testimony. That does not justify jettisoning the account, but it provides only the most slender basis for inferring that fear of losing pagan converts to Judaism motivated Tiberius' decree. One must observe that here too, whatever the motives or pretexts for expulsion, Jews were not singled out. Worshippers of Isis and perhaps others departed as well.[60] And, once again they could hardly have been away long, if many of them left at all. According to Philo's narrative, Tiberius' praetorian prefect Sejanus leveled charges against Jews in Rome a few years later, but the emperor subsequently dismissed them as false slanders.[61] There is very little here to sustain the idea that missionary actions generated Roman anxieties.

The third episode is the most infamous of them, and certainly the one over which most ink has been spilled. As is well known, Suetonius reports that the emperor Claudius expelled from Rome the Jews who were persistently causing upheaval at the instigation of Chrestus.[62] The passage has been parsed innumerable times with a vast variety of interpretations. Happily, we do not need to pause over it. The motives for this banishment can be debated forever. But the text says not a word about conversion. And once more the "exiles" were back in Rome in short order.[63] In brief, the very few episodes of Jewish expulsion, widely scattered and more symbolic than effective, give little foothold to those who wish to argue for pagan dread of Jewish proselytism.[64]

The very idea of Judeophobia seems counter-intuitive. That there should be widespread apprehension about a Jewish menace among the denizens of Greek cities or the officialdom of the Roman empire is highly implausible on the face of it. Certainly the snide remarks about alien practices or the quips of clever satirists do not remotely suggest anxiety about Jewish infiltration. And the supposed concern about proselytism is largely a red herring.

---

60 Tac. *Ann.* 2.85; Suet. *Tib.* 36; cf. Jos. *A. J.* 18.65 – 84.
61 Philo, *Legat.* 159 – 160; *Flacc.* 1, 161.
62 Suet. *Claud.* 25.4: *Iudaeos impulsore Chresto assidue tumultuantis Roma expulit.*
63 Cf. Paul, Rom. 16:3 – 4.
64 One other passage has often been used to make a case for Jewish missionary activity: Matt. 23:15. Jesus rebukes "scribes and Pharisees" for crossing land and sea to make a single proselyte. But the reference may well be to the recruitment of Pharisees rather than to any general mission to convert gentiles to Judaism. See M. Goodman "Jewish Proselytizing in the First Century," in J. Lieu, J. North, and T. Rajak, *Jews Among Pagans and Christians in the Roman Empire* (London, 1992), 60 – 63; *idem Mission and Conversion: Proselytizing in the Religious History of the Roman Empire* (Oxford, 1994), 68 – 72; cf. W. Huss "Zu den Ursprüngen des antiken Antijudaismus," in J.-F. Eckholt, M. Sigismund, and S. Sigismund, *Geschehen und Gedächtnis: Die hellenistische Welt und ihre Wirkung* (Münster, 2009), 170 – 171.

But this does not settle the matter. We need to return to the violent outbursts against Jews noted at the beginning of this paper: the massacres in Alexandria, Seleucia, and Caesarea. And they were by no means the only ones. In the course of the Jewish war against Rome, the inhabitants of Skythopolis slaughtered 13,000 Jews and seized their property.[65] At Ascalon, 2500 Jews fell, 2000 at Ptolemais, comparable numbers at Tyre, and in cities throughout Syria.[66] Renewed fighting broke out in Alexandria in 66 C.E. The pattern was a familiar one. A *melée* in the amphitheater between Greeks and Jews led to the intervention of the Roman prefect with two legions. They performed their "peace-keeping" operations by spreading carnage throughout the Jewish community of the city. And even when the Roman commander, Ti. Julius Alexander, who was a former Jew, called off the troops, the Alexandrian citizenry, driven, says Josephus, by excess of hatred, indulged themselves in mutilation of Jewish corpses.[67] Equally grim events occurred in Damascus. The citizens cooped up Jews in the gymnasium, ostensibly for purposes of security, and subsequently butchered them all, more than 10,000 within an hour.[68] Even the people of Antioch, normally congenial, turned on the Jews in their midst in 70. They abolished Sabbath observance, forced Jews to conduct Greek sacrifices, and then made Jews a collective scapegoat for a fire in the city.[69] The episode contains some chilling modern overtones. The numbers supplied by Josephus are suspiciously round, and all numbers in ancient manuscripts are unreliable or subject to exaggeration. But the bloated figures do not cast doubt upon the events themselves.

No easy explanations exist for such events. And those offered by modern interpreters are somewhat strained and implausible. So, for example, Greek anti-Judaism has been analyzed as anti-Romanism in disguise. Since Rome accorded privileges to Jews in various communities, as in Alexandria, so it is argued, attacks on Jews would be an indirect but safer way to vent their wrath against the Romans.[70] That answer is singularly unsatisfactory. Would a massacre of

---

65 Jos. *B. J.*, 2.466 – 468.
66 Jos. *B. J.*, 2.477 – 478.
67 Jos. *B. J.*, 2.487 – 498: δι' ὑπερβολὴν μίσους.
68 Jos. *B. J.*, 2.599 – 561.
69 Jos. *B. J.*, 7.41 – 60.
70 E.M. Smallwood *The Jews under Roman Rule from Pompey to Diocletian: A Study in Political Relations* (Leiden, 1981), 233 – 234; Gager *The Origins of Anti-Semitism*, 44, 49 – 50; Yavetz *Judenfeindschaft in der Antike*, 103 – 104. In addition to Jewish civic rights in Alexandria, Greek interference with Jewish privileges in cities of Asia Minor can also be seen as indirect clashes with Roman guarantors of those privileges; cf. Barclay *Jews in the Mediterranean Diaspora*, 266 – 278; M. Pucci Ben Zeev *Jewish Rights in the Roman World: The Greek and Roman Documents Quoted by Josephus Flavius* (Tübingen, 1998), 271 – 272, 412 – 429.

Jews in Alexandria be reckoned as an affront to Rome? Apart from turmoil which a Roman governor would be expected to repress, there is little to reason to believe that Roman interests would be damaged by an attack on Jews. One might note indeed that, after the assaults on the Jewish community in Alexandria in 38, a Jewish delegation to the emperor Caligula was greeted with derision.[71] Roman prestige was plainly not at stake. A different interpretation turns this one on its head. It proposes that pagan propaganda against the Jews actually represents an effort to curry the favor of the Romans. On this view Greeks employed tactics to blacken Jews in the eyes of Rome, thus to prove to their Roman overlords that the Hellenized people of the east were more reliable allies than the untrustworthy Semites.[72] That reconstruction is hardly any more plausible than the reverse. How likely is it that the Romans would be impressed by Hellenic assaults on the Jews? When complaints about mistreatment or loss of privileges came to Roman officials from Jews in the Greek cities of Asia Minor, the decisions in fact normally favored the complainant.[73]

Reconstructions of this sort suffer from two major drawbacks. First, they over-rationalize or over-intellectualize incidents that were actually driven by more emotional—and more destructive—passions. And, secondly, they err in searching for some general phenomenon, some sweeping explanation that underlay all of the particular outbursts. Surely, the massacre of 10,000 trapped Jews (or whatever the actual number may have been) in Damascus, for instance, cannot be accounted for by cold political calculation—let alone by the depiction of Jews in pagan literature.[74] The intensity of feelings in such communities suggests local conflicts and narrowly based animosities. Herein may lie the critical clue.

---

71 Philo, *Legat.* 355–373.
72 Yavetz "Judeophobia in Classical Antiquity," 21–22. For many recent scholars, Josephus' lengthy *apologia* for the Jews in his *Contra Apionem* was designed in large part to stress the similarities of Roman and Jewish values and ideals, thereby to refute Greek attackers who pointed to discrepancies between Jewish and Roman ways of life; see, e.g., G. Haaland "Jewish Laws for a Roman Audience: Toward an Understanding of *Contra Apionem*," in J.U. Kalms and F. Siegert, *Internationales Josephus-Kolloquium 1998* (Münster, 1999), 282–304; K. Berthelot "The Use of Greek and Roman Stereotypes of the Egyptians by Hellenistic Jewish Apologists, with Special Reference to Josephus' *Against Apion*,"in J.U. Kalms, *Internationales Josephus-Kolloquium Aarhus, 1999* (Münster, 2000), 185–221; J.M.G. Barclay "Judaism in Roman Dress: Josephus' Tactics in the *Contra Apionem*," in J.U. Kalms, *Internationales Josephus-Kolloquium Aarhus 1999* (Münster, 2000), 231–245; *idem Flavius Josephus* v.10, 362–369.
73 See below.
74 For the slaughter in the gymnasium at Damascus, see Jos. *B. J.*, 2.559–561.

We need to seek answers at the local level. A noteworthy text can serve as an illustration. One fragmentary papyrus from the 1st century B.C.E., too damaged to disclose the circumstances and situation, nonetheless contains a pregnant phrase. It makes reference to the Egyptian community of Tebtunis and to the priest of that community, and it adds the statement "you know how they loathe the Jews."[75] The particulars that generated this comment are elusive. But the text evidently indicates a local resentment of some sort. That is where the spotlight must be directed.

Josephus supplies some vital documentation here. He preserves a series of Roman decrees sent to individual cities in Asia Minor, the islands of the Aegean, Syria, Phoenicia, Palestine, and Cyrene in North Africa, a range of communities around the Mediterranean. The decrees repeatedly affirm Roman protection of Jewish rights.[76] Of course, Josephus may have had his own apologetic purposes in transmitting these documents. But that does not compromise their authenticity or diminish their value as evidence. What matters for our purposes is the fact that the edicts had to be issued by Roman magistrates and other officials because various cities had evidently interfered with or curtailed Jewish exercise of traditional practices. That issue, in one form or another, arises again and again.

One might take as an example the edict of the Roman governor of Asia to the city of Ephesus. It directs the officialdom of that city to exempt Jews from military service because they cannot bear arms on the Sabbath and cannot obtain the food required by their dietary prescriptions.[77] A similar document went out to the city of Tralles in Asia Minor demanding that its leaders cease attacking Jews and preventing them from observing the Sabbath and other traditions.[78] The emperor Augustus subsequently affirmed to the provinces of Asia and Cyrene that Jews should be free to practice their rituals, that their contributions to the Temple in Jerusalem were inviolable, and that no one was permitted to steal their sacred books or monies.[79] Several other letters, decrees, and edicts to various cities and states of Greece and the Near East were collected and preserved by Josephus. It stands to reason that such documents would not have been issued unless those communities had placed curbs on Jewish worship,

---

75 *CPJ*, I, #141. Cf. J.M. Mélèze Modrezejewski *The Jews of Egypt from Ramses II to Emperor Hadrian* (Philadelphia, 1995), 154–157.

76 See the thorough treatment by Pucci Ben Zeev *Jewish Rights in the Roman World*, *passim*; cf. Gruen *Diaspora*, 84–104.

77 Jos. *A. J.* 14.26; Pucci Ben Zeev *Jewish Rights in the Roman World*, 139–148.

78 Jos. *A. J.* 14.244–246; Pucci Ben Zeev *Jewish Rights in the Roman World*, 199–205.

79 Jos. *A. J.* 16.160–164; Pucci Ben Zeev *Jewish Rights in the Roman World*, 233–261.

had interfered with observance of the Sabbath, had hijacked Jewish contributions to the Temple, and had even stolen Jewish prayer books. All of this plainly had been prompted at the local level.

Why did the Roman imperial government choose to intervene at all? The emperor or his appointees could hardly have seen themselves as great champions of Jewish rights and privileges—whatever Josephus might wish us to believe. Particular conditions and circumstances called forth the interventions. Insofar as they reflected general policy, that would stem from the desire to maintain stability, order, and tranquility in the empire. Romans frowned on local disturbances and tensions that upset the smoothness of administration. Official policy, however, was not always satisfactorily implemented on the ground. When the Roman governor was distant or occupied, or indeed occasionally collaborative, regional hostilities played themselves out, sometimes with deleterious effects. What needs to be emphasized, however, is that these were local events, triggered by individual circumstances, not some ideological commitment to anti-semitism, let alone an official campaign of persecution. The events that prompted particular outbursts varied from community to community. They might involve a competition for civic rights in one city, rivalry for judicial privileges in another, resentment over tax benefits in another, anger over draft exemptions in still another.[80] The episodes were occasioned by social, economic, and political circumstances that differed from place to place, rather than conforming to some uniform, overall pattern.

Another point requires strong stress. The outbursts were not regular features of the historical landscape. If one surveys the long stretch of time from Alexander the Great to the outbreak of the Great Revolt, they claimed only a tiny portion of that period. The documents collected by Josephus signaling conflicts over privileges for Jews in Greek cities are almost entirely concentrated in the period of Caesar and Augustus when political and military circumstances produced unusual tensions.[81] The so-called Alexandrian "pogrom" arose from the combustible mix of rivalries among Greeks, Egyptians, and Jews in that city, triggered by the special situation in which the Roman prefect found himself.[82] And most of the ferocious attacks on Jews in the cities of Syria, Palestine, and Phoenicia came in the course of the Great Revolt itself when loyalties were put to their

---

80 These and other issues are documented in the decrees, edicts, and exchange of communications between Roman officials and Greek cities concerning the rights and privileges of Jewish communities, conveniently collected and commented upon by Pucci Ben Zev *Jewish Rights in the Roman World*, 25 – 357.

81 See Gruen *Diaspora*, 84 – 104.

82 See above, n. 3.

most severe test and the need felt by many communities to distinguish themselves from the rebels was at its most intense. These are not to be taken as representative of Jewish experience in the Hellenistic and Roman periods.

The anti-semitism or Judeophobia that we associate with the medieval and modern worlds has no real counterpart in antiquity. We do not find ideological fixation, consistent caricatures, religious intolerance, racial stereotypes, or elaborate justifications for oppression. If we are ever to understand the attacks that loom so large in the accounts, we must focus attention on local quarrels and community rivalries, on internal friction over political rights, civic privileges, economic claims, or social distinctions that varied from place to place—and on the individual circumstances that brought latent tensions to the surface.

Even if all this be granted, however, the matter is not closed. Contingency may indeed explain much. But why is it that Jews are the ones who are so frequently victimized in these situations? Why not Gauls, or Egyptians, or Thracians, or Sardinians? They too were frequently lampooned by Greek and Roman writers, but do not turn up as regular prey for violent assault.

There is no easy answer. But two avenues toward partial understanding might be considered. First, the nature of our information. We happen to possess Josephus' history of the Jewish experience in antiquity. There is no Thracian Josephus, no Celtic Josephus, no Sardinian Josephus. Had there been, we would have a fuller and more balanced view of inner conflicts and regional rivalries elsewhere. The Jews might not seem to be singular targets. Second, there is perhaps something especially notable about the Jews. They (or at least a significant proportion of them) held tenaciously to traits and observances that marked out their particular heritage. And, paradoxically, the more they became an integral part of pagan society, the greater the need they may have felt to maintain their own traditions and practices, in order to assert the distinctiveness of their identity. This was, to be sure, a source of pride—but it could also be a risk and a hazard. Through much of the time this commitment to singularity engendered nothing worse than amusement or irritation, and the Jews were left untroubled. In periods of crisis, however, whether political upheaval or regional conflict, local tensions become intensified. Under such circumstances, cultural differences, usually ignored or just scorned, can leap to the surface and take on sudden relevance. Under such conditions, the outsider becomes more obvious and vulnerable, an easy object for scapegoating, and eccentric traits become characterized as undesirable and unwelcome. The Jews' insistence upon their special attributes and observances gave them a firmer sense of self-esteem, but it also meant that, when crises came, they were readily identifiable—and an inviting target for victimization. When internal divisions in a community spilled over into confrontation, Jews were conspicuous and convenient casualties.

In that sense the experience of Jews in classical antiquity does have an interesting, illuminating, and indeed disturbing, resemblance to some events in the modern world.

15. Hellenism and Persecution: Antiochus IV and the Jews

The reign of Antiochus IV brought momentous upheaval to the land of the Jews. Judaea had, for nearly a century and a half, enjoyed a relatively untroubled existence under the suzerainty first of the Ptolemies, then of the Seleucids. But turmoil struck in the 170 s B.C.E., followed by civil strife and then a hideous persecution. Antiochus IV Epiphanes, it appears, endeavored to extirpate Judaism altogether from the Holy Land. That endeavor, stunning and memorable, stands in dramatic contrast to all that had gone before. Early Greek attitudes toward the Jews, insofar as they can be discerned, were more often favorable than unfavorable. The Jews, in turn, became increasingly familiar with and adaptive to Hellenism.[1] Seleucid rule in Palestine had been respectful and protective of Jewish institutions.[2] Antiochus' reversal of form thereby becomes the more striking— and the more baffling.

The issue has ramifications well beyond the circumstances and events of the persecution. The Jews, to be sure, played only a small part on the grand stage of the Hellenistic world—or even in the vast realm nominally under the hegemony of the Seleucid kings. An imbalance of information, it can be claimed, brings undue notice to the Jewish nation, obscuring the fact that in the sphere of high politics and amidst the titanic clashes of the Hellenistic monarchies the Jews were hardly more important than the denizens of Pontus or Cyrene. True enough—up to a point. Yet no apologies need be made for reopening the subject. It carries significance on a broad front and for substantial reasons: not only because of the long-range religious and cultural influence of Judaism for which this persecution—and the reaction it provoked, the Maccabean revolt—proved to be a pivotal moment in history, but also because the episode presents our best-documented example of the tensions between Hellenism and native traditions in the Near East, and the strains inherent in imperial rule over disparate societies in the Hellenistic Age. The drive to resolve this intractable puzzle remains potent, and justifiably so: why did Antiochus IV break sharply with the long-standing policy of both the Ptolemies and the Seleucids in Palestine and engage in a brutal re-

---

1 Texts on early Greek views of the Jews are conveniently collected by M. Stern, *Greek and Latin Authors on Jews and Judaism*, 2d ed. (Jerusalem, 1974), 1–96. On Hellenic influence in Palestine, see, most significantly, M. Hengel, *Judaism and Hellenism* (London, 1974).
2 See, especially, the declarations of Antiochus III; Jos. *A. J.* 12.138–46. For his successor Seleucus IV, note 2 Macc. 3.2–3.

pression with such fateful consequences for Jewish history and for Hellenism in the East?

It will be prudent first to review the salient facts. Not all, of course, can be detailed, and many are controversial as to precise chronology and meaning. But an outline of the principal events leading to and surrounding the persecution is vital.

The Seleucids gained supremacy in Palestine through the victories of Antiochus III in the Fifth Syrian War at the beginning of the second century B.C.E.[3] The king entrenched his success by showing favor to the Jews for their assistance against his Ptolemaic rivals. He expressed gratitude through a number of measures that bestowed privileges and promised tangible assistance. These included aid in rebuilding the war-battered city of Jerusalem, repair of the damaged temple, the restoration of exiles, subsidies for sacrificial expenses, various exemptions from and reductions of taxes, an endorsement of traditional Jewish religious prescriptions, and an express declaration that the Jews were to govern themselves under their own ancestral laws and institutions.[4] Those benefactions set the tone for three decades of cordial collaboration between the Seleucid regime and the Jewish nation. Greek *poleis* flourished in Palestine, and Jewish intellectuals felt the influence of Hellenic culture.[5] Appointment of the high priest, it appears, was subject to the approval of the Seleucid monarch.[6] But that office remained in the hands of the Oniads, the family that previously controlled it; and its occupant in the early third century, Simon the Just, both cooperated with Antiochus III in implementing the restoration of Temple and city and received high praise in the contemporary work of Ben Sira, a prominent advocate of traditionalist Jewish values.[7] Mutual advantage in the relations between Jewish leaders and the Seleucid overlord persisted in the years of Onias III, successor to

---

3 For sources and discussion of the Fifth Syrian War, see M. Holleaux, *Études d'épigraphie et d'histoire grecques* (Paris, 1968) 3:317 – 35; F. W. Walbank, *A Historical Commentary on Polybius* (Oxford, 1967), 2:523 – 25, 546 – 47; and D. Gera, "Ptolemy, Son of Thraseas, and the Fifth Syrian War," *Anc. Soc.* 18 (1987): 63 – 73.

4 Jos. *A. J.* 12.138 – 46. On the authenticity of these decrees, see E. Bickerman, "La Charte seleucide de Jerusalem," *REJ* 100 (1935): 4 – 35; cf. the discussion of V. Tcherikover, *Hellenistic Civilization and the Jews* (New York, 1959), 82 – 89. And see T. Fischer, *Seleukiden und Makkabäer* (Bochum, 1980), 1 – 10.

5 Tcherikover, *Hellenistic Civilization and the Jews*, 90 – 116; Hengel, *Judaism and Hellenism*, 58 – 106. One should not, of course, undervalue the continuities of Jewish traditions, as rightly noted by F. Millar, "The Background to the Maccabean Revolution," *JJS* 29 (1978): 1 – 21.

6 Cf. Jos. *A. J.* 12.237.

7 See Tcherikover, *Hellenistic Civilization and the Jews*, 80 – 81; Fischer, *Seleukiden und Makkabäer*, 6 – 8.

Simon the Just, and Seleucus IV, heir to Antiochus III. Jerusalem, so the author of II Maccabees reports, enjoyed complete peace and exemplary administration of the laws through the piety of Onias and the generous subsidies of Seleucus.[8]

The serenity did not last. Trouble began late in Seleucus' reign, stemming from individual ambitions and family rivalries within the Jewish state. A quarrel erupted between the High Priest Onias III and a certain Simon, financial overseer of the Temple. The latter, so the hostile account in II Maccabees implies, sought to extend his responsibilities to regulation of the market, thereby prompting appeal to the king's representatives and a suggestion that the funds contained in the Temple treasury be made available to the Seleucid regime.[9] The climax of the clash is told in the wonderful tale of Heliodorus, the royal minister who endeavored to confiscate the Temple funds. Heliodorus, impervious to human pleas, was turned back at the Temple gates by the arrival of a magnificent horse which kicked him and two gloriously handsome young men who beat him to a pulp—causing the wretched minister to be carted off in a litter acknowledging the sovereignty of the Jewish god.[10] The story, of course, is apocryphal. But there is no reason to question the underlying facts and circumstances: a split in the Jewish leadership, appeals to the arbitration of Seleucus, and the attractiveness of Jewish finances for the Seleucid monarch who still had the burden of a heavy indemnity owed to Rome. But he evidently stopped short of confiscation—doubtless a matter of policy, not the result of intervention by two angelic youths and the hooves of a golden horse.

Civil strife, however, intensified. Simon escalated his attacks upon Onias III, and one of the High Priest's supporters was murdered, thus causing him to seek the intervention of Seleucus. The timing proved unfortunate for Onias. His trip to Antioch came at or very near the time that Seleucus himself was assassinated in 175, the throne passing now to his brother Antiochus IV, newly arrived in Syria after nearly fifteen years as a hostage in Rome. Worse still for Onias, his removal to Antioch left him vulnerable at home. His own brother Jason seized the occasion to aim for the High Priesthood. The new ruler in Antioch concurred. Jason shrewdly offered cash, a bribe as represented by II Maccabees, in fact a promise to increase revenues through higher taxes. That proposition would appeal to An-

---

8 2 Macc. 3.1–3.
9 2 Macc. 3.4–7.
10 2 Macc. 3.8–30. Analysis of the story in E. Bickerman, *Studies in Greek and Christian History* (Leiden, 1980) 2:159–91; J. Goldstein, *II Maccabees* (New York, 1983), 198–215.

tiochus, who needed funds to bolster his image and to finance his ambitious plans.[11]

The Jewish leader, who had already changed his given name from Jesus to Jason, had a further proposition that Antiochus would find attractive. What he now suggested was a dramatic advance in the Hellenization of Jerusalem. He offered yet more cash for the authority to institute a gymnasium and an ephebate and to register the "Antiochenes" in Jerusalem.[12] What is meant by that last phrase is much disputed and need not be resolved here. Scholars have interpreted it either as the installation of a Greek *politeuma* of Hellenized Jews within the city of Jerusalem or as the wholesale conversion of Jerusalem into a Greek *polis*, a new "Antioch-at-Jerusalem."[13] It is hard to imagine just what would be meant by the latter. Certainly Jerusalem did not adopt a full panoply of Greek political institutions, nor did she abandon her traditional structure of governance. The "Antioch-at-Jerusalem" comprised, at most, a select body of individuals keen on the promotion of Hellenism. The discernible consequences lie in the sphere of culture rather than politics. The gymnasium soon materialized, attracting the elite of Jerusalem's youth and even enticing many in the priestly class who became patrons of the *palaestra*. For the author of II Maccabees that constituted the apogee of Hellenism in Jerusalem.[14]

The euphoria did not last. Jason held sway as High Priest for little more than three years. He had entertained Antiochus lavishly at Jerusalem, producing even a torchlight parade in his honor to show Jewish support for the king's prospective conflict with Egypt. He displayed continuous dedication to the furtherance of Hellenism, even dispatching an embassy to Tyre with cash to finance sacrifi-

---

11 2 Macc. 4.1–8; an inaccurate version in Jos. *A. J.* 12.237. On Antiochus IV's accession, see O. Mørkholm, *Antiochus IV of Syria* (Copenhagen, 1966), 38–50; Walbank, *Historical Commentary*, 3:284–85. To take the monetary transaction as an outright bribe is to adopt the bias of the author of II Maccabees; cf. Goldstein, *II Maccabees*, 227.

12 2 Macc. 4.9: πρὸς δὲ τούτοις ὑπισχνεῖτο καὶ ἕτερα διαγράφειν πεντήκοντα πρὸς τοῖς ἑκατόν, ἐὰν ἐπιχορηγηθῇ διὰ τῆς ἐξουσίας αὐτοῦ γυμνάσιον καὶ ἐφηβίαν αὐτῷ συστήσασθαι καὶ τοὺς ἐν Ἱεροσολύμοις Ἀντιοχεῖς ἀναγράψαι; cf. 1 Macc. 1.14; Jos *A. J.* 12.240–41.

13 For the *politeuma*, see E. Bickerman, *Der Gott der Makkabäer* (Berlin, 1937), 59–65. For the *polis*, see Tcherikover, *Hellenistic Civilization and the Jews*, 161–69; Hengel, *Judaism and Hellenism*, 277; E. Schürer, *The History of the Jewish People in the Age of Jesus Christ*, rev. ed. by G. Vermes and F. Millar (Edinburgh, 1973), 1:148. K. Bringmann, *Hellenistische Reform und Religionsverfolgung in Judäa* (Gottingen, 1983), 84–92, argues vigorously for the *polis* but recognizes that only a select number of Jerusalemites would be enrolled as members by Jason and that the continuation of Jewish institutions would produce a hybrid form. A moderate view in E. Will and C. Orrieux, *Ioudaismos-Hellenismos* (Nancy, 1986), 117–19.

14 2 Macc. 4.11–15; cf. 1 Macc. 1.14–15; Jos. *A. J.* 12.241.

ces to Heracles at the quinquennial games attended by the king. And in 172 or 171 he sent another mission to provide funds urgently requested by Antiochus, presumably for purposes of mobilization against the Ptolemies. The High Priest had acted with exemplary loyalty and cooperation.[15] It was not enough. Internal rivalries in Judaean ruling circles resurfaced. Menelaus, the envoy sent by Jason with revenues for the king, lusted after supreme power himself. He took a leaf from Jason's book, promised Antiochus more money than his superior had provided, and won the king's consent for his own appointment as High Priest.[16] The new appointee was outside the family of the Oniads which had held a monopoly on the office, thus marking a sharp break with Jewish tradition. Antiochus, however, was on the brink of a major and expensive campaign. The intricacies of Jewish political rivalries did not much concern him. Augmented revenues were decisive.

Menelaus' tenure as High Priest intensified turmoil and civil upheaval. The new High Priest, we are told, acted in an arbitrary and tyrannical fashion, even expropriating gold plate from the Temple treasury—a credible report in view of the income he had contracted to raise for the crown. Jason was forcibly exiled from Judaea and sought refuge in Transjordan. Menelaus, brother of that Simon who had harassed the earlier High Priest Onias III, now finished his brother's job, arranging for Onias' assassination. He accomplished the deed, so II Maccabees reports, through the connivance of Andronicus, one of the king's chief ministers. Reaction from the populace was sharp and unusually aggressive: not only indignation at the murder of Onias but a growing resentment at the heavy exactions imposed by Menelaus. Popular feelings burst to the surface. They issued first in a petition to the king to punish Onias' assassin, and later in a lynching of Menelaus' brother Lysimachus. The latter had plundered the treasury, probably to pay arrears owed to Antiochus. Pressure extended even to the Jewish Council of Elders, which began proceedings against Menelaus and brought charges before Antiochus. The king intervened twice in this tumultuous series of events: to order the execution of Andronicus, accused assassin of Onias, and to acquit Menelaus of the charges leveled against him. Antiochus would have preferred a more stable situation in Judaea, but his attention was concentrated upon Egypt. Menelaus, at least, was beholden to the crown and more likely to remain loyal than any alternative leaders. The result was to

---

15 2 Macc. 4.18 – 23.
16 2 Macc. 4.23 – 24. A garbled version in Jos. *A. J.* 12.237 – 38.

leave Menelaus in power but also, no doubt, to harden Jewish resentment against the Seleucid throne.[17]

Antiochus had gathered resources and recruits for an assault on Egypt. The king conducted two major campaigns, the first in 170/69, the second in 168, with the intent of bringing the Ptolemaic realm under his suzerainty. The initial thrust earned considerable success, a smashing victory over Egyptian forces, capture of territory, and the enthronement of a young Ptolemy who would be a client of Antiochus Epiphanes. The blatant power play, however, encountered stiff resistance in Alexandria. Antiochus returned to Syria in late 169, perhaps to build additional resources and fire power. He readied another invasion for spring 168, which resulted in notable advances for the Syrian cause. Egyptian opposition crumbled, Antiochus seized the ancient city of Memphis, became Lord of Upper Egypt, and set his sights on Alexandria itself. It was a high-water mark for Seleucid authority in the region. But not for long. The colossus from the west had just concluded a decisive victory over Macedon at the battle of Pydna. News of that victory released the Roman mission headed by C. Popillius Laenas and charged with terminating the Sixth Syrian War. Popillius arrived in Alexandria at the opportune moment. Antiochus' forces had just reached the outskirts of the city at the suburb of Eleusis. In one of the most celebrated episodes of antiquity, the Roman envoy confronted Antiochus Epiphanes and delivered the *senatus consultum* that demanded an end to hostilities. The king hesitated and requested a recess for consultation with his staff. Popillius Laenas, in a stunning display of arrogance, took a stick, drew a circle in the sand around Antiochus, and asked for a reply before he stepped out of it. This time, it was clear, the Roman meant business. Antiochus meekly evacuated his troops from Egypt and his fleet from Cyprus. The "Day of Eleusis," as it came to be known, cast a dark cloud over Seleucid aspirations and the reputation of Antiochus Epiphanes.[18]

---

17 2 Macc. 4.25 – 50. Whether Andronicus was, in fact, the murderer of Onias III has often been doubted. He is probably the same Andronicus executed by Antiochus in 170 for the slaying of the king's young nephew; DS 30.7.2. This does not itself diminish the likelihood of Andronicus' responsibility for Onias' death. But it does supply a more plausible motive for his own execution. Antiochus was more concerned with affairs of his court than with rivalries in Judaea. Cf. Tcherikover, *Hellenistic Civilization and the Jews*, 469 n. 40; Mørkholm, *Antiochus IV*, 45, 141; Schürer, *History of the Jewish People*, 150 n. 31; Hengel, *Judaism and Hellenism* 2:185 – 86 n. 142; Goldstein, *II Maccabees*, 238.

18 On the events and chronology of the Sixth Syrian War, see sources and discussion by W. Otto, "Zur Geschichte der Zeit des 6 Ptolemäers," *ABAW* 11 (1934): 40 – 81; E. Bickerman, "Sur la chronologie de la sixième guerre de Syrie," *Chron. d'Ég.* 27 (1952): 396 – 403; Mørkholm, *Antiochus IV*, 64 – 101; Walbank, *Historical Commentary* 3:352 – 63. A briefer review, with fur-

What impact did these dramatic events have upon the history of Palestine and the nation of the Jews? A contemporary Jewish source provides the most direct testimony, in the form of prophecy—which its author knew to have been fulfilled. The Book of Daniel reports Antiochus' endeavors in the Sixth Syrian War, his devious dealings with the Ptolemaic royal house, and the two campaigns against Egypt, each followed by an assault upon Judaea.[19] Those statements can be fleshed out by information in I and II Maccabees and in Josephus. The specifics of chronology remain very much in dispute, but the general outlines are relatively clear.[20]

The mixed successes of the first Egyptian campaign brought Antiochus back home in late 169. The need to shore up his finances seemed especially critical. The Temple at Jerusalem proved to be an inviting target. Since the High Priest Menelaus had himself requisitioned some of its wealth for the Seleucid cause, Antiochus did not scruple to march troops into the holy city, enter the Temple, and cart off priceless treasures to Syria, thus causing widespread lament and embitterment.[21]

The enriched resources enabled the king to undertake his second invasion of Egypt in spring 168. But his absence then gave occasion for renewed civil conflict

---

ther bibliography, in E. S. Gruen, *The Hellenistic World and the Coming of Rome* (Berkeley, 1984), 650–60.

19 Dan. 11.24–31. See L. F. Hartman and A. A. DiLella, *The Book of Daniel* (New York, 1978), 296–99.

20 A fundamental uncertainty arises over the question of whether dates in I Maccabees, given according to the Seleucid era, follow the Macedonian or the Babylonian calendar. The first year of the former runs from c. October 312 to October 311, the latter from c. April 311 to April 310. The author of I Maccabees may indeed have employed both systems, thus compounding the confusion; cf. Bickerman, *Gott der Makkabäer*, 155–68; Mørkholm, *Antiochus IV*, 160–61; J. Goldstein, *I Maccabees* (New York, 1976), 21–25, 540–43. Bringmann's recent argument, *Hellenistische Reform und Religionsverfolgung*, 15–28, that the author consistently used the Macedonian system, is attractive but unpersuasive.

21 1 Macc. 1.20–28; Dan. 11.28; cf. Jos. *A. J.* 12.249, Jos. *C. Ap.* 2.83–84. The author of I Maccabees sets the event in the year 143, which would translate to October 170–October 169 by the Macedonian system or April 169–April 168 by the Seleucid system. Either one would suit a return after the campaign of 169. Schürer, *History of the Jewish People*, 152–53 n. 37, combines this testimony with that of 2 Macc. 5.11–21. But the latter is explicitly dated after Antiochus' second departure for Egypt; 2 Macc. 5.1: τὴν δευτέραν ἄφοδον... εἰς Αἴγυπτον. It will not do to interpret this as "the second phase of the campaign," Schürer, *History of the Jewish People*, 128–29, nor to see it as Jason of Cyrene's effort to validate the prophecies of Daniel, Goldstein; *I Maccabees*, 45–51, *II Maccabees*, 246–47. This is not, of course, to deny that some elements in II Maccabees do, in fact, refer to the Temple robbery of 169; notably 2 Macc. 5.15–16, 21. Cf. J. Dancy, *A Commentary on I Maccabees* (Oxford, 1954), 67–71. On the chronological problems, see the summary in Will and Orrieux, *Ioudaismos-Hellenismos*, 138–41.

in Judaea, this time at a yet higher level of violence. A report reached Palestine that Antiochus had been slain in battle, thus inspiring dissidents to grasp at opportunity. Jason returned from exile, crossing the Jordan with a thousand men, and attacked Jerusalem. The regime of Menelaus had doubtless suffered opprobrium and unpopularity because of the High Priest's compliance with Antiochus' looting of the treasury. Menelaus, so Josephus remarks, had the backing of Judaea's premier commercial magnates, the family of the Tobiads, whereas the bulk of the populace stood by Jason. But Jason squandered his advantage. He took control of the city, forcing Menelaus and his supporters to seek refuge in the citadel, but wreaked vengeance for his setbacks by conducting murderous purges of his fellow citizens. The slaughter generated a sharp reaction that drove Jason back to Transjordan and sent his fortunes into a tailspin. He concluded his career as a wretched outcast in Sparta, where he perished unburied and unmourned. Menelaus resumed control of his war-torn nation.[22]

The "Day of Eleusis" fell upon Antiochus Epiphanes in the summer of 168. The king had to beat a retreat from Egypt; he had heard, also, of the upheaval and violence that wracked Palestine in his absence. Antiochus, so the Jewish sources assert, returned to Jerusalem in a fury, ordering his soldiers to conduct a massacre in the city, the outcome of which, according to II Maccabees, was the death of 40,000 Jews and a like number sold into slavery. His authority was to be established unambiguously and ruthlessly. Before withdrawing to Syria, the king installed officials, presumably with garrisons, to keep the Jews under heel: Philip in Jerusalem and Andronicus at Mount Gerizim in Samaria. They would also provide a bulwark for the regime of Menelaus.[23]

---

22 2 Macc. 5.5 – 10; Jos. *A. J.* 12.239. Tcherikover, *Hellenistic Civilization and the Jews*, 186 – 92, argues that Jason's coup was foiled by a rising of the Jewish populace rather than by resistance from Menelaus and his supporters, an attractive hypothesis but unattested and unverifiable. The entire episode is often transferred to 169 on grounds of II Maccabees' reference to the plundering of the Temple in subsequent verses; 2 Macc. 5.15 – 16, 21; Schürer, *History of the Jewish People*, 153. And the coup has even been seen as supplying the motive for Antiochus' return from Egypt in 169; Goldstein, *II Maccabees*, 249 – 53. But the contamination of II Macc. 5 with some data that belong to 169 is insufficient to remove the tale of Jason's coup, explicitly placed in Antiochus' second campaign, to that year. Jos., *A. J.* 12.240, indicates that Menelaus and the Tobiads went to Antiochus for assistance against Jason, an item accepted as fact by Hengel, *Judaism and Hellenism,* 281. But Josephus is here plainly confused, for he has Menelaus petition the Seleucid king for a gymnasium and other Hellenic institutions, a policy actually initiated by Jason seven years earlier; 2 Macc. 4.7 – 17.

23 Dan. 11.29 – 30; 2 Macc. 5.11 – 14, 22 – 23. The intervening lines probably refer to the expropriation of Temple treasures in 169, but it is not impossible that Antiochus extracted yet more cash from that source. 2 Macc. 5.11 associates Antiochus' rage at Judaea with receipt of

Those measures were only the beginning. Antiochus prepared even more drastic moves toward the subjection of Judaea. Some time in 167 he dispatched Apollonius, commander of mercenaries from Mysia, with a force of 22,000 men, to terrorize the populace of Jerusalem.[24] His orders, according to II Maccabees, were to massacre all adult males and sell women and children into slavery. Such instructions, of course, cannot possibly have been carried out, since Jews continued to inhabit the city. But rumors of wholesale terror may well have been encouraged, thereby to cow the populace into submission. Apollonius stayed his hand for a time, lulling the Jerusalemites into false confidence, then launched an attack on the Sabbath when unsuspecting crowds had gathered on his invitation to review a military parade. Numerous innocent citizens were slain, the city ransacked, and parts of it set on fire.[25] The temporary terror was then succeeded by a more permanent presence. Seleucid forces occupied a citadel, the Akra (site uncertain) and installed there a military colony, an "abode of aliens" according to I Maccabees, a place for "a sinful race and lawless men." In all likelihood, the garrison expanded with the addition of renegade Jews, the "Antiochenes" enrolled by Jason as citizens of the *polis* or *politeuma* a few years earlier; and foreign settlers, the "people of a foreign god" as designated by the author of Daniel.[26] The Akra would serve as a rampart of Seleucid strength in Jerusalem for the next quarter of a century. Dissident Jews took the only recourse

---

word that the land was in rebellion. Whether this refers to Jason's coup or to the whole sequence of events concluding with his ouster cannot be determined.

24 1 Macc. 1.29 fixes the time as two years after Antiochus' seizure of the Temple treasury, i.e., 143 of the Seleucid era, probably by Macedonian reckoning from April 167 to April 166. There is no sound reason to place the event in 168, as does Bickerman, *Gott der Makkabäer*, 161–68; Tcherikover, *Hellenistic Civilization and the Jews*, 188–89. See Goldstein, *II Maccabees*, 263–64. For Apollonius' title, see II Macc. 5.24. The text of I Macc. 1.29 has him as a chief financial official, but this may be due to a mistranslation of the original Hebrew; F.-M. Abel, *Les Livres des Maccabées* (Paris, 1949), 15; Goldstein, *I Maccabees*, 211–12.

25 1 Macc. 1.29–42; 2 Macc. 5.24–26; cf. Jos. *A. J.* 12.248. The thesis of Tcherikover, *Hellenistic Civilization and the Jews*, 188–89, that a Jewish revolt preceded and prompted Apollonius' appointment, has no textual support.

26 1 Macc. 1.33–40; Dan. 11.39; Jos. *A. J.* 12.252. On the site of the citadel, much disputed, see Schürer, *History of the Jewish People*, 154–55 n. 39; Goldstein, *I Maccabees*, 214–19; Will and Orrieux, *Ioudaismos-Hellenismos*, 168–69 n. 58. Goldstein, *I Maccabees*, 123–24, argues that Antiochus' idea stemmed from the example of Roman military colonies. But the Greek institution of a cleruchy or a *katoikia* supplied a more direct and more appropriate model; see I Macc. 1.38: κατοικία ἀλλοτρίων; cf. Tcherikover, *Hellenistic Civilization and the Jews*, 188–89. The actual ethnic composition of the *katoikia* remains uncertain; cf. Bringmann, *Hellenistische Reform und Religionsverfolgung*, 128; Goldstein, *II Maccabees*, 106–12; extensive bibliography in Fischer, *Seleukiden und Makkabäer*, 32–33.

remaining to them: flight, escape to the desert and mountains, and preparations for guerilla resistance.[27]

Antiochus IV Epiphanes now readied his most extreme measures. Installation of the physical presence of Seleucid force would be followed by direct interference in the spiritual realm. All previous policy by his predecessors was cast to the winds. To the shock and consternation of the Jews, Antiochus seemed determined to stamp out their religion itself. The king implemented this extraordinary scheme through a series of drastic decrees in the latter part of 167.[28] If the author of I Maccabees is to be believed, Antiochus laid the basis for his moves with a broad edict, issued throughout his realm, which commanded conformity in law and religion. Its authenticity, certainly in the form given, is questionable. But it may well represent a general call for allegiance in the Seleucid kingdom.[29] In any case, Antiochus directed subsequent measures quite specifically at Jewish practices, in damaging and disastrous fashion. He forbade burnt offerings, sacrifices, and libations in the Temple; he ordered the erection of altars, shrines, and images, the sacrifice of pigs and other impure animals, the elimination of circumcision, the burning of the Torah, and a range of activities that would require violation of Jewish practices and profanation of religious life. The dictates applied not just to Jerusalem but to the towns of Judaea generally, and evidently also to Samaria. Disobedience brought the death penalty.[30]

Nor did the king confine himself to proclamations. He saw to their implementation. His agents entered the Temple, defiled it with illicit intercourse, piled unclean offerings upon the altar, and compelled Jews to eat pagan sacrificial victims and to parade with wreaths of ivy at Dionysiac festivals. The Temple itself was now rededicated to Zeus Olympios and the sanctuary at Mount Gerizim to Zeus Xenios.[31] The fateful day of the "abomination of desolation," probably

---

27 1 Macc. 1.38; 2 Macc. 5.27.
28 1 Macc. 1.54 places the climactic deed on the 15th of Kislev in 145, i.e., December 167. Bringmann's endeavor, *Hellenistische Reform and Religionsverfolgung*, 29 – 40, to set all the preceding events, from Jason's coup through the "abomination of desolation" in 168 is unconvincing. He fails to account for the statement in 1 Macc. 1.29 that Apollonius' appointment came two years after Antiochus' plundering of the Temple in 169.
29 1 Macc. 1.41 – 43. Cf. *Hengel, Judaism and Hellenism*, 284 – 87. For Goldstein, *I Maccabees*, 119 – 21, Antiochus promulgated the edict at the beginning of his reign, without explicit attention to the Jews as such. Dancy, *Commentary*, 76 dismisses it too summarily as "fantastic."
30 1 Macc. 1.44 – 51, 56; Jos. *A. J.* 12.251, 253 – 54. Antiochus' agent in delivering the message is described as γέροντα Ἀθηναῖον in 2 Macc. 6.1. Whether this means "the old Athenian," "Geron the Athenian," "the old Athenaeus," or "an elder of Athens" need not be decided. On the Samaritans, see Jos. *A. J.* 12.257 – 60; elsewhere, 2 Macc. 6.8.
31 2 Macc. 6.2 – 9.

the introduction of a pagan altar into the Temple at Jerusalem, was the fifteenth day of Kislev, December of 167. Ten days later came the first sacrifice of a pig on that altar, an act of unspeakable desecration for the people of Judaea.[32] There was valiant resistance among many of the citizenry. But the soldiers of Antiochus ruthlessly punished dissent, torturing and executing those who preferred martyrdom to capitulation.[33] The measures of the king were devastating and calamitous. They represented a total reversal, of Seleucid policy—and a watershed for Jewish history. It is hardly surprising that scholars through the ages have offered a wide variety of explanations for this astounding turn of events—or that the puzzle remains unresolved. A review of the proposed solutions will be salutary; to be followed by a new attempt.

A favorite answer prevailed through most of the earlier scholarship, and still claims adherents: that Antiochus saw himself as a crusader for Hellenism, and attempted to impose conformity on his realm. On this view, Jewish recalcitrance became a sore point and an embarrassing aberration; the king resorted to compulsion to enforce compliance.[34]

The thesis receives support in certain key texts. First and foremost, the decree of Antiochus, cited above, declaring to his entire kingdom that all were to become one people and each would abandon his own customs.[35] That explanation is buttressed by two subsequent passages in II Maccabees. The order to enforce Antiochus' extremist measures against the Jews in 167 includes a sanction for executing those who did not choose to convert to Greek practices.[36] Also, a later letter by Antiochus V, reversing his father's policy, describes it as seeking a transformation of Jews to the ways of Greece.[37] Josephus adds a letter of Epiphanes, responding to a petition from the Samaritans, which acquits them of charges leveled against the Jews, since they elected to live in accordance with Hellenic

---

32 1 Macc. 1.54, 1.59; Dan. 11.31; Jos. *A. J.* 12.253; *BJ* 1.34; DS 34/5.1. It is not absolutely clear to what the "abomination of desolation" refers; Will and Orieux, *Ioudaismos-Hellenismos*, 147–51.
33 1 Macc. 1.57, 60–64; 2 Macc. 6.10–11; Jos. *A. J.* 12.255–56.
34 See, e.g., E. Bevan, *The House of Seleucus* (London, 1902) 2:162–74; Schürer, *History of the Jewish People* 1:147–48; *SEHHW*, 2d ed. 2:703–5; H. Bengtson, *Griechische Geschichte* (Munich, 1960), 482.
35 1 Macc. 1.41: καὶ ἔγραψεν ὁ βασιλεὺς πάσῃ τῇ βασιλείᾳ αὐτοῦ εἶναι πάντας εἰς λαὸν ἕνα καὶ ἐγκαταλιπεῖν ἕκαστον τὰ νόμιμα αὐτοῦ.
36 2 Macc. 6.9: τοὺς δὲ μὴ προαιρουμένους μεταβαίνειν ἐπὶ τὰ Ἑλληνικὰ κατασφάζειν.
37 2 Macc. 11.24: τοὺς Ἰουδαίους μὴ συνευδοκοῦντας τῇ τοῦ πατρὸς ἐπὶ τὰ Ἑλληνικὰ μεταθέσει.

customs.[38] From the perspective of two and a half centuries later, Tacitus offered a similar interpretation: Antiochus strove to stamp out the Jewish superstition and to introduce the institutions of the Greeks.[39]

How plausible is that motive? Antiochus IV certainly projected himself as a great benefactor of the Greeks. His generosity is well attested and widespread. Benefactions extended to Athens, Delphi, Delos, Argos, Achaea, Arcadia, Boeotia, Rhodes, Byzantium, Chalcedon, and Cyzicus. He earned his reputation as foremost among Hellenistic kings for patronage of Greek cities and cults.[40] Antiochus' assiduous efforts in this regard, of course, carried practical value, lending substantial prestige to the king in the international world of the second century. But dedications in shrines and subsidies for public events or institutions at various ancient Greek sites by no means betoken a drive to spread Hellenism to the Near East. The equation is facile and misguided.

The royal edict recorded in I Maccabees that required all nations to forsake their own traditions and become one people carries little credibility, at least in that form. Still less credible is the author's immediately subsequent statement that nations everywhere complied with the directive. The available evidence shows the contrary to be true. Eastern cities and territories under the suzerainty of the Seleucid kingdom continued to mint coinage with local symbols and types; the great temples at Uruk and Babylon betray no trace of Hellenization; and the priests and officialdom of the ancient sites retained native titles and responsibilities.[41]

The king, so some have argued, promoted his own worship as an incarnation of Zeus Olympios and visualized imposition of a syncretistic cult that could unify the peoples of his dominion.[42] However, that notion also finds little support in the ancient testimony. Antiochus did pay special attention to Olympian Zeus, and he employed the title of *Theos Epiphanes* for his own epithet; but there are no grounds to infer that the monarch identified himself with Zeus Olympios, let alone that he strove to employ ruler cult as a means of consolidation in his

---

38 Jos. *A. J.* 12.263: ὅτι μηδὲν τοῖς τῶν Ἰουδαίων ἐγκλήμασι προσήκουσιν, ἀλλὰ τοῖς Ἑλληνικοῖς ἔθεσιν αἱροῦνται χρώμενοι ζῆν.

39 Tac. *Hist.* 5.8: rex Antiochus demere superstitionem et mores Graecorum dare adnisus.

40 Plb. 26.1.10, 29.24.13; Livy, 41.20.5. See, especially, Mørkholm, *Antiochus IV*, 51–63; cf. Walbank, *Historical Commentary* 3:287–88; E. S. Gruen, *Hellenistic World*, 189–90.

41 Bickerman, *Gott der Makkabäer*, 90–92; Dancy, *Commentary*, 75–76. See now the collection of material and discussion by S. Sherwin-White, A. Kuhrt, and R. J. van der Spek, in A. Kuhrt and S. Sherwin-White, *Hellenism in the Near East* (Berkeley, 1987), 1–31, 48–52, 57–74.

42 Cf. Dan. 11.37–38; Bevan, *House of Seleucus* 2:154–55; W. W. Tarn, *The Greeks in Bactria and India*, 3d ed. (Chicago, 1984), 190–91; *SEHHW* 2:704; Dancy, *Commentary*, 47.

realm. The worship of that deity in Seleucid lands preceded Antiochus IV, and the king showed favor to a variety of gods and cults.[43] The fact that the worship inaugurated in the Temple at Jerusalem in 167 was that of Zeus Olympios does not imply unity and uniformity. For at the same time Antiochus ordered the sanctuary at Mount Gerizim to be dedicated to Zeus Xenios.[44] In any event, the establishment of the new cult came late in the series of events, at the time of Antiochus' most savage repression; it does not exemplify a long-standing policy of Hellenization to which the Jews objected. Nor had the king determined to eradicate Judaism as an aberration. His measures applied only to Judaea and Samaria. Nothing suggests an extension to the Jews of the Diaspora.[45] We can then safely and happily discard the notion of Antiochus Epiphanes as crusader for Hellenism, driven by the resolve to have Greek civilization penetrate throughout the Near East, or to unify his holdings through a cultural and religious homogeneity that was upset by recalcitrant Jews. Ideological fervor did not characterize the schemes of Antiochus IV.

A more plausible approach prefers pragmatism to ideology. The king, on this analysis, concerned himself more with concrete advantages than with lofty goals. The question of money arises repeatedly in the story, a motivating force and a determining factor. A crushing indemnity had been assessed against Syria by Rome in 188, thus putting severe strain on her resources and limits on her aspirations. Income from Judaea represented a critical source of revenue. That fact manifests itself in the reign of Seleucus IV, when the Jewish minister Simon offered to release cash from the Temple for the king, and when Heliodorus considered forced entry into the sanctuary for the same purpose. Antiochus' ambitious

---

43 See the evidence and discussion in O. Mørkholm, *Studies in the Coinage of Antiochus IV of Syria* (Copenhagen, 1963), 7–75; Mørkholm, *Antiochus IV,* 130–33; Hengel, *Judaism and Hellenism,* 284–86; J. G. Bunge, "'Theos Epiphanes' in den ersten fünf Regierungsjahren des Antiochos IV Epiphanes," *Historia* 23 (1974): 57–85, 24 (1975): 164–88.

44 1 Macc. 6.2. Cf. Goldstein, *II Maccabees,* 272–73. According to Dan. 11.37–38, the deity was not even reckoned among the ancestral gods of the Seleucid house; hence perhaps a blend with the Syrian god—and hardly a means to foster Hellenism. On the nature of the god and his cult, much discussed, see the incisive analysis of Bickerman, *Gott der Makkabäer,* 92–116; scholarly literature collected by Fischer, *Seleukiden und Makkabäer,* 35–38. Bickerman's view of the cult as syncretistic and assimilationist is criticized by Millar, "Background," 12–13, and Will and Orrieux, *Ioudaismos-Hellenismos,* 149–51.

45 1 Macc. 1.51; Jos. *A. J.* 12.257–63. A possible exception lies in 2 Macc. 6.8, referring to extension of the persecution to Jews in the "neighboring Greek cities," at the instigation of the "citizens of Ptolemais"—or perhaps "of Ptolemy." On either reckoning, this applies to local circumstances within or in the vicinity of Judaea. It in no way implies extension to the Diaspora. Cf. Abel, *Livres des Maccabees,* 363–64; Hengel, *Judaism and Hellenism,* 287.

ventures, it could be argued, helped give rise to conflict within Judaea, as rival leaders bid for his favor through offers of increased tribute and immediate cash subsidy. The king backed first Jason, then Menelaus, for the tangible returns that would support his aggressive expansionism. Hostility within Judaea to Menelaus and his party only bound Antiochus more closely to them. Expropriation of funds from the Temple, with Menelaus' direct assistance, gave the Seleucid monarch the boost needed for his renewed invasion of Egypt. The backlash against Menelaus, however, caused consternation. Jason's attempted coup threatened not only Menelaus but the pro-Seleucid elements in Palestine generally. Antiochus, after his forced evacuation of Egypt, had no choice but to shore up the regime of Menelaus with every means available; hence the citadel, the garrison, and the intimidation of the populace. But Menelaus needed more to retain his hold on power: a thorough cowing of the opposition. This would strengthen the hand of Menelaus' followers by giving them control of the cult and protect Antiochus' interests by keeping his partisans in central authority. So Menelaus persuaded his patron to crush dissidents through religious oppression. The motives that drove Antiochus were practical and political: cash for his military adventures and security for his position in Palestine. Such, in brief, is the gist of the pragmatic thesis, recently and forcefully argued.[46]

The case clearly has merit—up to a point. Additional cash was always welcome. Higher tribute payments would fuel Seleucid schemes of aggrandizement. And Antiochus' seizure of Temple funds in 169 surely had the Egyptian venture in view. But financial considerations do not tell the whole story, and it would be hazardous to place too much weight upon them. The indemnity imposed by Rome had evidently not crippled Seleucid resources. Antiochus, as we have already noted, was liberal in his benefactions; much of the Greek world profited from his gifts, donations, and subsidies.[47] Further, one must recall what is often forgotten: Antiochus had paid off the last installment on the indemnity in 173—four years before his assault on Jerusalem.[48] Financial demands from Rome were no longer at issue, and the kingdom was solvent.

The political motivation is as fragile as the economic. Conjecture has it that Antiochus committed himself to Menelaus as the principal bastion of strength for Seleucid interests in Palestine and that the offensive against Jewish traditions

---

46 See Bringmann, *Hellenistische Reform und Religionsverfolgung*, 111–40; more briefly in "Die Verfolgung der jüdischen Religion durch Antiochos IV: Ein Konflikt zwischen Judentum und Hellenismus," *Antike und Abendland* 26 (1980): 176–90.
47 See above.
48 Livy 42.6.6–7.

aimed to smash Menelaus' rivals and to keep him in power.[49] A single statement in Josephus alone can be cited. And it applies to the year 163, after the death of Antiochus Epiphanes, in the midst of the Maccabean rebellion. Lysias, chief minister to the new boyruler Antiochus V, advised the king to authorize the slaying of Menelaus, who, he claimed, had persuaded Epiphanes to force Jewish abandonment of their ancestral faith and was thereby the source of troubles for the Seleucid realm.[50] That text cannot, in fact, bear the weight set upon it. Lysias had his own reasons for seeking the elimination of Menelaus, and the young monarch was in no position to check the accuracy of his allegations. One may doubt, in fact, that Lysias even charged Menelaus with having instigated the religious persecution. Josephus plainly drew his data from a parallel passage in II Maccabees. Lysias there also prods the wrath of Antiochus V against Menelaus, denouncing him as responsible for all the troubles in the kingdom. But nothing is said in that passage about Menelaus prompting religious repression; this was an inference added by Josephus.[51] Nor is it likely that Menelaus, a Jew from the upper echelons of society, and one well aware of the proclivities of his countrymen, would foster a policy calculated to spark explosive upheaval—an upheaval that threatened to sweep him away with the debris. Persecution of the faithful hardly seems a prudent means to secure Menelaus' hold on power. Quite the contrary. Pragmatic politics cannot explain the decision.

A very different theory has Antiochus look not to Greeks or to Jews, but to Romans. Therein lay his inspiration. The Seleucid had resided for more than a dozen years in Rome, technically as a hostage for the good behavior of his father and his brother, in practice treated as an honored guest.[52] Those years allowed for observation and instruction. The later actions of the king in his own homeland have been traced to events and institutions experienced in Rome. The establishment of a *polis* or an enclave of "Antiochenes" in Jerusalem in 175 had, it can be argued, certain analogies with Roman extension of citizenship to Italian communities or segments of Italian communities. Antiochus conceived the idea, with Roman practice in mind, to grant privileges to "Antiochenes" in various cities who would serve as centers of loyalty to the Seleucid regime. The later introduction of a garrison, the Akra, in 167 had as its goal protection and enhancement of the "Antiochenes" in Jerusalem, while adding new soldier-settlers who would

---

49 Bringmann, *Hellenistische Reform und Religionsverfolgung,* 126 – 35.
50 Jos. *A. J.* 12.384: τοῦτον γὰρ ἄρξαι τῶν κακῶν, πείσαντ᾽ αὐτοῦ τὸν πατέρα τοὺς Ἰουδαίους ἀναγκάσαι τὴν πάτριον θρησκείαν καταλιπεῖν.
51 2 Macc. 13.4: Λυσίου ὑποδείξαντος τοῦτον αἴτιον εἶναι πάντων τῶν κακῶν.
52 The year of his arrival in Rome is not certain—189 or 188; Mørkholm, *Antiochus IV,* 22 – 23. On his honored status at Rome, see Livy 42.6.9; Asconius 13 Clark.

also obtain citizen privileges. And the outlawing of the Jewish religion, with the accompanying measures of persecution and ferocious repression, also has a Roman analogy: the fierce measures taken by the government against the Bacchanalian cult in 186—one of the years in which the Seleucid prince resided in Rome. The senate and magistrates demolished places of worship, punished the sect's adherents, and severely curtailed its activities. Antiochus, like his former mentors, could claim to be suppressing degenerate rites and restoring a purer, pristine religion.[53]

The idea is ingenious and alluring, but also fanciful and farfetched. Nothing in the evidence suggests that the stay in Rome had so profound an impact on Antiochus' actions and policies. It is difficult to imagine that the young hostage would have gained so intimate an acquaintance with the principles of Roman colonial policy—or indeed that he had access to the decision-making process that implemented it.[54] The conjecture that Antiochus created the "Antiochenes in Jerusalem" as a form of Roman citizen colony, founders on the fact that the initiative for the move came not from Antiochus but from Jason, the Jewish would-be High Priest—a man who had never had experience of Rome.[55] As for the presumed parallel between suppression of the Bacchants and the assault on Judaism, differences loom much larger than similarities. Most significantly, the Romans professed to be cracking down on an alien creed, foreign to national traditions, whereas Antiochus imposed an alien creed while seeking to eradicate a national tradition. No testimony alludes to the desire or even the claim to revive ancestral practice in a purer form. And if experience of the Bacchic affair had an influence on Antiochus' policy, it is most peculiar that among the grievous burdens imposed on the Jews was the obligation to don ivy wreaths and join the procession at the festival of Dionysus![56] The Roman hypothesis can be confidently abandoned.

Ancient testimony on the king includes numerous incidents of eccentricity and oddity. The monarch who could lavish gifts upon communities in most grandiose fashion also disported himself in most unlikely ways. Observers wondered

---

53 So Goldstein, *I Maccabees,* 104–60; somewhat modified, with the basic thesis intact, in *II Maccabees,* 104–12.

54 Goldstein's proposals that Antiochus enjoyed the patronage and friendship of various highly placed Roman political families, *I Maccabees,* 105–7, are pure speculation.

55 Goldstein attempts to get around this objection by placing Antiochus' general decree inviting conformity at the beginning of the reign and seeing Jason's move as a response to that invitation; *I Maccabees,* 120–21. This simply multiplies the conjectures and, in any case, undermines the putative link to the Roman experience. Did Antiochus suddenly recall that experience only when Jason proposed to register "Antiochenes"?

56 3 Macc. 6.7.

about his sanity. And jokesters played with his epithet, changing *Epiphanes* to *Epimanes* ("madman"). Antiochus regularly violated court etiquette and took pleasure in roaming the streets, exchanging shoptalk with artisans and craftsmen, conversing and carousing with commoners and riffraff. He showed up unannounced at parties, sometimes to take personal charge of the entertainment, bringing his own instrument and musicians, while astonished guests headed for the exits. He could be equally amusing on public occasions. The Roman experience may not have inspired persecution, but it did inspire mimicry. Antiochus delighted in shocking onlookers by removing royal attire, donning the white toga of a Roman candidate, and circulating among the public to solicit votes as if running for the aedileship or the tribunate. And he would carry the charade to its conclusion, performing like a Roman magistrate, presiding over lawsuits, and delivering judgments in mock solemnity. The king was endlessly inventive in surprising his countrymen. He snubbed friends but stopped strangers in the street and plied them with gifts. He embarrassed the highborn with childish toys, but would transform an unsuspecting commoner into an instant millionaire. His visits to the public baths gave occasion for revelry and practical jokes, which included the pouring of priceless ointment that had Antiochus and his fellow bathers slipping and sliding in hilarious frolic.[57]

Should one then abandon rational explanations for the assault on Judaism? Perhaps it was just another example of aberrant behavior by a monarch who gloried in the unorthodox and the bizarre? That would be an easy solution, but not a very satisfactory one. The political, diplomatic, and military successes that stand to Antiochus' credit belie the representation of him as a demented crackpot.[58] Moreover, the ruthless and thorough measures taken to stamp out Judaism possess a character altogether different from the quirky, idiosyncratic, playful, and topsy-turvy behavior designed to shock and amuse. An answer to the puzzle must be sought elsewhere.

An influential scholarly thesis affixes blame not on Antiochus, but on the Jews—or rather a segment of the Jews. Initiative for the reform movement came from the Jewish leadership itself and reflected internal conflict within its ranks. This was no Seleucid scheme. Jason brought the idea of a gymnasium and ephebate to Antiochus. As delineated by the author of I Maccabees, it rep-

---

57 Plb. 26.1 offers the most reliable catalogue of Antiochus' eccentricities. See further Livy 41.20.1–4; DS 29.32, 31.16. Mørkholm, *Antiochus IV*, 181–86, questions Polybius' authority here, without compelling reason. The mimicry of the Romans has been taken seriously by some scholars; e. g., Bunge, "'Theos Epiphanes'," 67; Walbank, *Historical Commentary*, 3:286.
58 See the treatment by Mørkholm, *Antiochus IV*, passim; in brief, Gruen, *Hellenistic World*, 647–63.

resented the efforts of lawless Jews to ingratiate themselves with the peoples surrounding them, for their separation had been the source of much suffering.[59] This set the Hellenizing trend in motion and also produced a rift between the Hellenizers and the traditionalists in Jewish society. Antiochus was the beneficiary rather than the instigator. Conversion of Jerusalem into a Greek *polis* or *politeuma* delivered a heavy blow to Jewish conservatives, effectively undermined ancestral practices, and stimulated other Jews to curry Seleucid favor by moving still further away from tradition. Hence Menelaus obtained power as a more "radical Hellenizer," generating a split with the faction of Jason. The extremist actions alienated much of public opinion in Judaea, making Menelaus ever more dependent upon Antiochus for his authority. Menelaus' urging, therefore, brought about the Seleucid garrison in Jerusalem, the intimidating terrorism of Apollonius, and even the sweeping prohibition of Jewish religious practices. The apostates pressed for abolition of Mosaic law and all ancestral ordinances ranging from dietary restrictions to circumcision. The insistence on full-scale assimilation would entail either forced conversion or elimination of their opponents. The "abomination of desolation" climaxed a concerted campaign to dissolve Judaism in its conventional form and replace it with a syncretistic worship suffused with Greek ideas and adapted to the Hellenistic world. The contest throughout represented a fundamental struggle between Judaism and Hellenism.[60]

The matter is, however, not so straightforward. Divisions among the leadership certainly plagued the course of Jewish history in this period. But did they open a genuine cleavage between Judaism and Hellenism? Did the escalation of tensions reflect an increasing push toward Hellenization that energized the support and encouragement of Antiochus? Did the initiative for change consistently come from Jewish reformers or apostates who were responsible not only for the injection and augmentation of Hellenism but for the persecution of Jews who clung to the old ways? Those issues merit serious review.

59 1 Macc. 1.11.
60 The classic statement of this position is to be found in Bickerman, *Gott der Makkabäer*, 117–36, reinforced and expanded by Hengel, *Judaism and Hellenism*, 277–309. Other scholars, who do not fully subscribe to this view, nevertheless concur in seeing Hellenization as responsible for the division among the leadership and in interpreting the contest as one between Hellenism and Judaism; e. g., Tcherikover, *Hellenistic Civilization and the Jews*, 152–74, 193–203; C. Habicht, "Hellenismus und Judentum in der Zeit des Judas Makkabäus," *Jhrb. Heid. Akad.* (1974), 97–104. A general discussion of the issue in Will and Orrieux, *Ioudaismos-Hellenismos*, 124–26, 149–51.

One might expect to find the confrontation of Judaism and Hellenism as a central and repeated theme in the contemporary or near-contemporary Jewish literature. In fact, it is almost altogether absent. The work of Ben Sira, composed in the early second century, reiterates traditional precepts and denounces those who yield to the temptations of wealth, who fall away from righteousness, who oppress the poor, who abandon fear of the Lord or the teachings of the Law. But he nowhere contrasts Jews and Greeks, and gives no hint that a struggle for the conscience of his fellow countrymen was being waged by Hellenizers and conservatives.[61] Nor does the Book of Daniel provide comfort for the theory. Written at the very time of the Maccabean revolt, the work's apocalyptic visions set the experience of the Jews squarely in the context of battles among the great Hellenistic powers: divine intervention and a last judgment will deliver the Jews from the foreign oppressor. This is not a cultural contest for the soul of Judaism.[62] Similarly, I Maccabees, although composed well after recovery of the Temple and the entrenchment of the Hasmonaean dynasty, does not express the discord as one between Judaism and Hellenism. The absence of this polarity becomes more striking.

The phrases do appear in II Maccabees, our fullest source on the relevant events. The author describes Jason's innovations as bringing his fellow Jews to a "Greek way of life." And the implementation of his reforms constitute the high point of "Hellenism."[63] The order to enforce the new cult in 167 authorized the king's agents to execute those who refused to convert to "Greek ways."[64] And, as earlier noted, Antiochus V's letter referred to Jews who resisted change to "Greek practices."[65] A few passages also designate "Judaism" as the principle upheld by rebellion against the Seleucids.[66] But the author nowhere juxtaposes

---

61 The quotations and summaries provided by Hengel, *Judaism and Hellenism*, 131–53, refute his own efforts to see Ben Sira as an opponent of "Hellenistic liberalism." None of the material makes any direct or indirect statement to that effect. A similar inference by A. Momigliano, *Alien Wisdom* (Cambridge, 1975), 95: "His book ... quietly reaffirmed Jewish traditional faith against the temptations of Hellenism." See now the proper skepticism of Goldstein, in E. P. Sanders, *Jewish and Christian Self-Definition* (Philadelphia, 1981) 2:72–73. Ben Sira's prayer for deliverance from foreign rule, 36.9–17, is, of course, a different matter.
62 Dan. 11.2–12.3. See Momigliano, *Alien Wisdom*, 109–12. The reference in 9.27 to Antiochus making alliance with many hardly implies a "Hellenizing party."
63 2 Macc. 4.10: πρὸς τὸν Ἑλληνικὸν χαρακτῆρα τοὺς ὁμοφύλους. 4.13: ἦν δ' οὕτως ἀκμή τις Ἑλληνισμοῦ.
64 2 Macc. 6.9: μεταβαίνειν ἐπὶ τὰ Ἑλληνικά.
65 2 Macc. 11.24: τοὺς Ἰουδαίους μὴ συνευδοκοῦντας τῇ τοῦ πατρὸς ἐπὶ τὰ Ἑλληνικὰ μεταθέσει.
66 2 Macc. 2.21, 8.1, 14.38.

the two phrases as opposites. The fact deserves emphasis. Were Judaism and Hellenism incompatible?

Jason introduced a gymnasium and the ephebate to Jerusalem, and he arranged for the registration of persons as "Antiochenes" in the city.[67] None of these measures involved elimination or alteration of religious rites. Nothing in the Hebrew Scriptures forbids gymnasia, military training for youths, or enrollment as citizens of a *polis* or *politeuma*. Although the author of II Maccabees brands the innovations as unlawful, he also provides material for his own refutation: the priests themselves welcomed the gymnasium and were eager to participate in exercises in the palaestra. They evidently did not consider it inconsistent with their sacerdotal functions.[68] Even Jason's closest allies would not cross the line from Hellenistic reform to religious compromise. The envoys he sent to Tyre with cash for sacrifice to Heracles at the quinquennial games declined to contribute to the pagan festival.[69] They shrank from idol worship and kept to the Law. The measures of Jason's High Priesthood stopped short of interference with traditional religion. The motive for those measures is accurately described in I Maccabees: a desire to foster good relations with neighboring peoples, isolation from whom had been the source of much evil.[70] The cultivation of Greek ways need not undermine the practice of Judaism.

Factional quarrels within the Jewish establishment brought turmoil and division. But where is the evidence that factions divided on the issue of Hellenism? Menelaus, it is commonly assumed, outbid Jason for Seleucid favor by out-Hellenizing the Hellenizer. The assumption lacks all foundation. Personal rivalry and political ambition alone can be inferred from the texts. Jewish sources brand Menelaus with venality, corruption, ruthlessness, treachery, murder, even sacrilege for expropriating Temple funds—but not with Hellenism.[71] Mene-

---

67 2 Macc. 4.9.

68 2 Macc. 4.14. It is often asserted that Hellenizing Jews had so far departed from tradition as to compete in the nude and even to undergo some form of reverse circumcision in order to conform to Greek practice. The silence of II Maccabees on this point is potent testimony against it. The most that the author can say is that they wore a Greek-style hat; 2 Macc. 4.12. So, rightly, Goldstein, in *Sanders, Jewish and Christian Self-Definition* 2:77–78. The reference in 1 Macc. 1.15 and Jos. *A. J.* 12.241 to the concealment of circumcision may perhaps apply to behavior after the repressive measures of 167—which included a ban on circumcision.

69 2 Macc. 4.18–20.

70 1 Macc. 1.11; cf. Bringmann, *Hellenistische Reform und Religionsverfolgung,* 189; Will and Orrieux, *Ioudaismos-Hellenismos,* 116–19.

71 2 Macc. 4.23–50. The fact is noted by Goldstein, *I Maccabees,* 159, and Millar, *JJS* 29 (1978): 10–11. Josephus' reference to Menelaus as petitioning Antiochus for a gymnasium is an obvious confusion with Jason; Jos. *A. J.* 12.240–41.

laus may indeed have had little sympathy with the Greek institutions sponsored by his rival Jason. Antiochus found him serviceable as a conduit for cash and an enforcer of loyalty in Judaea. The king did not require Hellenic credentials from his Jewish supporters.

The actions taken by Antiochus against the Jews belong in an entirely separate category. He seized moneys from the Temple after his first Egyptian campaign, with the collaboration of Menelaus. And after the second campaign, he implemented those extreme measures, ranging from the massacre of citizens to the prohibition of religion, that put all previous behavior in the shade. What reason is there to believe that the party of Menelaus put him up to it? Once the putative link between Menelaus and Hellenism is severed, the main prop for the conventional theory falls. That Menelaus exerted any influence over Antiochus may be seriously questioned. One item only suggests it: Lysias' later allegation to young Antiochus V that Menelaus bore responsibility for all the realm's troubles, an allegation intended to justify his elimination.[72] The statement lacks both specifics and objectivity. Lysias had an ax to grind and no facts to provide.[73] It is unlikely in the extreme that Menelaus prodded the Seleucid ruler to eradicate Judaism and terrorize its adherents. The one relevant piece of testimony points in the opposite direction. Three years after the outbreak of the Maccabean revolt, Menelaus helped to arrange an amnesty for the disaffected rebels and to restore to Jews the privilege of adhering to their dietary laws. The man responsible for the repression of Judaism would hardly have been used as intermediary for reconciliation.[74]

Blame for the persecution can be lifted from the shoulders of the Jews themselves. They aggravated their own difficulties with internal divisiveness, but the divisions did not break down neatly into Hellenizers and traditionalists. Personal and familial quarrels played a role, as did private ambitions and possibly political sympathies.[75] But the idea of a stark confrontation between Judaism and Hellenism should be discarded—and with it, the thesis that ardent Hellenizers

---

72 2 Macc. 13.4.

73 Josephus' statement, Jos. *A. J.* 12.384, is derivative and unreliable. See above.

74 The fact is recorded in a letter by Antiochus IV in 164 to the Jewish council and people: 2 Macc. 1.27–33. The proper sequence of letters in that collection is disputed; see the discussion in C. Habicht, "Royal Documents in Maccabees II," *HSCP* 80 (1976): 1–18. Goldstein, *II Maccabees*, 418–20, drew the proper conclusions with regard to Menelaus. So also Bringmann, "Verfolgung," 182.

75 Jos., *A. J.* 12.239–40, reports that the Tobiads backed Menelaus, while a majority of Jews supported Jason. Elsewhere, Josephus suggests that conflict in Judaea divided partly along pro-Seleucid and pro-Ptolemaic lines; *BJ* 1.31–32. That passage, however, is a hodgepodge of confusion. Bringmann, "Verfolgung," 185, assigns it more weight than it deserves.

prodded the king of Syria into persecuting their coreligionists, banning their creed, and inflicting an alien cult upon the temple. II Maccabees, in fact, reckons the Hellenizers as among the victims of the king.[76] Apart from Lysias' partisan and tainted allegation, our evidence is unanimous: it is Antiochus Epiphanes who must take responsibility for the savage onslaught against Judaism.[77]

Where then to turn for an answer? Until the final, ferocious act of the drama, the king had played a relatively passive or evenhanded role. Jason instigated the Hellenistic reform, Antiochus merely endorsing and benefiting from it. He benefited further when Menelaus contracted to raise the tribute and thereby won the Seleucid's backing as High Priest. Antiochus intervened when requested in immediately subsequent years, acquitting Menelaus at his trial, but condemning his own minister Andronicus. He did not pursue an activist policy in Palestine. Even the sequestering of funds from the Temple in 169 may have come at the suggestion of Menelaus, who had exploited that source once before, and now accompanied the king in stripping most of what remained. In any case, the objective was war on Egypt, not punishment of Jews. Antiochus had hitherto taken only a secondary interest in Palestinian affairs. But the measures implemented after the second Egyptian campaign created a wholly new situation. They cannot be explained in terms of Hellenization, intra-Jewish rivalries, or even pragmatic advantages. Stationing of a garrison, mass executions, terrorism, prohibition of the faith, and sweeping persecution shifted matters onto an altogether different plane. They did not evolve smoothly or logically out of what came before. Something happened in 168 to convert Antiochus Epiphanes into a rampaging monster.

II Maccabees offers an ostensible explanation. Jason raised an insurrection in that year, while Antiochus was campaigning in Egypt. The attempted coup against Menelaus ignited a civil war in Judaea. When news reached the king, so reports the text, he reckoned it as rebellion, flew into a fury, and made Jerusalem a prize of war. There followed the succession of terrorist measures that culminated in the "abomination of desolation."[78] The rage of Antiochus is plausible

---

76 2 Macc. 4.15 – 16.

77 Dan. 11.30 states only that Antiochus stayed his hand with regard to those Jews who abandoned the holy covenant—not that he was acting on their advice and instigation. That the king took the initiative is clear from Dan. 11.32.

78 2 Macc. 5.11: προσπεσόντων δὲ τῷ βασιλεῖ περὶ τῶν γεγονότων διέλαβεν ἀποστατεῖν τὴν Ἰουδαίαν. Cf. Abel, *Livres des Maccabees*, 352 – 53. In the view of Tcherikover, *Hellenistic Civilization and the Jews*, 186 – 203, Antiochus' anger directed itself not against Jason and his followers, whose coup had already failed, but against a popular rising that had expelled Jason, intimidated Menelaus, and seized control of the situation.

enough, but cannot suffice as explanation. Rebellion in his rear might inspire retaliation and subjugation; but it hardly accounts for the brutally thorough and detailed prescriptions which, if adhered to, would be tantamount to the abolition of Judaism. Those measures ran the risk of alienating even the king's staunchest supporters in Judaea. Investigation reaches an impasse. One eminent scholar announced despair, and declared an understanding of Antiochus' deeds to be beyond reach.[79]

The despair may be premature. One contemporary source addresses the question directly, and must be attended to. The author of the Book of Daniel asserts that "the king of the north" in his second invasion of the south will suffer a different outcome from the first. The ships of the Kittim will come against him, causing the king's withdrawal. He will then loose his wrath upon the Holy Covenant, taking care only for those who forsake that covenant. His armed forces will defile the sanctuary and the pious, and he will impose the "abomination of desolation."[80] Interpretation of the text is not controversial. Daniel plainly refers to Antiochus Epiphanes' second campaign against Egypt, its abortive conclusion when Rome intervened, the ignominious retreat, and then the oppressive and devastating measures inflicted upon the Jews.[81]

The explanation has both psychological and political plausibility. Antiochus was compelled to abandon his Egyptian adventure at Popillius Laenas' brusque command and infamous swagger stick.[82] Not only did the withdrawal terminate Antiochus' long-cherished dream of extending suzerainty over the Ptolemaic realm; it also came under humiliating circumstances that threatened to shatter the king's reputation throughout the lands of the Near East.[83] The rage of Anti-

---

79 Millar, "Background," 16–17: "There seems no way of reaching an understanding of how Antiochus came to take a step so profoundly at variance with the normal assumptions of government in his time."

80 Dan. 11.29–31. On the date of the work, see Hartman and DiLella, *Book of Daniel*, 9–18; Schürer, *History of the Jewish People*, vol. 3, pt. 1, 245–50.

81 The Septuagint even translates the Hebrew *kittim* as "Romans." See further Hartman and DeLella, *Book of Daniel*, 270–71.

82 For Popillius' intervention, see Plb. 29.27.1–10; Livy 45.12.3–8; DS 31.2; App. *Syr.* 66; Just. 34.3.1–4; Cic. *Phil.* 8.23; Vell. Pat. 1.10.1; Val. Max. 6.4.3; Porphyr. *FGrH* 260 F50; Plin. *NH* 34.24; Plut. *Mor.* 202F. See also, for Egyptian evidence, J. D. Ray, *The Archive of Hor* (London, 1976), 127–28.

83 Not that Rome herself intended to humiliate Antiochus. Popillius' intervention ended in amicable fashion; Plb. 29.27.6; DS 31.2.2; Livy 45.12.6; see E. S. Gruen, "Rome and the Seleucids in the Aftermath of Pydna," *Chiron* 6 (1976): 76–77. But the perception of a forced withdrawal could do serious damage to Seleucid prestige and authority.

ochus IV is readily intelligible. It could not, of course, be vented against Rome.[84] But the upheaval in Judaea came at a convenient time and offered a suitable target. The introduction of a garrison and the intimidation of the populace by state terrorism had a larger design than simply to punish the Jews. It would announce Antiochus Epiphanes' resumption of control to the diverse peoples and nations nominally under the Seleucid regime. The "Day of Eleusis" was to be buried under a barrage. Antiochus would answer any potential questions about his withdrawal from Egypt by taking the offensive in Palestine.[85]

The initial measures, however, did not suffice for the king's purpose. He determined to stamp out Judaism. The reasons can hardly have been religious or ideological. Nor can an outburst of anger explain the sweeping actions that took place a year later. Judaea would serve as a conspicuous showcase for Seleucid power. The antiquity of the Jewish faith and the tenacity with which its adherents clung to it were well known to Greeks and natives alike in the Near East. Whether they voiced approval or disapproval, they acknowledged the strength and endurance of Jewish traditions.[86] Eradication of the creed and forcible conversion of the faithful would send a message throughout the ancestral kingdom of the Seleucids—the message that Antiochus had accomplished what no ruler before him had hoped to achieve: the abandonment of Jewish belief at Seleucid command. Antiochus Epiphanes would put the "Day of Eleusis" behind him for good.

The concern for image and reputation can be illustrated further. In the immediately subsequent year Antiochus staged a dazzling demonstration at Daphne, a suburb of Antioch. Invitations were issued to towns all over the Greek world, in order to ensure a diverse and widespread audience. The king put on a splendid show: a grand parade of armed forces including both nationals under his control and mercenaries in his pay. Infantry, cavalry, chariots, and elephants marched in procession. More than 50,000 men displayed armor, weaponry, and handsome accoutrements. The nonmilitary aspects of the parade were equally impressive: 800 ephebes with gold-crowns, 1,000 cattle for sacrifice, numerous images of gods, lesser divinities, and heroes, 200 women sprinkling perfume from gilded jugs upon the crowd of onlookers, and vast quantities of silver

---

84 Indeed Antiochus soon dispatched a mission to Rome to offer congratulations for Pydna and thus regained Roman favor; Livy 45.13.2–3, 45.13.6.

85 Cf. also Jos *A: J.* 12.246, who relates the return from Egypt, through fear of the Romans, directly to the assault on Jerusalem: ὑποστρέψας γὰρ ἀπὸ τῆς Αἰγύπτου διὰ τὸ παρὰ Ῥωμαίων δέος ὁ βασιλεὺς Ἀντίοχος ἐπὶ τὴν Ἱεροσυλυμιτῶν πόλιν ἐξεστράτευσε.

86 See the texts collected by Stern, *Greek and Latin Authors*, 20–130.

and gold plate—much of it from Egypt—carted by the attendants of the king. As is obvious, Antiochus presented a pageant to exhibit the power and wealth of his kingdom, a signal to the Hellenic world of east and west that he had withdrawn from Egypt only to collect resources of awesome extent for even greater ventures. Projection and propaganda dominated.[87] The spectacle was very much in character. It fitted Antiochus' repeated practice of dedicating objects and bestowing gifts upon shrines and cities of Hellas to advertise his means. The calculated elevation of his stature evidently worked. A Greek inscription from the Near East hails him as "savior of Asia," and Diodorus identifies him as the strongest of all kings in his day.[88] Antiochus exploited the image in the closing years of his life to overawe his subjects, consolidate his realm, and engage in further aggrandizement.[89]

Persecution of the Jews belongs in this category. The complicated tale had many facets. Inner turmoil began with clashing ambitions among the Jewish leadership, contests for power entangled by the introduction of Hellenic institutions and aggravated by financial obligations to the Seleucids. Those elements can explain the civil strife, the fierce divisions, and the compromise of traditions that characterized relations between the warring factions and the king. But the savagery and repression of 167 require a different explanation. Here responsibility rests with Antiochus Epiphanes. The persecution did not grow out of factional quarrels, ideological divisions, or financial needs. It served the ends of the king as a display of might, a sign that he had suffered no setback, indeed had emerged with greater strength. The international image of the ruler and his dominion were at stake. Antiochus victimized the Jews in a Seleucid power play.

But the power play, in the end, backfired. Antiochus acknowledged his error too late. The persecution galvanized Jewish resistance, issuing in the Maccabean revolt that ultimately liberated the victims and gave independence to the nation.

---

87 Plb. 30.25 – 26; DS 31.16. See Mørkholm, *Antiochus IV,* 97 – 100; J. G. Bunge, "Die Feiern Antiochos' IV. Epiphanes in Daphne im Herbst 166 v.Chr.," *Chiron* 6 (1976): 53 – 71; Walbank, *Historical Commentary* 3:448 – 53.

88 The Near Eastern inscription: *OGIS* 253; improved text by M. Zambelli, "L'ascesa in trono di Antioco IV Epifane di Siria," *Riv. Filol.* 88 (1960): 374 – 80; cf. Bunge "Feiern," 58 – 64; S. Sherwin-White, "A Greek Ostracon from Babylon of the Early Third Century B.C.," *ZPE* 47 (1982): 65 – 66. On Antiochus' power, DS 31.17a.

89 DS 31.17a; App. *Syr.* 45, 66; Porphyr. *FGrH* 260 F56 (subjugation of Armenia); 1 Macc. 3.31, 3.37; 2 Macc. 9.1 – 2; Jos. *A. J.* 12.293 – 97; cf. Plb. 31.9.1 (campaign in Persis).

16. The Origins and Objectives of Onias' Temple

Some time in the mid-2nd century B.C.E., Jewish leaders in exile from Palestine installed a new temple in Egypt. The decision derived from high authority. Onias, heir to the venerable Zadokite clan of High Priests in Jerusalem, founded the shrine himself, with the sanction of the Ptolemaic king of Egypt. The structure rose in the Heliopolite nome, not far from Memphis, at a site referred to as Leontopolis. As a center for Jewish worship, the temple stood for well over two centuries until its destruction at Roman hands after the Great Revolt. Abolition of the site, however, did not eradicate its memory. Rabbinic sources still preserve echoes of the temple of Onias.

A question arises immediately. The strong Biblical pronouncement about worship of the Lord at a single site and the prohibition of ritual ceremonies elsewhere would seem to deny legitimacy to religious centers outside the Temple in Jerusalem.[1] On the face of it, Onias' house of worship was schismatic, a breakaway cult, and a challenge to the authorities in Palestine.[2] The mid-2nd century certainly constituted a turbulent time for Judaism in the homeland. The persecutions unleashed by Antiochus IV had sullied the Temple, terrorized the populace, and created or exacerbated divisions among Jewish factions and sects. The office of High Priest had been compromised more than once, some of its occupants of dubious lineage and loyalty. The Maccabaean rebellion, while successful in restoring the Temple, opened additional rifts within Judaean politics and society. And the Hasmonaean regime that followed in its wake generated challenges to its own authority by conducting a complex policy that veered between the autonomy of the Temple and collaboration with Hellenistic princes and pretenders. How then does one interpret the meaning of Leontopolis? Did Onias' religious center represent an alternative to Jerusalem, a refuge for Palestinian Jews disenchanted with or in flight from the turmoil at home, the creation of a new temple uncontaminated by political compromise and the questionable credentials of the Jerusalem leadership?

Such is the interpretation applied by Josephus, the principal and almost sole substantive source on the events underlying the genesis of the new shrine. But the evidence conveyed by Josephus, unfortunately, is confused and inconsistent, a major muddle even for that historian. Any conclusions, however tentative, must rest on careful and critical evaluation of his text.

---

1 Deut. 12.4 – 18.
2 So, e.g., U. Kahrstedt, *Syrische Territorien in hellenistischer Zeit* (Berlin, 1926), 132 – 145; E. Cavaignac, *RHR*, 130 (1945), 49; A. Momigliano, *Alien Wisdom* (Cambridge, 1975), 118.

The subject of Leontopolis surfaces in Josephus' *Bellum Judaicum*. Indeed it neatly frames the entire work. The historian brings it up right at the outset of his narrative. He sets Antiochus IV Epiphanes' assault on Judaea in the context of quarrels amidst the Jewish leadership. Onias, a High Priest, gained the upper hand over his rivals, who then took refuge with the Seleucid king. They in turn encouraged Antiochus in his attack on Jerusalem and on the Jewish sympathizers with his enemy Ptolemy VI Philometor of Egypt. Onias consequently fled to Egypt under the protection of Ptolemy, and from him gained permission to construct a temple in the Heliopolite nome similar to that in Jerusalem.[3] Josephus then drops the subject, promising to return to it later. He keeps that promise only at the very end of his work. After narrating the fall of Masada, Josephus turns to a final uprising by Jewish survivors of the Great Revolt who had managed to escape to Egypt. The result was an imperial order to destroy the sanctuary of Onias. This gave Josephus the occasion to revert to the origins of that house of worship. Onias son of Simon, he asserts, a High Priest in Jerusalem, fled his native land as consequence of Antiochus' invasion, gained refuge in Alexandria, and, upon promise to Ptolemy that he would swing all Jewish support to him, received permission to build a temple in the nome of Heliopolis. He went on to erect an impressive edifice, more like a tower than its counterpart in Jerusalem, and received from the king an extensive area of land whose income could support the temple and its priesthood. Josephus proceeds to append his own explanation of Onias' motives. They were not altogether respectable: Onias sought to win an advantage over the Jews in Jerusalem whom he blamed for his exile and hoped to draw a substantial number away to his own temple; moreover, he claimed to be fulfilling a prophecy made by Isaiah that a sanctuary would be raised in Egypt by a Jew.[4]

A fundamental difficulty stands in the way of Josephus' account. By identifying Onias as son of Simon, he apparently refers to Onias III, High Priest and successor to Simon the Just who held office in the first part of the 2nd century.[5] But Onias III had a very different fate in the narrative of our earliest source, II Maccabees. The author of that work has Onias deposed from office by his brother Jason ca. 175 B.C.E., and, three years or more later, when Menelaus

---

3 Jos. *B. J.* 1.31–33.
4 Jos. *B. J.* 7.421–432. F. Parente, in F. Parente and J. Sievers, *Josephus and the History of the Greco-Roman Period: Essays in Honor of Morton Smith* (Leiden, 1994), 75–76, oddly contrasts this negative portrayal of Onias with the allegedly positive one in Jos. *A. J.* 1.31–33. But there is nothing particularly positive in the latter; see 1.31: ἡ φιλοτιμία δ᾽ ἦν αὐτοῖς περὶ δυναστείας. ἑκάστου τῶν ἐν ἀξιώματι μὴ φέροντος τοῖς ὁμοίοις ὑποτετάχθαι.
5 Cf. Jos. *A.J.* 12.224.

had usurped the High Priesthood, Onias was slain in Daphne by Andronicus, an official of the Seleucid king, on the initiative of Menelaus.[6] What reason then is there to value Josephus' version over that of II Maccabees?

Some scholars have found reasons. The tale in II Maccabees contains questionable elements. Onias, according to the narrative, sought asylum at Daphne, presumably in a pagan temple—not the most likely sanctuary for a Jewish High Priest. He was then treacherously lured out of the shrine and murdered by Andronicus.[7] But Andronicus, so independent testimony informs us, was the assassin of Antiochus IV's nephew and potential rival.[8] Hence, it has been argued, the story is sheer fabrication, a romantic tale designed to provide a dramatic demise for Onias. The wicked Andronicus could serve as suitable villain for this invention, although his real victim was an altogether different person. Other texts have also been brought into the reckoning. The 5th-century scholar Theodore of Mopsuestia follows the account in II Maccabees through Jason's accession to power and his Hellenic reforms, but then has Onias III, disgusted with these developments, depart for Egypt and erect his temple.[9] Rabbinic evidence too would seem to lend support. The "House of Onias" appears in both Talmuds, on each occasion with Onias labeled as son of "Simon the Just."[10] This assemblage of texts and arguments has led a number of scholars to prefer Josephus' account in *Bellum Judaicum* to II Maccabees: Onias III did not perish at the hands of an assassin, but survived to found the temple at Leontopolis.[11]

The case, however, is weak and unconvincing as most investigators have long since realized. The author of II Maccabees stood much closer to the events, his text composed probably within two generations of Onias III's death—or indeed rather less if Onias actually survived to establish the Heliopolitan temple

---

6 2 Macc. 4.4 – 7, 4.31 – 34. A slightly different dating in J.G. Bunge, *JSJ*, 6 (1975), 4 – 5.

7 2 Macc. 4.33 – 34.

8 Diod. 30.7.2 – 3; John of Antioch, fr. 58.

9 Theodore of Mopsuestia, *Comm. in Ps. 54*, edited by R. Devreesse in *Studi e testi*, 93 (1939), 351 – 3.

10 Menahot, 109b; y. Yoma, 6.3.

11 S.A. Hirsch, *Jews' College Jubilee Volume* (London, 1906), 52 – 77, makes a case for Talmudic confirmation of the *BJ* account, but he ignores the evidence of II Maccabees altogether. Efforts to discredit II Maccabees occur periodically: A. Bouché-Leclercq, *Histoire des Seleucides, 323 – 64 av. Chr.* (Paris, 1913), I, 250 – 1; A. Momigliano, *Prime linee di storia della tradizione maccabaica* (Rome, 1930), 38 – 9; I.L. Seeligmann, *The Septuagint Version of Isaiah* (Leiden, 1948), 91 – 4. O. Murray, *JTS*, 18 (1967), 364 – 6; V. Keil, *ZAW*, 97 (1985), 222 – 6. The fullest treatment can be found in Parente, *Josephus and the History of the Greco-Roman Period*, 69 – 98.

several years later.[12] Dubious elements do indeed occur in the narrative, most notably Antiochus IV's public weeping at the death of a Jewish High Priest and the fervor with which he carried out the execution of Andronicus.[13] But embellishments do not discredit the kernel of the tale. Much more striking is the fact that II Maccabees describes the death of Onias quite briefly, in sober and restrained fashion.[14] The author does not provide the drama of a martyr tale that we might expect—and that exists elsewhere in his text.[15] If he simply invented a fable here, he missed a good bet. Andronicus, to be sure, had another dastardly deed to his discredit. Yet he could well have been the agent in both assassinations. The slaying of Onias provided the king with a convenient pretext to eliminate the man who had done his dirty work.[16] Theodore of Mopsuestia adds little weight to the argument. He appears simply to have conflated the version found in Josephus with the narrative of II Maccabees. That hardly counts as independent confirmation of Josephus.[17] As for the rabbis, they had no access to historical records and no interest in historical research. That they adopted a modified form of the story conveyed in Josephus' Bellum Judaicum does not lend any further au-

---

12 A massive bibliography exists on the date of II Maccabees. Important titles collected in E. Schürer, The History of the Jewish People in the Age of Jesus Christ, III.1 (rev. ed. by G. Vermes, F. Millar, and M. Goodman, Edinburgh, 1986), 536–7. See further the sensible and sober remarks of B. Bar-Kochva, Judas Maccabaeus (Cambridge, 1989), 182–5; J. Sievers, The Hasmoneans and their Supporters (Atlanta, 1990), 4–7.

13 2 Macc. 4.37–38.

14 2 Macc. 4.34.

15 Cf. 2 Macc. 6.18–7.41. That the High Priest might seek refuge in a pagan temple at a time of emergency should hardly be surprising. The situation can be paralleled in rabbinic sources; see now R. Wilk, Sinai, 108 (1991), 185–7 (Hebrew). It is noteworthy that II Maccabees makes no issue of the fact: 2 Macc. 4.3. Some scholars even postulated that Onias' sanctuary in Daphne was a synagogue; cf. V. Tcherikover, Hellenistic Civilization and the Jews (New York, 1959), 469; J. Bunge, Untersuchungen zum zweiten Makkabäerbuch (Bonn, 1971), 560.

16 See the cogent remarks of M. Stern, Zion, 25 (1960), 4–5 (Hebrew). A similar conclusion reached by F.M. Abel, Les Livres des Maccabées (Paris, 1949), 343–4; Tcherikover, Hellenistic Civilization and the Jews, 469–70; Bunge, Untersuchungen, 559–60; J. Goldstein, II Maccabees (Garden City, 1983), 238–9.

17 Seeligmann, The Septuagint Version, 91–94, noted an ostensible gap between 2 Macc. 4.6 and 4.7, and argued that the story of Onias III's flight to Egypt and establishment of the temple was deliberately omitted by the epitomator. The thesis has now gained further elaboration at the hands of Parente, REJ, 154 (1995), 434–5, who maintains that Theodore's version derived from a lost ms. of II Maccabees which included the story. On his view, the interpolator who excised the flight also substituted the fiction of the murder. The case rests on sheer speculation. No glaring gap between 4.6 and 4.7 strikes the reader of II Maccabees. And, if the alleged tamperer removed Onias' flight and inserted his invented murder, why leave the purported gap?

thority to it.[18] The account in II Maccabees can stand. Onias III perished in Daphne and could not have led a Jewish exile community to Heliopolis.[19]

Josephus himself supplies a rather different rendition in the *Antiquitates*. Here he acknowledges the death of Onias III early in the reign of Antiochus Epiphanes and the successive occupation of the High Priesthood by Jason and Menelaus.[20] It was the son of Onias, a mere infant upon his father's death, who remained to witness the slaying of Menelaus and the installation of a non-Zadokite Alcimus as High Priest, an act which prompted his flight to Egypt. Young Onias IV came under the protection of Ptolemy and his wife Cleopatra, receiving from them a place in the nome of Heliopolis where he built a temple similar to that in Jerusalem.[21] Josephus takes up the story again later in the *Antiquitates,* this time providing a more detailed treatment. Onias IV, having fled to Ptolemy Philometor, dwelled for some time in Alexandria, and then requested permission from the king and queen to build a temple like that in Jerusalem and to appoint Levites and priests of his own nation. He gave as justification the prophecy of Isaiah that a Jew will build a temple to God in Egypt.[22] Josephus proceeds to quote a letter of Onias to Ptolemy and Cleopatra recounting his services to the royal couple during a war in Coele-Syria and Phoenicia and seeking authorization for a new temple in Leontopolis. Onias explains the choice of site as one containing a shrine in ruins, filled with trees and sacred animals,

---

18 The tortuous efforts of J. Brand, *Yavneh,* 1 (1939), 76–84 (Hebrew), to wring authentic data out of the rabbinic traditions amount to little more than imaginative conjecture. The Talmudic tales, by contrast with Josephus, have Onias install his sanctuary in Alexandria. The error, however, may arise from the fact that "Alexandria" was an alternative designation for Leontopolis in the early Byzantine period—a point persuasively argued, with characteristic erudition, by A. Wasserstein, *Illinois Classical Studies,* 18 (1993), 124–8. That great scholar's passing has left many persons intellectually and personally bereft.
19 The *Bellum Judaicum* version, in fact, is not even internally self-consistent. The beginning of the work has Onias build a temple similar to that in Jerusalem, whereas the description at the end explicitly denies that the ναός resembles its Jerusalemite counterpart; Jos. *BJ* 1.33: πολίχνην τε τοῖς Ἱεροσολύμοις ἀπεικασμένην καὶ ναὸν ἔκτισεν ὅμοιον; Jos. *BJ,* 7.427: τὸν μὲν ναὸν οὐχ ὅμοιον... τῷ ἐν Ἱεροσολύμοις. See the discussion by G. Bohak, *Joseph and Aseneth and the Jewish Temple in Heliopolis* (Atlanta, 1996), 27–30. The matter would be definitively settled if Daniel's allusion, 9.26, to "an anointed one cut down" refers to Onias III, as most commentators conclude; e.g., L.F. Hartman and A.A. Di Lella, *The Book of Daniel* (Garden City, 1978), 251–2; J.J. Collins, *Daniel* (Minneapolis, 1993), 356–7. But that conclusion is plausible rather than decisive. For Keil, *ZAW,* 97 (1985), 226–8, Daniel's statement does not refer to assassination. Similarly inconclusive is another passage often cited in this connection: 1 Enoch, 90.8.
20 Jos. *A. J.* 12.237–239.
21 Jos. *A. J.* 12.237, 12.387–388, 20.236.
22 Jos. *A. J.* 13.62–64.

and needing restoration. He proposed to construct a temple to the Lord of the same dimensions as that in Jerusalem, a shrine that would be a religious center for the Jews of Egypt and a place where they could serve the interests of the king. Onias then concluded by citing the forecast of Isaiah.[23] A return letter followed from Ptolemy and Cleopatra. They rebuked Onias for his transgression and violation of the law and questioned whether a site so wild and crowded with sacred animals would be pleasing to God. Nonetheless, in view of Isaiah's prophecy, they granted the petition, fearing lest they appear to have offended the Lord.[24] Having received authorization, Onias constructed the temple, erected an altar comparable to but smaller than that in Jerusalem, and assigned Levites and priests to administer it.[25]

The ascription of the temple's establishment to Onias IV rather than to Onias III carries greater plausibility. And it has drawn the endorsement of most scholars.[26] Yet the story in *Antiquitates* too is riddled with problems. A blunder occurs right at the outset, with regard to the relationship of the High Priests. Josephus has Menelaus as brother of Onias III and Jason, all sons of Simon.[27] Menelaus, however, was not a Zadokite, as II Maccabees informs us, but of a different priestly clan.[28] The fact is significant, for it means that Menelaus, not Alcimus, broke the Oniad hold on the High Priesthood, thus undermining Josephus' explanation for the flight of Onias IV to Egypt. The muddle gets worse. Onias IV was a mere child, even an infant, upon the death of his father, so Josephus reports more than once.[29] Yet, after arrival in Egypt, he obtained high hon-

---

23 Jos. *A. J.* 13.65–68.

24 Jos. *A. J.* 13.69–71.

25 Jos. *A. J.* 13.72–73, 20.236.

26 E. g., Tcherikover, *Hellenistic Civilization and the Jews*, 275–7; Stern, *Zion*, 25 (1960), 1–16 (Hebrew); M. Delcor, *RevBibl*, 75 (1968), 188–93; Bunge, *Untersuchungen*, 555–61; H. Hegermann, in W.D. Davies and L. Finkelstein, *The Cambridge History of Judaism*, II (Cambridge, 1989), 141–2.

27 Jos. *A. J.* 12.237–238; cf. 20.235–236.

28 2 Macc. 3.4, 4.23–25. The tribe of Menelaus' brother Simon is given as Benjamin in the Greek text, but is almost certainly to be emended to Balgea on the basis of the Latin and Armenian manuscripts. See Abel, *Les Livres des Maccabées*, 316–7; Tcherikover, *Hellenistic Civilization and the Jews*, 403–4; Goldstein, *II Maccabees*, 201. This would give Menelaus priestly status, but evidently not Zadokite lineage. On Josephus' confusion here, see Bunge, *JSJ*, 6 (1975), 6–9.

29 Jos. *A. J.* 12.237: νήπιος ἦν ἔτι; 12.387: ἔτι παῖδα. Parente's interpretation of these texts in *Josephus and the History of the Greco-Roman Period*, 79, is without foundation. On the same page he has Onias III die both in 175 and in 170. And his claim that Onias IV was about twenty-three when he fled to Egypt lacks any textual authority. An anonymous referee suggests that Onias IV's youth was invented by Josephus to account for the High Priesthood going to Onias

ors from Ptolemy VI Philometor, and, according to his letter, as quoted by Josephus, he gave substantial military aid to the king for his war in Coele-Syria and Phoenicia.[30] On that version, Onias would have had to reach a swift maturity, establish credentials as a military leader, and round up a significant force to make a difference in Ptolemy's war. Not very likely. And what war was it anyway? Surely not that between Ptolemy and Antiochus IV which took place between 170 and 168 when Onias was a boy—and well before he went to Egypt on Josephus' own account. Ptolemy VI did, to be sure, engage in subsequent contests with his brother and rival Ptolemy VIII Euergetes over the next two decades. But none of these struggles occurred in Coele-Syria or Phoenicia.[31] The reliability of Josephus becomes increasingly suspect.

Only the most determined or committed will find anything of historical value in the exchange of letters between Onias and Ptolemy, supplied by Josephus. As we have seen, Onias claimed to have provided sizable military assistance for what was, in fact, a non-existent war.[32] His justification for asking leave to build a temple strikes a further discordant note. Onias alleged that he found numerous Jewish communities in Egypt with improper shrines and engaged in mu-

---

III's brother Jos. *A. J.* 12.237. But this would not explain Jos. *A. J.* 12.387, set in a different context. No good reason exists for questioning Josephus on this point.

30 Jos. *A. J.* 12.388, 13.65.

31 For the battles between the Ptolemies in this period, see W. Otto, *AbhMünch,* 11 (1934), 88 – 133. A. Kasher, *The Jews in Hellenistic and Roman Egypt* (Tubingen, 1985), 133 – 4, implausibly proposes that Onias' services came in the war between the Seleucid rivals Demetrius I and Alexander Balas ca. 150, on the grounds that Balas was an ally of the Ptolemies. Even less likely is Bunge's speculation that this refers to an otherwise unattested backing by Onias and Ptolemy of Jason's "Putsch" in 169; *JSJ,* 6 (1975), 10. Philometor did interfere in Syrian politics and moved forces into Palestine in the mid 140s; 1 Macc. 11.1 – 19; Jos. *A. J.* 13.103 – 119; Diod. 32.9c – 10.1; Livy, *Per.* 52. But that came at the end of Philometor's life, not a war for which Onias could later gain the king's blessing for construction of a temple.

32 The evidence of Jos. *C. Ap.,* 2.49 – 50, is regularly brought up in this connection: Philometor and Cleopatra appointed Jewish commanders, Onias and Dositheus, to head the entire royal army. The statement is, on any reckoning, a gross exaggeration. But one can go further. The common scholarly presumption that Onias the general and Onias the temple-founder are one and the same is far from certain. Josephus makes no such identification or suggestion. The Onias of *C. Apionem* is simply a στρατηγός, not heir to the line of High Priests. And Onias IV, who was only a child at the time of his father's death ca.172, would be little more than thirty by the death of Philometor in 145—hence hardly an experienced commander of armies. Yet the identification of general and priest has gone almost entirely unquestioned; see, e.g., Tcherikover, *Hellenistic Civilization and the Jews,* 276 – 9; Delcor, *RevBibl,* 75 (1968), 192; Bunge, *Untersuchungen,* 578 – 579; J.A. Goldstein, *I Maccabees* (Garden City, 1976), 35; Hegermann, *Cambridge History of Judaism,* II, 142; Parente, *Josephus and the History of the Greco-Roman Period,* 80; Bohak, *Joseph and Aseneth,* 24.

tual hostilities, comparable to the religious diversities and disagreements among Egyptians. He then sought a royal mandate to refurbish the ruined temple at Leontopolis, a neglected site still filled with animals sacred to the Egyptians. This revived sanctuary would unify the Jews of Egypt and provide a center of support for the Ptolemaic regime—in addition to fulfilling the prophecy of Isaiah.[33] Why Onias selected a location with such pagan reverberations goes unexplained. Nor are we told why Ptolemy should be expected to welcome the establishment of a strong and united Jewish seat of authority in the vicinity of Memphis. The reply of Ptolemy and Cleopatra appears more extraordinary still. The royal couple rebuked Onias for selecting a spot sacred to Egyptians and thus displeasing to the Lord, a violation of the law, but acceded to his request anyway on the authority of Isaiah.[34] Ptolemy and his sister-wife, in short, are represented as more pious than Onias, protectors and promoters of Jewish law and traditions. The portrayal mirrors other texts that present Hellenistic rulers as respecters of the faith and champions of Jewish interests, most notably the *Letter of Aristeas*. In this instance, however, praise of the Ptolemies comes at the expense of Onias, a gratuitous slap at the founder of Leontopolis. Josephus' narrative is shot through with tendentiousness.[35]

The character and inconsistencies of the evidence render efforts to establish a firm chronology largely fruitless and pointless. The dates of Onias' departure from Judaea for Egypt and his construction of the temple in the Heliopolite nome remain elusive. Josephus' version in the *Bellum Judaicum* has Onias escape from his homeland in the wake of Antiochus Epiphanes' invasion, plundering, and desecration of the Temple, hence ca. 168.[36] How long an interval passed between that event and the erection of a new sanctuary receives no indication in this narrative. Josephus' brief account, in fact, suggests that Onias' request to Ptolemy Philometor occurred not long after the Jewish leader had taken refuge in Alexandria, and construction proceeded with no apparent delay.[37] Acceptance of this tale would place the founding of the temple in the mid 160s, a date adopted by many.[38] But the text also identifies the founder as Onias III, a conclusion

---

33 Jos. *A. J.* 13.65 – 68.

34 Jos. *A. J.* 13.69 – 71: τὴν γὰρ ἁμαρτίαν καὶ τὴν τοῦ νόμου παράβασιν εἰς τὴν Ὀνίου κεφαλὴν ἀνέθεσαν ... διὸ καὶ θαυμάζομεν εἰ ἔσται τῷ θεῷ κεχαρισμένον.

35 In the view of L. Robert, *Études épigraphiques et philologiques* (Paris, 1938), 235, Josephus' use of the term θρησκεία (Jos. *A. J.* 13.66) suffices to discredit the correspondence, for its usage is unattested prior to the Roman period. Thanks are due to G. Bohak for this reference.

36 Jos. *B. J.* 1.32, 7.421.

37 Jos. *B. J.* 7.421 – 422.

38 So, e.g., Cavaignac, *RHR*, 130 (1945), 48 – 49; Bunge, *Untersuchungen,* 567 – 72; Parente, *Josephus and the History of the Greco-Roman Period,* 95 – 7.

already shown to be most dubious and implausible. Once that identification falls, a date for the temple in the 160s falls with it.[39]

The *Antiquitates* name a more likely founder in Onias IV. But the rest of the text leaves much to be desired. Josephus here dates Onias' self-exile to the time of Alcimus' appointment as High Priest, i.e. 162.[40] There followed a stay in Alexandria of unspecified length, until Onias, distressed by evils wrought upon Judaea by Hellenistic kings, asked for authorization to build a temple in Egypt.[41] This version provides little secure ground for chronology. Struggles between Seleucid commanders and Jewish forces, and then between princes and pretenders, plagued the land of Israel repeatedly from the late 160s through the 140s. And the year 162 as the supposed time of Onias' withdrawal depends upon the motive ascribed by Josephus: that elevation of Alcimus brought a non-Oniad to the post. Since Menelaus' appointment, however, had already broken the Oniad monopoly a decade earlier, this motive loses meaning, and, with it, the date. So we are no closer to chronological confidence.

A more tangible pointer has been found in an intriguing letter on papyrus, dating to 164. The *dioiketes* Herodes in Memphis addressed the missive ostensibly to a certain Onias. Given the very polite formula at the outset, which includes reference to the health of the entire royal family, one may infer that the addressee was a man of considerable prestige and standing. The temptation is strong to identify the recipient of the letter with the scion of Judaea's high priestly clan, recently arrived in Egypt.[42] The identification, however, creates more problems than it solves. If Onias were already ensconced in Egypt by 164, this wrecks Josephus' chronology in the *Antiquitates* which brings him to that land only after 162. An appeal to the *Bellum Judaicum* does not help much. That account has Onias depart for Egypt ca. 168, but he spent some time in Alexandria before gaining permission to build his sanctuary in Heliopolis. Its construction, however swiftly undertaken, would not likely be complete by 164 when the addressee of the papyrus was evidently well established and well respected somewhere in the *chora*. Moreover, the recipient's stature is not readily compatible with

---

39 A common view has it that Onias' temple could only have been built between 168 and 165, i.e. between Antiochus' sacrilege and the cleansing of the Temple by Judas; see previous note. But this presumes that a shrine in Leontopolis would otherwise violate a prescription that no second temple was legitimate—which begs the question.
40 Jos. *A. J.* 12.387.
41 Jos. *A. J.* 13.62–63.
42 So, e.g., V. Tcherikover and A. Fuks, *Corpus Papyrorum Judaicarum*, I (Cambridge, Mass., 1957), 244–6, no. 132; Murray, *JTS*, 18 (1967), 366; Delcor, *RevBibl*, 75 (1968), 192–3; Bunge, *Untersuchungen*, 562–3; Parente, *Josephus and the History of the Greco-Roman Period*, 84; a more guarded view by Bohak, *Joseph and Aseneth*, 21.

that of young Onias IV—who was still a pre-teen in 164. The document itself may well be a red herring in this context. The reading of "Onias" as addressee is far from certain; only a single letter of the name is clearly legible.[43] And even if one accepts the conjecture, it falls well short of proving the identification: the name Onias occurs with some frequency in the Egyptian diaspora. Hence, the papyrus letter fails to advance the quest for a timetable.

One other chronological item has generated some discussion. At the end of the *Bellum Judaicum*, Josephus records the closing down of Onias' temple by the Romans in 73 C.E., and adds the peculiar datum that the structure had lasted 343 years.[44] What can one make of this? The reckoning, if accurate, would take the founding of the sanctuary back to 270 B.C.E., a date far earlier than any suggested by the available testimony, and altogether at odds with the contexts supplied by Josephus himself.[45] A more promising approach led to emendation. By altering the numeral from 343 to 243, scholars reached a foundation date of 170 B.C.E., which does indeed approximate the time elsewhere supplied in the *Bellum Judaicum*, namely the period of Antiochus Epiphanes' persecutions.[46] The idea is attractive, but, in fact, gets us nowhere. Even if correct, the emendation shows only that Josephus was internally consistent in the *Bellum Judaicum*. It does not make the date, ca. 170 B.C.E., any more plausible than it had been before—a date vitiated by the fact that Onias III was dead and Onias IV still a small child. A third theory has had appeal as well: the number 343 possesses symbolic significance, seven jubilees, i.e. seven times seven sabbatical years ($7 \times 7 \times 7 = 343$). Hence a mystical connotation rather than temporal chronology explains the figure.[47] Perhaps so. But this leaves the actual foundation date as elusive as ever.

The results of this discussion need to be faced. The inconsistencies, inaccuracies, and wild improbabilities in Josephus' two versions shake faith in any re-

---

43 The reading was first proposed by U. Wilcken, *UPZ*, 110, who claimed to see Ὀνί[αι]; accepted, e. g., by J. Mélèze-Modrzejewski, *RevHistDroit*, 72 (1994), 7 – 8. An earlier conjecture by Letronne, *P. Per.* 63, I-VII, offered [θέο]νι. Mahaffy, *P. Petrie*, iii, 15, more cautiously, printed only [...]ν[.]. Skepticism on Wilcken's reconstruction is expressed by Tcherikover, *Hellenistic Civilization and the Jews*, 498—a shift from his earlier position in *CPJ*, I, 245 – 6. See also Kasher, *Jews in Hellenistic and Roman Egypt*, 60 – 1.
44 Jos. *B. J.* 7.436.
45 This has not prevented some scholars from embracing that date; e. g., Hirsch, *Jews' College Jubilee Volume*, 54 – 6, 74 – 7; M.A. Beek, *Oudtestamentische Studiën*, 2 (1943), 126 – 9.
46 Jos. *BJ* 1.33, 7.421 – 423. The emendation has been widely adopted; see a summary of opinions by Hirsch, *Jews' College Jubilee Volume*, 54 – 5; also Murray, *JTS*, 18 (1967), 365, n. 2. Jerome gives a similar figure, 250 years for the lifetime of the temple; *In Dan.* 3.11.14.
47 See R. Hayward, *JJS*, 33 (1982), 436 – 7, with earlier bibliography.

construction. It does not help to adopt the tale in *Antiquitates* as against that in *Bellum Judaicum,* or vice-versa, since each is independently confounded and muddled. Josephus exercised few analytic powers in scrutinizing his sources and paid little attention to the incongruities of his own narratives. They provide neither a clear chronology of events nor a meaningful understanding of the circumstances.

We turn now to Josephus' ascription of motives to Onias. Do they carry any greater authority?

Characteristically, Josephus supplies more than one motive, with confusing and incompatible results. To summarize once again in brief the reasons that he puts into the head of Onias (III or IV) for abandoning Palestine and creating a sanctuary in Egypt: the *Bellum Judaicum* has Onias enmeshed in internal Palestinian politics, his enemies gaining success through alliance with Antiochus Epiphanes, thereby prompting his own flight to Ptolemy.[48] The building of the temple constituted an element in the power struggle: Onias promised that a center for Jewish worship would galvanize support of Jews everywhere behind the Ptolemaic contest with Antiochus.[49] And Onias had a private grudge of his own to indulge: his new temple would attract Palestinian Jews away from rivals in the homeland who had brought about his exile.[50] The *Antiquitates* give a somewhat different set of purposes—though hardly any more to the credit of Onias. The young heir to the high priestly line headed for Egypt when the Seleucid king removed his clan from the office and installed Alcimus.[51] Onias' drive to build a temple in Heliopolis stemmed not only from distress at seeing the travails of his native land caused by Macedonians and their monarchs, but also from desire for permanent reputation and glory of his own.[52] Still another motivation surfaces in Onias' supposed letter to Ptolemy. He expresses the aim of a central and uniform worship, to supersede the diverse, questionable, and mutually antagonistic Jewish communities in Egypt—and also to form a solid core of backing for the Ptolemaic regime.[53]

Little reason exists for confidence in any of these excogitated motives. Josephus' demonstrable confusion over the facts hardly renders him trustworthy

---

48 Jos. *B. J.* 1.31–33, 7.421–423.
49 Jos. *B. J.* 7.424–425: οὕτως γὰρ Ἀντιόχῳ μὲν ἔτι μᾶλλον ἐκπολεμώσεσθαι τοὺς Ἰουδαίους … πρὸς αὐτὸν δ’ εὐνοικωτέρως ἕξειν.
50 Jos. *B. J.* 7.431: καὶ τοῦτο τὸ ἱερὸν ἐνόμιζε κατασκευάσας εἰς αὐτὸ περισπάσειν ἀπ ἐκείνων τὸ πλῆθος.
51 Jos. *A. J.* 12.387.
52 Jos. *A. J.* 13.62–63: βουλόμενος αὑτῷ μνήμην καὶ δόξαν αἰώνιον κατασκευάσαι.
53 Jos. *A. J.* 13.65–67.

when he supplies explanation for them. The account in *Bellum Judaicum* lumps together internal dissension, a contest for political supremacy between Oniads and their opponents, and the larger international conflict between Seleucids and Ptolemies. The analysis reduces itself to a gross simplification. Whatever the truth of the factional strife in Judaea, the situation had changed markedly by the time Onias established his position in Egypt and could expect authorization for a temple. Antiochus IV had been ordered out of Egypt by a Roman directive, the Maccabaean movement led resistance to the Seleucids and their surrogates in Judaea (while stirring up animosities to themselves among other communities in Palestine), and internal rivalries within both the Ptolemaic and Seleucid houses consumed their energies in the mid 160s.[54] Given those turbulent circumstances, the notion that Onias built his temple as retaliation against the foes who had brought about his exile seems peculiarly senseless. Nor would Ptolemy VI have had much use for it against the Seleucids who had their hands full in Syria and Palestine, while he was occupied by contests within his own family.[55] Josephus' conclusions collapse.

Recourse to the *Antiquitates* does not improve matters. As we have seen, the Oniad stranglehold on the High Priesthood ended with the occupancy of that office by Menelaus. The subsequent installation of Alcimus, therefore, hardly accounts for Onias' precipitate departure. Nor is it obvious why a temple in Leontopolis should ease Onias' anxieties about the assaults on Judaea by the Macedonians. Nothing suggests that the new sanctuary provided a refuge for exiles and fugitives from the homeland. Onias may well have looked to increase his prestige and promote his reputation for posterity, perfectly reasonable impulses —though no more than speculation by Josephus. But they alone cannot explain the authorization, backing, and endurance of the temple. The assertion in Onias' letter to Ptolemy and Cleopatra that he would end divisiveness among Egyptian Jews and unite them behind the regime has ostensible logic. Yet one wonders how much value a Jewish temple in the remote district of Heliopolis, far from the Ptolemaic capital of Alexandria, would have for rulers whose power was in jeopardy.[56] Josephus' hypotheses about motivation have no greater credibility than his reconstruction of events or his confused chronology.

---

54 Principal evidence on these matters in 1 Macc. 3 – 9; 2 Macc. 8 – 15.

55 See Bouché-Leclercq, *Histoire des Séleucides*, I, 262 – 322; Otto, *AbhMünch*, 11 (1934), 82 – 124; cf. E.S. Gruen, *Chiron*, 6 (1976), 76 – 93; *idem, The Hellenistic World and the Coming of Rome* (Berkeley, 1984), 692 – 702.

56 Tcherikover' s idea, *CPJ*, I, 45, that Ptolemy hoped to use the temple as anti-Seleucid propaganda among the Jews in Palestine, is far-fetched. G. Bohak, *JSJ*, 26 (1995), 36 – 8, proposes that Ptolemy needed a strong and loyal military commander in Heliopolis to ward off foreign

What then is the significance of Onias' temple? Some have been tempted to downplay it altogether: a mere shrine attached to what was essentially a military colony.[57] But that theory fails to account for the endurance of the sanctuary, its importance as a center of Jewish resistance as late as the Great Revolt, and, even more telling, its continued reputation, long after the Romans put it out of commission, in rabbinic literature. What reason is there to believe that Onias had established credentials as a military leader at all? His claim in the purported letter to have performed many great services in a war in Coele-Syria and Phoenicia carries no weight.[58] No such war was fought, Onias was too young anyway, and the letter is a fabrication. It is methodological madness to base any inferences on that information. To be sure, two Jewish generals, one of them named Onias, led armies in support of Queen Cleopatra against Ptolemy Physcon after the death of Ptolemy Philometor in 145.[59] But, despite unanimity among scholars in identifying this Onias with the founder of the temple, there is no hint in the texts to support such an identification.[60] The actions of Onias, both diplomatic and military, took place in Alexandria. Did Cleopatra call up a garrison all the way from Heliopolis to rescue her from the hostility of the Alexandrians? Or had Onias' ministry at the temple been so impressive that Philometor and Cleopatra transferred him earlier to take charge of the royal armies in or near the capital? It will not do to pile hypothesis upon hypothesis. The notion of Onias the soldier-priest is essentially a modern concoction.[61]

---

foes and help to control restive natives. But Onias' prior background would hardly seem to fit that description.

57 So Tcherikover, *Hellenistic Civilization and the Jews*, 278–80; S. Safrai, *Die Wallfahrt im Zeitalter des zweiten Tempels* (Dusseldorf, 1981), 79–81; J. Mélèze-Modrzejewski, *The Jews of Egypt* (Philadelphia, 1995), 128.

58 Jos. *A. J.* 13.65: πολλὰς καὶ μεγάλας ὑμῖν χρείας τετελεκὼς ἐν τοῖς κατὰ πόλεμον ἔργοις … ἔν τε τῇ κοίλῃ Συρίᾳ καὶ Φοινίκῃ.

59 Jos. *C. Ap.*, 2.49–52.

60 See above, n. 23.

61 Josephus does elsewhere refer to two Jewish generals, Chelkias and Ananias, whom he designates as sons of the Onias who built the temple in Heliopolis. The historian cites Strabo for the information that they remained steadfastly loyal to Cleopatra III in the contest with her son Ptolemy Lathyrus; Jos. *A. J.* 13.284–287. For this war, see E. Van't Dack, et al., *The Judaean-Syrian-Egyptian Conflict of 103–101 B.C.* (*Collectanea Hellenistica*, I, Brussels, 1989), *passim*; J. Whitehorne, *Cleopatras* (London, 1994), 138–44. The father of these generals is likely to have been the man who commanded the forces in Alexandria for Cleopatra's mother, Cleopatra I. But Josephus may simply have assumed that Onias the father was identical with the founder of the temple. That datum certainly did not come from Strabo; cf. M. Stern, *Greek and Latin Authors on Jews and Judaism*, I (Jerusalem, 1976), 269–70. It is noteworthy that Josephus says nothing in the *Antiquitates* about Onias the priest as a Ptolemaic general, and, conversely, nothing in the

The installation of a temple in the Heliopolite nome had religious and cultural meaning, no simple appendage to a soldiers' settlement. Its implications need to be explored. The existence of Jewish places of worship in Egypt was nothing new in the 2nd century B.C.E. Even the spurious letter of Onias to the Ptolemaic court alludes to various Jewish communities with sanctuaries of whose practices he disapproves.[62] And documentary evidence discloses a number of synagogues in a variety of Egyptian locations.[63] The Idumaeans too established houses of worship in Egypt in the 2nd and 1st centuries B.C.E., setting up local ethnic communities, particularly in Memphis and Hermopolis.[64] From the Ptolemaic vantage point, Onias' temple may not have seemed out of the ordinary. But Onias had quite a different vision. This structure would be consciously modeled on the Temple in Jerusalem, a parallel shrine to minister to the spiritual needs of all Egyptian Jews, and presided over by a member of the most august family, next in succession to the Zadokite line of High Priests. This sets the Heliopolite sanctuary outside conventional categories. Onias' temple would make a bold statement.

We arrive now at the heart of the matter. Did the new shrine represent a schismatic Judaism, a challenge to usurpers in Jerusalem, an appeal for Palestinian Jews to escape the woes of the homeland and join the faithful in the more authentic community of Leontopolis? We have observed already that Josephus' interpretations along these lines rest on unfounded and unreliable surmise. Better to scrap them and confront the issue anew.

That Jews everywhere looked to the Temple in Jerusalem as the seat of religious authority is clear and uncontroversial. Numerous biblical and post-biblical references attest to it. The *locus classicus* occurs in Deuteronomy: Moses asserts

---

Contra Apionem about Onias the general as a priest in Heliopolis. A certain Chelkias is mentioned, perhaps as a στρατηγός, in a fragmentary inscription from the Heliopolite nome; *CPJ*, III, 1450 = W. Horbury and D. Noy, *Jewish Inscriptions of Greco-Roman Egypt* (Cambridge, 1992), #129, with full references. See the discussions of Stern, *Greek and Latin Authors*, I, 270; Kasher, *Jews in Hellenistic and Roman Egypt*, 61, 123, n. 55; G. Cohen, in E. Van' t Dack, et al., *The Judaean-Syrian-Egyptian Conflict*, 123, n. 47, with further bibliography. This does not prove, despite the term τεμέ[νει] in the document, that the Jewish temple served as a military stronghold governed by Onias and his heirs. Little can be made of "Chelkias the *strategos*" in P. Med. inv. 69.59; see A. di Bitonto, *Aegyptus*, 54 (1974), 20–1; D. Hagedorn and P.J. Sijpesteijn, *ZPE*, 65 (1986), 103–4. Neither date nor provenance is known—nor is the name itself certain.

62 Jos. *A. J.* 13.66: πλείστους εὑρὼν παρὰ τὸ καθῆκον ἔχοντας ἱερά.

63 See the summary record by Tcherikover, *CPJ*, I, 8. An extensive discussion by Kasher, *Jews in Hellenistic and Roman Egypt*, 106–67.

64 Evidence and discussion in U. Rappaport, *RevPhil*, 43 (1969), 73–82; D.J. Thompson, *Memphis under the Ptolemies* (Princeton, 1988), 99–103.

that the Lord will choose a dwelling for his worship across the Jordan where all sacrifices and ritual offerings are to be made.[65] Deuteronomic historiography reinforced the principle by hailing kings who stamped out sacrifices at the "high places," and denouncing those who encouraged them.[66] Later writers, like Philo and Josephus, transformed the pronouncement of Deuteronomy into the unambiguous assertion that no site other than Jerusalem can have an altar or temple.[67]

How then could Onias expect to get away with his new foundation? Did he fly directly in the face of biblical prohibitions, a deliberate break with Jerusalem? Not a likely proposition. Onias needed to attract and build a constituency of Jews who were presumably familiar with scriptural traditions. And he held some cards that could be played. The prophecy of Isaiah supplied strong authority. Isaiah's forecast that an altar to Yahweh would someday rise in the midst of Egypt doubtless bolstered Onias' purpose.[68] If he faced any criticism based on Deuteronomy 12, he would not lack responses. Ambiguity, as so often, inheres in the biblical verses, giving rise to divergent exegetical interpretation. Moses issued a prohibition against sacrificing burnt offerings wherever one wishes, permitting them only in a place that the Lord has chosen. The rabbinical commentary on that passage allows that the ritual can be performed in any place that a prophet directs.[69] To Egyptian Jews eager for a holy shrine of their own, a similar rationalization might well suffice. Onias could indeed stretch a point and claim that what really mattered in regard to sacrifice was the recipient of the offerings, not the location of the practice, a claim for which biblical authority was available.[70] The strict interpretation of Deuteronomy 12 delivered by Philo and Josephus may not have prevailed in the age of the Maccabees. And, more striking still, even Josephus, in his varied accounts of Onias' temple, nowhere states or implies that the institution violated Jewish law or practice.[71] Onias had a defen-

---

65 Deut. 12.4 – 18; cf. Jeremiah, 7.3 – 15; Ezekiel, 24.21. Other references usefully collected by Wasserstein, *Illinois Classical Studies,* 18 (1993), 120, n. 2.

66 E.g. 2 Kgs., 12.4, 14.4, 15.4, 15.35, 16.4, 16.10 – 16, 17.7 – 12, 18.1 – 4, 21.2 – 3, 23.8 – 20.

67 Philo, *De Spec. Leg.* 1.67; Jos. *A. J.* 4.200 – 201; Jos. *C. Ap.*, 2.193.

68 Note that, in Josephus' account, Onias plainly expanded on Isaiah to suit his own ends. The biblical text forecasts an altar to the Lord in Egypt; Isaiah, 19.19. Onias interpreted it as a temple to be erected by a Jew; Jos. *B. J.* 7.432; Jos. *A. J.* 13.62 – 64.

69 Deut. 12.13 – 14. See the Sifre to Deuteronomy, Pisqa 70, translated by J. Neusner, *Sifre to Deuteronomy: An Analytical Translation* (Atlanta, 1987), vol. 1, 203.

70 Cf. 2 Chron. 33.17; see M. Smith, *Palestinian Parties and Politics that Shaped the Old Testament* (New York, 1971), 139 – 40.

71 It is particularly noteworthy that Josephus juxtaposes to his narrative of the Onias/Ptolemy correspondence a report that representatives of Jews and Samaritans disputed the legitimacy of

sible case to make. Imitation of the temple in Jerusalem need not constitute defiance or schism.

The "house of Onias," surprisingly and revealingly, continued to be a topic of discussion and a source of dispute among the rabbis. The Mishnah cites R. Simeon as stating that priests who ministered in the temple of Onias could not serve in the temple of Jerusalem. But he clearly distinguished them from idolators. That opinion is confirmed in the Babylonian Talmud which asserts that Onias' shrine was no idolatrous one.[72] To be sure, the consensus of rabbis set Onias' sanctuary below the level of Jerusalem. But they did not reckon it as a breakaway alternative.[73] Onias' creation, as is obvious, was still taken seriously in Talmudic times. Whatever the upshot of rabbinic opinion, however, it has no direct bearing upon attitudes in the mid-2nd century B.C.E. Onias did not have to contend with the pronouncements of the sages.

---

one another's temples in a debate before Ptolemy in Alexandria: the king ruled on behalf of the temple in Jerusalem; Jos. *A. J.* 13.74–79. The historicity of this story is more than dubious. Why should such a quarrel be arbitrated in Alexandria? And what force would Ptolemy's ruling have at a time when Palestine was outside his authority? The matter cannot here be explored in detail. Whatever the authority of the tale, however, it is remarkable that the issue of a rival temple to Jerusalem, the central question regarding the Samaritans on Mt. Gerizim, does not arise at all in the adjoining passage on Leontopolis. The Samaritan temple, located within easy reach of Jerusalem, naturally offended Hasmonaean sensibilities, leading to its destruction at the hands of John Hyrcanus in 128 B.C.E.; Jos. *A. J.* 13.254–256. But the temple of Onias, far off in the region of Memphis, remote from any Hasmonaean influence, would not have been a comparable irritant.

72 Menahot, 13.10; b. Menahot, 109b; cf. t. Menahot, 13.12–15. And see Parente, *Josephus and the History of the Greco-Roman Period*, 77, 81. The discussion itself has interesting implications. The fact that Jewish sages still debated the propriety of actions in the temple of Onias long after its demise plainly indicates a stature well beyond that of a mere local shrine, as some have described it; see above n. 57.

73 Differences among the rabbis surfaced with regard to the origins of the Egyptian temple. The tale, conveyed in slightly different versions in both the Palestinian and the Babylonian Talmuds, depicts a quarrel between the two sons of Simon the Just over succession to the High Priesthood, a quarrel resulting in Onias' flight to Egypt where he would build a new shrine. Onias appears in the story as a less than admirable figure. But his Temple drew mixed responses from the Talmudic sages. R. Meir considered the new religious center to be idolatrous, but R. Judah observed that Onias had the authority of Isaiah 19.19. See b. Menahot, 109b; p. Yoma, 6.3. Discussions of the talmudic material in Hirsch, *Jews' College Jubilee Volume*, 60–70; Brand, *Yavneh*, 1 (1939), 76–84 (Hebrew); B.Z. Luria, *Beit Miqra*, 31 (1967), 65–81 (Hebrew); Parente, *Josephus and the History of the Greco-Roman Period*, 77, 81. R. Yankelevich, in A. Oppenheimer, I. Gafni, and M. Stern, *Jews and Judaism in the Second Temple, Mishnaic, and Talmudic Periods* (Jerusalem, 1993), 107–15 (Hebrew), plausibly proposes that the rabbinic arguments reflect a dispute between Palestine and the Diaspora communities over the source of legitimacy after the destruction of the Temple and the failure of the Bar Kochba revolt.

Reactions contemporary or near contemporary to the founding of the temple escape record, a source of high frustration. Yet indirect testimony supplies some clues. The text of II Maccabees contains two letters attached as a preface and quite independent of the body of the work. Both are addressed by Jews in Jerusalem and Judaea to their kinsmen in Egypt. The epistles abound in problems and difficulties, stimulating a veritable library of modern scholarship.[74] This is not the place to enter that particular thicket. We concentrate upon the possible relevance of the letters for relations between the temples in Jerusalem and Leontopolis.

The first letter carries a date of year 188 of the Seleucid era, i.e. 124 B.C.E. Its prescript brings the greetings of Jews in Jerusalem and in the country of Judaea to their "brothers" in Egypt.[75] The purpose is to report their prayers to God, asking that he be reconciled to the Egyptian Jews, that he open their hearts to his commandments, and that he not forsake them in an evil time.[76] Further, the writers request that their Egyptian kinsmen celebrate with them the Hanukkah festival, here termed the "feast of Tabernacles of the month of Kislev," as it was indeed known at the outset.[77] The text notes also that an earlier message too had been sent, dating to the year 169 (143 B.C.E.) and recounting the distress that Palestinian Jews had suffered in the time of the persecutions.[78]

The second letter in the text is far longer. It purports to date from the time of Judas Maccabaeus himself, directed to Aristobulus who is described as tutor of king Ptolemy and a member of the high priestly clan, and to the Jews of Egypt generally.[79] The epistle reports a version of the death of Antiochus Epiphanes and announces the Jews' rescue by God from their perils.[80] Like the other letter, it invites the Egyptian Jews to celebrate the purification of the Temple by honoring the feast of Tabernacles on the 25th of Kislev.[81] The epistle proceeds to a

---

74 See particularly the treatments in Abel, *Les Livres des Maccabees*, 285–310; Bunge, *Untersuchungen*, 32–152; C. Habicht, 2. *Makkabaerbuch* (*Jüdische Schriften aus hellenistisch-römischer Zeit*, I) (Gütersloh, 1976), 199–207; R. Doran, *Temple Propaganda: The Purpose and Character of 2 Maccabees* (Washington, 1981), 3–12; Goldstein, *II Maccabees*, 137–88. Extensive bibliographical citations can be found in B.Z. Wacholder, *HUCA*, 49 (1978), 89–133.
75 2 Macc. 1.1: τοῖς ἀδελφοῖς τοῖς κατ' Αἴγυπτον Ἰουδαίος χαίρειν οἱ ἀδελφοὶ οἱ ἐν Ἱεροσολύμοις Ἰουδαῖοι καὶ οἱ ἐν τῇ χώρᾳ τῆς Ἰουδαίας εἰρήνην ἀγαθήν.
76 2 Macc. 1.2–6.
77 2 Macc. 1.9.
78 2 Macc. 1.7–8.
79 2 Macc. 1.10.
80 2 Macc. 1.11–17.
81 2 Macc. 1.18: μέλλοντες ἄγειν ἐν τῷ Χασελευ πέμπτῃ καὶ εἰκάδι τὸν καθαρισμὸν τοῦ ἱεροῦ δέον ἡγησάμεθα διασαφῆσαι ὑμῖν. ἵνα καὶ αὐτοὶ ἄγητε σκηνοπηγίας καὶ τοῦ πυρός.

lengthy and largely fanciful account of the background to the festival, linking it to miraculous occurrences connected with the foundation and dedication of the First and Second Temples.[82] The authors claim documentary authority, citing the scrupulous collection of records by Nehemiah and the assemblage of scattered materials by Judas himself—all of which the Egyptian Jews are welcome to consult.[83] The letter concludes by reiterating the importance of the festival: it commemorates the fulfillment of God's promise to restore to the Jews control over their religious and political heritage. The authors once again call upon Egyptian Jews to honor that festival. And they express the hope that God will speedily regather his people from everywhere to his holy place.[84]

What implications do these epistles have for the image of Onias' temple in the eyes of Palestinian Jews? A distinguished assemblage of scholars has interpreted the letters as anti-Oniad propaganda, a polemic against the temple in Heliopolis: they aimed to rebuke the schismatic Jews of Egypt and to regather the faithful under the umbrella of the establishment in Jerusalem.[85] The analysis lacks textual support and rests on infirm foundations. To begin, the letters make no explicit reference to Onias, Leontopolis, or any rival temple in the Heliopolite nome. The first letter does suggest a need for reconciliation to God by Egyptian Jews and a revival of obedience to divine law and precepts.[86] This evidently alludes to troubled times in Egypt and sufferings by Jews, circumstances that, as is customary in Biblical traditions, are ascribed to a falling away from adherence to God's commands. But nothing implies that this stems from a schismatic temple. The Jews of Judaea had to request more than once, so it is claimed, that their Egyptian kinsmen celebrate the Hanukkah festival. Does this then imply recalcitrance on the part of Onias' followers who preferred independence

---

82 2 Macc. 1.19–2.12.

83 2 Macc. 2.13–15.

84 2 Macc. 2.16–18: μέλλοντες οὖν ἄγειν τὸν καθαρισμὸν ἐγράψαμεν ὑμῖν. καλῶς οὖν ποιήσετε ἄγοντες τὰς ἡμέρας … ἐλπίζομεν γὰρ ἐπὶ τῷ θεῷ ὅτι ταχέως ἡμᾶς ἐλεήσει καὶ ἐπισυνάξει ἐκ τῆς ὑπὸ τὸν οὐρανὸν εἰς τὸν ἅγιον τόπον.

85 So, in various formulations, Kahrstedt, *Syrische Territorien*, 133–45; E. Bickermann, *ZNW*, 32 (1933), 250–51 = *Studies in Jewish and Christian History* (Leiden, 1980), 2, 154–5; Momigliano, *Prime Linee*, 93–4; *CP*, 70 (1975), 82–3; Abel, *Les Livres des Maccabées*, xliv; Cavaignac, *RHR*, 130 (1945), 42–3, 48–52; Habicht, 2. *Makkabäerbuch*, 186; Bunge, *Untersuchungen*, 595–602; Goldstein, *I Maccabees*, 34–6, 545–50; *II Maccabees*, 24–6. The thesis is rightly questioned by D. Arenhoevel, *Die Theokratie nach dem 1. und 2. Makkabäerbuch* (Mainz, 1967), 100–2; Doran, *Temple Propaganda*, 11–2; J.J. Collins, *Between Athens and Jerusalem* (New York, 1983), 73–9; A. Kasher, in M. Mor, *Eretz Israel, Israel and the Jewish Diaspora* (Lanham, 1991), 30–2.

86 2 Macc. 1.2–6.

and disengagement?[87] The inference is unfounded. Reference to a letter in 143 B.C.E. gives no indication of its contents. It need not have included a request to celebrate Hanukkah. Nor do we know that it was addressed to Leontopolis anyway. The recipients may well have been the Jews of Alexandria. Certainly the second letter was purportedly sent to Aristobulus in Alexandria, still reckoned as the proper destination for transmittal to the Jews of Egypt. The thesis of "anti-Oniad propaganda" evaporates.

The festal letters may nonetheless bear some relevance. A scholarly consensus accepts the authenticity of the letter dated to 124 and the existence of a prior one in 143.[88] The second extant letter is more dubious. Judas Maccabaeus had little occasion to dictate missives of historical interest in the wake of cleansing the Temple, with numerous enemies and much fighting still ahead.[89] But, whatever the date of the epistle, its author or forger had it reinforce the message of the other, a significant reflection of Judaean opinion in the late 2nd or early 1st century. The urging of an Egyptian celebration of Hanukkah communicates unity between Palestinian and Diaspora Judaism. Restoration and purification of the Temple held high symbolic value as expression of that unity. The letters do not represent an imperialist extension of authority by Jerusalem over the separatist sect of Onias. The concluding wish in the second epistle of a regathering of the faithful at the Holy Place may well articulate the sentiments of Oniad and Jerusalemite alike.

This idea finds support in the body of II Maccabees itself. The work, as is well known, places Jerusalem at the center and celebrates the exploits of Judas Maccabaeus, resolute champion of its cult.[90] At the same time, II Maccabees evinces great regard and admiration for Onias III. He emerges as a model of piety and righteousness, the upholder of ancient traditions against the machinations of Seleucid officials, a man of broad sympathies and unsullied reputa-

---

87 2 Macc. 1.7. Collins, *Between Athens and Jerusalem,* 78 – 9, rightly rejects the idea of the letters as anti-Oniad propaganda, but he believes nonetheless that the Oniads had estranged themselves from the Jerusalem Temple and that the festal letters endeavored to bring them back into the fold.

88 The consensus rests on an influential article by Bickermann, *ZNW,* 32 (1933), 233 – 54 = *Studies,* 2, 136 – 58.

89 The genuineness of the letter has been argued by Bunge, *Untersuchungen,* 32 – 55; Wacholder, *HUCA,* 49 (1978), 89 – 133; Th. Fischer, *Seleukiden und Makkabäer* (Bochum, 1980), 86 – 100; D. Flusser, in Gafni, Oppenheimer, and Schwartz, *Jews in Hellenistic-Roman World,* 55 – 82. But see Habicht, 2. *Makkabäerbuch,* 201; Goldstein, *II Maccabees,* 157 – 9.

90 For Doran, *Temple Propaganda, passim,* the Temple cult itself is the principal focus of the text. But see D.R. Schwartz, in M. Poorthuis and Ch. Safrai, *The Centrality of Jerusalem* (Kampen, Netherlands, 1996), 122 – 3.

tion. His assassination triggered the horrors that were about to befall the Jewish people.[91] The climax and conclusion of the book underscore the author's attitude most dramatically. On the eve of Judas' greatest victory, the culminating contest with Nicanor, a vision appeared in his dream. The figure of Onias himself, the very emblem of temperance and gentleness and the embodiment of the good life, materialized in the dream and introduced the aged prophet Jeremiah who extended to Judas a golden sword that would assure his triumph.[92] This striking passage pointedly denies any cleavage between the clan of the Oniads and the ruling dynasty of Judaea. II Maccabees was composed in the latter part of the 2nd century, at a time when the Hasmonaeans controlled the High Priesthood in the homeland and heirs of the Oniads held sway in Leontopolis. The message delivered by II Maccabees articulates a harmony of purpose. The two branches had a common commitment to Jewish unity.

Only sparse evidence survives for the later history of the Oniad temple,[93] But that remainder helps to confirm the above interpretation. Cleopatra III gained the advantage in the war with her son Ptolemy Lathyrus at the end of the 2nd century. Lathyrus had had to give up his gains in Judaea and withdraw from the land. The Hasmonaean High Priest Alexander Jannaeus, much relieved and restored to his holdings, sent gifts of gratitude to Cleopatra, on whose favor he now relied. The queen, however, with the advice of some of her counselors, contemplated invasion of the country herself, prepared to put it under Ptolemaic suzerainty. The plan might have been implemented but for the intervention of Ananias, the Jewish general who, together with Chelkias, had been a consistently loyal and successful commander for Cleopatra. Ananias advised the queen against invasion, pointing out the injustice of attacking an ally and, most importantly, declaring that an injustice done to the Jewish High Priest would make all Jews her enemies.[94] This is telling testimony. If Ananias was really the son of Onias IV, as Josephus states, his advice becomes all the more remarkable. It signals solidarity between the house of Onias and the Hasmonaean regime in

---

91 2 Macc. 3.1–5, 3.31–34, 4.1–6, 4.32–38.
92 2 Macc. 15.11–16.
93 See the summary of epigraphic testimony by D. Noy, in J.W. van Henten and P.W. van der Horst, *Studies in Early Jewish Epigraphy* (Leiden, 1994), 162–72. The texts are set out with translations and commentaries now by Horbury and Noy, *JIGRE*, 51–196 (#29-#115).
94 Jos. *A. J.* 13.352–354: οὐ γὰρ ἀγνοεῖν βούλομαί σε. φησίν. ὅτι τὸ πρὸς τοῦτον ἄδικον ἐχθροὺς ἅπαντας ἡμᾶς σοι τοὺς Ἰουδαίους καταστήσει. Cf. Stern, *Zion*, 50 (1985), 101–2 (Hebrew).

Jerusalem.[95] But even if the general comes from another clan of Egyptian Jews, his assertion of Jewish unanimity everywhere behind the High Priesthood carries real significance. It coheres with the rest of our evidence, denies any schismatic movement among Egyptian Jews, and affirms harmony between the homeland and the Diaspora.

One other piece of testimony can be brought into the reckoning. When Julius Caesar was besieged in Alexandria during the civil war in 48/7, a contingent of Jewish forces under Antipater made its way from Palestine to assist in his rescue. The troops were held up, however, in the "land of Onias," blocked by the Jews who dwelled there and prevented their progress. Antipater, however, appealed not only to their common kinship but, more significantly, to their allegiance to the High Priesthood. He displayed a letter from Hyrcanus II, High Priest in Jerusalem, who exhorted them to support Antipater's contingent and take the side of Caesar. The wish of the High Priest sufficed. Jews both in the Oniad district and in the vicinity of Memphis joined in the cause of Antipater.[96] The episode provides still one more instance of unquestioned loyalty by the inhabitants of Oniad land to the temple in Jerusalem.[97]

The favorable portrait conveyed in II Maccabees did not monopolize subsequent opinion. A less flattering depiction of the temple founder surfaced in later years. It found its way into Josephus' analysis which assigned somewhat disreputable motives for Onias' departure from Palestine and his religious shrine in Egypt—even reckoning Ptolemy's respect for Jewish traditions as more genuine than Onias' own. That ensuing generations may have had reason to question the Oniad achievement is plausible enough. Onias might seem in retrospect to have abandoned the Jewish cause in Palestine too hastily and prematurely. It was easy to manufacture selfish motives or to imagine a conflict with personal rivals. Disputes over the interpretation of the Deuteronomic text, analogous to those which embroiled the rabbis, may have surfaced by the time of Josephus.

---

95 For Ananias and Chelkias as sons of Onias, see Jos. *A. J.* 13.285 – 7. But his testimony is not decisive; see above, n. 51. Bohak, *Joseph and Aseneth*, 83 – 7, interprets Ananias' advice in terms of pragmatic calculation.

96 Jos. *A. J.* 14.127 – 132: καὶ οἱ μὲν ὡς ἑώρων τὸν Ἀντίπατρον καὶ τὸν ἀρχιερέα συνθέλοντας ὑπήκουον. A briefer version in Jos. *BJ* 1.190.

97 As is well known, Jews everywhere made regular contributions to the Temple in Jerusalem, a practice enjoined by Biblical prescription and widely attested; Exodus, 30.11 – 15; Philo, *Leg. ad Gaium*, 156 – 157, 216, 291, 311 – 316; Jos. *A. J.* 14.110, 16.166 – 171; Cic. *Pro Flacco*, 67; Tac. *Hist.* 5.5. Egyptian Jews were certainly no exception. The notion of S.L. Wallace, *Taxation in Egypt from Augustus to Diocletian* (Princeton, 1938), 174 – 5, that Jews in Egypt paid their tax to Onias' temple rather than to Jerusalem has no textual support and little probability; see E.M. Smallwood, *The Jews under Roman Rule from Pompey to Diocletian* (Leiden, 1981), 368.

Priestly attitudes in Jerusalem, perhaps reflected in the historian's analysis, could have contributed to the negative tradition on Onias. It does not follow, however, that critics at the time stigmatized Leontopolis as a schismatic sect that rejected the authority of Jerusalem.[98]

Dispute over Onias' reputation in posterity has also been read by scholars in variants that occur in the text of Isaiah. Onias cited a verse in Isaiah to justify the building of his temple: the prophet had foretold that a sanctuary to God would be raised in Egypt by a Jew.[99] The claim rests on Isaiah 19.19 which looks ahead to an altar of the Lord in the heart of Egypt. The expansion on that text which appears in Josephus, authorizing construction of the temple by a "Jewish man" may well derive from circles favorable to the Oniads. A similar inference has been made regarding the Septuagint version of Isaiah 19.18, the immediately preceding verse, which speaks of five cities in Egypt, one of which was to be called "City of Destruction"—so, at least, most of the manuscripts of the Massoretic text have it. The Septuagint preferred a positive rendition: "City of Righteousness," thus bringing the verse into line with Isaiah 1.26 and making it a mirror of Jerusalem. Translators of the Septuagint, on this view, altered the Biblical phrase in order to enhance the stature of Onias' foundation. Or, as an alternative hypothesis, the process can be reversed. Perhaps the Septuagint reflects an earlier reading of the Hebrew text, whereas the extant manuscripts incorporate an "anti-Oniad" revision.[100] In fact, the matter is more complicated and undermines confidence in simplistic speculation. Our earliest version of Isaiah, in a Qumran text, has "City of the Sun." If that is indeed the correct reading, Oniad apologists should have seized upon it as an obvious buttress for a sanctuary in Heliopolis.[101] The appearance of "City of Righteousness" in the Septuagint need have nothing to do with followers of the Oniads, nor the variant "City of

---

98 As we have seen, Josephus himself, who believed that Jews were prohibited from having more than one temple (Jos. *A. J.* 4.200–201; Jos. *C. Ap.* 2.193), did not attack Onias' institution on that score. The thesis of S.H. Steckoll, *Revue du Qumran*, 21 (1967), 55–69, that priests at Qumran came from the temple at Leontopolis, has been adequately refuted by Delcor, *RevBibl*, 75 (1968), 196–9, with a postscript by R. de Vaux, *loc. cit.*, 204–5.

99 Jos. *B. J.* 7.432; Jos. *A. J.* 13.64, 13.68.

100 On all this, see the discussions of G.B. Gray, *A Critical and Exegetical Commentary on Isaiah, I-XXVII*, I (Edinburgh, 1912), 332–9; Seeligmann, *The Septuagint Version of Isaiah*, 68; Luria, *Beit Miqra*, 31 (1967), 65–81 (Hebrew); Delcor, *RevBibl*, 75 (1968), 199–201; Bunge, *Untersuchungen*, 585–8; Hayward, *JJS*, 33 (1982), 438–41; Bohak, *Joseph and Aseneth*, 22–3, 90–1.

101 Acutely noted by Murray, *JTS*, 18-(1967), 365, n. 1. The text is IQ Isᵃ.

Destruction" with their opponents. The notion of a tug of war between pro and anti-Leontopolis propaganda has bedevilled scholarship for too long.[102]

The temple in Heliopolis deserves a better press than it has received in the pages of Josephus. The historian's tendentious presentation clouds our vision of the founder, date, and motive for the new sanctuary. Neither the circumstances nor the consequences of its creation suggest that it represented defiance of the Temple in Jerusalem. Chronology remains murky. The specific occasion of Onias' exit from Palestine eludes our grasp. It may indeed have come shortly after the assassination of his father in 172, a murder engineered by Menelaus and his Seleucid supporters. The life of young Onias could well have been in danger, and a precipitate departure quite intelligible. Insofar as it was an act of rejection, it rejected the current occupant of the High Priesthood and the Seleucid regime—but not the authority of the Temple. Construction of a shrine in the Heliopolite nome came at an unspecified later time, after some years in Alexandria and, presumably, a process of maturation by Onias. The situation in Judaea had altered markedly by then. Judas Maccabaeus' recapture and purification of the Temple had not resolved the situation. A Seleucid garrison remained in the Akra, Seleucid influence still permeated the land of Palestine, an appointee of the king took over as High Priest, and the Maccabaean movement resolved itself into warfare with neighboring peoples and periodic compromises with Hellenistic princes. A lesser replica of the Jerusalem Temple in the Heliopolite nome would provide a center of worship for pious Jews in Egypt for whom the fate of their homeland must have seemed to be in grave jeopardy. A new temple would serve as a beacon announcing that the faith remained alive and strong.[103]

---

102 Murray, *JTS*, 18 (1967), 365 – 6, unfortunately, also falls prey to this tendency, labeling the different accounts in Josephus as "pro-Leontopolis" or "anti-Leontopolis," depending upon whether they identify Onias III or Onias IV as founder. Cf. also Beek, *Oudtestamentische Studiën*, 2 (1943), 121 – 5. Bunge, *Untersuchungen*, 589 – 94, reckons every reference to Heliopolis or "On" in the Septuagint as representing polemic against the temple of Onias—an extreme position. Reference to the sanctuary at Leontopolis has also been found in the fifth book of the Sibylline Oracles, 501 – 503, compiled probably in the early 2nd century C.E. The verses speak of a great holy temple in Egypt whose residents are sanctioned by God and who sacrifice to him there. If this is meant to signify Leontopolis, it is a most favorable allusion. But the author may simply be elaborating upon Isaiah 19.19; cf. J. Geffcken, *Komposition und Entstehungszeit der Oracula Sibyllina* (Leipzig, 1902), 26.

103 One can, of course, raise the question of why Heliopolis and not Alexandria. Cf. Tcherikover, *Hellenistic Civilization and the Jews*, 277 – 8. But the decision need not have been Onias's. It is appropriate to recall that permission was needed from Ptolemy. And Ptolemy may well have

When might such an event have taken place? A novel postulate perhaps deserves consideration: some time between 159 and 152, when the High Priesthood stood vacant in Jerusalem.[104] Leontopolis would thereby carry the message that religious continuity remained despite upheavals in the homeland. The house of Onias directed its defiance to the enemies of the Jews, not to Jerusalem. Nor would the conferral of the High Priesthood upon Jonathan in 152 deprive the Egyptian sanctuary of its *raison d'être*. Onias indeed very likely avoided the title of High Priest in Egypt, thus to shun even ostensible conflict.[105] The symbolic significance had greater force than any personal advantage for Onias. A common purpose between Hasmonaeans and Oniads received evocative expression in II Maccabees. And unity of the faith had practical application as well: in the advice of Ananias to Cleopatra III, and in the allegiance of Egyptian Jews to the High Priesthood at the time of Julius Caesar. The Jewish sanctuary in Egypt was a reinforcement, not a rival, of Jerusalem.[106]

---

preferred a Jewish center remote from the capital, where it would not upset the Alexandrian Greeks.

104 1 Macc. 9.54, 10.21; Jos. *A. J.* 20.237, Josephus' contradictory notices that Judas was named High Priest upon the death of Alcimus (Jos. *A. J.* 12.413–414, 12.419, 12.434) are plainly false. Judas, in fact, died before Alcimus; 1 Macc. 9.54–56. The thesis of H. Stegemann, *Die Entstehung der Qumrangemeinde* (Bonn, 1971), 210–25, followed by Bunge, *JSJ,* 6 (1975), 27–8, 43–7, argues that there was no *interregnum*. He contends that the "Teacher of Righteousness" who appears in the Qumran texts held the High Priesthood until ousted by Jonathan. The conjecture has little to recommend it. See the refutation by H. Burgmann, *JSJ,* 11 (1980), 135–76; cf. J. Sievers, *The Hasmoneans and their Supporters* (Atlanta, 1990), 75–7.

105 Such a possibility has never been considered by modern scholars. Yet the evidence points in that direction. Only in his summary of the roster of High Priests at the end of the *Antiquitates* does Josephus say that Onias asked Philometor and Cleopatra to name him High Priest; Jos. *A. J.* 20.236. There is no hint of that in his narratives of events. Indeed, Josephus elsewhere has Onias appoint others to minister to the cult in Heliopolis; Jos. *A. J.* 13.63, 13.73.

106 Despite numerous differences in interpretation, this paper has gained much profit from correspondence with and from the fine study of G. Bohak, *Joseph and Aseneth and the Jewish Temple in Heliopolis* (Atlanta, 1996). Analysis of the Talmudic texts owes a debt to consultations with Professor Daniel Boyarin. A valuable conversation with Daniel Stoekl resulted in some salutary changes. The acute suggestions of referees for *SCI* prompted additional improvements—which is not to say that they will now concur with the conclusions. Most important, the meticulous reading (more than once) and the incisive advice of Professor Daniel Schwartz deserve special commendation.

17. Herod, Rome, and the Diaspora

The Roman Empire in the Near East at the time of Augustus was a patchwork rather than a system. It constituted not so much an organized structure as a circuitry of relationships and dependencies. The influence of Rome manifested itself most conspicuously in provinces and governors. But that was only part of the grid. An intricate set of associations was also held with what we conventionally term "client kings". The institution was malleable and fluid, a matter of mutual interest. No formal duties, no uniform constitutional principles underpinned the responsibilities of the parties to such arrangements. Only conventional practices, still in process of evolution in the Augustan Age, linked a number of rulers, especially in the east, to Roman hegemony.[1] In this nebulous network, Herod has served as chief exemplar. Modern reconstructions regularly depict him as the quintessential instance of the client king, a loyal and trustworthy satellite of empire.[2] The assessment can benefit from further scrutiny.

One item deserves notice before proceeding. The phrase "client king" is almost never employed by the Romans—let alone, by the kings. Customary usage took a much more polite form: *socius et amicus populi Romani* (ally and friend of

---

1 Some scholars have endeavored to set "client kingship" into a constitutional frame, with common features and prescribed obligations; see, e.g., E. Schürer *The History of the Jewish People in the Age of Jesus Christ*, vol. I (rev. and ed. by G. Vermes and F. Millar, Edinburgh: T. and T. Clark, 1973), 316–7; U. Baumann *Rom und die Juden* (Frankfurt: Peter Lang, 1983), 228–37; A. Schalit *König Herodes: der Mann und sein Werk* (Berlin: De Gruyter, 2001, first published 1969), 155–67. D.C. Braund "Client Kings," in D. C. Braund, ed. *The Administration of the Roman Empire* (Exeter: University of Exeter Press, 1988), 69–78 properly advocates a more flexible understanding. The statements of Suetonius (*Aug.* 48, 60) delivered from the distant perspective of the High Empire under Hadrian, envision a tighter set of interconnections in the Augustan age than the evidence would support.
2 M. Grant *Herod the Great* (New York: American Heritage Press, 1971), 11, 94–7, 225–6; Schürer *The History of the Jewish People*, 316–20; E.M. Smallwood *The Jews under Roman Rule* (Leiden: E. J. Brill, 1976), 82–90; Baumann *Rom und die Juden*, 228–37; P. Richardson *Herod: King of the Jews and Friend of the Romans* (Columbia, South Carolina: University of South Carolina Press, 1996), 226–34; J. Geiger "Herodes *Philorhomaios*," *Ancient Society*, 28 (1997), 75–88; Schalit *König Herodes*, 154–67, 421–24, 554–62. D.C. Braund *Rome and the Friendly King: The Character of Client Kingship* (Beckenham, Kent: Groom Helm, 1984), 136–44, 182–3 applies the Roman concept of *tutela*. See also D.M. Jacobson "Three Roman Client Kings: Herod of Judaea, Archelaus of Cappadocia and Juba of Mauretania," *Palestine Exploration Quarterly*, 133 (2001), 22–7, who makes useful comparisons with Archelaus of Cappadocia and Juba of Mauretania.

the Roman people).[3] Some kings did refer to themselves as *philorhomaioi*. But this need signify nothing more than the reciprocal response to the label *amicus populi Romani*.[4] The eastern rulers gained great advantage from association with the western power. But they did not normally represent themselves (nor consider themselves) as mere lackeys of Rome.

Herod, the ruler of whom we know most, had numerous constituencies to take into account. Within Judaea alone sectarian divisions could complicate matters. Pharisees, Sadducees, and Essenes had their own agendas. The Hasmonaean legacy—and indeed the surviving members of the Hasmonaean dynasty —added further complications. And the wider Herod's kingdom became, the more multi-ethnic were the communities that had a place in his realm. The king had to walk a fine line. The goodwill and, occasionally, the material and military resources of Rome played a critical role in Herod's acquisition and maintenance of authority. He could not and would not cross the western power. Yet to be perceived as a Roman puppet carried its own hazards. It might foster resentment and discord at home from subordinates for whom too tight an embrace by Rome was less than fully welcome. Contemporary circumstances suffice to remind us of that form of dilemma. A number of current rulers or leaders need to walk a comparable fine line between dependency upon American power on the one hand and reassurances to diverse constituencies on the other that they do not take orders from the U.S.

Herod had his problems in this regard. One need refer only to the incident of the trophies. The theatre or amphitheatre built by Herod in Jerusalem contained a number of inscriptions honoring Augustus and trophies seized from various foes that attested to the *princeps'* victories. This struck some of Herod's subjects as undesirable, indeed intolerable. They convinced themselves—or at least claimed—that the trophies concealed images to be worshipped. The idea that some form of homage to the Emperor as divinity might be introduced into Jerusalem naturally provoked alarm. Herod's attempts to set the minds of the objectors at rest proved unavailing. The king had to order the trophies stripped of decoration to show that they contained nothing but bare wood and could house no images. This appeased most of those who were angry and even provoked some laughter—perhaps at Herod's expense. But a number of die-hards remained ob-

---

3 P.C. Sands *The Client Princes of the Roman Empire under the Republic* (Cambridge: Cambridge University Press, 1908), 10–40; M.R. Cimma *Reges Socii et Amid Populi Romani* (Milan: A. Giuffrè, 1976), 21–32; Braund *Rome and the Friendly King*, 22–37. J. Richardson *Roman Provincial Administration, 227 BC to AD 117* (London: Macmillan, 1976), 13 wrongly states that the rulers were called client kings.

4 Cf. Braund *Rome and the Friendly King*, 105–7.

durate. Ten of them plotted to assassinate Herod, thwarted only by an informer. And, although the conspirators were executed by the government, the informer himself was torn limb from limb by private parties, in an act witnessed by numerous Judaeans who did not disapprove.[5] Passions plainly ran high. Herod's links to Roman power stirred fierce hostility in some quarters. Whatever Herod's intent here, he obviously faced the ire of many in Jerusalem who found that his cozying up to the emperor had become unendurable and had violated traditional practices and principles.

More dramatic still was the episode of the golden eagle on a gate of the Temple. How long it had sat on that site remains unknown. But near the end of Herod's life, when illness had severely debilitated him, his foes used it to demonstrate against the weakened king. A group of young men, prodded by their learned teachers, pulled down the massive eagle and chopped it to bits. Herod, surprisingly, recovered from what had been thought to be his deathbed, sent out an armed force to disperse the crowd and arrest the perpetrators, and had them executed, some of them burned alive.[6] The ferocity of the response points once again to deep-rooted bitterness among certain circles. Whether or not Herod had actually violated religious prohibitions, Jewish sensitivities clearly expressed themselves here.[7] And it is no accident that the golden eagle was perceived as emblematic of Roman power.[8]

Perceptions mattered. Herod had to engage in some fancy footwork. He needed the backing of Augustus, to be sure, as he had that of Antonius before him. And he did not hesitate to advertise that backing. But it risked offence and diminishment to be judged simply as an instrument of Rome. Relationship with the Romans carried inherent complexities that resist reductionism. The patron-client concept is inadequate as a characterization, and perhaps even misleading. Mutual manipulation comes closer to the mark. Herod strove to present himself as Rome's collaborator, not its agent. He had a broader image to project: that of a ruler in command of his own realm—and a figure of genuinely international stature.

---

5 Jos. *A. J.* 15.272 – 91. The precise date of this event is unknown.
6 Jos. *B. J.* 1.648 – 55; Jos. *A. J.* 17.149 – 67.
7 P. Richardson *Herod: King of the Jews and Friend of the Romans*, 15 – 8, somewhat minimizes this event; similarly, Schalit 2001, 638.
8 Smallwood *The Jews under Roman Rule*, 99. Cf. Schalit *König Herodes*, 734, who also finds Jewish connections for the eagle; and see now G. Fuks "Josephus on Herod's Attitude towards Jewish Religion: The Darker Side," *Journal of Jewish Studies* 53, (2002), 241 – 2.

Herod's extraordinary building program in his own kingdom has received much attention and scrutiny.[9] The plethora of palaces, fortresses, religious structures, theatres, amphitheaters, gymnasia, hippodromes, and even cities to Herod's credit is quite staggering. They drew on a combination of influences: Hellenistic, Hasmonaean, Roman, and, indeed, Augustan.[10] To what degree Herod's subjects could actually discern these refined architectural distinctions and ascertain their political and cultural implications we may well question. The subtle messages detected by scholars may not always have reached the consciousness of the inhabitants of Palestine. But they did not miss the import of names applied to the structures by Herod. The fortress that Herod reconstructed as protection for the Temple in Jerusalem was named Antonia, after M. Antonius (Jos. *B. J.* 1.401; Jos. *A. J.* 15.292, 15.409). The king also restored a Hasmonaean palace in Jericho, with the addition of new structures. He made a point of naming the two new buildings after Augustus and Agrippa (Jos. *B. J.* 1.331, 407). In his own palace in Jerusalem, Herod erected two large and handsome structures also named for Augustus and Agrippa respectively (Jos. *B. J.* 1.402; Jos. *A. J.* 15.318). Even more conspicuously, Herod rebuilt the ancient city of Samaria, transformed it as a new settlement, and renamed it Sebaste (Jos. *B. J.* 1.403; Jos. *A. J.* 15.292, 296–8), in honour of Augustus (*Sebastos*). And, of course, at the site of Straton's tower on the Mediterranean coast, Herod erected his magnificent city and harbor, now to be designated as Caesarea, echoing the name of Caesar Augustus.[11] The king went further still. He ordered the construction of temples to Roma and Augustus in his new foundations at Sebaste and Caesarea (Jos. *B. J.* 1.403, 414; Jos. *A. J.* 15.298, 339). And he added a third one near the sources of the Jordan in the region of the Paneion dedicated to the pagan deity Pan.[12]

---

9 A convenient catalogue of the buildings can be found in P. Richardson *Herod: King of the Jews and Friend of the Romans*, 197–202. See further the studies of the building program by D.W. Roller *The Building Program of Herod the Great* (Berkeley: University of California Press, 1998), 76–124 and A. Lichtenberger *Die Baupolitik Herodes des Grossen* (Wiesbaden: Harrassowitz = Abhandlungen des deutschen Palästina-Vereins, 26, 1999), 17–175.
10 For the influences on Herod's architectural works, see Roller *The Building Program of Herod the Great*, 85–119, who stresses the impact of Roman forms and institutions. See also Geiger "Herodes *Philorhomaios*," 80–5, with additional bibliography.
11 Jos. *B. J.* 1.156, 408–14; Jos. *A. J.* 14.76; 15.293; 15.331–2. According to Suetonius *Aug.* 60, this was standard procedure among kings who were friends and allies of Rome.
12 Jos. *B. J.* 1.404; Jos. *A. J.* 15.363–4. See the valuable discussion of J.F. Wilson *Caesarea Philippi: Banias, the Lost City of Pan* (London: I. B. Tauris, 2004), 9–16, who sees the temple as part of Herod's effort to appeal to local non-Jewish populations in his kingdom.

To what do we attribute this flurry of activity? Acts of homage, piety, and allegiance to his patrons in Rome?[13] Perhaps so. But that misplaces the emphasis. How much notice was Augustus likely to pay to these moves by the ruler of a distant and minor principality? It is notorious that the *princeps* in his autobiographical memoir, the *Res Gestae*, while taking note of numerous cities, states, peoples, and monarchs, never once mentions Judaea, the Jews, or Herod. Augustus received divine homage abroad but had no policy of actively encouraging public worship or promoting what we call the "Imperial Cult" in the East.[14] Hence, as a means of currying favor with the emperor, Herod's actions would have had limited value. The fact that Herod renamed cities for Augustus was unlikely to have had much impact in Rome—not to mention buildings or parts of buildings carrying the names of Augustus or Agrippa.[15]

The impact came at home. The gleaming new cities, temples, and structures with the names of Roman leaders advertised to his subjects Herod's links to the great colossus in the west. Internal turmoil, sectarian discontents, and widespread hostility to the regime motivated the king to exhibit those links. By parading his association with Roman authority and asserting the favor of Augustus and his family Herod shaped his message primarily for internal consumption. Herod projected himself less as client of Rome than as benefactor. The structures that rose in Jerusalem and elsewhere in his realm put on display the wealth and resources of the king, as well as his ties to the rulers of the Mediterranean who stood behind him.

Similar purposes held for the other major building projects in the land. Herod, as is well known, produced a proliferation of palaces. They emerged in

---

13 Baumann *Rom und die Juden*, 201 – 5; Geiger "Herodes *Philorhomaios*," 79 – 80; Lichtenberger *Die Baupolitik Herodes des Grossen*, 91 – 2, 152 – 3, 186 – 7.

14 He could also place certain restraints upon divinization and state cults where appropriate (Suet., *Aug.* 52; Dio 51.20.7 – 9); cf. I. Gradel *Emperor Worship and Roman Religion* (Oxford: Oxford University Press, 2002), 109 – 16. This did not, of course, prevent local and regional authorities, especially in the east, from conferring divine honors upon Augustus; cf. S. Price *Rituals and Power: The Roman Imperial Cult in Asia Minor* (Cambridge: Cambridge University Press, 1984), 54 – 62. See the lengthy catalogue of sites, with texts and discussion, by H. Hänlein-Schäfer *Veneratio Augusti: Eine Studie zu den Tempeln des ersten römischen Kaisers* (Rome: Georgio Brettschneider, 1985), 113 – 265.

15 Agrippa, we are told, was mightily impressed by the Temple in Jerusalem and by structures built elsewhere in Palestine by Herod (Philo, *Legat.* 295; Jos. *A. J.* 16.12 – 15). But this came in the course of Agrippa's trip to the region, a visit carefully scripted by Herod—see below. The one notice of Augustus' interest occurs in Josephus' report that he and Livia provided a handsome sum to help finance the games held to celebrate completion of work on Caesarea (Jos. *A. J.* 16.138 – 9). This, of course, carried greater significance for Herod than for Augustus.

Jerusalem, Masada, Jericho, Herodion, Caesarea, and Sepphoris.[16] It is improbable in the extreme that the king required all of these edifices for his own creature comforts or those of his family. He could not have had enough vacation time to make much use of all these facilities. But they certainly served to publicize his riches, grandeur, and authority, a means of overawing his restive subjects. One can say much the same about the fortresses that Herod installed in a variety of places in his dominions: at the Temple in Jerusalem, on the walls of the city, in Masada, and at Herodion, Sebaste, and Caesarea.[17] As a means to ward off foreign foes in defence of the land, they would not have been mightily effective. And what foreign foes did Herod really have to worry about? The Parthian menace had faded after defeats by M. Antonius's generals in the early 30s B.C.E., and certainly after Augustus' recovery of the military standards in a peaceful exchange in 20 B.C.E.[18] Relations with the Nabataeans, though strained, did not usually issue in hostilities and, when they did, Herod tended to be the aggressor.[19] The fortresses were not needed to defend the land from external enemies. They served primarily to intimidate Herod's internal adversaries. The exhibition of affluence and possessions could dismay potential rivals.[20] Herod's building projects, of course, provided employment for those who might otherwise be unhappy with the regime. The king kept his eye trained upon his own subjects.

---

16 See the discussions of P. Richardson *Herod*, 179–183; Roller *The Building Program of Herod*, 140, 164–8, 171–3, 176, 187–9, 212–3; Lichtenberger 1999, 23–34, 56–68, 93–112, 122–124, 162; Schalit *König Herodes*, 344–58, 371–2, 397–403; E. Netzer *The Palaces of the Hasmoneans and Herod the Great* (Jerusalem: Yad Ben-Zvi Press, 2001), 40–61, 117–22.

17 Roller *The Building Program of Herod*, 143, 166–7, 175–6, 179–81, 187–90; Lichtenberger *Die Baupolitik Herodes*, 21–39, 80–92, 99–112, 131–42; Schalit *König Herodes*, 328–97; Netzer *The Palaces of the Hasmoneans*, 79–116.

18 On Rome and Parthia in this period, see K.–H. Ziegler *Die Beziehungen zwischen Rom und dem Partherreich* (Wiesbaden: Franz Steiner, 1964), 45–57; B. Campbell "War and Diplomacy: Rome and Parthia, 31 BC–AD 235," in J. Rich and G. Shipley, eds. *War and Society in the Roman World* (London: Routledge, 1993), 220–8.

19 On Herod's relations with the Nabataeans, see G.W. Bowersock *Roman Arabia* (Cambridge, Mass.: Harvard University Press, 1983), 39–44, 49–53; J. Retsö *The Arabs in Antiquity: Their History from the Assyrians to the Umayyads* London: Routledge, 2003), 372–5.

20 Cf. Jos. *A. J.* 15.330. The sources of Herod's wealth remain a matter of speculation; see A. Momigliano *Giudea Romano* (Amsterdam: Hakkert, 1967, first published 1934), 41–52; E. Netzer "Herod's Building Program: State Necessity or Personal Need?" *Jerusalem Cathedra*, 1 (1981), 484–61; E. Gabba "The Finances of King Herod," in A. Kasher, U. Rappaport and G. Fuks, eds. *Greece and Rome in Eretz Israel* (Jerusalem, 1990), 160–8; J. Pastor "Herod: King of Jews and Gentiles: Economic Policy as a Measure of Evenhandedness," in M. Mor et al., eds. *Jews and Gentiles in the Holy Land* (Jerusalem, Yad Ben-Zvi Press, 2003), 152–64.

Herod preferred to be perceived as Rome's partner in the Near East rather than its client. The stature afforded by displaying connections to Rome demonstrated that he was a player on the international stage. That aspect of Herod's image deserves emphasis. How did it play but in the countless communities of Jews scattered in the Mediterranean Diaspora? They would seem to be obvious constituents before whom Herod could exhibit his largesse and liberality. For many scholars indeed, Herod's stance as champion of Diaspora Jews exemplifies his posture as international figure.[21] The proposition, however, needs serious re-examination.

A connection among Rome, the Judaean ruler, and the Jews of the Diaspora is, on the face of it, logical and mutually beneficial. It goes back to the time of Julius Caesar. A series of decrees recorded by Josephus granted prestige and authority to Hyrcanus II, the Jewish High Priest who had aided the Caesarian cause in the wars of Alexandria and Asia Minor. Caesar's edicts in 47 B.C.E. confirmed Hyrcanus as High Priest and added the title of Ethnarch. More importantly, they named him and his future offspring as "Ethnarchs of the Jews" and "High Priests of the Jews" (Jos. *A. J.* 14.194). The phraseology plainly indicates more than mere territorial dominion. Hyrcanus had authorization to hold sway not simply in Judaea but over Jews in general. A subsequent *senatus consultum* reasserted his status. It ratified Caesar's edict and declared that Hyrcanus and his children should rule over the *ethnos* of the Jews and serve as protector of Jews who suffered injustice (Jos. *A. J.* 14. 196). The measures evidently endorsed Hyrcanus' ascendancy in the Diaspora.[22] And Hyrcanus was not slow to act on this endorsement. He interceded with Roman authorities on behalf of Jews in the cities of Asia Minor to reaffirm their rights and privileges in the communities in which they dwelled (Jos. *A. J.* 14.223–4, 241–3). Caesar's generosity, we may be sure, came not altogether out of gratitude or magnanimity. The Roman dictator, still engaged in a contest with the sons and followers of Pompey, would benefit from an ally who had responsibility for a people scattered through the eastern Mediterranean. The Judaean leader's foothold in the Diaspora would be a source of support and stability.

---

21 Grant *Herod the Great*, 175–82; Schürer *The History of the Jewish People*, 319; Smallwood *The Jews under Roman Rule*, 82; P. Richardson *Herod*, 264–6, 270–2; L. Levine *Judaism and Hellenism in Antiquity* (Seattle: University of Washington Press, 1998), 51–4; S. Schwartz *Imperialism and Jewish Society 200 BCE to 640 CE* (Princeton: Princeton University Press, 2001), 46.
22 M. Pucci Ben Zeev *Jewish Rights in the Roman World: The Greek and Roman Documents Quoted by Josephus Flavius* (Tübingen: Mohr Siebeck, 1998), 49–50, 65–6, with bibliography; E.S. Gruen *Diaspora: Jews Amidst Greeks and Romans* (Cambridge, Mass.: Harvard University Press, 2002), 88–9; cf. Jos. *A. J.* 14.199.

It could also supply a prototype for Herod. An episode of very high profile stands as the chief exhibit. In the year 15 B.C.E.; M. Agrippa, son-in-law and chief confidante of Augustus, took a trip to the east to oversee affairs in that region. Herod immediately seized the opportunity to meet him *en route* and invite him to his kingdom. There Herod gave Agrippa the grand tour, showing off the recently founded cities and the spanking new buildings at Sebaste, Caesarea, and elsewhere. The highlight, of course, took place in Jerusalem itself where Herod paraded Agrippa before the assembled populace, dressed in his finery and greeted with great applause. The Roman leader concluded with a conspicuously magnanimous gesture: he sacrificed a hecatomb to the Jewish god and hosted a feast for the people of Jerusalem (Jos. *A. J.* 16.12–5; Philo, *Legat.* 295).

Careful orchestration had doubtless preceded this whole set of events. Agrippa's endorsement of Herod shored up a ruler who could be a source of strength and security for the Near East. And Herod's ostentatious pageant aimed to portray that collaborative relationship with Rome that could entrench and perpetuate his own power at home. Reciprocal benefits, not a patron-client relationship, held centre stage.

The episode that came on the heels of this visit, though not as showy, carries even greater import. The account in Josephus this time suggests less orchestration than improvisation. Agrippa had sailed back to Ionia before the onset of winter, 15/14 B.C.E., to prepare for an expedition to the Bosporus. When spring arrived in 14, Herod raced to catch up with Agrippa, finally reaching him in Pontus (Jos. *A. J.* 16.16–26). The king made a point of accompanying Agrippa in work and in relaxation, regularly at his side and a conspicuous associate as they wended their way through Anatolia. Herod projected himself as a significant benefactor to the cities through which he passed, and prompted Agrippa to comparable generosity. There followed the most telling event, evidently unplanned. A large number of Jews arrived from Ionia to seek assistance from this beneficent duo. They complained of various indignities suffered and restraints imposed upon them by cities of Ionia in violation of Roman guarantees of their privileges. Herod swiftly took up their cause. Agrippa agreed to hold a hearing together with his *consilium* that included a number of kings and dynasts who happened to be present (Jos. *A. J.* 16. 27–30). Herod asked his counsellor and friend, Nicolaus of Damascus, to deliver a speech on behalf of the Ionian Jews, a speech obviously included in Nicolaus' work and transmitted by Josephus. How closely it adhered to what was actually said we cannot know.[23] The version we have, in any case,

---

23 Many take the speech as a genuine reflection of Nicolaus' words [B.Z. Wacholder *Nicolaus of Damascus* (Berkeley: University of California Press, 1962), 28–9; J.-M. Roddaz *Marcus Agrippa*

waxed eloquent on the virtues of the Jews, their unstinting loyalty and gratitude to Rome, their unjust victimization, and the services performed for Rome by both Herod and his father Antipater before him (Jos. *A. J.* 16.30 – 57).[24] Agrippa's verdict was unequivocal. He granted everything that the Jewish petitioners and their spokesman requested. Moreover and more strikingly, he asserted that he did so because of Herod's goodwill and friendship towards him. A final flourish then followed. Herod and Agrippa embraced publicly, and the Roman *imperator* did so in a fashion to suggest that the two of them were on an equal level (Jos. *A. J.* 16.60 – 1)—a most striking gesture. Herod then returned to Jerusalem in an exultant mood. He summoned all the inhabitants of the city, and a large number from the countryside joined them. He laid out the tale of the entire trip to them, noting in particular his role in protecting the prerogatives of the Jews in Asia Minor. And just to underscore his generosity, Herod announced a remission of one quarter of the citizens' taxes for that year (Jos. *A. J.* 16.62– 5).

This arresting sequence of events harmonizes nicely with the posturing of Herod that we have already seen elsewhere. The king underscored his association with the Roman regime. And he directed the message once again primarily to the inhabitants of his own realm. Equally significant, the representation took the form of a collaborative endeavor, not a patron-client relationship. Agrippa conspicuously embraced Herod as an equal. By claiming that his favorable verdict was due to Herod's intervention, he gave the patronage honors essentially to the king of the Jews.[25]

The meaning of these gestures requires close analysis. Do they signify that Herod fostered the image not only of powerful ruler in Palestine, with international connections, but of patron, protector, and champion of Diaspora Jews everywhere? So it is often stated.[26] Yet the evidence will not easily bear the weight of that conclusion. Where else do we have testimony to Herod's solicitude for Diaspora Jews? The episode in Ionia stands out as exceptional rather than exemplary. It served Herod's purpose, not as a signal to Jews dwelling in gentile com-

---

(Rome: École Française de Rome, 1984), 458; J.M.G. Barclay *Jews in the Mediterranean Diaspora from Alexander to Trajan (323 BCE– 117 CE)* (Edinburgh: T. and T. Clark, 1996), 268 – 9.] Proper skepticism in M. Stern *Greek and Latin Authors on Jews and Judaism* (Jerusalem: The Israel Academy of Sciences and Humanities, 1976), I, 231 – 2.

24 On the ideological underpinnings here, see Schalit *König Herodes*, 424 – 50.

25 On Roman motivations here, see Gruen *Diaspora*, 96 – 100.

26 Grant *Herod the Great*, 178 – 82; Smallwood *The Jews under Roman Rule*, 82, 140 – 1; P. Richardson *Herod*, 270 – 2. Schalit *König Herodes*, 424 – 8 sees Herod's posture as buying into a broader Roman framework of patronage of the *oikoumene*.

munities outside the land of Palestine but as a mark of the king's authority and connections in order to make a point to the folks at home.

Herod, to be sure, was active and energetic in distributing benefits abroad. Indeed that activity constituted an elaborate advertisement of his resources and his magnanimity on the international stage. But the benefactions fell upon gentile communities and in the form of gentile institutions. One can cite examples large in number and extensive in geography. In Phoenicia and Syria Herod made ostentatious, gifts to the cities of Antioch, Damascus, and Laodicea, to Tyre, Sidon, Beirut, Byblos, Tripolis, and Ptolemais.[27] To be sure, there were Jews living in all these cities. But the contributions provided by Herod were certainly not earmarked for them. They included gymnasia, temples, theatres and aqueducts. Antioch, we are told, received marble paving and colonnades for its main street, thus notably enhancing its appearance (Jos. *B. J.* 1.425; Jos. *A. J.*16.148). Undoubtedly the Jews of Antioch could enjoy strolling on that street. But it was hardly built with them primarily in mind. At Rhodes Herod paid out of his own pocket to restore the damaged temple of Apollo and rebuild it on a grander scale (Jos. *B. J.* 1.424; Jos. *A. J.* 14.378; 16.147). At Elis in the Peloponnesus he made the grandiose gesture of a handsome endowment for the Olympic Games that had fallen into arrears. As a consequence he received the signal honor of being named as president of the games (Jos. *B. J.* 1.426–7; Jos. *A. J.* 16.149). That gesture plainly spoke to the deepest traditions of the Hellenic world. If there were Jews of any number in the city of Elis we certainly do not know of them. Herod awarded gifts, endowments, or tax relief to a range of communities. These included places in Cilicia, Lycia, and every district of Ionia (Jos. *B. J.* 1.425, 428; Jos. *A. J.* 16.24); also the great Hellenistic city of Pergamum, and the Aegean islands of Cos, Chios, and Samos.[28] And Herod made sure to embellish celebrated Greek cities with the most glorious of pasts, Athens and Sparta (Jos. *B. J.* 1.425). The wealth and generosity of Herod held high profile in all of this.[29] But gymnasia, temples, porticoes, not to mention Olympic Games, carried only marginal appeal to most Diaspora Jews.

Herod went further. He took on the task of constructing most of the public buildings at Nicopolis, the city founded to commemorate Augustus' victory at Ac-

---

27 Jos. *B. J.* 1.422. Note also the significant benefactions to Ascalon mentioned, here, which in the view of N. Kokkinos *The Herodian Dynasty: Origins, Role in Society and Eclipse* (Sheffield: Sheffield Academic Press, 1998), 112–28 underscore a close connection between that city and the family of Herod.
28 Pergamum (Jos. *B. J.* 1.425); Cos, Chios and Samos (Jos. *B. J.* 1.423, 425; Jos. *A. J.* 16.18–9, 26).
29 See the discussion of Lichtenberger *Die Baupolitik Herodes*, 168–175.

tium (Jos. *B. J.* 1.425; Jos. *A. J.* 16.137). This gave broad publicity to Herod's close link to the Augustan regime.[30] But, equally important, it proclaimed the vast wealth and bounteous generosity of the Jewish king. There were, of course, no Diaspora Jews dwelling in Nicopolis. In addition to the evidence of Josephus, a number of fragmentary inscriptions attest to dedications by Herod or honors paid to him for his benefactions in Athens and Delos, even a statue of Herod dedicated at the Nabataean temple of Ba'al Shamim at Sia in southern Syria.[31]

The king had a tightrope to walk on this score as well. Lavish bounty outside his own dominions could dismay the denizens of Judaea. Josephus describes the dilemma. He has Herod explain himself to Jews at home by claiming the directives of Rome, while professing to the Romans that he preferred to honor them than to adhere to his own native traditions (Jos. *A. J.* 15.328–30). The protestations were disingenuous on both fronts. They illustrate the repeated need to present different faces to different constituencies. But Diaspora Jews held little interest for the king.

Herod's action on behalf of the Jews of Ionia was altogether atypical. It can hardly count as a defining moment for Herodian policy. Herod may have been a great sponsor of pagan temples, theatres, amphitheatres, gymnasia, and civic structures. But we have no reference to him building, endowing, or furnishing a synagogue anywhere in the Diaspora. The episode in Ionia appears to have been an *ad hoc* event, unplanned and unprepared for. The Jews of Ionia brought their grievances to Agrippa, the emperor's representative, not to Herod. The king simply happened to be there, taking the part of Agrippa's companion and counsellor. Naturally he seized the occasion, urging Agrippa to give them a hearing, and he advocated their cause.[32] But one needs to bear in mind (what is generally overlooked) that Herod had been playing that sort of role all along on the trip with Agrippa. He not only showered benefactions upon various cities at which he stopped during that voyage. He also made a point of prodding Agrippa into hearing the petitions and granting the wishes of those who sought his favors (Jos. *A. J.* 16.24–5). So, for example, Herod smoothed relations between Agrippa and the people of Ilium with whom he had become angry, while he relieved the Chians by settling their debts and releasing them from tribute payments (Jos. *A. J.* 16.26). The Ionian Jews, in other words, did not receive special attention. And it is worth noting that the long speech of Nicolaus of Damascus, while it stresses

---

30 Cf. Braund *Rome and the Friendly King*, 77.
31 *OGIS*, 414, 415, 427; *SEG*, 12.150.
32 Jos. *A. J.* 16.29–30. Cf. Braund *Rome and the Friendly King*, 82.

the good deeds performed by Herod's family for Rome and the house of Augustus, makes no mention of the king as champion of Diaspora Jews.

Herod's principal posture needs to be seen in a different light. He shunned the perception of a toady of Rome. That he was a friend of Augustus and supported by Roman power was, of course, vital. But Herod made sure to present himself more as patron than as client. Nor did he cast himself in the role of sponsor of Jewish interests abroad. Diaspora Jews had little to offer him—and they got little from him. Herod projected a different and far wider image. He strutted the international stage primarily in the mould of a Hellenistic king.

Alexander the Great had dramatically expanded the horizons of the Greek world in the Near East. The monarchs who followed in his wake had vaulting ambitions on a scale unmatched in the crabbed confines of mainland Greece. Power and authority rested only in part on the big battalions. Self-representation demanded at least as much attention. On that score, splendor and magnanimity held central place. Nothing better exemplifies this feature than the pattern of royal donations, endowments, and gifts to cities and communities not only within but well beyond the king's own dominions. These could range from dedications in temples to the construction of buildings and even the foundation of cities. The monarch's benefactions advertised his success—and his reach.[33] The prevalence of this practice permeated the Hellenistic world.[34] Insofar as Herod pursued an impact upon the Mediterranean community outside his own realm, Hellenistic monarchy supplied the logical and appropriate context.[35]

Two models spring most readily to mind. The Attalid rulers of Pergamum not only embellished their own capital with buildings of stunning magnificence.

33 See the valuable overview by K. Bringmann "The King as Benefactor: Some Remarks pn Ideal Kingship in the Age of Hellenism," in A. Bulloch, et al., eds. *Images and Ideologies: Self-Definition in the Hellenistic World* (Berkeley: University of California Press = *Hellenistic Culture and Society,* XII, 1993), 7 – 24.
34 The extensive testimonia, with translations and commentary, are gathered by K. Bringmann & H. von Steuben *Schenkungen hellenistischer Herrscher an griechische Städte und Heiligtümer,* Teil I (Berlin: Akademie Verlag, 1995); see further the analysis and historical interpretation of the material in two subsequent volumes by K. Bringmann *Geben und Nehmen: Monarchische Wohltätigkeit und Selbstdarstellung im Zeitalter des Hellenismus,* Teil II.1 (Berlin: Akademie Verlag, 2000) and B. Schmitt-Dounas *Geschenke erhalten die Freundschaft: Politik und Selbstdarstellung im Spiegel der Monumente,* Teil II.2 (Berlin: Akademie Verlag, 2000).
35 Herod's imitation of Hellenistic kings as founder and benefactor of cities was rightly noted by D.M. Jacobson "King Herod's 'Heroic' Public Image," *Revue Biblique* 95 (1988), 394 – 5; *idem* "Three Roman Client Kings," 30 – 3; see also Lichtenberger *Die Baupolitik Herodes,* 181, 186). Kokkinos *The Herodian Dynasty,* 112 – 28, 342 – 52, sees Herod's actions as consonant with a background rooted in the Hellenised environment of Idumaea.

They also spread their wealth and enhanced their reputations widely in Hellas. The kings distributed their endowments to Greek cities like Athens, Delos, Delphi, and Thespiae to announce their magnanimity to the great shrines and centres of the Hellenic world generally.[36] A second paradigm is still more striking—and replete with irony. Antiochus IV Epiphanes represents the very embodiment of villainy in Jewish tradition. Yet as a Hellenistic ruler he epitomized the magnanimous monarch who bestowed benefactions upon communities across the Greek world. Epigraphic evidence aplenty attests to that notorious Seleucid king's favors to and bonds with states like Athens, Delos, Delphi, Argos, Rhodes, Byzantium, and others.[37] Antiochus Epiphanes, however horrendous his actions in Jerusalem, cultivated a paternalistic image in Hellas as a whole.

It does not follow, of course, that Herod modeled himself consciously upon Antiochus—nor even indeed upon the Attalids. But the Jewish ruler fitted into the Hellenistic framework. Eminence and splendor announced his international authority. He was a friend of Augustus and stood on a level with Agrippa. He was benefactor of the multiethnic peoples of Palestine. And he emblematized the magnificence and munificence of a Hellenistic monarch abroad.[38]

---

36 On Attalid policy, see H.-J. Schalles *Untersuchungen zur Kulturpolitik der pergamenischen Herrscher im dritten Jahrhundert vor Christus* (Tübingen: Ernst Warmuth = Istanbuler Forschungen, 36, 1985), 33 – 68, 104 – 43; E.S. Gruen "Culture as Policy: The Attalids of Pergamon," in N. T. de Grummond and B. S. Ridgway, eds. *From Pergamon to Sperlonga: Sculpture and Context* (Berkeley: University of California Press = *Hellenistic Culture and Society*, XXXIV, 2000), 17 – 31.
37 On Antiochus' benefactions, see O. Morkholm *Antiochus IV of Syria* (Copenhagen: Gyldendal, 1966), 51 – 63.
38 This paper has been markedly improved by the acute comments and suggestions of David Jacobson and Nikos Kokkinos—even if it has not altogether won their assent.

18. Caligula, The Imperial Cult, and Philo's *Legatio*

Jewish experience in the early Roman Empire was not always a smooth and untroubled one. But one event stands out with high drama and great notoriety. It represented a terrifying, memorable, and, in many ways, inexplicable act on the part of the imperial power: the emperor Gaius Caligula's order to install a statue in the Temple in Jerusalem. The episode left a deep impression upon Philo, a contemporary of this shattering decision, who recounted it at length in his *Legatio ad Gaium*. The account, fascinating and frustrating, presents numerous problems, only a few of which can be addressed here—and even fewer solved.[1] But they do afford a valuable avenue for an assessment of Philo as a historian and the nature of his narrative.

A summary of the relevant text is in order.[2] Two fundamental motifs run through Philo's interpretation of events: Gaius's virulent hatred of Jews and his insatiable desire to demonstrate and broadcast his divinity. The two incentives combined when the emperor issued instructions to place a statue of himself in the Temple. A particular incident provided the pretext. Recent gentile immigrants to Jamnia, a city of mixed population, sought to ingratiate themselves with the emperor by setting up a makeshift altar of brick, a deliberate affront to the Jewish inhabitants. As expected, the Jews tore it down. Word reached Herennius Capito, procurator in the region, who sent off a report to Rome. Caligula, after prompting from his most dubious advisers, the freedman Helikon and the actor Apelles, reacted with over-kill. He would teach the Jews a lesson. Instead of the paltry altar in Jamnia, he would set a statue in the holy sanctuary itself in

---

1 For some discussions of the subject, see John P. V. D. Balsdon, *The Emperor Gaius* (Oxford: Clarendon Press, 1934), 135–140; Arnold H. M. Jones, *The Herods of Judea* (Oxford: Clarendon Press, 1938), 196–203; E. Mary Smallwood, "The Chronology of Gaius' Attempt to Desecrate the Temple." *Latomus* 16 (1957): 3–17; Emil Schürer, *The History of the Jewish People in the Age of Jesus Christ*, vol. I (rev. ed. by Geza Vermes and Fergus Millar (Edinburgh: T&T Clark, 1973), 394–397; E. Mary Smallwood, *The Jews under Roman Rule* (SJLA 20; Leiden: Brill, 1981), 174–180; Per Bilde, "The Roman Emperor Gaius (Caligula)'s Attempt to Erect his Statue in the Temple of Jerusalem." *StudTheol* 32 (1978): 67–93; Anthony A. Barrett, *Caligula: the Corruption of Power* (London: Batsford, 1989), 188–191; Daniel R. Schwartz, *Agrippa I* (TSAJ 23; Tubingen: Mohr Siebeck, 1990), 18–23, 77–89; Monika Bernett, *Der Kaiserkult in Judäa unter den Herodiern und Römern* (WUNT 203; Tubingen: Mohr Siebeck, 2007), 264–287. And see the valuable text and commentary of the *Legatio ad Gaium* by E. Mary Smallwood, *Philonis Alexandrini, Legatio ad Gaium* (Leiden: Brill, 1961).
2 Philo, *Legat.* 184–346.

Jerusalem. And he would make his statement quite unequivocally. The princeps gave orders by letter to P. Petronius, governor of Syria, to take half his army, two full legions, to implement this directive.[3]

Petronius was caught in a bind. He could hardly disobey a direct mandate from the emperor, especially one convinced of his divinity who would brook no opposition. Yet he also knew that Jewish resistance would be ferocious and horrific, not only from those dwelling in Judaea but from the countless multitudes in the diaspora, thereby setting off a conflagration that could be overwhelming. The legate had one piece of good luck. Caligula did not send a statue from Rome nor did he demand that one already available in Syria be transported to Jerusalem. This allowed Petronius to commission a new work of art from expert craftsmen in Sidon, providing a welcome respite and giving time for reflection and reconsideration. The Roman governor called upon Jewish leaders and appealed to sweet reason. Much better to yield on this issue than to risk massacre. Of course, the priests and elders would not hear of it. No compromise was possible with so fundamental a principle at the very core of their existence and identity. A vast multitude of Jews descended upon Petronius' headquarters in Phoenicia, unarmed but defiant, ready to lay down their lives, men, women, and children alike, rather than suffer the unspeakable horror of the Temple's defilement.[4]

Instead of pushing matters to the brink, Jews requested of Petronius that he permit them to send an embassy to Rome, thus to dissuade the emperor of his purpose. Petronius declined the plea but, being a reasonable and sympathetic man, said that he would write a letter to the emperor himself. The missive advised Caligula to delay his purpose. Since harvest time approached, why run the risk of Jews burning the crops and ravaging the land, especially as Caligula planned a trip to the Near East with his vast entourage which needed to be fed and housed in style? The arrival of the letter in Rome sparked a fit of rage. The emperor fumed at his appointee's insubordination. He fired off a letter in return, one that concealed his fury, couched in pleasant and encouraging tones, but reiterating, his desire to have the statue installed as soon as possible. Disaster still seemed inevitable.[5]

A fortuitous or providential event then intervened. Agrippa I, grandson of Herod, a friend and successful courtier of Gaius who had recently been awarded rule over much of the land of Palestine, was in Rome when matters came to a

---

3 Philo, *Legat.* 198–207.
4 Philo, *Legat.* 209–238.
5 Philo, *Legat.* 239–260.

head. The emperor informed him of his decision and denounced Agrippa's fellow Jews as being the only nation to deny his divinity. Agrippa, stunned and shocked in disbelief, fell into a coma.[6] After recovery, he could not face Caligula but wrote him a long letter, recounted in Philo's text. The king outlined Jewish loyalty to Rome, including sacrifices on behalf of the emperors, and detailed Roman favors over the years to Jews, including support for and handsome gifts to the Temple. And he made clear the deep significance of attachment to ancestral traditions which keep the Temple inviolate, expressing readiness to give up all possessions and life itself rather than witness its desecration.[7]

The emperor greeted this letter with mixed response. He retained his wrath toward the Jewish nation, the one people who refused to recognize his divinity. But he made the key concession to his friend Agrippa. Gaius rescinded his order to Petronius and sent a letter that terminated any further action that might undermine the authority of the Temple. The letter, however, contained an added clause that bound the Jews in turn. Anyone in the areas near Jerusalem who wished to set up altars, shrines, images, or statues in honor of the emperor should be allowed to do so. If Jews should seek to prevent this, Petronius had full authority to punish them or to send them to Rome for punishment.[8]

That would seem to settle the matter. But not quite. Caligula shortly thereafter regretted his compliance, resurrected his earlier decision, and directed the construction of a new colossal image in Rome to be shipped by sea and erected surreptitiously before the Jewish people realized what was happening. This would involve transformation of the Temple into a shrine dedicated to Gaius himself.[9] So ends the narrative, somewhat abruptly and disconcertingly, as Philo returns to his discussion of the *legatio* on behalf of the Alexandrian Jews. As we know, the plans for the Temple did not materialize because Gaius conveniently died before they could be implemented. We know this, however, not from Philo but from Josephus—whose account is still more problematical. That will not be treated here.[10] We stick to Philo. He provides us with more than enough problems.

---

6 Philo, *Legat.* 261–269.
7 Philo, *Legat.* 270–329. Solomon Zeitlin, "Did Agrippa Write a Letter to Gaius Caligula?" *JQR*, 56 (1965/6): 22–31, doubts that such a letter could have been written in the fashion presented in Philo's account. But this rests on his presumption that Gaius was a maniacal believer in his own divinity and that Agrippa would not have dared use the language attributed to him.
8 Philo, *Legat.* 331–334.
9 Philo, *Legat.* 337, 346.
10 Jos. *B. J.* 2.184–203; Jos. *A. J.* 18.256–309. See the comparisons of Philo's and Josephus's accounts in the works listed above, n. 1. See also Steve Mason, *Flavius Josephus, Judean War 2*

Why should Caligula have a deep-seated hatred of Jews? What would prompt immigrants to Jamnia to provoke Jews by setting up an altar to the emperor? How provocative really was that? Was it enough to justify destroying the altar and defying the emperor? Did this deed suffice in turn to rouse the fury of Gaius to such an extent that he ordered a statue to be placed in the Temple, an altogether unprecedented act? And to implement it, did he require the force of two Roman legions, removing half the garrison of the province of Syria? Would P. Petronius, governor of the province, drag his feet, risk the wrath of the emperor, and become weak-kneed at the idea of diaspora Jews coming from all over the Mediterranean and from beyond the Euphrates to encircle his troops and assault them? Was it a heavenly blessing that Gaius did not send an already constructed statue but gave Petronius time to arrange for a new one, thus providing respite for reconsideration? Did a huge throng of Jews show up in Phoenicia, baring their throats, and persuade Petronius to alter the resolve of his sovereign? Did Agrippa fortuitously happen to be in Rome at this crucial moment, in time to dissuade Caligula from his dastardly deed? Did the emperor, having reversed himself at the importuning of his friend, then reverse himself again almost immediately thereafter, and order a new statue to be enshrined secretly in the Temple?

It is not impossible, I suppose, that any individual piece in this plethora of puzzles could be explained to someone's satisfaction. Indeed few of the pieces have even been challenged, in the face of Philo's contemporary testimony. Yet the collection of implausibilities should surely give us pause.

This lengthy portion of Philo's narrative is patently theatrical, over-dramatized, and replete with embellishments and imaginings. The portrait of the princeps as obsessed with his own divinity and driven by a ferocious hostility to Jews underpins the entire exposition. Philo fits events into that structure and has the characters behave in accordance with that motif.

As preamble to the story, Philo offers a long rehearsal of Gaius's extravagant behavior. He likened himself to the gods and heroes, dressed up as Heracles, Dionysus, or the Dioscuri, appeared in public as Hermes with staff, cloak, and sandals, as Apollo with sun rays on his head, bow and arrows in one hand and images of the Graces in the other, or as Ares with sword, helmet, and shield.[11] And animosity to the Jews is traced to the fact that, while all the other nations of the

---

(Flavius Josephus: Translation and Commentary, Volume 1B; Leiden: Brill, 2008), 156–168. For chronological discrepancies between them and efforts to reconstruct the chronology, see Balsdon, *Gaius,* 19–24; Smallwood, "The Chronology," 3–17; Bilde, "The Roman Emperor Gaius," 89–92; Schwartz, *Agrippa I,* 78–80.
11 Philo, *Legat.* 75–97.

world acknowledged his divinity, the Jews alone rejected it out of principle and devotion to their own supreme deity. Hence the emperor determined to wage a great war against that people.[12] In a brief digression on the events in Alexandria, Philo observes that the enemies of the Jews there felt that they could attack them with impunity because of the well known hatred of the emperor toward that people.[13] The allegation comes just before the story of the statue, a suitable frame for Philo's narrative. The impulse for installing an image in the Temple is Caligula's drive to be acknowledged as a god, to appropriate the Temple for his ends, and to inflict grievous injury upon the recalcitrant Jews.[14] Like the Alexandrians, the gentile immigrants to Jamnia were also spurred to action by the knowledge of Gaius's unrelenting hatred of Jews and insatiable desire for deification. Hence, the setting up of the brick altar seemed a logical ploy, guaranteed to stir Jewish reaction, and then imperial retaliation. The whole scheme was concocted by the procurator Capito, just waiting his opportunity to report on events —and to exaggerate them—in a message to the emperor.[15] Just how Philo could have known this is beyond comprehension. But it suited his scenario of a building clash between a tyrannical monarch and a pious people whom he was determined to oppress.

The villainous ruler and his despicable advisors are juxtaposed in the tale with the admirable Petronius. The legate, while wary of Caligula's fury, respected the values of the Jews, moved by their piety and commitment to principle, impressed by the vast numbers who turned up and declared their determination to die for their beliefs, and even somewhat schooled, if we credit Philo, in Jewish philosophy and religious traditions.[16] The stark contrast between the virtuous and the wicked in Philo's morality tale is further punctuated by histrionics. The Jews who gathered in multitudes to make their case to Petronius came in structured groups of children, adults, and the elderly of both sexes, with weeping, wailing, and smiting of breasts. They exposed their throats and insisted that no Roman armies were needed. If the order for the statue were not rescinded, the Jews would voluntarily commit mass suicide, each family slaughtering its own members, and bathing themselves in their own blood. The theatrical character of all this is expressly asserted by Philo himself who states that it would require the language of the tragic poets to describe the tragic sufferings that they faced.[17]

---

12 Philo, *Legat.* 114–119.
13 Philo, *Legat.* 133.
14 Philo, *Legat.* 198.
15 Philo, *Legat.* 201.
16 Philo, *Legat.* 245.
17 Philo, *Legat.* 233–235.

Equally histrionic is the scene in which Agrippa receives the news of Caligula's decision to erect the statue. The king now turned a variety of colors from deep pale to fiery red in a matter of seconds, suffered a violent seizure in every part of his body, collapsed into a coma, and had to be carried off in a stretcher. He lay unconscious for a day and a half, and then took a few more days for recuperation before he realized where he was and what was happening. That did not, however, prevent him from ordering a writing tablet and composing a long, windy letter to the emperor in hopes of deflecting his purpose.[18]

Philo's tale, in short, is shaped around his message: a clash between virtue and vice, the devout Jews stand up to the anti-semitic despot, the reasonable Roman governor delays the emperor's design, and the pious Jewish prince dissuades him from it. Caligula, according to Philo, was still hatching evil schemes to the end, but, as his readers knew, the emperor's own death guaranteed that they would come to naught.

None of this means that Philo created the story out of whole cloth. But it certainly counsels caution about purported motives and unfulfilled intentions that the author ascribes to the princeps. Did Gaius Caligula conduct a campaign against the Jews? Nothing in the classical sources drops a hint on that score. Indeed the absence of evidence here merits emphasis. The whole episode of the statue goes unmentioned apart from a single line in Tacitus's *Histories*. The Roman historian observes that, when ordered by Gaius to set up an image in the Temple, Jews preferred to take up arms, an uprising terminated only by the death of the emperor.[19] He certainly did not get this from Philo, nor from Josephus, neither of whom speaks of armed rebellion, only passive resistance. Suetonius and Dio ignore the whole episode. It hardly counted as a matter of high importance to Rome. Of course, we cannot tell what Tacitus might have said about it in the missing portion of the *Annales* that recounted Gaius's reign. But the idea of an embittered hatred toward the Jews is difficult to fathom. What motive would there have been? Even in the *In Flaccum,* where Philo deals in detail with the riots in Alexandria, he lays no blame at the doorstep of the emperor. Caligula's one act of significance in that treatise was to remove the offending Roman prefect, Avillus Flaccus, from office, a deed that can only have been welcomed by Jews.[20] The fearsome hostility toward that nation appears only in the *Legatio* where it receives no origin, explanation, or interpretation. It is a mere Leitmotif for Philo's drama.

---

18 Philo, *Legat.* 261–276. The contrived character of Philo's picture of Agrippa here is recognized by Bilde, "The Roman Emperor," 83–86. See also Schwartz, *Agrippa I,* 85–87.
19 Tacitus, *Hist.* 5.9.
20 Philo, *Flacc.* 109–115; cf. *Flacc.* 5.

The aspiration to divinity, of course, receives much more play in the ancient sources. Philo dwells on the emperor's penchant for imitating gods and demi-gods, dressing in their garb, and brandishing their accoutrements. He ascribes it to Gaius's lunatic drive for superhuman ascendancy.[21] Other authors go further in describing his extravagant impersonations of divinity. In the accounts of Suetonius and Dio Cassius, Caligula not only paraded about in the costume of gods like Jupiter, Apollo, or Dionysus but clothed himself as Juno, Diana, or Venus. No sexual discrimination here. He employed wigs, false beards, and various female accessories, sported a trident or a thunderbolt or the hunting equipment of Diana. And the sacrifices he ordered in his honor were equally excessive. No rams, oxen, or pigs; instead, flamingos, peacocks, and pheasants, exotic imports rather than homegrown products.[22]

Far from seeing these acts as a serious claim on divinity, however, the sources reckon them, for the most part, as comic publicity stunts.[23] They stand on a par with Gaius placing himself next to a statue of Jupiter and asking an onlooker to declare which of the two is the greater.[24] Or his challenge to Jupiter: "either raise me up, or I'll raise you up."[25] Or his declaration of having had intercourse with Selene, the moon-goddess.[26] Or his creation of a mechanical contrivance which, whenever lightning and thunder came from the sky, would send off his own answering peals.[27] All of this seems more like mockery of the gods than emulation of them. Philo, writing from a Jewish perspective, presented such behavior as deadly serious—not to mention seriously deadly. The classical authors took a more sardonic view. Suetonius lists Gaius's rivalry with Jupiter among his practical jokes.[28] And Dio reports an incident in which a Gallic shoemaker, having

---

21 Philo, *Legat.* 75–97.
22 Suetonius, *Cal.* 22, 52; Dio, 59.5–8; Donna Hurley, *A Historical and Historiographical Commentary on Suetonius' Life of C. Caligula* (American Classical Studies 32; Atlanta: Scholars Press, 1993), 81–91, 186–189; David Wardle, *Suetonius' Life of Caligula* (Collection Latomus 225; Brussels: Collection Latomus, 1994), 203–217, 336–341.
23 Cf. Balsdon, *The Emperor Gaius*, 160–162; Barrett, *Caligula*, 146; Aloys Winterling, *Caligula: Eine Biographic* (Munich: C.H. Beck, 2003), 144–152. Ittai Gradel, *Emperor Worship and Roman Religion* (Oxford Classical Monographs; Oxford: Oxford University Press, 2002), 146–149, takes them more seriously as expressions of status. Cf. also Hurley, *A Historical Commentary*, 186–188; Wardle, *Suetonius' Life of Caligula*, 205–208; Manfred Clauss, *Kaiser und Gott: Herrscherkult im römischen Reich* (Munich: K.G. Saur, 2001), 89–94.
24 Suetonius, *Cal.* 33.
25 Suetonius, *Cal.* 22.4; Dio, 59.28.6. Cf. Seneca, *De Ira*, 1.20.8–9.
26 Dio, 59.26.5, 59.27.6.
27 Dio, 59.28.6.
28 Suetonius, *Cal. 33: inter varios iocos*.

witnessed the emperor dressed as Jupiter and delivering oracular pronouncements, burst into laughter. When Caligula confronted him and asked "what do
I seem to you?," the shoemaker replied, "one big piece of nonsense." And the
man got off scot-free.[29] One might observe also that nothing in the inscriptions,
coinage, or archaeological evidence in Italy shows any trace of official acknowledgment of Gaius's divinity.[30] This hardly looks like a determined effort to compel worship as a god. Rather, a wicked sense of humor.

Why then seek to impose his worship upon the Jews, which neither of his
predecessors had dreamed of doing? Or did he? Not exactly. It is worth observing—what is rarely noted—that the statue designated for the Temple was apparently not one of Gaius at all but one of Jupiter. Philo states this explicitly on two
separate occasions.[31] And when he speaks of the emperor's intentions for the
Temple, he alleges that it would be named for him as representing the new
Zeus Epiphanes.[32] Not that this would make it any easier on the Jews. But it
may take the episode outside the context of the emperor's supposed obsession
with his own divinity. Whatever the situation in Rome, the imperial cult or
cults in the east had strong roots dating from the Augustan era, indeed even earlier, on the initiative of the easterners themselves. The association of the emperor
with a divinity housed in an eastern shrine would not itself be surprising.[33] Gaius
may have been a little more active in this regard than his predecessors. According to Dio, he directed that the temple to Apollo being constructed at Miletus
should embrace him as well.[34] This could help to promote a more consistent
and uniform mode of expressing loyalty to the crown among the subjects of
the eastern Mediterranean.[35]

---

29 Dio, 59.26.8–9.
30 Gradel, *Emperor Worship*, 149–159, interprets the literary testimony to mean that the cult to
Gaius in Rome was private rather than public.
31 Philo, *Legat.* 188: ἀνδριάντα ... Γάιος προσέταξε Διὸς ἐπίκλησιν αὐτοῦ; *Legat.* 265: ἐμοῦ
κελεύσαντος ἐν τῷ ἱερῷ Διὸς ἀνδριάντα ἀνατεθῆναι.
32 Philo, *Legat.* 346: μετεσχημάτιζεν εἰς οἰκεῖον ἱερόν, ἵνα Διὸς Ἐπιφανοῦς Νέου χρηματίζῃ
Γαΐου. On Gaius and Jupiter, see Smallwood, *Philonis Alexandrini*, 315–316. C. J. Simpson,
"The Cult of the Emperor Gaius," *Latomus* 40 (1981): 492–501, sees the relationship as one
of rivalry, at least in Rome.
33 Stefan Weinstock, *Divus Iulius* (Oxford: Clarendon Press, 1971), 304; Mary Beard, John
North, and Simon Price, *Religions of Rome* (Cambridge: Cambridge University Press, 1998),
348–363.
34 Dio, 59.28.1–2.
35 On the imperial cult as a means of expressing allegiance and gratitude, see Keith Hopkins,
Conquerors and Slaves (Sociological Studies in Roman History 1; Cambridge: Cambridge Univer-
sity.Press, 1978), 197–242; Simon Price, *Rituals and Power: The Roman Imperial Cult in Asia
Minor* (Cambridge: Cambridge University Press, 1984), *passim*; J. E. Lendon, *Empire of Honour:*

Might not Gaius have thought simply of extending this practice to Judaea, of having Jupiter or Gaius in the guise of Jupiter share the holy shrine of Jahweh? Temples to Roma and Augustus, of course, already stood in Palestine, the fruit of Herod's collaboration with Roman authority.[36] Agrippa I himself represented not only Caligula but even his sisters on the coinage of Caesarea Philippi.[37] If expansion of the imperial cult were to be general policy in the east, exemption for the Jews could cause serious difficulty for that nation itself since it would only stir resentment against them by other peoples in that part of the world.[38] Establishing some form of the imperial cult in Jerusalem did not entail, from the Roman point of view, suppression of the worship of Yahweh, indeed it was quite compatible with it. From the Jewish perspective, of course, the conjunction was impossible and anathema, thus prompting the stark drama depicted by Philo. The directive by Gaius, however, need not have been aimed at punishing Jews but at promoting paths to pay homage to the imperial power.

Such promotion might help to explain the affair at Jamnia. Philo, of course, accounts for it by word having reached the Jamnians of Gaius's passion for deification and his deep malevolence toward Jews.[39] The second point is highly dubious. But the first is not without some basis, if one understands it as response to messages, direct or indirect, from Rome encouraging acts of reverence to the emperor as expressions of loyalty and unity. The erection of a modest altar was a perfectly reasonable show of such allegiance. That it represented a deliberate provocation of Jews, anticipating forceful reaction, and then retaliation by Rome, the flames fanned by the Roman procurator, is part of Philo's schema, but carries little plausibility for historical reconstruction. Why should Jews have found this makeshift shrine offensive? They were not being asked to worship at it. At most, a group of extremists, showing their zeal for the faith, pulled it down, and the whole episode was exaggerated in the report to Rome, as Philo himself acknowledges.[40] It strains credulity to believe that this minor incident in

---

The Art of Government in the Roman World (Oxford: Clarendon Press, 1997), 160–172. And see the recent collection of essays by Jeffrey Brodd and Jonathan L. Reed, *Rome and Religion: A Cross-Disciplinary Dialogue on the Imperial Cult* (SBLWGRWSupp Series 5; Atlanta: Society of Biblical Literature).

36 See the thorough study of Bernett, *Der Kaiserkult*, 28–170, with extensive references to bibliography at 1–15.

37 Bernett, *Der Kaiserkult*, 271–272, 284–285.

38 Cf. Jos. *B. J.* 2.193–194.

39 Philo, *Legat.* 201.

40 Philo, *Legat.* 202. Bilde, "The Roman Emperor," 74–75, considers this a serious act of disloyalty, justifying strong Roman reaction. A comparable view in Schwartz *Agrippa I*, 80–83, who goes further to see the act at Jamnia as representing a fundamental clash between Jewish prin-

Jamnia triggered a momentous decision to violate and desecrate the sacred Temple in Jerusalem, an event that barely left a trace in the classical sources—which had few kind words for Gaius Caligula. It is much easier to conclude that the depth and force of Jewish reaction to the introduction of the imperial cult into Jerusalem was unforeseen, a miscalculation by the emperor rather than a retribution.

A critical question arises. Could Caligula possibly have been ignorant of the likely consequences of his order for a statue in the Temple? Does not the command to Petronius to bring half of the Syrian garrison to Palestine imply the anticipation of massive rebellion by the Jews? Perhaps. Yet no such Jewish rebellion had ever surfaced in the past. When opposition rose to the offensive acts of Pontius Pilate, it was passive resistance, the baring of throats and the willingness to perish for principle.[41] The same sort of demonstration occurred, as we have seen, in the appeal to Petronius. It is noteworthy too that Jewish leaders sought permission for an embassy to the emperor so that they could make their case and explain their commitment to tradition. This gesture implies both that they felt the need to instruct Gaius about Jewish beliefs and obligations of which he was otherwise ignorant and that they did not regard him as an implacable foe.

Why then did Petronius mobilize two legions? No easy answer to that. One might note, however, that there was more going on in the region than just the anticipated shipment of a statue. Tension and conflict within the Herodian house, itself no novel feature, became increasingly problematic in these years. Herod Antipas, the tetrarch in Galilee, had recently fought an unnecessary war with the Nabataeans, suffering a grievous defeat and forcing the Romans to intervene, with only mixed success. The Parthians still loomed across the Euphrates, and Antipas's involvement in negotiations with them drew the ire of Vitellius, the Roman governor of Syria, thus rendering Antipas's situation precarious and throwing the whole region into potential peril. Rivalry between Antipas and his nephew Agrippa soon came to a head. Caligula, shortly after accession to the throne in 37, awarded territories to Agrippa in Palestine and accorded him the title of king which had been denied to Antipas. Reports came back to Rome, fostered by Agrippa, about alleged collusion between Antipas and the Parthians. Antipas lost his tetrarchy and went off into exile, his region

---

ciples and the interests of the Roman empire. Cf. Barrett, *Caligula*, 190–191; Bernett, *Der Kaiserkult*, 278–280. Are we to imagine then that no other gentiles in Judaea ever set up offerings without incurring the fearsome wrath of the Jewish populace who regarded it as violating the sanctity of the holy land?

41 Jos. *B. J.* 2.169–177; Jos. *A. J.* 18.55–62.

now also granted to Agrippa.[42] This can only have intensified friction in the homeland. And it may also explain why Agrippa, after only a short sojourn in his new kingdom, soon found himself back in Rome. Antipas's former subjects may not have given the new king a warm welcome, the Nabataeans remained recalcitrant across the Jordan, and Parthian power always posed a potential menace. Further, the episode in Jamnia demonstrated that raw nerves existed among some Jews and gentiles even in the heartland. If Caligula wished to extend the imperial cult and underscore Roman religious authority in so volatile a region, it was prudent to have a large army at the ready.[43] Its mandate, one might surmise, was to assure order and stability and to intimidate possible dissidents, not to punish Jews.

A final question. If Caligula's purpose were to extend the imperial cult as a symbol of uniform Roman rule in the east and the stability of the empire, why did he persist in this aim in the face of a determined opposition that could only undermine that stability? The answer is that he did not persist. That may be the one reasonable certainty in this whole morass of uncertainties. On Philo's own showing, Agrippa's plea to the emperor dissuaded him from his aim of setting a statue in the Temple. Gaius sent a letter to Petronius countermanding his previous order and directing him to take no action that might subvert the sanctity of the Jewish Temple.[44] This, of course, does not fit readily with Philo's portrait of the tyrannical monster. Hence, he has Gaius make the decision grudgingly and reluctantly, out of admiration for Agrippa's candor, while continuing to harbor deep resentment against the Jews.[45] Philo had put a similar spin upon the emperor's earlier letter to Petronius praising the governor for his sound policy and for his meticulous caution in preparing for future developments. But he adds that Caligula simply masked his real anger at Petronius with this friendly exterior and waited his opportunity for retaliation.[46]

The second letter, after instructing the legate to refrain from any offensive measures against the Jews, concluded with an admonition. If persons in the areas bordering on the metropolis of the Jews should wish to set up altars, shrines, images, or statues on the emperor's behalf, they should be free to do so, and Petronius was enjoined to punish those who sought to obstruct

---

42 For the circumstances and course of events, see the summaries in Jones, *The Herods*, 176– 203; Smallwood, *Jews under Roman Rule,* 183–193. More detailed analysis in Schwartz, *Agrippa I,* 53–74.
43 Cf. Bernett, *Der Kaiserkult,* 280.
44 Philo, *Legat.* 333.
45 Philo, *Legat.* 331–332.
46 Philo, *Legat.* 259–260.

them.[47] That was a perfectly reasonable addendum. The princeps encouraged such expressions of loyalty and would not wish them to be interfered with, as some Jews had done at Jamnia. The Jewish Temple was to be respected, and Jews in turn should respect the religious offerings of their neighbors to the emperor. An appropriate quid pro quo.

Philo, however, does not leave it at that. He surmises the real—and insidious—motives of the scheming Caligula. Such an injunction, he supposes, would inspire gentiles all over the area to erect countless numbers of such offerings, thus provoking Jews to tear them down everywhere, affording the emperor his desired pretext to penalize the offenders and revive his order for a statue in the Temple.[48] Philo may have had access to good sources for the letters themselves. But he had no access to the interior of Caligula's mind. His comments on the emperor's diabolic motives and intent were part of the artistic construct.

Even that was not enough for Philo. In his vision the embittered and fearsome tyrant repented of his own repentance. Why wait for others to provide a pretext? He issued orders for another statue, this a colossal one of bronze arid gold, to be fashioned in Rome, then shipped secretly to Jerusalem, where it would be installed, and then discovered only as a *fait accompli*.[49] Philo abandons the story there. Of course, nothing of the sort ever happened. The very idea of erecting a colossal statue in the Temple without anyone's knowing about it until after it occurred is preposterous. Nor would the Jewish reaction be any less violent and vociferous afterward than before. Philo simply could not leave the tale with a generous act on the part of Caligula. So he imagined a more wicked one in the offing. The testimony of the letters is a safer guide. The rest is concoction.[50]

It has not been my intent to whitewash Caligula or to turn this eccentric megalomaniac into a benevolent despot of sweet reasonableness. But insofar as the statue episode has been taken as an exemplary instance of despotic lunacy,

---

47 Philo, *Legat.* 334.
48 Philo, *Legat.* 335.
49 Philo, *Legat.* 337.
50 For similar skepticism about this last project of Gaius, see Bilde, "The Roman Emperor," 87 – 88. As is well known, Josephus conceived an even more dramatic conclusion to the whole affair. He has Gaius change his mind and send a blistering letter to Petronius, demanding that the governor pay for his insubordination by committing suicide. But, by a great act of providence, the letter was slightly delayed and reached Petronius only after word came of the emperor's death; Jos. *B. J.,* 2.203; Jos. *A. J.* 18.302 – 309. It was a breathtaking "nick-of time" tale. God had intervened to spare the virtuous and destroy the vicious. Cf. Bilde, "The Roman Emperor," 88 – 89. Schwartz, *Agrippa I,* 87 – 88, is prepared to believe it. Similarly, Bernett, *Der Kaiserkult,* 283 – 284.

stemming from irrational hatred of Jews and consuming passion for divinity, it might be prudent to take a more measured view. Gaius's supposedly virulent anti-semitism has no obvious basis and nowhere receives explanation, and his spread of the imperial cult may owe more to eastern policy than maniacal self-absorption. But Philo had a tale to tell. And his portrait did much to shape the tradition. The philosopher-historian conveyed a vivid narrative with dramatic force, driven by loathing for the emperor who had mocked and summarily dismissed his embassy on behalf of the Alexandrian Jews. He may have obtained some reliable information, including accounts of the correspondence between Gaius and his appointee in Syria. But imputed motivation and purported objectives were a different matter. Philo divined them to suit his portrait. They do not qualify as responsible reportage. And it is high time to question their authority.

Jewish Literary Constructs

19. The *Letter of Aristeas* and the Cultural Context of the Septuagint

The tale of the Hebrew Bible's translation into Greek is familiar and fascinating. Our earliest text on the subject, the *Letter of Aristeas*, offers the most elaborate version, one that had a deep influence upon all subsequent retellings, however divergent they were.[1] According to the author, the initiative for this enterprise came from the top. Ptolemy II Philadelphus, ruler of Egypt, commissioned the work, on the prompting of his chief librarian Demetrius of Phalerum. Demetrius made his case persuasively and compellingly. To the king he extolled the value of having a Greek version of the "laws of the Jews" on the shelves of the great library in Alexandria. Ptolemy unhesitatingly sanctioned the venture, and a select group of Jewish scholars, brought from Jerusalem, lavishly welcomed and hosted in Alexandria, carried out the task.

Such is the skeleton of the story. Debate and controversy have long swirled about the question of how much to believe. Many scholars have found the narrative to be little more than creative fiction, an attractive fantasy without foundation in fact. On that view, the impetus for a Greek rendition of the Scriptures came not from the king of Egypt but from the Jews themselves. Pragmatic motives prompted the process. The Jewish community in Alexandria had lost fluency and familiarity with Hebrew. Hence, whether for religious or educational purposes, or some combination thereof, they required a Greek text to serve the needs of diaspora existence. This interpretation has long held sway in the scholarship.[2] Some recent contributions, however, accord greater respect to the Aristeas narrative, or at least to the core of the tale, namely that the inspiration for the Septua-

---

1 The date of the *Letter* remains controversial. Scholars put it at various times in the 2nd century BCE, between a half century and a century and a half after the events recorded; cf. M. Hadas, *Aristeas to Philocrates (Letter of Aristeas)* (JAL) (New York 1951), 9 – 18; S. Jellicoe, *The Septuagint and Modern Study* (Oxford, 1968), 47 – 49; F. Parente, "La lettera di Aristea come fonte per la storia del Giudaismo Alessandrino durante la prima meta del 1 secolo a.C.", AnnPisa 2.1 (1972) 177 – 237; 2.2 (1972) 517 – 567, 182 – 185, 189 – 190; P.M. Fraser, *Ptolemaic Alexandria*. 3 vols. (Oxford, 1972), II, 970 – 972; E. Schürer, *The History of the Jewish People in the Age of Jesus Christ*. A New English Version rev. by G. Vermes/F. Millar/M. Goodman, vol. III. (Edinburgh, 1986), 679 – 684. The most valuable edition of the work, with fullest commentary, remains that of R. Tramontano, *La Lettera di Aristea a Filocrate* (Naples, 1931). On the variations and subsequent legacy of the tale, see A. Wasserstein/D. Wasserstein, *The Legend of the Septuagint From Classical Antiquity to Today* (Cambridge, 2006).
2 E.g., Fraser, *Ptolemaic Alexandria* I, 690; II, 957 – 958; Schürer, *History*, 491 – 492, with bibliography; see also Wasserstein/Wasserstein, *Legend*, 4 – 13.

gint came from the Ptolemaic court. On one theory, such a translation would give the ruling power access to Jewish law, thus providing a means whereby the Torah could take its place among legal codes governing the diverse ethnic groups that made up the Ptolemaic kingdom, a matter of convenience for the administration of the realm.[3] Or on another, perhaps more plausible, analysis, the stimulus arose from the cultural interests of Ptolemy Philadelphus, a renowned patron of literature and the arts, a man keenly devoted to intellectual matters, and one who shared the burgeoning Greek interest in eastern peoples and eastern traditions.[4] *The Letter of Aristeas* certainly presents him in this guise. And Philo offers an even more elaborate and flattering portrait of Ptolemy's devotion to the life of the mind.[5] A translated edition of the Hebrew Bible (or, more precisely, the Pentateuch) would lend further distinction to the King's repute as a promoter of high culture.

The question of motive admits of no easy answer.[6] And it has perhaps been too much bound up in the effort to ascertain the historicity of circumstances described in the *Letter*. Even those scholars who are most inclined to find some reality behind the traditions of the translation do not accept as historical the colorful details and embellishments purveyed by the narrative of "Aristeas." Few, for example, would endorse the legend of seventy two translators completing their work in precisely seventy two days, or the High Priest's lecture on Jewish practices to the envoys of Ptolemy, or the long and tedious interrogation of the Jewish elders at a Greek symposium in Alexandria. But all agree that the celebrated saga recounted in the *Letter of Aristeas* comes from the pen of a Jewish author, a writer clearly at home in Ptolemaic Alexandria, familiar with the protocols of the court, even with the formulas of diplomatic correspondence – yet also deeply committed to the principles of Judaism and the faith of the fathers. We can consequently forgo pronouncing upon the degree of historicity that resides in the story of the origins of the Septuagint. The tale itself matters. It constitutes a document of high historical importance. The value of the narrative lies not in extract-

---

3 E. Bickerman, *Studies in Jewish and Christian History* I (Leiden, 1976), 167–175; J. Mélèze-Modrzejewski, *The Jews of Egypt: From Rameses II to Emperor Hadrian* (Philadelphia, 1995), 99–106.
4 W. Orth, "Ptolemaios II. und die Septuaginta-Übersetzung," in *Im Brennpunkt: Die Septuaginta. Studien zur Entstehung und Bedeutung der Griechischen Bibel* I, hrsg. v. H.-J. Fabry and U. Offerhaus (BWANT 153) (Stuttgart u.a., 2001), 97–114, 106–112; T. Rajak *Translation and Survival: The Greek Bible of the Ancient Jewish Diaspora* (Oxford; New York: Oxford University Press, 2009).
5 Philo, *Mos.* 2.29–30.
6 For a summary of competing opinions, see J.M. Dines, *The Septuagint (Understanding the Bible and its World)* (London/New York 2004), 42–61.

ing nuggets of fact from a largely fictional facade, but in employing the text as a window upon the Jewish mentality in the circumstances of a diaspora community in Ptolemaic Alexandria. It offers an avenue toward understanding the self-fashioning of a Jewish image in the intellectual and cultural world of Hellenistic society.[7] The origin of the Septuagint, or rather the legend in which that origin is recounted, needs to be seen in a broader context. It belongs to Jewish experience in the cultural environment of Alexandria, in relation to contemporary or near contemporary writings that endeavor to articulate Jewish identity and to its wider connections with the literate society of the Hellenistic world. That constitutes the essence of this investigation.

First, a few words about the place of Jews in the social scene of Alexandria. The subject suffers from poor documentation. But, enough survives to indicate a relatively comfortable and untroubled existence. What brought Jews there in the first place remains a matter of dispute in conflicting sources. The *Letter of Aristeas* reports that some had been deported from Judaea by the Persians, but that the bulk came when Ptolemy I Soter, after subduing the whole of Coele-Syria and Phoenicia, forcibly removed up to 100,000 Jews to Egypt. He then installed 30,000 of them in garrisons and fortresses throughout his realm.[8] A rosier portrait derives from the pen of a Jewish author, writing under the pseudonym of Hecataeus: Soter was such a gentle and kindly conqueror that Jews followed him voluntarily to Egypt, there to share in the affairs of that land.[9] Whatever the truth of the matter and however inflated the numbers may be, the fact of Jewish soldiers serving in the Ptolemaic armies is amply attested in the literary, epigraphic, and papyrological record. Jews were not confined to garrison duty. They served in regular units of the army could rise to officer rank, and received land grants like others enlisted in the ranks of the king's forces.[10] Inscriptions in Aramaic and Greek from Alexandrian cemeteries dating to the early Ptolemaic period record Jews, probably as mercenary soldiers, buried alongside Greeks from all parts of the Hellenic world.[11] One does not have to believe Josephus when he claims that Ptolemy VI entrusted his entire kingdom to Jews.[12] But there can

---

7 Cf. V. Tcherikover, "The Ideology of the Letter of Aristeas," HTR 51 (1958) 59–85; E.S. Gruen, *Heritage and Hellenism: The Reinvention of Jewish Tradition* (Berkeley, 1998), 206–222, with bibliography; S.R. Johnson, *Historical Fictions and Hellenistic Jewish Identity: Third Maccabees in its Cultural Context* (Berkeley, 2004), 34–38.

8 *Let. Aris.*, 12–14, 20–23, 35–36. Cf. Jos. *C. Ap.* 1.186; Jos. *A. J.* 12.8.

9 Jos. *C. Ap.* 1.186–189; Jos. *A. J.* 12.8.

10 See the documents collected in CPJ, I, 18–32. See also JIGRE, no. 115; P. Köln, III, 144.

11 JIGRE, nos. 1–8. See the discussion of Mélèze-Modrzejewski, *The Jews of Egypt*, 77–80.

12 Jos. *C. Ap.* 2.49; cf. Jos. *A. J.* 13.285–287, 13.349.

be little doubt that Jews in substantial numbers could be found in the military ranks of the king.[13] Jews, in fact, turn up, even in our scanty evidence, at various levels of the Ptolemaic administration in Egypt, as tax-farmers and tax collectors, as bankers and granary officials.[14] Philo records Alexandrian Jews as shop-owners, merchants, shippers, traders, and artisans.[15] No obvious barriers prevented their engagement in the social and economic world of Ptolemaic Alexandria.

Furthermore, Jews evidently had free rein in establishing their own religious institutions. Literary sources report a plethora of synagogues in Alexandria.[16] Among them was the structure that Philo labeled as the largest and most celebrated of synagogues, one that was subsequently described in elaborate fashion by rabbinic sources.[17] Documentary testimony confirms the textual evidence. Important inscriptions attest to standard but revealing formulas, through which Jews exhibited due respect to the overlordship of the Ptolemies while maintaining the traditions of their forefathers. Documents record the dedication of Jewish synagogues, *proseuchai*, in honor of the king or the royal family of Egypt. Several of them survive from the Ptolemaic period, including two from Alexandria itself, and the earliest from Schedia in the near vicinity of Alexandria. As the latter inscription asserts, the Jewish dedicators set up their *proseuche* on behalf of King Ptolemy, Queen Berenike, and their children.[18] The formula closely parallels those to be found in pagan dedications.[19] Jews felt no hesitation in paying tribute

---

13 See, e. g., Jos. *C. Ap.*, 1.200–204, 2.64; Jos. *A. J.* 14.99, 14.131–132; *B. J.* , 1.175, 1.190–192.

14 CPJ, 48–124, 127, 132, 137; cf. Jos. *A. J.* 20.147. See the valuable treatment by A. Kasher, *The Jews in Hellenistic and Roman Egypt. The Struggle for Equal Rights* (TSAJ 7) (Tübingen, 1985), 58–63.

15 Philo, *Flacc.* 56–57; Philo *Legat.* 129; cf. 3 Macc. 3.10; Jos. *A. J.* 18.159.

16 Philo, *Flacc.* 41, 45, 48, 53; Philo *Legat.* 132, 134, 137–138, 152, 191, 346; *Mos.* 2.216; Cf. 3 Macc. 2.28, 3.29, 4.18, 7.20; Philo, *Somn.* 2.127; Jos. *A. J.* 13.65–66.

17 Philo, *Legat.* 134. See Kasher, *The Jews in Hellenistic and Romnan Egypt*, 349–351; L.I. Levine, *The Ancient Synagogue: The First Thousand Years* (New Haven, 2000), 84–89.

18 JIGRE, no. 22. See also nos. 9 and 13.

19 Among many treatments, see P.M. Fraser, *Ptolemaic Alexandria* I, 282–285; II, 440–444; Kasher, *The Jews in Hellenistic and Roman Egypt*, 106–119; idem, "Synagogues as 'Houses of Prayer' and 'Holy Places' in the Jewish Communities of Hellenistic and Roman Egypt," in: *Ancient Synagogues: Historical Analysis and Archaeological Discovery*, eds. D. Urman/P.V.M. Flesher, vol. I (StPB 47/1) (Leiden, 1995), 205–220; J.G. Griffiths, "Egypt and the Rise of the Synagogue," in: *Ancient Synagogues: Historical Analysis and Archaeological Discovery* (see above) I, 3–16; Mélèze-Modrzejewski, *The Jews of Egypt*, 87–98; D. Binder, *Into the Temple Courts: The Place of the Synagogues, in the Second Tentple, Perio*d (SBL.DS 169) (Atlanta, 1999), 233–252.

to the gentile rulers of the land while simultaneously dedicating their synagogues to the "Most High God." The two actions were perfectly consistent with
one another. Royal favor extended to the Jewish places of worship, even granting
them the privilege of *asylia*, the formal status of asylum commonly accorded to
pagan temples, a notable mark of official approval.[20]

The evidence is slender, and conclusions must be tentative. But it does appear that Jews enjoyed productive and rewarding lives in Alexandria, the queen
of Hellenistic cities. Integration in the social and economic life of the city lay
open to them – and they took advantage of that opening. Jews served in the armies, obtained administrative posts, played a role in commerce, shipping, finance, farming, and every form of occupation, and reached posts of some prestige and importance. Juridically, the Jews, like other Greek-speaking immigrants
to Egypt, were reckoned among the "Hellenes."[21]

The nature of Jewish civic status in Alexandria remains obscure and controversial. This is not the appropriate place to discuss that complex matter in the
detail that it requires.[22] It suffices to say that the Jews did enjoy an acknowledged
political position of some sort in the Alexandrian community. Whether it goes
back to Alexander the Great or to Ptolemy I, as Josephus reports, can be left
aside questionable speculation or a biased agenda.[23] But the Jews had certainly
obtained an acknowledged civic position in Alexandria by the end of the 1st century BCE, and probably much earlier. The Greek geographer Strabo attests to it,
and he had no reason to fabricate or exaggerate on this score. Strabo reports that
the Jews had a large portion of the city allotted to them, and that they possessed
their own official, an ethnarch, to govern disputes and oversee contracts and decrees, as if he headed an autonomous political entity.[24] The text plainly implies
that Jews governed their internal affairs while also being part of a larger Alexan-

---

20 JIGRE, no. 125.
21 Cf. J. Mélèze-Modrzejewski, "How to be a Greek and Yet a Jew in Hellenistic Alexandria," in
Diasporas in Antiquity, eds. S.J.D. Cohen/E.S. Frerichs (BJSt 288) (Atlanta, 1993), 65–92, 79–
80; idem, *The Jews of Egypt*, 81–83; W. Clarysse, "Jews in Trikomia," Proceedings of the
XXth International Congress of Papyrologists (Copenhagen, 1994), 193–203.
22 See, e.g., W. Ameling, "'Market-Place' und Gewalt: Die Juden in Alexandrien 38 n. Chr,"
Würzburger Jahrbücher 27 (2003) 71–123: 85–100, with extensive bibliographical citations.
The subject receives full treatment in Bradley Ritter, *Judeans in the Greek Cities of the Roman Empire: Rights, Citizenship and Civil Discord* Supplements to the Journal for the Study of Judaism
(Leiden; Boston: Brill, 2015).
23 Jos. *A. J.* 12.8; Jos. *C. Ap.* 2.35. Cf. V. Tcherikover *Hellenistic Civilization and the Jews* (Philadelphia, 1959), 120–124; J.M.G. Barclay, *Jews in the Mediterranean Diaspora from Alexander to
Trajan* (323 BCE–117 CE) (Edinburgh, 1996), 70.
24 Strabo, apud Jos. *A. J.* 14.117. Cf. 19.283.

drian entity to which they owed allegiance. *The Letter of Aristeas* (310) refers to this corporate body as *politeuma*. The text offers no specifics on its structure and organization. But some idea can be had from a comparable Jewish institution at Heracleopolis in Middle Egypt, only recently revealed by a most important papyrological find.[25] Whatever the nature of the Alexandrian *politeuma* and the reach of its authority, Jews did not huddle themselves in an isolated ghetto. They lived in all parts of the city (Philo, *Flacc.* 55), and they felt free to term themselves "Alexandrians."[26] The emperor Augustus reportedly referred to them on a bronze stele as Ἀλεξανδρέων πολῖται. And Philo intriguingly makes reference to the Alexandrian Jews' "sharing in political rights" (*Flacc.* 53). Although we do not possess precision, it seems clear that Jews had some claim on civic prerogatives in Alexandria, just as they had on the social and economic life of the city.

So far as our evidence goes, therefore, Jews did not suffer oppression or subjugation by the Ptolemies.[27] They enjoyed freedom to perform traditional rites and to worship the divinity in their own way. And they possessed civic privileges in the larger community. It would be prudent to avoid loaded terms like "assimilation" or "accommodation," which could have negative connotations. Jews did not abandon or compromise their own traditions while functioning successfully in the society of Hellenistic Alexandria. Nor did the Ptolemaic government require conformity. The Jews, within the limits of our testimony, led a contented and largely untroubled existence which must have promoted a sense of self-confidence and security.[28]

---

25 The texts are edited by J.M.S., Cowey/K. Maresch. *Urkunden des Politeuma der Juden von Herakleopolis (144/3 – 133/2 b. Chr.) (P. Polit. Iud).* *Papyri aus den Sammlungen von Heidelberg, Köln, München und Wien* (Abhandlungen der Nordrhein-Westfälischen Akademie der Wissenschaften. Sonderreihe Papyrologica–Coloniensia 29) (Wiesbaden, 2001). See the review essay of S. Honigman; "The Jewish Politeuma at Heracleopolis." *SCI* 22 (2002) 251 – 266. On the Alexandrian *politeuma* see the discussion by Ameling, 'Market-Place' und Gewalt, 88 – 92.

26 Philo, *Legat.* 183, 194; Jos. *A. J.* 2.38 – 39. Cf. Kasher, *The Jews in Hellenistic and Roman Egypt*, 233 – 261; D. Delia, *Alexandrian Citizenship during the Roman Principate* (Atlanta, 1991), 23 – 28.

27 We can leave out of account the fictional tale of 3 Maccabees – which, in any case, had a happy ending for the Jews. See below.

28 For overviews of the Jews' experience in Alexandria along these lines, see E.S. Gruen, *Diaspora: Jews amidst Greeks and Romans* (Cambridge, MA 2002), 68 – 78; H.-J. Gehrke, "Das sozial- und religionsgeschichtliche Umfeld der Septuaginta," in *Im Brennpunkt: Die Septuaginta. Studien zur Entstehung und Bedeutung der Griechischen Bibel* II, hrsg.v. S. Kreuzer/I.P. Lesch (BWANT 161) (Stuttgart u. a., 2004), 44 – 60, with bibliography. The extensive study of Kasher, *The Jews in Hellenistic and Roman Egypt*, remains essential reading.

More significantly for our purposes, Jews had access even to the upper echelons of the Alexandrian intelligentsia. Jewish authors were well versed in most, perhaps all, forms of Hellenic writing. They worked and wrote in a wide range of Greek literary genres. Those conversant with the conventions include epic poets like Theodotus and Philo, tragic dramatists like Ezekiel, writers of history like Demetrius, philosophers like Artistobulus, those who engaged in cosmology and mythography like Pseudo-Eupolemus and the *Sibylline Oracles*, and composers of novellas and historical fiction like the authors of *3 Maccabees* – and indeed the *Letter of Aristeas*. A moment's consideration makes it obvious (though it is rarely remarked upon) that the capacity to produce such works demonstrates that their authors could partake of higher education and engage deeply with the Hellenic literary and cultural traditions available in Ptolemaic Alexandria. Those Jewish authors were themselves part and parcel of the Alexandrian intelligentsia.

Jewish authors, in short, showed a wide familiarity with the genres, forms, and styles of Greek literature. They wrote in Greek and they adapted Greek literary modes. But they employed those conventions to their own ends. Jewish intellectuals may have embraced Hellenic forms but they had no interest in recounting the tale of Troy, the labors of Heracles, the house of Atreus, or the Greco-Persian wars, let alone the myths of the Olympian gods. Their heroes were Abraham, Joseph, and Moses. They appropriated Hellenism to the goals of rewriting biblical narratives, recasting the traditions of their forefathers, reinvigorating their ancient legends, and shaping a distinctive sense of Jewish character within the larger world of Hellenic culture.

The story of the Septuagint's creation exemplifies that drive for refashioning Jewish identity in the circumstances of Ptolemaic Alexandria. The *Letter of Aristeas* constitutes a centerpiece of the endeavor. Its narrative has traditionally served as the prime document of a harmonious and mutually beneficial interchange between Greek and Jew. The work, in fact, is no real letter. It purports to be a communication from a certain Aristeas to his brother Philocrates. Both ostensibly served in the court of Ptolemy II Philadelphus, ruler of Egypt in the first half of the 3rd century BCE. The author describes his communication as a *diegesis*, an unspecific and widely applicable term signifying a literary prose narrative (1, 8, 322). It could signify any number of genres. The *Letter* does not fit neatly into any category. It could count as a piece of historical fiction, a monograph, or even a novella. Individual features of the work have close affinities with a whole range of Hellenic writings. The author plainly had a strong education in the literature of Hellas. But the treatise as a whole is *sui generis*. "Aristeas" did not aim for historical accuracy. Nor, on the other hand, did he seek to deceive readers with the pretense of a verifiable narrative. He offered verisimilitude rather than history, employing known figures and plausible circumstances to present a picture of mutual benefits enjoyed by Jewish learning and Hellenic patronage.[29] None can doubt, however, that the composer of the *Letter* was a Jew cloaked in the garb of a learned official at the court of Ptolemy II. The agenda is a decidedly Jewish one.[30]

The story of the translation provides a frame for the narrative. But only a frame. It introduces the treatise and closes it. But much transpires within that frame that has little or nothing to do with rendering the Hebrew Bible into Greek. In fact, the segments dealing with the process and results of the translation constitute only about one sixth of the whole. The author plainly had more in mind than recounting the creation of the Septuagint. The *Letter of Aristeas* provides a showpiece for the familiarity of Jewish intellectuals with diverse currents of literature practiced in the Hellenistic era.[31] For example, the lengthy portion on Aristeas' visit to Jerusalem, with its detailed description of the features of the landscape, the setting of the citadel, the terrain of the city, the geography of its surroundings, the appointments of the Temple, and the garb of the priests, much of it remote from reality, would remind readers of the geographical treatises and the utopian literature common in this period (83–120).[32] The High Priest Eleazar's exegesis of peculiar Jewish customs in turn provides parallels to the ethnographic excursuses that also appear frequently in Greek writings (128–170). The *Letter* frequently cites and quotes documents, whether royal decrees, memoranda/administrative reports, or letters, a practice regularly found in Greek historiography. The extended symposium, the formal seven-day banquet described in the book, was a thoroughly Hellenic institution, and most of the Jewish sages respond to the king's questions with answers drawn (at least super-

---

29 Cf. Gruen, *Heritage and Hellenism*, 208–210; S. Honigman, *The Septuagint and Homeric Scholarship in Alexandria: A Study in the Narrative of the Letter of Aristeas* (London, 2003), 29–35, 65–81; Johnson, *Historical Fictions*, 34–38; Wasserstein/Wasserstein, *Legend of the Septuagint*, 19–25.

30 See in general, with different emphases, Hadas, *Aristeas to Philocrates*, 61–64; Tcherikover, "Ideology", 59–85; C.R. Holladay, "Jewish Responses to Hellenistic Culture in Early Ptolemaic Egypt," in *Ethnicity in Hellenistic Egypt*, ed. P. Bilde et al. (Aarhus, 1992), 139–163: 147–149; Barclay, *Jews in the Mediterranean Diaspora*, 38–150; Gruen, *Heritage and Hellenism*, 202–222; J.J. Collins, *Between Athens and Jerusalem: Jewish Identity in the Hellenistic Diaspora*, 2nd ed. (Grand Rapids, 2000), 191–195; E. Birnbaum, "Portrayals of the Wise and Virtuous in Alexandrian Jewish Works: Jews' Perceptions of Themselves and Others," in *Ancient Alexandria Between Egypt and Greece*, ed. W.V. Harris and G. Ruffini (CSCT 26) (Leiden, 2004), 125–160. 131–438.

31 Honigman *Septuagint and Homeric Scholarship*, 13–35.

32 See, for instance, the fantastic tales of Iambulus and Euhemerus; Diod.2.55–60, 5.41–46, 6.1.

ficially) from Greek philosophy or political theory (187–294). The High Priest, in recounting the significance of Jewish dietary prescriptions, explains them in good Greek style, either as having a rational basis or as requiring allegorical interpretation (128–171). He receives description, in fact, in terms befitting a Greek aristocrat, a man of *kalokagathia* (3). The text includes learned allusions to Greek intellectuals like Menedemus, Hecataeus, Theopompus, and Theodectes. The author is plainly steeped in Hellenic culture. Perhaps most striking is the process of translation itself as presented in the narrative. The project arose when the librarian found Hebrew copies to be deficient and inadequate (29–30). And the Jewish scholars, when they set about their task, in comfortable quarters supplied by Ptolemy, did so by dividing labors, comparing results, and arriving at an agreed upon text (301–312, 317–321). This surely replicates, at least in principle, the type of subsidized scholarship promoted by the court and carried out in the Museum.[33]

The author is a cultivated Hellene. Adopting the pose of "Aristeas" came naturally and easily. He begins with a notice that extant copies of the Hebrew Bible had been carelessly transcribed and ends with a definitive Greek text subject to no further revision (29–30, 311). That implies a sanction of the Septuagint that supersedes the Hebrew original.[34] And, in a famous statement, Aristeas declared to Ptolemy that the Jews revere God, overseer and creator of all, who is worshipped by all including the Greeks, except that they give him a different name: Zeus (16). On the face of it, the *Letter of Aristeas* appears to be the most telling attestation of a cultural convergence between Judaism and Hellenism – at least as viewed from the Jewish side.[35] It certainly articulates the convergence.

But that does not tell the whole tale. The author, while fully familiar with Hellenic literary genres and the Alexandrian scholarly scene, adapted that knowledge to advertise the advantages of Jewish tradition. The distinctiveness of the Jews is never in question. The god to whom all bear witness, even though the Greeks may call him Zeus, is the Jewish god (cf. 42). Eleazar the High Priest happily sends Jewish scholars to Alexandria to render the Bible into Greek but he

---

33 Honigman, *Septuagint and Homeric Scholarship*, 42–49, 119–127.

34 On the sanctity of the text, and its replication of the original (in the eyes of "Aristeas"), see the remarks of H.M. Orlinsky, "The Septuagint as Holy Writ and the Philosophy of the Translators," *HUCA* 46 (1975) 89–114: 89–103, and B.G. Wright, "The Letter of Aristeas and the Reception History of the Septuagint," *BIOCS* 39 (2006) 47–67, with bibliography.

35 M. Hengel, *Judaism and Hellenism: Studies in their Encounter in Palestine during the Early Hellenistic Period.* 2 vols., (London, 1974), I, 264–265; Barclay, *Jews in the Mediterranean Diaspora*, 138–150; Collins, *Between Athens and Jerusalem*, 191–195; G.W.E. Nickelsburg, *Jewish Literature between the Bible and the Mishnah.* 2nd ed. (Minneapolis, 2005), 196–199.

reminds Aristeas of the superiority of Jewish monotheism, ridiculing those who worship idols of wood and stone fashioned by themselves, and he insists that Mosaic law insulated the Hebrews from outside influences, erecting firm barriers to prevent the infiltration of tainted institutions (134 – 142). The learned librarian Demetrius of Phalerum declared the wisdom of the Pentateuch to be both holy and highly philosophical, citing other Greek intellectuals for confirmation (312 – 316). The seven-day symposium, in which the Jewish scholars were interrogated, may have been a fundamentally Hellenic practice. But the scholars answered every query put by the king with swift and pithy answers, adding a reference to God in each response, and earning the admiration not only of Ptolemy and his courtiers but of all the Greek philosophers in attendance who acknowledged, their inferiority to the sagacity of the guests (200 – 210, 235, 296). The king's deference to the Hebrew scrolls and the Jerusalemite sages underscores the superiority of Jewish tradition and learning. Further, it is the Lord of the Jews who guided the king's actions and kept his kingdom secure so as to achieve his ends. And the High Priest observed that the Jews offer sacrifices to God to insure the peace and renown of the Ptolemaic kingdom – a neat reversal of the patron-client relationship (45). In short, the *Letter of Aristeas*, that quintessential text of Jewish Hellenism, testifies most eloquently to the appropriation of Hellenistic culture to express the preeminence of Jewish values.

Indeed one can go further than that. The *Letter of Aristeas* exhibits a remarkable self-assurance and a sense of comfort and belonging in the realm of Ptolemaic intellectual society that have rarely been recognized. "Aristeas" delivers his narrative in a sober and serious tone. Yet a closer reading can detect an undertone of oblique mockery and even mild subversiveness. And, on this score, it shows a linkage not only with other Jewish literature of this era, but with the wider literary scene of Ptolemaic Alexandria.

The portrait of Ptolemy II Philadelphus that looms so large in the text serves as the central exhibit. When scrutinized with care, it turns out to be more complex, problematic, and intriguing than scholars have realized. "Aristeas" presents an image that is overwhelmingly positive. Ptolemy is a wise gentle, and generous ruler. He is also a man of deep cultivation and learning Ptolemy took a personal interest and exercised direct oversight in the crafting of the elaborate gifts that were sent to Jerusalem, a man devoted to the arts (51, 56, 80 – 81). He filled his court with distinguished men, and he spent money freely in order to enjoy the company of the erudite and the wise (43, 124 – 125, 321). He evinced great reverence for the holy scriptures of the Jews and paid much honor to the High Priest and the Jewish scholars. He spared no expense in the construction of the furniture and art objects that would go to the Temple, and he spent unstintingly for the comfort and entertainment of his visitors from Jerusalem.

All this to the good. The remarks represent flattery of the king for his sterling qualities and for the honor he paid to Jewish practices and principles. So it seems on the surface. Yet the text, on second look, contains an undertone that compromises that impression. The generosity of Ptolemy could slide into excess and extravagance. In planning the dimensions of the table that he would offer as a gift to the Temple, his initial inclination was to order one of immense size, a testament to his grandiose authority.[36] He subsequently had second thoughts and inquired about the proportions of the previous table, but even then his preference was to build on a still larger scale – indeed five times the size of the earlier table. Only then did he realize that so huge an object might be unsuitable for the priestly ritual to be performed on it; and he backed down. But not before insisting that, if he had had leeway, he would have spared no expense (53 – 55). It is difficult to avoid the sense that "Aristeas" is here mocking the royal pretentiousness. Philadelphus' appetite for building on a lavish scale is known from other texts and other circumstances outside the Jewish context. The contemporary Alexandrian poet Posidippus spoke of a massive couch or table (3.22 – 23). And the grand procession in Alexandria, described by another contemporary Callixeinus, that exhibited the king's opulence included a tent with one hundred thirty gold couches (Athenaeus, 5.197 A). The *Letter*'s emphasis on self-promotion and ostentatious flamboyance has implications that are less than flattering.

The elaborate and detailed descriptions of Ptolemy's gifts, the *ekphrasis* portion of the text, reflect the king's munificence – but also his grandiose self-display. "Aristeas" makes a point of emphasizing the cost of these presents (80, 82). The very spectacle was designed to dazzle observers (77). And the artists strove to have everything project the exalted glory of the king (79). That puts the matter quite bluntly.[37] The author ends his *ekphrasis* by asserting that the expenditure in materials and craftsmanship amounted to five times the value of the gold (82). This quantification once more suggests a disproportionate extravagance.[38]

---

36 *LetAris*, 52. Notice the author's use of the term (ὑπέροπλόν) suggesting not just a colossal size but one that exhibited excess and arrogance.

37 In similar fashion, Callixeinus emphasized the ostentatious exhibit of splendor that marked Philadelphus' pageant in Alexandria; Athenaeus, 5.197C–203B. The encomium to Philadelphus composed by the contemporary poet Theocritus further highlights the king's wealth, in which he exceeds all other monarchs, and his lavish generosity; *Idylls*, 17.95 – 111.

38 It is noteworthy that Jos. *A. J.* 12.84, perhaps preferring not to inject a critical tone, omits this passage.

The king thought of everything "in a lordly manner," according to "Aristeas" (56: σεμνῶς). That sounds like a positive assessment. But a lordly monarch could also act in peremptory and authoritarian fashion. The decision to render the Hebrew Scriptures into Greek came on Philadelphus's orders (38). He commissioned the task and he simply "summoned" the Jewish scholars from Jerusalem to do the job – a clear sign of who was in charge.[39] Eleazar the High Priest had reason to feel some anxiety on this score. As the text has it, he knew of the king's penchant to seek out men of education and intellect; and he evidently worried that the Jewish elders might be induced to stay in Alexandria, even swearing an oath that he would not have allowed them to go were it not for the common benefit of his own nation (124; 126; cf. 46). This reflects on Ptolemy's cultivation – but also on his cultural acquisitiveness. The point recurs at the very end of the work when Ptolemy does release the scholars but encourages them to return and urges Eleazar not to prevent it (321). That is a telling conclusion. The author leaves readers with the final impression that the king could hijack learned visitors for his own cultural purposes.

At the week-long symposium Ptolemy put questions to each of the seventy two Jewish sages and received numerous gratifying and adulatory answers.[40] But the attentive reader would also find subtle allusions to some characteristics less appealing or admirable. An ironic comment may be detected at the very outset, surely no coincidence. The king's first question asked how he could maintain his kingdom intact to the end. His Jewish guest recommended that he exercise great patience with wrong-doers and treat them with greater indulgence than they merit (187–188; cf. 207). That advice stands sharply at odds with Eleazar's earlier praise of Philadelphus for executing informers, a practice which the character Aristeas heartily approves, even adding that the king imposes torture and grisly executions (166–167). Thus, the first piece of advice by a Jewish interlocutor at the banquet calls indirect attention to the cruelty of the king. That is un-

---

39 *LetAris*, 124: (μεταπέμπεσθαι). The Greek verb here implies a command rather than a request, thus hinting at Ptolemy's authoritarianism. This is reflected also in a much later story of Ptolemy's sending for the renowned Athenian comic dramatist Menander to join his court, an invitation that Menander declined. The story appears in the 3rd century CE writer Alciphron; *Letter*, 4.18. See the illuminating discussion of T. Rajak, "An invitation from Ptolemy; Aristeas, Alciphron, and Collective Memory," in *For Uriel: Studies in the History of Israel in Antiquity Presented to Professor Uriel Rappaport*, eds. M. Mor et al., (Jerusalem, 2005), 145–164: 152–162.
40 O. Murray, "Aristeas and Ptolemaic Kingship," *JTS* 18 (1967) 337–371: 344–361, remains a most important treatment of the symposium, but does not discuss the issues raised here. See also Parente, "La lettera di Aristea," 549–563; D. Mendels, "'On Kingship' in the 'Temple' Scroll and the Ideological Vorlage of the Seven Banquets in the 'Letter of Aristeas to Philocrates,'" *Aegyptus* 59 (1979) 127–136.

likely to be accidental. The subject comes up again later in the symposium with still more ominous implications: Ptolemy addresses a Jewish sage with the query of how he might avoid resort to rage. The Jew reminded him that he possesses absolute authority, including the power of life and death, but counseled that multiple executions, just because he had the power to order them, would be disadvantageous and dire (253). One is tempted here to see a reflection upon the absolutist regime. The very fact that the author regards large-scale executions by Ptolemy as a possibility against which he needs to be warned is sufficiently suggestive. And it may be significant that the Jewish elder followed this statement with a reference to God's clemency and asserted that this is a model that the king *must* follow.[41] He thus moves from admonition to directive. The language is unusually strong, a bold pronouncement by the author–and conveys the idea that Ptolemy requires this reminder.

Allusions to flaws in the king's makeup or accomplishments occur periodically in the interchange, not conspicuous criticism but subtle subversion. So, for instance, Ptolemy's question of what he needs do to remain rich hardly casts him in a favorable light. And the interlocutor's answer that he should avoid unnecessary expenses suggests a bit of mockery (204–205). A whimsical tone exists also in ascribing to Ptolemy a question on how to cure insomnia. The learned Jewish scholar professes to reply in sober fashion but in fact, gives a rambling response that has only marginal relevance to the query (213–216). This too is hard to take seriously. A comparable instance occurs when the king asks how he can avoid doing something unworthy of himself. The scholar replies that he should look at all times to his own glory and prominence since everybody always talks about him. That, in effect, bids Ptolemy to keep polishing his public image, not altogether noble counsel. And the Jew proceeds to advise Ptolemy that he be sure not to appear inferior to actors who have to play a consistent role (217–219). The comparison alone is demeaning, since actors held a rather low status in society. "Aristeas" may well be speaking tongue-in-cheek. One might note also the query that Philadelphus makes as to how to build structures that would endure. The interlocutor offers a numbingly obvious reply: make them great and awesome (258). As if anyone had to tell Philadelphus to construct majestic buildings! And the Jew adds the noteworthy advice that laborers on the buildings should be paid a decent wage and others should not be coerced into doing the job without remuneration (258–259). This is either an obliquely critical comment or an amusing reflection on Ptolemy's building program. Unmistakably whimsical is an exchange prompted by the king's question of how he might have a cordial

---

41 *LetAris:* 254: (τούτῳ δὲ κατακολουθεῖν ἀναγκαῖόν ἐστί σε).

relationship with his wife. The Jewish scholar replies with a litany of stereotypes about female fickleness, emotional instability, poor reasoning powers, and natural weakness. The best way to handle them, he proposes, is to avoid starting a quarrel (250). The author plainly indulges in some fun here. The question he puts in Ptolemy's mouth suggests problems in his marital situation – which no king, of course, would have put out to public scrutiny.[42] And one cannot fail to see a sardonic twist when, near the end of the last day of the prolonged symposium, the king asks how one should conduct himself in symposia (286). Since he had already spent seven days posing questions in tedious and often repetitive fashion to seventy different individuals, it seems a bit late now to wonder about the proprieties of symposium behavior.

Other comments are less frivolous, but perhaps more subversive. Philadelphus puts to a guest the question of what is the strongest rule. The initial answer, to rule oneself and not allow the passions to rule, is good Stoic doctrine. But the guest adds that most men are led astray by desire for food, drink, and pleasure, whereas kings are motivated by acquisition of territory and fame; moderation in all matters, however, is best (222–223). Philadelphus, in fact, prided himself upon and was lauded by the poets for the vast imperial holdings he had brought under his sway.[43] Under the circumstances, a reference to the acquisitiveness of kings and the need for moderation would seem to have a critical edge.

A large proportion of the answers involve some flattery of the king. But in more than one case, the flattery goes beyond expected bounds. When the interlocutor asserts that it is impossible for Ptolemy to make a false step, in reply to a question of how the king might regain his glory after stumbling; the adulation is excessive and unnecessary in the context (230). It may indeed hint at the sycophancy that was encouraged at the court of Philadephus. The issue arises more directly somewhat later in the symposium. When the king asks how he might recognize those who engaged in deceit in their dealings with him, the Jewish sage suggested that he watch out for those who went further than necessary in their compliments to him and in the rest of their behavior (246). "Aristeas" here again draws attention to the fawning blandishments called forth at ceremonial occa-

---

42 Philadelphus sister-wife Arsinoe II was a notoriously powerful woman, involved even in Ptolemaic foreign policy decisions. See Syll. 3.434–5; lines. 15–18: "Aristeas" may very well be making an oblique allusion to his.
43 Theocritus, 17.82–94; Posidippus, 45.1, 46.2, 47.5, 54.3; Athenaeus, 5.197B–203B.

sions and official functions. By placing the practice in the context of a question on guile and deceit, he offers a still darker image of court demeanor.[44]

This is no incidental comment. "Aristeas" brings up the same subject later in the banquet when the king asks a parallel question about how he could avoid being deceived. The Jewish speaker gives a pragmatic and calculated response: the best tactic is to interrogate the suspected double-dealer at different times with the same question and judge the reaction (275–276). The query itself suggests a ruler anxious about intrigue and opposition within his own ranks, thus implying the existence of dissent, something that few kings would wish to disclose in public. It is noteworthy that the speaker does not deny, rather assumes the presence of dissimulation among Ptolemy's courtiers. His advice about persistent interrogation exposes a cynical view of relations within the king's inner circle.

Ptolemy's next to last query also merits notice. He wondered whether it is better for the people to have a king who rose from the ranks of the citizenry or one born of royal blood. The Jewish scholar offered a judicious response, noting that kings who stem from other kings can be harsh and savage with their subjects, although those who were commoners by birth could be worse (288–289). The statement about harsh and savage monarchs of royal stock is a general one and meant to be understood as such. Yet by placing the remark in the ostensible setting of Philadelphus' court (where the interrogator was the only example of a king sprung from a king), the author must have expected his readers to draw a conclusion about that monarch. The very last question about what constitutes the greatest thing in royalty drew the reply that subjects should live in peace. And the speaker concluded by expressing confidence that this was bound to come about because God accorded Philadelphus a mind pure and unsullied by any evil (291–292). The flattery once again is transparently immoderate, doubtless deliberately so. But there may be more to it than that. The juxtaposition of this fulsome characterization by the final speaker of Ptolemy's irreproachable intellect with the previous speaker's reference to royal (his) cruelty and inhumanity ends the banquet on a decidedly sardonic note.

The cumulative evidence is strong and compelling. Amidst all the praise and accolades heaped upon Ptolemy by the Jewish sages who received lavish hospitality at his hands, an undertone of nuanced cynicism pervades the narrative of the symposium. The speakers allude in recurrent fashion to the king's extrava-

---

44 Cf. also *LetAris*, 270, where the Jewish speaker contrasts those who serve the king out of good will and those who do so from fear or self interest. The latter operate from calculations of profit and amount to traitors. This looks like a hint of what is going on in court.

gance, ostentation, acquisitiveness, suspicious nature, harshness, and insecurity.

Nor is this all. The *Letter* portrays Ptolemy II as a man of great generosity, beneficence, and sensitivity toward the Jews. One needs mention only the liberality he displayed in emancipating (according to the text) more than one hundred thousand Jews who had been brought to Egypt as war captives by his father (17–20). Even here, however, the author, ever so slightly, compromises this act of magnanimity. The king, presented for the first time near the beginning of the treatise, does not conceive the deed himself. Aristeas had to suggest it to him. Ptolemy hesitated at first, evidently not ready to leap at the chance to bestow this benefaction. It took God's intervention to persuade the king. The language of the text, in fact, is quite strong. Aristeas prayed to God in order that Ptolemy be *compelled* to fulfill his request. And he did so under constraint.[45] It was God who *empowered* the king to perform his acts of munificence.[46]

Ptolemy, to be sure, exhibits throughout the narrative his respect for and deference to the Jews, to their practices, their traditions, and their God. Yet the undercurrent here as well may flow in a different direction. "Aristeas" carries this portrait somewhat beyond the sober and the plausible. Ptolemy, to be sure, is deferential, but perhaps deferential to a fault. Upon the arrival in Alexandria of the Jewish elders from Jerusalem, the king promptly canceled all other matters of state, dismissed all official personnel, and gave sole attention to his new guests, a procedure altogether exceptional in royal protocol (174–175). The exaggeration is patent. That Ptolemy would put a delegation from Jerusalem ahead of all business of the realm and accord them signal privileges is sheer fantasy. And the implausibility only deepens. It is one thing to pay due respect to the Jewish divinity and sacred books. It is quite another to perform *proskynesis* no fewer than seven times to the Hebrew scrolls once they reached the shores of Alexandria – and then to proclaim that the date of their arrival would henceforth be celebrated as an annual festival (176–180). That stretches the point beyond plausibility and borders on parody.

Further, the very inclusion of the symposium in the treatise and the manner in which it was conducted appear to derive from a mischievous sense of humor. And the king can be seen as its principal target. Quite apart from the oblique criticisms that emerge in individual exchanges already discussed, the circum-

---

45 *LetAris*, 17: (ἵνα συναναγκασθῇ, καθὼς ἠξίουν, ἐπιτελέσαι); 20: (τοῦ θεοῦ ... συναναγκάσαντος αὐτόν).
46 *LetAris*, 21: (τοῦ θεοῦ κατισχύοντος αὐτόν).

stances and proceedings have little claim on credibility. The festivities went on for a full week, with Ptolemy straining to provide a different question for each of the seventy-two Jewish elders. When the answers came, they were swift, brief, often repeating Greek philosophical commonplaces, and usually rather banal. Many of them bore only a marginal relation to the question asked.[47] In each case, the Jewish sages inserted a reference to God as the ultimate authority, repeated in various ways but with much the same message, almost to the point of monotony. And in a large portion of instances, the allusion to divine power bore no relevance to the question or the answer; but constituted a mechanical tag line that only increased the tedium of the mounting responses.[48] And yet to every sage who spoke Philadelphus dutifully commended his wisdom and sagacity – no matter how conventional or repetitive the reply. The author struggled to find enough variation in his vocabulary to characterize praise by the king for each of the seventy-two interlocutors. The fact that Ptolemy lauds them all hardly attests to his discrimination or discernment. When he asked how he might be invincible in warfare, he heard that he should forget about military numbers or power and just rely on God (193). That answer would not be found in Greek political philosophy. It comes strictly from Jewish tradition (e.g. Psalms, 104:27). Nor would Ptolemy follow advice that had him go to the battlefield with prayers rather than arms. The notion that he acclaimed the speaker for this recommendation borders on the ludicrous. "Aristeas," even without direct criticism, repeatedly underscores the gullibility of the king.

What stands out in all this is the liberty that the author of the *Letter* felt in poking fun at the ruler. None of it necessarily constitutes hostility or ill-will. Ptolemy remains a generally sympathetic figure. But he could also be the subject of reproach or the butt of humor. That suggests a level of comfort and satisfaction enjoyed by Jewish intellectuals in the society of Ptolemaic Alexandria. The *Letter of Aristeas* could both exhibit the integration of Jewish culture in the Hellenic community and emphasize its superiority – and do so with a sense of humor. On this score the work takes its place among a number of Jewish-Hellenistic writings composed (or probably composed) in Alexandria that exhibit similar characteristics and reinforce the picture of circumstances suitable to the flourishing

---

47 So, for instance, when Ptolemy asks "what is the nature of piety?" the respondent reminds the king that no act of injustice escapes God's notice (210). Or his inquiry about the noblest aim of life receives the answer that God guides all mens' actions (195).
48 As an example, the reply to Ptolemy's query about the advantages of kinship concludes with advice to pray to God (241–242). Or, most noticeably, when the sage answered Ptolemy's request about how to live harmoniously with his wife, he threw in a line regarding the invocation of God as a steersman for one's life (250–251). Numerous other instances could be cited.

of literary activity. This is not the place for a detailed recapitulation of such works. But reference to a few instances can make the point.

Aristobulus, a 2nd century BCE Jew of philosophic education and pretensions, played with what became a favored Jewish fiction: that Hellenic ideas derived from Hebraic roots.[49] Aristobulus' work, it appears, was cast in the form of a dialogue between the Jewish philosopher and Ptolemy VI Philometor in the mid 2nd century. That frame may be a literary conceit. But the effort to link his writing to the Alexandrian court, as in the *Letter of Aristeas*, reflects the context in which Aristobulus sought to place himself. In his imaginative construct, Moses provided stimulus for Hellenic philosophers and poets. The ideas of Pythagoras and Plato, for example, followed the path laid out by Mosaic legislation (Eus. *PE*, 13.12.1). Even Socrates' divine voice allowing him to contemplate the creation of the cosmos, arose from the words of Moses. As if that were not enough, Aristobulus affirmed that a universal consensus existed among philosophers that only pious opinions should be held about God, and since that view is embedded in Mosaic law, it follows that Jewish conceptualizing supplied the wellspring for Hellenic philosophizing (Eus. *PE*, 13.12.3–4, 8). Aristobulus further extended the work of the Jews from philosophy to poetry. He conjured up Orpheus, the legendary singer and source of Greek poetics. By interpreting his supposed verses on God as all-encompassing power, origin of life, and supreme being in light of Jewish precepts, Aristobulus could claim the father of Hellenic song as well for the camp of Moses' followers (Eus. *PE*, 13.12.4). Aristobulus had thus harnessed some of the most celebrated Greek thinkers and artists, legendary or real, to the antique traditions of the Jews. There is a sense of playfulness in this endeavor, not a fierce rivalry between Greek and Jew. The Jewish claim on precedence need not be taken as altogether serious. But it represents a mode of prideful expression in a diaspora community that both asserted its connection to the Greek achievement and displayed its own self-assurance.

A similar orientation can be found, with even greater exuberance and wit, in the imaginative writer Artapanus, a Hellenized Jew from Egypt in the 2nd or 1st century BCE.[50] His creative rewriting of biblical stories includes an elaborate ac-

---

49 See the thorough and invaluable treatment of C.R. Holladay, *Fragments from Hellenistic Jewish Authors.* Vol. III: Aristobulus. (Atlanta, 1995). Subsequent discussions appear in Barclay, *Jews in the Mediterranean Diaspora*, 150–158; Gruen, *Heritage and Hellenism*, 246–251; Collins, *Between Athens and Jerusalem*, 186–190.

50 On Artapanus, see the edition and commentary of C.R. Holladay, *Fragments from Hellenistic Jewish Authors.* Vol. I: The Historians (Chico, 1983), 189–243. More treatments by Barclay, *Jews in the Mediterranean-Diaspora*, 127–132; Gruen, *Heritage and Hellenism*, 155–160; Collins,

count of Moses' exploits that goes well beyond any scriptural foundation. Apart from ascribing to Moses the inception of a host of Egyptian institutions and technologies, he adds a Greek connection. The name Moses, so Artapanus claims, induced Greeks to identify him with Musaeus, the legendary poet and prophet from Attica, son or pupil of Orpheus, who stands at the dawn of Hellenic song and wisdom. Artapanus, however, gives a slight but significant twist to the legend. He has Musaeus as mentor of Orpheus rather than the other way around. Moses therefore becomes the father of Greek poetic and prophetic traditions (Eus. *PE*, 9.27.3 – 4). Artapanus neither rejects nor disparages those Greek traditions. He simply goes them one better and counts them as part of a Hebrew heritage. The fragments of Artapanus disclose a humorous quality that also characterizes the work of other Jewish texts. They claim Jewish priority and precedence, but they do so with a light touch that owes more to caprice than to polemics.

That quality appears also in a fragment from an unknown Jewish writer Josephus cites him as Hecataeus of Abdera, a well known Greek historian, but the quotations from his work make it nearly certain that he is an Egyptian Jew who adopted the pseudonym "Hecataeus," just as the composer of the *Letter* employed the pseudonym "Aristeas." The author delivered a most favorable account of Ptolemy I and his generous attitude toward Jews whose migration to Egypt he had encouraged by his gentleness and humanitarianism (Jos. *CAp*, 1.186 – 189). This did not, however, prevent Pseudo-Hecataeus from inserting an amusing tale that exhibited superior Jewish skill and intelligence (Jos. *CAp*, 1.200 – 204).[51] The anecdote speaks of a Jewish archer, Mosollamos, in the service of the Ptolemaic army. The author describes him as the best of bowmen, whether Greek or non-Greek, and a man who combined physical and intellectual prowess. As the tale has it, the army stalled on its march because a Greek seer observed the movements of a bird to discern whether the soldiers should advance, retreat, or delay. Mosollamos then calmly brought out his bow and arrows and shot the bird dead. When confronted by the shocked and angry Greeks who demanded to know why he did so, Mosollamos had a witty reply: "If the bird were so smart and could foretell the future, why did he show up here and fail to foresee that he would be shot by the arrow of Mosollamos the Jew?" The episode, surely an invention by Pseudo-Hecataeus, mocked the incompetence of the Greek seer and the credulity of Ptolemy's Greek forces. The able Jew showed himself more adept and knowledgeable than any other member of the king's troops.

Between Athens and Jerusalem, 37 – 46; Johnson, *Historical Fictions*, 95 – 108; P. Bourgeaud, *Aux origines de l'histoire des religions* (Paris, 2004), 125 – 134.
51 See the discussion of B. Bar-Kochva, *Pseudo-Hecataeus, "On the Jews" Legitimizing the Jewish Diaspora* (Hellenistic Culture and Society 21) (Berkeley, 1996), 57 – 71.

The whimsical story contained an indirect slap at the Ptolemaic ruler for relying upon somewhat thick-headed military men and seers who were charlatans, instead of more pragmatic, accomplished, and smart Jews. Once again, the narrative contains more wit than animosity, an index of Jewish pride in their people's own cleverness and achievements.

A somewhat darker quality appears in the remarkable text called 3 Maccabees – but perhaps only on the surface. The story represents a Ptolemaic ruler, in this case Ptolemy IV Philopator, as determined to eradicate all the Jews in his kingdom. The task was to be effected by having them trampled by five hundred elephants motivated by heavy doses of frankincense and unmixed wine. The wicked plot, however, was foiled by the intervention of God, twice through afflicting Ptolemy with sudden sleep and amnesia, and finally by having the elephants turn about and crush the forces of the king, leaving the Jews safe and sound. Philopator at last acknowledged the power of the Jewish god, heaped honor upon the Jews, scorned their enemies, and established a festival to celebrate their liberation. The narrative is often seen as reflecting a deep hostility between the crown and the Jewish community. But that adopts too somber and serious an interpretation of the text. It does, after all, deliver a happy ending in which king and Jews express harmony and concord and Jewish success is commemorated on the orders of the king. In fact, those who opposed the Jews are largely a court cabal, whereas the Alexandrian Greeks offered them sympathy, encouragement, and even clandestine assistance (3.8 – 10). Nor is Ptolemy represented simply as a fierce monster struck down by the Lord to bring about the salvation of the Jews. Rather, the author of 3 Maccabees shows a sardonic humor that makes the king more a baffled buffoon than a fiendish villain. And the scenes carry more hilarity than terror. So, for instance, the king abandoned the registration of Jews because his clerks ran out of pen and paper (4.20). And he failed to execute his plans, first because he fell asleep, and second because he could not remember what orders he had given (5.10 – 20, 5.26 – 32). Indeed, the very idea of rounding up five hundred elephants and drugging them with massive quantities of frankincense and wine only underlines the absurdity of the tale. The fact that the great animals had to be drugged three times before they began their stampede, and then they turned in the wrong direction, can only have been designed as comic farce. The text once again demonstrates the marvelous self-assurance of Hellenistic Jews in Alexandria who could frame a tale that reinforced their cordial connection to the throne while making the occupant the target of good-natured caricature.[52]

---

52 This summarizes the analysis of Gruen, *Heritage and Hellenism*, 222 – 236. See the thorough

More telling still, the Jews in this regard fitted perfectly into the conventions of pagan Alexandrian literary society. Even the poets who enjoyed royal subsidy and support in the Alexandrian Museum and who naturally presented the monarch in a favorable light could occasionally slip in a sly dig at the man on the throne.

One might note as an illustration Theocritus, the famed composer of pastoral poetry who had the warm backing of Ptolemy Philadelphus, a direct contemporary of the period about which "Aristeas" wrote. Theocritus, in addition to his poems of shepherds and singers, composed an *Encomium to Ptolemy Philadelphus*. The poem of course, celebrates Ptolemy's deeds and achievements. Yet the poet also makes sure to put him in his place. He opens the piece by stating that he begins and ends with Zeus (12.1–2). Poets in former times, he says, had demi-gods to sing of; he has Ptolemy (17.5–8). And at the end of the poem, Theocritus hails king Ptolemy, but adds that the quest for virtue must come from Zeus (137). Moreover, in a work couched as an encomium, there as strikingly little reference to any accomplishments – or virtues for that matter – of the ruler. Theocritus alludes to Ptolemy's territorial holdings and his skill with the sword (85–94, 102–103). But this could only remind readers that Philadelphus had no reputation or record as a warrior. Theocritus' comparison of Ptolemy's marriage with his sister Arsinoe to the wedding of Zeus and Hera had a double edge (17.128–135). Some readers did not approve of that incestuous union (cf. Athenaeus, 621 A). And a comparison with the stormy relationship of Zeus and Hera may not have been an altogether flattering one.

In a different poem, Theocritus has an Alexandrian praise the king's virtues to his friend. They include his kindliness, love of culture, and generosity. But he also refers to Ptolemy as ἐρωτικός (14.61–65). In itself that is no negative remark. In the circumstances, however, it was bound to bring to readers' minds Philadelphus' notorious flings with his mistresses (Athenaeus, 13:576 E–F). And the speaker also notes the limits to Ptolemy's generosity. He advises his friend that, although Ptolemy does not refuse when he is asked, "don't ask him for everything" (65).

In yet another poem, Theocritus also offers some circuitous criticism. When two women venture out in the crowded streets of Alexandria, one of them praises Philadelphus for having cleared out many of the criminal elements, the robbers, pick-pockets, and beggars who had been left by his father Soter. But just at that

---

and incisive study of Johnson, *Historical Fictions*, 122–216. Different interpretations in Barclay, *Jews in the Mediterranean Diaspora*, 192–203; Collins, *Between Athens and Jerusalem*, 122–131; Nickelsburg, *Jewish Literature*, 199–202.

point the woman is suddenly reminded of the unruly crowds still in the city, as she is crushed by a mob and almost trampled by a horseman in the cavalry of the king (15.46 – 53). The poet may have been a loyal client of the monarchy. But that did not prevent him from delivering subtle thrusts at the flaws of the king and his regime.

This form of disguised dissent can be found elsewhere. In Herodas' mime about the matchmaker, also in the time of Philadelphus, the speaker pauses to recount the numerous and varied advantages of living in Egypt (1.26 – 31). They include wealth, gymnasia, power, glory, spectacles, philosophers, young men, the Museum, endless numbers of beautiful women; in short everything one could wish. Amidst this catalogue of delights, there is just a single passing mention of the "good king" – and that appears in conjunction with the shrine of the brother-sister gods. The monarch is nothing more than one of the sights to see in Alexandria. Herodas' allusion hardly serves as a great compliment, and plainly comes tongue-in-cheek.

The great Alexandrian poet and prolific writer Callimachus composed a hymn to Delos that contains a passage worth noticing in this connection (4.171 – 195). Callimachus has Apollo predict a future contest between Greeks and the barbaric Gauls. He makes reference here to the celebrated defeat of the Gauls who sought to capture the shrine of Apollo at Delphi but were thwarted by the god. In the same passage, Apollo predicts the birth of Ptolemy Philadelphus and a parallel victory over the Gauls. To be sure, Ptolemy did indeed contend with Gauls, but they were his own hired mercenaries who then plotted to seize Egypt, and he managed to foil the plot only by inducing them to occupy a desert island where they died of hunger or at one another's hands (Pausanias, 1.7.2). That was far from a glorious victory for Ptolemy. The juxtaposition of that tawdry event with the fabled rescue of Delphi from Gallic attack could only diminish by comparison Ptolemy's feat and his reputation.

None of these examples, of course, constitutes an open and direct attack upon the king. Artists dependent on the court would not likely run the risk of giving offense. In each case, the writer couched his allusion in the form of praise and admiration – or at least ostensible praise and admiration. But the poets evidently exercised the liberty of inserting indirect innuendoes and insinuations that gave an ironic twist to their encomiums, a marked feature of Alexandrian literature. In this important regard, Jewish writers in Alexandria seem to have enjoyed a similar privilege. They too could pepper their writings with subtle and clever jabs at men in power, while simultaneously and superficially paying homage to them. They fitted well into the intellectual environment of Hellenistic Alexandria. Their works could exhibit that same freedom of expression, delivered in forms that reinforced their standing in the society and culture of that city. Such works served to articulate their status – and the fact that they belonged.

Did this combination of self-esteem and integration in the community, exemplified by the *Letter of Aristeas*, help to motivate the creation of the Septuagint itself? One can give no decisive answer. The *Letter* was composed at least a half century, perhaps more than a century, after the translation of the Pentateuch. And the other Jewish texts discussed here were no earlier. They speak to the cultural environment of the 2nd century. The circumstances of the actual translation elude our grasp. Ptolemy Philadelphus may or may not have played a role in the project. He had the reputation of a cultivated and learned man and he might well have taken an interest in making accessible an important piece of alien wisdom. But it is precisely that reputation that would have made him a logical figure to whom a later Jewish author could attribute such a project. In similar fashion, Demetrius of Phalerum's reputation as a wide-ranging intellectual made him a logical person to be imagined as a collaborator in the undertaking. In any case, it seems quite unlikely that either Ptolemy or Demetrius conceived this enterprise. The impetus may have come from below, as is usually thought: the Jews of Alexandria had largely lost their command of Hebrew.[53] Even if that is the case, however, the job had to be done by an intellectual elite, i.e. those who retained fluency in both tongues – and they did not have the same motivation. There is more to this than the need for an intelligible text.

The project may best be seen as a means of exhibiting Jewish pride and self-confidence. Having the holy books rendered into Greek carried considerable symbolic meaning. It signified that Jews had a legitimate claim on a place in the prevailing culture of the Mediterranean.[54] Their Scriptures did not belong to an isolated and marginal group. They expounded the traditions and principles of a people whose roots went back to distant antiquity but who also maintained their prestige and authority in a contemporary society – and a contemporary language. Like their pagan counterparts in Alexandrian literary circles; they developed the self-assurance to praise the ruler of their land – and also gently to tease

---

53 That remains the prevailing view; e.g. Fraser, *Ptolemaic Alexandria*, I, 690; II, 957–958, and, much too confidently, Gruen, *Heritage and Hellenism*, 208–210, with further bibliography. See also S. Kreuzer, "Entstehung und Publikation der Septuagint im Horizont frühptolemäischer Bildungs- und Kulturpolitik," in *Im Brennpunkt: Die Septuaginta*. II (see Footnote 28), 61–75; Wasserstein/Wasserstein, *Legend of the Septuagint*, 4–13.

54 For somewhat analogous suggestions, based on quite different arguments, see Honigman, *Septuagint and Homeric Scholarship*, 137–138; Rajak *Translation and Survival*. Dines, *The Septuagint*, 60–61, sees the project as a natural result of Jews living in the cultivated, bookish society of Alexandria.

him and mock him. That may be the clearest sigh that Jews perceived themselves as an integral part of the Hellenistic cultural world.

20. The Twisted Tales of Artapanus: Biblical Rewritings as Novelistic Narrative

Artapanus defies categories and classification. Efforts to assign a label have won no consensus. The author slips swiftly out of our grasp. And the application of tags may well be beside the point. Artapanus does not readily fit molds and ought not to be squeezed into them. His name suggests Persian origins, he composed in Greek, and his subject matter stems from the Hebrew Bible—though much massaged and manipulated. Arguments over whence he came, when he lived, and why he wrote have been many, with few results. Yet Artapanus continues to stir interest. His idiosyncratic tales, entertaining and amusing, with a mixture of piety and irreverence, verisimilitude and fantasy, naturally lure investigators, even when they lead to bafflement and perplexity.

Only three fragments survive from Artapanus' work, the Περὶ Ἰουδαίων, yet another source of frustration. But the fragments intrigue inquirers and disclose an inventive mind. The 1st century BCE Greek polymath, Alexander Polyhistor, quoted them, whence they came to Eusebius whose *Praeparatio Evangelica* preserved them for posterity.[1] Like many Hellenistic Jewish texts, the treatise was ignored or scorned by the rabbis but proved more congenial to Christian churchmen to whom we owe what survives. Two of the fragments, those on Abraham and Joseph, are too brief for extended comment. But the third, on Moses, gives more to chew upon, a substantial chunk that conveys an involved and engaging tale and justifies analysis in the context of creative fiction.

A summary of the extant text will facilitate matters. The brief extract concerning Abraham has him move with his entire household to Egypt, stay there for twenty years, teach astrology to the Pharaoh, and then return home, while many in his entourage remained to enjoy the prosperity of the land.[2] That is all we have. But even so condensed a citation shows that Artapanus departed freely from the text of Genesis. The latter gives a very different story about Abraham's visit to Egypt where he deviously represented his wife as his sister in order to save his own neck, makes no allusion to astrology, and says nothing about so long a stay.[3] Further, Artapanus provides the provocative (and unique) notice that the Jews originally carried the designation of "Hermiouth" which translates to "Ioudaioi" in Greek, only later receiving the appellation of "Hebrews" from the

---

1 For the title, see Eus. *PE*, 9.23.1; Clement, *Strom.* 1.23.154.2. An alternative, ἐν τοῖς Ἰου-δαικοῖς, appears in Eus. *PE*. 9.18.1

2 Eus. *PE*, 9.18.1.

3 See Gen. 12:10 – 13.1.

time of Abraham. Whatever one makes of that most peculiar observation, it certainly signals the author's idiosyncrasy.

The saga of Joseph reaches us in equally truncated form. Artapanus has his own take on the quarrel between Joseph and his brothers, presenting him as a discerning young man who anticipates his brothers' (ostensibly unmotivated) plot, enlists neighboring Arabs to help him escape to Egypt, and rapidly becomes finance minister for the Pharaoh's whole realm. His wisdom and sense of justice brought economic equity to the land, introduced knowledge of measures, and gained him the affection of the Egyptian people, among whom he dwelled, took a bride, and fathered children. He subsequently welcomed his father and brothers who came to settle in Egypt, built temples in two different sites, and multiplied rapidly. Joseph's tenure as czar of finance made him, in effect, ruler of the nation.[4] This abridged version leaves out some of the juicier parts of the Genesis narrative, including Joseph's time in prison, his interpretation of dreams, and the attempted seduction by Potiphar's wife. Nor is this merely a feature of selectivity by the excerptor. Artapanus' picture of Joseph has a decidedly different flavor from that of the biblical account. His Joseph takes the initiative in the dispute with his brothers, no mere victim but an anticipator of events. He swiftly gained the confidence of the Pharaoh, and took over the affairs of the land with resoluteness and success. While Genesis has Joseph serve the king and entrench royal power on the backs of the Egyptian peasantry, Artapanus makes him into an authentic reformer, ending exploitation of the weak by the strong, and acting in the interests of the nation as a whole.[5] A much rosier depiction than that of the Bible where Joseph is a more ambiguous and occasionally less admirable character. Artapanus once more goes his own way.

The bulk of Artapanus as bequeathed by Eusebius consists of a long fragment that conveys the Moses story. The narrative intersects at various points with the Book of Exodus. But the author gave full rein to his imagination. Moses, in his version, becomes a cultural progenitor of the Egyptians and, to some extent, of all mankind. Although a Jew, he was raised by a daughter of the pharaoh and swiftly became the central figure of Egyptian society. The Greeks transformed the name Moses into Musaeus, thus giving him mythological status as teacher of Orpheus. That association granted him wide knowledge and authority, allowing him to accord to humankind numerous benefactions, such as naval vessels, hauling equipment, weaponry, hydraulic devices—and even phi-

---

4 Eus. *PE*, 9.23.1 – 4.
5 For the biblical account of Joseph and his brothers, see Gen. 37:2 – 36. For that of his administration in Egypt, see Gen. 47:13 – 26.

losophy. More immediately, Moses had responsibility for creating the administrative districts called nomes, for assigning the god to be worshipped in each, specified as cats, dogs, and ibises, and for distributing sacred writings, as well as land, to the priests. All this Moses accomplished in order to assure stability for the realm of the pharaoh Chenephres. He earned the favor of the people, received honors equivalent to a god from the priests, and gained the name Hermes because of his skill in interpreting sacred scriptures.[6] Very little of this parallels anything to be found in the Book of Exodus. Conspicuous for its omission is any mention of Moses as lawgiver for the Hebrews. Artapanus reinvents Moses as the fount of Egyptian institutions, even of hieroglyphics and animal worship, and as cultural benefactor to all of humankind.

The author then reverts to the narrative of an adventure tale—and an altogether novel one. Chenephres the Pharaoh, jealous of Moses' accomplishments, took a dislike to him, and sent him off to war against the Ethiopians with a makeshift band, expecting to see the last of him. But Moses proved to be as successful a military hero as a bringer of culture. He conducted a ten year war of epic proportions and not only returned victorious but won the hearts of the Ethiopians themselves, even introducing them to the fine art of circumcision.[7] That bit of whimsy gives a clue to Artapanus' mindset: a writer of some mischief.

The wicked Chenephres pretended to welcome Moses' homecoming, even asking his advice on the best breed of oxen to plow the fields, whence came the origin of Apis worship among the Egyptians. But, all the while, he plotted against the hero. He appointed assassins, most of whom declined the task, and the one who agreed was duly overpowered by the swifter and keener Moses. The adventures accumulate. A sojourn in Arabia brought Moses to the attention of an Arab leader whose daughter he married but whose importunings to march on Egypt he declined out of regard for his countrymen. Moses returned to his homeland only when the conniving Chenephres perished of elephantiasis, a fitting end, for he was the initial victim of that disease.[8]

Now, for the first time, God enters the picture. Hitherto, the story was strictly secular—apart from Egyptian divinities whom Moses himself had introduced. Echoes from Exodus resonate here. Moses seeks assistance from God to rescue his people from oppression in Egypt. And the burning bush duly blazes. The hero, briefly frightened, then receives reassurance from a divine voice that urges him to take up arms against the Egyptians, which he proceeds to do.[9] Ar-

---

6 Eus. *PE*, 9.27.1 – 6.
7 Eus. *PE*. 9.27.7 – 10.
8 Eus. *PE*, 9.27.11 – 20.
9 Eus. *PE*, 9.27.21 – 22.

tapanus' version here, even while alluding to Exodus, gives it his own twist, and quite a striking one. God never orders a military expedition in the Bible, only remonstrations with pharaoh. The warrior credentials of Moses take precedence in this retelling.

What came of the war disappeared from the record.[10] Domestic intrigue, however, supervened. The new pharaoh imprisoned Moses, hoping to silence him. It was a futile resistance to the inevitable. Prison doors miraculously opened, guards proved helpless, some of them asleep, some dead, their weapons broken, and Moses calmly sauntered into the palace. Pharaoh, roused from sleep, demanded that Moses tell him what god had sent him. That was poor miscalculation on his part. Moses whispered the divine name in the king's ear, thus causing him to collapse in a heap, reviving only when Moses picked him up. An Egyptian priest was not so fortunate. He had a look at the divine name that had been inscribed on a tablet by Moses, treated it mockingly, and immediately suffered a convulsion that terminated his life.[11] It need hardly be said that the Bible breathes not a hint of any of this. Artapanus constructed his own tale with Moses as magician and God as mowing down Egyptians.

The rest of Artapanus' narrative does bear a closer resemblance to the account in Exodus, but far from a replica. He plays willfully with the tale of the plagues, including some, omitting others, reshuffling and reordering them, and inserting some noteworthy novelties.[12] So, for instance, Moses strikes the Nile with his rod, not to turn the waters into blood but to have the Nile flood its banks. The author proudly announces that this act initiated the regular flooding of the Nile, the very lifeline of the nation, yet another feat of magnitude and magnanimity by the culture-hero Moses.[13] Not exactly what Exodus had in mind. Various plagues followed at Moses' behest, corresponding only occasionally and erratically with those found in the biblical account. The mischievous Artapanus juxtaposes the plague of hail with one of earthquakes (the latter makes no appearance in Exodus) and presents Egyptians as darting about to escape the one, only to be felled by the other.[14] Pharaoh remained resolute. For Artapanus,

---

10 The battle itself does not appear in the text, and there is no follow-up of Moses' resolve to wage war. That ostensible gap in the narrative may mean that Alexander Polyhistor left it out of his summary. It is noteworthy that Josephus' rewriting of Exodus has the divine voice enjoin Moses to become commander of the Hebrew hosts but also provides no battle narrative; *Ant.* 2.268.

11 Eus. *PE*, 9.27.23 – 26.

12 Eus. *PE*, 9.27.27 – 33.

13 Eus. *PE*, 9.27.27 – 28.

14 Eus. *PE*, 9.27.33.

arrogance impelled him. No mention of God hardening his heart.[15] And a still more startling omission cannot fail to have been noticed by any knowledgeable reader. Artapanus leaves out the fatal tenth plague: death of the Egyptian first-born. He would tell his own tale, with a surprise at almost every turn.

The final portion corresponds loosely with Exodus. Pharaoh at last let the Hebrews go. They gathered some necessities and valuables from the Egyptians and headed for the Red Sea which they reached in three days.[16] But Artapanus cannot resist some touches of his own. The Exodus tale blends two distinct versions of the crossing of the sea without acknowledging the difference: the drying up of the waters to enable passage and the separation of the sea into two walls of water through which the Israelites could move safely.[17] Atrapanus rightly presents them as two independent explanations. He ascribes them, however, not to the Bible, but to two Egyptian variants, one from the Memphians and one from the Heliopolitans.[18] This was hardly an innocent insertion. By offering alternative interpretations (one of which has Moses rationally plan the crossing in advance by waiting for the ebb tide) and assigning each to different Egyptian sources, he casts a cloud on the whole tale. Artapanus subtly signals his irreverence.

The account ends in highly condensed fashion. It covers the destruction of the Egyptians, the forty years in the desert, the miraculous sustenance from heaven, and a final description of Moses in a single paragraph.[19] That may be the choice of the epitomator rather than the author. But Artapanus does include one last addition of his own. He has the pursuing Egyptians halted not only by the sea but by a burst of flame. Drowning in the waters was not enough. Artapanus has them consumed by both fire and flood.[20] Even the end has a twist.

How should one understand a work of this kind? Why did a Hellenistic Jew take familiar stories about the patriarchs and Moses and reshape them to his own taste? Why did an intellectual steeped in the Scriptures choose to manipulate them in a fashion that left them recognizable but skewed and perplexing? Why did a man grounded in the faith choose to remodel Moses from a Hebrew lawgiver to an inventor of Egyptian traditions and institutions—including even animal worship? If answers can be found, they may shed light upon the literary

---

15 Eus. *PE*, 9.27.31.
16 Eus. *PE*, 9.27.34. Even this departs from the biblical text which has the Israelites "plunder" the Egyptians; Exod. 12:36. Josephus offers still more of a whitewash, alleging that Egyptian willingly bestowed gifts upon the Hebrews; *Ant.* 2.314.
17 Exod. 14:21 – 22.
18 Eus. *PE*, 9.27.35.
19 Eus. *PE*, 9.27.37.
20 Eus. *PE*, 9.27.37.

and cultural environment in which Jewish thinkers found themselves in the Hellenistic diaspora, the traditions within which they worked, and the expectations that they aroused.

The paradox looms large. For some scholars, the idea of a Jew who looked favorably upon animal worship is incomprehensible and quite unthinkable.[21] Best to deny that Artapanus was a Jew at all. If he can present Moses as one who advocates dogs, cats, and ibises as divinities, he must have been a pagan. That would cut the knot nicely.[22] But it is too soft a solution. What would stimulate a pagan not simply to repeat biblical stories (that might have some entertainment value) but to remold them liberally, thus enhancing and elevating Hebrew heroes? To be sure, some gentile intellectuals commented favorably (or ambiguously) on the Jews in passing or as part of treatises devoted largely to other matters.[23] A sustained fragment appears in Hecataeus of Abdera, but the favorable assessment is tempered by more questionable observations, and the treatment of Jews occurs only within a broader study of Egypt.[24] And Alexander Polyhistor, a good pagan whose researches preserved the words of Artapanus that we possess, was interested enough to collect the writings of Hellenistic Jews.[25] But none of this bears comparison with the combination of biblical narrative and inventive intrusions that feature the idiosyncratic text of Artapanus. The twists on the tales have little force unless the reader is familiar with the traditional version. This holds for Artapanus' take on Abraham's sojourn in Egypt, on Joseph's character, shrewdness, and rise to authority, and on

---

21 The fundamental study of Artapanus by J. Freudenthal *Alexander Polyhistor* (Breslau, 1874–75), 147–174, makes a powerful case for the writer as a Jew. But Freudenthal was nonetheless quite uncomfortable with the features of the work that seemed starkly at odds with Jewish tradition. Hence he offered the bold hypothesis that Artapanus, though Jewish, adopted a pagan pseudonym as cover for his un-Jewish conceptualizations; cf. P. Dalbert *Die Theologie der hellenistisch-jüdischen Missions-Literatur unter Ausschluss von Philo und Josephus* (Hamburg, 1954), 44. The idea of a Jewish ventriloquist with a pagan persona, however, adds an unnecessary complication to an already tangled issue. What motive would he have had for such a deception?
22 The idea was tendered cautiously by P.M. Fraser *Ptolemaic Alexandria*, 3 vols. (Oxford, 1972), I, 706; II, 985, and L.H. Feldman *Jew and Gentile in the Ancient World* (Princeton, 1993), 208. See also, H. Jacobson '*Artapanus Judaeus*', JJS 57 (2006), 210–221, argued it at greater length.
23 One might note the remarks of Theophrastus, Megasthenes, Clearchus of Soli, and Hermippus of Smyrna. The fragments are conveniently collected by M. Stern *Greek and Latin Authors on Jews and Judaism* (Jerusalem, 1974), # IV, VII, VIII, XV.
24 Stern (1974), # V. See the discussion of E.S. Gruen *Heritage and Hellenism: The Reinvention of Jewish Tradition* (Berkeley, 1998), 49–54, with bibliography. See, especially, B. Bar-Kochva *Pseudo-Hecataeus,"On the Jews": Legitimizing the Diaspora* (Berkeley, 1996), 18–43.
25 Freudenthal *Alexander Polyhistor* (1874–75), *passim*.

Moses' role as military leader, adventure hero, miracle worker, Egyptian benefactor, and bearer of culture to humankind. The whole account depends on extensive acquaintance with the biblical version, so as to render meaningful the deviations, departures, and whimsical expansions to an audience who would appreciate them.[26] That would include very few gentiles. Artapanus was plainly part of a Jewish intellectual circle that both knew the tradition and would recognize the massaging it received.

What implications arise in acknowledging that a Jew could treat the Scriptures so cavalierly and produce a form of romance that has his hero enmeshed in Egyptian culture and Greek mythology? One might resolve the issue by deconstructing Judaism. If it constituted a multi-layered system permitting a range of accommodations to diverse beliefs and cults, Artapanus would not stand out as a sore thumb. His blending of Moses with Hermes, Thoth, or Musaeus simply represented a form of syncretism that would be inoffensive to a Jewish readership. He could even be characterized as "both a monotheist and a polytheist."[27] Artapanus, on this view, would be part of a "liberal" wing of Judaism that flourished in the Diaspora, cheek by jowl with gentile communities, and could readily assimilate pagan features to Jewish tradition.[28] The idea has some force. Judaism was certainly no monolithic institution, and the diaspora experience naturally engendered borrowing, overlapping, and interconnection. But the whole concept of "liberal" and "orthodox" Jewish communities is anachronistic and unhelpful. Indeed this mode of reasoning tends to judge Artapanus' work as an expression of his religious outlook and a manifesto of his faith, a particularly unfortunate misperception. This was no didactic treatise, announcing a position somewhere along the extended spectrum of Jewish belief. Artapanus hardly advocated the embrace of animal cults. No Jew was that "liberal." His work provided a quirky take on biblical tradition, not an articulation of religious doctrine.

Others have strained to skirt the problem. For some, Egyptian reverence for animals does not amount to worship, but only to "consecration," because of their usefulness to society. That would take Moses off the hook in Jewish

---

26 So also H. Zellentin 'The End of Jewish Egypt: Artapanus and the Second Exodus', in *Antiquity in Antiquity: Jewish and Christian Pasts in the Greco-Roman World*, eds. G. Gardner and K. L. Osterloh. (Tübingen, 2008), 31–32.

27 J.M.G. Barclay *Jews in the Mediterranean Diaspora from Alexander to Trajan (323 BCE – 117 CE)* (Edinburgh, 1996), 131–132; cf. G.E. Sterling *Historiography and Self-Definition: Josephos, Luke-Acts, and Apologetic Historiography* (Leiden, 1992), 167.

28 C. Holladay *Fragments from Hellenistic Jewish Authors*, vol. I. (Chico, 1983), 193.

eyes.[29] In a different formulation, Artapanus' "theology" or "piety" could express itself in a positive evaluation of Egyptian deities so long as they were subordinate to the Jewish god, a gentle nod toward Hellenistic paganism that would not offend Jewish sensibilities.[30] Or the matter can be put in less gentle fashion. The author, in some interpretations, sought to show the inferiority of Egyptian religious traditions. Moses had a hand in founding them only because he regarded them as adequate for Egyptians, by contrast with the higher form of belief in Yahweh. The superiority of the god of Israel to pagan deities is underscored by the fact that his agent Moses created them in the first place. On that reckoning Artapanus' position can be described as "monolatry."[31] But the whole approach misses the main point. Artapanus was not here taking a theological stance that could reconcile biblical pronouncements with pagan practices. Nor did he make a case for the acceptability of animal cults, whether or not on Jewish initiative. One might observe that he has the pharaoh chase the Hebrews all the way to the Red Sea with images of his sacred animals in hand. And all were consumed by fire and the closing of the waters.[32] That is hardly an endorsement for the effectiveness of the animal gods.

What then prompted this highly irregular rewriting of the Bible in which the author enhances the characters of Abraham and Joseph and blows up Moses' deeds to the level of world-historical accomplishment? The favorite answer, often repeated and still dominant in the scholarship, reckons Artapanus as an apologist for his countrymen. He took up the pen in response to gentile authors who vilified Jews, retailing stories of their hostility to pagan cults, their pollution, and their failure to bring anything of intellectual or cultural value to the world of learning. Artapanus thus carried on a noble fight to restore Jewish pride in boasting of the achievements of their ancestors, embellishing and ele-

---

29 E. Schürer *The History of the Jewish People in the Age of Jesus Christ* , vol. III, eds. G, Vermes, F. Millar, and M. Goodman. (Edinburgh, 1986), 523. Cf. D. Flusser and S. Amorai-Stark 'The Goddess Thermutis, Moses, and Artapanus', *JSQ* 1(1993/4), 227 – 229.

30 J.J. Collins Artapanus', in *The Old Testament Pseudepigrapha*, ed. J. H. Charlesworth, vol. 2. (Garden City, 1985), 893 – 894; *idem, Between Athens and Jerusalem*, 2ⁿᵈ ed. (Grand Rapids, 2000), 42 – 43.

31 E. Koskenniemi 'Greeks, Egyptians, and Jews in the Fragments of Artapanus', *JSP*, 13 (2002), 24 – 31; similarly, Flusser and Amorai-Stark, 'The Goddess Thermutis, Moses, and Artapanus' 227 – 231; R. Kugler 'Hearing the Story of Moses in Ptolemaic Egypt: Artapanus Accommodates the Tradition', in *The Wisdom of Egypt*, eds. A. Hilhorst and G. H. van Kooten. (Leiden, 2005), 75 – 78. For C. Holladay *Theios Aner in Hellenistic Judaism* (Missoula, 1977), 214, 216, Artapanus saw Judaism as in serious competition with Egyptian cults and was motivated to denigrate them.

32 Eus. *PE*, 9.27.35 – 37.

vating them precisely in retort to the criticisms. Far from animosity to gentile religion in Egypt, their leader was responsible for putting it into place. Far from rejecting animal worship, he inaugurated it. Far from lacking cultural attainments, he introduced them to the Egyptians and made them available for all mankind. Artapanus' work went well beyond a religious treatise to a trumpeting of Jewish values and exploits. Indeed, in most interpretations, the Περὶ Ἰουδαίων constituted a direct reply to the malicious characterization of Jews by the Egyptian-Hellenistic writer Manetho who portrayed them as enemies of Egyptian religion and as lepers who had to be expelled from the land.[33] Artapanus in short engaged in "competitive historiography," the composition of a counter-attack not only to restore the Exodus story to its proper place but to improve and amplify it, thereby going one better than the distorted accounts by gentile foes.[34]

But the whole conceptualization is faulty. The alleged rebuttals of Manetho have only indirect and incidental force. Even if readers of Artapanus had a text of Manetho in front of them for comparison—an altogether fanciful idea—they would hardly have found these subtle allusions (if that is what they were) to be refutations of Manetho. Indeed, Manetho's own work, the *Aegyptiaka* concerned itself with the chronology, history, and traditions of Egypt. His comments on Jews loom large in modern discussions but constituted only a minor portion of his text—and much of that may not have been composed by Manetho himself.[35] Are we really to imagine that the audience for Artapanus' biblical re-creations would feel relieved or uplifted because they recognized them as contradicting a supposedly malevolent text that few would ever have read or heard of? That imaginary scenario needs at long last to be expunged. The extant fragments of Artapanus' composition nowhere possess the character of a polemic. He had different objectives in mind.

33 The number of scholars who have taken this line is legion. Freudenthal (1875), 160–162, as so often, was the fountainhead. A select but substantial bibliography can be found in E.S. Gruen *Diaspora: Jews Amidst Greeks and Romans* (Cambridge, Mass, 2002), 332, n. 83. Add also S.R. Johnson *Historical Fictions and Hellenistic Jewish Identity* (Berkeley, 2004), 102–106.

34 So, Collins 'Artapanus', 891–892; *idem, Between Athens and Jerusalem* 39–40. Sterling *Historiography and Self-Definition*, 182–183, juxtaposes various charges by Manetho against the Jews to items in Artapanus' text that might be taken as replies. Cf. also M. Braun *History and Romance in Graeco-Oriental Literature* (Oxford, 1938), 26–31; A.J. Droge *Homer or Moses?* (Tübingen, 1989), 30–32; Johnson *Historical Fictions*, 102–105.

35 Cf. Gruen *Heritage and Hellenism*, 55–61, with bibliography. On Manetho generally, see R. Laqueur 'Manethon', *RE* 14 (1928), 1061–1101; W.G. Waddell *Manetho* (Cambridge, Mass, 1940); G.P. Verbrugghe and J.M. Wickersham *Berossos and Manetho, Introduced and Translated* (Ann Arbor, 1996), 95–182; J. Dillery 'The First Egyptian Narrative History: Manetho and Greek Historiography', *ZPE*, 127(1999), 93–116.

It would be salutary to move out of the realms of patriotism, polemic, and propaganda. The readers of Artapanus need not have been searching for solace in oppressive circumstances or struggling to assert their own cultural superiority in a situation where they were devalued by the majority culture. The surviving fragments of his work, small but significant, suggest that entertainment value counted for more than the bolstering of self-esteem.

Entertainment takes precedence in this work over theology or didacticism. Whether one applies to the Περὶ Ἰουδαίων the label of novel, romance, or similar form of narrative fiction matters little. The ancients had no term for "novel," and the ascription of a particular work to that category is inevitably artificial. A groping after genre usually leads to frustration. Not that one cannot group works with similar themes, patterns, modes of expression, or objectives for heuristic purposes. But the fitting of a particular item into a constructed category affords limited illumination.

A comparison with Greek novels naturally arises in this inquiry. But it is hazardous to infer overlap, influence, or even parallel paths. None of the extant Greek novels is as early as Artapanus' composition, nor do we have reason to believe that older ones, if there were any, formed an integral part of the literary context in which he wrote. The usual motifs in Hellenic romances, an erotic story line, visits to exotic places, the separation of lovers, their numerous adventures or misadventures, whether kidnapping, shipwrecks, or the amorous designs of third parties, play no part in Artapanus' text.

Other possibilities can be canvassed. It has long been noted that elements in his Moses story echo deeds and exploits in Near Eastern legends, especially those involving the great Assyrian rulers Ninus and Semiramis and the Egyptian conqueror Sesostris.[36] One can find intriguing parallels in the traditions on Sesostris in particular. His vast conquests included Ethiopia, whose people practiced circumcision; he divided up the land of Egypt into the nomes; he founded temples, consecrating each to the god of the region; and he brought a variety of benefactions to his countrymen.[37] Artapanus ascribes somewhat comparable achievements to Moses. The Babylonian traditions about the accomplished Ninus and his even more celebrated wife and successor Semiramis may also have some resonance. Ninus made himself lord of many lands and founded the city of Nineveh; Semiramis extended Assyrian conquests still further, went

---

36 The classic study is that of Braun *History and Romance in Graeco-Oriental Literature*, 1–31; see also D.L. Tiede *The Charismatic Figure as Miracle Worker* (Missoula, 1972), 149–168.
37 See the brief account, stemming from near eastern sources, in Herodotus, 2.102–110. The fuller version appears in Diodorus, 1.53–58.

as far as India, founded the city of Babylon, constructed numerous buildings and statues of divinities, and subdued Ethiopia.[38] Here the parallels are looser. And in neither case need one postulate that Artapanus plucked items from near eastern embellishments of their heroes to impose them on the Moses story. A familiarity by the Jewish author in Egypt with the folk-tales and legends of that land would hardly be surprising. And borrowings, whether consciously or unconsciously, from the tales associated with Sesostris might well be expected. But the idea of a heroic conqueror, a benefactor to the nation, a framer of institutions, or a founder of cities was widespread in antiquity. Artapanus wrote within a cultural context in which traditions circulated and overlapped not only about Semiramis and Sesostris, but a host of other figures, like Osiris, Isis, Hermes-Thoth, and Nectanebos, who filled similar roles.[39] The Egyptian-Jewish intellectual could bring a rich range of legends to bear.

A different literary setting, however, offers a better route to understanding. Artapanus may not have been familiar with the Greek novel or heavily engaged with near eastern legends. But he was steeped in biblical tradition. And the Bible or its offshoots had a wealth of novelistic narratives that could provide stimulus.[40]

One need think only of the narrative of Esther. It possesses all the elements of a captivating novel that one could desire: a fatuous king, a beautiful heroine, a treacherous villain, a wicked plot, the near annihilation of a nation, a stunning turnabout, the taking of revenge, and a happy ending.[41] Some of these features turn up in Artapanus' rewriting of the Exodus material. Moses too clashed with a monarch, defeated his villainous agents, saved his people from destruction, and exacted vengeance upon his enemies. These do not, of course, constitute close parallels or duplicates. But they provide a vital background for the enterprise of Artapanus and the expectations of his readership.

The Book of Daniel provides additional illumination. The text took its final form in the 160 s BCE, a time probably very close to that of Artapanus himself. The first six chapters of the work, familiar and fascinating, provide notable complements. Daniel entered the service of king Nebuchadnezzar of Babylon, gained his favor as interpreter of dreams, and swiftly outstripped the magicians, sorcer-

---

38 The principal surviving narrative of this hero and heroine is found in Diodorus, 2. 1 – 20, drawing primarily on Ctesias; see Diod. 2.2.2, 2.20.3.
39 So, rightly, Holladay *Theios Aner in Hellenistic Judaism*, 209 – 212,
40 On the Jewish novellas, quite different from the later Greek novel, see L.M. Wills 'The Jewish Novellas', in *Greek Fiction: The Greek Novel in Context*, eds. J. R. Morgan and R. Stoneman (London, 1994), 223 – 237; *idem, The Jewish Novel in the Ancient World* (Ithaca, 1995), *passim*.
41 Esther, *passim*.

ers, and exorcists at court. The king himself acknowledged the power and authority of Daniel's god and promoted Daniel to the highest offices of the land. Of course, jealousy and intrigue followed in the court. Daniel's rivals denounced his fellow Jews for failing to worship the golden image erected on Nebuchadnezzar's orders, leading to the episode of the fiery furnace from which the Jews emerged unscathed. The intrepid interpreter explained yet another dream that boded ill for the monarch, reduced him to repentance, explained the handwriting on the wall at Belshazzar's feast, and, after incurring the wrath of another king's ministers, was hurled into a lion's den only to escape harm miraculously while his accusers were devoured even before they hit the ground.[42] That last item injects a somewhat comic note—a characteristic that takes more conspicuous form in Artapanus.

The Greek version of Daniel in the Septuagint included some additions to the biblical tale. A noteworthy one, the amusing "Bel and the Dragon," has Daniel foil the hapless ruler Cyrus and his advisers by exposing the folly first of worshipping an idol, then of paying homage to a reptile.[43] Another, the famous story of Susanna, recounts the means whereby Daniel outwitted the lecherous voyeurs, brought the villains to justice, rescued the virtuous damsel, and restored her to the good graces of her husband.[44] Ingenuity rather than eroticism takes center stage here.

The Book of Judith, another Hellenistic text that was incorporated in the Septuagint, invented a figure otherwise unknown to the biblical tradition. Judith, a demure widow, came out of retirement to rebuke and to rally her dispirited fellow Jews, about to capitulate to Nebuchadnezzar's general Holofernes. Judith's seduction, then beheading of the general, turned the whole situation around, stimulated the Jews to victory, and permitted her to return to a quiet and chaste retirement.[45]

None of these texts carries a one-to-one correspondence to episodes, themes, or structure in Artapanus' work. But they disclose the narrative traditions he would have known and the literary ambience within which he worked.

It does not follow that Artapanus looked only to the Bible and to Jewish-Hellenistic writings for inspiration. But the Jewish framework remains the most telling one. And the author's talent directed itself principally toward capturing an

---

42 Dan. 1–6.
43 Dan. 14:1–27. See L.M. Wills *The Jew in the Court of the Foreign King: Ancient Jewish Court Legends* (Minneapolis, 1990), 131–133; Gruen *Heritage and Hellenism*, 168–172, with bibliography.
44 Dan. 13:1–64.
45 Judith, *passim*.

audience with familiar biblical narratives presented in fresh, innovative, diverting, and often surprising ways. The whimsical character of Artapanus' additions and alterations emerges frequently in this text.

A number of instances illustrate Artapanus' proclivity. His identification of Moses with Musaeus is more than syncretism. He inverts the Hellenic myth that has Orpheus as teacher of Musaeus, thus to make Moses the fountainhead of music and literature. Victory over the Ethiopians turned them from foes to friends and even induced them to take up circumcision. He employs the burning bush episode to energize Moses for a military invasion of Egypt. He has the pharaoh fall in a dead faint upon hearing the name of the Jewish god—only to be revived again by Moses. As if there were not enough plagues, Artapanus adds an earthquake to the hailstorm so as to have Egyptians hopping from calamity to calamity. Moses' prowess with the rod prompted the envious Egyptians to set up a rod in each of their temples, and his successful advocacy of oxen to plow the land resulted in Egyptian worship of the Apis bull—while pharaoh scrambled to bury the evidence that this came on Moses' suggestion.

Whimsy and mischief are more prominent than polemic, apologetics, or theology. What sort of readership would Artapanus target for such a rewriting of the Bible that upset expectations at every turn? The idea that a work designed to amuse and entertain was a form of "popular culture," appealing primarily to a level of society below the elite and the cultivated, no longer holds sway. Literacy was not widespread in the ancient world, and, although oral recitation might reach a larger number, it required patience, time, and attention. Nor, on the other hand, should one assume that the educated classes scorned texts that aimed at distraction and enjoyment. Yet it would be simplistic to rule out the attraction of prose fiction to a wider audience than the narrow circle of the intelligentsia.[46] Artapanus' clever, witty, and unanticipated divergences from the standard narrative presumed a readership that would catch them. But his composition works on more than one plane and could appeal to a diverse readership. Knowledge of the Bible, at least in its Greek version, extended to many Jews, who would recognize

---

46 On the readership for Greek prose fiction, a topic much discussed, see the assessments of S.A. Stephens 'Who Read Ancient Novels?', in *The Search for the Ancient Novel*, ed. J. Tatum. (Baltimore, 1994), 405–418; E. Bowie 'The Readership of Greek Novels in the Ancient World', in *The Search for the Ancient Novel*, ed. J. H. Tatum. (Baltimore, 1994), 435–449; T. Hägg Orality, 'Literacy and the "Readership" of the Early Greek Novel', in *Contexts of Pre-Novel Narrative: The European Tradition*, ed. R. Eriksen. (Berlin, 1994), 47–81; C. Ruiz-Montero 'The Rise of the Greek Novel', in *The Greek Novel in the Ancient World*, ed. G. Schmeling. (Leiden, 1996), 80–85; R. Hunter 'Ancient Readers', in *The Cambridge Companion to the Greek and Roman Novel*, ed. T. Whitmarsh. (Cambridge, 2008), 261–271; T. Whitmarsh 'Class', in *The Cambridge Companion to the Greek Novel*, ed. T. Whitmarsh. (Cambridge, 2008), 72–87.

departures from the tradition—whatever they might have thought of them. A more discerning comprehension, however, would require some familiarity with Hellenic figures like Hermes, Orpheus, and Musaeus, and an ability to detect allusions to Egyptian and even Assyrian legends of Osiris, Sesostris, and Semiramis. Not everyone will have had such a repertoire. But Artapanus' work indicates reception by an indeterminate number of Jews who could appreciate the leavening of biblical tradition by Greek myth and near eastern folklore. Both the populace and the intellectual classes, moreover, could take pleasure in the narrative charm and mischievous inversions of Artapanus.

21. Jews, Greeks, and Romans
in the Third Sibylline Oracle

Jewish appropriation of pagan traditions took a multitude of forms. The Sibylline Oracles constitute an instance of the first order. No more dramatic example of the practice exists than the adaptation and recreation of those texts. Collections of the Sibyl's pronouncements, duly edited, expanded, or invented, had wide circulation in the Graeco-Roman world—long before Jewish writers exploited them for their own purposes. But circumstances of transmission, as so often, produce peculiar ironies. The pagan originals that served as models have largely been lost, surviving only in fragments or reconstructions. The extant corpus of Sibylline Books, drawing upon but refashioning those models, derives from Jewish and Christian compilers who had their own agenda to promote. The role of Hellenized Jews in this development is pivotal. Rehabilitation of the originals may no longer be possible, but assessment of the means and motives for the transformation raises even more significant issues of Jewish self-image.

In this quest, the Third Sibylline Oracle possesses special importance. It contains the earliest material in the collection and its composition is predominantly Jewish. That much can confidently be stated. Beyond it lies controversy, dispute, and division. A large and burgeoning scholarly literature daunts the researcher, with innumerable disagreements in detail. And irony enters here as well. A few issues do command a broad consensus, issues of centrality and importance, thus affording an ostensible reassurance. Yet the very ground on which that consensus rests is shaky, and may well have clouded rather than clarified understanding. The areas of agreement touch on fundamental matters that have not been subjected to adequate scrutiny. The time is overdue for a closer look.

First, the matter of unity or diversity of composition. Opinions vary widely on specifics. But a heavy majority of scholars have always discerned a main corpus or a principal core produced or redacted at a particular historical time. Earlier material might have been incorporated and accretions subsequently added, but the body of the work, so most have claimed, can be tied to identifiable historical circumstances that called it forth. The favored times, each boasting notable champions, are the mid-second century BCE, the early first century BCE, and the later first century BCE.[1] Second, and in close conjunction with the first, var-

---

1 In the first edition of real importance and influence, C. Alexandre *Oracula Sibyllina*, 2 vols. (Paris, 1841–56) assigned well over half of the text to a Jewish redactor of *c*.168 BCE. The notion of a principal author dating to the mid-2nd cent. prevailed until the sustained assault by J. Geffcken *Komposition und Entsthungszeit der Oracula Sibyllina* (Leipzig, 1902*b*), 1–17, which

ious pointers in the text to what appear to be historical episodes have regularly been taken as disclosing the *Sitz-im-Leben* of the text—a sign of the author's attitude to contemporary leaders, nations, or events. The most common referents identified by interpreters are Antiochus Epiphanes, the Maccabees, Ptolemy VI or VIII, Mithridates, the triumvirs, and Cleopatra.[2] And third, a firm unanimity among scholars holds that the bulk of Book III derives from the Jewish community in Egypt, whether in Alexandria or Leontopolis. The Egyptian provenance, so

---

has had wide impact in the scholarship. Geffcken, as a committed pluralist, dissected the Third Book with scrupulous care but excessive confidence, labeling various segments as products of the Babylonian Sibyl, the Persian Sibyl, the Erythraean Sibyl, or the Jewish Sibyl. Even his atomistic structure, however, includes a Jewish composer from the Maccabaean period for nearly a quarter of the lines and a Jewish revision of the Erythraean Sibyl, constituting more than a third of the Whole, in the early 1st cent. BCE. W. Bousset 'Sibyllen und Sibyllinische Bücher', in *Real-Encyclopädie für protestantische Theologie und Kirsche*, (1906), 270–1, detected divisions in, places other than those noted by Geffcken, but ascribed more than half the text to an author living in the early 1st cent. E. Schürer *Geschichte des jüdischen Volkes im Zeitalter Jesu Christi*, ii (Leipzig, 1886), 794–9, believed that almost all came from the pen of a Jewish writer in the mid-2nd cent. Similar judgments were expressed by H. Lanchester, in R.H. Charles *The Apocrypha and Pseudepigrapha of the Old Testament*, ii (Oxford, 1913), 371–2, and A. Rzach 'Sibyllinischer Orakel', *PWRE* (1923) II.A.2:2127–8. A. Peretti *La Sibilla babilonese nella propaganda ellenistica* (Florence, 1943), 96–9, 143–7, 317–40, 350–1, 397–9, 459–68, holds that the core of the text was composed in the early 1st cent., and certainly prior to 63 BCE, the taking of Jerusalem by Pompey, and then subject to subsequent accretions. The strongest argument for unity came from V. Nikiprowetzky *La Troisème Sibylle* (Paris, 1970), 195–225, who set almost the entire work in the time of the later 1st cent., the period of Cleopatra VII and the triumvirate. That verdict has not found favor among more recent commentators. The current consensus inclines to the composite interpretation of Geffcken, but discerns a main corpus, encompassing more than two-thirds of the whole, as a product of the mid-2nd cent. That is the conclusion of J.J. Collins who has written extensively on the subject (Collins *The Sibylline Oracles of Egyptian Judaism* (Missoula, 1974a), 21–33; id. in J.H. Charlesworth *The Old Testament Pseudepigrapha*, I (Garden City, N.Y., 1983), 354–5; id. in M.E. Stone *Jewish Writings of the Second Temple Period* (Philadelphia, 1984), 365–71; id. 'The Development of the Sibylline Tradition', *ANRW* (1987), 430–6). Similarly, P.M. Fraser *Ptolemaic Alexandria*, 2. Vols. (Oxford, 1972), 1. 709, 711. The position has been endorsed in recent works; e.g. J.D. Newsome *Greeks, Romans, Jews* (Philadelphia, 1992); 93–7; L.H. Feldman *Jew and Gentile in the Ancient World* (Princeton, 1993), 294; cf. M. Delcor, in Davies and Finkelstein *The Cambridge History of Judaism*, ii (Cambridge, 1989), 487–9. A more pluralistic interpretation by M. Goodman, in Schürer *The History of the Jewish People in the Age of Jesus Christ*, iii. I. rev. G. Vermes, *et al.* (Edinburgh, 1986), 632–8. Arguments about the Sibylline Oracles generally began already among Renaissance humanists; see A. Grafton *Defenders of the Text* (Cambridge, Mass., 1991), 172–7.

2 No need to rehearse the bibliography here. Specifics will emerge in subsequent discussions.

it is asserted or assumed, accounts for the attitudes expressed and the general thrust of, at least, the main corpus of the work.[3]

The modern literature, in short, has sought to locate the Third Sibyl in time and place. The aim is logical and laudable enough. Yet the search for historical specificity may miss the essence of the Sibyl's message, its apocalyptic character, and its significance for the interaction of Judaism and Hellenism. A reconsideration of the three propositions outlined above is in order.

Is there, in fact, a 'main corpus' in Book III, in which earlier oracles were incorporated and later material tacked on? The idea runs into trouble from the start. Chronological indicators are few, scattered, and usually ambiguous. The problem can be readily illustrated. Verse 46 speaks of a time when Rome ruled Egypt, a passage that can hardly be earlier than the battle of Actium.[4] A mention of Beliar who comes from the Sebastenoi occurs in verse 63. The Sebastenoi very likely signify the line of Roman emperors or Augusti, and the arrogant Beliar who comes to a bad end probably denotes Nero. Hence, this passage evidently post-dates 68 CE.[5] The sequence of kingdoms given in lines 156–61 places Rome after Egypt, again implying a date after 30 BCE, the fall of Egypt into Roman hands.[6] By contrast, the following oracle, offering yet another series of kingdoms that will rise and fall, sets the Romans after the Macedonians, gives Macedon as their prime victim, and, in describing them as 'white, many-headed, from the western sea', obviously alludes to the Republic and, presumably, to the defeat of Macedon in 168 or 148.[7] The fierce hostility and rage directed against Rome and the vengeance promised from Asia in verses 350–80 belong more suitably to the late Republic when Roman expansionism and imperial exactions had left deep scars in the east.[8] Yet the oracle that appears next in the text reverts

---

3 See e.g. Collins *The Sibylline Oracles of Egyptian Judaism*, 35–55.

4 *Sib. Or.* 3. 46: αὐτὰρ ἐπεὶ Ῥώμη καὶ Αἰγύπτου βασιλεύσει. The suggestion of Lanchester, in Charles *The Apocrypha and Pseudepigrapha*, 371, that this may allude to Popillius Laenas' mission to Egypt in 168 BCE, is out of the question. Rome exercised no sovereignty over Egypt at that time. Nor after the bequests of either Ptolemy Apion or Ptolemy Auletes, the other possibilities canvassed by Lanchester.

5 So Collins *The Sibylline Oracles of Egyptian Judaism*, 80–7, citing as parallel Ascension of Isaiah 4: 1. Beliar, however, can have other connotations; see Nikiprowetzky *La Troisème Sibylle*, 138–43.

6 Collins *The Sibylline Oracles of Egyptian Judaism*, 26, implausibly prefers the 2nd cent. BCE on the grounds that Rome was already a world empire by that time. That skirts the significance of the sequence of empires, each kingdom replacing or subduing the previous.

7 *Sib. Or.* 3. 162–90, esp. 176: λευκὴ καὶ πολύκρανος ἀφ᾽ ἑσπερίοιο θαλάσσης.

8 That conclusion is generally accepted, although commentators differ as to whether the lines allude to the Mithridatic war or to Cleopatra's resistance to Rome: cf. W. Bousset 'Sibyllen und

to an earlier time, lamenting the mighty power of Macedon and the sorrows it brings, and looking ahead to its demise.[9] Later, the Sibyl proclaims the dire fate of Italy as consequence not of foreign war but of civil bloodshed, and refers also to a murderous man from Italy, the destroyer of Laodicea. Those verses must recall the Roman Social and civil wars, of the early first century BCE and the ravages by Sulla in the east that fell in that very period.[10] Yet the succeeding lines raise the spectre of a previous time, two generations earlier, that witnessed the eradication of Carthage and Corinth.[11] And the Sibyl could also recall a much earlier era, when savage Gauls devastated Thrace in the early third century BCE.[12] One could proceed to passages of more speculative date. But no need. It seems clear that Book III of the Sibylline Oracles constitutes a conglomerate, a gathering of various prophecies that stem from different periods ranging from the second century BCE through the early Roman empire. To postulate a main corpus or a primary redaction reflecting special circumstances does not get us far.[13] The composition has a broader significance.

The ostensible historical pointers in the text require reassessment. Cornerstone for the idea of a principal edition in the second century rests upon three references to a seventh king of Egypt: verses 193, 318, 608. Since he is explicitly described in two of the three passages as 'from the race of the Greeks', the allusion is apparently to a Ptolemaic, monarch. Scholars have wrangled over how to calculate the sequence of kings. Does Alexander the Great count as the first or not? Does one include the short and overlapping reign of Ptolemy VII Philopator? The uncertainties have caused some argument over whether 'the seventh king' is Ptolemy VI Philometor (180–145), Ptolemy VII Philopator (145–144), or Ptolemy VIII Euergetes (145–116). The first stands as favorite, but near unanimity, in any case, prevails in identifying the period in question as the mid-second century.[14] That has engendered the further conclusion that this work repre-

---

Sibyllinische Bücher', 271; A. Peretti *La Sibilla babilonese*, 329–57; Collins *The Sibylline Oracles of Egyptian Judaism*, 57–64. On this, see below.

9 *Sib. Or.* 3. 381–400.

10 *Sib. Or.* 3.464–73.

11 *Sib. Or.* 3.484–8.

12 *Sib. Or.* 3.508–10.

13 The conglomerate mixture is reflected also in the confused and overlapping manuscript transmission. The tangled strands permit no neat stemma, suggesting a number of layers built over time by diverse interests and sources. See J. Geffcken *Die Oracula Sibyllina* (Leipzig, 1902a), xxi–liii; Rzach 'Sibyllinischer Orakel', 2119–22; Goodman, in Schürer *The History of the Jewish People*, 628–31.

14 The conclusion is taken for granted by Lanchester, in Charles *The Apocrypha and Pseudepigrapha*, 382. A fuller discussion by Collins *The Sibylline Oracles of Egyptian Judaism*, 28–32;

sents the propaganda of Egyptian Jews to ingratiate themselves with the Ptolemaic dynasty and to express a common basis for relations between Jews and Gentiles in Egypt.[15] How legitimate is that analysis?

The first mention of the 'seventh king' causes misgivings right away. It follows upon the Sibyl's recounting of the rise and fall of kingdoms. Among them the Greeks are singled out as arrogant and impious and the Macedonians as bringing a fearsome cloud of war upon mortals. The God of Heaven, however, will eradicate them, paving the way for Roman rule, the ascendancy of the many hoary-headed men from the western sea, whose dominion too will prove oppressive, whose morals will degenerate, who will provoke hatred, and who will engage in every form of deceit until the time of the seventh kingdom when an Egyptian monarch of Greek lineage will be sovereign.[16] Do these really suit the era of Ptolemy VI or Ptolemy VII? No *ex eventu* forecast could have set the fall of Roman power to that period, a time when its might was increasing and its reach extending. Nor can one imagine the Sibyl (or her recorder) making such a pronouncement in the reigns of Philometor or Euergetes themselves when its falsity was patent. The idea collides abruptly with reality.[17] The Sibyl must be looking forward to a demise of Rome that had not yet occurred. Hence the 'seventh king' can hardly refer to a present or past scion of the Ptolemaic dynasty.

(1974b), 1 – 5. See also Rzach 'Sibyllinischer Orakel', 2127 – 8; Fraser (1972), 2. 992; Goodman, in Schürer *The History of the Jewish People*, 635 – 6. The sole dissenter is Nikiprowetzky *La Troisème Sibylle*, 208 – 17, whose proposal that the seventh king is Cleopatra has rightly found no takers.

15 So Collins, in Charlesworth *The Old Testament Pseudepigrapha*, i.356; Collins 'The Development of the Sibylline Tradition', 432.

16 *Sib. Or.* 3.165 – 95; see esp. 191 – 3: μῖσος δ' ἐξεγερεῖ καὶ πᾶς δόλος ἔσσεται αὐτοῖς, ἄχρι πρὸς ἑβδομάτην βασιληίδα, ἧς βασιλεύσει Αἰγύπτου Βασιλεύς, ὃς αφ' Ελλήνων γένος ἔσται.

17 Geffcken *Die Oracula Sibyllina*, 58, recognized the problem and simply bracketed lines 192 – 3, thus removing the seventh kingdom from the passage. Peretti *La Sibilla babilonese*, 178 – 96, took a different route, separating out the verses on Roman conquest (lines 175 – 8), and seeing the rest of the segment as a denunciation of Macedonian imperialism. Such dissection, however, is unwarranted and implausible. Geffcken's solution is arbitrary, and Peretti's reconstruction ignores the problem of the Macedonian realm coming to an end at the time when Egypt was ruled by a king of Macedonian lineage. The unity of the whole passage is ably defended by Nikiprowetzky *La Troisème Sibylle*, 209 – 13. Collins *The Sibylline Oracles of Egyptian Judaism*, 31 – 2, argues that an anti-Roman attitude by Egyptian Jews might well have been prompted by Ptolemy Philometor who had reason to feel aggrieved at the Romans. The suggestion carries little conviction. No evidence exists for any animosity on Philometor's *part* toward Rome, let alone for any prodding of Jews by him for this purpose. Even if the conjecture were right, however, it fails to address the question of how the collapse of Roman power could be set in Philometor's reign.

The Sibyl's next reference to a seventh king comes in the midst of numerous woeful prophecies. She dwells on the grievous fate that has either overtaken or will eventually overtake a number of nations. Egypt indeed is among them, with a mighty blow to come, unanticipated and dreadful, in the seventh generation of kings—and then she will rest.[18] The oracle proceeds to detail the evils that will befall numerous other places, reiterating once more that the baleful race of Egypt is approaching its own destruction.[19] In the context of so dire a set of predictions, with the afflictions of Egypt doubly noted, it strains the point to place emphasis upon a single line alluding to a pause in the seventh generation. Nothing in the passage gives any reason to evoke the era of Philometor and Euergetes.[20] Indeed, what is predicted for the seventh generation is dispersal, death, and famine, and only subsequently will it cease.[21] The apocalyptic visions predominate in the long string of verses. A search for historical specificity misses the point.

The third passage is still more problematic. It too lies embedded in an eschatological prophecy. The oracle foresees calamity, war, and pestilence inflicted by the Immortal upon those who fail to acknowledge his existence and persist instead in the worship of idols. Destruction will fall upon Egypt in the time of the young (or new) seventh king reckoned from the rule of the Greeks. And the divine instrument is named: a great king from Asia whose infantry and cavalry will despoil the land, spread every evil, overthrow the Egyptian kingdom, and cart off its possessions over the sea. Then they will bow their knees to God, the great king, the immortal one, while all handmade works collapse in a flame of fire.[22] A standard line has it that the Asian invader is Antiochus IV Epiphanes and the young Egyptian king is Ptolemy Philometor, victim of the Se-

---

18 *Sib. Or.* 3. 295 – 318. See esp. 314 – 18: ἥξει σοι πληγὴ μεγάλη, Αἴγυπτε, πρὸς οἴκους, δεινή, ἣν οὔπω ποτ᾽ ἐξήλπισας ἐρχομένην σοι … θάνατος καὶ λιμὸς ἐφέξει ἑβδομάτῃ γενεῇ βασιλήων, καὶ τότε παύσῃ.

19 *Sib. Or.* 3. 319 – 49. See 348: ἴσθι τότ᾽ Αἰγύπτου ὀλοὸν γένος ἐγγὺς ὀλέθρου.

20 That the allusion in line 316 to a sword passing through their midst refers to civil conflict between Philometor and Euergetes is pure conjecture, made even less substantial by the fact that the line itself is corrupt. The conjecture was offered by Lanchester, in Charles *The Apocrypha and Pseudepigrapha*, 384; endorsed by Fraser *Ptolemaic Alexandria*, 1. 710; 2. 994; Collins *The Sibylline Oracles of Egyptian Judaism*, 31; rightly dismissed by Nikiprowetzky *La Troisème Sibylle*, 198. The Sibyl could indeed appeal to biblical authority for civil strife in Egypt; Isaiah 19: 2.

21 *Sib. Or.* 3. 316, quoted above, n. 18.

22 *Sib. Or.* 3.601 – 18.

leucid's assault.[23] Again, however, the effort to find direct historical allusions encounters serious stumbling-blocks. If the Sibyl intended Antiochus IV as the Asian king, her timing would have to be very precise indeed. Seleucid success and deposition of the Ptolemies came as a consequence of Epiphanes' first invasion in 170; the second, in 168, was thwarted by Rome and followed by reinstatement of Ptolemaic authority. An *ex eventu* prophecy would make no sense except in that narrow corridor of time—far too tight a squeeze. The idea of a direct allusion to Antiochus Epiphanes can be discarded. Threats to Egypt from Asia were endemic in Egyptian history and lore. The Sibyl simply fastened upon the traditional foe as anticipated ravager of the land, not a particular monarch, nor an identifiable invasion.[24] The passage also provides little comfort to those who argue that a cordial relationship between Ptolemy Philometor and the Jews and the elevation of Jewish leaders under his aegis justify a dating of the oracle to his reign. On the contrary, the relevant verses hold no brief, indeed hold no hope, for the seventh king. The invasion will come in his time, bringing with it not only devastation and pestilence but the fall of the Egyptian kingdom that had been founded by Macedonians.[25] Far better then to divorce these verses

---

23 See Lanchester, in Charles *The Apocrypha and Pseudepigrapha*, 389; Fraser *Ptolemaic Alexandria*, 2. 998 – 9; A. Momigliano *Sesto contributo alla storia studi classici*, ii (Rome, 1980), 557. Collins *The Sibylline Oracles of Egyptian Judaism*, 29 – 30, shrinks from too narrow or definite a judgment on the Asian king, but adheres to the view that Egypt's monarch must be Philometor or Euergetes: if the term νέος in line 608 means 'young', it could suit the youthful Philometor at the time of Antiochus' invasion; if the meaning is 'new', this might be the product of an oracle issued late in either king's reign. Collins leaves the options open. One might even consider the possibility of an allusion to the title of Ptolemy Neos Philopator. Goodman, in Schürer *The History of the Jewish People*, 636, declines to take a stand.

24 This is correctly noted by Collins *The Sibylline Oracles of Egyptian Judaism*, 29 – 30, 39 – 40, who points to invasions by Hyksos and Persians and to oracular pronouncements in the Potter's Oracle and elsewhere. But he still considers Epiphanes' invasion as a prod for the Sibyl's forecast. On Antiochus' two military expeditions into Egypt, see E.S. Gruen *The Hellenistic World and the Coming of Rome* (Berkeley, 1984), 651 – 60, with bibliography. Antiochus did, allegedly, acknowledge the power of the Jewish god at the end, as recounted by 2 Macc. 9: 11 – 17; cf. 1 Macc. 6: 12 – 13. But this is certainly not alluded to by *Sib. Or.* 3. 616 – 17, where those who will bend a knee to God are clearly repentant Egyptians. Peretti's notion *La Sibilla babilonese*, 389 – 93, that the Asian king represents the coming Messiah, drastically misconceives his role in the text—which is that of destroyer, not reclaimer.

25 *Sib. Or.* 3. 608 – 15: ὁππόταν Αἰγύπτου βασιλεὺς νέος ἕβδομος ἄρχῃ τῆς ἰδίης γαίης ἀριθμούμενος ἐξ Ἑλλήνων ἀρχῆς, ἧς ἄρξουσι Μακηδόνες ἄσπετοι ἄνδρες. ἔλθῃ δ' ἐξ Ἀσίης βασιλεὺς μέγας ... ῥίψει δ' Αἰγύπτου Βασιλήιον. The opposition here between an Asian ruler and a kingdom founded by Macedonians makes it even less likely that the former could be a Seleucid. Collins 'The Development of the Sibylline Tradition', 431 – 2, remarks upon 'the enthusiasm for the Egyptian king in *Sib. Or.* III'. There is certainly no sign of it here. If anything, the reverse.

from the particular events that marked the reign of Ptolemy VI—or anyone else for that matter. The Sibyl predicts catastrophe for Egyptian idolators, laid low by the hand of God through the agency of an Asian conqueror, and then redeemed when they prostrate themselves before the true Immortal. The model should more properly be sought in something like the thunderings of Isaiah than in the special circumstances of a Ptolemaic reign.[26] Once again, the eschatology holds central place and drives the entire passage. In this context it looks ahead to the smashing of idolatry, to transformation, conversion, and redemption. A narrow political interpretation would be simplistic and distorting.[27]

A noteworthy point demands attention, one missed by all those who have written on the subject. Designations like Ptolemy VI or Ptolemy VII may be a convenience for modern scholars, but they lack ancient authority. The Greek rulers of Egypt nowhere identified themselves by numbers. One will look in vain for such a title in official documents, whether on stone, papyri, or coinage. Petitions to the crown do not address the kings in this fashion, nor are they so referred to indirectly in transactions between private persons. The Ptolemies, of course, regularly appear with cult titles (Soter, Euergetes, Philometor, and the like), other epithets of dignity and honor, and patronymics, but they did not place themselves in a numerical sequence.[28] Perhaps more striking, our fullest and most reliable Hellenistic literary source, the historian Polybius, refers to the Ptolemies regularly and frequently, but never attaches numbers to them.[29] One can go further still. Jewish sources, contemporary or nearly contemporary with the Ptolemaic monarchy, namely 1, 2, and 3 Maccabees, and the *Letter of Aristeas*, speak of the Egyptian kings—but not by number.[30] The same indeed holds for Josephus' *Antiquitates* which employs cult titles, no numerals.[31] In a word, neither the technical language in documents nor the less formal designations by literary sources, whether pagan or Jewish, employ any numbering system to distin-

---

26 Nikiprowetzky *La Troisème Sibylle*, 208, rightly points to parallels between Isaiah 2: 18 – 21, 30: 22 – 4, and *Sib. Or.* 3. 604 – 7, 616 – 23.

27 Cf. the reference to a coalition of kings organized for a concerted assault on the Temple; *Sib. Or.* 3. 657 – 68. No historical circumstance has been suggested or can be found for that purported episode. Cf. Psalms 2: 1 – 2.

28 To take only the most celebrated examples, see the titulature exhibited in the Canopus decree, the Rosetta Stone, and Ptolemy Euergetes' will that bequeathed his kingdom to Rome; *OGIS* 56, 90; *SEG* IX. 7.

29 See e.g. Plb. 5. 34. 1: Πτολεμαῖος ὁ κληθεὶς Φιλοπάτωρ; 14. 3 – 4, 31. 10.

30 See 1 Macc. 10: 51, 10: 55, 11: 8; 2 Macc. 1: 10, 4: 21; 3 Macc. 1: 1, 3: 12, 7: 1; *Let. Aris.* 13. 35, 41.

31 e.g. Jos. *A. J.* 12. 2 – 3, 11, 118, 235, 243; 13. 62, 79 – 80, 103, 285, 328, 370. An exception in *C. Apion.* 2. 48: τρίτος Πτολεμαῖος—but this is not a technical designation. Cf. *War* 1. 31.

guish the Ptolemies. When the Sibyl makes mention of a seventh king, she could hardly expect her readers to recognize a specific Ptolemy. The number seven possessed high symbolic import for the Jews.[32] It must be understood in that broad and spiritual sense, not as denotation of a royal tenure.

One further passage needs treatment in this connection. The Sibyl describes a dismal period of civil strife, cataclysmic warfare among kings and peoples, seizure of territory and riches, foreign rule over the Greek world, the destructive power of greed for wealth that terminates in utter ruin, death, and devastation. But rescue will come when God sends a king from the sun to put an end to war, slaying some and binding others with oaths of loyalty—an end achieved not by private counsel but by obeying the worthy precepts of the great God.[33] This image too has been associated with the Ptolemies, and 'the king from the sun' reckoned as identical with the 'seventh king'.[34] Precedents and parallels in the Egyptian material ostensibly lend credence to the association. The nearest analogy, however, appears in the Potter's Oracle which looks to a king from the sun appointed by the goddess Isis. And that is an expression of Egyptian nationalist sentiment, certainly not advocacy of Ptolemaic rule.[35] To be sure, connection of the king with the sun might well be appropriated by the Ptolemies too. But the relationship has its roots in Pharaonic imagery and ancient Egyptian religion. These lines in the Third Sibylline Book represent Jewish adaptation of Egyptian lore to forecast a Messiah who will stamp out strife and restore tranquility. The 'king from the sun' is an emissary of God, not a Ptolemaic monarch. In short, the standard theory of a central core for the Third Sibyl in the mid-second century is a ramshackle structure on the most fragile foundations.

Similar historical markers have been discerned (or imagined) for the later first century BCE—most notably in alleged allusions to the 'second triumvirate' and to Cleopatra VII, last of the Ptolemies. They do not easily survive scrutiny.

A verse in the early part of the text furnishes the sole basis for finding the 'second triumvirate'—amidst the Sibylline pronouncements. The oracle speaks

---

32 Cf. Gen. 41; 1 Enoch 91: 12 – 17, 93: 3 – 10; and see *Sib. Or.* 3. 280, 3. 728.

33 *Sib. Or.* 3. 635 – 56.

34 A strong argument for this identification is made by Collins 'The Provenance and Date of the Third Sibyl', *Bulletin of the Institute of Jewish Studies*, (1974b) 2:5 – 8; *The Sibylline Oracles of Egyptian Judaism*, 40 – 4; *Between Athens and Jerusalem* (New York, 1983), 68 – 70. Accepted by O. Camponovo *Königherrschaft und Reich Gottes in den frühjüdischen Schriften* (Freiburg, 1984), 344 – 5. But Collins's claim that 'the identification is inevitable' greatly overstates the case. Momigliano *Sesto contributo alla storia studi classici*, 556, rightly questions the connection. See also the comments of Nikiprowetzky *La Troisème Sibylle*, 133 – 7.

35 See the text in L. Koenen 'Die Prophezeiungen des "Töpfers"', *ZPE* (1968), 206, lines 38 – 41.

of a time when Rome will rule over Egypt, when the greatest kingdom of the immortal king will materialize among men, when the holy sovereign will take universal dominion. At that time, inexorable anger will fall upon the men of Latium, and three with woeful destiny will rain destruction upon Rome. And all will perish in their own abodes when a cataract of fire rushes from Heaven.[36] Scholars regularly repeat identification of the cryptic 'three'—with the triumvirate of Antony, Octavian, and Lepidus.[37] But the text itself provides grave difficulties for that hypothesis. The opening line of the passage has Rome exercising dominion over Egypt, an explicit statement that makes sense only after annexation of the land as a Roman province in 30 BCE. But the triumvirate no longer existed at that time: Lepidus had been dropped, Antony was dead, and Octavian unopposed. Furthermore, the forecast that the trio will destroy Rome hardly applies to the triumvirate. Rome stood intact, and the empire had expanded. No *ex eventu* oracle could have uttered such patently false phrases. And a genuine prediction would hardly have conceived Rome's destruction at the hands of the triumvirate after the conquest of Egypt.[38] Nor is it likely that the Sibyl projects, three future rulers of Rome who will cause the destruction of the empire.[39] She foresees the destruction of Rome as the deed of the deathless monarch, the holy prince as sovereign over all the earth, doubtless a reference to the divinity. The three who administer the mournful fate to Rome should therefore be agents of God, not identifiable personages from Roman history.[40]

Does Cleopatra appear in the Third Sibylline Book? Many have found her in lines that describe the world as being in the hands of a woman, a world governed

---

36 *Sib. Or.* 3. 46–54: αὐτὰρ ἐπεὶ Ῥώμη καὶ Αἰγύπτου βασιλεύσει... τρεῖς Ῥώμην οἰκτρῇ μοίρῃ καταδηλήσονταί.

37 So e. g. Geffcken *Komposition und Entsthungszeit*, 13–14; A. Kurfess *Sibyllinische Weissagungen* (Berlin, 1951), 288; Peretti *La Sibilla babilonese*, 342–5. Doubts expressed by M. Simon, in D. Hellholm *Apocalypticism in the Mediterranean World and the Near East* (Tübingen, 1983), 224.

38 The remark of W.W. Tarn 'Alexander Helios and the Golden Age', *JRS* (1932), 142, that once Roman rule was established over Egypt, it could itself be used as a date, is unfathomable. Collins *The Sibylline Oracles of Egyptian Judaism*, 65, rightly sees that the oracle must have been composed after Actium but fails to recognize the implications for any reference to the triumvirate.

39 So Nikiprowetzky *La Troisème Sibylle*, 150–4, who usefully points to the motif of three Roman kings in Jewish apocalyptic.

40 Note *Sib. Or.* 3. 533–6, which refers to 'five' who will arouse a mighty wrath and who will shamelessly engage one another in frightful and tumultuous war, bringing joy to their enemies but woe to the Greeks. The author evidently blended an echo of Isaiah 30: 17 with an allusion to Roman civil wars. The number 'five', it is clear, lacks any specific denotation here. And there is no more reason to assign specificity to the number 'three' in *Sib. Or.* 3. 52.

and obedient in every regard. The Sibyl goes on to characterize the woman as a widow, reigning over all the universe, hurling gold and silver into the deep, as well as the brass and iron of ephemeral men. Then all parts of the cosmos will be bereft when God rolls up the sky like a scroll and the heavens themselves fall upon the earth, followed by a cataract of fire to burn earth and sea, eradicating daylight and nightfall, as well as all the seasons, a terrible divine judgement.[41] Only guesswork can offer an identity for the 'woman' and the 'widow'. And there has been plenty of that. Many scholars, both early and recent, favor Cleopatra.[42] The reasons fall well short of compelling. Cleopatra, to be sure, was a widow after the death of her brother-husband Ptolemy XIII. But her widowhood was hardly conspicuous at a time when she ruled much of the east together with and largely as a consequence of her consort Mark Antony. Nor is it likely that the widow allusion refers to Cleopatra's association with Isis, on the grounds that Isis lost her husband Osiris every year (only to regain him again) and that Cleopatra was twice widowed. That is far-fetched, and out of tune with the context of the passage. The widow in question rules the world—not simply the lands of the east on the sufferance of a Roman dynast.[43] Only one power fits that description: Rome itself. Characterization of the great city as a widow has parallels in biblical prophecies about Babylon.[44] The metaphorical bereavement of the super-power may signify the loss of divine support, presaging an imminent demise, which indeed follows shortly thereafter in the passage. That sense is reinforced by repetition of the widow metaphor in connection with the divine judgment: all elements of the universe will be bereft when God rolls up the heavens.[45] The oracle, like so much else in the Third Book, directs itself against Rome, not Cleopatra.[46]

---

41 *Sib. Or.* 3.75–92.
42 e.g. Tarn 'Alexander Helios and the Golden Age', 142: 'That the widow is Cleopatra ... seems certain'; Collins *The Sibylline Oracles of Egyptian Judaism*, 66–70; Goodman, in Schürer *The History of the Jewish People*, 641.
43 *Sib. Or.* 3. 75–7: καὶ τότε δὴ κόσμος ὑπὸ ταῖς παλάμῃσι γυωαικός ... ἔνθ' ὁπόταν κόσμου παντὸς χήρη βασιλεύσῃ. Indeed κόσμος appears yet a third time in line 81.
44 Isaiah 47: 8–9; Apocalypse of John 17–18. This was acutely noted by Nikiprowetzky *La Troisème Sibylle*, 146–9.
45 *Sib. Or.* 3. 80–2: τότε δὴ στοιχεῖα πρόπαντα χηρεύσει κόσμου, ὁπόταν θεὸς αἰθέρι ναίων οὐρανὸν εἱλίξῃ.
46 The idea of Rome as the referent here was suggested long ago but has found little favor in the last century. See Alexandre *Excursus ad Sibyllina* (Paris, 1856), 517; Lanchester, in Charles *The Apocrypha and Pseudepigrapha*, 371. Rzach 'Sibyllinischer Orakel', 2131, rules out Cleopatra and reckons the widow as an apocalyptic figure. The argument of Nikiprowetzky *La Troisème*

Another oracle involves an explicit attack on Rome. This too has been identified with Cleopatra, only here she takes the positive role as the avenger of Roman misdeeds. Such at least is the theory.[47] The passage itself makes that conclusion less than obvious. In the Sibylline pronouncement, vengeance will fall upon Rome, a threefold exaction taken by Asia, previously its victim, now its conqueror, and a twentyfold return in Italian slaves for the Asians once enslaved by Rome, a down payment on a debt of myriads. Rome, the virgin, often intoxicated with numerous suitors, will be wed unceremoniously as a slave. The mistress will frequently snip her locks and, passing judgment, will cast her from heaven to earth and then again from earth to heaven. After destruction, however, will come reconciliation, peace, and prosperity, a time of concord and the flight of all evils.[48] Is Cleopatra the *despoina*, the mistress? Does this represent a Jewish reflection of the Ptolemaic queen's propaganda against Rome? Not a likely inference. The oracle pits Asia against Rome, unambiguously favoring the former and projecting an eventual era of harmony. Depiction of the struggle between Cleopatra and Octavian as one between east and west was, of course, the product of propaganda from Rome, a blackening of the shameless and power-mad woman who leads barbaric hordes against the valiant Italians.[49] It is quite unthinkable that Cleopatra herself would embrace that distorted portrait. Egypt had suffered no depradation from Rome, Cleopatra had no reason to seek reparations or exact revenge for past iniquities. The notion that she looked toward conquest of Rome itself rests on a hostile and thoroughly unreliable tradition.

Sibylle, 146–9, that the widow represents the Messiah or the coming of New Jerusalem, confusingly amalgamates both the world-ruler and the dominion which follows, the divine destruction.

47 So Tarn 'Alexander Helios and the Golden Age', 135–41; H. Jeanmaire La Sibylle et la retour de l'âge d'Or (Paris, 1939), 55–61. Collins *The Sibylline Oracles of Egyptian Judaism*, 57–64, questions many of Tarn's arguments, but adopts his conclusion.

48 *Sib. Or.* 3. 350–80. See esp. 356–60: ὦ χλιδανὴ ζάχρυσε Λατινίδος ἔκγονε Ῥώμη, παρθένε, πολλάκι σοῖσι πολυμνήστοισι γάμοισιν οἰνωθεῖσα, λάτρις νυμφεύσεαι οὐκ ἐνὶ κόσμῳ, πολλάκι δ' ἀβρὴν σεῖο κόμην δέσποινά τε κείρει ἠδὲ δίκην διέπουσα ἀπ' οὐρανόθεν ποτὶ γαῖαν ῥίψει, ἐκ δὲ γαίης πάλιν ορανὸν εἰς ἀνεγείρει.

49 Cf. Hor. *Epod.* 9; *Carm.* 1. 37; Verg. *Aen.* 8. 675–728; Prop. 3. 11, 4. 6. To be sure, the war of Actium is portrayed as a clash of Europe against Asia also by Philo, *Leg.* 144, a point stressed by Collins *The Sibylline Oracles of Egyptian Judaism*, 60. But Philo, whose objective in this section of his work was to contrast the virtues of Caligula's predecessors with his own megalomania, clearly took up the Augustan line and represents no independent Jewish viewpoint—let alone a reflection of Cleopatra's attitude. His account, in fact, omits any allusion to the Ptolemaic queen, depicting the contest as one headed by rival Romans: ἡγεμόνας ἔχουσι καὶ προαγωνιστὰς Ῥωμαίων τοὺς ἐν τέλεσι δοκιμωτάτους. Moreover, Augustus appears not as leader of Rome against a Greek ruler but as champion of Hellenism and civilizer of the barbarians; Philo, *Leg.* 147.

The queen's ambitions in fact directed themselves toward revival of the Ptolemaic empire—with the assistance of Rome. Once again, the Sibyl's meaning transcends a specific historical circumstance. The mistress who shears the head of Roma, the newly enslaved servant, may well be Asia itself, a broad and vague allusion to the sufferings of the east at Roman hands, now to be reversed and compensated for many times over.[50] The forecast, plainly a wishful hope for a future that never came to pass, expresses fierce eastern resentment against Roman exploitation and looks ahead to a happier time when the empire will be crushed, its reparations plenteous, and the outcome one of concord. Cleopatra has no place here.

Similar doubts need to be applied to other inferences about historical events or personages lurking behind the Sibyl's dark pronouncements. The very passage just discussed has been ascribed to the time of the Mithridatic wars, an anticipated vengeful retaliation by Mithridates against Romans who had despoiled the east.[51] But Mithridates would hardly qualify as a 'mistress'. And his fearsome war against Romans and Italians would certainly not suit a prediction of subsequent peace and harmony.

Elsewhere, a cryptic oracle regarding Macedonian terrors unleashed upon Asia has stimulated a wealth of scholarly speculation. The Sibyl bewails afflictions imposed upon Asia, and even upon Europe, by the horrific Macedon becoming mistress of all lands under the sun, climaxed by the conquest of Babylon. The evils wrought upon Asia are ascribed to an untrustworthy man, clad in purple cloak, characterized as barbaric and fiery, who came to place Asia under a wicked yoke. Ultimately, however, so the Sibyl forecast, the very race he sought to destroy will bring, about the destruction of his own race. A still more cryptic pronouncement follows: the destroyer provides a single root which he will cut off from ten horns and will leave another side-shoot; then, after slaying the warrior progenitor of a purple race, he will perish at the hands of his sons, and the side-horn will rule.[52] Opinions divide on the identity of the malignant Macedonian conqueror whose race will perish by the hand of those whom he oppressed. Some opt for Alexander the Great, some for Antio-

---

50 So Peretti *La Sibilla babilonese*, 351–4.
51 So Bousset 'Sibyllen und Sibyllinische Bücher', 271; Lanchester, in Charles *The Apocrypha and Pseudepigrapha*, 372; Peretti *La Sibilla babilonese*, 329–40; Geffcken *Komposition und Entsthungszeit*, 8–9. Goodman, in Schürer *The History of the Jewish People*, 636, declines to choose between Mithridates and Cleopatra.
52 *Sib. Or.* 3. 381–400. The oracle is often divided into two, with a break after line 387. But even if the division is justified, the forecasts are closely related and belong together.

chus IV Epiphanes.[53] Or, as almost all commentators now seem to concur, the original oracle had Alexander as its villain but was then reworked by a Jewish Sibyllist who directed its fire against Antiochus Epiphanes, archenemy of the Jews, and saw the collapse of Macedonian power in the internecine warfare of the Seleucid house.[54] Again, however, focus upon historical personages and their actions veers away from the central significance. The purple-clad invader of Asia may well be Alexander the Great, but he is cited as emblematic of Macedonian power and ruthlessness, not with regard to specific deeds of the individual. The one explicit reference to conquest of Babylon should have made that clear to commentators: Alexander did gain control of Babylon, but postured as its liberator, respected its religion and traditions, and treated it with generosity.[55] The Sibyl is concerned with the broader consequences of Macedonian dominance, not with historical particulars. By the same token, the narrow interpretation of the oracle's conclusion by seeking to identify individuals in the house of Antiochus Epiphanes has little point. To be sure, the Sibyl here has adopted the image of the ten horns and their offshoot that can be found in Daniel 7: 7–8, but it does not follow that the image carries the same significance—even if we knew for certain to what Daniel does refer. What matters here is the sharp hostility to Hellenic overlordship in the east, at least as exercised by savage rulers, and the prediction of its violent demise. The thrust of the oracle is out of tune with much else in the Third Book. Knowledge of Daniel implies a Jewish hand at work. But the message contains no hint of divine retribution or intervention. And this is the one segment in the Third Book in which Macedonians, rather than the more usual Romans, are the targets of oracular venom. In so far as Jewish authorship is involved, whether in origin or as redaction, it is best seen as expressing resent-

---

53 For Antiochus, see e.g. Lanchester, in Charles *The Apocrypha and Pseudepigrapha*, 385; H.H. Rowley 'The Interpretation and Date of the Sibylline Oracles III 388–400', *Zeitschrift für die Alttestamentliche Wissenschaft*, (1926), 324–7; Fraser *Ptolemaic Alexandria*, 2. 995–6. The argument for Alexander, at least as the initial figure in lines 388–91, was forcefully made by Bousset 'Die Beziehungen der ältesten jüdischen Sibylle zur chaldäischen Sibyll', *Zeitschrift für die Neutestamentliche Wissenschaft*, (1902), 3:34–41, followed by many in subsequent years.

54 Peretti *La Sibilla babilonese*, 372–4; S.K. Eddy *The King is Dead* (Lincoln, 1961), 11–14; Collins *The Sibylline Oracles of Egyptian Judaism*, 27; Goodman, in Schürer *The History of the Jewish People*, 634. The dispute over whether the first part of the forecast, in lines 381–7, derives from a 'Persian Sibyl', a 'Babylonian Sibyl', or neither one need not be exploited here. See the valuable discussion, with bibliography, by Nikiprowetzky 'La Sibylle juive depuis Charles Alexandre', *ANRW* (1987), 474–5; 524–8.

55 Arrian 3. 16. 3–5-, 7. 17. 1–2. See also Ps. Hecataeus in Joseph. *C. Apion*. 1. 192, for a favorable Jewish view of Alexander at Babylon; cf. 2. 43.

ment against foreign oppression, wherever it manifests itself in the east. The quest for historical specificity has led researchers astray.[56]

A comparable quest for geographical specificity may be equally delusive. The favored provenance is Egypt, with the Hellenized Jews of Alexandria or Leontopolis as principal sites for authors.[57] The theory connects closely with the idea that a cozy relationship between Jews and the Ptolemies of mid-second-century Egypt finds voice in the utterances of the Third Sibyl. The weakness of that reconstruction has already been indicated above. And the corollary correspondingly falls. Since no unequivocal reference to the relevant Ptolemies exists in the text, further speculation about the significance of an alleged Jewish—Egyptian provenance lacks warrant.

In fact, many of the Sibyl's pronouncements would dishearten the devotees of Ptolemaic Egypt. Almost the very opening lines of the Third Book denounce Egyptians for their idolatry that includes not only the erection of stone statues to people, but the worship of snakes, and the rendering of sacrifice to cats.[58] The early verses, to be sure, may actually belong to Book II, and hence have no bearing on the-attitude of the authors of the Third Sibyl.[59] But it is perhaps not irrelevant that those who ordered the extant edition found ostensible congruence. In any event, later passages are comparably uncomplimentary to Egyptians. When God's wrath falls upon the nations, Egypt will suffer together with others, indeed doubly so.[60] The Egyptians are characterized as a destructive race.[61] The Sibyl brackets them, together with Phoenicians, Romans, and others, as moral transgressors, indulging in homosexual vice.[62] And it is noteworthy that

---

56 See the sensible general remarks of Simon, in Hellholm *Apocalypticism in the Mediterranean World*, 224 – 5.
57 The case is made most fully by Collins 'The Provenance and Date of the Third Sibyl', 1 – 18; *The Sibylline Oracles of Egyptian Judaism*, 35 – 55. Collins's argument for Leontopolis as the principal site of composition, however, has little force. The absence of any allusion to Leontopolis in the text fatally weakens the idea, forcing Collins to postulate a very narrow corridor of time for the composition: after Onias's arrival in Egypt but before he built the temple at Leontopolis. However, the recent immigration of Onias and his followers from Judaea and their relatively conservative ideology, which Collins himself acknowledges, make them the least likely persons to embrace the quintessentially Hellenic form of Sibylline prophecy to convey their message.
58 *Sib. Or.* 3. 29 – 45.
59 See Geffcken *Komposition und Entsthungszeit*, 47 – 53; Bousset 'Sibyllen und Sibyllinische Bücher', 273 – 4; Rzach 'Sibyllinischer Orakel', 2123, 2130.
60 *Sib. Or.* 3. 314 – 18, 348 – 9.
61 *Sib. Or.* 3.348 – 9: Αἰγύπτου ὀλοὸν γένος.
62 *Sib. Or.* 3.596 – 600.

the projected time of peace and prosperity will come *after* the collapse of Egypt, destroyed by an Asian king.[63]

That some verses in the collection stem from Hellenized Jews in Egypt can be readily acknowledged. The denunciations of Egypt noted above belong in that category. So do the lines that give Egypt prominence in the sequence of empires, singling out its royal rule twice.[64] And one may plausibly infer Egyptian provenance for the passage on the 'king from the sun', a Jewish reworking of material rooted in their adopted land.[65] All of this, however, amounts to no more than a fraction of the 829 verses in Book III. Much of the remainder could just as readily derive from Palestinian Jews.[66] And parts indeed need not even be Jewish in origin.[67] In short, it is hazardous to see the centrality of Egypt in the work, let alone Jewish favor toward Ptolemy VI or Ptolemy VIII as stimulus for its composition.[68]

The Sibyl has a wider canvas. Her realm of concern stretches to the world at large, at least the word as she knew it, the lands of the Mediterranean. And there the dominant power was Rome, ruthless, tyrannical, and appalling. Rome is the prime villain of the verses, overwhelmingly so. Only misguided scholarly ingenuity has obscured that otherwise conspicuous fact.

The evils of Rome, Romans, and the Roman empire recur repeatedly. A forecast near the outset of Book III issues a severe condemnation. When the imperial power stretches over Egypt, its days become numbered. Despite all the splendid cities with their temples, stadia, fora, and statuary, the empire stands doomed, to be destroyed by the fiery cataract of the Supreme Being who will reign over the earth.[69] The very next oracle directs itself against Beliar from the Sebastenoi, the latter probably signifying the line of Roman emperors and the former perhaps Nero, who will lead men away from God but will perish by divine fire, as will those who put trust in him.[70] There follows the passage in which 'the widow', quite probably Rome, who rules the entire world, will herself be swept away

---

63 *Sib. Or.* 3.611–23.

64 *Sib. Or.* 3.156–61.

65 *Sib. Or.* 3.619–56.

66 e.g. *Sib. Or.* 3. 63–74, 97–155, 196–294, 381–400, 489–600, 657–808.

67 350–80, 401–88.

68 A similar criticism with regard to reductive interpretations of the *Oracula Sibyllina*, Book 7 was delivered by J.G. Gager 'Some attempts to label the Oracula Sibylla, Book 7', *HTR* (1972), 91–7.

69 *Sib. Or.* 3. 46–62.

70 63–74. On Beliar as Nero, see Collins *The Sibylline Oracles of Egyptian Judaism*, 80–7. *Contra:* Nikiprowetzky *La Troisème Sibylle*, 138–43; cf. Goodman, in Schürer *The History of the Jewish People*, 640–1.

by the mighty wrath of a divine judgement.[71] Not long thereafter in the text, a list of kingdoms culminating in Rome provokes a prophecy whereby the imperial forces of the Roman Republic will wreak widespread destruction only to fall foul of their own arrogance, impiety, and moral corruption.[72] A harsher fate for Rome is proclaimed later in the text: retribution threefold for exactions made from Asia, twentyfold for the numbers enslaved, and ten thousand fold for debts imposed; vengeance will reduce Rome to a mere street.[73] Yet another oracle bewails the devastation and destruction to be wrought by Romans upon the east but also foretells civil war that will tear Italy apart, the land described not as mother of good men but as nurse of wild beasts.[74] Finally, the large barbarian horde, which will devastate the Greeks, rampage, lay waste the earth, enslave and rape the conquered, and place a heavy yoke upon the Hellenes until God unleashes his deadly fire, unquestionably refers to the Romans.[75]

The divine judgment that will eventually blast the Romans to perdition is, of course, a triumphant vindication of Jewish faith. Ultimate glory for the Jews is a repeated refrain of the Third Sibyl.[76] A noteworthy feature, however, needs emphasis here. Whereas the oracle mounts a heavy assault upon Roman wickedness, no comparable attacks are leveled at the Greeks. To the contrary. The Sibyl reaches out to the Hellenic world, exhorting its people to repentance, urging acknowledgment of the true God, and offering hope of salvation. Oracular verses expose the folly of trust in mortal leaders and resort to idolatry, proclaiming instead the need to recognize the great God, thereby to escape the woes that will fall upon Hellas.[77] A further call to repentance comes several lines later, prescribing sacrifices, prayers, and righteous behavior to earn divine favor.[78] The disasters to befall Greece will eventually be lifted by God through the agency of a king from the sun.[79] And the Sibyl subsequently repeats her appeal to unhappy Hellas to abandon haughtiness and embrace the true God—which will

---

71 *Sib. Or.* 3. 75–92. See above.
72 *Sib. Or.* 3.156–95.
73 *Sib. Or.* 3.350–64.
74 *Sib. Or.* 3.464–88; see 469: ἔσσῃ δ' οὐκ ἀγαθῶν μήτηρ, θηρῶν δὲ τιθήνη.
75 *Sib. Or.* 3.520–44. The suggestion that this may allude to the Gallic invasion of Greece is ruled out by line 530 which states that the Greeks will have no one to give them a little aid in war and to preserve their lives.
76 Cf. *Sib. Or.* 3, 211–17, 282–94, 573–600, 669–731, 767–808.
77 *Sib. Or.* 3.545–72.
78 *Sib. Or.* 3.624–34. Since these lines follow, directly upon a passage that speaks of Graeco-Macedonians bending a knee to God who then, brings about peace and prosperity, 601–23, the exhortation must be directed to Greeks.
79 *Sib. Or.* 3. 635–56.

bring a share in the blissful peace to come.[80] In so far as the Third Book contains negative aspersions upon Greeks, it includes them among wayward peoples whose failure to see the truth has led them into arrogance, impiety, and immorality, thus provoking divine vengeance.[81] But Greeks alone are singled out for encouragement to enter the fold of the true believers.[82]

The gesture of the Sibyl is noble and magnanimous. It should not, however, be mistaken for a conscious campaign of proselytism. Readership of the Books would consist largely of Hellenized Jews, with but a sprinkling of Gentiles. The message had symbolic import, not a manifesto for missionary activity. It asserted common cultural bonds that could encompass both communities.

The appeal to the Greeks constitutes a striking feature of the text. It may also help to solve a peculiar puzzle. The Sibyl directs her fire against Rome, against the terror, destructiveness, and corruption of the Roman empire. Her verses, of course, are no political clarion call. Efforts to locate the message in precise time and place, with concrete intent and expectation, lead to blind-alleys. The fall of Rome will come only through a cataclysmic divine intervention. But the vitriol against Rome itself demands explanation. Jews did not suffer at Roman hands in the Hellenistic period prior to the advent of Pompey, and rarely thereafter before the time of Caligula. Indeed, they generally enjoyed tolerance, alliance, and signal favor. Why then should a Jewish Sibyl of this era blast the Romans? The question, a difficult and troubling one, seldom even arises in the scholarship. A possible, at least partial, answer may lurk in the features outlined above. Oracular forebodings of doom delivered by a Jewish voice through a Greek medium signaled a solidarity between the two cultures. The verbal assault on

---

80 *Sib. Or.* 3.732–61.
81 *Sib. Or.* 3.196–219, 295–365, 594–600. Only the anti-Macedonian prophecy of lines 381–400, with its parallel to the forecast of Daniel, gives no ostensible hope for reconciliation. But the reference is to the aggressions of royal imperialists, not to the Hellenistic people as such. The thesis of E. Kocsis 'Ost-West Gegensatz in den jüdischen Sibyllinen', *Novum Testamentum* (1962), 105–10, that the oracles drew a sharp contrast between the favored east and the savage west, is simplistic: One needs only to cite the destructive king from Asia in *Sib. Or.* 3. 611–18.
82 The Sibyl's hostile comments about Egyptian practices might be thought to reflect ill upon the Hellenic masters of that land. Not so. The opening verses unambiguously condemn the idolatry of native Egyptians, worship of snakes and reverence for cats; *Sib. Or.* 3. 29–45. Later, the baleful race of Egypt whose doom is nigh is evidently contrasted with the Alexandrians who seem to be put in a different category; *Sib. Or.* 348–9: ἴσθι τότ' Αἰγύπτου ὀλοὸν γένος ἐγγὺς ὀλέθρου, καί τότ' Ἀλεξανδρεῦσιν ἔτος τὸ παρελθὸν ἄμεινον. That the Sibyl did not subsume Greeks under Egypt is plain from lines 594–600. The cryptic allusions to the seventh king of Egypt remain elusive, but clearly imply no reproach of the Hellenic dwellers in that land; *Sib. Or.* 3. 191–5, 314–18, 608. See above.

Rome would suitably fit that context. The Greeks had indeed been victimized by the western power, especially in the later Hellenistic era. Greek resentment bursts out with pointed force in lines preserved by the Third Sibyl herself and plainly deriving from Hellenic circles.[83] Adoption of the anti-Roman line by Hellenized Jews who helped to shape this compilation symbolized the conjoining of Greek experience and Jewish aspirations.

Eschatology is the central ingredient throughout. Reference both to past disasters and to ills still to come issue in forecasts of terrifying divine judgments and usually the glorious elevation of the Jewish faithful. That is surely the significance of the 'king from the sun', not a historical personage but a Messianic figure.[84] And eschatological overtones may be caught also in lines that allude to construction of the Second Temple but also carry deeper meaning embodied in a king sent by the Lord to deliver judgment in blood and fire.[85]

The message of the Third Sibyl transcends the political realm. Its resonance is religious and cultural. The roots of the Sibyl's utterances reside in biblical prophecy, not the official functionaries who advised kings or participated in cult, but the powerful voices who denounced contemporaries and heralded destruction from the skies: an Amos, a Hosea, or an Isaiah. No less potent in inspiration for the Sibyl was the apocalyptic literature of Hellenistic Judaism: Daniel, 1 Enoch, Jubilees, 4 Ezra, and a variety of other texts, now further illuminated by the Qumran documents. The Sibylline pronouncements fit snugly within that setting, a complex of thoroughly Jewish traditions.[86] At the same time, of course,

---

83 The bitterness is unmistakable in *Sib. Or.* 3. 350–80, 464–88, which are surely of Greek origin.

84 *Sib. Or.* 3. 652–6; see above.

85 *Sib. Or.* 3.282–94, esp. 286–7: καὶ τότε δὴ θεὸς οὐράνιος πέμψει βασιλῆα, κρινεῖ δ' ἄνδρα ἕκαστον ἐν αἵματι καὶ πυρὸς αὐγῇ. Cf. Peretti *La Sibilla babilonese*, 393–5, whose speculations about the influence of Iranian eschatology, however, need to be taken with caution. The Messianic interpretation of these lines is not in fashion; cf. Nikiprowetzky *La Troisème Sibylle*, 133–7; Collins *The Sibylline Oracles of Egyptian Judaism*, 38–9. J. Nolland 'Sib. Or. III. 265–94, An Early Maccabean Messianic Oracle', *JTS* (1979), 158–66, with valuable bibliography, rightly endeavored to revive it. But his effort to pinpoint it to the early Maccabaean period, despite the absence of any Maccabaean allusion, is unpersuasive. Cf. Collins *Between Athens and Jerusalem*, 66–8. Nothing in the Third Book gives any hint of Jewish resistance to the Seleucid persecutions. That resounding silence also undermines the thesis of Momigliano, *Sesto contributo alla storia studi classici*, 553–6, that lines 194–5, predicting the future strength *of* the Jews, refer to the success of the Maccabaean uprising.

86 This emerges forcefully in Nikiprowetzky's discussion *La Troisème Sibylle*, 95–9, 127–37, 160–76, 248–67. The lengthy and repetitive treatment by Peretti *La Sibilla babilonese*, 363–444, tracing the apocalyptic statements to Iranian eschatology, as exemplified by the Oracle of Hystaspes, is altogether speculative.

the authors or compilers of this collection, whether from Palestine or the Diaspora, purposefully and pointedly donned the cloak of the pagan Sibyl. Declarations issuing forth from oracular shrines, subsequently assimilated, expanded, or fabricated in written form, had long been a feature of Hellenic religious culture. They could even take shape as a full-scale piece of literature, as in the case of Lycophron's *Alexandra*. Sibylline prophecies constituted an important part of this development, widely circulated in private hands, available for consultation by public authorities, and the basis for literary invention. The authority of the Sibyls spread through much of the Greek world, most especially the prophetess at Erythrae, but also a number of others located at various Mediterranean sites.[87] Jewish intellectuals tapped into the tradition and embraced the Hellenic oracular form. A Hebrew Sibyl eventually took her place among the venerable female seers acknowledged by pagan writers. Verses in the extant Third Book that concern the tower of Babel, the reign of the Titans, and the myth of Chronos and his sons are attributed to the Sibyl by Alexander Polyhistor already in the first century BCE.[88] By the second century CE Pausanias could make specific reference to a Sibyl of the Hebrews in Palestine alongside the Erythraean, Libyan, and Cumaean Sibyls.[89]

The Jews successfully appropriated the Hellenic medium. The Jewish Sibyl speaks in proper Homeric hexameters. She pronounces her prophecies under divine prodding, a mouthpiece, even a somewhat reluctant one, of the greater power who speaks through her.[90] She has a grasp of Greek mythology and the epic tradition.[91] Indeed she forecasts both the fall of Troy and the Exodus from Egypt.[92] Employment of Hellenic forms, language, and themes in the service of advancing Judaic ideas enlivened the intellectual circles of Hellenistic Judaism. The composers of the Third Sibylline Oracle stand shoulder to shoulder with Ezekiel the tragedian, the historians Demetrius and Eupolemus, and the imaginative reinventors of a Hebraic—Hellenic past like Artapanus, Aristobulus, and Pseudo-Eupolemus.

---

87 On the Sibyls and Sibylline oracles, see Alexandre *Oracula Sibyllina*, 2. 1 – 101; Rzach 'Sibyllinischer Orakel', 2073 – 183; H.W. Parke *Sibyls and Sibylline Prophecy in Classical Antiquity* (London, 1988), 1 – 50; D. Potter *Prophets and Emperors* (Cambridge, Mass., 1994), 71 – 93.
88 See Euseb. *Chron.* 1. 23 (Schoene).
89 Paus. 10. 12; cf. Schol. Pl. *Phdr.* 315. See Nikiprowetzky *La Troisème Sibylle*, 37 – 53; Peretti *La Sibilla babilonese*, 53 – 69.
90 See *Sib. Or.* 3. 1 – 7, 162 – 4, 196 – 8, 295 – 9, 489 – 91, 698 – 9.
91 *Sib. Or.* 3.110 – 55, 401 – 32.
92 *Sib. Or.* 3.248 – 56, 414 – 18.

Preparation for the Eschaton marks a blending of Hebrew and Hellene. The Sibylline declarations extend a hand to Greeks and a promise of divine deliverance—an invitation to link the two heritages. The Jewish authors express a cultural solidarity with Greeks, but one in which the precedence of their own traditions is clear. Greeks who show themselves worthy are invited to partake of the values of the Jews. The provenance of the Third Sibyl makes the point unambiguously. She presents herself as daughter-in-law of Noah, hence a claim on the most distant antiquity and the hoariest biblical and Near-Eastern legacies. The Hellenic connection is a secondary one. The Sibyl moved from Babylon to Greece, there to be associated with Erythrae. But her memory stretches back to the Flood, a divine prescience, infallible as the gift of God.[93] Here is appropriation indeed. The Sibyl's origins precede even Babel. She thus asserts a universal heritage, embodying Hebrew traditions and later subsuming the authority of the Erythraean Sibyl, most venerated of the Hellenic prophetesses. Jewish identity stands in the forefront here. The keepers of the faith who had also absorbed pagan learning, literature, and legends claimed a place in both worlds but held firm to their core. The oracular voice promises a happy fate for the Chosen People—and also extends a compassionate embrace to those Greeks touched by their values and ideals.

---

93 *Sib. Or.* 3.809–29.

22. Subversive Elements in Pseudo-Philo

Second Temple Jews found a fascination for retelling biblical tales in multiple modes. This might take the form of adapting, altering, adding to, or subtracting from traditional stories, creating new ones, or parodying familiar ones. Occasionally the enterprise issued in rewriting of an extended portion of biblical narrative, as in Chronicles, Jubilees, the Genesis Apocryphon, and, in fullest form, Josephus' *Jewish Antiquities*. None of the authors, of course, expected to replace or supersede the biblical text; all took it for granted and could assume familiarity with it by most of their readers.[1] Nor did the works function (primarily) to interpret or explicate the accepted accounts. They provided alternative versions, expanded or contracted, from diverse angles and with diverse objectives, depending upon the perspectives of the writers. The *Liber Antiquitatum Biblicarum* (*LAB*) of "Pseudo-Philo" belongs in this company.

LAB provides a narrative of events from the advent of Adam to the eve of David's monarchy. The text is firmly based on the Bible, but adds some material and omits much more. The author (so it appears) will forever elude us. Discussions of date, provenance, and orientation rest largely—and inescapably—upon conjecture. No purpose in adding to the speculation here. A general consensus holds that the extant Latin text derived from a Hebrew original, via a Greek translation, that composition came in the 1st or 2nd century CE, and that the author dwelled in Palestine. Those conclusions need not be challenged. Nor is there compelling reason to find sectarian sympathies, political motivation, or an ideological campaign in the work. Pseudo-Philo had his own agenda.

A brief study cannot pretend to address all aspects, let alone to elucidate the whole.[2] Yet a central item on the agenda requires reconsideration. General agreement holds that the author's principal objective was to reinforce implicit faith in the ways of the Lord. Israel strayed repeatedly from God's Law, suffering penalty for waywardness and sin. Lack of commitment to God again and again brought

---

1 One should note, however, that, according to B.Z. Wacholder, *The Dawn of Qumran* (Cincinnati, 1983), pp. 1 – 32, 41 – 62, the Temple Scroll from Qumran did actually endeavor to provide another Torah more authoritative than the Mosaic archetype, and the author of Jubilees preferred that version to the Torah of Moses. But the reconstruction is highly speculative, and would certainly not apply to Pseudo-Philo.

2 On the structure, compositional techniques, and hermeneutical approach of *LAB*, matters not discussed here, see, especially, E. Reinmuth, *Pseudo-Philo und Lukas* (Tübingen, 1994), pp. 3 – 127. On intertextuality and use of Scripture, see now B.N. Fisk, *Do You Not Remember? Scripture, Story, and Exegesis in the Rewritten Bible of Pseudo-Philo* (Sheffield, 2001), *passim.* (hereafter: Fisk, *Do You Not Remember?*)

leaders and people into catastrophe. The fault lay not with the divine but with humanity. God remains firm and constant. Those who obey his precepts will prosper, the disobedient will fall. A divine plan governs the universe, determining the fate of the faithful and the sinner alike. On this analysis, God holds responsibility for both success and suffering. Although figures like Abraham, Moses, Joshua, and Deborah place implicit trust in the Lord, the absence of trust prevails. Iniquity and infidelity mark much of the history of Israel. God rewards and punishes in accordance with a consistent scheme. However fierce his rage and terrible his retaliation, he remains true to the covenant with Israel. His special concern for his people resurfaces even after the darkest of times, his purposes undeviating, his promises fulfilled, his plan accomplished. The Israelites may be devastated by divine wrath, but they are never altogether abandoned. The covenant will ultimately be upheld. The main message of Pseudo-Philo then seems clear. He calls upon Jews to maintain unremitting reliance on the Lord, to obey his precepts and follow his Law, to give themselves into his hand, and to acknowledge the unchallengeable authority of his will.[3]

This reconstruction holds the field, and numerous passages in the text can be marshalled to support it. Yet a monolithic interpretation here is curiously unsatisfying. The image of a steadfast God, of discerning figures who place their trust in him, and of wayward souls who court disaster does not do justice to the ambiguities and equivocations of the text. Pseudo-Philo may, in the final analysis, be an advocate of faith and obedience. But the work contains its doubts and queries, its challenges and criticisms, its uncertainties about God, even its subtle subversions.

One might note first of all that God needs to be reminded, more than once, about adherence to the covenant. Moses himself responds sharply to a divine tirade against the faithlessness of the Israelites, as if he were himself being charged with failure to keep his flock in tow: did I set them on their paths before you

3 See, e.g., L. Cohn, *JQR*, 10 (1898), p. 322; M.R. James, *The Biblical Antiquities of Philo* (New York, 1971), 2nd ed; first published 1917, pp. 33–34; C. Dietzfelbinger, *JSHRZ*, II.2, 91–92, 97–99; C. Perrot and P.-M. Bogaert, *Pseudo-Philon, Les Antiquités Bibliques* (Paris, 1976), II, pp. 28–52; G.W.E. Nickelsburg, in G.W.E. Nickelsburg and J.J. Collins (eds.), *Ideal Figures in Ancient Judaism* (Chico, CA, 1980), pp. 60–64; D.J. Harrington, J.H. Charlesworth (eds.), *The Old Testament Pseudepigrapha*, II, (Garden City, 1984), pp. 300–301; F.J. Murphy, *Pseudo-Philo: Rewriting the Bible* (New York, 1993), pp. 223–228, 244–246, 263; H. Jacobson, *A Commentary on Pseudo-Philo's Liber Antiquitatum Biblicarum*, I, (Leiden, 1996), pp. 241–246 (hereafter: Jacobson, *Commentary*); Fisk, *Do You Not Remember?*, pp. 45–53, 191–193. A whole range of possible motives for the author is scrupulously canvassed by L. Feldman, "Prolegomenon," to James, *Biblical Antiquities*, xxxiii–l—without opting for any. Fisk, *Do You Not Remember?*, pp. 34–45, ably summarizes subsequent contributions and wisely remains non-committal.

took the seed with which to make mankind upon the earth?[4] And he follows this immediately by pointing out to God that he owes mercy and consideration to his people to the end of days. "If you do not show mercy, who will be protected?"[5] This type of rebuke, an effort to put God back on track, is by no means an isolated instance. As another example, Pseudo-Philo has Gideon complain pointedly about the Lord's neglect of his own promises to the patriarchs.[6] And one might further note the reproach by the Israelites, accusing God of the unfulfilled promise to lead them to the land of milk and honey.[7]

Elsewhere Moses needs to reason with God, so as to point out to him where his real interests lie. After the Israelites lapsed and created the golden calf, thus prompting Moses' fury, he knew that his people had reason to worry about the vengeance of the Lord. Moses' plea thus emphasizes what God has to gain by refraining from destruction of the faithless Israelites. He observes that if they should be wiped out, all of God's work will have been in vain and he will have no one left to glorify him. Even worse, any future people on whom he might bestow his favor would distrust him, since he had demolished the Israelites. If he abandons the world now, who will be left to act in accordance with the divine will?[8] The argument is a strictly pragmatic one. God has to be told that a hasty act against Israel will cost him his constituency and will make it impossible to produce another to trust him, let alone to sing his praises. If God knows what is good for him, he will spare the Israelites.[9]

---

4 *LAB* 15.7: *Numquid, antequam semen acciperes quo hominem faceres super terram, ego constitui vias eorum?* Jacobson, *Commentary*, I, 551, sees the influence of Numbers 12, 11.

5 *LAB* 15.7: *Et ideo nunc sustineat nos misericordia tua usque in finem, et pietas tua in longitudinem dierum, quoniam nisi tu miserearis quis procreabitur?* On *procreabitur*, possibly corrupt, see Jacobson, *Commentary*, I, 552–553. Reinmuth (above, note 2), p. 56, sees only an assertion of God's clemency by Moses.

6 *LAB* 35.2: *et ecce modo tradidit nos, et oblitus est sponsionum quas dixit patribus nostris.*

7 *LAB* 15.4. On this passage, see the discussion by Fisk, *Do You Not Remember?*, pp. 195–199.

8 *LAB* 12.9: *Si ergo non misertus fueris vinee tue, omnia Domine in vano facta sunt, et non habebis qui te glorificet. Nam etsi aliam vineam plantaveris, nec hec tibi credet, eo quod priorem dissipasti. Si enim relinquens reliqueris seculum, et quis faciet tibi quod locutus es tamquam Deus?* Cf. Dietzfelbinger, *JSHRZ*, II.2, 136; E. Reinmuth, "'Nicht vergleiblich' bei Paulus und Pseudo-Philo, Liber Antiquitatum Biblicarum," *NT*, 33 (1991), pp. 112–116. The corresponding passage in Exod. 32.11–13 also appeals to God's self-interest, but in a different way. Moses raises the possibility that the ruin of Israel would give the Egyptians cause to infer that God brought the Israelites out of their land only to destroy them in the mountains. A somewhat comparable lament appears in 2 Bar. 3.5–7, in which the prophet asks God who will sing his praises if Israel is destroyed. But the motif does not reappear in that work.

9 An interesting twist on this comes in *LAB* 18.6, when God confronts the Mesopotamian seer Balaam who had been asked by the king of Moab to curse the Israelites. God reminds him of

Moses expresses himself similarly on his death-bed. He reminds the Lord that no man can escape sin, and that unless he extends patience and mercy his legacy will be shaky.[10] He advises God to correct the Israelites for a time, but not in anger.[11] This is more, than a plea or a prayer. Moses serves as counsellor to God, no mere servant of his will. He offers recommendation on what is to God's own advantage: live up to your promises or your inheritance will suffer.

Such statements represent part of a pattern. Pseudo-Philo's characters frequently have to advise God to pay heed to his reputation. Moses makes the point when the children of Israel face destruction at the Red Sea. Others had suggested suicide, surrender, or resistance. But Moses shouted out to the Lord with a reproach for having led his people to the edge of the sea, their enemies now upon them: "think about your reputation!"[12] Joshua provides comparable counsel. As the days of his life drew to a close and the future of Israel lay in the balance, Joshua quotes to God the words of Jacob regarding continuity for the nation's leadership: "the sceptre will not depart from Judah, nor the ruler's rod from between his feet." God evidently needed the reminder. And Joshua proceeds to underscore the issue by insisting that God fulfill Jacob's prediction so that all the peoples and tribes of the world can learn that he is immortal.[13] Joshua had shown similar sensitivity to the perception of God by other peoples when first he took over for Moses. He exhorted the Israelites to adhere to God's precepts, lest they be crushed and thus allow the gentiles to conclude that the Lord could not free his people.[14] Once again the Lord's repute is at stake. This form of exhortation occurs in biblical texts.[15] For Pseudo-Philo, however, it is a special favorite.

Nor is it Israelite leaders alone who show concern about the impression that others might have about God. The humble Hannah, long infertile and frustrated, mocked by Peninnah, her husband's other wife, utters a moving prayer to the

---

comparable consequences: if he curses Israel, he will have none to bless him. One might well wonder whether Pseudo-Philo is being deliberately playful here.

10 *LAB* 19.9: *Et nisi permaneat longanimitas tua, quomodo constabilietur hereditas tua si non misertus fueris eis?*

11 *LAB* 19.9: *Emendabis autem eos in tempore, et non in ira.*

12 *LAB* 10.3 – 4: *et tu Domine memor esto nominis tui,*

13 *LAB* 21.5: *Et nunc confirma predictos sermones ut discant gentes terre et tribus orbis quoniam tu sempiternus es.* For Jacob's prediction, see Gen. 49, 10. Jacobson, *Commentary*, p. 684, cites Jos. 7, 9, a biblical instance of Joshua reminding God to consider his reputation.

14 *LAB* 20.4. In this instance, however, he adds that the gentiles may have second thoughts once they realize that God chose no other people, but punished his own for their sins.

15 Cf. Num. 14.15 – 16; Jer. 14.7; Ps. 25.11; 31.4. Rightly noted by Jacobson, *Commentary*, I, pp. 439 – 440.

Lord. Affirming her unswerving fidelity, Hannah asks him to allow her to conceive, lest she perish without issue. But she takes care to pray silently, not an open plea like everyone else. Why? Pseudo-Philo explains. If she were overheard, not only would she be taunted yet again by her tormenter Penninah. Worse still, others who discovered what she was praying for and finding her prayers unanswered, would concur with Penninah that God heard no prayers, and they would indulge in blasphemy.[16] Nothing comparable to that explanation appears in the parallel biblical passage. Pseudo-Philo presses the point here. And commentators have missed the underlying significance. Hannah expresses anxiety about how God's inaction might be interpreted by those who witnessed it, thus suggesting his ineffectualness. Hannah, in short, doubts that her prayers will, in fact, be answered. And God will consequently (and rightly?) suffer in the public esteem.

Even more striking, God himself has reason to worry about his reputation. The issue arises in the *LAB* version of the Gideon story. The Israelite leader, buoyed by the support of the Lord, gains a smashing victory over the Midianites. In the biblical tale, he then inexplicably indulges in idolatry. God shows no concern, and Gideon goes unpunished.[17] Pseudo-Philo offers a much abbreviated narrative of Gideon's career but is evidently concerned about accounting for its conclusion—in particular, about God's neglect in failing to react to infidelity. The author thus fills in the gap in the Bible and supplies an explanation. God considered chastising Gideon, but thought better of it. At the time when Gideon had destroyed the altar of Baal, everyone said that Baal will eventually avenge himself. God concluded that if he should now punish Gideon, they would all ascribe it to Baal's doing, not to his own. He thus preferred that Gideon die of old age, so that people will have nothing to talk about.[18] This is exegesis, but quite remarkable exegesis. Pseudo-Philo presents God as worried about his image in the public eye. He will forgo penalizing the most flagrant act of disloyalty (at least during Gideon's lifetime) lest he be seen as outdone by Baal! This is hardly the conventional portrait of the omnipotent deity.

God, it appears, had reason to worry about his repute. Several characters in Pseudo-Philo's narrative lacked full confidence in counting on him. This might

---

16 *LAB* 50.1 – 5. See, especially 50, 5. *Nam qui scierint quod oravi, si cognoverint quod non exaudior in oratione mea, blasphemabunt.* The parallel biblical passage is 1 Sam. 1.1 – 13.

17 Judg. 8.24 – 32.

18 *LAB* 36.4: *Et dixit Deus* (speaking to himself): *Una via posita est, ut non redarguam Gedeonem in vita sua, eo quod dissipaverat sacrarium Baal, quia dixerunt tunc omnes: Vindicet se Baal. Erit nunc si castigavero eum propter quod inique gessit in me, dicitis: Non Deus castigavit eum sed Baal, quoniam ante peccavit in eum. Et ideo nunc morietur Gedeon in bona senectute, ut non habeant quod loquantur.*

be expected for the wayward or the wicked. But it holds also for some of the author's heroes and heroines. That makes it all the more meaningful.

The tale of Hannah, noted above, gives a pointed illustration. Hannah, the very epitome of the steadfast and faithful servant of the Lord, is quite dubious that her fidelity will earn her any success at all. Of course, the episode has a happy ending. Hannah conceives and gives birth to Samuel. But the maxim that trust in God will earn its reward is tempered by Pseudo-Philo's subtle suggestion that even the most faithful have reason to question the efficacy of reliance on the Lord.

The motif occurs right near the outset. Abram, the future patriarch, represents in modern interpretation the prime virtue advocated by *LAB*: unstinting obedience to the Lord and firm faith in its reward. Pseudo-Philo inserts Abram in a tale completely concocted—or, at least, without biblical precedent. The patriarch takes part in an imaginative narrative tacked on to the Tower of Babel story. When the arrogant builders seek to recruit associates for the construction, twelve men alone refused to cooperate, Abram among them. Leaders of the scheme condemned the dissidents to a fiery death. But one of the chiefs hatched a plot to rescue the twelve by hiding them away in the mountains until their enemies abandoned their murderous plan. Eleven of them leaped at the idea. Abram alone rejected this form of rescue. He placed his trust in God alone. The results, of course, vindicated Abram's constancy. He emerged unscathed from the fiery furnace while the flames rushed to consume his enemies—all 83,500 of them![19] No wonder that this tale has been taken as the paradigm for the author's main message: uncompromising faith in God and in him alone is the central obligation of man. That seems clear enough. Yet even in the case of Abram, Pseudo-Philo includes a slight twist. When the benevolent leader sketched out the rescue plan, Abram, as lone holdout, did not dismiss it strictly on the grounds of certainty that God would intercede on his behalf. His retort was more cynical: flight to the mountains would simply put him at the mercy of wild beasts or starvation; he might as well take his chances with the furnace. If God chose to save him, it would be as likely in the one place as in the other.[20] This implies no diminution of Abram's belief. But it injects a note of sardonic pragmatism that complicates the paradigm.

Other instances underscore the author's questioning attitude on this count. Moses' father Amram rejects the advice of his people's leaders that they cease to

---

19 *LAB* 6.1 – 18.
20 *LAB* 6.11. Cf. Perrot and Bogaert (above, note 3), II, p. 96. Fisk, *Do You Not Remember?*, p. 295, sees only Abraham's solitary trust in God here. So also F.J. Murphy, "Divine Plan, Human Plan, a Structuring Theme in Pseudo-Philp," *JQR*, 77 (1986), pp. 5 – 10.

produce children, all of whom, are doomed by the Pharaoh's policy. He advocates concealed pregnancy instead. Of course, one can only conceal it for so long. What happens then? Amram has hope in God, but well short of full confidence. "Who knows?" he says, "if God might be prompted to zealous action on this score so as to free us from our humiliation."[21] Amram feels rather less than altogether secure.

Kenaz, the first of Israel's judges in *LAB*, is almost entirely a creature of Pseudo-Philo's making. Although he receives brief mention in the Bible, the author turns him into a full-blown figure—and a quite positive one. He also weaves a lengthy narrative around him. Kenaz, with God's authority, extracts confessions from members of all the tribes about their respective offenses, and condemns them all to death for transgressing the Law of the Lord. The tribe of Asher had committed the sin of idolatry by stealing the golden images of the Amorites together with the precious stones set upon them. After their condemnation, Kenaz wondered whether the stones themselves might be preserved and dedicated to God. But he received reprimand instead. God retorted sharply that if he were to accept forbidden items for himself, what would stop men from doing so?[22] Kenaz may well have felt chastened, yet not entirely convinced. God ordered Kenaz to arrange the stones and the mysterious books of the Amorites for their destruction. He would have his angel eliminate the stones by sinking them into the sea, since fire could not consume them nor iron cut them, and he would dispose of the books, whose words no water could erase, by dew from a cloud and the lightning flash of the Lord. Kenaz obeyed instructions— but not right away. He needed to persuade himself first by testing the words of God. So Kenaz tossed the stones into the fire (the flames were extinguished), then hacked them with an iron sword (the iron melted), then poured water on the books (the water congealed). It took all that to persuade him.[23] Pseudo-Philo was obviously not presenting a man of unfailing faith.

Nor did this erase Kenaz's doubts. His men gained a major victory on the battlefield against the Amorites, but he was criticized for not entering the fray himself. So Kenaz gathered a small group for a clandestine attack at night. He prefaced his adventure with a prayer to God. His faith in the Lord, however, needed a

---

21 *LAB* 9.6: *Et, quis sciet si pro hoc zelabitur Deus, ut liberet nos de humiliatione nostra?*

22 *LAB* 25.1 – 26, 2. See 26, 2: *Si Deus aliquid accipit in nomine suo de anathemate, quid faciet homo?*

23 *LAB* 26.3 – 6. Jacobson, *Commentary*, II, p. 765, maintains that these actions are modeled on Gideon's behavior in Judges, 6, 17 – 23, 36 – 40. But the circumstances are not comparable. F.J. Murphy, "God in Pseudo-Philo," *JSJ*, 19 (1988), pp. 3 – 4, oddly sees Kenaz acting solely on God's instructions.

sign from above before he could be completely confident. Hence the prayer did more than ask for divine assistance; Kenaz outlined a specific sign that he requested God to provide, and only then would he proceed with his plan.[24]

This too turns out to be a motif. Yael, when she schemed to deceive and to execute Sisera, the, general of Hazor, on behalf of the Israelites, spoke first with the Lord. Her speech, however, was less a prayer to God than advice as to why he should assist her.

Yael reminds him that he had chosen Israel as his special flock and, in effect, *instructs* him as to the sign she wants in order to go ahead with her plan.[25] And, even after she gets it and has Sisera almost at her mercy, she requests still another sign, spelling it out for God to supply, so that she could feel quite secure in finishing off the general.[26] Yael plainly needed double reassurance, with concrete testimony. Mere faith in the Lord would not do the trick.

LAB includes a similar feature in the Gideon material. When the angel of the Lord singled out Gideon as his choice to lead Israelite forces against the Midianites, Gideon at first shrinks from the assignment, then asks for a divine sign that God really wants him for the job – and that he could count on success. The angel duly supplies it.[27] This is no invention, by Pseudo-Philo. The corresponding biblical narrative already contains Gideon's request and the angel's response.[28] But its inclusion, when so much is omitted, in the Gideon story, surely has significance. The recurrence of the motif suggests that even characters fighting the good fight needed confidence that God was on their side, and sought explicit tokens to tell them that it was so. Pseudo-Philo's figures did not rely on faith and obedience alone.

In a very different context, the tribe of Benjamin too raised a doubt about God's reliability. They wondered about the authenticity of Torah. Did God really compose it or had Moses taught these laws on his own?[29] Pseudo-Philo may have his tongue in cheek here. But the questioning of God's trustworthiness repeats the recurring refrain.

---

24 *LAB* 27.7.
25 *LAB* 31.5. Jacobson, *Commentary*, II, pp. 852 – 853, finds a parallel with Abraham's servant (Gen. 24, 14).
26 *LAB* 31.7. That Pseudo-Philo here borrows elements from the Judith story is well known; cf. Murphy (above, note 3), pp. 141 – 143; Jacobson, *Commentary*, II, pp. 853 – 854.
27 *LAB* 35.6 – 7.
28 Judg. 6, 17 – 22.
29 *LAB* 25.13: *Nos voluimus in hoc tempore librum legis perscrutari utrum manifeste Deus scripsisset que erant in eo aut Moyses docuisset ea per se.*

Nor does God always appear in full control. The periodic insistence by individuals that he carry out his covenantal obligations, as we have seen, implies neglect, forgetfulness, or even limitations. Matters came to a head when the Israelite people as a whole reached the point of exasperation. The era of the judges had closed and no leader emerged to take the people in hand. Even the casting of lots proved unavailing, for the man upon whom the lot fell refused it unequivocally, prepared indeed to commit suicide rather than to take up that onerous task. The people then challenged God directly, demanding a reason for his abandonment of them in a time of need. They even quote his own words back to him. "If the provisions that you established with our fathers are true, when you said 'I shall multiply your seed,' then it would have been preferable to say to us 'I cut off your seed,' rather than neglect our root."[30] The expression as transmitted is tortured and convoluted, but the sense is arresting. The Israelites are fed up with God's apparent disregard of their interests. And they do not mince words. God's reply is still more revealing. He admits to being at a loss. His personal inclination would be to pay them no heed, in view of the evil deeds they have perpetrated. Yet he is not altogether a free agent. "What shall I do," says the Lord, "since my own name comes to be invoked upon you?"[31] He concedes the necessity of providing a leader for the nation. The omnipotence of God, in short, has its boundaries. Acknowledgment of limits on the divine had cropped up earlier, as we have seen: God's self-restraint in withholding punishment of Gideon's idolatry —for it might suggest that Baal, and not he, was responsible.[32]

Criticisms of God form no small part of the text of *LAB*. And they come from sympathetic characters. Young Samuel, for example, called upon to do the Lord's Work, had reason to complain. A divine message reached him through a dream, when Samuel was just eight years old. God assigned him the task of informing his own mentor, the priest Eli, that he will suffer the wrath of the Lord for failing to control and chastise his sinful sons. The boy Samuel, with great reluctance, carries out his chore and informs Eli of his fate. The narrative closely follows the parallel text of the Bible.[33] But Pseudo-Philo inserts a significant addition not to be found in the Scriptures. He has Samuel lament this unhappy assign-

---

30 *LAB* 49.6: *Si enim vere sunt dispositiones quas disposuisti patribus nostris dicens: Semen vestrum amplificabo et hoc scient, tune profuerat nobis dicere: Abscido vestrum semen, quam negligas radicem nostram.*
31 *LAB* 49.7: *Et dixit ad eos Deus: Si redderem secundum mala vestra, oportuerat me nec intendere ad genus vestrum. Et quid faciam, quoniam veniet nomen meum ut invocetur in vos?* Cf. Dietzfelbinger, *JSHRZ*, II.2, p. 234.
32 *LAB* 36.4.
33 *LAB* 53.1 – 13. The corresponding biblical text is 1 Sam. 3, 1 – 18.

ment and question God's judgment in imposing such a task upon his young minister. Samuel bemoans the fact that the inception of his prophetic career must come with prophesying the ruin of the very man who nourished him. "Is this why I was given in answer to my mother's plea?" The boy's censure of God is pointed and unmistakable: "Why does he who appointed me command me to spread evil tidings?"[34] Pseudo-Philo did not include this by accident.

Joshua, another of God's favorites, also felt free to censure him. When Joshua reached old age, with death approaching, God informed him of the future wickedness of his people and announced that he would forsake them, just as he had predicted to Moses. The announcement provoked an outburst from Joshua that has no model in the Bible. Joshua charged that God had known this all along. How could he not? "You know the sentiments of all generations before they are born." The Israelite leader offers some sound and obvious advice: give your people a wise heart and a prudent mind; then when you instruct them, they won't sin and you won't have to be angry.[35] The rebuke is clear. Joshua holds God himself responsible for the wickedness of his flock that could easily have been avoided. And, in case he missed the point, Joshua delivers it with unconcealed irritation. "Didn't I tell you all this before?"[36] Here Pseudo-Philo alludes to a biblical passage, but not one that he had himself earlier placed in his text. Joshua castigates the Lord in no uncertain terms, asking why it would not have been better for the Israelites to perish in the Red Sea or the wilderness than to be delivered into the hands of the Amorites and thus be destroyed forever.[37] God, one might observe, makes no reply.

Perhaps the most striking reproach of God comes in an altogether different context. The Bible conveys the tale of a Levite's concubine who was raped, abused, and left to die by the Benjamites, an episode that brought about war between Benjamites and Israelites. The latter had the worst of it at first, suffering

---

34 *LAB* 53.11: *Si sic obiaverit iuventuti mee, ut prophetizem a perditione nutritoris mei? Et nunc quomodo datus sum in petitione matri mee? Et quis me suscepit? Quomodo me precepit ut evangelizem mala?* Of course, the motif of the reluctant prophet who feels inadequate to the task occurs frequently in the Bible. Jeremiah indeed pleads inadequacy precisely because he is just a child; Jer. 1, 6. But Samuel's complaint is quite different and more pointed: he is imposed upon to deliver bad tidings to his own tutor.

35 *LAB* 21.2: *Tu scis sensum omnium generationum antequam nascantur. Et nunc, Domine, largire populo tuo cor sapientie et sensum prudentie, et erit cum dabis hereditatibus tuis dispositiones istas, non peccabunt coram te, et tu non irasceris eis.* Joshua's penchant for speaking freely to God is remarked on by Josephus, *Ant.* 5, 38.

36 *LAB* 21.3: *Nonne hec verba sunt que locutus sum ante conspectum tuum, Domine.*

37 Josh. 7.7. The biblical passage does not contain the sharpness that Pseudo-Philo puts in Joshua's mouth.

grievous losses, but eventually prevailed. Pseudo-Philo picks up the story and repeats it in condensed form.[38] But he gives it a telling twist that places the Lord in a notably harsh light. He advised the Israelites to go into battle with the tribe of Benjamin, promising them victory, on two separate occasions. Both contests ended in disaster. Over ninety thousand Israelites fell in the initial battles with the enemy, causing widespread mourning and despair, not to mention great puzzlement regarding what the children of Israel might have done to merit such a grievous fate. They wondered aloud as to why God should have deluded them into catastrophe: did he want the innocent to perish with the wicked?[39] The priest Phinehas emerges as spokesman for the people and reproves God in unrestrained language: "What kind of deception is this whereby you have led us astray, O Lord? If the sons of Benjamin have done right in your eyes, why didn't you tell us, so that we could have understood? But if they did not find favor in your sight, why did you allow us to fall before them?"[40]

In fact, God had deliberately led the Israelites into a trap. It was punishment, as Pseudo-Philo notes, for the transgressions committed by the sons of Israel earlier under the leadership of the evil idolator Micah. The Lord had sworn vengeance on them all at that time.[41] But the author in no way justifies the magnitude of God's retaliation.[42] And he certainly condemns the deceitfulness with which he went about it. The biblical narrative from which this account derives does have God encourage the Israelites to engage in battle. But it does not suggest deviousness or an ulterior motive.[43] Pseudo-Philo places a far darker construction upon the events. The language employed leaves no doubt about it. Three times he puts the word *seductio* or *seducere* (deception, deceive) in the

---

38 *LAB* 45 – 47; cf. Jud. 19 – 21.

39 *LAB* 46.4: *Numquid voluit Deus seducere populum suum? Aut numquid ita constituit propter id quod factum est malum, ut equaliter cadant tam innoxii quam hi qui faciunt iniqua?*

40 *LAB* 46.4: *Que est seductia hec qua seduxisti nos Domine? Si iustum est ante conspectum tuum que fecerunt filii Benjamin, quare nobis non renuncidsti ut intenderemus? Si autem non erat placitum in conspectu tuo, quare nos permisisti ut caderemus ante eos?*

41 *LAB* 44. This represents an extensive and much harsher revision of Judges 17.

42 Pseudo-Philo does have God explain his decision to his "adversary" (*anteciminum*), perhaps Satan, as stemming from Micah's misdeeds. Indeed he evidently commissions the "adversary" to do his dirty work for him (45, 6). But this hardly constitutes justification. Even if a current opinion had it that Satan played a role (as is suggested by Jacobson, *Commentary* (above, note 2), II, 1037 – 1038;, cf. L. Feldman, "Josephus' Portrayal ('Antiquities' 5.136 – 174) of the Benjaminite Affair of the Concubine and its Repercussions (Judges 19 – 21)," *JQR*, 90 (2000), pp. 280 – 281), *LAB* does not put it forward as apologetics. The text holds God responsible, and the "adversary" appears nowhere else in the work. On the "adversary," see Perrot and Bogaert (above, note 3), II, pp. 203 – 204.

43 Judg. 20.18 – 25.

mouths of the Israelites or Phinehas in characterizing the actions of the Lord—the same term he uses with regard to Micah![44] Phinehas, proceeds to even stronger words. He observes that God's Urim and Tummim are said to utter lies in his sight. And he challenges the Lord to explain why he has committed *iniquitas* (injustice).[45] Pseudo-Philo does not simply hide behind the phrases of others. He delivers, the same phrases in his own voice: "God himself deceived them so as to fulfill his words."[46] That does not leave much to the imagination. But Pseudo-Philo puts, an exclamation upon it in the most direct fashion. He has God himself declare that he had duped (*fefelli*) the people of Israel and led them into destruction![47]

How does one interpret all this? The *Liber Antiquitatum Biblicarum* is hardly a revolutionary tract designed to annul traditional practice and belief. Indeed it takes tradition for granted, assumes acquaintance with the Bible in its readership, expands or abbreviates its narratives, and alludes frequently to those portions omitted as a familiar part of the common heritage. A dominant theme pervades the text: the power and authority of God, the command he possesses over human destiny, the value inherent in obedience to the precepts of the Lord and a trust that, despite the sins of man and the ferocity of divine wrath, God will adhere to the covenant and maintain special care for his chosen people.

But to leave it at that does not suffice. Nor does it do justice to the author. Pseudo-Philo stops well short of advocating passive compliance or portraying an infallible deity. Leading characters like Moses, Joshua, and Kenaz and sympathetic figures like Hannah, Samuel, and Phinehas occasionally reprimand God, remonstrate with him, remind him of his promises, or worry themselves about his reputation. They and others find reasons to doubt his word, check up on his pledges, seek reassurances, or even denounce his actions. God himself sometimes drops his guard, seems at a loss, or feels concern about his public image. Such features do not predominate in the text. But they occur too frequently to be explained away. The subversive elements in *LAB* complicate but also enrich the narrative. They suggest that the Jews' obligation goes beyond obedience. They

---

44 *LAB* 46.4: *Numquid voluit Deus seducere populum suum? ...Que est seductio hec qua seduxisti nos Domine?* Cf. *LAB* 45.6, on Micah: *seduceret populum.*

45 *LAB* 47.2: *Et nunc dicunt quia manifestationes tue et veritates mentiantur coram te ...renuntia nobis propter quid fecisti in nos iniquitatem istam.* The phraseology at the end is especially pointed: "that injustice of yours."

46 *LAB* 46.1: *Ipse autem seduxit eos, ut compleret verba sua.* Cf. Perrot and Bogaert (above, note 3), II, p. 205.

47 *LAB* 47.8: *Propterea fefelli vos et dixi: Tradam vobis illos. Et nunc disperdidi vos, qui tunc tacuerunt.*

have a right to question and to challenge, to prod the Lord and to insist that he too live up to obligations. Pseudo-Philo does not preach docility. He presents the relationship between man and god as a dynamic one, subject to mutual recriminations, but also to mutual reinforcement. The treatise is a pre-eminently dialogic one.[48]

48 It is a pleasure to dedicate this piece to Uri Rappaport, a first-class scholar and human being, who helped to organize an excellent group at the Institute for Advanced Studies in Jerusalem a few years ago, in which I was privileged to participate. I am grateful too for the valuable comments made on an earlier draft of this paper by Louis Feldman, George Nickelsburg, and Ron Hendel who bear no responsibility for its remaining flaws.

23. Jewish Literature and the Second Sophistic

The Jews saw themselves as a people apart. The Bible affirmed it, and the nation's experience seemed to confirm it. As God proclaimed in the Book of Leviticus, "You shall be holy to me, for I the Lord am holy, and I have set you apart from other peoples to be mine".[1] The idea is echoed in Numbers: "There is a people that dwells apart, not reckoned among the nations."[2] Other biblical passages reinforce the sense of a chosen people, selected by the Lord (for both favor and punishment) and placed in a category unto themselves.[3] This notion of Jewish exceptionalism recurs with frequency in the Bible, most pointedly perhaps in the construct of the return from the Babylonian Exile when the maintenance of endogamy loomed as paramount to assert the identity of the nation.[4]

The image was more than a matter of self-perception. Greeks and Romans also characterized Jews as holding themselves aloof from other societies and keeping to their own kind. The earliest Greek writer who discussed Jews at any length, Hecataeus of Abdera, described them (in an otherwise favorable account) as somewhat xenophobic and misanthropic.[5] That form of labeling persisted through the Hellenistic period and well into the era of the Roman Empire. One need only cite Tacitus and Juvenal for piercing comments on the subject: Jews are fiercely hostile to gentiles and spurn the company of the uncircumcised.[6]

Whatever the perceptions or the constructs, however, they did not match conditions on the ground. Jews dwelled in cities and nations all over the eastern Mediterranean, spilling over also to the west, particularly in Italy and North Africa. The diaspora population far outnumbered the Palestinian, and the large majority of the dispersed grew up in lands of Greek language and culture—and Roman political dominance.[7] Isolation was not an option.

Indeed the Hellenic world of the Roman empire was part and parcel of the Jewish experience, no alien setting or foreign intrusion. It had been so for a long time. Jewish intellectuals showed familiarity with and engagement in the genres

---

1 Lev. 20:26.
2 Num. 23:9.
3 eg. Gen. 12:1–3; Exod. 6:7, 33:16; Deut. 7:6, 10:15, 14:2.
4 Ezra, 9–10; Neh. 10:29–31; 13:1–3, 23–30.
5 Hecataeus, *apud* Diod. Sic. 40.3.4.
6 Tac. *Hist.* 5.5.1–2, 5.8.1; Juv. 14.103–104.
7 John Barclay, *Jews in the Mediterranean Diaspora: From Alexander to Trajan (323 BCE–117 CE)* (Edinburgh, 1996); E.S. Gruen, *Diaspora: Jews amidst Greeks and Romans* (Cambridge, Mass., 2002).

and forms of Greek literature from the later 3rd century BCE. Jewish writers composed tragic drama, epic poetry, history, philosophy, and even prose fiction in Greek with some frequency (far more than we know, since we have but a fraction of it). By the time of the Second Sophistic, they were steeped in Hellenic literary traditions, many of them probably knew no language other than Greek (the Hebrew Bible had long since been translated into Greek), and they were fully comfortable with the intellectual horizons of the Hellenic Mediterranean.

Did this produce strain and tension? Did working within well established Greek literary conventions in a world under Roman sway require compromise of Jewish principles and values that had an even longer history and a more compelling hold on the consciousness of the Jews? A revealing clue lies in the subject matter that pervades Jewish writings in Greek of every form from the beginning. Epic, tragedy, history, and prose fiction did not celebrate the exploits of Zeus, Herakles, Odysseus, or Aeneas. Their heroes were Abraham, Joseph, and Moses. The genres of classical cultures were put to use to retell in new shapes and guises the ancient tales on which Jews founded their faith. The Hellenic mode served as a means of expression rather than an adoption of ideology.

That does not, however fully resolve the issue. The pride in isolation and distinctiveness on the one hand and immersion in Hellenic culture on the other hardly made for a cozy fit. Tensions and strains must have existed as Jewish writers grappled with the amalgam of ideas and formulations at the intersection of the cultures. The literary output constituted a rich and diverse mix, and no brief survey can do it justice. Some salient examples will have to suffice.

Philo of Alexandria

Philo of Alexandria stands out as the most prominent and conspicuous instance of the Jewish intelligentsia steeped in Greek learning. His output was vast, and his corpus (of which most, though not by any means all, survives) defies summary. He held a position of high esteem in the Jewish community of Alexandria in the period of the early Roman Empire, living into the reign of Claudius.[8] The diversity and variety of his writings reflect a lifetime of learning of which only a small hint can be given here.[9] Philo was a devoted student and adherent of

---

8 Daniel Schwartz, "Philo, his Family, and his Times." In A. Kamesar, ed. *The Cambridge Companion to Philo* (Cambridge, 2009), 9–31.
9 Jenny Morris, "The Jewish Philosopher Philo." In E. Schürer, *The History of the Jewish People in the Age of Jesus Christ*. Rev. and ed. by G. Vermes, F. Millar, and M. Goodman, vol. III.2: 809–

the Hebrew Bible in its Greek version (he knew little or no Hebrew), and he dedicated much of his energy to biblical exegesis. Interpretation of the Pentateuch, often elaborate allegorical interpretation, represented his principal métier and drove his mission throughout. But he brought to that task a wealth of erudition in Greek literature and, especially, Greek philosophy.[10]

Philo's deep engagement with Hellenic culture is no better illustrated than by his treatise, *Quod Omnis Probus Liber Sit* ("Every Good Man is Free"). The work tackles a familiar Stoic "paradox," the proposition that the Stoic wise man alone is free, regardless of material condition, oppressed circumstances, or even servile status. Philo follows Stoic doctrine in insisting that freedom is a quality of mind or soul, an inward certitude of virtue, unaffected by anything external. Only the sage is rich, no matter how poverty-stricken, and only he is sovereign, no matter his fetters, brands of servitude, and enduring enslavement.[11] Genuine *eleutheria* comes from scorning the claims of the passions, resisting the blandishments of wealth, reputation, and pleasure, and renouncing human frailties. The wise man is thus immune to the shifts of fortune and unaffected by avarice, jealousy, ambition, fear, or even pain.[12] Philo assigns due credit to the fountainhead of Stoicism, Zeno, as the peerless practitioner of true virtue, even defending his doctrines against critics and skeptics. Zeno was the preeminent advocate of living life in accord with nature.[13] But Philo's exposition went beyond Stoicism. The sources he cites and the illustrations he employs show a wide acquaintance with Hellenic history, literature, tradition, and mythology. Philo does not hesitate to appeal to Pythagorean teachings, to Plato, to other philosophers like Antisthenes, Anaxarchus, Zeno the Eleatic, and Diogenes, to Sophocles, and indeed to Homer.[14] He makes reference to the constitutions of Athens and Sparta, and to their lawgivers Solon and Lycurgus, he includes anecdotes about Alexander the Great, and he praises the sentiments and actions of the hero Herakles as conveyed by Euripides.[15] And he freely employs tales from Greek history, drama, and legend to reinforce his philosophical

---

889. (Edinburgh, 1987) in particular 819 – 870; James Royse, "The Works of Philo." In A. Kamesar, ed. *The Cambridge Comanion to Philo* (Cambridge, 2009), 32 – 64.

10 H.A. Wolfson, *Philo: Foundations of Religious Philosophy in Judaism, Christianity, and Islam*, 2 vols. (Cambridge, Mass.,1948): *passim*; John Dillon, *The Middle Platonists: A Study of Platonism, 80 B.C. to A.D. 220.* (London, 1977): 145 – 183; Maren Niehoff, *Philo on Jewish Identity and Culture.* (Tübingen, 2001): 137 – 158.

11 Philo, *Prob.*, 8 – 10, 59 – 61.

12 Philo, *Prob.*, 17 – 25.

13 Philo, *Prob.*, 53 – 56, 97, 108, 160.

14 Philo, *Prob.*, 2, 13, 19, 28, 31, 106 – 109, 121 – 125, 157.

15 Philo, *Prob.*, 47, 92 – 96, 99, 101 – 103, 114.

propositions.[16] All of this shows Philo comfortable, quite unselfconsciously so, in the culture of the Hellenes.

Yet the comfort level was incomplete. Reading between the lines shows that the cultivated philosopher did not altogether escape a sense of tension in negotiating the relationship of his ancestral tradition to the intellectual world of Hellas. Philo felt obliged to remind his readers that the lawgiver of the Jews went beyond the praise of inner virtue to celebrate love of the divine that makes the devout similar to gods among men.[17] The passage fits ill in its context, almost an afterthought or an insertion, suggesting a need to reassert foundational principles, however incongruous in the setting. And Philo goes further still to propose that Zeno himself drew on the Torah for some of his precepts.[18] That proposition was not novel. Earlier Jewish thinkers too had advanced the idea that the best in Greek philosophy was prompted by the Bible—and none was deterred by the fact that the Greek translation was unavailable to Zeno or any of his predecessors.[19] Philo cites Moses more than once for statements that supposedly anticipated the Stoics.[20] He occasionally takes potshots at Greek sophists, mere wordsmiths absorbed in logic-chopping and petty quibbling.[21] And he identifies as the very embodiment of ascetic existence and devotion to spiritual life the Jewish sect of the Essenes. They need no philosophical justification, only the piety that stems from adherence to the laws of the fathers.[22] The digression on the Essenes looks very much like an intrusion in the treatise, hardly a smooth transition. Although (or perhaps because) this work is as thoroughly Hellenic as any item in Philo's large corpus, the author felt obliged to reassure readers, even at the cost of consistency, that his commitment to Jewish teachings remained unshaken.

The motif that Jewish learning lies behind the Hellenic intellectual achievement appears with some frequency in Philo's other writings. In different contexts he has Heraclitus, Socrates, Zeno, and various Greek lawgivers owe their insights to the laws of Moses.[23] In the *Life of Moses*, Philo goes further still, asserting that Jewish law has earned the respect of Hellenic communities everywhere and gentiles generally who, among other things, have embraced the Sabbath and the Day

---

16 Philo, *Prob.*, 125–146.
17 Philo, *Prob.*, 43.
18 Philo, *Prob.*, 57.
19 Erich Gruen, *Heritage and Hellenism: The Reinvention of Jewish Tradition* (Berkeley, 1998)
20 Philo, *Prob.*, 68–70
21 Philo, *Prob.*, 80, 88, 96; cf. *Mos.* 2.211–212.
22 Philo, *Prob.*, 75–88.
23 Philo, *Leg. All.* 1.108; *Q Genesis*, 2.6; Philo *Spec.* 4.59–61; *Mut.* 152; *Somn.* 2.244.

of Atonement as nearly universal practices.²⁴ No Greek legislator comes close to the supreme accomplishments of Moses.²⁵ Philo even accounts for the translation of the Hebrew Bible into Greek by a Hellenic desire to emulate the ways of the Jews.²⁶ Extravagant claims of this sort leave more than a hint of the disquiet that accompanied the embrace of Hellas even for this most Hellenic of Jews.

Philo devoted a whole treatise, *De Congressu*, to discussing the value of the various branches of educational training. He ranges over grammar, geometry, astronomy, rhetoric, dialectic, music, and the whole span of subjects that belong to the traditional curriculum of the Hellenic elite. He even provides some autobiographical notices of his own educational experience that proceeded through these forms of instruction, for all of which he expressed praise and admiration.²⁷ The combination of disciplines leads the mind inexorably toward its true goal, the acquisition of wisdom through philosophy.²⁸ Philo underscores throughout the contrast between the formation of the mental faculties and the ultimate objective, employing the analogy of Hagar and Sarah, and including a host of biblical allusions and allegories.²⁹ But there are no theological overtones here. The work provides as thoroughly Hellenic a presentation as one could wish for the Stoic doctrine of preliminary teachings that lead to the embrace of philosophy.³⁰ Yet it is not the whole story.

A remarkable passage encapsulates both Philo's firm attachment to Hellenic education and his need to go beyond it. He provides a strikingly idiosyncratic version of Moses' own primary and secondary education. For Philo, the Hebraic founder of the faith had Egyptian teachers at the outset, followed by masters summoned from Greece to advance his intellectual training. Egyptians took him through the initial stages in arithmetic, geometry, rhythm, harmony and astrology, and Greeks carried him to higher learning, evidently literature, rhetoric, and philosophy. Lest readers conclude, however, that Moses was fully formed by educators beyond the biblical borders, Philo adds that the young man's inner genius allowed him swiftly to transcend his teachers, who had no more to give

---

24 Philo, *Mos.* 2.17–24, 2.44.
25 Philo, *Mos.* 2.12–14.
26 Philo, *Mos.* 2.25–27, 2.43.
27 Philo, *Congr.* 11–18, 74–76, 144.
28 Philo, *Congr.* 77–80, 146–148.
29 Sarah Pearce, *The Land and the Body.* (Tübingen, 2007), 170–175;
30 Monique Alexandre, *De Congressu Eruditionis Gratia.* (Paris, 1967), *passim*; Alan Mendelson, *Secular Education in Philo of Alexandria* (Cincinnati, 1982), *passim*.

him—as if he drew more on his own recollection than on anyone's instruction.[31] Philo's blend of Hellenism and Judaism was less a smooth process than a tense negotiation.

4 Maccabees

A complex interweaving of Greek philosophy and Jewish precepts appears also in a treatise that our textual tradition labels as *4 Maccabees*. The genre of the work does not conform readily to a single or standard model. Its form suggests, at least on the face of it, a diatribe, expounding on a philosophic position and defending it against objections.[32] The opening of the treatise indicates that its topic will be the mastery of devout reason over the passions, and that motif holds, in various ways, throughout. Yet the bulk of *4 Maccabees* treats, often in graphic detail, the noble resistance and the cruel fate of Jewish martyrs in the persecutions that led to the Maccabean rebellion. This might recall the genre of the encomium, a eulogy of praiseworthy persons, often in the form of a funeral oration.[33] It carries echoes of lofty rhetoric, the epideictic speech, performative oratory that stemmed from Classical Greece and enjoyed a vogue in the era of the Second Sophistic. *4 Maccabees* appears to be something a hybrid, a rare combination of the diatribe and the encomium, or, more likely, an entity of its own, not a conscious mixture of genres and not easily subject to classification. Whatever label one applies, however, Hellenic features predominate.

The peculiar work not only defies categorization but baffles inquiry into author, provenance, and date. There is little point in probing beyond its anonymity which leads nowhere. And the author's location could be anywhere in the Jewish diaspora. Asia Minor or Antioch is a favored guess because of the "Asianism" of the author's style.[34] But "Asianism" is largely a pejorative term flung about by

---

31 Philo, *Mos.* 1.21–24.

32 Eduard Norden, *Die antike Kunstprosa vom VI Jahrhundert v. Chr. bis in die Zeit der Renaissance* (Leipzig, 1923), 303–304, 416–420; Moses Hadas, *The Third and Fourth Books of Maccabees.* (New York, 1953), 101–2.

33 J.C.H. Lebram, "Die literarische Form des vierten Makkabäerbuches" *VC* (1974) 28: 81–96; Jan Willem Van Henten, *The Maccabean Martyrs as Saviours of the Jewish People: A Study of 2 and 4 Maccabees.* (Leiden, 1997), 60–67; David deSilva, *4 Maccabees* (Sheffield, 1998), 26–28, 46–49, 76–97.

34 Norden, *Die antike Kunstprosa* I, 416–420; Hadas, *The Third and Fourth Books of Maccabees,*110–113; H. Anderson, "4 Maccabees.' In J.H. Charlesworth, ed. *The Old Testament Pseudepigrapha.* Vol. 2:531–573. (Garden City, 1985), 534–535; H.-J. Klauck, "4. Makkabäer-

critics who prefer a more direct "Attic" style, and has little to do with geography.[35] A rough date, on the other hand, is slightly more accessible. Language and vocabulary, as well as historical arguments, have induced most scholars to place it anywhere between the mid 1st and mid 2nd centuries CE.[36] Similarities with philosophical treatises and with rhetorical pieces of the Second Sophistic, in any case, place the work snugly within that cultural context.

Much ink has spilled over the question of whether the author owes more to Plato or to the Stoics.[37] None of the arguments has compelling force. The issue of reason's control over the emotions, with which the text opens, was a standard Stoic topic, as is the claim that reason is mind choosing with right judgment the life of wisdom, and wisdom, in turn, being the knowledge of things divine and human and their causes.[38] But the Stoics had no monopoly on such precepts. *4 Maccabees'* insistence on the four cardinal virtues, good sense, justice, courage, and self-control, can be traced back to Plato and Aristotle, and numerous thinkers that followed, including Philo.[39] The author need not and should not be pinned down. Some have plausibly dubbed him an eclectic, though one might as easily see him as the purveyor of philosophic clichés.[40] The work, on any reckoning, resonates with Hellenic philosophy. The encounter between Antiochus, the Hellenistic monarch who was determined to bend Jews to Greek ways, and Eleazer, the elderly Jewish sage of priestly stock and deep legal training, turns into a philosophic dialogue.[41] Antiochus indeed challenges Eleazer by asserting that he cannot be a true philosopher if he adheres to the observances of the Jews, and he brands his beliefs as "foolish philosophy." Eleazer responds in kind, affirming that it is precisely his philosophy that teaches self-

buch." *JSHRZ* (1989) 3.6:666–667; Barclay, *Jews in the Mediterranean, 370;* Van Henten, *The Maccabean Martyrs,* 78–81; deSilva, *4 Maccabees,* 18–21.

35 Van Henten, *The Maccabean Martyrs,* 59–60.

36 A. Dupont-Sommer, *Le Quatrième Livre des Machabées.* (Paris, 1939); U. Breitenstein, *Beobachtungen zu Sprache, Stil und Gedankengut des vierten Makkabäerbuches.* 2nd ed. (Basel, 1978), 75; Anderson, "4 Maccabees', 533–534; Barclay, *Jews in the Mediterranean,* 449; Van Henten, *The Maccabean Martyrs,* 73–78; deSilva, *4 Maccabees,* 14–18; J.J. Collins, *Between Athens and Jerusalem: Jewish Identity in the Hellenistic Diaspora.* 2nd ed. (Grand Rapids, 2000), 203–204.

37 Hadas, *The Third and Fourth Books of Maccabees,* 115–118; R. Renehan, "The Greek Philosophic Background of Fourth Maccabees." *RhM* (1972) 115: 224–232; Breitenstein, *Beobachtungen,* 132–133; Anderson, "4 Maccabees', 537–539; Klauck," 4 Makkabäerbuch", 665–666; Collins, *Between Athens and Jerusalem,* 205–6.

38 *4 Macc.* 1.1–3, 1.15–16.

39 *4 Macc.* 18; cf. Philo, *Leg. All.* 1.71–72.

40 Barclay, *Jews in the Mediterranean Diaspora,* 370–372.

41 Van Henten, *The Maccabean Martyrs,* 275–278.

restraint, justice, and courage, the traditional Hellenic virtues, but adds to them the requirement of piety, thus best to worship the sole god in properly magnificent fashion.[42]

The philosophic character of the piece predominates. The author proceeds to detail the tortures and death inflicted by the tyrannical monarch not only upon the aged Eleazer but upon a steadfast and devout mother and her seven stalwart sons, horror scenes that occupy most of the treatise. But the horror serves a larger purpose. These actions, for the author, represent exemplary instances of the exercise of philosophic principle in the face of autocracy and injustice.[43] The text indeed repeats these points, almost to excess, as recurrent themes that bind together the story and remind readers of its meaning. After Eleazer's noble death, the author declares that it represented the triumph of devout reason over the passions.[44] Only a man of wisdom and courage, like Eleazer, can be lord of his emotions.[45] The author delivers the same verdict upon the seven brave sons who defied the king and went proudly to their deaths. They showed that reason is sovereign over the passions, and that right reasoning can overcome suffering.[46] Reasoning powers, so declares the author, are more kingly than kings and freer than free men.[47] Even the superiority of the martyrs' convictions over royal power and persecution is described in terms of a Greek athletic contest, with competitors contending for prizes and the winners metaphorically crowned as spiritual victors.[48]

In all this the Hellenic element prevails, readily recognizable, even stereotypical, for any reader conversant with Greek philosophy and rhetoric in the age of the Second Sophistic. Indeed, the treatise refrains from theology, and it alludes only vaguely to any precepts or practices that could be identified as Jewish. The term "Judaism" appears just once in the text, and "Hebrews" also just once, apart from references to Hebrew as a language spoken by characters in the story. The author does state that Antiochus sought to have the people renounce their "Judaism" and take up a "Greek form of life," and he refers to an epitaph that praises the martyrs for resisting the tyrant who had resolved to destroy the polity of "the Hebrews."[49] But the treatise shows little interest in pitting

---

42 *4 Macc.* 5.1–38.
43 deSilva, *4 Maccabees,* 65–74.
44 *4 Macc.* 6.31–35.
45 *4 Macc.* 8.23.
46 *4 Macc.* 13.1–5.
47 *4 Macc.* 14.2.
48 *4 Macc.* 17.11–16.
49 *4 Macc.* 4.26, 8.7–8, 17.9–10.

Hellenism against Judaism. *4 Maccabees* does not depict an ideological war. The focus is on philosophical principles that are thoroughly Greek, rather than on matters of religion.

Yet the author engaged in no pretense or disguise. His heritage stands out unequivocally. The story dwelled on the Maccabean martyrs, not on abstract theory. We may not be able to identify precise Greek texts on which the author drew for his philosophic ideas. But we do know that he employed the tale of the origins of the Maccabean rebellion as found in *2 Maccabees*, although he rewrote it for his own purposes, giving little space to the historical background recounted by *2 Maccabees*, while dwelling at length upon and significantly expanding the narrative of the martyrdoms. And, although he avoided depicting a clash of cultures or religions, he injected a feature that left no doubt about the special piety of his people. The "reason" (λογισμὸς) to which the text repeatedly refers is frequently accompanied by the adjective εὐσεβὴς.[50] Thus, "devout reason," a coinage of the author, is the driving force of the treatise. And reference to piety, εὐσεβεία, occurs throughout as prime motif and motivation for the actions of the characters.[51] Although the particulars of the author's religion are not spelled out, the fundamental principle, that adherence to the Law, i.e. Mosaic law, inspires the steadfastness of its believers, dominates the work.[52] Further, the author appeals regularly to the exemplars of his nation's past, the figures of the Bible, Abraham, Isaac, Jacob, Joseph, Moses, David, Daniel, and others.[53] Most notably, the text describes Eleazer as "philosopher of the divine life" and as advocate of "divine philosophy".[54] The wise and courageous man who masters his own passions is the philosopher who lives in accord with the rule of philosophy—and has trust in God. Control of the passions comes through reverence for God.[55] The author, in effect, equates true philosophy with the faith of his fathers.

4 Maccabees holds enduring interest as a document of Jewish intellectual engagement with the cultural world of the Greeks. How best to characterize that engagement poses a challenging task. The aim has been described as "wrapping its (Jewish) message in attractive philosophic garb".[56] That formulation may not have it quite right. The philosophic garb is the author's own. His familiarity

---

50 e.g., *4 Macc.*1.1, 6.31, 7.16, 8.1, 13.1, 16.1, 18.2.
51 e.g. *4 Macc.* 5.38, 6.22, 7.3 – 4, 12.11, 13.7 – 8, 15.1 – 3.
52 e.g. *4 Macc.* 1.17, 2.5 – 6, 3.20, 5.16 – 36, 6.18 – 21, 7.7, 9.1 – 4, 11.27, 15.8 – 10.
53 *4 Macc.* 2.2 – 3, 2.17 – 19, 3.6 – 16, 7.19, 13.9, 13.17, 15.28, 16.3, 16.20 – 22, 18.10 – 19.
54 *4 Macc.* 7.7, 7.9.
55 *4 Macc.* 7.21 – 23.
56 Barclay, *Jews in the Mediterranean,* 379.

with currents of philosophy and rhetoric swirling in the world of the Second Sophistic suggests a writer thoroughly at home in that world, not one who needed to borrow its accouterments for an artificial construct. He conceived his work as a "most philosophical one."[57] Its lessons would be conveyed in the form and style in which he had been trained through the Hellenic *paideia* of his diaspora community. *4 Maccabees* was no mere façade, nor was it a piece of apologetic literature designed to justify the ways of Jews to Gentiles. The mode of expression was deeply ingrained. But so also was the religious conviction that underlay it. The blend of the two may not always have been easy. Stoic *logismos* was transformed into a "devout *logismos.*" The exercise of reason became equivalent to obedience to the Law. The four cardinal virtues were appropriated, but Jewish piety held center stage. Laudatory rhetoric celebrated heroic deeds, but the praise went to murdered martyrs rather than military heroes. Ultimate authority—and triumph—rested not with tyrants and despots but with the God-given Law.

Pseudo-Phocylides

A very different text in a very different genre speaks to a very similar issue: the expression of Jewish precepts in the language, culture, and modalities of Hellenism. The Greek gnomic poet Phocylides dates to the 6th century BCE, in the archaic age of Hellenic literature. His reputation in subsequent generations was high and impressive. Yet only a few fragments of his writings survive, an unfortunate, probably quite a significant, loss. What we do have, however, is a poem of 230 lines in dactylic hexameters attributed to Phocylides but composed probably half a millennium or more later. And this set of verses was written by a Jew.

No firm date can be fixed. The text contains a number of words unattested prior to the 1st century BCE. And parallels with Stoic writings of the early imperial era, like those of Musonius Rufus and Seneca, offer a clue that might put it in the 1st century CE.[58] Further precision eludes us. But the poem likely falls somewhere in the era inhabited by Philo and the author of *4 Maccabees*. And it serves further to illustrate Jewish adaptation to the wider world of the Second Sophistic.

The work raises a number of fascinating questions. If one digs below the surface, certain telltale signs identify it unmistakably as a Jewish composition. Yet

---

57 *4 Macc*, 1.1.
58 P.W. van der Horst, *The Sentences of Pseudo-Phocylides* (Leiden, 1978), 81–83; Pascale Derron, *Pseudo-Phocylide: Sentences* (Paris, 1986), lxi–lxvi.

there are few signs of Judaism that could be detected by the most determined researcher, and even fewer by any contemporary. The author appears to have covered his tracks. To what purpose? Why produce a work in a palpably Greek mode, ascribe it to a well-known Greek poet, but use it to convey Jewish thinking? Was this an elaborate disguise or a charade? Whom was the author seeking to fool, and why? Did the poem represent an effort to bring Jewish ideas to the attention of a wider Greco-Roman world? Or did the reverse hold, a demonstration that the ways of that world impinged productively upon Jewish consciousness?

The work conventionally carries the designation of *The Sentences of Pseudo-Phocylides*. That label alludes to the form, a series of *sententiae* or statements, set in verse, delivering moral maxims or aphorisms, a genre known in Greek as *gnomai*. Gnomic poetry, brief and pithy sayings for the edification or education of the readership, had its origin in archaic Greece, with Hesiod, Theognis—and Phocylides. The reputation of the last in antiquity made him a logical figure to whom to attach the work that we possess.[59] There is little doubt, however, that the author is a Jew. Parallels in Septuagint pronouncements can readily be found. Although many are generic and not exclusively tied to Jewish precepts, others have a specificity that is hard to dismiss. So, for example, the opening lines of the text, admonishing readers to refrain from adultery, murder, theft, falsehoods, or covetousness of others' property, while honoring God and parents, plainly paraphrase parts of the Decalogue.[60] In similar fashion, the author's stress on concern for the poor and the laborer, on charity to the needy, and on philanthropy by the fortunate echoes biblical pronouncements.[61] So also does the noble injunction to hold strangers as equal to citizens.[62] More tellingly still, the author's reference to the physical resurrection of the dead, a concept quite foreign to Greco-Roman thought, has a direct predecessor in the Book of Daniel.[63] Scholars have rightly pointed to many other parallels.[64]

The connection can be reinforced. Overlappings exist between Pseudo-Phocylides' remarks on sexual behavior, condemnation of homosexuality, marriage

---

59 van der Horst, *The Sentences of Pseudo-Phocylides*, 60–63.

60 Ps-Phoc. 3–8; Exodus, 20:12–14.

61 Ps-Phoc. 10, 19, 22–29; Deut. 24:14–15; Isaiah, 58:7; Prov. 3:27–28.

62 Ps-Phoc. 39–41; Exod. 23:9; Lev. 19:34, 24:22.

63 Ps-Phoc. 103–104; Dan. 12:22–3.

64 van der Horst, *The Sentences of Pseudo-Phocylides*, 65; Johannes Thomas, *Der jüdische Phokylides* (Göttingen, 1992), 161–179; Walter Wilson, *The Sentences of Pseudo-Phocylides* (Berlin, 2005), 17–19.

practices, and attitudes toward the elderly and the poor on the one hand and those expressed by Philo and Josephus in their summaries of Jewish law on the other.[65] The correspondence can occur even in the smallest detail, as in the case of the prohibition against taking the mother-bird from her nest.[66] Whether or not all three drew on the same source, the Jewish inspiration for the pronouncements is undeniable. The form itself of the work, the staccato-like delivery of maxims and lessons for behavior, readily recalls the Book of Proverbs, as well as the 2nd century BCE Jewish writer of ethical and practical counsel, Ben Sira. The whole tradition of Jewish Wisdom literature lies in the background. In addition to Proverbs and Ben Sira, Kohelet deserves mention, and the Wisdom of Solomon also contains comparable adages and aphorisms in a text that may be approximately contemporary with Pseudo-Phocylides. God himself gains repeated mention. He is the one god, wise and powerful, judge of the wicked, scourge of the perjurer, provider of prosperity, the bestower of reason, whose spirit and image is granted to mortals, and who is to be honored first above all.[67]

All that said, however, the poem hardly wears its Judaism on its sleeve. The name of Israel appears nowhere in the text, and the distinguishing characteristics of Jews that were most familiar to pagans, such as circumcision, dietary laws, observance of the Sabbath, and prohibition of idolatry, go altogether without mention. It causes little surprise that the ascription to Phocylides himself went unquestioned not only in antiquity but until the late 16th century. The piece plainly had close affinities with the Greek gnomological tradition. Precedents exist in Hesiod's *Works and* Days, in Theognis, Isocrates, Menander, and elsewhere in Greek literature. The authors provided ethical and practical advice, with didactic objectives, in some instances perhaps deliberately designed for pedagogical purposes. Gnomic poetry enjoyed a vogue in the Hellenistic period, employed most notably by the Cynics, embraced also by other philosophers, and used by a range of other authors. Gnomic sayings generated wide enough interest even to prompt collections and anthologies, a veritable industry of *gnomologia*.[68] Philosophic, especially Stoic, teachings can be found among the

---

65 Jos. *C. Ap.* 2.190 – 219; Philo, *Hyp.* 7.1 – 9; Wilson, *The Sentences of Pseudo-Phocylides*, 19 – 22.

66 Ps-Phoc. 84 – 85; Philo, *Hyp.* 7.9; Jos. *C. Ap.* 2.213.

67 Ps-Phoc. 8, 11, 17, 29, 54, 106, 128.

68 Derron, *Pseudo-Phocylide*, vii-xxxi; Thomas, *Der jüdische Phokylides,* 287 – 313; Walter Wilson, *The Mysteries of Righteousness* (Tübingen, 1994), 18 – 33.

Sentences of Pseudo-Phocylides. The praise of moderation, self-restraint, resistance to pride, anger, or excess of any sort take prominence in the treatise.[69]

The *Sentences* falls within a well-established Greek tradition of supplying wise counsel for the instruction of its constituencies. Resonance occurs in a text conveniently reflective of the Second Sophistic. Dio Chrysostom's third oration on monarchy, directed probably to the emperor Trajan, expounds on the qualities and principles desirable in a ruler and offers generous advice on how that ruler should comport himself. The counsel provided by Dio includes embrace of the familiar virtues of courage, self-restraint, and justice, only taken to a higher level since the king must serve as a model for his subjects. A shepherd to his flock, the monarch takes full responsibility for their welfare and security, exercising sound judgment, scorning flattery and false glorification, preferring duty to self-indulgence, adhering to law, and following the guidance of the divine.[70] In that company, pagan readers would have found the *Sententiae* of Pseudo-Phocylides a recognizable parallel. The Jewish roots of the text would have been difficult to detect.

How then should one understand the aims of the *Sentences?* Did Pseudo-Phocylides address himself to a gentile readership, suppressing his Jewishness, presenting his principles as entirely consistent with pagan philosophical and ethical teachings, and thus seeking to secure a welcome place for Jews within the larger Greco-Roman society? Or was his audience a Jewish one, the intellectual elite who enjoyed a Greek *paideia* but needed assurance that they could participate in the broader culture because the precepts of the Torah were consonant with Hellenic tenets? Or did he have an intermediate segment in mind, the "god-fearers," that category of gentiles who were sympathetic to and shared many practices and beliefs of the Jews, without seeking full conversion? Or did the text express a form of universalizing Judaism, symbolized by the donning of a gentile mask?[71] None of the suggestions has compelling force. If the author endeavored to win Jewish acceptance by gentile society because of the correspondence of their doctrines or concepts, why present them in strictly Greek guise and attribute them to a celebrated Greek writer? There would be little point in covering up his Jewishness if he wished to exhibit its consonance with Hellenism. An appeal to fellow-Jews makes more sense if he hoped to reassure them that they could fully embrace Greco-Roman culture without deviating from their own tra-

---

69 Ps-Phoc. 36, 53, 57, 59–64,76, 118, 122.
70 Dio Chrys. *Orat.* 3, *passim.*
71 Cf. van der Horst, *The Sentences of Pseudo-Phocylides,* 70–76; *idem* 1988, 3–30; Derron, *Pseudo-Phocylide,* xxxviii-li; Thomas, *Der jüdische Phokylides,* 231–235, 352–361; Barclay, *Jews in the Mediterranean,* 343–346; Collins, *Between Athens and Jerusalem,* 173–174.

ditions. Yet the message would seem to be over-subtle and too indistinct for readers to catch the meaning when Torah teachings take on pagan trappings, Jewish practices are nowhere in sight, and the author of the tract has the persona of an ancient Greek gnomic poet. As for the "god-fearers," we have only the haziest sense of their mind-set, we know little or nothing of their aspirations, and we have no reason to believe that they took any interest in this form of literature. A resort to their membership as either authors or audience is a mere stab in the dark.

A different approach might be salutary. Pseudo-Phocylides need not have been on a mission at all. The composition of a gnomic poem places him as part of a literary tradition. By the age of the Second Sophistic, Jewish intellectuals had long since been participants in a shared culture, without needing to calculate a balance of Hellenism and Judaism or consciously brewing a cultural blend. The Jewish author worked within the known genre of the didactic poem, possessing a deep familiarity with both Jewish Wisdom literature and Hellenic gnomic poetry. The mix may well have been ingrained for generations in the circles of the Jewish intelligentsia. It did not require a deliberate scheme to win over gentiles or comfort Jews. The *Sentences* of Pseudo-Phocylides embodies the unselfconsciousness of Jewish participation in Greco-Roman intellectual culture.

Why then the application of a pseudonym, and recourse to a renowned writer dating to many centuries earlier? Was it camouflage or deception? One might consider instead a simpler answer: the name was chosen because it exemplified a master of the genre. The real author perhaps indulged in a bit of whimsy.

Joseph and Aseneth

Yet another genre serves as illuminating instance of Jewish interaction with Greek literature in the age of the Roman Empire. The "novel" had its heyday in that era, a literary type difficult to define, somewhat easier to illustrate. Labels and categories are inevitably artificial, requiring repeated exceptions, modification, and reformulation. The ancients themselves had no word for "novel," a disconcerting fact that needs to be borne in mind. But we do like to think that we know one when we see one. The novel, in general, takes form as a piece of prose fiction that narrates an entertaining and/or edifying tale that can also communicate values, ideas, and guidance. In antiquity, the standard examples normally cited fall somewhere in the period of the 1st through the 4th century CE, though none can be dated with any precision. The extant Greek novels of that period are ascribed to Chariton, Xenophon of Ephesus, Achilles Tatius, Longus, and Heliodorus. Two celebrated Latin novels, by Petronius and Apuleius, much influenced by Greek models, serve also as prime exemplars of the category. It held favor over an extensive stretch of time and possessed appeal not only in the realm of "popular culture," often transmitted orally, but also possessed subtleties and complexities, while assuming knowledge of earlier literature and intellectual traditions that could appeal to more sophisticated audiences.

Ancients may not have had a name for the genre. But certain common features among these works (even if those features are occasionally parodied) do suggest a pattern that readers came to expect and found welcome: the separation of lovers, their adventures or misadventures, whether kidnapping, shipwrecks, or the amorous designs of third parties, and eventual reuniting with a happy ending. The repeated motifs, themes, and narrative techniques give a unity to the genre, without inhibiting the great variety and diversity in which they were expressed.[72]

One Jewish "romance" falls recognizably within the umbrella of these prose narratives. It evidently partook of their popularity in the age of the Roman Empire. *Joseph and Aseneth* shares a number of features with the other novels. Among them, alas, is deep uncertainty as to its provenance and date. The story takes place in ancient Egypt, unsurprisingly so, since Joseph is a principal figure, but that need not be a clue to its place of composition. And the work has been situated anywhere from the Ptolemaic period to late antiquity, although most scholars put it in the 1st or 2nd century CE.[73] In any case, it belongs in the company of the extant Greek and Latin novels, whether as imitation or model. They thrived in a common intellectual atmosphere.

The narrative of *Joseph and Aseneth* can receive only the briefest summary here. It has but a small basis in Scripture. Genesis reports that the patriarch Joseph took as wife a certain Aseneth, daughter of an Egyptian priest by whom she bore two children.[74] The novel employs that short notice as launching pad for a full-scale fantasy. It divides into two quite different parts. The first takes the form

---

72 T. Hägg, *The Novel in Antiquity* (Oxford, 1983); Graham Anderson, *Ancient Fiction: The Novel in the Graeco-Roman World.* (London, 1984); Bryan Reardon, *The Form of Greek Romance* (Princeton, 1991); Tim Whitmarsh, "Introduction." In T. Whitmarsh, ed. *The Cambridge Companion to the Greek and Roman Novel* (Cambridge, 2008), 1 – 14; Simon Goldhill, "Genre."In T. Whitmarsh, ed. *The Cambridge Companion to the Greek and Roman Novel* (Cambridge, 2008), 185 – 200.
73 Randall Chesnutt, *From Death to Life: Conversion in Joseph and Aseneth* (Sheffield, 1995), 80 – 85; Ross Kraemer, *When Aseneth Met Joseph* (New York, 1998), 225 – 244; Edith Humphrey, *Joseph and Aseneth* (Sheffield, 2000), 28 – 37; Collins, *Between Athens and Jerusalem*, 104 – 110.
74 Gen. 41:45, 41:50 – 52, 46:20.

of an erotic tale in which Joseph meets and rejects the beautiful teenager Aseneth until she abandons her idolatrous ways through a mystical revelation,
thus paving the way for a marriage between them sanctioned by the Pharaoh
himself.[75] The second consists of an adventure story in which the embittered
son of Pharaoh endeavors to murder Joseph and carry off Aseneth, sparking a
split among Joseph's brothers and a fierce battle in which Aseneth emerges victorious with the assistance of some of Joseph's brothers while magnanimously
sparing the others. The narrative concludes with Pharaoh's appointment of Joseph to rule the land of Egypt.[76]

Affinities exist with certain Greek or Roman novels. A plot set in the distant
past, the virginal status of the lovers, their separation and then uniting, and the
attempted kidnapping of the heroine by a rival lover all strike familiar chords. So
also does Aseneth's dramatic conversion to the faith of Joseph and his fathers
through a mysterious vision which bears comparison to mystical tales and sacred
epiphanies, as in Apuleius' *Metamorphoses*.[77] The author was surely familiar
with the motifs and devices that occur in pagan romances.[78]

But parallels do not provide the full picture. *Joseph and Aseneth* has its own
characteristics and peculiarities that set it apart from the mainstream. The erotic
features central to most of the novels play a subordinate role in this one. Separation of the lovers was a voluntary rather than an involuntary one, a dramatic
tension between the priggish Joseph and the haughty Aseneth.[79] And the fantasy,
imaginative and inventive though it be, did employ a known setting, that of the
biblical narrative of the patriarch in Egypt. The Jewish author, moreover, had
other novelistic texts as forerunners, Jewish texts quite independent of the
Greco-Roman tradition, the tales of Judith, Esther, and Tobit which also combined marriage narratives with adventure stories.[80] Both Hebraic and Hellenic

---

75 *Jos. Asen.* 1–21.
76 *Jos. Asen.* 22–29.
77 *Jos. Asen.* 14–18; Howard Clark Kee, "The Socio-Cultural Setting of Joseph and Aseneth."
NTS (1983) 229: 394–413.
78 Stephanie West, *"Joseph and Asenath: A Neglected Greek Romance."* CQ (1974) 68: 70–81;
Richard Pervo, "Aseneth and her Sisters: Women in Jewish Narrative and in the Greek Novels" in
A.J. Levine, ed. *'Women Like This': New Perspectives on Jewish Women in the Greco-Roman World*
(Atlanta, 1991), 145–160; Lawrence Wills, *The Jewish Novel in the Ancient World* (Ithaca, 1995),
16–28, 170–184; Chesnutt, *From Death to Life,* 85–93; Angela Standhartinger, *Das Frauenbild
im Judentum der hellenistischen Zeit: Ein Beitrag anhand von 'Joseph und Aseneth.'* (Leiden,
1995), 20–26; Humphrey, *Joseph and Aseneth,* 38–46.
79 *Jos. Asen.* 2–9.
80 Richard Pervo, "Joseph and Asenath and the Greek Novel." *SBL Seminar Papers* (Missoula,
1976) 171–181.

strands intertwined in this remarkable text. It would be misleading to isolate them—or indeed to imagine that the author consciously combined them. The work reflects a mixed milieu.

As with the other authors and writings discussed here, a subtle tension swirls below the surface in *Joseph and Aseneth*. Joseph's insistence upon the purity of the faith and the pollution of idolatry, Aseneth's abject debasement and violent break with her past to achieve absolution, and the favor of God supporting the faithful against their idolatrous opponents all seem to suggest a stark dichotomy between the forces of good and evil, and a sharp distancing of Jew from gentile.[81] The relationship, however, is more nuanced and complex. The fact that the wedding of Joseph and Aseneth takes place under the auspices of Pharaoh, who had not himself become a convert, holds central symbolic significance. The enemies of the faithful were forgiven, harmony and reconciliation followed, and the gentile ruler of Egypt placed his kingdom in the power of the immigrant from Israel. Indeed it is noteworthy that no mention of "Jew" or "gentile" occurs anywhere in the text. Aseneth's transformation amounted essentially to abandonment of idolatry. This is no simple tale of cultural clash. Distinctions between the people hold at one level in the novel, but they are overcome at another. *Joseph and Aseneth* exemplifies the duality stressed throughout this chapter. The Jewish author perpetuated a literary tradition that stemmed from his forefathers, while at the same time he bought into (or perhaps helped to shape) a Hellenic literary tradition that reached its apogee in the empire of the Romans.

---

81 Barclay, *Jews in the Mediterranean*, 204–216; Collins, *Between Athens and Jerusalem*, 231–232.

List of Abbreviations

Hebrew Bible
Gen.   = Genesis
Exod.   = Exodus
Lev.   = Leviticus
Num.   = Numbers
Deut.   = Deuteronomy
Josh.   = Joshua
Judg.   = Judges
1–2 Sam. = 1–2 Samuel
1–2 Kgs. = 1–2 Kings
1–2 Chr. = 1–2 Chronicles
Neh.   = Nehemiah
Esth.   = Esther
Ps.   = Psalm/Psalms
Isa.   = Isaiah
Jer.   = Jeremiah
Dan.   = Daniel
Zech.   = Zechariah
Ezek.   = Ezekial
Prov.   = Proverbs

New Testament
Matt.   = Matthew
Rom.   = Romans
1–2 Cor. = 1–2 Corinthians
Gal.   = Galatians
Col.   = Colossians

Deuterocanonical Works, Septuagint and Pseudepigrapha
Bar.   = Baruch
2 Bar.   = 2 Baruch
1–2 Esd.   = 1–2 Esdras
Add. Esth. = Additions to Esther
Jdt.   = Judith
Jos.Asen. = *Joseph and Aseneth*

Jub.   = *Jubilees*
LAB   = Pseudo-Philo, *Liber Antiquitatum Biblicarum*
Let. Aris.   = *Letter of Aristeas*
Ps. Sol.   = *Psalms of Solomon*
1 Macc.   = 1 Maccabees
2 Macc.   = 2 Maccabees
3 Macc.   = 3 Maccabees
4 Macc.   = 4 Maccabees
Sib.Or.   = *Sibylline Oracles*
T. Ash.   = *Testament of Asher*
T. Dan   = *Testament of Dan*
T. Iss.   = *Testament of Issachar*
T. Job.   = Testament of Job
T. Jud.   = Testament of Judah
T. Levi   = Testament of Levi
T. Naph.   = *Testament of Naphtali*
T. Reu.   = Testament of Reuben
T. Zeb.   = *Testament of Zebulun*
Tob.   = Tobit
Wis.   = Wisdom of Solomon

Josephus

Jos. A.J.   = Flavius Josephus, *Antiquitates judaicae*
Jos. B.J.   = Flavius Josephus, *Bellum judaicum*
Jos. C. Ap.   = Flavius Josephus, *Contra Apionem*

Philo

Philo, Abr.   = *De Abrahamo*
Philo, Aet.   = *De aeternitate mundi*
Philo, Cher.   = *De Cherubim*
Philo, Conf.   = *De confusione linguarum*
Philo, Congr.   = *De congressueru ditionis gratia*
Philo, Decal.   = *De decalogo*
Philo, Deus   = *Quod Deus sit immutabilis*
Philo, Ebr.   = *De ebrietate*
Philo, Flacc.   = *In Flaccum*
Philo, Fug.   = *De fuga et inventione*
Philo, Her.   = *Quis rerum divinarum heres sit*

Philo, Hypoth. = *Hypothetica*
Philo, Leg. All. = *Legum allegoriae*
Philo, Legat. = *Legatio ad Gaium*
Philo, Migr. = *De migratione Abrahami*
Philo, Mos. = *De vita Mosis*
Philo, Mut. = *De mutatione nominum*
Philo, Plant. = *De plantatione*
Philo, Praem. = *De praemiis et poenis*
Philo, Prob. = *Quod omnis probus liber sit*
Philo, QG = *Quaestiones et solutiones in Genesin*
Philo, Somn. = *De somniis*
Philo, Spec. = *De specialibus legibus*

Classical Sources

Apollod. Bibl. = Pseudo-Apollodorus, *Library*
App. Syr. = Appian, *Syrian Wars*
Aristot. Met. = Aristotle, *Metaphysics*
Aristot. Pol. = Aristotle, *Politics*
Arr. An. = Arrian, *Anabasis*
Augustine, CD = Augustine, *Christian Doctrine*
Augustine, Civ.Dei. = Augustine *De Civitate Dei*
Call.Del. = Callimachus, *Hymn to Delos*
Cic. Flacc. = Cicero, *Pro Flacco*
Cic. Phil. = Cicero, *Philippics*
Clement, Protr. = Clement of Alexandria, *Protrepticus*
Clement, Strom. = Clement of Alexandria, *Stromateis*
Curt. = Curtius, *Historiarum Alexandri Magni*
D.H. = Dionysius of Halicarnassus, *Antiquitates Romanae*
Diod. = Diodorus Siculus, *Historical Library*
Diogenes Laertius = Diogenes Laertius, *Vitae philosophorum*
Eus. Chron. = Eusebius, *Chronicle*
Eus. HE = Eusebius, *Historia Ecclesiastica*
Eus. PE = Eusebius, *Praeparatio Evangelica*
Frontinus, Strat. = Frontinus, *Stratagems*
Gel. = Gellius, *Noctes Atticae*
Hdt. = Herodotus, *Histories*
Hes.Th. = Hesiod, *Theogony*
Hom. Il. = Homer, *Iliad*
Hom. Od. = Homer, *Odyssey*

Hor. Carm.	= Horace, *Carmen Saeculare*
Hor. Epod.	= Horace, *Epodes*
Iamblichus, VP	= Iamblichus, *Vita Pythagorae*
Isoc. 11	= Isocrates, *Busiris*
Juv. *Sat.*	= Juvenal, *Satires*
Liv.	= Livy, *History of Rome*
Longin, *De Subl.*	= Longinus, *De Sublimate*
Macrob. Sat.	= Macrobius, *Saturnalia*
Mart.	= Martial, *Epigrammata*
Origen, C.C.	= Origen, *Contra Celsum*
Paus.	= Pausanias, *Description of Greece*
Petr. Fr.	= Petronius, *Fragments*
Petr.	= Petronius, *Satyricon*
Plat. Rep.	= Plato, *Republic*
Plat. Tim.	= Plato, *Timaeus*
Plb.	= Polybius, *Histories*
Pliny, *NH*	= Pliny the Elder, *Naturalis Historia*
Plut. Agis	= Plutarch, *Agis*
Plut. Alex.	= Plutarch, *Alexander*
Plut. Cam.	= Plutarch, *Camillus*
Plut. Cat. Ma.	= Plutarch, *Marcus Cato*
Plut. De Iside	= Plutarch, *Isis and Osiris*
Plut. Flam.	= Plutarch, *Titus Flamininus*
Plut. Lyc.	= Plutarch, *Lycurgus*
Plut. Mor.	= Plutarch, *Moralia*
Plut. Pyrrh.	= Plutarch, *Pyrrhus*
Plut. Quaes. Conv.	= Plutarch, *Quaestiones Convivales*
Plut. Rom.	= Plutarch, *Romulus*
Plut. Sert.	= Plutarch, *Sertorius*
Plut. Sol.	= Plutarch, *Solon*
Porphyry Abst.	= Porphyry, *De Abstinentia*
Porphyry VP	= Porphyry, *Vita Pythagorae*
Prop.	= Sextus Propertius, *Elegies*
Ps-Phoc.	= Pseudo-Phocylides
Sen. Ira.	= Seneca, *de Ira*
Serv. A.	= Servius, *Commentary on the Aeneid of Vergil*
Strab.	= Strabo, *Geography*
Strab.	= Strabo, *Geography*
Suet, Dom.	= Suetonius, *Domitianus*
Suet. Aug.	= Suetonius, *Divus Augustus*

Suet. Cal.	= Suetonius, *Caligula*
Suet. Cl.	= Suetonius, *Divus Claudius*
Suet. Tib.	= Suetonius, *Tiberius*
Tac. Ag.	= Tacitus, *Agricola*
Tac. Ann.	= Tacitus, *Annales*
Tac. Ger.	= Tacitus, *Germania*
Tac. Hist.	= Tacitus, *Historiae*
Tatian, Orat. Ad. Graec.	= Tatian, *Oratio ad Graecos*
Tert. Haer.	= Tertullian, De Prescriptione Haereticorum
Theoc. Id.	= Theocritus, *Idylls*
Thuc.	= Thucydides, *Histories*
V. Max.	= Valerius Maximus, *Facta et Dicta Memorabilia*
Verg. A.	= Vergil, *Aeneid*

Non-Biblical Jewish Sources
M. Abod. Zar. = Mishnah Avodah Zarah

Secondary Sources

AA	= *Antiquités Africaines*
A Class	= *Acta Classica*
AB	= *Anchor Bible*
AGJU	= *Arbeiten zur Geschichte des antiken Judentums und des Ur-christentums*
AHR	= *American Historical Review*
AJS Review	= *Association for Jewish Studies Review*
AJPh	= *American Journal of Philology*
ANRW	= *Aufstieg und Niedergang der römishchen Welt*
ANS	= *American Numismatic Studies*
AOAT	= *Alter Orient und Altes Testament*
BEHE	= *Bibliothèque de l'Ecole des hautes études*
BEFAR	= *Bibliothèque de l'Ecole Francaise de Rome*
BIOSCS	= *Bulletin of the International Organization for Septuagint and Cognate Studies*
BIS	= *Biblical Interpretation Series*
BJSt	= *Brown Judaic Studies*
BWANT	= *Beiträge zur Wissenschaft vom Alten und Neuen Testament*
ChrEg	= *Chronique d'Égypte*

CP	= *Classical Philology*
CPG	= *Corpus Papyrorum Judaicarum*
CQ	= *Classical Quarterly*
CSCT	= *Columbia Studies in the Classical Tradition*
FGrH	= *Die Fragmente der griechischen Historiker*
FJCD	= *Forschungen zum jüdisch- christlichen Dialog*
GTA	= *Göttinger theologische Arbeiten*
Hist.E	= *Historia Einzelschriften*
HSCP	= *Harvard Studies in Classical Philology*
HTR	= *Harvard Theological Review*
HUCA	= *Hebrew Union College Annual*
JAOS	= *Journal of the American Oriental Society*
JBL	= *Journal for Biblical Literature*
JEA	= *Journal of Egyptian Archaeology*
Jhrb. Heid. Akad.	= *Jahrbuch der Heidelberger Akademie*
JIGRE	= *Jewish Inscriptions of Graeco-Roman Egypt: With an Index of the Jewish Inscriptions of Egypt and Cyrenaica*
JJS	= *Journal of Jewish Studies*
JNES	= Journal of Near Eastern Studies
JQR	= Jewish Quarterly Review
JRS	= Journal of Roman Studies
JSHRZ	= Jüdische Schriften aus hellenistisch-römischer Zeit
JSJ	= Journal for the Study of Judaism
JSJSup	= Supplements to the *Journal for the Study of Judaism*
JSNT	= *Journal for the Study of the New Testament*
JSOT	= *Journal for the Study of the Old Testament*
JSOTSup	= *Journal for the Study of the Old Testament Supplement Series*
JSP	= *Journal for the Study of the Pseudepigrapha*
JSPSup	= *Journal for the Study of the Pseudepigrapha Supplement Series*
JSS	= *Journal of Semitic Studies*
JTS	= *Journal of Theological Studies*
LCL	= *Loeb Classical Library*
MJSt	= *Münsteraner Judaistische Studien*
NovTSup	= *Supplements to Novum Testamentum*
NT	= *Novum Testamentum*
NTS	= *New Testament Studies*
OBO	= *Orbis biblicus et orientalis*
OPA	= *Les Oeuvres de Philon d'Alexandrie*
PalEQ	= *Palestine Exploration Quarterly*

P.Petrie III	= *The Flinders Petrie Papyri III*
PEQ	= *Palestine Exploration Quarterly*
PVTG	= *Pseudepigrapha Veteris Testamento Graece*
RE	= *Realencyclopädie der klassischen Altertumswissenschaft*
REJ	= *Revue des Études Juives*
RevHistDroit	= *Revue d'histoire de droit francais et étranger*
RevPhil	= *Revue de Philologie*
RGRW	= *Religions in the Graeco-Roman World*
RhM	= *Rheinisches Museum für Philologie*
RHR	= *Revue de l'histoire des religions*
SBLDS	= *Society of Biblical Literature Dissertation Series*
SBLSCS	= *Society of Biblical Literature Septuagint and Cognate Studies*
SBLWGRWSup	= *Society of Biblical Literature Writings from the Greco-Roman World Supplement Series*
SCI	= *Scripta Classica Israelica*
SPhilA	= *Studia Philonica Annual*
StPB	= *Studia post-Biblica*
TSAJ	= *Texte und Studien zum Antiken Judentum*
UPZ	= *Urkunden der Ptolemäerzeit*
VC	= *Vigiliae Christianae*
VT Sup	= *Supplements to Vetus Testamentum*
WSAMA.T	= *Wallberger Studien der Albertus-Magnus-Akademie-Theologishe*
WUNT	= *Wissenschaftliche Untersuchungen zum Neuen Testament*
YCS	= *Yale Classical Studies*
ZABR	= *Zeitschrift für altorientalische und biblische Rechtsgeschichte*
ZAW	= *Zeitschrift für die alttestamentliche Wissenschaft*
ZNW	= *Zeitschrift für die neutestamentliche Wissenschaft*
ZPE	= *Zeitschrift für Papyrologie und Epigraphik*

Bibliography

Abel, F.M. *Les livres des Maccabées*. Paris: Gabalda, 1949.

Ackroyd, P.R. *Israel under Babylon and Persia*. Oxford: Oxford University Press, 1970.

Ahearne-Kroll, P.D. "Constructing Jewish Identity in Ptolemaic Egypt: The Case of Artapanus," in *The "Other" in Second Temple Judaism*, edited by D. Harlow, K.M. Hogan, M. Goff, and J.S. Kaminsky, 434–456. Grand Rapids: W.B. Eerdmans Pub. Co., 2011.

Aitken, J.K. "Review Essay on Hengel, *Judaism and Hellenism*," *JBL* 123 (2004): 331–41.

Albertz, R. *Die Exilzeit, 6. Jahrhundert v.Chr.* Biblische Enzyklopäide 7. Stuttgart: Kohlhammer, 2001.

Alexandre, C. *Oracula Sibyllina*. 2 vols. Paris: Didot, 1841–56.

——. *Excursus ad Sibyllina*. Paris: Didot, 1856.

Alexandre, M. *De Congressu Eruditionis Gratia*. OPA 16. Paris: Cerf, 1967.

Alter, R. *The Art of Biblical Narrative*. New York: Basic Books, 1981.

Ameling, W. "'Market-Place' und Gewalt: Die Juden in Alexandrien 38 n. Chr," *Würzburger Jahrbücher für die Altertumswissenschaft Neue Folge* 27 (2003): 71–123.

——. *Inscriptiones Judaicae Orientis*, Vol. II: *Kleinasien*. Tübingen: Mohr Siebeck, 2004.

Amir, Y. "Philo's Version of the Pilgrimage to Jerusalem," in *Jerusalem in the Second Temple Period: Abraham Schalit Memorial Volume*, edited by A. Oppenheimer, U. Rappaport, and M. Stern, 154–165. [Hebrew] Jerusalem: Yad Izhak Beu-Zvi, 1980.

——. "Θεοκρατία as a Concept of Political Philosophy: Josephus' Presentation of Moses' *Politeia*," *SCI* 8–9 (1985–8): 83–105.

Arenhoevel, D. *Die Theokratie nach dem 1. und 2. Makkabäerbuch*. WSAMA.T Reihe 3. Mainz: Matthias-Grünewald, 1967.

Anderson, G. *Ancient Fiction: The Novel in the Graeco-Roman World*. London: Croom Helm/Barnes & Noble, 1984.

Anderson, H. "3 Maccabees," in *The Old Testament Pseudepigrapha*, edited by J. H. Charlesworth, 2.509–529. Garden City, N.Y.: Doubleday, 1985.

——. "4 Maccabees," in *The Old Testament Pseudepigrapha*, edited J. H. Charlesworth, 2.531–564. Garden City, N.Y.: Doubleday, 1985.

Atkinson, J.E. "Ethnic Cleansing in Roman Alexandria in 38," *A Class* 49 (2006): 31–54.

Attridge, H.W. "Josephus and His Works," in *Jewish Writings of the Second Temple Period: Apocrypha, Pseudepigrapha, Qumran Sectarian Writings, Philo, Josephus*, edited by M. Stone, 185–232. Philadelphia: Fortress Press, 1984.

——. "Fragments of Pseudo-Greek Poets," in *The Old Testament Pseudepigrapha*, edited J.H. Charlesworth, 2:824–30. Garden City, N.Y.: Doubleday, 1985.

Avidov, A. *Not Reckoned among Nations: The Origins of the so-called "Jewish Question" in Roman Antiquity*. TSAJ 128. Tübingen: Mohr Siebeck, 2009.

Aziza, C. "L'utilisation polémique du récit de l'Exode chez les écrivains alexandrins," *ANRW* II.20.1 (1987): 53–63.

Baer, Y.F. *Galut*. New York: Schocken, 1947.

Balsdon, J.– P.V.D. *The Emperor Gaius (Caligula)*. Oxford: Clarendon Press, 1934, 1964.

Baltzer, K. *Deutero-Isaiah: A Commentary on Isaiah 40–55*, edited by P. Machinist, translated by M. Kohl. Hermeneia. Minneapolis: Fortress Press, 2001.

Balch, D. "Two Apologetic Encomia: Dionysius on Rome and Josephus on the Jews," *JSJ* 13 (1982): 102–122.

Bakhos, C. *Ishmael on the Border: Rabbinic Portrayals of the First Arab.* Albany: State University of New York Press, 2006.

Barclay, J.M.G. *Jews in the Mediterranean Diaspora: From Alexander to Trajan (323 BCE–17 CE)* Edinburgh: T&T Clark, 1996.

——. "Josephus v. Apion," in *Understanding Josephus: Seven Perspectives,* edited by S. Mason, 194–221. Sheffield: Sheffield Academic Press, 1998.

——. "Judaism in Roman Dress: Josephus' Tactics in the *Contra Apionem*," in *Internationales Josephus-Kolloquium Aarhus 1999,* edited by J.U. Kalms and F. Siegert, 231–245. Münster: LIT, 2000.

——. "The Politics of Contempt: Judaeans and Egyptians in Josephus's *Against Apion*," in *Negotiating Diaspora: Jewish Strategies in the Roman Empire,* edited by J. M. G. Barclay, 109–127. London: T&T Clark, 2004.

——. *Flavius Josephus: Translation and Commentary,* vol. 10: *Contra Apionem.* Leiden: Brill, 2007.

Bar-Kochva, B. *Judas Maccabaeus: The Jewish Struggle Against the Seleucids.* Cambridge: Cambridge University Press, 1989.

——. "The Hellenistic 'Blood-Libel'– Content, Origins, and Transformations," *Tarbiz* 65 (1995/6): 347–374 [Hebrew].

——. *Pseudo-Hecataeus on the Jews: Legitimizing the Jewish Diaspora.* Hellenistic Culture and Society 21. Berkeley: University of California Press, 1996a.

——. "An Ass in the Jerusalem Temple: The Origins and Development of the Slander," in *Josephus' Contra Apionem: Studies in its Character and Context with a Latin Concordance to the Portion Missing in Greek,* edited by L.H. Feldman and J.R. Levison, 310–326. Leiden: Brill, 1996b.

——. "Aristotle, the Learned Jew, and the Indian Kalanoi," *Tarbiz* 67 (1997/8): 435–481 [Hebrew].

——. "The Anti-Jewish Treatise of Apollonius Molon," *Tarbiz* 69 (1999–2000a): 5–58 [Hebrew].

— "Lysimachus of Alexandria and the Hostile Traditions Concerning the Exodus," *Tarbiz* 69 (1999–2000b): 471–506 [Hebrew].

——. *The Image of the Jews in Greek Literature: The Hellenistic Period.* Hellenistic Culture and Society 51. Berkeley: University of California Press, 2010.

Baron, S. "Population," in *Encyclopedia Judaica 13,* edited by Cecil Roth, 866–903. Jerusalem: Keter Publishing House, 1971.

Barrett, A.A. *Caligula: the Corruption of Power.* London and New Haven: B.T. Batsford Ltd. and Yale University Press, 1989.

Barrett, D.S. "Tacitus, *Hist.* 5.13.2 and the Dead Sea Scrolls Again," *RhM* 119 (1976): 366.

Baumann, U. *Rom und die Juden: Die römisch-jüdischen Beziehungen von Pompeius bis zu Tide des Herodes (63 v. Chr-4 v. Chr.).* Frankfurt: Peter Lang, 1983.

Beard, M., J. North, and S. Price, *Religions of Rome.* Cambridge: Cambridge University Press, 1998.

Bedford, P.R. *Temple Restoration in Early Achaemenid Judah.* JSJSup 65. Leiden: Brill, 2001.

Beek, M.A. "Relations entre Jérusalem et la Diaspora égyptienne au deuxième siècle avant Jésus-Christ," *Oudtestamentische Studiën* 2 (1943): 119–43.

Bellinger, A.R. *Essays on the Coinage of Alexander the Great.* Numismatic Studies 11. New York: American Numismatic Studies, 1963.

Benbassa, E. and J.C. Attias, *The Jew and the Other.* Ithaca: Cornell University Press, 2004.

Bengtson, H. *Griechische Geschichte von den Anfängen bis die römische Kaiserzeit.* Munich: Beck, 1960.

Berg, S.B. *The Book of Esther: Motifs, Themes, and Structures.* Missoula, Mt.: Scholars Press, 1979.

Berger, P.-R. "Der Zyroszylinder mit dem Zusatzfragment BIN II, 32 und die akkadischen Personennamen im Danielbuch," *Zeitschrift für Assyriologie* 64 (1975): 192–234.

Bergren, T.A. "Nehemiah in 2 Maccabees, 1:10–2:18," *JSJ* 28 (1997): 249–70.

Bernal, M. *Black Athena: The Afroasiatic Roots of Classical Civilization,* vol. 1: *The Fabrication of Ancient Greece,* 1785–1985. New Brunswick, NJ: Rutgers University Press, 1987.

——. *Black Athena: The Afroasiatic Roots of Classical Civilization,* vol. 2: *The Archaeological and Documentary Evidence.* New Brunswick, NJ: Rutgers University Press, 1991.

——. "Responses to critical reviews of *Black Athena,* volume 1," *Journal of Mediterranean Archaeology* 3 (1990): 111–137.

——. "Response to Edith Hall," *Arethusa* 25.1 (1992): 203–214.

Bernays, J. *Theophrastos' Schrift über Frömmigkeit: Ein Beitrag zur Religionsgeschichte.* Berlin: Verlag von Wilhelm Hertz, 1866.

Bernett, Monika *Der Kaiserkult in Judäa unter den Herodiern und Römern.* WUNT 203. Tubingen: Mohr Siebeck, 2007.

Bertholet, A. *Die Stellung der Israeliten und der Juden zu den Fremden.* Freiburg: J. C. B. Mohr, 1896.

Berthelot, K. "The Use of Greek and Roman Stereotypes of the Egyptians by Hellenistic Jewish Apologists, with Special Reference to Josephus' *Against Apion,*" in *Internationales Josephus-Kolloquium Aarhus, 1999,* edited by J.U. Kalms, 185–221. Münster: LIT, 2000.

——. *Philanthropia Judaica: Le débat autour de la "misanthropie" des lois juives dans l'Antiquité.* JSJSup 76. Leiden: Brill, 2003.

——. "The Original Sin of the Canaanites," in *The "Other" in Second Temple Judaism,* edited by D. Harlow, K.M. Hogan, M. Goff, and J.S. Kaminsky, 49–66. Grand Rapids: Eerdmans, 2011.

Bevan, E. *The House of Seleucus.* London: Arnold, 1902.

Bickerman, E.J. "Ein jüdischer Festbrief vom Jahre 124 v. Chr.," *ZNW* 32 (1933): 233–54.

——. "La Charte seleucide de Jerusalem," *REJ* 100 (1935): 4–35.

——. *Der Gott der Makkabäer: Untersuchungen über Sinn und Ursprung der makkabäischen Erhebung.* Berlin: Schocken Books, 1937.

——. "The Edict of Cyrus in Ezra 1," *JBL* 65 (1946): 249–275.

——. "Origenes Gentium," *CP* 47 (1952): 65–81.

——. "Sur la chronologie de la sixième guerre de Syrie," *ChrEg* 27 (1952): 44–54.

——. *Studies in Jewish and Christian History* vol. I. Leiden: Brill, 1976.

——. "Ritualmord und Eselkult: Ein Beitrag zur Geschichte antiker Publizistik," in *Studies in Jewish and Christian History,* vol. 2, edited by E. Bickermann, 225–55. Leiden: Brill, 1980.

——. *The Jews in the Greek Age.* Cambridge, MA: Harvard University Press, 1988.

Bilde, P. "The Roman Emperor Gaius (Caligula)'s Attempt to Erect his Statue in the Temple of Jerusalem," *Studia Theologica* 32 (1978): 67–93.

——. *Flavius Josephus between Jerusalem and Rome: His Life, His Works, and Their Importance.* JSPSup 2. Sheffield: Sheffield Academic Press, 1988.

——. "*Contra Apionem* 1.28–56: Josephus' View of his own Work in the Context of the Jewish Canon," in *Josephus' Contra Apionem: Studies in its Character and Context*, edited by L.H. Feldman and J.R. Levison, 94–114. Leiden: Brill, 1996.

Bilde, P., T. Engberg-Pedersen, L. Hannestad, and J. Zahle, eds. *Religion and Religious Practice in the Seleucid Kingdom*. Studies in Hellenistic Civilization 1. Aarhus: Aarhaus University Press, 1990.

Binder, D. D. *Into the Temple Courts: The Place of the Synagogues in the Second Temple Period*. SBLDS 169. Atlanta, Ga.: Society of Biblical Literature, 1999.

Birnbaum, E. "Portrayals of the Wise and Virtuous in Alexandrian Jewish Works: Jews' Perceptions of Themselves and Others," in *Ancient Alexandria Between Egypt and Greece*, edited by W.V. Harris and G. Ruffini, 125–160. CSCT 26. Leiden: Brill, 2004.

Blenkinsopp, J. *Ezra-Nehemiah: A Commentary*. Philadelphia: Westminster, 1988.

——. *Isaiah 40–55: A New Translation with Introduction and Commentary*. New York: DoubleDay, 2000.

Bloch, R.S. "Geography without Territory: Tacitus' Digression on the Jews and its Ethnographic Context," in *Internationales Josephus-Kolloquium*, edited by J.U. Kalms, 38–54. Münster: LIT, 2000.

——. *Antike Vorstellungen vom Judentum: Der Judenexkurs des Tacitus im Rahmen der griechisch-römischen Ethnographie*. Hist.E 160. Stuttgart: Franz Steiner, 2002.

Boccaccini, G. *Middle Judaism: Jewish Thought, 300 B.C.E. to 200 C.E.* Minneapolis: Fortress Press, 1991.

Bohak, G. "CPJ III, 520: The Egyptian Reaction to Onias' Temple," *JSJ* 26 (1995): 32–41.

——. *Joseph and Aseneth and the Jewish Temple in Heliopolis*. Atlanta: Scholars Press, 1996.

Bollansée, J. *Hermippos of Smyrna and His Biographical Writings: A Reappraisal*. Leuven: Peeters, 1999.

Borgen, P. "'There Shall Come Forth a Man': Reflections on Messianic Ideas in Philo," in *The Messiah: Developments in Earliest Judaism and Christianity*, edited by J.H. Charlesworth, 341–361. Minneapolis: Fortress Press, 1992.

Bouché-Leclercq, A. *Histoire des Seleucides, 323–64 av. Chr.* 2 vol. Paris: Leroux, 1913–14.

Bourgeaud, P. *Aux origines de l'histoire des religions*. Paris: Seuil, 2004.

Bousset, W. "Die Beziehungen der ältesten jüdischen Sibylle zur chaldäischen Sibyll," *ZNW* 3:23–49.

——. "Sibyllen und Sibyllinische Bücher," in *Real-Encyclopädie für protestantische Theologie und Kirsche* (1906): 18:265–80.

Bowersock, G. W. *Roman Arabia*. Cambridge, Mass.: Harvard University Press, 1983.

Bowie, E. 'The Readership of Greek Novels in the Ancient World,' in *The Search for the Ancient Novel*, ed. J. H. Tatum, 435–459. Baltimore: John Hopkins University Press, 1994.

Brand, J. "The Temple of Onias," *Yavneh* 1 (1939): 76–84 [Hebrew].

Braun, M. *History and Romance in Graeco-Oriental Literature*. Oxford: Blackwell, 1938.

Braund, D. C. *Rome and the Friendly King: The Character of Client Kingship*. Beckenham, Kent: Groom Helm, 1984.

——. "Client Kings," in *The Administration of the Roman Empire*, edited by D. C. Braund, 69–96. Exeter: University of Exeter Press, 1988.

Breitenstein, U. *Beobachtungen zu Sprache, Stil und Gedankengut des vierten Makkabäerbuches*. 2nd ed. Basel: Schwabe, 1978.

Brenner, A. *A Feminist Companion Esther, Judith, and Susanna.* A Feminist Companion to the Bible 7. Sheffield: Sheffield Academic Press, 1995.

——. "Ruth as a Foreign Worker and the Politics of Exogamy," in *Ruth and Esther,* ed. A Feminist Companion to the Bible Second Series 3. Sheffield: Sheffield Academic Press, 1999.

Bresciani, E. "The Persian Occupation of Egypt," in *The Cambridge History of Iran* vol. 2, edited by I. Gershevitsh, 503–528. Cambridge: Cambridge University Press, 1985.

Briant, P. "Histoire impériale et histoire régionale à propos de l'histoire de Juda dans l'empire achéménide," *Congress Volume Oslo 1998,* edited by A. Lemaire and M. Saebo, 235–245. VT Sup 80. Leiden: Brill, 2000.

Briend, J. "L'édit de Cyrus et sa valeur historique," *Transeu* 11 (1996): 33–44.

Bringmann, K. "Die Verfolgung der jüdischen Religion durch Antiochos IV: Ein Konflikt zwischen Judentum und Hellenismus," *Antike und Abendland* 26 (1980): 176–90.

——. *Hellenistische Reform und Religionsverfolgung in Judäa: Eine Untersuchung zur jüdisch-hellenistichen Geschichte.* Gottingen: Vandenhoeck & Ruprecht, 1983.

——. "The King as Benefactor: Some Remarks on Ideal Kingship in the Age of Hellenism," in *Images and Ideologies: Self-Definition in the Hellenistic World,* edited by A. Bulloch, et al., 7–24. Hellenistic Culture and Society 12. Berkeley: University of California Press, 1993.

——. *Geben und Nehmen: Monarchische Wohltätigkeit und Selbstdarstellung im Zeitalter des Hellenismus,* Teil II.1. Berlin: Akademie Verlag, 2000.

Bringmann, K. and H. von Steuben, *Schenkungen hellenistischer Herrscher an griechische Städte und Heiligtümer,* Teil I. Berlin: Akademie Verlag, 1995.

Brodd, J. and J.L. Reed, *Rome and Religion: A Cross-Disciplinary Dialogue on the Imperial Cult.* SBLWGRWSup 5. Atlanta: Society of Biblical Literature, 2011.

Bunge, J. G. *Untersuchungen zum zweiten Makkabäerbuch.* Bonn: Ph.D. Dissertation, Rheinische Friedrich-Wilhelms-Universität zu Bonn, 1971.

——. "'Theos Epiphanes' in den ersten fünf Regierungsjahren des Antiochos IV Epiphanes," *Historia* 23 (1974): 57–85; 24 (1975): 164–88.

——. "Zur Geschichte und Chronologie des Untergangs der Oniaden und des Aufsteigs der Hasmonäer" *JSJ* 6 (1975): 1–46.

——. "Die Feiern Antiochos' IV. Epiphanes in Daphne im Herbst 166 v.Chr.," *Chiron* 6 (1976): 53–71.

Burchard, C. *"Joseph et Aséneth: Questions actuelles,"* in La *littérature juive entre Tenach et Mischna,* edited by W.C. van Unnik, 84–96. Leiden: Brill, 1974.

——. *Untersuchungen zur Joseph und Aseneth.* Tubingen: Mohr, 1965.

Burgmann, H. "Das umstrittene Intersacerdotium in Jerusalem 159–152 v.Chr." *JSJ* 11 (1980): 135–76.

Burstein, S. M. *Agatharchides of Cnidus: On the Erythraean Sea.* London: The Hakluyt Society, 1989.

Campbell, B. "War and Diplomacy: Rome and Parthia, 31 BC–AD 235," in *War and Society in the Roman World,* edited by J. Rich and G. Shipley, 213–240. London: Routledge, 1993.

Campbell, E. F. Jr., *Ruth.* AB 7. New York: Doubleday, 1975.

Camponovo, O. *Königherrschaft und Reich Gottes in den frühjüdischen Schriften.* OBO 58. Freiburg: V&R, 1984.

Cardauns, B. "Juden und Spartaner," *Hermes* 95 (1967): 317–24.

Carroll, R.P. "Exile! What Exile? Deportation and the Discourses of Diaspora," in *Leading Captivity Captive: "The Exile" as History and Ideology,* edited by L. Grabbe, 62–79. JSOTSup 278. Sheffield: Sheffield Academic Press, 1998.

Cartledge, P. and A. Spawforth, *Hellenistic and Roman Sparta: A Tale of Two Cities.* London: Routledge, 1989.

Catastini, A. "Le testimonianze di Manetone e la 'storia di Giuseppe' (Genesis 37–50)," *Henoch* 17 (1995): 279–300.

Cavaignac, E. "Remarques sur le deuxième livre des 'Macchabées'," *RHR* 130 (1945): 42–58.

Charles, R.H. ed. *The Apocrypha and Pseudepigrapha of the Old Testament,* 2 vols. Oxford: Clarendon Press, 1913.

Charlesworth, J.H. ed. *The Old Testament Pseudepigrapha* 2 vols. Garden City, N.Y.: Doubleday, 1983–1985.

Chesnutt, R. *From Death to Life: Conversion in Joseph and Aseneth.* Sheffield: Sheffield Academic Press, 1995.

Chilver, G.E.F. *A Historical Commentary on Tacitus' Histories IV and V.* Oxford: Oxford University Press, 1985.

Cimma, M. R. *Reges Socii et Amid Populi Romani.* Milan: A. Giuffrè, 1976.

Clarysse, W. "Jews in Trikomia," *Proceedings of the XXth International Congress of Papyrologists.* Copenhagen: Museum Tusculanum Press, 1994.

Clauss, M. *Kaiser und Gott: Herrscherkult im römischen Reich.* Munich: K.G. Saur, 2001.

Clifford, J. *Routes: Travel and Translation in the Late Twentieth Century.* Cambridge, Mass.: Harvard University Press, 1997.

Cohen, A.A. and P. Mendes-Flohr, eds., *Contemporary Jewish Religious Thought.* New York: Free Press, 1987.

Cohen, S. J. D. "Alexander the Great and Jaddus the High Priest According to Josephus," *AJS Review* 78 (1982–1983): 41–68.

——. *From the Maccabees to Mishnah.* Philadelphia: Westminster Press, 1987.

—."History and Historiography in the *Against Apion* of Josephus," in *Essays in Jewish Historiography,* edited by A. Rapoport-Albert, 1–11. History and Theory, Studies in the Philosophy of History Beiheft 27. Middleton, CT: Wesleyan University, 1988.

——. "Religion, Ethnicity, and 'Hellenism' in the Emergence of Jewish Identity in Maccabean Palestine," in *Religion and Religious Practice in the Seleucid Kingdom,* edited by P. Bilde, T. Engberg-Pedersen, L. Hannestad, and J. Zahle, 204–23. Aarhus: Aarhaus University Press, 1990.

——. *The Beginnings of Jewishness: Boundaries, Varieties, Uncertainties.* Berkeley: University of California Press, 1999.

Cohn, L. "An Apocryphal Ascribed to Philo of Alexandria," *JQR* 10 (1898): 227–332.

Cohn, R. L. "Before Israel: The Canaanites as Other in Biblical Tradition," in *The Other in Jewish Thought and History: Constructions of Jewish Thought and Identity,* edited by L. Silberstein and R.L. Cohn, 74–90. New York: New York University Press, 1994.

Collins, J. J. *The Sibylline Oracles of Egyptian Judaism.* Missoula: Scholars Press, 1974a.

——. "The Provenance and Date of the Third Sibyl," *Bulletin of the Institute of Jewish Studies,* (1974b): 2:1–18.

——. "The Sibylline Oracles," *The Old Testament Pseudepigrapha,* ed. J. H. Charlesworth, 1.354–405. Garden City, N.Y.: Doubleday, 1983.

——. "Artapanus," in *The Old Testament Pseudepigrapha,* ed. J. H. Charlesworth, 2.889–903. Garden City, N.Y.: Doubleday, 1985.

——. "The Development of the Sibylline Tradition," *ANRW* (1987): II.20.I: 421–59.
——. "'The King has become a Jew' The Perspective on the Gentile World in Bel and the Snake," in *Diaspora Jews and Judaism: Essays in Honor of, and in Dialogue with A. Thomas Kraabel,* ed. J.A. Overman and R.S. MacLennan, 335–345. Atlanta: Scholars Press, 1992.
——. *Daniel: A Commentary on the Book of Daniel.* Hermeneia. Minneapolis: Fortress Press, 1993.
——. *Between Athens and Jerusalem: Jewish Identity in the Hellenistic Diaspora.* 2d ed. Grand Rapids: Eerdmans, 2000.
——. "Cult and Culture: The Limits of Hellenization in Judea," in *Hellenism in the Land of Israel,* edited by J. J. Collins and G. E. Sterling, 38–61. Notre Dame, IN: University of Notre Dame Press, 2001.
——. *Jewish Cult and Hellenistic Culture: Essays on the Jewish Encounter with Hellenism and Roman Rule.* Leiden: Brill, 2005.
Cowey, J.M.S., K. Maresch. *Urkunden des Politeuma der Juden von Herakleopolis (144/3–133/2 b. Chr.) (P. Polit. Iud).* Papyri aus den Sammlungen von Heidelberg, Köln, München und Wien. Papyrologica Coloniensia 29. Wiesbaden: Westdeutscher Verlag, 2001.
Crowley, A.E. *Aramaic Papyri of the Fifth Century B.C.* Oxford: Clarendon Press, 1923.
Curty, O. "A propos de la parenté entre juifs et spartiates," *Historia* 41 (1992): 246–48.
——. *Les parentés legéndaires entre cités grecques.* Geneva: Droz, 1995.
Dack, E. van't. "La date de la letter d'Aristée," *Studia Hellenistica* 16 (1968): 263–78.
Dalbert, P. *Die Theologie der hellenistisch-jüdischen Missions-Literatur unter Ausschluss von Philo und Josephus.* Hamburg: Herbert Reich, 1954.
Dancy, J.C. *A Commentary on I Maccabees.* Oxford: Blackwell, 1954.
Daniel, J.L. "Anti-Semitism in the Hellenistic-Roman World," *JBL* 98 (1979): 45–65.
Davies, W.D. *The Territorial Dimension of Judaism.* Berkeley: University of California Press, 1982.
Davies, W.D., and Finkelstein, L. eds. *The Cambridge History of Judaism 2: The Hellenistic Age.* Cambridge: Cambridge University Press, 1989.
Delcor, M. "Le temple d'Onias en Egypte," *Revue Biblique* 75 (1968): 188–205.
——. *Le livre de Daniel.* Paris: J. Gabalda, 1971.
Delia, D. *Alexandrian Citizenship during the Roman Principate.* Atlanta: Scholars Press, 1991.
Delling, G. "Die Begegnung zwischen Hellenismus und Judentum," *ANRW* II.20.1 (1987a): 3–39.
——. *Die Bewältigung der Diasporasituation durch das hellenistische Judentum.* Göttingen: Vandenhoeck & Ruprecht, 1987b.
Denis, A.-M. *Fragmenta Pseudepigraphorum Quae Supersunt Graeca.* PVTG 3. Leiden: Brill, 1970.
Derron, P. *Pseudo-Phocylide: Sentences.* Paris: Société d'Édition "Les Belles Lettres," 1986.
deSilva, D. *4 Maccabees.* Sheffield: Sheffield Academic Press, 1998.
de Jonge, M. ed. *The "Testaments of the Twelve Patriarchs": A Critical Edition of the Greek Text.* PVTG 1, 2. Leiden: Brill, 1978.
Develin, R. and J. C. Yardley *Justin: Epitome of the Philippic History of Pompeius Trogus.* Atlanta: Scholars Press, 1994.
Devreesse, R. *Le Commentaire de Théodore de Mopsueste sur les Psaumes (I-LXXX).* Studi e testi 93. Città del Vaticano: Biblioteca Apostolica Vaticana, 1939.

Diamond, F.H. "Hecataeus of Abdera and the Mosaic Constitution," in *Panhellenica: Essays in Ancient History and Historiography in Honor of Truesdell S. Brown,* edited by S. M. Burstein and L. A. Okin, 77–95. Lawrence, KS: Coronado, 1980.

di Bitonto, A. "Papiri documentary dell' Universita Cattolicà di Milano," *Aegyptus,* 54 (1974): 34–39.

Dietzfelbinger, C. ed. *Pseudo-Philo, Antiquitates Biblicae.* JSHRZ II.2. Gütersloh: Gütersloher Verlagshaus, 1976.

Dillery, J. "The First Egyptian Narrative History: Manetho and Greek Historiography," *ZPE* 127 (1999): 93–116.

——. "Putting him Back Together Again: Apion Historian, Apion *Grammatikos,*" *CP* 98 (2003): 383–390.

Dillon, J.M. *The Middle Platonists: A Study of Platonism, 80 B.C. to A.D. 220.* London: Duckworth, 1977.

Dines, J.M. *The Septuagint: Understanding the Bible and its World.* London: T&T Clark, 2004.

Doran, R. *Temple Propaganda: The Purpose and Character of 2 Maccabees.* Washington: The Catholic Biblical Association, 1981.

——. "Cleodemus Malchus," in *Old Testament Pseudepigrapha,* edited by J. H. Charlesworth, 2.883–87. New York: Doubleday, 1985.

——. "Pseudo-Eupolemus," in *Old Testament Pseudepigrapha,* edited by J. H. Charlesworth, 2.873–82. New York: Doubleday, 1985.

Dorothy, C.V. *The Books of Esther: Structure, Genre, and Textual Integrity.* JSOTSup 187. Sheffield: Sheffield Academic Press, 1997.

Dothan, T. and R. Cohn, "The Philistine as Other: Biblical Rhetoric and Archaeological Reality," in *The Other in Jewish Thought and History,* edited by L. Silberstein and R. Cohn, 61–73. New York: New York University Press, 1994.

Droge, A.J. *Homer or Moses? Early Christian Interpretations of the History of Culture.* Tübingen: Mohr Siebeck, 1989.

——. "Josephus between Greeks and Barbarians," in *Josephus' Contra Apionem: Studies in its Character and Context with a Latin Concordance to the Portion Missing in Greek,* edited by L. H. Feldman and J. R. Levinson, 115–142. Leiden: Brill, 1996.

Dupont-Sommer, A. *Le Quatrième Livre des Machabées.* Paris: Champion, 1939.

Eddy, S.K. *The King is Dead: Studies in the Near Eastern Resistance to Hellenism 334–31 B.C.E.* Lincoln, NE: University of Nebraska, 1961.

Ehrenberg, V. "Sparta (Geschichte)," *RE* IIIA.2 (1929): 1373–1453.

Eisen, A.M. *Galut: Modern Jewish Reflection on Homelessness and Homecoming.* Bloomington: Indiana University Press, 1986.

Enslin, M.S. and S. Zeitlin. *The Book of Judith.* Leiden: Brill, 1972.

Eph'al, I. "Ishmael and 'Arab(s)': A Transformation of Ethnological Terms," *JNES* 35 (1976): 225–35.

Ezrahi, S. D. "Our Homeland, the Text … Our Text, the Homeland: Exile and Homecoming in the Modern Jewish Imagination," *Michigan Quarterly Review* 31 (1992): 463–97.

Feldman, L. H. "Prolegomenon," to the reprint of *The Biblical Antiquities of Philo,* M.R. James, ix-clxix. New York: KTAV, 1971.

——. "Hengel's *Judaism and Hellenism* in Retrospect," *JBL 96* (1977): 371–82.

——. "Anti-Semitism in the Ancient World," in *History and Hate: The Dimensions of Anti-Semitism,* edited by D. Berger, 15–42. Philadelphia: Jewish Publication Society, 1986.

——. "Pro-Jewish Intimations in Anti-Jewish Remarks Cited in Josephus' *Against Apion*," *JQR* 78 (1988–89): 187–251.

——. "Pro-Jewish Intimations in Tacitus' Account of Jewish Origins," *REJ* 150 (1991): 331–60.

——. *Jew and Gentile in the Ancient World: Attitudes and Interactions from Alexander to Justinian*. Princeton, N.J.: Princeton University Press, 1993.

——. "Reading Between the Lines: Appreciation of Judaism in Anti-Jewish Writers," in *Josephus' Contra Apionem: Studies in its Character and Context with a Latin Concordance to the Portion Missing in Greek*, edited by L.H. Feldman and J.R. Levison, 250–270. Leiden: Brill, 1996.

——. "The Concept of Exile in Josephus," in *Exile: Old Testament, Jewish, and Christian Conceptions*, edited by J.M. Scott, 145–172. JSJSup 56. Leiden: Brill, 1997.

——. "Did Jews Reshape the Tale of the Exodus?" *Jewish History* 12 (1998): 123–127.

——. *Flavius Josephus: Translation and Commentary*, III: *Judean Antiquities 1–4*. Leiden: Brill, 2000a.

——. "Josephus' Portrayal ('Antiquities' 5.136–174) of the Benjaminite Affair of the Concubine and its Repercussions (Judges 19–21)," *JQR* 90 (2000b): 255–92.

Fischer, T. *Seleukiden und Makkabäer*. Bochum: Studienverlag Brockmeyer, 1980.

Fishbane, M. *Biblical Interpretation in Israel*. Oxford: Oxford University Press, 1985.

Fisk, B.N. *Do You Not Remember? Scripture, Story, and Exegesis in the Rewritten Bible of Pseudo-Philo*. Sheffield: Sheffield Academic Press, 2001.

Fitzmyer, J.A. and D. Harrington, *A Manual of Palestinian Aramaic Texts*. Rome: Biblical Institute, 1978.

Flusser, D., and Amorai-Stark, S. "The Goddess Thermuthis, Moses, and Artapanus," *JSQ* 1 (1993–94): 217–33.

Fox, M.V. *Character and Ideology in the Book of Esther*. Columbia, SC: University of South Carolina Press, 1991.

Frankfurter, D. "Lest Egypt's City be Deserted: Religion and ideology in the Egyptian Response to the Jewish Revolt (116–117 C.E.)," *JJS* 43 (1992): 203–220.

——. *Elijah in Upper Egypt: The Apocalypse of Elijah and Early Egyptian Christianity*. Minneapolis: Fortress Press, 1993.

Fraser, P. M. *Ptolemaic Alexandria*. 3 vols. Oxford: Clarendon, 1972.

Frei, P. "Die persische Reichsautorisation," *ZABR* 1 (1995): 1–35.

Freudenthal, J. *Hellenistische Studien 1 und 2: Alexander Polyhistor und die von ihm erhaltenen Reste judäischer und samaritanischer Geschichtswerke*. Breslau: H. Skutsch, 1874–5.

Frick, C. *Chronica Minora*. Leipzig: Teubner, 1892.

Fuks, G. "Josephus on Herod's Attitude towards Jewish Religion: The Darker Side," *JJS* 53 (2002): 238–245.

Funkenstein, A. "Anti-Jewish Propaganda: Pagan, Christian, and Modern," *The Jerusalem Quarterly* 19 (1981): 56–75.

——. *Perceptions of Jewish History*. Berkeley: University of California Press, 1993.

Gabba, E. "The Growth of Anti-Judaism or the Greek Attitude Towards the Jews," in *The Cambridge History of Judaism*, Vol. 2: *The Hellenistic Age*, edited by W. D. Davies and L. Finkelstein, 614–56. Cambridge: Cambridge University Press, 1989.

——. "The Finances of King Herod," in *Greece and Rome in Eretz Israel*, edited by A. Kasher, U. Rappaport and G. Fuks, 160–168. Jerusalem: Jerusalem Exploration Society, 1990.

Gafni, I. M. "Reinternment in the Land of Israel: Notes on the Origin and Development of the Custom," *The Jerusalem Cathedra* 1 (1981): 96–104.

——. *Land, Center, and Diaspora: Jewish Constructs in Late Antiquity.* JSPSup 21. Sheffield: Sheffield Academic Press, 1997.

Gager, J.G. *Moses in Greco-Roman Paganism.* Nashville: Abingdon Press, 1972a.

——. "Some attempts to label the Oracula Sibylla, Book 7," *HTR* 65 (1972b): 91–7.

——. *The Origins of Anti-Semitism: Attitudes toward Judaism in Pagan and Christian Antiquity.* Oxford: Oxford University Press, 1985.

——. "Some Thoughts on Greco-Roman Versions of the Exodus Story," *Jewish History* 12 (1998): 129–132.

Gambetti, S. *The Alexandrian Riots of 38 C.E. and the Persecution of the Jews: A Historical Reconstruction.* Leiden: Brill, 2009.

Gardner, A.E. "The Purpose and Date of I Esdras," *JJS* 37 (1986): 18–27.

Gauger, J. –D. *Beiträge zur jüdischen Apologetik.* Cologne and Bonn: Hanstein, 1977.

——. "Zitate in der jüdischen Apologetik und die Authentizität der Hekataios-Passagen bei Flavius Josephus und im Ps. Aristeas-Brief," *JSJ* 13 (1982): 6–46.

Geffcken, J. *Die Oracula Sibyllina.* Leipzig: Hinrichs, 1902a.

——. *Komposition und Entstehungszeit der Oracula Sibyllina.* Leipzig: Hinrichs, 1902b.

Gehrke, H.-J. "Das sozial- und religionsgeschichtliche Umfeld der Septuaginta," in *Im Brennpunkt: Die Septuaginta. Studien zur Entstehung und Bedeutung der Griechischen Bibel* II, edited by S. Kreuzer and I.P. Lesch, 44–60. BWANT 161. Stuttgart: Kohlhammer, 2004.

Geiger, J. "Herodes *Philorhomaios*," *Ancient Society* 28 (1997): 75–88.

Gera, D. "Ptolemy, Son of Thraseas, and the Fifth Syrian War," *Ancient Society* 18 (1987): 63–73.

——. "On the Credibility of the History of the Tobiads," in *Greece and Rome in Eretz Israel,* edited by A. Kasher, U. Rappaport, and G. Fuks, 21–38. Jerusalem: Israel Exploration Society, 1990.

Gerber, C. *Ein Bild des Judentums für Nichtjuden von Flavius Josephus: Untersuchungen zu seiner Schrift Contra Apionem.* Leiden: Brill, 1997.

Gibson, E. L. *The Jewish Manumission Inscriptions of the Bosporus Kingdom.* Tübingen: Mohr Siebeck, 1999.

Ginsburg, M.S. "Sparta and Judaea," *CP* 29 (1934): 117–22.

Golan, D. "Der Besuch Alexanders in Jerusalem," *Berliner Theologische Zeitschrift* 8.1 (1991): 19–30.

Goldhill, Simon. "Genre," in *The Cambridge Companion to the Greek and Roman Novel,* edited by T. Whitmarsh, 185–200. Cambridge: Cambridge University Press, 2008.

Goldstein, J.A. "The Tales of the Tobiads," in *Christianity, Judaism, and Other Greco-Roman Cults: Studies for Morton Smith at Sixty* III, edited by J. Neusner, 85–123. Leiden: Brill, 1975.

——. *I Maccabees: A New Translation with Introduction and Commentary.* New York: Doubleday, 1976.

——. "Jewish Acceptance and Rejection of Hellenism," in *Jewish and Christian Self-Definition* Vol. 2, edited by E.P. Sanders, 64–87. Philadelphia: Fortress Press, 1981.

——. *II Maccabees: A New Translation with Introduction and Commentary.* New York: Doubleday, 1983.

——. *Peoples of an Almighty God: Competing Religions in the Ancient World*. New York: Doubleday, 2002.

Goodman, M. "Jewish Proselytizing in the First Century," in *Jews Among Pagans and Christians in the Roman Empire*, edited by J. Lieu, J. North, and T. Rajak, 53–78. London: Routledge, 1992.

——. *Mission and Conversion: Proselytizing in the Religious History of the Roman Empire*. Oxford: Oxford University Press, 1994.

——. "Josephus' Treatise *Against Apion*," in *Apologetics in the Roman Empire: Pagans, Jews, and Christians*, edited by M. Edwards, M. Goodman, and S. Price, 45–58. Oxford: Oxford University Press, 1999.

——. "The Pilgrimage Economy of Jerusalem in the Second Temple Period," in *Jerusalem: Its Sanctity and Centrality to Judaism, Christianity, and Islam*, edited by L. I. Levine, 69–76. New York: Continuum, 1999.

——. *Rome and Jerusalem: The Clash of Ancient Civilizations*. London and New York: Allen Lane, 2007.

Gorman, P. "Pythagoras Palestinus," *Philologus* 127 (1983): 33–36.

Goudriaan, K. "Ethnical Strategies in Graeco-Roman Egypt," in *Ethnicity in Hellenistic Egypt*, edited by P. Bilde, 74–99. Aarhus: Aarhaus University Press, 1992.

Goulder, M. "Ruth, a Homily on Deuteronomy 22–25?" in *Of Prophets' Visions, and the Wisdom of Sages: Essays in Honour of R. Norman Whybray on His Seventieth Birthday*, edited by H. A. McKay and D.J.A. Clines, 307–19. JSOTSup 162. Sheffield: Sheffield Academic Press, 1993.

Grabbe, L. L. *Judaism from Cyrus to Hadrian*. 2 vols. Minneapolis: Fortress Press, 1992.

——. *Ezra and Nehemiah* London: Routledge, 1998.

Gradel, I. *Emperor Worship and Roman Religion*. Oxford: Clarendon Press, 2002.

Grafton, A. *Defenders of the Text: The Traditions of Scholarship in an Age of Science, 1450–1800*. Cambridge: Harvard University Press, 1991.

Grant, M. *Herod the Great*. New York: American Heritage Press, 1971.

Gray, G.B. *A Critical and Exegetical Commentary on Isaiah, I-XXVII*. Edinburgh: T&T Clark, 1912.

Green, P. *Alexander to Actium: The Historical Evolution of the Hellenistic Age*. Berkeley: University of California Press, 1990.

Griffiths, J.G. "Tacitus, *Hist.* 5.13.2 and the Dead Sea Scrolls," *RhM* 113 (1970): 363–368.

——. "Tacitus and the *Hodayot* in the Dead Sea Scrolls," *RhM* 122 (1979): 99–100.

——. "Apocalyptic in the Hellenistic Era," in *Apocalypticism in the Mediterranean World and the Near East*, edited by D. Hellholm, 273–293. Tübingen: Mohr Siebeck, 1983.

——. "Egypt and the Rise of the Synagogue," in *Ancient Synagogues: Historical Analysis and Archaeological Discovery*, edited by D. Urman and P.V.M. Flesher, I.3–16. StPB 47. Leiden: Brill, 1995.

Gruen, E.S. "Rome and the Seleucids in the Aftermath of Pydna," *Chiron* 6 (1976): 73–95.

——. *The Hellenistic World and the Coming of Rome*. 2 vols. Berkeley and Los Angeles: University of California Press, 1984.

——. *Studies in Greek Culture and Roman Policy*. Cincinnati Classical Studies N.S. 7. Leiden: Brill, 1990.

——. *Culture and National Identity in Republican Rome*. Cornell Studies in Classical Philology 52. Ithaca, NY and London: Cornell University and Duckworth, 1992.

——. "The Purported Jewish-Spartan Affiliation," in *Transitions to Empire: Essays in Greco-Roman History, 300–146 B. C. in Honor of E. Badian,* edited by R. W. Wallace and E. M. Harris, 254–69. Oklahoma Series in Classical Culture 21. Norman: University of Oklahoma Press, 1996.

——. "The Origins and Objectives of Onias' Temple," *SCI* 16 (1997): 47–70.

——. *Heritage and Hellenism: The Reinvention of Jewish Tradition.* Hellenistic Culture and Society 30. Berkeley: University of California Press, 1998a.

——. "The Use and Abuse of the Exodus Story," *Jewish History* 12 (1998b): 93–122.

——. "Culture as Policy: The Attalids of Pergamon," in *From Pergamon to Sperlonga: Sculpture and Context,* edited by N. T. de Grummond and B. S. Ridgway, 17–31. Hellenistic Culture and Society 34. Berkeley: University of California Press, 2000.

——. *Diaspora: Jews Amidst Greeks and Romans.* Cambridge, Mass.: Harvard University Press, 2002a.

——. "Roman Perspectives on the Jews in the Age of the Great Revolt," in *The First Jewish Revolt: Archaeology, History, and Ideology,* edited by A.M. Berlin and J.A. Overman, 27–42. London and New York: Routledge, 2002b.

——. "Greeks and Jews: Mutual Misperceptions in Josephus' *Contra Apionem,*" in *Ancient Judaism in Its Hellenistic Context,* edited by C. Bakhos, 31–51. JSJSup. 95. Leiden: Brill, 2005.

——. "The Letter of Aristeas and the Cultural Context of the Septuagint," in *Die Septuaginta – Texte, Kontexte, Lebenswelten,* edited by M. Karrer and W. Kraus, 134–56. WUNT 219. Tübingen: Mohr Siebeck, 2008.

——. *Rethinking the Other in Antiquity.* Martin Classical Lectures. Princeton: Princeton University Press, 2011.

——. "Cicero and the Alien," in *Roman Literature, Gender and Reception,* edited by D. Lateiner, B.K. Gold, and J. Perkins, 13–27. New York: Routledge, 2013.

Grunauer-von Hoerschelmann, S. *Die Munzprägung der Lakedaimonier.* Berlin: De Gruyter, 1978.

Gudeman, A. "Lysimachos," RE 14 (1928): 32–39.

Gutman, Y. "Philo the Epic Poet," *Scripta Hierosolymitana* 1 (1954): 36–63.

——. *The Beginnings of Jewish-Hellenistic Literature [ha-Sifrut ha-Yehudit-ha-Helenistit lifnei tekufat ha-hashmonaim]* 2 vols. Jerusalem. [Hebrew]. Jerusalem: Bialik, 1958–1963.

Gutschmid, A. von, *Kleine Schriften,* vol. 4. Leipzig: Teubner, 1893.

Haaland, G. "Jewish Laws for a Roman Audience: Toward an Understanding of *Contra Apionem,*" in *Internationales Josephus-Kolloquium Brüssel 1998,* edited by J.U. Kalms and F. Siegert, 282–304. MJSt 4. Münster: LIT, 1999.

Habicht, C. "Hellenismus und Judentum in der Zeit des Judas Makkabäus," *Jhrb. Heid. Akad.* (1974): 97–104.

——. *2 Makkabäerbuch.* Jüdische Schriften aus hellenistisch-römischer Zeit, vol. 1, part 3. Gütersloh: G.Mohn, 1976a.

——. "Royal Documents in Maccabees II," *HSCP* 80 (1976b): 1–18.

Hadas, M. "Aristeas and III Maccabees," *HTR* 42 (1949): 175–84.

——. *Aristeas to Philocrates.* Dropsie College Series. New York: Harper, 1951.

——. *The Third and Fourth Books of Maccabees.* Dropsie College Series. New York: Harper, 1953.

Hagedorn, D. and P.J. Sijpesteijn, "Die Stadtviertel von Herakleopolis," *ZPE* 65 (1986): 101–105.

Hägg, T. *The Novel in Antiquity*. Oxford: Basil Blackwell, 1983.

——. "Orality, Literacy and the "Readership" of the Early Greek Novel," in *Contexts of Pre-Novel Narrative: The European Tradition*, edited by R. Eriksen, 47–81. Berlin: De Gruyter, 1994.

Hall, E. "When is a Myth not a Myth? Bernal's 'Ancient Model'," *Arethusa* 25 (1992): 181–201.

Hall, R. G. "Josephus' *Contra Apionem* and Historical Inquiry in the Roman Rhetorical Schools," in *Josephus' Contra Apionem: Studies in its Character and Context*, edited by L.H. Feldman and J.R. Levison, 229–249. Leiden: Brill, 1996.

Halpern-Amaru, B. "Land Theology in Josephus' *Jewish Antiquities*," *JQR* 71 (1980/81): 201–229.

——. "Land Theology in Philo and Josephus," in *The Land of Israel: Jewish Perspectives*, edited by L. A. Hoffmann, 65–93. Notre Dame: Center for the Study of Judaism and Christianity, 1986.

——. "Exile and Return in Jubilees," in *Exile: Old Testament, Jewish, and Christian Conceptions*, edited by J.M. Scott, 127–144. JSJSup 56. Leiden: Brill, 1997.

Hänlein-Schäfer, H. *Veneratio Augusti: Eine Studie zu den Tempeln des ersten römischen Kaisers*. Archaelogica 39. Rome: Georgio Brettschneider, 1985.

Harker, A. *Loyalty and Dissidence in Roman Egypt: The Case of the Acta Alexandrinorum*. Cambridge: Cambridge University Press, 2008.

Harland, P. A. "Acculturation and Identity in the Diaspora: A Jewish Family and 'Pagan' Guilds at Hierapolis," *JJS* 57 (2006): 222–44.

Harmatta, J. "The Literary Pattern of the Babylonian Edict of Cyrus," *Acta Antiqua* 19 (1971): 217–249.

Harrington, D.J. "Pseudo-Philo," in *The Old Testament Pseudepigrapha*, edited by J.H. Charlesworth, 2.297–377. Garden City, N.Y.: Doubleday, 1985.

Hartman, L.F. and A.A. Di Lella, *The Book of Daniel*. Garden City, N.Y.: Doubleday, 1978.

Hata, G. "The Story of Moses Interpreted within the Context of Anti-Semitism," in *Josephus, Judaism, and Christianity*, edited by L.H. Feldman and G. Hata, 180–97. Leiden: Brill, 1987.

Hayes, J. H., and S. R. Mandell. *The Jewish People in Classical Antiquity from Alexander to Bar Kochba*. Louisville, Ky.: Westminster/ John Knox, 1998.

Hayward, R. "The Jewish Temple at Leontopolis: A Reconsideration," *JJS* 33 (1982): 429–443.

Hecht, R.D. "Philo and Messiah," in *Judaisms and their Messiahs at the Time of the Christian Era*, edited by J. Neusner, W. S. Green, and E. Frerichs, 139–68. Cambridge: Cambridge University Press, 1987.

Hegermann, H. "The Diaspora in the Hellenistic Age," in *The Cambridge History of Judaism* II, edited by W.D. Davies and L. Finkelstein, 115–66. Cambridge: Cambridge University Press, 1989.

Heinemann, I. "The Relationships between the Jewish People and Its Land in Jewish-Hellenistic Literature," *Zion* (1948): 13–14 [Hebrew].

Heinen, H. *Untersuchungen zur hellenistischen Geschichte des 3. Jahrhunderts v. Chr. Zur Geschichte der Zeit des Ptolemaios Keraunos und zum chremonideischen Krieg*. Historia Einzelschriften 20. Wiesbaden: Steiner, 1972.

Hellholm, D. *Apocalypticism in the Mediterranean World and the Near East: Proceedings of the International Colloquium on Apocalypticism, Uppsala August 12–17, 1979*. Tübingen: Mohr Siebeck, 1983.

Hengel, M. *Judaism and Hellenism: Studies in Their Encounter in Palestine during the Early Hellenistic Period.* 2 vols. Philadelphia: Fortress Press, 1974.

——. "Judaism and Hellenism Revisited" in *Hellenism in the Land of Israel,* edited by J.J. Collins and G.E. Sterling, 6–37. Notre Dame, IN: University of Notre Dame Press, 2001.

Henten, J. W. van. *The Maccabean Martyrs as Saviours of the Jewish People: A Study of 2 and 4 Maccabees.* JSJSup 57. Leiden: Brill, 1997.

Henten, J.-W. van and R. Abusch, "The Jews as Typhonians and Josephus' Strategy of Refutation in *Contra Apionem,*" in *Josephus'* Contra Apionem: *Studies in its Character and Context,* edited by L.H. Feldman and J.R. Levison, 271–309. Leiden: Brill, 1996.

Herholt, V. *Antisemitismus in der Antike.* Mörlenbach: Computus, 2009.

Heubner, H. and W. Fauth, *P. Cornelius Tacitus: Die Historien Band V: Fünftes Buch.* Heidelberg: Carl Winter-Universitätsverlag, 1982.

Himmelfarb, M. "Judaism and Hellenism in 2 Maccabees," *Poetics Today* 19 (1998): 19–40.

Hirsch, S.A. "The Temple of Onias," *Jews' College Jubilee Volume* (1906): 39–80.

Holladay, C.R. *Theios Aner in Hellenistic Judaism: A Critique of the Use of This Category in New Testament Christology.* SBLDS 40. Missoula: Scholars Press, 1977.

——. *Fragments from Hellenistic Jewish Authors: Vol. I: Historians.* Chico, CA.: Scholars Press, 1983.

——. *Fragments from Hellenistic Jewish Authors: Vol. II: The Poets.* Atlanta: Scholars Press, 1989.

——. "Jewish Responses to Hellenistic Culture in Early Ptolemaic Egypt," in *Ethnicity in Hellenistic Egypt,* edited by P. Bilde, 139–163. Aarhus: Aarhaus University Press, 1992.

——. *Fragments from Hellenistic Jewish Authors,* Vol. III: *Aristobulus.* Atlanta: Scholars Press, 1995.

——. *Fragments from Hellenistic Jewish Authors.* Volume IV: *Orphica.* Atlanta: Scholars Press, 1996.

Holleaux, M. *Études d'épigraphie et d'histoire grecques* I-VI . Paris: Librarie d'Amerique et d'Orient Adrien Maisonneuve, 1952–1968.

Honig, B. "Ruth, the Model Emigrée: Mourning and the Symbolic Politics of Immigration," in *Ruth and Esther,* ed. A. Brenner, 50–74. A Feminist Companion to the Bible Second Series 3. Sheffield: Sheffield Academic, 1999.

Honigman, S. "The Jewish Politeuma at Heracleopolis," SCI 22 (2002): 251–266.

——. *The Septuagint and Homeric Scholarship in Alexandria: A Study in the Narrative of the Letter of Aristeas.* London: Taylor & Francis, 2003.

Hopkins, K. *Conquerors and Slaves.* Sociological Studies in Roman History 1. Cambridge: Cambridge University Press, 1978.

Horbury, W. and D. Noy. *Jewish Inscriptions of Graeco-Roman Egypt: With an Index of the Jewish Inscriptions of Egypt and Cyrenaica.* Cambridge: Cambridge University Press, 1992.

Hornblower, J. *Hieronymus of Cardia.* Oxford: Oxford University Press, 1981.

Howard, G.E. "The Letter of Aristeas and Diaspora Judaism," *JTS* 22 (1971): 337–48.

Humphrey, E. *Joseph and Aseneth.* Sheffield: Sheffield Academic Press, 2000.

Hunter, R. "Ancient Readers," in *The Cambridge Companion to the Greek and Roman Novel,* edited by T. Whitmarsh, 261–271. Cambridge: Cambridge University Press, 2008.

Hurley, Donna *A Historical and Historiographical Commentary on Suetonius' Life of C. Caligula.* American Classical Studies 32. Atlanta: Scholars Press, 1993.

Huss, W. "Zu den Ursprüngen des antiken Antijudaismus," in *Geschehen und Gedächtnis: Die hellenistische Welt und ihre Wirkung,* edited by J.-F. Eckholt, M. Sigismund, and S. Sigismund, 161–176. Münster: LIT, 2009.

Ilan, T. *Jewish Women in Greco-Roman Palestine: An Inquiry into Image and Status.* Tübingen: Mohr Siebeck, 1995.

Isaac, B. *The Invention of Racism in Classical Antiquity.* Princeton: Princeton University Press, 2004.

——. "The Ancient Mediterranean and the pre-Christian Era," in *Antisemitism: A History,* edited by A.S. Lindemann and R.S. Levy, 34–46. Oxford: Oxford University Press, 2010.

Isaac, J. *Genèse de l'antisémitisme.* Paris: Calmann-Lévy, 1956.

Jacobson, D. M. "King Herod's 'Heroic' Public Image," *Revue Biblique* 95 (1988): 386–403.

——. "Three Roman Client Kings: Herod of Judaea, Archelaus of Cappadocia and Juba of Mauretania," PEQ 133 (2001): 22–38.

Jacobson, H. "Hermippus, Pythagoras, and the Jews," *REJ* 135 (1976): 145–49.

——. *The Exagoge of Ezekiel.* Cambridge: Cambridge University Press, 1983.

——. *A Commentary on Pseudo-Philo's Liber Antiquitatum Biblicarum,* 2 vol. Leiden: Brill, 1996.

——. "*Artapanus Judaeus,*" *JJS* 57 (2006): 210–221.

Jacoby, F. "Hekataios," *RE* 7.2 (1912): 2667–2750.

——. *Die Fragmente der griechischen Historiker.* Leiden: Brill, 1943.

Jaeger, W. "Greeks and Jews: The First Greek Records of Jewish Religion and Civilization," *Journal of Religion* 18 (1938a): 127–43.

——. *Diokles von Karystos: die griechische Medizin und die Schule des Aristoteles.* Berlin: De Gruyter, 1938b.

James, M.R. *The Biblical Antiquities of Philo.* 2nd ed. New York: Ktav, 1971.

Jeanmaire, H. *La Sibylle et la retour de l'âge d'Or.* Paris: E. Leroux, 1939.

Jellicoe, S. "The Occasion and Purpose of the Letter of Aristeas: A Reexamination," *NTS* 12 (1965/66): 144–50.

——. *The Septuagint and Modern Study.* Oxford: Clarendon Press, 1968.

Jeremias, J. *Jerusalem in the Time of Jesus.* Philadelphia: Fortress Press, 1969.

Jobes, K.H. *The Alpha-Text of Esther: Its Character and Relationship to the Masoretic Text.* SBLDS 153. Atlanta: Scholars Press, 1996.

Johnson, S. R. *Historical Fictions and Hellenistic Jewish Identity: Third Maccabees in Its Cultural Context.* Hellenistic Culture and Society 43. Berkeley: University of California Press, 2004.

Jones, A.H.M. *The Herods of Judea.* Oxford: Clarendon Press, 1938.

Jones, C. P. *Kinship Diplomacy in the Ancient World.* Revealing Antiquity 12. Cambridge: Harvard University Press, 1999.

Jones, K. R. "The Figure of Apion in Josephus," *JSJ* 36 (2005): 278–315.

Juster, J. *Les juifs dans l'empire romain,* 2 vols. Paris: Librairie Paul Geuther, 1914.

Kahrstedt, U. *Syrische Territorien in hellenistischer Zeit.* Berlin: Weidmann, 1926.

Kasher, A. "The Propaganda Goals of Manetho's Accusations in the Matter of the Low Origins of the Jews," in *Studies in the History of the Jewish People and the Land of Israel* v.3, edited by B. Oded et al. 69–84. Haifa, 1974 [Hebrew].

——. "Jerusalem as 'Metropolis' in Philo's National Consciousness," *Cathedra* 11 (1979): 45–56 [Hebrew].

——. "Jewish Emigration and Settlement in Diaspora in the Hellenistic-Roman Period" in *Emigration and Settlement in Jewish and General History*, edited by A. Shinan, 65–91. Jerusalem: Zalman shazat Center, 1982 [Hebrew].

——. *The Jews in Hellenistic and Roman Egypt:The Struggle for Equal Rights*. TSAJ 7. Tübingen: Mohr Siebeck, 1985.

——. *Jews and Hellenistic Cities in Eretz-Israel*. Tübingen: Mohr Siebeck, 1990.

——. "Political and National Connections Between the Jews of Ptolemaic Egypt and their Bretheren in Eretz Israel," in *Eretz Israel, Israel and the Jewish Diaspora: Mutual Relations*, edited by M. Mor, 24–41. Lanham: University Press of America, 1991.

——. "Synagogues as 'Houses of Prayer' and 'Holy Places' in the Jewish Communities of Hellenistic and Roman Egypt," in: *Ancient Synagogues: Historical Analysis and Archaeological Discovery*, edited by D. Urman and P.V.M. Flesher, I.205–225. StPB 47/1. Leiden: Brill, 1995.

——. "Polemic and Apologetic Methods of Writing in *Contra Apionem*," in *Josephus' Contra Apionem: Studies in its Character and Context with a Latin Concordance to the Portion Missing in Greek*, edited by L. H. Feldman and J. R. Levinson, 143–186. Leiden: Brill, 1996.

Katzoff, R. "Jonathan and Late Sparta," *AJPh* 106 (1985): 485–89.

Kaufmann, Y. *Exile and Estrangement: A Socio-Historical Study on the Issue of the Fate of the Nation of Israel from Ancient Times Until the Present*, 2 vols. Tel Aviv: Dvir, 1962 [Hebrew].

Kee, H.C. "The Socio-Cultural Setting of Joseph and Aseneth," *NTS* 229 (1983): 394–413.

Keil, V. "Onias III – Märtyrer oder Templegründer?" *ZAW* 97 (1985): 221–33.

Kennell, N.M. *The Gymnasium of Virtue: Education and Culture in Ancient Sparta*. Chapel Hill: University of North Carolina Press, 1995.

Kerkeslager, A. "Jewish Pilgrimage and Jewish Identity in Hellenistic and Early Roman Egypt," in *Pilgrimage and Holy Space in Late Antique Egypt*, edited by D. Frankfurter, 99–225. RGRW 134. Leiden: Brill, 1998.

——. "The Absence of Dionysios, Lampo, and Isidoros from the Violence in Alexandria in 38 C.E," *SPhilA* 17 (2005): 49–94.

Klauck, H.-J. "4 Makkabäerbuch," *JSHRZ* 3.6 (1989): 645–763.

Knauf, E. A. *Ismael. Untersuchungen zur Geschichte Palästinas und Nordarabiens im 1 Jahrtausend v. Chr.* Wiesbaden: Abhandlungen des deutschen Palästinavereins, 1985.

Kocsis, E. "Ost-West Gegensatz in den jüdischen Sibyllinen," *Novum Testamentum* 5 (1962): 105–10.

Koenen, L. "Die Prophezeiungen des 'Töpfers'," *ZPE* 2 (1968): 178–209.

Kokkinos, N. *The Herodian Dynasty: Origins, Role in Society and Eclipse*. JSPSup 30. Sheffield: Sheffield Academic Press, 1998.

Koskenniemi, E. "Greeks, Egyptians, and Jews in the Fragments of Artapanus," *JSP* 13 (2002): 17–31.

Kossmann, R. *Die Esthernovelle vom Erzählten zur Erzählung: Studien zur Traditons- und Redaktionsgeschichte des Estherbuches*. VT Sup 79. Leiden: Brill, 2000.

Kraabel, A.T. "Unity and Diversity among Diaspora Synagogues," in *The Synagogue in Late Antiquity*, edited by L. Levine, 49–60. Philadelphia: American Schools of Oriental Research, 1987.

Kraemer, R.S. "On the Meaning of the Term "Jew" in Greco-Roman Inscriptions," *HTR* 82 (1989): 35–53.

—. "Jewish Tuna and Christian Fish: Identifying Religious Affiliation in Epigraphic Sources," *HTR* 84 (1991): 141–62.

—. *When Aseneth Met Joseph: A Late Antique Tale of the Biblical Patriarch and His Egyptian Wife.* Oxford: Oxford University Press, 1998.

Kreuzer, S. "Entstehung und Publikation der Septuagint im Horizont frühptolemäischer Bildungs- und Kulturpolitik," in *Im Brennpunkt: Die Septuaginta. Studien zur Entstehung und Bedeutung der Griechischen Bibel* II, edited by S. Kreuzer and J. Lesch. BWANT 161. Stuttgart: Kohlhammer, 2004.

Kugler, R. "Hearing the Story of Moses in Ptolemaic Egypt: Artapanus Accommodates the Tradition," in *The Wisdom of Egypt: Jewish, Early Christian, and Gnostic Essays in Honour of Gerard P. Luttikhuizen,* edited by A. Hilhorst and G. H. van Kooten, 67–80. Leiden: Brill, 2005.

Kuhrt, A. "The Cyrus Cylinder and Achaemenid Imperial Policy," *JSOT* 25 (1983): 83–97.

—. "Nabonidus and the Babylonian Priesthood," in *Pagan Priests: Religion and Power in the Ancient World,* edited by M. Beard and J. North, 117–155. Ithaca: Cornell University Press, 1990.

A. Kuhrt, A. and S. Sherwin-White, *Hellenism in the East: The Interaction of Greek and Non-Greek Civilizations from Syria to Central Asia after Alexander.* Berkeley: University of California Press, 1987.

Kurfess, A. *Sibyllinische Weissagungen.* Berlin: Tusculum, 1951.

LaCocque, A. *The Feminine Unconventional: Four Subversive Figures in Israel's Tradition.* Minneapolis: Fortress Press, 1990.

—. *Ruth: A Continental Commentary.* Minneapolis: Fortress Press, 2004.

Lane, E.N. "Sabazius and the Jews in Valerius Maximus: A Re-examination," *JRS* 69 (1979): 35–38.

Laqueur, R. "Manetho," *RE* 14 (1928): 1060–1101.

Le Bohec, Y. "Inscriptions Juives et Judaisantes de l'Afrique Romaine," *AA* 17 (1981): 165–207.

Lebram, J.C.H. "Die literarische Form des vierten Makkabäerbuches," *VC* 28 (1974): 81–96.

Letronne, M. *Lettres a M. Letrone: Les Papyrus Bilingues et Grecs, et sur Quelques Autres Monumens Gréco-Egyptiens.* I-VII. A Leide: Musée D'Antiquités de Université de Leide, 1830.

Levenson, J.D. *Esther.* Louisville: Westminster John Knox, 1997.

—. "The Universal Horizon of Biblical Particularism," in *Ethnicity and the Bible,* edited by M.G. Brett, 143–169. BIS 19. Leiden: Brill, 1996.

Lévi, I. "La dispute entre les Égyptiens et les Juifs," *REJ* 63 (1912): 211–215.

Levi, Y. "Cicero on the Jews," *Zion* 7 (1942): 109–34.

Levine, A. -J. "Sacrifice and Salvation: Otherness and Domestication in the Book of Judith," in *"No One Spoke Ill of Her": Essays on Judith,* edited by J. C. VanderKam, 17–30. Atlanta: Scholars Press, 1992.

Levine, E. "The Jews in Time and Space," in *Diaspora: Exile and the Contemporary Jewish Condition,* edited by E. Levine, New York: Shapolsky Books, 1986.

Levine, L. *Judaism and Hellenism in Antiquity.* Seattle: University of Washington Press, 1998.

—. *The Ancient Synagogue: The First Thousand Years.* New Haven: Yale University Press, 2000.

Levine, M.M. "Multiculturalism and the Classics," *Arethusa* 25 (1992): 215–220.

—. "The Use and Abuse of Black Athena," *AHR* 97 (1992): 440–464.

Levine, M.M. and J. Peradotto "The Challenge of 'Black Athena'" special issue *Arethusa* 22.1 1989.

Levinskaya, I. *The Book of Acts in Its Diaspora Setting*. Grand Rapids: Eerdmans, 1996.

Lévy, I. "Tacite et l'origine du peuple juif," *Latomus* 5 (1946): 331–340.

Lewis, D.M.L. "The First Greek Jew," *JSS* 2 (1957): 264–66.

Lewy, H. "Aristotle and the Jewish Sage According to Clearchus of Soli," *HTR* 31 (1938): 216–21.

Lewy, Y. "Tacitus on the Jews," in *Binah*, vol. 1: *Studies in Jewish History*, edited by J. Dan, 15–46. New York: Praeger, 1989.

Lichtenberger, A. *Die Baupolitik Herodes des Grossen*. Wiesbaden: Harrassowitz = Abhandlungen des deutschen Palästina-Vereins, 1999.

Lloyd-Jones, H. and P. Parsons, *Supplementum Hellenisticum* Berlin: De Gruyter, 1983.

Luria, B.Z. "Mihu honio?" *Beit Miqra* (1967): 65–81 [Hebrew].

Mahaffy, J.P. and J.G. Smyly. *The Flinders Petrie Papyri III*. Dublin: The Royal Irish Academy, 1905.

Marasco, G. *Sparta agli inizi dell'età ellenistica: Ilregno di Areo I*. Florence: Cooperativa Editrice Universita, 1980.

Marshall, A.J. "Flaccus and the Jews of Asia (Cicero, *Pro Flacco* 28.67–69)," *Phoenix* 29 (1975): 139–54.

Mason, S. "The *Contra Apionem* in Social and Literary Context: An Invitation to Judean Philosophy," in *Josephus'* Contra Apionem: *Studies in its Character and Context with a Latin Concordance to the Portion Missing in Greek*, edited by L. H. Feldman and J. R. Levinson, 187–228. Leiden: Brill, 1996.

——. *Flavius Josephus, Translation and Commentary*, Volume 1B; *The Judean War 2*. Leiden: Brill, 2008.

McCown, C.C. "Hebrew and Egyptian Apocalyptic Literature," *HTR* 18 (1925): 357–411.

Meecham, H.G. *The Letter of Aristeas: A Linguistic Study with Special References to the Greek Bible*. Manchester: Manchester University Press, 1935.

Meisner, N. "Aristeasbrief," *JSHRZ* 2.1 (1973): 35–87.

Mélèze-Modrzejewski, J. "L'Image du Juif dans la pensée grecque vers 300 avant notre ère," in *Greece and Rome in Eretz Israel: Collected Essays*, edited by A. Kasher, et al., 105–18. Jerusalem: Yad Izhak Ben-Zvi, 1990.

——. "How to Be a Greek and Yet a Jew in Hellenistic Alexandria," in *Diasporas in Antiquity*, edited by S.J.D. Cohen and E.S. Frerichs, 65–92. BJSt 288. Atlanta: Scholars Press, 1993.

——. "La détention des en Egypte au premier millénaire avant J.-C.," *RevHistDroit* 72 (1994): 193–202.

——. *The Jews of Egypt: From Rameses II to Emperor Hadrian*. Philadelphia: The Jewish Publication Society, 1995.

——. "The Exodus Traditions: Parody or Parallel Version?" *Jewish History*, 12 (1998): 133–136.

Mellor, R. *Tacitus*. London and New York: Routledge, 1993.

Mendels, D. "'On Kingship' in the 'Temple' Scroll and the Ideological Vorlage of the Seven Banquets in the 'Letter of Aristeas to Philocrates,'" *Aegyptus* 59 (1979): 127–136.

——. "Hecataeus of Abdera and a Jewish *patrios politeia* of the Persian Period (Diodorus Siculus XL, 3)," *ZAW* 95 (1983): 96–110.

——. *The Land of Israel as a Political Concept in Hasmonean Literature*. Tübingen: Mohr Siebeck, 1987.

——. "Creative History in the Hellenistic Near East in the Third and Second Centuries BCE: The Jewish Case," *JSP* 2 (1988): 13–20.

——. "The Polemical Character of Manetho's *Aegyptiaca*," *Studia Hellenistica* 30 (1990): 91–110.

——. *The Rise and Fall of Jewish Nationalism: Jewish and Christian Ethnicity in Ancient Palestine*. New York: Doubleday, 1992.

Mendelson, A. *Secular Education in Philo of Alexandria*. Cincinnati: Hebrew Union College Press, 1982.

Meyer, E. *Aegyptische Chronologie*. Berlin: Abhandlungen der Konigl. Preuss. Akademie der Wissenchaften, 1904.

Michell, H. *Sparta*. Cambridge: Cambridge University Press, 1952.

Milikowsky, C. "Notions of Exile, Subjugation, and Return in Rabbinic Literature," in *Exile: Old Testament, Jewish, and Christian Conceptions*, edited by J.M. Scott, 266–78. JSJSup 56. Leiden: Brill, 1997.

Millar, F. "The Background to the Maccabean Revolution: Reflections on Martin Hengel's 'Judaism and Hellenism,'" *JJS* 29 (1978): 1–21.

——. "Hagar, Ishmael, Josephus, and the Origins of Islam," *JJS* 44 (1993): 23–45.

Miranda, E. "La comunità giudaica di Hierapolis di Frigia," *Epigraphica Anatolica* 31 (1999): 109–55.

Momigliano, A. *Prime linee di storia della tradizione maccabaica*. Rome: Società Editrice del "Foro Italico", 1930.

——. "Intorno al *Contro Apione*," *Rivista di Filologia* 59 (1931): 485–503.

——. *Giudea Romano*. Amsterdam: Hakkert, 1967, first published Bologna, 1934.

——. " The Second Book of Maccabees," *CP* 70 (1975a): 81–88.

——. *Alien Wisdom: The Limits of Hellenization*. Cambridge: Cambridge University Press, 1975b.

——. "Flavius Josephus and Alexandre's Visit to Jerusalem," *Athenaeum* 57 (1979): 442–8.

——. *Sesto contributo alla storia degli studi classici e del mondo antico*, V.II. Rome: Edizioni de Storia e Letteratura, 1980.

——. *Settimo contributo alla storia degli studi classici e del mondo antico*. Rome: Edizioni de Storia e Letteratura, 1984.

——. *Essays on Ancient and Modern Judaism*, edited and with an Introduction by S. Berti and translated by M. Masella-Gayley. Chicago: University of Chicago Press, 1994.

Moore, C.A. *Daniel, Esther, and Jeremiah: The Additions*. AB 44. Garden City: Doubleday, 1977.

——. *Judith: A New Translation with Introduction and Commentary*. AB 40. Garden City: Doubleday, 1985.

——. *Tobit: A New Translation with Introduction and Commentary*. AB 40 A. Garden City: Doubleday, 1996.

Moreau, J. "Le troisième livre des Maccabées," *ChrEg* 16 (1941): 111–22.

Moretti, L. *Iscrizioni storiche ellenistiche* V.I. Florence: La nuova Italia, 1967.

Mørkholm, O. *Studies in the Coinage of Antiochus IV of Syria*. Copenhagen: Munksgaard, 1963.

——. *Antiochus IV of Syria*. Copenhagen: Gyldendal, 1966.

Morris, J. "The Jewish Philosopher Philo," in *The History of the Jewish People in the Age of Jesus Christ*, edited by E. Schürer and G. Vermes, III.2:809–889. Edinburgh: T&T Clark, 1987.

Motzo, B. "Il κατὰ Ἰουδαίων di Apione," *Atti della R. Accademia delle scienze di Torino* 48 (1912–13): 459–468.

Murphy, F.J. "Divine Plan, Human Plan: A Structuring Theme in Pseudo-Philo," *JQR* 77 (1986): 5–14.

——. *Pseudo-Philo: Rewriting the Bible.* Oxford: Oxford University Press, 1993.

Murray, O. "Aristeas and Ptolemaic Kingship," *JTS* 18 (1967): 337–371.

——. "Hecataeus of Abdera and Pharaonic Kingship," *JEA* 56 (1970): 141–171.

Mussies, G. "The Interpretatio Judaica of Thoth-Hermes," in *Studies in Egyptian Religion: Dedicated to Professor Jan Zandee,* edited by M. Voss, 87–120. Leiden: Brill, 1982.

Myers, J.M. *I and II Esdras.* AB 42. Garden City: Doubleday, 1974.

Netzer, E. "Herod's Building Program: State Necessity or Personal Need?" *Jerusalem Cathedra* 1 (1981): 484–61.

——. *The Palaces of the Hasmoneans and Herod the Great.* Jerusalem: Yad Ben-Zvi Press, 2001.

Neusner, J. *Sifre to Deuteronomy: An Analytical Translation.* Atlanta: Scholars Press, 1987a.

——. *Self-Fulfilling Prophecy: Exile and Return in the History of Judaism.* Boston: Beacon Press, 1987b.

——. "Exile and Return as the History of Judaism," in *Exile: Old Testament, Jewish, and Christian Conceptions,* edited by J. M. Scott, 221–238. Leiden: Brill, 1997.

Newsome, J.D. *Greeks, Romans, Jews: Currents of Culture and Belief in the New Testament World.* Philadelphia: Trinity Press International, 1992.

Nickelsburg, G.W.E. "Good and Bad Leaders in Pseudo-Philo's Liber Antiquitatum Biblicarum," in *Ideal Figures in Ancient Judaism: Profiles and Paradigms,* edited by G.W.E. Nickelsburg and J.J. Collins, 49–65. SBLSCS 12. Chico & Michigan: Scholars Press, 1980.

——. *Jewish Literature Between the Bible and Mishnah: A Historical and Literary Introduction.* Philadelphia: Fortress Press, 1981. [2nd ed. 2005].

——. *1 Enoch 1: A Commentary on the Book of 1 Enoch, Chapters 1–36; 81–108.* Minneapolis: Fortress Press, 2001.

Niehoff, Maren. *Philo on Jewish Identity and Culture.* TSAJ 86. Tübingen: Mohr Siebeck, 2001.

Nikiprowetzky, V. *La Troisème Sibylle.* Paris: Mouton, 1970.

——. "La Sibylle juive depuis Charles Alexandre," *ANRW* (1987) II.20.I: 460–542.

Nirenberg, D. *Anti-Judaism: The Western Tradition.* New York: Norton & Company, 2013.

Nock, A.D. *Conversion: The Old and the New in Religion from Alexander the Great to Augustine of Hippo.* Oxford: Oxford University Press, 1933.

Nolland, J. "Proselytism or Politics in Horace, *Satires,* I,4,143?" *Vigiliae Christianae* 33 (1979): 347–355.

——. "*Sib. Or.* III. 265–94, An Early Maccabean Messianic Oracle," *JTS* 30 (1979): 158–66.

Norden, E. *Die antike Kunstprosa vom VI Jahrhundert v. Chr. bis in die Zeit der Renaissance.* Leipzig: Teubner, 1923.

North, C.R. *The Second Isaiah.* Oxford: Clarendon, 1964.

Noy, D. "The Jewish Communities of Leontopolis and Venosa," in *Studies in Early Jewish Epigraphy,* edited by J.W. van Henten and P.W. van der Horst, 162–88. AGJU 21. Leiden: Brill, 1994.

Noy, D., H. Bloedhorn, and A. Panayotov. *Inscriptiones Judaicae Orientis,* vol. 1: *Eastern Europe.* TSAJ 101. Tübingen: Mohr Siebeck, 2004.

Noy, D. and H. Bloedhorn. *Inscriptiones Judaicae Orientis*, vol. 3: *Syria and Cyprus*. TSAJ 102. Tübingen: Mohr Siebeck, 2004.

Oilier, F. *Le mirage spartiate: étude sur l'idéalisation de Sparte dans l'antiquité grecque du début de l'école cynique jusqu'à la fin de la cité*, 2 vols. Annales de l'Université de Lyon. Troisième série, Lettres 13. Paris: E. de Boccard, 1933–43.

O'Gorman, E. *Irony and Misreading in the Annals of Tacitus*. Cambridge: Cambridge University Press, 2000.

Oliva, P. *Sparta and Her Social Problems*. Amsterdam: Hakkert, 1971.

Orlin, E. M. *Foreign Cults in Rome: Creating a Roman Empire*. Oxford: Oxford University Press, 2010.

Orlinsky, H.M. "The Septuagint as Holy Writ and the Philosophy of the Translators," *HUCA* 46 (1975): 89–114.

Orrieux, Cl. "La 'parenté' entre juifs et spartiates," in *L'étranger dans le monde grec: Actes du colloque organisé par l'Institut d'Études Anciennes*, edited by R. Lonis, 169–91. Nancy: Presses Universitaires de Nancy, 1987.

Orth, "Ptolemaios II. und die Septuaginta-Übersetzung," in *Im Brennpunkt: Die Septuaginta. Studien zur Entstehung und Bedeutung der Griechischen Bibel* I, edited by H.-J. Fabry and U. Offerhaus, 107–114. BWANT 153. Stuttgart: Kohlhammer, 2001.

Otto, W. *Zur Geschichte der Zeit des 6 Ptolemäers. Ein Beitrag zur Politik und zum Staatsrecht des Hellenismus*. München: Akademie der Wissenschaften, 1934.

Ozick, C. "Ruth," in *Reading Ruth: Contemporary Women Reclaim a Sacred Story*, edited by J.A. Kates and G. Twersky, 211–232. New York: Ballantine, 1994.

Parente, F. "La lettera di Aristea come Fonte pen la storia del Giudaismo Alessandrino durante la prima meta del I secolo a. C.," *Annali della Scuola Normale Superiore di Pisa*, 2, *Classe di Lettere e Filosofa*. 2.1 (1972): 177–237; 2.2 (1972) 517–567, 182–190.

——. "The Third Book of Maccabees as Ideological Document and Historical Source," *Henoch* 10 (1988): 143–82.

——. "Le témoignage de Théodore de Mopsueste sur le sort d'Onias III et la fondation du temple de Léontopolis," *REJ* 154 (1995): 429–436.

Parente, F. and J. Sievers, *Josephus and the History of the Greco-Roman Period: Essays in Honor of Morton Smith*. Leiden: Brill, 1994.

Parke, H. W. *Sibyls and Sibylline Prophecy in Classical Antiquity*. London and N.Y.: Routledge, 1988.

Pastor, J. "Herod: King of Jews and Gentiles: Economic Policy as a Measure of Evenhandedness," in *Jews and Gentiles in the Holy Land*, edited by M. Mor, A. Oppenheimer, J. Pastor, and D.R. Schwartz, 152–164. Jerusalem: Yad Ben-Zvi Press, 2003.

Paul, A. "Le troisième livre des Macchabées," *ANRW* II.20.1 (1987): 298–336.

Pearce, S. "Belonging and Not Belonging: Local Perspectives in Philo of Alexandria," in *Jewish Local Patriotism and Self Identification in the Graeco-Roman Period*, edited by S. Jones and S. Pearce, 79–105. Sheffield: Sheffield Academic Press, 1998.

——. *The Land and the Body: Studies in Philo's Representation of Egypt*. WUNT 208. Tübingen: Mohr Siebeck, 2007.

Pelletier, A. *Lettre d'Aristée à Philocrate*. Paris: Cerf, 1962.

Peretti, A. *La Sibilla babilonese nella propaganda ellenistica*. Biblioteca di Cultura 21. Florence: La Nuova Italia Editrice, 1943.

Perrot, C. and P.-M. Bogaert, *Pseudo-Philon, Les Antiquités Bibliques*. Paris: Cerf, 1976.

Pervo, R. "Joseph and Asenath and the Greek Novel," *Society for Biblical Literature 1976 Seminar Paper Series*, edited by G. MacRae, 171–181. Missoula: Scholars Press, 1976.
——. "Aseneth and her Sisters: Women in Jewish Narrative and in the Greek Novels," in *'Women Like This': New Perspectives on Jewish Women in the Greco-Roman World*, edited by A.J. Levine, 145–160. Early Judaism, and Its Literature 1. Atlanta: Scholars Press, 1991.
Petuchowski, J.J. "Diaspora Judaism–An Abnormality," *Judaism* 9 (1960): 17–28.
Pfeiffer, R.H. *History of New Testament Times and an Introduction to the Apocrypha*. New York: Harper, 1949.
Philonenko, M. *Joseph et Aséneth, Introduction, texte critique, traduction et notes*. StPB 13. Leiden: Brill, 1968.
Piper, L.J. *Spartan Twilight*. New Rochelle: Caratzas, 1986.
Plass, P. *Wit and the Writing of History: The Rhetoric of Historiography in Imperial Rome*. Madison: Wisconsin University Press, 1988.
Pohlmann, K.F. *Studien zum dritten Ezra*. Göttingen: Vandenhoeck & Ruprecht, 1970.
Porten, B. *Archives from Elephantine: The Life of an Ancient Jewish Military Colony*. Berkeley: University of California Press, 1968.
Potter, D. *Prophets and Emperors: Human and Divine Authority from Augustus to Theodosius*. Cambridge: Harvard University Press, 1994.
Pressler, C. *Joshua, Judges, and Ruth*. Louisville: Westminster John Knox, 2002.
Price, J. "The Jewish Diaspora of the Graeco-Roman Period," *SCI* 13 (1994): 169–86.
Price, S. *Rituals and Power: The Roman Imperial Cult in Asia Minor*. Cambridge: Cambridge University Press, 1984.
Pritchard, J.B. *The Ancient Near East: An Anthology of Texts and Pictures*. Princeton: Princeton University Press, 1958.
Pucci Ben Zeev, M. "The Reliability of Josephus Flavius: The Case of Hecataeus' and Manetho's Accounts of Jews and Judaism," *JSJ* 24 (1993): 215–34.
——. "Greek and Roman documents from Republican Times in the *Antiquities:* What was Josephus' source? *SCI* 13 (1994): 46–59.
——. *Jewish Rights in the Roman World: The Greek and Roman Documents Quoted by Josephus Flavius*. Tübingen: Mohr Siebeck, 1998.
Rad, G. von. *Genesis: A Commentary*. Translated by J. Marks. Philadelphia: Westminster, 1972.
Rajak, T. *The Jewish Dialogue with Greece and Rome: Studies in Social and Cultural Interaction*. Leiden: Brill, 2001.
——. "An invitation from Ptolemy; Aristeas, Alciphron, and Collective Memory," in *For Uriel: Studies in the History of Israel in Antiquity Presented to Professor Uriel Rappaport*, eds. M. Mor, J. Pastor, I. Ronen, and Y. Ashkenazi, 145–164. Jerusalem: Zalman Shazar Center for Jewish History, 2005.
——. *Translation and Survival: The Greek Bible of the Ancient Jewish Diaspora*. Oxford: Oxford University Press, 2009.
Rappaport, U. "Les Iduméens en Egypte," *RevPhil* 43 (1969): 73–82.
——. "Relations between the Jews of Eretz-Yisrael and the Jewish Diaspora in the Hellenistic and Hasmonaean Period," *Te'uda* 12 (1996–97) [Hebrew]
Rawson, E. *The Spartan Tradition in European Thought*. Oxford: Oxford University Press, 1969.
Ray, J.D. *The Archive of Hor*. London: Egypt Exploration Society, 1976.

Reardon, B. *The Form of Greek Romance*. Princeton: Princeton University Press, 1991.

Redford, D.B. *Pharaonic King-Lists, Annals, and Day Books: A Contribution to the Study of the Egyptian Sense of History*. Mississauga, Ontario: Benben Pub., 1986.

Reinmuth, E. "'Nicht vergeblich' bei Paulus und Pseudo-Philo, Liber Antiquitatum Biblicarum," *NT* 33 (1991): 97–123.

——. *Pseudo-Philo und Lukas*. WUNT 74. Tübingen: Mohr Siebeck, 1994.

Reinach, T. *Flavius Josèphe, Contre Apion*. Paris: Les Belles Lettres, 1930.

Renehan, R. "The Greek Philosophic Background of Fourth Maccabees," *RhM* 115 (1972) : 223–238.

Retsö, J. *The Arabs in Antiquity: Their History from the Assyrians to the Umayyads*. London: Routledge, 2003.

Ritter, B. *Judeans in the Greek Cities of the Roman Empire: Rights, Citizenship and Civil Discord*. JSJSup 170. Leiden: Brill, 2015.

Ritti, T. "Nuovi dati su una nota epigrafe sepolcrale con stefanotico da Hierapolis di Frigia," *Scienze dell' antichità storia archeologia antropologia* 6–7 (1992–93): 41–68.

Robert, L. *Études épigraphiques et philologiques*. BEHE 272. Paris: E. de Boccard, 1938.

——. "Arsinoè de Kéos," *Hellenica* 11–12 (1960): 146–60.

Robin, P. *L'Ironie chez Tacite*. Paris: Lille, 1973.

Rochette, B. "Juifs et Romains: Y a-t-il eu un antijudaisme romain?" *REJ* 160 (2001): 1–31.

Roddaz, J.-M. *Marcus Agrippa*. BEFAR 253. Rome: École Française de Rome, 1984.

Rokeah, D. "Tacitus and Ancient Antisemitism," *REJ* 154 (1995): 281–294.

Roller, D. W. *The Building Program of Herod the Great*. Berkeley: University of California Press, 1998.

Rosen, K. "Der Historiker als Prophet: Tacitus und die Juden," *Gymnasium* 103 (1996): 107–126.

Rowley, H.H. "The Interpretation and Date of the Sibylline Oracles III 388–400," *ZAW* 44 (1926): 324–7.

——. *Darius the Mede and the Four World Empires in the Book of Daniel* (2nd ed.), Cardiff: University of Wales Press, 1959.

Royse, J. "The Works of Philo," in *The Cambridge Companion to Philo*, edited by A. Kamesar, 32–64. Cambridge: Cambridge University Press, 2009.

Ruether, R. *Faith and Fratricide: The Theological Roots of Antisemitism*. New York: Seabury Press, 1974.

Ruiz-Montero, C. "The Rise of the Greek Novel," in *The Greek Novel in the Ancient World*, edited by G. Schmeling, 29–85. Leiden: Brill, 1996.

Rutgers, L.V. *The Jews in Late Ancient Rome: Evidence of Cultural Interaction in the Roman Diaspora*. RGRW 126. Leiden: Brill, 1995.

——. "Attitudes to Judaism in the Greco-Roman Period: Reflections on Feldman's *Jew and Gentile in the Ancient World*," *JQR* 85 (1995): 361–395.

Rüttersworden, U. "Die persische Reichsautorisation der Thora: Fact or Fiction?" *ZABR* 1 (1995): 47–61.

Rzach, A. "Sibyllinischer Orakel," *RE* (1923): II.A.2:2073–2183.

Safrai, S. "Relations between the Diaspora and the Land of Israel," in *The Jewish People in the First Century: Historical Geography, Political History, Social, Cultural and Religious Life and Institutions.*, edited by S. Safrai and M. Stern, I. 186–91. Philadelphia: Fortress Press, 1974.

——. *Die Wallfahrt im Zeitalter des Zweiten Tempels*. FJCD 3. Neukirchen-Vluyn: Neukirchener Verlag, 1981.

Safrai, S., and M. Stern. *The Jewish People in the First Century*. 2 vols. Philadelphia: Fortress Press, 1974.

Safran, W. "Diasporas in Modern Societies: Myths of Homeland and Return," Diaspora 1 (1991): 83–99.

Sanders, E.P. ed. *Jewish and Christian Self-Definition*. 3 vols. Philadelphia: Fortress Press, 1980–1.

Sands, P. C. *The Client Princes of the Roman Empire under the Republic*. Cambridge: Cambridge University Press, 1908.

Satlow, M.L. "Theophrastus's Jewish Philosophers," *JJS* 59 (2008): 1–20.

Schäfer, P. "The Exodus Tradition in Pagan Greco-Roman Literature," in *The Jews in the Hellenistic-Roman World: Studies in Memory of Menahem Stern*, edited by I. M. Gafni, A. Oppenheimer, and D. R. Schwartz, 9–38. Jerusalem: Zalman Shazar Center for Jewish History, 1996.

——. *Judeophobia: Attitudes toward the Jews in the Ancient World*. Cambridge, Mass.: Harvard University Press, 1997.

Schalit, A. *König Herodes: der Mann und sein Werk*. Berlin: De Gruyter, 2001.

Schaller, B. "Philon von Alexandreia und das 'Heilige Land,'" in *Das Land Israel in biblischer Zeit*, edited by G. Strecker, 172–187. GTA 25. Gottingen: Vandenhoek & Ruprecht, 1983.

Schalles, H.-J. *Untersuchungen zur Kulturpolitik der pergamenischen Herrscher im dritten Jahrhundert vor Christus*. Istanbuler Forschungen 36. Tübingen: Ernst Warmuth, 1985.

Schaublin, C. "Josephus und die Griechen," *Hermes* 110 (1982): 316–341.

Schaudig, H. *Die Inschriften von Nabonids Babylon und Kyros' des Grossen samt den in ihren Umfeld entstandenen Tendenzschriften: Textausgabe und Grammatik*. AOAT 256. Münster: Ugarit-Verlag, 2001.

Scheiber, S. *Jewish Inscriptions in Hungary, from the 3rd Century to 1686*. Leiden: Brill, 1983.

Scheller, M. "σάββω und σαββάτωσις," *Glotta* 34 (1955): 298–300.

Schmitt-Dounas, B. *Geschenke erhalten die Freundschaft: Politik und Selbstdarstellung im Spiegel der Monumente*, Teil II.2. Berlin: Akademie Verlag, 2000.

Schüller, S. "Some Problems Connected with the Supposed Common Ancestry of Jews and Spartans and Their Relations during the Last Three Centuries B.C.," *JSS* 1 (1956): 257–68.

Schüpphaus, J. "Das Verhältnis von LXX- und Theodotion-Text in den apokryphen Zusätzen zum Danielbuch," *ZAW* 83 (1971): 49–72.

Schürer, E. *Geschichte des jüdischen Volkes im Zeitalter Jesu Christi*, II. Leipzig: J.C. Hinrichs, 1886.

——. *The History of the Jewish People in the Age of Jesus Christ (175 B.C.–A. D. 135)* Vol. 3.1. Revised and edited by G. Vermes, F. Millar, and M. Goodman. Edinburgh: T&T Clark, 1986.

Schwartz, D.R. *Agrippa I: The Last King of Judaea*. TSAJ 23. Tubingen: Mohr Siebeck, 1990.

——. "Temple or City: What did Hellenistic Jews See in Jerusalem?" in *The Centrality of Jerusalem: Historical Perspectives*, edited by M. Poorthuis and Ch. Safrai, 114–127. Kampen: Kok Pharos, 1996.

——. "The Jews of Egypt between Onias' Temple, the Jerusalem Temple, and the Heavens," *Zion* 62 (1997): 5–22. [Hebrew]

——. "Diodorus Siculus 40.3—Hecataeus or Pseudo-Hecataeus?" in *Jews and Gentiles in the Holy Land in the Days of the Second Temple, the Mishnah, and the Talmud*, edited by A. Oppenheimer and M. Mor, 181–198. Jerusalem: Yad Ben-Zvi, 2003.

——. "Philo, His Family, and His Times," in *The Cambridge Companion to Philo*, edited by A. Kamesar, 9–31. Cambridge: Cambridge University Press, 2009.

Schwartz, R.M. *The Curse of Cain: The Violent Legacy of Monotheism*. Chicago: University of Chicago Press, 1997.

Schwartz, S. "Gamaliel in Aphrodite's Bath: Palestinian Judaism and Urban Culture in the Third and Fourth Centuries," in *The Talmud Yerushalmi and Graeco-Roman Culture* 3 vols., edited by P. Schäfer, I.203–17. Tübingen: Mohr Siebeck, 1998.

——. *Imperialism and Jewish Society 200 BCE to 640 CE*. Princeton: Princeton University Press, 2001.

Schwyzer, H.R. *Chairemon*. Klassisch-philologische Studien 4. Leipzig: Harrassowitz, 1932.

Scott, J.M. "Philo and the Restoration of Israel," *SBL Seminar Papers* (1995): 553–75.

——. "Exile and the Self-Understanding of Diaspora Jews," in *Exile: Old Testament, Jewish, and Christian Conceptions*, edited by J.M. Scott, 173–218. JSJSup 56. Leiden: Brill, 1997.

Seeligmann, I.L. *The Septuagint Version of Isaiah*. Leiden: Brill, 1948.

Sevenster, J. N. *The Roots of Pagan Anti-Semitism in the Ancient World*. NovTSup 41. Leiden: Brill, 1975.

Shavit, Y. *Athens in Jerusalem: Classical Antiquity and Hellenism in the Making of the Modern Secular Jew*. London: Littman Library of Jewish Civilization, 1997.

Sherwin-White, S. "A Greek Ostracon from Babylon of the Early Third Century B.C.," *ZPE* 47 (1982): 51–70.

Sievers, J. *The Hasmoneans and Their Supporters: From Mattathias to the Death of John Hyrcanus*. Atlanta: Scholars Press, 1990.

Silberstein, L. J. and R. L. Cohn, *The Other in Jewish Thought and History: Constructions of Jewish Culture and Identity*. New York: New York University Press, 1994.

Simcox, C.E. "The Role of Cyrus in Deutero-Isaiah," *JAOS* 57 (1937): 158–171.

Simon, M. *Verus Israel: A Study of the Relations between Christians and Jews in the Roman Empire*. Oxford: Littman Library of Oxford University Press, 1986.

Simpson, C.J. "The Cult of the Emperor Gaius," *Latomus* 40 (1981): 489–511.

Sirat, C. "The Jews," in *Perceptions of the Ancient Greeks*, edited by K. Dover, 54–78. Oxford: Blackwell, 1992.

Skehan, P.W. and A. A Di Lella. *The Wisdom of Ben Sira: A New Translation with Notes*. New York: Doubleday, 1987.

Slingerland, H.D. *Claudian Policymaking and the Early Imperial Repression of Judaism at Rome*. Atlanta: Scholars Press, 1997.

Smallwood, E.M. "The Chronology of Gaius' Attempt to Desecrate the Temple," *Latomus* 16 (1957): 3–17.

——. *Philonis Alexandrini, Legatio ad Gaium*. Leiden: Brill, 1961.

——. *The Jews under Roman Rule from Pompey to Diocletian: A Study in Political Relations*. Leiden: Brill, 1981.

Smith, M. *Palestinian Parties and Politics that Shaped the Old Testament*. New York: Columbia University Press, 1971.

Smith-Christopher, D.L. "The Mixed Marriage Crisis in Ezra 9–10 and Nehemiah 13: A Study of the Sociology of the Post-Exilic Judaean Community," in *Second Temple Studies*, II:

Temple Community in the Persian Period, edited by T. C. Eskenazi and K. H. Richards, II.243 – 65. Sheffield: Sheffield Academic, 1994.

———. *A Biblical Theology of Exile.* Minneapolis: Fortress, 2002.

Speiser, E. A. *Genesis.* AB 1. New York: Doubleday, 1964.

Sperling, A.G. *Apion der Grammatiker und sein Verhältnis zum Judentum.* Dresden: Lehmann, 1886.

Spina, F. A. *The Faith of the Outsider: Exclusion and Inclusion in the Biblical Story.* Grand Rapids, MI: Eerdmans, 2005.

Staden, H. von. "Affinities and Elisions: Helen and Hellenocentrism," *Isis* 83 (1992): 578 – 595.

Standhartinger, A. *Das Frauenbild im Judentum der hellenistischen Zeit: Ein Beitrag anhand von 'Joseph und Aseneth.'* Leiden: Brill, 1995.

Stanley, C. "'Neither Jew nor Greek': Ethnic Conflict in Graeco-Roman Society," *JSNT* 64 (1996): 101 – 24.

Steckoll, S.H. "Qumran and the Temple of Leontopolis," *Revue du Qumran* 21 (1967): 55 – 69.

Stegemann, H. *Die Entstehung der Qumrangemeinde.* Bonn: published privately, 1971.

Steiner, G. "Our Homeland, The Text," *Salmagundi* 66 (1985): 4 – 25.

Stephens, S.A. "Who Read Ancient Novels?" in *The Search for the Ancient Novel,* edited by J. Tatum, 405 – 418. Baltimore: John Hopkins University Press, 1994.

Sterling, G.E. *Historiography and Self-Definition: Josephos, Luke-Acts, and Apologetic Historiography.* Supplements to Novum Testamentum 64. Leiden: Brill, 1992.

Stern, M. " The Death of Onias III," *Zion* 25 (1960): 1 – 16. [Hebrew]

———. "A Fragment of Greco-Egyptian Prophecy and the Tradition of the Jews' Expulsion from Egypt in Chaeremon's History," *Zion* 28 (1963): 223 – 227. [Hebrew]

———. *Greek and Latin Authors on Jews and Judaism,* 3 vols. Jerusalem: Israel Academy of Sciences & Humanities, 1974, 1980, 1984.

———. "The Jewish Diaspora," in *The Jewish People in the First Century,* edited by S. Safrai and M. Stern, I:117 – 83. Philadelphia: Fortress Press, 1974.

———. "Relations between the Hasmoneans and Ptolemaic Egypt in Light of the International Relations of the Second and First Centuries," *Zion* 50 (1985): [Hebrew]

Steussy, M.J. *Gardens in Babylon: Narrative and Faith in the Greek Legends of Daniel.* SBLDS 141. Atlanta: Scholars Press, 1993.

Stone, D.D. "Matthew Arnold and the Pragmatics of Hebraism and Hellenism," *Poetics Today* 19:2 (1998): 179 – 98.

Stone, M. E. *Jewish Writings of the Second Temple Period: Apocrypha, Pseudepigrapha, Qumran, Sectarian Writings, Philo, and Josephus.* Philadelphia: Fortress Press, 1984.

Syme, R. *Tacitus,* 2 vols. Oxford: Clarendon Press, 1958.

Talschir, Z. *I Esdras: From Origin to Translation.* SBLSCS 47. Atlanta: Society of Biblical Literature, 1999.

———. *I Esdras: A Text Critical Commentary.* SBLSCS 50. Atlanta: Society of Biblical Literature, 2001.

Tarn, W.W. "Alexander Helios and the Golden Age," *JRS* (1932) 22: 135 – 60.

———. *The Greeks in Bactria and India,* 3d ed. Chicago: Ares Pub., 1984.

Tcherikover, V. "Jewish Apologetic Literature Reconsidered," *Eos* 48 (1956): 169 – 193.

———. "The Ideology of the Letter of Aristeas," *HTR* 51 (1958): 59 – 85.

———. *Hellenistic Civilization and the Jews.* Philadelphia: Jewish Publication Society of America, 1959.

Tcherikover, V. and A. Fuks, *Corpus Papyrorum Judaicarum,* 3 vols. Cambridge, Mass.: Harvard University Press, 1957–1964.

Te Velde, H. *Seth. God of Confusion: A Study of his Role in Egyptian Mythology and Religion.* Leiden: Brill, 1967.

Thomas, J. *Der jüdische Phokylides: formgeschichte Zugänge zu Pseudo-Phokylides und Vergleich mit der neutestamentlichen Paränese.* Göttingen: Vandenhoeck & Ruprecht, 1992.

Thompson, D.J. *Memphis under the Ptolemies.* Princeton: Princeton University Press, 1988.

Thompson, L.A. "Domitian and the Jewish Tax," *Historia* 31 (1982): 329–342.

Thompson, T.L. "The Exile in History and Myth: A Response to Hans Barstad," in *Leading Captivity Captive: "The Exile" as History and Ideology,* edited by L. Grabbe, 101–18. Sheffield: Sheffield Academic Press, 1998.

Tiede, D.L. *The Charismatic Figure as Miracle Worker.* Missoula: Society of Biblical Literature, 1972.

Tigerstedt, E.N. *The Legend of Sparta in Classical Antiquity,* 3 vols. Stockholm Studies in History of Literature 9, 15, 21. Stockholm: Almqvist & Wiksell, 1965, 1974, 1978.

Torrey, C.C. *Ezra Studies.* Chicago: University of Chicago Press, 1910.

Tracy, S. "III Maccabees and Pseudo-Aristeas," *YCS* 1 (1928): 241–52.

Tramontano, R. *La Lettera di Aristea a Filocrate.* Naples: Ufficio succursale della civiltà cattolica, 1931.

Trebilco, P. *Jewish Communities in Asia Minor.* Cambridge: Cambridge University Press, 1991.

Troiani, L. "Sui frammenti di Manetone nel primo libro del Contra Apionem di Flavio Giuseppe," *Studi classici e orientali* 24 (1975): 97–126.

——. "Ii libro di Aristea ed il giudaismo ellenistico," *Studi Ellenistici* 2 (1987): 31–61.

Urbach, E.E. "Center and Periphery in Jewish Historical Consciousness: Contemporary Implications," in *World Jewry and the State of Israel,* edited by M. Davis, 217–35. New York: Arno, 1977.

van der Horst, P. W. *The Sentences of Pseudo-Phocylides.* Leiden: Brill, 1978.

——. *Chaeremon: Egyptian Priest and Stoic Philosopher: The Fragments Collected and Translated with Explanatory Notes.* Leiden: Brill, 1984.

——. *Ancient Jewish Epitaphs: An Introductory Survey of a Millennium of Jewish Funerary Epigraphy (300 BCE – 700 CE).* Kampen: Kok Pharos Pub. House, 1991.

——. "'Thou Shalt Not Revile the Gods": The LXX Translation of Ex. 22:28," *SPhilA* 5 (1993): 1–8.

——. "Who was Apion?" in *Japheth in the Tents of Shem: Studies in Jewish Hellenism in Antiquity,* P.W. van der Horst, 207–221. Leuven: Peeters, 2002.

——. *Philo's Flaccus: The First Pogrom.* Leiden: Brill, 2003.

VanderKam, J. C. *An Introduction to Early Judaism.* Grand Rapids: Eerdmans, 2001a.

——. *The Book of Jubilees.* Sheffield: Sheffield Academic, 2001b.

Van Henten, J.W. *The Maccabean Martyrs as Saviours of the Jewish People: A Study of 2 and 4 Maccabees.* JSJSup 57. Leiden: Brill, 1997.

Van Henten, J.-W. and R. Abusch, "The Jews as Typhonians and Josephus' Strategy of Refutation in *Contra Apionem*," in *Josephus' Contra Apionem,* edited by L.H. Feldman and J.R. Levison, 271–309. Leiden: Brill, 1996.

Van't Dack, E. et al., *The Judaean-Syrian-Egyptian Conflict of 103–101 B.C.* Collectanea Hellenistica I. Brussels: Koninklijke Academie voor Wetenschappen, 1989.

van Unnik, W.C. *Das Selbstverständnis der jüdischen Diaspora in der hellenistisch-römischen Zeit.* Leiden: Brill, 1993.

Vaux, R. de. *The Bible and the Ancient Near East.* Garden City: Doubleday, 1971.

Verbrugghe, G. P. and J. M. Wickersham. *Berossos and Manetho, Introduced and Translated: Native Traditions in Ancient Mesopotamia and Egypt.* Ann Arbor: University of Michigan Press, 1996.

Vital, D. *The Origins of Zionism.* Oxford: Clarendon Press, 1975.

Wacholder, B.Z. *Nicolaus of Damascus.* Berkeley: University of California Press, 1962.

——. "Pseudo-Eupolemus' Two Greek Fragments on the Life of Abraham," *HUCA* 34 (1963): 83–113.

——. *Eupolemus: A Study of Judaeo-Greek Literature.* Cincinnati: Hebrew Union College, 1974.

——. "The Letter from Judah Maccabee to Aristobulus: Is 2 Maccabees 1:10b-2:18 authentic?" *HUCA* 49 (1978): 89–133.

——. *The Dawn of Qumran: The Sectarian Torah and the Teacher of Righteousness.* Cincinnati: Hebrew Union College Press, 1983.

Waddell, W.G. *Manetho.* LCL 350. Cambridge: Harvard University Press, 1940.

Walbank, F.W. *A Historical Commentary on Polybius,* 3 vols. Oxford: Clarendon Press, 1957–79.

Wallace, S.L. *Taxation in Egypt from Augustus to Diocletian.* Princeton: Princeton University Press, 1938.

Walter, N. *Der Thoraausleger Aristobulos.* Berlin: Akademie-Verlag, 1964.

——. *Jüdische Schriften aus hellenistisch-römischer Zeit,* I.2. Gütersloh: Gütersloher Verl.-Haus Mohn, 1973.

——. "Fragmente jüdish-hellenistischer Exegeten: Aristobulos, Demetrios, Aristeas," *JSHRZ* 3.2 (1975): 257–96.

——. "Kleodemos Malchas," *JSHRZ* 1.2 (1976).

Wardle, D. *Suetonius' Life of Caligula: A Commentary.* Collection Latomus 225. Brussels: Collection Latomus, 1994.

Wardy, B. "Jewish Religion in Pagan Literature during the Late Republic and Early Empire," *ANRW* II.19.1 (1979): 592–644.

Wasserstein, A. "Notes on the Temple of Onias at Leontopolis," *Illinois Classical Studies* 18 (1993): 119–29.

Wasserstein, A. and D. Wasserstein, *The Legend of the Septuagint From Classical Antiquity to Today.* Cambridge: Cambridge University Press, 2006.

Watts, J.W. *Persia and Torah: The Theory of Imperial Authorization of the Pentateuch.* Atlanta: Society of Biblical Literature, 2001.

Wehrli, F. *Die Schule des Aristoteles,* Vol. III: *Klearchos.* Basel: Schwabe, 1948.

Weinfeld, M. *The Promise of the Land: The Inheritance of the Land of Canaan by the Israelites.* Berkeley: University of California Press, 1993.

Weinstock, S. *Divus Iulius.* Oxford: Clarendon Press, 1971.

West, S. "Joseph and Aseneth: A Neglected Greek Romance," *CQ* 24 (1974): 70–81.

Westermann, C. *Isaiah 40–66: A Commentary,* Philadelphia: Westminster, 1969.

——. *Genesis, II: 12–36: A Continental Commentary.* Minneapolis: Augsburg, 1985.

Whitehorne, J. *Cleopatras.* London and New York: Routledge, 1994.

Whitmarsh, T. "Introduction," in *The Cambridge Companion to the Greek and Roman Novel,* edited by T. Whitmarsh, 1–14. Cambridge: Cambridge University Press, 2008.

——. "Class," in *The Cambridge Companion to the Greek and Roman Novel*, edited by T. Whitmarsh, 72–87. Cambridge: Cambridge University Press, 2008.

Wiesehöfer, J. "'Reichsgesetz' oder 'Einzelfallgerechtigkeit'? Bemerkungen zu P. Freis These von der Achämenidischen 'Reichsautorisation,'" *ZABR* 1 (1995): 36–46.

——. *Ancient Persia: From 550 BC to 650 AD*. London: Tauris, 1996.

——. "The Medes and the Idea of the Succession of Empires in Antiquity," in *Continuity of Empire (?): Assyria, Media, and Persia*, ed. G. Lanfranchi and R. Rollinger, 391–396. Padova: Sargon, 2003.

Wilcken, U. *Urkunden der Ptolemäerzeit*, 2 vols.. Berlin: De Gruyter, 1927–57, 1977 re-print.

Wilk, R. "Onias in Daphne," *Sinai* 108 (1991): 185–7. [Hebrew]

Wilken, R.L. *The Land Called Holy: Palestine in Christian History and Thought*. New Haven: Yale University Press, 1992.

Will, E. and Cl. Orrieux, *Ioudaismos-Hellenismos: Essai sur le judaisme judéen à l'époque hellénistique*. Nancy: Presses Universitaires de Nancy, 1986.

Williams, M.H. "Domitian, the Jews, and the 'Judaizers' – A Simple Matter of Cupiditas and Maiestas?" *Historia* 39 (1990): 196–211.

——. "Review of Yavetz, *Juden feindschaft* and Schäfer, *Judeophobia*," *JRS* 89 (1999): 213.

Williamson, H.G.M. *Ezra, Nehemiah*. Word Biblical Commentary 16. Waco: Word Books, 1985.

Wills, L.M. *The Jew in the Court of the Foreign King: Ancient Jewish Court Legends*. Minneapolis: Fortress Press, 1990.

——. "The Jewish Novellas," in *Greek Fiction: The Greek Novel in Context*, edited by J. R. Morgan and R. Stoneman, 223–238. London: Routledge, 1994.

——. *The Jewish Novel in the Ancient World*. Ithaca: Cornell University Press, 1995.

Wilson, J.F. *Caesarea Philippi: Banias, the Lost City of Pan*. London: I.B. Tauris, 2004.

Wilson, W. *The Mysteries of Righteousness: The Literary Composition and Genre of the Sentences of Pseudo-Phocylides*. Tübingen: Mohr Siebeck, 1994.

——. *The Sentences of Pseudo-Phocylides*. Berlin: De Gruyter, 2005.

Winston, D. *The Wisdom of Solomon*. Garden City: Doubleday, 1979.

Winterling, A. *Caligula: Eine Biographic*. Munich: C.H. Beck, 2003.

Wirgin, W. "Judah Maccabee's Embassy to Rome and the Jewish-Roman Treaty," *PalEQ* 101 (1969): 16–20.

Wolfson, H.A. *Philo: Foundations of Religious Philosophy in Judaism, Christianity, and Islam*, 2 vols. Cambridge: Harvard University Press, 1948.

Wright, B.G. "The Letter of Aristeas and the Reception History of the Septuagint," *BIOSCS* 39 (2006): 47–67.

Yankelevich, R. "Onias," in *Jews and Judaism in the Second Temple, Mishnaic, and Talmudic Periods: Studies in Honor of Shmuel Safrai*, edited by A. Oppenheimer, I. Gafni, and M. Stern, . Jerusalem: Yad Itzhak Ben-Zvi, 1993.

Yavetz, Z. "Judeophobia in Classical Antiquity: A Different Approach," *JJS* 44 (1993): 1–22.

——. *Judenfeindschaft in der Antike*. München: C.H. Beck, 1997.

——. "Latin Authors on Jews and Dacians," *Historia* 47 (1998): 77–107.

Yerushalmi, Y.M. *Diener von Königen und nicht Diener von Dienern: einige Aspekte der politischen Geschichte der Juden*. München: Siemens Stiftung, 1995.

Yoyotte, J. "L'Égypte ancienne et les origines de l'antijudaisme," *RHR* 163 (1963): 133–43.

Zakovitch, Y. *Das Buch Rut: Ein jüdischer Kommentar*. Stuttgarter Bibelstudien 177. Stuttgart: Katholisches Bibelwerk, 1999.

Zambelli, M. "L'ascesa in trono di Antioco IV Epifane di Siria," *Riv. Filol.* 88 (1960): 374–80.

Zeitlin, S. "Did Agrippa Write a Letter to Gaius Caligula?" *JQR* 56 (1965/6): 22–31.
Zellentin, H. "The End of Jewish Egypt: Artapanus and the Second Exodus," in *Antiquity in Antiquity: Jewish and Christian Pasts in the Greco-Roman World*, edited by. G. Gardner and K. L. Osterloh, 27–73. Tübingen: Mohr Siebeck, 2008.
Ziegler, K.-H. *Die Beziehungen zwischen Rom und dem Partherreich: Ein Beitrag zur Geschichte des Völkerrechts*. Wiesbaden: Franz Steiner, 1964.

Index of People, Places and Subjects

Index of Primary Sources

Hebrew Bible

New Testament

Deuterocanonical Works, Septuagint and Pseudepigrapha

Josephus

Philo

Classical Sources

Non-Biblical Jewish Sources

www.ingramcontent.com/pod-product-compliance
Lightning Source LLC
Chambersburg PA
CBHW020146090426
42734CB00008B/714